EVERYMAN, I will go with thee,

and be thy guide,

In thy most need to go by thy side

JOSEPH ADDISON

Born at Milston in Wiltshire, 1672; educated at Lichfield Grammar School, the Charterhouse and Magdalen College, Oxford, where he was a Demy and Fellow. M.P. for Malmesbury, Under-Secretary of State, Secretary of the Irish Government and Secretary of State in England, he died in 1719 at Holland House, his wife's London residence.

SIR RICHARD STEELE

Born at Dublin in 1672; educated at the Charterhouse and Merton College, Oxford. He was elected M.P. for Stockbridge in 1713, for Boroughbridge in 1715 (in which year he was knighted) and for Wendover in 1722. He died at Llangunnor in 1729.

ADDISON & STEELE
AND OTHERS

The Spectator

IN FOUR VOLUMES · VOLUME THREE

EDITED BY
GREGORY SMITH

INTRODUCTION BY
PETER SMITHERS, D.PHIL.(OXON.)

DENT: LONDON
EVERYMAN'S LIBRARY
DUTTON: NEW YORK

No. 166   Hardback ISBN 0 460 00166 3
No. 1166 Paperback ISBN 0 460 01166 9

CONTENTS

THOMAS Earl of WHARTON.

My LORD,

THE Author of the *Spectator* having prefixed before each of his Volumes the Name of some great Person to whom he has particular Obligations, lays his Claim to Your Lordship's Patronage upon the same Account. I must confess, my Lord, had not I already receiv'd great Instances of Your Favour, I should have been afraid of submitting a Work of this Nature to Your Perusal. You are so throughly acquainted with the Characters of Men, and all the Parts of Humane Life, that it is impossible for the least Misrepresentation of them to escape Your Notice. It is Your Lordship's particular Distinction, that You are Master of the whole Compass of Business, and have signalized Your Self in all the different Scenes of it. We admire some for the Dignity, others for the Popularity of their Behaviour; some for their Clearness of Judgment, others for their Happiness of Expression; some for the laying of Schemes, and others for the putting of them in Execution: It is Your Lordship only who enjoys these several Talents united, and that too in as great Perfection as others possess them singly. Your Enemies acknowledge this great Extent in Your Lordship's Character, at the same Time that they use their utmost Industry and Invention to derogate from it. But it is for Your Honour that those who are now Your Enemies were always so. You have acted in so much Consistency with Your Self, and promoted the Interests of Your Country in so uniform a Manner, that even those who would misrepresent Your generous Designs for the Publick Good, cannot but approve the Steadiness and Intrepidity with which You pursue them. It is a most sensible Pleasure to me that I have this Opportunity of professing my self one of Your great Admirers, and, in a very particular Manner,

My Lord,

Your Lordship's most Obliged,

and most Obedient, Humble Servant,

THE SPECTATOR.

THE SPECTATOR.

VOL. V.

No. 322.
[STEELE.]

Monday, March 10, 1712.

. . . *Ad humum maerore gravi deducit & angit.*—Hor.

It is often said, after a Man has heard a Story with extra-ordinary Circumstances, it is a very good one if it be true: But as for the following Relation, I should be glad were I sure it were false. It is told with such Simplicity, and there are so many artless Touches of Distress in it, that I fear it comes too much from the Heart.

'Mr. Spectator,

Some Years ago it happened that I lived in the same House with a young Gentleman of Merit; with whose good Qualities I was so much taken, as to make it my Endeavour to shew as many as I was able in my self. Familiar Converse improved general Civilities into an unfeigned Passion on both Sides. He watched an Opportunity to declare himself to me; and I, who could not expect a Man of so great an Estate as his, received his Addresses in such Terms as gave him no Reason to believe I was displeased with them, tho' I did Nothing to make him think me more easy than was decent. His Father was a very hard worldly Man, and proud; so that there was no Reason to believe he would easily be brought to think, there was any Thing in any Woman's Person or Character that could ballance the Disadvantage of an unequal Fortune. In the mean Time the Son continued his Application to me, and omitted no Occasion of Demonstrating the most disin-terested Passion imaginable to me; and in plain direct Terms offer'd to marry me privately, and keep it so 'till he should be so happy as to gain his Father's Approbation, or become possessed of his Estate. I passionately loved him, and you will believe I did not deny such a one what was my Interest also to grant. However I was not so young, as not to take the Precaution of carrying with me a faithful Servant, who had been also my Mother's Maid, to be present at the Ceremony. When that was over, I demanded a Certificate, signed by the Minister, my Husband, and the Servant I just now spoke of.

After our Nuptials we conversed together very familiarly in the same House; but the Restraints we were generally under, and the Interviews we had being stolen and interrupted, made our Behaviour to each other have rather the impatient Fondness which is visible in Lovers, than the regular and gratified Affection which is to be observed in Man and Wife. This Observation made the Father very anxious for his Son, and press him to a Match he had in his Eye for him. To relieve my Husband from this Importunity, and conceal the Secret of our Marriage, which I had Reason to know would not be long in my Power in Town, it was resolved that I should retire into a remote Place in the Country, and converse under feigned Names by Letter. We long continued this Way of Commerce; and I with my Needle, a few Books, and Reading over and over my Husband's Letters, passed my Time in a resigned Expectation of better Days. Be pleased to take Notice, that within four Months after I left my Husband I was delivered of a Daughter, who died within few Hours after her Birth. This Accident, and the retired Manner of Life I led, gave criminal Hopes to a neighbouring Brute of a Country Gentleman, whose Folly was the Source of all my Affliction. This Rustick is one of those rich Clowns, who supply the Want of all Manner of Breeding by the Neglect of it, and with noisy Mirth, half Understanding, and ample Fortune, force themselves upon Persons and Things without any Sense of Time and Place. The poor ignorant People where I lay concealed, and now passed for a Widow, wondered I could be so shy and strange, as they called it, to the Squire; and were bribed by him to admit him whenever he thought fit. I happened to be sitting in a little Parlour which belonged to my own Part of the House, and musing over one of the fondest of my Husband's Letters, in which I always kept the Certificate of my Marriage, when this rude Fellow came in, and with the nauseous Familiarity of such unbred Brutes, snatched the Papers out of my Hand. I was immediately under so great a Concern, that I threw my self at his Feet, and begged of him to return them. He, with the same odious Pretence to Freedom and Gayety, swore he would read them. I grew more importunate, he more curious; 'till at last, with an Indignation arising from a Passion I then first discovered in him, he threw the Papers into the Fire, swearing that since he was not to read them, the Man who writ them should never be so happy as to have me read them over again. It is insignificant to tell you my Tears and Reproaches made the boisterous Calf leave the Room ashamed and out of Countenance, when I had Leisure to ruminate on this Accident with more than ordinary Sorrow:

However such was then my Confidence in my Husband, that I writ to him the Misfortune, and desired another Paper of the same Kind. He deferred writing two or three Posts, and at last answered me in general, That he could not then send me what I asked for, but when he could find a proper Conveyance, I should be sure to have it. From this Time his Letters were more cold every Day than other, and as he grew indifferent I grew jealous. This has at last brought me to Town, where I find both the Witnesses of my Marriage dead, and that my Husband, after three Months Cohabitation, has buried a young Lady whom he married in Obedience to his Father. In a Word, he shuns and disowns me. Should I come to the House and confront him, the Father would join in supporting him against me, though he believed my Story; should I talk it to the World, what Reparation can I expect for an Injury I cannot make out? I believe he means to bring me, through Necessity, to resign my Pretensions to him for some Provision for my Life; but I will die first. Pray bid him remember what he said, and how he was charmed when he laughed at the heedless Discovery I often made of my self; let him remember how aukward I was in my dissembled Indifference towards him before Company; ask him how I, who could never conceal my Love for him, at his own Request can part with him for ever? Oh, Mr. SPECTATOR, sensible Spirits know no Indifference in Marriage; what then do you think is my piercing Affliction— I leave you to represent my Distress your own Way, in which I desire you to be speedy, if you have compassion for Innocence exposed to Infamy.

T

Octavia.'

No. 323.
[ADDISON.] Tuesday, March 11.

   . . . *Modo vir, modo femina* . . .—Ovid.

THE Journal with which I presented my Reader on *Tuesday* last, has brought me in several Letters with Account of many private Lives cast into that Form. I have the *Rake's Journal*, the *Sot's Journal*, the *Whoremaster's Journal*, and among several others a very curious Piece, entituled, *The Journal of a Mohock*. By these Instances I find that the Intention of my last *Tuesday's* Paper has been mistaken by many of my Readers. I did not design so much to expose Vice as Idleness, and aimed at those Persons who pass away their Time rather in Trifle and Impertinence, than in Crimes and Immoralities.

Offences of this latter Kind are not to be dallied with, or treated in so ludicrous a Manner. In short, my Journal only holds up Folly to the Light, and shews the Disagreeableness of such Actions as are indifferent in themselves, and blameable only as they proceed from Creatures endow'd with Reason.

My following Correspondent, who calls herself *Clarinda*, is such a Journalist as I require: She seems by her Letter to be placed in a modish State of Indifference between Vice and Virtue, and to be susceptible of either, were there proper Pains with her. Had her Journal been filled with Gallantries, or such Occurrences as had shewn her wholly divested of her natural Innocence, notwithstanding it might have been more pleasing to the Generality of Readers, I should not have published it; but as it is only the Picture of a Life filled with a fashionable Kind of Gayety and Laziness, I shall set down five Days of it, as I have received it from the Hand of my fair Correspondent.

'*Dear Mr.* SPECTATOR,

You having set your Readers an Exercise in one of your last Week's Papers, I have perform'd mine according to your Orders, and herewith send it you enclosed. You must know, Mr. SPECTATOR, that I am a maiden Lady of a good Fortune, who have had several Matches offered me for these ten Years last past, and have at present warm Applications made to me by a very pretty Fellow. As I am at my own Disposal, I come up to Town every Winter, and pass my Time in it after the Manner you will find in the following Journal, which I began to write upon the very Day after your *Spectator* upon that Subject.

TUESDAY *Night*. Could not go to Sleep 'till one in the Morning for Thinking of my Journal.

WEDNESDAY. *From Eight till Ten*. Drank two Dishes of Chocolate in Bed, and fell asleep after them.

From Ten to Eleven. Eat a Slice of Bread and Butter, drank a Dish of Bohea, read the *Spectator*.

From Eleven to One. At my Toilette, try'd a new Head. Gave Orders for *Veny* to be combed and washed. *Mem*. I look best in Blue.

From One 'till Half an Hour after Two. Drove to the *Change*. Cheapned a Couple of Fans.

'*Till Four*. At Dinner. *Mem*. Mr. *Froth* passed by in his new Liveries.

From Four to Six. Dressed, paid a Visit to old Lady *Blithe* and her Sister, having before heard they were gone out of Town that Day.

From Six to Eleven. At Basset. *Mem.* Never set again upon the Ace of Diamonds.

THURSDAY. *From Eleven at Night to Eight in the Morning.* Dream'd that I punted to Mr. *Froth.*

From Eight to Ten. Chocolate. Read two Acts in *Aurenzebe* abed.

From Ten to Eleven. Tea-Table. Sent to borrow Lady *Faddle*'s *Cupid* for *Veny.* Read the Play-Bills. Received a Letter from Mr. *Froth.* *Mem.* locked it up in my strong Box.

Rest of the Morning. Fontange, the Tire-woman, her Account of my Lady *Blithe*'s Wash. Broke a Tooth in my little Tortoise-shell Comb. Sent *Frank* to know how my Lady *Hectick* rested after her Monkey's leaping out at Window. Looked pale. *Fontange* tells me my Glass is not true. Dressed by Three.

From Three to Four. Dinner cold before I sat down.

From Four to Eleven. Saw Company. Mr. *Froth*'s Opinion of *Milton.* His Account of the *Mohocks.* His Fancy of a Pin-cushion. Picture in the Lid of his Snuff-Box. Old Lady *Faddle* promises me her Woman to cut my Hair. Lost five Guineas at Crimp.

Twelve a Clock at Night. Went to bed.

FRIDAY. *Eight in the Morning.* Abed. Read over all Mr. *Froth*'s Letters. *Cupid* and *Veny.*

Ten a Clock. Stay'd within all Day, not at home.

From Ten to Twelve. In Conference with my Mantua-Maker. Sorted a Suit of Ribbands. Broke my blue *China* Cup.

From Twelve to One. Shut my self up in my Chamber, practised Lady *Betty Modely*'s Skuttle.

One in the Afternoon. Called for my flower'd Handkercheif. Worked half a Violet Leaf in it. Eyes aked, and Head out of Order. Threw by my Work, and read over the remaining Part of *Aurenzebe.*

From Three to Four. Dined.

From Four to Twelve. Changed my Mind, dressed, went abroad, and play'd at Crimp 'till Midnight. Found Mrs. *Spitely* at home. Conversation. Mrs. *Brilliant*'s Necklace false Stones. Old Lady *Loveday* going to be married to a young Fellow that is not worth a Groat. Miss *Prue* gone into the Country. *Tom Townly* has red Hair. *Mem.* Mrs. Spitely whispered in my Ear that she had something to tell me about Mr. *Froth.* I am sure it is not true.

Between Twelve and One. Dreamed that Mr. *Froth* lay at my Feet, and called me *Indamora*.

SATURDAY. Rose at Eight a Clock in the Morning. Sat down to my Toilette.

From Eight to Nine. Shifted a Patch for Half an Hour before I could determine it. Fixed it above my left Eye-brow.

From Nine to Twelve. Drank my Tea, and dressed.

From Twelve to Two. At Chappel. A great Deal of good Company. *Mem.* The third Air in the new Opera. Lady *Blithe* dressed frightfully.

From Three to Four. Dined. Miss *Kitty* called upon me to go to the Opera before I was risen from the Table.

From Dinner to Six. Drank Tea. Turned off a Footman for being rude to *Veny*.

Six a Clock. Went to the Opera. I did not see Mr. *Froth* till the Beginning of the second Act. Mr. *Froth* talked to a Gentleman in a black Wig. Bowed to a Lady in the front Box. Mr. *Froth* and his Friend clapt *Nicolini* in the third Act. Mr. *Froth* cried out *Ancora*. Mr. *Froth* led me to my Chair. I think he squeezed my Hand.

Eleven at Night. Went to Bed. Melancholly Dreams. Methought *Nicolini* said he was Mr. *Froth*.

SUNDAY. Indisposed.

MONDAY. *Eight a Clock.* Waked by Miss *Kitty*. *Aurenzebe* lay upon the Chair by me. *Kitty* repeated without Book the eight best Lines in the Play. Went in our Mobbs to the dumb Man, according to Appointment. Told me that my Lover's Name began with a G. *Mem.* the Conjurer was within a Letter of Mr. *Froth*'s Name, *&c.*

Upon looking back into this my Journal, I find that I am at a Loss to know whether I pass my Time well or ill; and indeed never thought of considering how I did it, before I perused your Speculation upon that Subject. I scarce find a single Action in these five Days that I can thoroughly approve of, except the Working upon the Violet Leaf, which I am resolved to finish the first Day I am at Leisure. As for Mr. *Froth* and *Veny*, I did not think they took up so much of my Time and Thoughts, as I find they do upon my Journal. The latter of them I will turn off if you insist upon it; and if Mr. *Froth* does not bring Matters to a Conclusion very suddenly, I will not let my Life run away in a Dream.

Your humble Servant,

Clarinda.'

To resume one of the Morals of my first Paper, and to confirm *Clarinda* in her good Inclinations, I would have her consider what a pretty Figure she would make among Posterity, were the History of her whole Life published like these five Days of it. I shall conclude my Paper with an Epitaph written by an uncertain Author on Sir *Philip Sidney's* Sister, a Lady who seems to have been of a Temper very much different from that of *Clarinda*. The last Thought of it is so very noble, that I dare say my Reader will pardon me the Quotation.

On the Countess Dowager of *Pembroke*.

Underneath this Marble Hearse
Lies the Subject of all Verse,
Sydney's *Sister,* Pembroke's *Mother;*
Death, ere thou hast kill'd another,
Fair and learn'd, and good as she,
Time shall throw a Dart at thee. L

No. 324.
[STEELE.]
Wednesday, March 12.

O curvae in terris animae & coelestium inanes.—Pers.

'Mr. SPECTATOR,
THE Materials you have collected together towards a general History of Clubs, make so bright a Part of your Speculations, that I think it is but a Justice we all owe the learned World to furnish you with such Assistances as may promote that useful Work. For this Reason I could not forbear communicating to you some imperfect Informations of a Set of Men (if you will allow them a Place in that Species of Being) who have lately erected themselves into a Nocturnal Fraternity, under the Title of *The Mohock Club*, a Name borrowed it seems from a Sort of *Cannibals* in *India*, who subsist by Plundering and Devouring all the Nations about them. The President is stiled *Emperor of the Mohocks*; and his Arms are a *Turkish* Crescent, which his Imperial Majesty bears at present in a very extraordinary Manner engraven upon his Forehead. Agreeable to their Name, the avowed Design of their Institution is Mischief; and upon this Foundation all their Rules and Orders are framed. An outragious Ambition of doing all possible Hurt to their Fellow-Creatures, is the great Cement of their Assembly, and the only Qualification required in the Members. In order to exert this Principle in its full Strength and Perfection, they take Care to drink themselves to a Pitch, that is, beyond the Possibility of attending to any Motions of Reason or Humanity; then make a general Sally, and attack

all that are so unfortunate as to walk the Streets through which they patroll. Some are knock'd down, others stabb'd, others cut and carbonado'd. To put the Watch to a total Rout, and mortify some of those inoffensive Militia, is reckon'd a *Coup d'eclat.* The particular Talents by which these *Misanthropes* are distinguished from one another, consist in the various Kinds of Barbarities which they execute upon their Prisoners. Some are celebrated for a happy Dexterity in Tipping the Lion upon them; which is perform'd by squeezing the Nose flat to the Face, and boring out the Eyes with their Fingers: Others are called the Dancing-Masters, and teach their Scholars to cut Capers by running Swords thro' their Legs; a new Invention, whether originally *French* I cannot tell: A third Sort are the Tumblers, whose Office it is to set Women upon their Heads, and commit certain Indecencies, or rather Barbarities, on the Limbs which they expose. But these I forbear to mention, because they can't but be very shocking to the Reader, as well as the SPECTATOR. In this Manner they carry on a War against Mankind; and by the standing Maxims of their Policy, are to enter into no Alliances but one, and that is Offensive and Defensive with all Bawdy-Houses in general, of which they have declared themselves Protectors and Guarantees.

I must own, Sir, these are only broken incoherent Memoirs of this wonderful Society, but they are the best I have been yet able to procure; for being but of late Establishment, it is not ripe for a just History: And to be serious, the chief Design of this Trouble is to hinder it from ever being so. You have been pleas'd, out of a Concern for the Good of your Countrymen, to act under the Character of SPECTATOR not only the Part of a Looker-on, but an Overseer of their Actions; and whenever such Enormities as this infest the Town, we immediately fly to you for Redress. I have Reason to believe, that some thoughtless Youngsters, out of a false Notion of Bravery, and an immoderate Fondness to be distinguished for Fellows of Fire, are insensibly hurry'd into this senseless scandalous Project: Such will probably stand corrected by your Reproofs, especially if you inform them, that it is not Courage for half a Score Fellows, mad with Wine and Lust, to set upon two or three soberer than themselves; and that the Manners of *Indian* Savages are no becoming Accomplishments to an *English* fine Gentleman. Such of them as have been Bullies and Scowrers of a long Standing, and are grown Veterans in this Kind of Service, are I fear too hardned to receive any Impressions from your Admonitions. But I beg you would recommend to their Perusal your ninth Speculation: They may there be taught to take Warning from the Club of Duellists; and be put in Mind, that the common Fate of those Men of Honour was to be hang'd.

I am,

March the 10th,　　　　　　　*Sir,*

　ʼ711–12.　　　　　　　　　*Your most humble Servant,*

Philanthropos.'

The following Letter is of a quite contrary Nature; but I add it here that the Reader may observe at the same View, how amiable Ignorance may be when it is shewn in its Simplicities, and how detestable in Barbarities.   It is written by an honest Countryman to his Mistress, and came to the Hands of a Lady of good Sense wrapped about a Thread-Paper, who has long kept it by her as an Image of artless Love.

'*To her I very much Respect,* Mrs. Margaret Clark.

Lovely, and oh that I could write loving Mrs. *Margaret Clark,* I pray you let Affection excuse Presumption.   Having been so happy as to enjoy the Sight of your sweet Countenance and comely Body, sometimes when I had Occasion to buy Treacle or Liquorish Powder at the Apothecary's Shop, I am so ᴇnamour'd with you, that I can no more keep close my flaming Desire to become your Servant.   And I am the more bold now to write to your sweet self, because I am now my own Man, and may match where I please; for my Father is taken away, and now I am come to my Living, which is Ten Yard Land, and a House; and there is never a Yard of Land in our Field but it is as well worth ten Pound a Year as a Thief is worth a Halter; and all my Brothers and Sisters are provided for: Besides I have good Household-stuff, though I say it, both Brass and Pewter, Linnen and Woollens; and though my House be thatched, yet, if you and I match, it shall go hard but I will have one Half of it slated.   If you think well of this Motion, I will wait upon you as soon as my new Cloaths is made and Hay-Harvest is in. I could, though I say it, have good . . .'   The rest is torn off; and Posterity must be contented to know that Mrs. *Margaret Clark* was very pretty, but are left in the Dark as to the Name of her Lover.　　　　　　　　　　　　　　　　　　　T

No. 325.

[BUDGELL.]　　　　　　　　　　　　Thursday, March 13.

. . . *Quid frustra simulacra fugacia captas?*
Quod petis, est nusquam: quod amas, avertere, perdes,
Ista repercussae, quam cernis, imaginis umbra est.

Nil habet ista sui; tecum venitque, manetque,
Tecum discedat, si tu discedere possis.—Ovid.

WILL HONEYCOMB diverted us last Night with an Account of a young Fellow's first Discovering his Passion to his Mistress. The young Lady was one, it seems, who had long before conceived a favourable Opinion of him, and was still in Hopes that he would some Time or other make his Advances. As he was one Day talking with her in Company of her two Sisters, the Conversation happening to turn upon Love, each of the young Ladies was, by way of Raillery, recommending a Wife to him; when, to the no small Surprize of her who languished for him in Secret, he told them with a more than ordinary Seriousness, That his Heart had been long engaged to one whose Name he thought himself obliged in Honour to conceal; but that he could shew her Picture in the Lid of his Snuff-Box. The young Lady, who found herself the most sensibly touched by this Confession, took the first Opportunity that offered of snatching his Box out of his Hand. He seemed desirous of recovering it, but finding her resolved to look into the Lid, begged her, that if she should happen to know the Person she would not reveal her Name. Upon carrying it to the Window she was very agreeably surprized to find there was Nothing within the Lid but a little Looking-Glass, in which, after she had view'd her own Face with more Pleasure than she had ever done before, she returned the Box with a Smile, telling him, She could not but admire at his Choice.

WILL fancying that his Story took, immediately fell into a Dissertation on the Usefulness of Looking-Glasses, and applying himself to me, asked, If there were any Looking-Glasses in the Times of the *Greeks* and *Romans*; for that he had often observed in the Translations of Poems out of those Languages, that People generally talked of seeing themselves in Wells, Fountains, Lakes, and Rivers: Nay, says he, I remember Mr. *Dryden* in his *Ovid* tells us of a swinging Fellow, called *Polypheme*, that made use of the Sea for his Looking-Glass, and could never dress himself to Advantage but in a Calm.

My Friend WILL, to shew us the whole Compass of his Learning upon this Subject, further informed us, that there were still several Nations in the World so very barbarous as not to have any Looking-Glasses among them, and that he had lately read a Voyage to the South-Sea, in which it is said, that the Ladies of *Chili* always dress their Heads over a Bason of Water.

I am the more particular in my Account of WILL's last Night's Lecture on these natural Mirrors, as it seems to bear some Relation to the following Letter, which I received the Day before.

'*Sir*,

I have read your last *Saturday*'s Observation on the Fourth
Book of *Milton* with great Satisfaction, and am particularly
pleased with the hidden Moral, which you have taken Notice
of in several Parts of the Poem.   The Design of this Letter is
to desire your Thoughts, whether there may not also be some
Moral couched under that Place in the same Book where the
Poet lets us know, that the first Woman immediately after her
Creation, ran to a Looking-Glass, and became so enamoured of
her own Face, that she had never removed, to view any of the
other Works of Nature, had not she been led off to a Man.   If
you think fit to set down the whole Passage from *Milton*, your
Readers will be able to judge for themselves, and the Quotation
will not a little contribute to the filling up of your Paper.

Your Humble Servant,

R. T.'

The last Consideration urged by my Querist is so strong, that
I cannot forbear closing with it.   The Passage he alludes to
is part of *Eve*'s Speech to *Adam*, and one of the most beautiful
Passages in the whole Poem.

> *That Day I oft remember, when from sleep*
> *I first awak'd, and found my self repos'd*
> *Under a shade of flowers, much wondring where*
> *And what I was, whence thither brought, and how.*
> *Not distant far from thence, a murmuring sound*
> *Of waters issu'd from a Cave, and spread*
> *Into a liquid Plain, then stood unmov'd*
> *Pure as the Expanse of Heav'n; I thither went*
> *With unexperienc'd thought, and laid me down*
> *On the green Bank, to look into the clear*
> *Smooth Lake, that to me seem'd another Skie.*
> *As I bent down to look, just opposite,*
> *A shape within the watry gleam appear'd*
> *Bending to look on me; I started back;*
> *It started back; but pleas'd I soon return'd;*
> *Pleas'd it return'd as soon, with answering looks*
> *Of sympathy and love; there I had fixt*
> *Mine Eyes till now, and pin'd with vain desire,*
> *Had not a Voice thus warn'd me: What thou seest,*
> *What there thou seest fair Creature is thy self;*
> *With thee it came and goes: but follow me,*
> *And I will bring thee where no shadow stays*
> *Thy coming, and thy soft Embraces; he*
> *Whose image thou art, him thou shalt enjoy*
> *Inseparably thine, to him shalt bear*
> *Multitudes like thy self, and thence be call'd*
> *Mother of humane Race: What could I do,*
> *But follow streight, invisibly thus led;*

> Till I espy'd thee, fair indeed and tall,
> Under a Platan, yet methought less fair,
> Less winning soft, less amiable mild,
> Than that smooth watry image; back I return'd;
> Thou following cry'dst aloud, Return fair Eve;
> Whom fly'st thou? whom thou fly'st, of him thou **art,**
> His flesh, his bone; to give thee being I lent,
> Out of my side to thee, nearest my heart,
> Substantial Life, to have thee by my side
> Henceforth an individual solace dear;
> Part of my Soul I seek thee, and thee claim
> My other half; with that thy gentle hand
> Seis'd mine; I yielded, and from that time see
> How beauty is excell'd by manly grace
> And wisdom, which alone is truly fair.
>   So spake our general Mother . . .

X

No. 326.
[STEELE.]   Friday, March 14.

> Inclusam Danaen turris ahenea,
> Robustaeque fores, & vigilum canum
> Tristes excubiae munierant satis
>   Nocturnis ab adulteris,
> Si non . . .—Hor.

'Mr. SPECTATOR,

YOUR Correspondent's Letter relating to Fortune-Hunters, and
your subsequent Discourse upon it, have given me Encouragement to send you a State of my Case; by which you will see,
that the Matter complained of is a common Grievance both to
City and Country.

I am a Country Gentleman of between five and six thousand
a Year. It is my Misfortune to have a very fine Park and an
only Daughter; upon which Account I have been so plagu'd
with Deer-Stealers and Fops, that for these Four Years past I
have scarce enjoy'd a Moment's Rest. I look upon my self to
be in a State of War; and am forc'd to keep as constant Watch
in my Seat, as a Governour would do that commanded a Town
on the Frontier of an Enemy's Country. I have indeed pretty
well secur'd my Park, having for this Purpose provided my self
of four Keepers, who are Left-handed, and handle a Quarter-
staff beyond any other Fellows in the Country. And for the
Guard of my House, besides a Band of Pensioner-Matrons and
an old Maiden Relation, whom I keep on constant Duty, I have
Blunderbusses always charged, and Fox-gins planted in private
Places about my Garden, of which I have given frequent Notice
in the Neighbourhood; yet so it is, that in spite of all my Care.

I shall every now and then have a sawcy Rascal ride by *re-connoitring* (as I think you call it) under my Windows, as sprucely drest as if he were going to a Ball. I am aware of this Way of Attacking a Mistress on Horseback, having heard that it is a common Practice in *Spain*; and have therefore taken Care to remove my Daughter from the Road-side of the House, and to lodge her next the Garden. But to cut short my Story; What can a Man do after all? I durst not stand for Member of Parliament last Election, for Fear of some ill Consequence from my being off of my Post. What I would therefore desire of you, is, to promote a Project I have set on Foot, and upon which I have writ to some of my Friends; and that is, that Care may be taken to secure our Daughters by Law as well as our Deer; and that some honest Gentleman of a publick Spirit, would move for Leave to bring in a Bill *for the better Preserving of the female Game. I am, Sir,*

Your humble Servant.'

'*Mr.* SPECTATOR,

Mile-End-Green, March 6, 1711–12.

Here is a young Man walks by our Door every Day about the Dusk of the Evening. He looks up at my Window as if to see me; and if I steal towards it to peep at him, he turns another Way, and looks frightned at finding what he was looking for. The Air is very cold; and pray let him know that, if he knocks at the Door, he will be carried to the Parlour Fire; and I will come down soon after, and give him an Opportunity to break his Mind.

I am,
Sir,
Your humble Servant,
Mary Comfitt.

If I observe he cannot speak, I 'll give him time to recover himself, and ask him how he does.'

'*Dear Sir,*

I beg you to print this without Delay, and by the first Opportunity give us the natural Causes of Longing in Women; or put me out of Fear that my Wife will one Time or other be delivered of something as monstrous as any Thing that has yet appeared to the World; for they say the Child is to bear a Resemblance of what was desired by the Mother. I have been married upwards of six Years, have had four Children, and my Wife is now big with the fifth. The Expences she has put me to, in procuring what she has longed for during her Pregnancy with them, would not only have handsomely defrayed the

Charges of the Month, but of their Education too; her Fancy being so exorbitant for the first Year or two, as not to confine it self to the usual Objects of Eatables and Drinkables, but running out after Equipage and Furniture, and the like Extravagancies. To trouble you only with a few of them: When she was with Child of *Tom* my eldest Son, she came home one Day just fainting, and told me she had been visiting a Relation, whose Husband had made her a Present of a Chariot and a stately Pair of Horses; and that she was positive she could not breathe a Week longer, unless she took the Air in the Fellow to it of her own within that time: This, rather than lose an Heir, I readily complied with. Then the Furniture of her best Room must be instantly changed, or she should mark the Child with some of the frightful Figures in the old-fashion'd Tapistry. Well, the Upholsterer was called, and her Longing saved that Bout. When she went with *Molly*, she had fixed her Mind upon a new Set of Plate, and as much China as would have furnished an *India* Shop: These also I chearfully granted, for Fear of being Father to an *Indian Pagod*. Hitherto I found her Demands rose upon every Concession; and had she gone on I had been ruined: But by good Fortune, with her third, which was *Peggy*, the Heighth of her Imagination came down to the Corner of a Venison-Pasty, and brought her once even upon her Knees to gnaw off the Ears of a Pig from the Spit. The Gratifications of her Palate were easily preferred to those of her Vanity; and sometimes a Partridge or a Quail, a Wheat-Ear or the Pestle of a Lark, were chearfully purchased; nay I could be contented though I were to feed her with green Pease in *April*, or Cherries in *May*. But with the Babe she now goes she is turned Girl again, and fallen to eating of Chalk, pretending 'twill make the Child's Skin white; and nothing will serve her but I must bear her Company, to prevent its having a Shade of my Brown. In this however I have ventured to deny her. No longer ago than Yesterday, as we were coming to Town, she saw a Parcel of Crows so heartily at Breakfast upon a Piece of Horse-flesh, that she had an invincible Desire to partake with them, and (to my infinite Surprise) begged the Coachman to cut her off a Slice as if 'twere for himself; which the Fellow did; and as soon as she came home she fell to it with such an Appetite, that she seemed rather to devour than eat it. What her next Sally will be I cannot guess; but in the mean Time my Request to you is, that if there be any Way to come at these wild unaccountable Rovings of Imagination by Reason and Argument, you'd speedily afford us your Assistance. This exceeds the Grievance of Pin-Money; and I think in every Settlement there ought to be a Clause inserted, that the Father should be answerable for the Longings of his Daughter. But I shall impatiently expect your Thoughts in this Matter; and am,

> Sir,
>
> > Your most obliged,
> >
> > > And most faithful
> > >
> > > > Humble Servant,
> > > >
> > > > > T. B.

Let me know whether you think the next Child will love Horses as much as *Molly* does China-Ware.' T

No. 327.
[ADDISON.] Saturday, March 15.

> . . . *Major rerum mihi nascitur ordo.*—Virg.

WE were told in the foregoing Book how the Evil Spirit practised upon *Eve* as she lay asleep, in order to inspire her with Thoughts of Vanity, Pride and Ambition. The Author, who shews a wonderful Art throughout his whole Poem, in preparing the Reader for the several Occurrences that arise in it, founds, upon the above-mention'd Circumstance, the First Part of the Fifth Book. *Adam* upon his Awaking finds *Eve* still asleep, with an unusual Discomposure in her Looks. The Posture in which he regards her, is described with a Tenderness not to be express'd, as the Whisper with which he awakens her is the softest that ever was conveyed to a Lover's Ear.

> *His wonder was to find unwaken'd Eve*
> *With tresses discompos'd, and glowing cheek*
> *As through unquiet rest; he on his side*
> *Leaning half-rais'd, with looks of cordial love*
> *Hung over her enamour'd, and beheld*
> *Beauty, which whether waking or asleep,*
> *Shot forth peculiar Graces; then with voice*
> *Mild, as when* Zephyrus *or* Flora *breathes,*
> *Her Hand soft touching, whisper'd thus: Awake*
> *My fairest, my espous'd, my latest found,*
> *Heaven's last best gift, my ever new delight.*
> *Awake, the morning shines, and the fresh field*
> *Calls us; we lose the prime, to mark how spring*
> *Our tended plants, how blows the Citron Grove,*
> *What drops the Myrrhe, and what the balmie Reed,*
> *How Nature paints her colours, how the Bee*
> *Sits on the bloom, extracting liquid sweet.*
> *Such Whispering wak'd her, but with startled Eye*
> *On* Adam, *whom embracing, thus she spake,*
>
> > *O Sole in whom my thoughts find all Repose,*
> > *My glory, my perfection, glad I see*
> > *Thy face, and morn return'd . .*

I cannot but take Notice that *Milton*, in the Conferences between *Adam* and *Eve*, had his Eye very frequently upon the Book of *Canticles*, in which there is a noble Spirit of Eastern Poetry, and very often not unlike what we meet with in *Homer*, who is generally placed near the Age of *Solomon*. I think there is no Question but the Poet in the preceding Speech remember'd those two Passages which are spoken on the like Occasion, and fill'd with the same pleasing Images of Nature.

My beloved spake, and said unto me, Rise up, my love, my fair one, and come away; For lo, the winter is past, the rain is over and gone; the flowers appear on the earth; the time of the singing of birds is come, and the Voice of the Turtle is heard in our Land. The fig-tree putteth forth her green figs, and the Vines with the tender grape give a good smell. Arise, my Love, my fair one, and come away.

Come, my beloved, let us go forth into the Field; let us get up early to the Vineyards, let us see if the Vine flourish, whether the tender Grape appear, and the Pomegranates bud forth.

His preferring the Garden of *Eden* to that

> . . . *Where the* Sapient *King*
> *Held Dalliance with his fair* Egyptian *Spouse,*

shews that the Poet had this delightful Scene in his Mind.

Eve's Dream is full of those *high Conceits engendring Pride*, which, we are told, the Devil endeavoured to instil into her. Of this Kind is that Part of it where she fancies herself awaken'd by *Adam* in the following beautiful Lines.

> *Why sleep'st thou* Eve? *now is the pleasant time,*
> *The cool, the silent, save where silence yields*
> *To the night-warbling bird, that now awake*
> *Tunes sweetest his love-labour'd song; now reigns*
> *Full orb'd the moon, and with more pleasing light*
> *Shadowy sets off the face of things: In vain,*
> *If none regard; Heav'n wakes with all his eyes*
> *Whom to behold but thee, Nature's desire,*
> *In whose sight all things joy, with ravishment*
> *Attracted by thy beauty still to gaze!*

An injudicious Poet would have made *Adam* talk thro' the whole Work, in such Sentiments as these. But Flattery and Falshood are not the Courtship of *Milton's Adam*, and could not be heard by *Eve* in her State of Innocence, excepting only in a Dream produc'd on purpose to taint her Imagination. Other vain Sentiments of the same Kind in this Relation of her Dream, will be obvious to every Reader. Tho' the catastrophe of the Poem is finely presaged on this Occasion, the Particulars of it are so artfully shadow'd, that they do not anticipate the Story which follows in the Ninth Book. I shall only add, that tho' the Vision it self is founded upon Truth, the Circumstances of it are full of that Wildness and Inconsistency which are natural to a Dream. *Adam*, conformable to his superior Character for Wisdom, instructs and comforts *Eve* upon this Occasion.

> *So chear'd he his fair Spouse, and she was chear'd,*
> *But silently a gentle tear let fall*
> *From either eye, and wip'd them with her hair;*
> *Two other precious drops that ready stood,*
> *Each in their chrystal sluice, he e'er they fell*
> *Kiss'd, as the gracious Signs of sweet remorse*
> *And pious awe, that fear'd to have offended.*

The Morning Hymn is written in Imitation of one of those Psalms, where, in the Overflowings of Gratitude and Praise, the Psalmist calls not only upon the Angels, but upon the most conspicuous Parts of the inanimate Creation, to joyn with him in extolling their Common Maker. Invocations of this Nature fill the Mind with glorious Ideas of God's Works, and awaken that divine Enthusiasm, which is so natural to Devotion. But if this Calling upon the dead Parts of Nature, is at all Times a proper Kind of Worship, it was in a particular Manner suitable to our first Parents, who had the Creation fresh upon their Minds, and had not seen the various Dispensations of Providence, nor consequently could be acquainted with those many Topicks of Praise which might afford Matter to the Devotions of their Posterity. I need not remark the beautiful Spirit of Poetry, which runs through this whole Hymn, nor the Holiness of that Resolution with which it concludes.

Having already mentioned those Speeches which are assigned to the Persons in this Poem, I proceed to the Description which the Poet gives of *Raphael*. His Departure from before the Throne, and his Flight thro' the Choirs of Angels, is finely imaged. As *Milton* every where fills his Poem with Circumstances that are marvellous and astonishing, he describes the Gate of Heaven as framed after such a Manner, that it open'd of it self upon the Approach of the Angel who was to pass through it.

> *. . . 'till at the gate*
> *Of Heav'n arriv'd, the gate self-open'd wide,*
> *On golden Hinges turning, as by work*
> *Divine the Sovereign Architect had framed.*

The Poet here seems to have regarded two or three Passages in the 18th *Iliad*, as that in particular, where, speaking of *Vulcan*, *Homer* says, that he had made twenty *Tripodes* running on Golden Wheels, which, upon Occasion, might go of themselves to the Assembly of the Gods, and, when there was no more Use for them, return again after the same Manner. *Scaliger* has rallied *Homer* very severely upon this Point, as M. *Dacier* has endeavoured to defend it. I will not pretend to determine, whether in this Particular of *Homer*, the Marvellous does not lose Sight of the Probable. As the miraculous Workmanship of *Milton's* Gates is not so extraordinary as this of the *Tripodes*, so I am perswaded he would not have mentioned it, had not he been supported in it by a Passage in the Scripture, which speaks of Wheels in Heaven that had Life in them, and moved of themselves, or stood still, in Conformity with the Cherubims, whom they accompanied.

There is no Question but *Milton* had this Circumstance in his Thoughts, because in the following Book he describes the Chariot of the *Messiah* with *living* Wheels, according to the Plan in *Ezekiel's* Vision.

> . . . *Forth rush'd with whirlwind sound*
> *The Chariot of Paternal Deity,*
> *Flashing thick flames, wheel within wheel undrawn,*
> *It self instinct with Spirit* . . .

I question not but *Bossu*, and the two *Daciers*, who are for vindicating every Thing that is censured in *Homer*, by something parallel in Holy Writ, would have been very well pleased had they thought of confronting *Vulcan's* *Tripodes* with *Ezekiel's* Wheels.

Raphael's Descent to the Earth, with the Figure of his Person, is represented in very lively Colours. Several of the *French*, *Italian*, and *English* Poets have given a Loose to their Imaginations in the Description of Angels: But I do not remember to have met with any so finely drawn, and so conformable to the Notions which are given of them in Scripture, as this in *Milton*. After having set him forth in all his heavenly Plumage, and represented him as alighting upon the Earth, the Poet concludes his Description with a Circumstance, which is altogether new, and imagined with the greatest Strength of Fancy.

> . . . *Like* Maia's *Son he stood*
> *And shook his plumes, that Heav'nly fragrance fill'd*
> *The Circuit wide.* . . .

Raphael's Reception by the Guardian Angels; his passing through the Wilderness of Sweets; his distant Appearance to *Adam*, have all the Graces that Poetry is capable of bestowing. The Author afterwards gives us a particular Description of *Eve* in her Domestick Employments.

> *So saying, with dispatchful looks in haste*
> *She turns, on hospitable thoughts intent,*
> *What choice to chuse for delicacy best,*
> *What order, so contriv'd as not to mix*
> *Tastes, not well joyn'd inelegant, but bring*
> *Taste after taste, upheld with kindliest change;*
> *Bestirs her then, &c. . . .*

Though in this, and other Parts of the same Book, the Subject is only the Housewifry of our First Parent, it is set off with so many pleasing Images and strong Expressions, as make it none of the least agreeable Parts in this Divine Work.

The natural Majesty of *Adam*, and at the same Time his submissive Behaviour to the superior Being, who had vouchsafed to be his Guest; the solemn Hail which the Angel bestows upon the Mother of Mankind, with the Figure of *Eve* ministring at the Table, are Circumstances which deserve to be admired.

Raphael's Behaviour is every Way suitable to the Dignity of his Nature, and to that Character of a sociable Spirit, with which the Author has so judiciously introduced him. He had received Instructions to converse with *Adam*, as one Friend converses with another, and to warn him of the Enemy, who was contriving his Destruction: Accordingly he is represented as sitting down at Table with *Adam*, and eating of the Fruits of *Paradise*. The Occasion naturally leads him to his Discourse on the Food of Angels. After having thus entered into Conversation with Man upon more indifferent Subjects, he warns him of his Obedience, and makes a natural Transition to the History of that fallen Angel, who was employed in the Circumvention of our first Parents.

Had I followed Monsieur *Bossu*'s Method, in my first Paper on *Milton*, I should have dated the Action of *Paradise Lost* from the Beginning of *Raphael*'s Speech in this Book, as he supposes the Action of the *Aeneid* to begin in the second Book of that Poem. I could allege many Reasons for my drawing the Action of the *Aeneid* rather from its immediate Beginning in the first Book, than from its remote Beginning in the second, and shew why I have considered the sacking of *Troy* as an *Episode*, according to the common Acceptation of that Word. But as this would be a dry unentertaining Piece of Criticism, and perhaps unnecessary to those who have read my first Paper, I shall not enlarge upon it. Whichever of the Notions be true, the Unity of *Milton*'s Action is preserved according to either of them; whether we consider the Fall of Man in its immediate Beginning, or proceeding from the Resolutions taken in the infernal Council, or in its more remote Beginning, or proceeding from the first Revolt of the Angels in Heaven. The Occasion which *Milton* assigns for this Revolt, as it is founded on Hints in Holy Writ, and on the Opinion of some great Writers, so it was the most proper that the Poet could have made use of.

The Revolt in Heaven is described with great Force of Imagination and a fine Variety of Circumstances.   The learned Reader cannot but be pleased with the Poet's Imitation of *Homer* in the last of the following Lines.

> *At length into the limits of the North*
> *They came, and Satan took his Royal Seat*
> *High on a Hill, far blazing, as a Mount*
> *Rais'd on a Mount, with Pyramids and Tow'rs*
> *From Diamond Quarries hewn, and Rocks of Gold,*
> *The Palace of great* Lucifer, *(so call*
> *That Structure in the Dialect of Men*
> *Interpreted)* . . .

Homer mentions Persons and Things, which he tells us in the Language of the Gods are call'd by different Names from those they go by in the Language of Men.   *Milton* has imitated him with his usual Judgment in this particular Place, wherein he has likewise the Authority of Scripture to justify him.   The Part of *Abdiel*, who was the only Spirit that in this infinite Host of Angels preserved his Allegiance to his Maker, exhibits to us a noble Moral of religious Singularity.   The Zeal of the Seraphim breaks forth in a becoming Warmth of Sentiments and Expressions, as the Character which is given us of him denotes that generous Scorn and Intrepidity which attends heroick Virtue.   The Author doubtless designed it as a Pattern to those who live among Mankind in their present State of Degeneracy and Corruption.

> *So spake the Seraph* Abdiel *faithful found,*
> *Among the faithless, faithful only he;*
> *Among innumerable false, unmov'd,*
> *Unshaken, unseduc'd, unterrify'd;*
> *His Loyalty he kept, his Love, his Zeal:*
> *Nor Number, nor Example with him wrought*
> *To swerve from Truth, or change his constant mind*
> *Though single.   From amidst them forth he pass'd,*
> *Long Way through hostile Scorn, which he sustain'd*
> *Superior, nor of Violence fear'd ought;*
> *And with retorted Scorn his Back he turn'd*
> *On those proud Tow'rs to swift Destruction doom'd.*

L

No. 328.

[ADDISON.]   Monday, March 17.

Nullum a labore me reclinat otium.—Hor.

'Mr. SPECTATOR,

As I believe this is the first Complaint that ever was made to
you of this Nature, so you are the first Person I ever could prevail upon my self to lay it before.   When I tell you I have a
healthy vigorous Constitution, a plentiful Estate, no inordinate
Desires, and am married to a very virtuous lovely Woman, who
neither wants Wit nor good Nature, and by whom I have
a numerous Offspring to perpetuate my Family, you will
naturally conclude me a happy Man.   But, notwithstanding
these promising Appearances, I am so far from it, that the
Prospect of being ruin'd and undone, by a Sort of Extravagance
which of late Years is in a less Degree crept into every fashionable Family, deprives me of all the Comforts of my Life, and
renders me the most anxious miserable Man on Earth.   My
Wife, who was the only Child and darling Care of an indulgent
Mother, employ'd her early Years in learning all those Accomplishments we generally understand by good breeding and a
polite Education.   She sings, dances, plays on the Lute and
Harpsichord, paints prettily, is a perfect Mistress of the *French*
Tongue, and has made a considerable Progress in *Italian*.   She
is besides excellently skill'd in all domestick Sciences, as Preserving, Pickling, Pastry, making Wines of Fruits of our own
Growth, Embroidering, and Needle-works of every Kind.
Hitherto you will be apt to think there is very little Cause of
Complaint; but suspend your Opinion till I have further explain'd my self, and then I make no Question you will come over
to mine.   You are not to imagine I find Fault that she either
possesses or takes Delight in the Exercise of those Qualifications
I just now mention'd; 'tis the immoderate Fondness she has
to them that I lament, and that what is only design'd for the
innocent Amusement and Recreation of Life, is become the
whole Business and Study of hers.   The six Months we are in
Town (for the Year is equally divided between that and the
Country) from almost Break of Day 'till Noon, the whole
Morning is laid out in practising with her several Masters; and
to make up the Losses occasion'd by her Absence in Summer,
every Day in the Week their Attendance is requir'd; and as
they are all People eminent in their Professions, their Skill and
Time must be recompensed accordingly: So how far these
Articles extend, I leave you to judge.   Limning, one would
think, is no expensive Diversion, but as she manages the

Matter, 'tis a very considerable Addition to her Disbursements; which you will easily believe when you know she paints Fans for all her female Acquaintance, and draws all her Relations' Pictures in Miniature; the first must be mounted by no Body but *Colmar*, and the other set by no Body but *Charles Mather*. What follows is still much worse than the former; for, as I told you, she is a great Artist at her Needle, 'tis incredible what Sums she expends in Embroidery: For besides what is appropriated to her personal Use, as Mantuas, Petticoats, Stomachers, Handkerchiefs, Purses, Pin-cushions, and Working-Aprons, she keeps four *French* Protestants continually employ'd in making divers Pieces of superfluous Furniture, as Quilts, Toilets, Hangings for Closets, Beds, Window-Curtains, easy Chairs, and Tabourets: Nor have I any Hopes of ever reclaiming her from this Extravagance, while she obstinately persists in thinking it a notable Piece of good Housewifry, because they are made at Home, and she has had some Share in the Performance. There would be no End of relating to you the Particulars of the annual Charge in furnishing her Store-room with a Profusion of Pickles and Preserves; for she is not contented with having every Thing, unless it be done every Way, in which she consults an hereditary Book of Receipts; for her female Ancestors have been always fam'd for good Housewifry, one of whom is made immortal by giving her Name to an Eye-Water and two Sorts of Puddings. I cannot undertake to recite all her medicinal Preparations, as Salves, Cerecloths, Powders, Confects, Cordials, Ratafia, Persico, Orange-flower, and Cherry-brandy, together with innumerable Sorts of simple Waters. But there is nothing I lay so much to Heart, as that detestable Catalogue of counterfeit Wines, which derive their Names from the Fruits, Herbs, or Trees of whose Juices they are chiefly compounded: They are loathsome to the Taste, and pernicious to the Health; and as they seldom survive the Year, and then are thrown away, under a false Pretence of Frugality, I may affirm they stand me in more than if I entertain'd all our Visiters with the best Burgundy and Champaign. Coffee, Chocolate, Green, Imperial, Peco, and Bohea Tea seem to be Trifles; but when the proper Appurtenances of the Tea-Table are added, they swell the Account higher than one would imagine. I cannot conclude without doing her Justice in one Article; where her Frugality is so remarkable I must not deny her the Merit of it, and that is in Relation to her Children, who are all confin'd, both Boys and Girls, to one large Room in the remotest Part of the House, with Bolts on the Doors, and Barrs to the Windows, under the Care and Tuition of an old Woman who had been dry Nurse to her Grandmother. This is their Residence all the Year round; and as they are never allow'd to appear, she prudently thinks it needless to be at any Expence in Apparel or Learning. Her eldest Daughter to this Day would have neither read nor writ, if it had not been for the Butler, who being the Son of a Country Attorney, has taught her such a Hand as is generally used for engrossing Bills in Chancery. By this Time I have sufficiently tried your Patience with my domestick Grievances; which I hope you will agree could not well be contain'd in a narrower Compass, when you consider what a Paradox I undertook to maintain in the Beginning of my Epistle, and which manifestly appears to be but too melancholy a Truth. And now I heartily wish the Relation I have given of my Misfortunes may be of Use and Benefit to the Publick. By the Example I have set before them, the truly virtuous Wives may learn to avoid those Errors which have so unhappily misled mine, and which are visibly these three. First, In mistaking the proper Objects of her Esteem, and fixing her Affections upon such Things as are only the Trappings and Decorations of her Sex. Secondly, In not distinguishing what becomes the different Stages of Life. And, Lastly, The Abuse and Corruption of some excellent Qualities, which, if circumscrib'd within just Bounds, would have been the Blessings and Prosperity of her Family, but by a vicious Extream are like to be the Bane and Destruction of it.' T

No. 329.
[ADDISON.]   Tuesday, March 18, 1712.

Ire tamen restat, Numa quo devenit & Ancus.—Hor.

My Friend Sir ROGER DE COVERLY told me t'other Night, that he had been reading my Paper upon *Westminster-Abbey*, in which, says he, there are a great many ingenious Fancies. He told me at the same Time, that he observed I had promised another Paper upon *the Tombs,* and that he should be glad to go and see them with me, not having visited them since he had read History. I could not at first imagine how this came into the Knight's Head, till I recollected that he had been very busy all last Summer upon *Baker*'s Chronicle, which he has quoted several Times in his Disputes with Sir ANDREW FREEPORT since his last coming to Town. Accordingly I promised to call upon him the next Morning, that we might go together to the *Abbey*.

I found the Knight under his Butler's Hands, who always shaves him. He was no sooner dressed, than he called for a

Glass of the Widow *Trueby*'s Water, which he told me he always
drank before he went abroad. He recommended to me a
Dram of it at the same Time, with so much Heartiness, that I
could not forbear drinking it. As soon as I had got it down I
found it very unpalatable, upon which the Knight observing
that I had made several wry Faces, told me that he knew I
should not like it at first, but that it was the best Thing in the
World against the Stone or Gravel.

I could have wished indeed that he had acquainted me with
the Virtues of it sooner; but it was too late to complain, and I
knew what he had done was out of Good-will. Sir ROGER told
me further, that he looked upon it to be very good for a Man
whilst he staid in Town, to keep off Infection, and that he got
together a Quantity of it upon the first News of the Sickness
being at *Dantzick :* When of a sudden turning short to one of
his Servants, who stood behind him, he bid him call an Hackney-Coach, and take Care it was an elderly Man that drove it.

He then resumed his Discourse upon Mrs. *Trueby*'s Water,
telling me that the Widow *Trueby* was one who did more Good
than all the Doctors and Apothecaries in the County: That she
distilled every poppy that grew within five Miles of her, that she
distributed her Water *gratis* among all Sorts of People; to which
the Knight added, that she had a very great Jointure, and that
the whole Country would fain have it a Match between him
and her; and truly, says Sir ROGER, if I had not been engaged,
perhaps I could not have done better.

His Discourse was broken off by his Man's telling him he had
called a Coach. Upon our going to it, after having cast his
Eye upon the Wheels, he asked the Coachman if his Axle-tree
was good; upon the Fellow's telling him he would warrant it,
the Knight turned to me, told me he looked like an honest
Man, and went in without further Ceremony.

We had not gone far, when Sir ROGER popping out his Head,
called the Coachman down from his Box, and upon his presenting himself at the Window, asked him if he smoaked; as I
was considering what this would end in, he bid him stop by the
Way at any good Tobacconist's, and take in a Roll of their
best *Virginia*. Nothing material happen'd in the remaining
Part of our Journey, till we were set down at the West-End
of the *Abbey*.

As we went up the Body of the Church, the Knight pointed
at the Trophies upon one of the new Monuments, and cry'd
out, A brave Man I warrant him. Passing afterwards by Sir
Cloudsly Shovel, he flung his Hand that Way, and cry'd Sir
Cloudsly Shovel! a very gallant Man! As we stood before
Busby's Tomb, the Knight utter'd himself again after the same

Manner, Dr. *Busby,* a great Man, he whipp'd my Grandfather, a very great Man. I should have gone to him my self, if I had not been a Blockhead, a very great Man!

We were immediately conducted into the little Chappel on the Right Hand. Sir ROGER planting himself at our Historian's Elbow, was very attentive to every Thing he said, particularly to the Account he gave us of the Lord who had cut off the King of *Morocco*'s Head. Among several other Figures, he was very well pleased to see the Statesman *Cecil* upon his Knees; and, concluding them all to be great Men, was conducted to the Figure which represents that Martyr to good Housewifry, who died by the Prick of a Needle. Upon our Interpreter's telling us, that she was a Maid of Honour to Queen *Elizabeth,* the Knight was very inquisitive into her Name and Family, and, after having regarded her Finger for some Time, I wonder, says he, that Sir *Richard Baker* has said Nothing of her in his Chronicle.

We were then convey'd to the two Coronation Chairs, where my old Friend, after having heard that the Stone underneath the most ancient of them, which was brought from *Scotland,* was called *Jacob's Pillar,* sat himself down in the Chair, and looking like the Figure of an old *Gothic* King, asked our Interpreter, What Authority they had to say, that *Jacob* had ever been in *Scotland?* The Fellow, instead of returning him an Answer, told him, that he hoped his Honour would pay his Forfeit. I could observe Sir ROGER a little ruffled upon being thus trapanned; but our Guide not insisting upon his Demand, the Knight soon recovered his good Humour, and whispered in my Ear, that if WILL WIMBLE were with us, and saw those two Chairs, it would go hard but he would get a Tobacco-Stopper out of one or t'other of them.

Sir ROGER, in the next Place, laid his Hand upon *Edward* III's Sword, and leaning upon the Pommel of it, gave us the whole History of the *Black Prince*; concluding, that in Sir *Richard Baker's* Opinion, *Edward* the Third was one of the greatest Princes that ever sate upon the *English* Throne.

We were then shewn *Edward* the Confessor's Tomb; upon which Sir ROGER acquainted us, that he was the first who touched for the Evil; and afterwards *Henry* the Fourth's, upon which he shook his Head, and told us, there was fine Reading in the Casualties of that Reign.

Our Conductor then pointed to that Monument, where there is the Figure of one of our *English* Kings without an Head; and upon giving us to know, that the Head, which was of beaten Silver, had been stolen away several Years since: Some Whig, I warrant you, says Sir ROGER; You ought to lock up your Kings better: They will carry off the Body too, if you don't take Care.

The glorious Names of *Henry* the Fifth and Queen *Elizabeth* gave the Knight great Opportunities of shining, and of doing Justice to Sir *Richard Baker*, who, as our Knight observed with some Surprize, had a great many Kings in him, whose Monuments he had not seen in the Abbey.

For my own Part, I could not but be pleased to see the Knight shew such an honest Passion for the Glory of his Country, and such a respectful Gratitude to the Memory of its Princes.

I must not omit, that the Benevolence of my good old Friend, which flows out towards every one he converses with, made him very kind to our Interpreter, whom he looked upon as an extraordinary Man; for which Reason he shook him by the Hand at Parting, telling him, that he should be very glad to see him at his Lodgings in *Norfolk-Buildings*, and talk over these Matters with him more at Leisure.   L

No. 330.
[STEELE.]   Wednesday, March 19.

Maxima debetur pueris reverentia . . .—Juv.

THE following Letters, written by two very considerate Correspondents, both under twenty Years of Age, are very good Arguments of the Necessity of taking into Consideration the many Incidents which affect the Education of Youth.

' *Sir*,

I have long expected, that in the Course of your Observations upon the several Parts of humane Life, you would one Time or other fall upon a Subject, which, since you have not, I take the Liberty to recommend to you. What I mean is the Patronage of young modest Men to such as are able to countenance and introduce them into the World. For Want of such Assistances, a Youth of Merit languishes in Obscurity or Poverty, when his Circumstances are low, and runs into Riot and Excess when his Fortunes are plentiful. I cannot make my self better understood, than by sending you an History of my self, which I shall desire you to insert in your Paper, it being the only Way I have of expressing my Gratitude for the highest Obligations imaginable.

I am the Son of a Merchant of the City of *London*, who, by many Losses, was reduced from a very luxuriant Trade and Credit to very narrow Circumstances, in Comparison to that of his former Abundance. This took away the Vigour of his Mind, and all Manner of Attention to a Fortune, which he now thought desperate, insomuch, that he died without a Will, having before buried my Mother in the Midst of his other Misfortunes. I was sixteen Years of Age when I lost my Father, and an Estate of 200*l.* a Year came into my Possession, without Friend or Guardian to instruct me in the Management or Enjoyment of it. The natural Consequence of this, was, (though I wanted no Director, and soon had Fellows who found me out for a smart young Gentleman, and led me into all the Debaucheries of which I was capable) that my Companions and I could not well be supplied without running in Debt, which I did very frankly 'till I was arrested, and conveyed with a Guard strong enough for the most desperate Assassine, to a Bayliff's House, where I lay four Days, surrounded with very merry, but not very agreeable Company. As soon as I had extricated my self from this shameful Confinement, I reflected upon it with so much Horror, that I deserted all my old Acquaintance, and took Chambers in an Inn of Court, with a Resolution to study the Law with all possible Application. But I trifled away a whole Year in looking over a thousand Intricacies, without Friend to apply to in any Case of Doubt; so that I only lived there among Men, as little Children are sent to School before they are capable of Improvement, only to be out of Harm's Way. In the Midst of this State of Suspense, not knowing how to dispose of my self, I was sought for by a Relation of mine, who, upon observing a good Inclination in me, used me with great Familiarity, and carried me to his Seat in the Country. When I came there he introduced me to all the good Company in the County, and the great Obligation I have to him for this kind Notice, and Residence with him ever since, has made so strong an Impression upon me, that he has an Authority of a Father over me, founded upon the Love of a Brother. I have a good Study of Books, a good Stable of Horses always at my Command; and though I am not now quite eighteen Years of Age, familiar Converse on his Part, and a strong Inclination to exert my self on mine, have had an Effect upon me that makes me acceptable wherever I go. Thus, Mr SPECTATOR, by this Gentleman's Favour and Patronage, it is my own Fault if I am not wiser and richer every Day I live. I speak this, as well by subscribing the initial Letters of my Name to thank him, as to incite others to an Imitation of his Virtue. It would be a worthy Work to shew what great Charities are to be done without Expence, and how many noble Actions are lost, out of Inadvertency in Persons capable of performing them, if they were put in Mind

of it. If a Gentleman of Figure in a County would make his
Family a Pattern of Sobriety, good Sense, and Breeding, and
would kindly endeavour to influence the Education and growing Prospects of the younger Gentry about him, I am apt to
believe it would save him a great Deal of stale Beer on a
publick Occasion, and render him the Leader of his Country
from their Gratitude to him, instead of being a Slave to their
Riots and Tumults in order to be made their Representative.
The same Thing might be recommended to all who have made
any Progress in any Parts of Knowledge, or arrived at any
Degree in a Profession; others may gain Preferments and
Fortunes from their Patrons, but I have, I hope, received from
mine good Habits and Virtues. I repeat to you, Sir, my
Request to print this, in Return for all the Evil an helpless
Orphan shall ever escape, and all the good he shall receive in
this Life; both which are wholly owing to this Gentleman's
Favour to,

> *Sir,*
>
> *Your most obedient humble Servant,*
>
> S. P.'

'*Mr.* SPECTATOR,

I am a Lad of about fourteen. I find a mighty Pleasure in
Learning. I have been at the *Latin* School four Years. I
don't know I ever play'd Truant, or neglected any Task my
Master set me in my Life. I think on what I read in School
as I go home at Noon and Night, and so intently, that I have
often gone half a Mile out of my Way, not minding whither I
went. Our Maid tells me, she often hears me talk *Latin* in my
Sleep. And I dream, two or three Nights in the Week I am
reading *Juvenal* and *Homer*. My Master seems as well pleased
with my Performances as any Boy's in the same Class. I
think, if I know my own Mind, I would chuse rather to be a
Scholar, than a Prince without Learning. I have a very good
affectionate Father; but, though very rich, yet so mighty near,
that he thinks much of the Charges of my Education. He
often tells me, he believes my Schooling will ruin him; that I
cost him God knows what in Books. I tremble to tell him I
want one. I am forced to keep my Pocket-Money, and lay it
out for a Book now and then that he don't know of. He has
ordered my Master to buy no more Books for me, but says he
will buy them himself. I asked him for *Horace* t'other Day,
and he told me in a Passion, he did not believe I was fit for it,
but only my Master had a Mind to make him think I had got
a great Way in my Learning. I am sometimes a Month
behind other Boys in getting the Books my Master gives
Orders for. All the Boys in the School, but I, have the classick

Authors *in usum Delphini*, gilt and letter'd on the Back. My Father is often reckoning up how long I have been at School, and tells me he fears I do little Good. My Father's Carriage so discourages me, that he makes me grow dull and melancholy. My Master wonders what is the Matter with me: I am afraid to tell him; for he is a Man that loves to encourage Learning, and would be apt to chide my Father, and, not knowing my Father's Temper, may make him worse. Sir, if you have any Love for Learning, I beg you would give me some Instructions in this Case, and perswade Parents to encourage their Children when they find them diligent and desirous of Learning. I have heard some Parents say, they would do any Thing for their Children, if they would but mind their Learning. I would be glad to be in their Place. Dear Sir, pardon my Boldness. If you will but consider and pity my Case, I will pray for your Prosperity as long as I live.

  London, Mar.   *Your humble Servant,*
T   2, 1711.   James Discipulus.'

No. 331.
[BUDGELL.]   Thursday, March 20.

  . . . *Stolidam praebet tibi vellere barbam.*—Pers.

WHEN I was last with my Friend Sir ROGER, in *Westminster-Abbey*, I observed that he stood longer than ordinary before the Bust of a venerable old Man. I was at a Loss to guess the Reason of it, when after some Time he pointed to the Figure, and asked me if I did not think that our Forefathers looked much wiser in their Beards than we do without them. For my Part, says he, when I am walking in my Gallery in the Country, and see my Ancestors, who many of them died before they were of my Age, I cannot forbear regarding them as so many old Patriarchs, and at the same Time looking upon my self as an idle smock-faced young Fellow. I love to see your *Abrahams*, your *Isaacs*, and your *Jacobs*, as we have them in old Pieces of Tapistry, with Beards below their Girdles, that cover Half the Hangings. The Knight added, if I would recommend Beards in one of my Papers, and endeavour to restore human Faces to their ancient Dignity, that upon a Month's Warning he would undertake to lead up the Fashion himself in a Pair of Whiskers.

I smiled at my Friend's Fancy; but after we parted, could not forbear reflecting on the Metamorphoses our Faces have undergone in this Particular.

The Beard, conformable to the Notion of my Friend Sir

ROGER, was for many Ages looked upon as the Type of Wisdom. *Lucian* more than once rallies the Philosophers of his Time who endeavoured to rival one another in Beard; and represents a learned Man who stood for a Professorship in Philosophy, as unqualified for it by the Shortness of his Beard.

Aelian, in his Account of *Zoilus*, the pretended Critick, who wrote against *Homer* and *Plato*, and thought himself wiser than all who had gone before him, tells us that this *Zoilus* had a very long Beard that hung down upon his Breast, but no Hair upon his Head, which he always kept close shaved; regarding, it seems, the Hairs of his Head as so many Suckers, which if they had been suffered to grow, might have drawn away the Nourishment from his Chin, and by that Means have starved his Beard.

I have read somewhere that one of the Popes refused to accept an Edition of a Saint's Works, which were presented to him, because the Saint, in his Effigies before the Book, was drawn without a Beard.

We see by these Instances what Homage the World has formerly paid to Beards; and that a Barber was not then allowed to make those Depredations on the Faces of the Learned, which have been permitted him of later Years.

Accordingly several wise Nations have been so extreamly jealous of the least Ruffle offered to their Beards, that they seem to have fix'd the Point of Honour principally in that Part. The *Spaniards* were wonderfully tender in this Particular. Don *Quevedo*, in his third Vision on the last Judgment, has carried the Humour very far, when he tells us that one of his vain-glorious Countrymen, after having received Sentence, was taken into Custody by a Couple of Evil Spirits; but that his Guides happening to disorder his Mustachoes, they were forced to recompose them with a Pair of Curling-Irons before they could get him to file off.

If we look into the History of our own Nation, we shall find that the Beard flourished in the *Saxon* Heptarchy, but was very much discouraged under the *Norman* Line. It shot out, however, from Time to Time in several Reigns under different Shapes. The last Effort it made seems to have been in Queen *Mary*'s Days, as the curious Reader may find, if he pleases to peruse the Figures of Cardinal *Poole* and Bishop *Gardiner*, tho' at the same Time, I think, it may be questioned, if Zeal against Popery has not induced our Protestant Painters to extend the Beards of these two Persecutors beyond their natural Dimensions, in order to make them appear the more terrible.

I find but few Beards worth taking Notice of in the Reign of King *James* the First.

During the Civil Wars there appeared one, which makes too great a Figure in Story to be passed over in Silence; I mean that of the redoubted *Hudibras,* an Account of which *Butler* has transmitted to Posterity in the following Lines:

> *His tawny Beard was th' equal Grace,*
> *Both of his Wisdom, and his Face.*
> *In Cut and Dye so like a Tyle,*
> *A sudden View it would beguile.*
> *The upper Part thereof was Whey,*
> *The nether Orange mixt with Grey.*

The Whisker continued for some Time among us after the Expiration of Beards; but this is a Subject which I shall not here enter upon, having discussed it at large in a distinct Treatise, which I keep by me in Manuscript, upon the *Mustachoe.*

If my Friend Sir ROGER's Project, of introducing Beards, should take Effect, I fear the Luxury of the present Age would make it a very expensive Fashion. There is no Question but the Beaux would soon provide themselves with false ones of the lightest Colours, and the most immoderate Lengths. A fair Beard, of the Tapistry-Size Sir ROGER seems to approve, could not come under twenty Guineas. The famous Golden Beard of *Esculapius* would hardly be more valuable, than one made in the Extravagance of the Fashion.

Besides, we are not certain that the Ladies would not come into the Mode, when they take the Air on Horseback. They already appear in Hats and Feathers, Coats and Perriwigs; and I see no Reason why we may not suppose that they would have their *riding Beards* on the same Occasion.

I may give the Moral of this Discourse in another Paper. X

No. 332.
[STEELE.]   Friday, March 21.

> . . . *Minus aptus acutis*
> *Naribus horum hominum* . . .—Hor.

'*Dear Short-Face,*

IN your Speculation of *Wednesday* last, you have given us some Account of that worthy Society of Brutes the *Mohocks;* wherein you have particularly specified the ingenious Performances of the Lion-Tippers, the Dancing-Masters, and the Tumblers: But as you acknowledge you had not then a perfect History of the whole Club, you might very easily omit one of the most notable Species of it, the Sweaters, which may be reckon'd a Sort of Dancing-Masters too. It is, it seems, the Custom for Half a Dozen, or more, of these well-disposed Savages, as soon as they have inclosed the Person upon whom they design the Favour of a Sweat, to whip out their Swords, and holding them parallel to the Horizon, they describe a Sort of Magick Circle round about him with the Points. As soon as this Piece of Conjuration is perform'd, and the patient without Doubt already beginning to wax warm, to forward the Operation, that Member of the Circle towards whom he is so rude as to turn his Back first, runs his Sword directly into that Part of the Patient wherein School-boys are punished; and, as it is very natural to imagine this will soon make him tack about to some other Point, every Gentleman does himself the same Justice as often as he receives the Affront. After this Jigg has gone two or three Times round, and the Patient is thought to have sweat sufficiently, he is very handsomly rubb'd down by some Attendants, who carry with them Instruments for that Purpose, and so discharged. This Relation I had from a Friend of mine, who has lately been under this Discipline. He tells me he had the Honour to dance before the Emperor himself, not without the Applause and Acclamations both of his Imperial Majesty and the whole Ring; though, I dare say, neither I nor any of his Acquaintance ever dreamt he wou'd have merited any Reputation by his Activity.

I can assure you, Mr. Spec, I was very near being qualified to have given you a faithful and painful Account of this walking Bagnio, if I may so call it, my self: For going the other Night along *Fleet-street*, and having, out of Curiosity, just enter'd into Discourse with a wandering Female who was travelling the same Way, a Couple of Fellows advanced towards us, drew their Swords, and cry'd out to each other: A Sweat! a Sweat! Whereupon, suspecting they were some of the Ring-leaders of the Bagnio, I also drew my Sword, and demanded a Parley; but finding none would be granted me, and perceiving others behind them filing off with great Diligence to take me in Flank, I began to sweat for Fear of being forced to it; but very luckily betaking my self to a Pair of Heels, which I had good Reason to believe wou'd do me Justice, I instantly got Possession of a very snug Corner in a neighbouring Alley that lay in my Rear; which Post I maintained for above Half an Hour with great Firmness and Resolution, tho' not letting this Success so far overcome me, as to make me unmindful of the Circumspection that was necessary to be observed upon my advancing again towards the Street; by which Prudence and good Management I made a handsome and orderly Retreat, having suffer'd no other Damage in this Action than the Loss of my Baggage, and the Dislocation of one of my Shoe-heels, which last I am just now inform'd is in a fair way of Recovery. These Sweaters, by what I can learn from my Friend, and by as near a View as I was able to take of them my self, seem to me to have at present but a rude Kind of Discipline amongst them. It is probable, if you wou'd take a little Pains with them, they might be brought into better Order. But I 'll leave this to your own Discretion; and will only add, that if you think it worth while to insert this by Way of Caution to those who have a Mind to preserve their Skins whole from this Sort of Cupping, and tell them at the same Time the Hazard of treating with Night-walkers, you will perhaps oblige others, as well as

Your very humble Servant,

Jack Lightfoot.

P. S. My Friend will have me acquaint you, That though he would not willingly detract from the Merit of that extra-ordinary Strokes-man Mr. *Sprightly*, yet it is his real Opinion, that some of those Fellows who are employ'd as Rubbers to this new-fashion'd Bagnio, have struck as bold Strokes as ever he did in his Life.

I had sent this Four and twenty Hours sooner, if I had not had the Misfortune of being in a great Doubt about the Orthography of the Word Bagnio. I consulted several Dictionaries, but found no Relief; at last having Recourse both to the Bagnio in *Newgate-street* and to that in *Chancery-lane*, and finding the original Manuscripts upon the Sign-Posts of each to agree literally with my own Spelling, I return'd Home, full of Satisfaction, in order to dispatch this Epistle.'

'Mr. SPECTATOR,

As you have taken most of the Circumstances of Humane Life into your Consideration, we, the underwritten, thought it not improper for us also to represent to you our Condition. We are three Ladies who live in the Country, and the greatest Improvement we make is by Reading. We have taken a small Journal of our Lives, and find it extreamly opposite to your last *Tuesday*'s Speculation. We rise by Seven, and pass the Beginning of each Day in Devotion and looking into those Affairs that fall within the Occurrences of a retired Life; in the Afternoon we sometimes enjoy the Company of some Friend or Neighbour, or else work or read; at Night we retire to our Chambers, and take Leave of each other for the whole Night at Ten a Clock. We take particular Care never to be sick of a *Sunday*. *Mr.* SPECTATOR, We are all very good

Maids, but are ambitious of Characters which we think more laudable, that of being very good Wives. If any of your Correspondents enquire for a Spouse for an honest Country Gentleman, whose Estate is not dipped, and wants a Wife that can save half his Revenue, and yet make a better Figure than any of his Neighbours of the same Estate with finer bred Women; You shall have further Notice from,

> *Sir,*
>
> *Your courteous Readers,*
>
> Martha Busie.
> Deborah Thrifty.
> Alice Early.'

T

No. 333.
[ADDISON.]   Saturday, March 22.

> . . . *Vocat in certamina divos.*—Virg.

WE are now entering upon the Sixth Book of *Paradise Lost*, in which the Poet describes the Battel of Angels; having raised his Reader's Expectation, and prepar'd him for it by several Passages in the preceding Books. I omitted quoting these Passages in my Observations on the former Books, having purposely reserved them for the Opening of this, the Subject of which gave Occasion to them. The Author's Imagination was so inflamed with this great Scene of Action, that wherever he speaks of it, he rises, if possible, above himself. Thus where he mentions Satan in the Beginning of his Poem.

> . . . *Him the Almighty Power*
> *Hurl'd headlong flaming from th' Etherial Skie,*
> *With hideous ruin and combustion down*
> *To bottomless perdition, there to dwell*
> *In Adamantine Chains and Penal Fire,*
> *Who durst defie the Omnipotent to Arms.*

We have likewise several noble Hints of it in the Infernal Conference.

> *O Prince, O Chief of many throned Powers,*
> *That led th' imbattel'd Seraphim to War . . .*
> *Too well I see and rue the dire event,*
> *That with sad overthrow and foul defeat*
> *Hath lost us Heav'n, and all this mighty host*
> *In horrible destruction laid thus low. . . .*
> *But see the angry Victor hath recall'd*
> *His Ministers of vengeance and pursuit*
> *Back to the gates of Heav'n: The sulphurous hail*
> *Shot after us in Storm, o'erblown hath laid*

> *The fiery Surge, that from the Precipice*
> *Of Heav'n receiv'd us falling; and the Thunder,*
> *Wing'd with red lightning and impetuous rage,*
> *Perhaps hath spent his Shafts, and ceases now*
> *To bellow through the vast and boundless Deep.*

There are several other very sublime Images on the same Subject in the First Book, as also in the Second.

> *What when we fled amain, pursu'd and strook*
> *With Heav'n's afflicting Thunder, and besought*
> *The Deep to shelter us; this Hell then seem'd*
> *A refuge from those wounds.*

In short, the Poet never mentions any thing of this Battel but in such Images of Greatness and Terrour as are suitable to the Subject. Among several others, I cannot forbear quoting that Passage where the Power, who is describ'd as presiding over the Chaos, speaks in the Third Book.

> *Thus Satan; and him thus the Anarch old*
> *With faultring speech and visage incompos'd*
> *Answer'd, I know thee, stranger, who thou art,*
> *That mighty leading Angel, who of late*
> *Made head against Heaven's King, tho' overthrown.*
> *I saw and heard; for such a numerous Host*
> *Fled not in Silence, through the frighted Deep*
> *With ruin upon ruin, rout on rout,*
> *Confusion worse confounded; and Heaven's Gates*
> *Pour'd out by Millions her victorious Bands*
> *Pursuing.*

It required great Pregnancy of Invention, and Strength of Imagination, to fill this Battel with such Circumstances as should raise and astonish the Mind of the Reader; and, at the same time, an Exactness of Judgment to avoid every thing that might appear light or trivial. Those who look into *Homer*, are surpriz'd to find his Battels still rising one above another, and improving in Horrour, to the Conclusion of the *Iliad*. *Milton's* Fight of Angels is wrought up with the same Beauty. It is usher'd in with such Signs of Wrath as are suitable to Omnipotence incensed. The first Engagement is carried on under a Cope of Fire, occasion'd by the Flights of innumerable burning Darts and Arrows which are discharged from either Host. The second Onset is still more terrible, as it is filled with those artificial Thunders, which seem to make the Victory doubtful, and produce a kind of Consternation even in the good Angels. This is follow'd by the tearing up of Mountains and Promontories; till, in the last Place, the Messiah comes forth in the Fulness of Majesty and Terrour. The Pomp of his Appearance, amidst the Roarings of his

Thunders, the Flashes of his Lightnings, and the Noise of his Chariot-Wheels, is described with the utmost Flights of Humane Imagination.

There is nothing in the first and last Day's Engagement which does not appear natural, and agreeable enough to the ideas most Readers would conceive of a Fight between two Armies of Angels.

The second Day's Engagement is apt to startle an Imagination, which has not been raised and qualified for such a Description, by the Reading of the ancient Poets, and of *Homer* in particular.   It was certainly a very bold Thought in our Author, to ascribe the first Use of Artillery to the Rebel Angels.   But as such a pernicious Invention may be well supposed to have proceeded from such Authors, so it entered very properly into the Thoughts of that Being, who is all along described as aspiring to the Majesty of his Maker.   Such Engines were the only Instruments he could have made use of to imitate those Thunders, that in all Poetry, both Sacred and Prophane, are represented as the Arms of the Almighty. The Tearing up the Hills was not altogether so daring a Thought as the former.   We are, in some measure, prepared for such an Incident by the Description of the Gyants' War, which we meet with among the ancient Poets.   What still made this Circumstance the more proper for the Poet's Use, is the Opinion of many Learned Men, that the Fable of the Gyants' War, which makes so great a Noise in Antiquity, and gave Birth to the sublimest Description in *Hesiod*'s Works, was an Allegory founded upon this very Tradition of a Fight between the good and bad Angels.

It may, perhaps, be worth while to consider with what Judgment *Milton*, in this Narration, has avoided every Thing that is mean and trivial in the Descriptions of the *Latin* and *Greek* Poets; and, at the same time, improv'd every great Hint which he met with in their Works upon this Subject. *Homer* in that Passage, which *Longinus* has celebrated for its Sublimeness, and which *Virgil* and *Ovid* have copied after him, tells us, that the Gyants threw *Ossa* upon *Olympus*, and *Pelion* upon *Ossa*.   He adds an Epithet to *Pelion* (εἰνοσίφυλλον) which very much swells the Idea, by bringing up to the Reader's Imagination all the Woods that grew upon it.   There is further a great Beauty in his singling out by Name these three remarkable Mountains, so well known to the *Greeks*. This last is such a Beauty as the Scene of *Milton*'s War could not possibly furnish him with.   *Claudian*, in his Fragment upon the Gyants' War, has given full Scope to that Wildness of Imagination which was natural to him.   He tells us, that

the Gyants tore up whole Islands by the Roots, and threw them
at the Gods. He describes one of them in particular taking
up *Lemnos* in his Arms, and whirling it to the Skies, with all
Vulcan's Shop in the midst of it.   Another tears up Mount
Ida, with the River *Enipeus*, which ran down the Sides of it;
but the Poet, not content to describe him with this Mountain
upon his Shoulders, tells us that the River flow'd down his
Back, as he held it up in that Posture.   It is visible to every
judicious Reader, that such Ideas savour more of Burlesque
than of the Sublime.   They proceed from a Wantonness of
Imagination, and rather divert the Mind than astonish it.
Milton has taken every thing that is Sublime in these several
Passages, and composes out of them the following great Image.

> *From their Foundations loosning to and fro*
> *They pluck'd the seated Hills with all their load,*
> *Rocks, Waters, Woods, and by the shaggy tops*
> *Up-lifting, bore them in their Hands.*

We have the full Majesty of *Homer* in this short Description, improved by the Imagination of *Claudian*, without its
Puerilities.

I need not point out the Description of the fallen Angels
seeing the Promontories hanging over their Heads in such a
dreadful Manner, with the other numberless Beauties in this
Book, which are so conspicuous, that they cannot escape the
Notice of the most ordinary Reader.

There are indeed so many wonderful Stroaks of Poetry in
this Book, and such a Variety of sublime Ideas, that it would
have been impossible to have given them a Place within the
Bounds of this Paper.   Besides that, I find it in a great measure
done to my Hand at the End of my Lord *Roscommon*'s Essay
on translated Poetry.   I shall refer my Reader thither for
some of the Master-Stroaks in the Sixth Book of *Paradise Lost*,
though at the same time there are many others which that
noble Author has not taken notice of.

Milton, notwithstanding the sublime Genius he was Master
of, has in this Book drawn to his Assistance all the Helps he
could meet with among the ancient Poets.   The Sword of
Michael, which makes so great a Havock among the bad
Angels, was given him, we are told, out of the Armory of God.

> . . . *But the Sword*
> *Of* Michael *from the Armory of God*
> *Was giv'n him temper'd so, that neither keen*
> *Nor solid might resist that edge: it met*
> *The Sword of* Satan *with steep force to smite*
> *Descending, and in half cut sheere;* . . .

This Passage is a Copy of that in *Virgil*, wherein the Poet tells us, that the Sword of *Aeneas*, which was given him by a Deity, broke into Pieces the Sword of *Turnus*, which came from a mortal Forge. As the Moral in this Place is Divine, so by the way we may observe, that the bestowing on a Man who is favour'd by Heaven such an Allegorical Weapon, is very conformable to the old Eastern Way of Thinking. Not only *Homer* has made use of it, but we find the *Jewish* Hero in the Book of *Maccabees*, who had fought the Battels of the chosen People with so much Glory and Success, receiving in his Dream a Sword from the Hand of the Prophet *Jeremiah*. The following Passage, wherein Satan is described as wounded by the Sword of *Michael*, is in Imitation of *Homer*.

> *The griding Sword with discontinuous wound*
> *Pass'd through him; but th' Ethereal substance closed,*
> *Not long divisible; and from the gash*
> *A stream of Nectarous humour issuing flow'd*
> *Sanguin, such as celestial Spirits may bleed,*
> *And all his Armour stain'd . . .*

Homer tells us in the same manner, that upon *Diomedes* wounding the Gods, there flow'd from the Wound an *Ichor*, or pure kind of Blood, which was not bred from mortal Viands; and that tho' the Pain was exquisitely great, the Wound soon closed up and healed in those Beings who are vested with Immortality.

I question not but *Milton* in his Description of his furious *Moloch* flying from the Battel, and bellowing with the Wound he had received, had his Eye on *Mars* in the *Iliad*, who, upon his being wounded, is represented as retiring out of the Fight, and making an Outcry louder than that of a whole Army when it begins the Charge. *Homer* adds, that the *Greeks* and *Trojans* who were engaged in a general Battel, were terrified on each Side with the bellowing of this wounded Deity. The Reader will easily observe how *Milton* has kept all the Horrour of this Image without running into the Ridicule of it.

> *. . . Where the might of* Gabriel *fought,*
> *And with fierce Ensigns pierc'd the deep array*
> *Of* Moloc, *furious King, who him defy'd,*
> *And at his Chariot wheels to drag him bound*
> *Threaten'd, nor from the Holy One of Heav'n*
> *Refrain'd his tongue blasphemous; but anon*
> *Down cloven to the waste, with shatter'd Arms*
> *And uncouth pain fled bellowing. . . .*

Milton has likewise raised his Description in this Book with many Images taken out of the Poetical Parts of Scripture. The

Messiah's Chariot, as I have before taken Notice, is form'd upon a Vision of *Ezekiel*, who, as *Grotius* observes, has very much in him of *Homer*'s Spirit in the Poetical Parts of his Prophecy.

The following Lines in that glorious Commission which is given the Messiah to extirpate the Host of Rebel Angels, is drawn from a sublime Passage in the Psalms.

> *Go then thou mightiest in thy Father's might,*
> *Ascend my Chariot, guide the rapid wheels*
> *That shake Heaven's basis, bring forth all my War,*
> *My Bow, my Thunder, my almighty Arms,*
> *Gird on thy Sword on thy puissant Thigh.*

The Reader will easily discover many other Stroaks of the same Nature.

There is no question but *Milton* had heated his Imagination with the Fight of the Gods in *Homer*, before he entered upon this Engagement of the Angels. *Homer* there gives us a Scene of Men, Heroes, and Gods mixed together in Battel. *Mars* animates the contending Armies, and lifts up his Voice in such a manner, that it is heard distinctly amidst all the Shouts and Confusion of the Fight. *Jupiter* at the same time thunders over their Heads; while *Neptune* raises such a Tempest that the whole Field of Battel and all the Tops of the Mountains, shake about them. The Poet tells us, that *Pluto* himself, whose Habitation was in the very Center of the Earth, was so affrighted at the Shock, that he leapt from his Throne. *Homer* afterwards describes *Vulcan* as pouring down a Storm of Fire upon the River *Xanthus*, and *Minerva* as throwing a Rock at *Mars*; who, he tells us, covered seven Acres in his Fall.

As *Homer* has introduced into his Battel of the Gods every thing that is great and terrible in Nature, *Milton* has filled his Fight of Good and Bad Angels with all the like Circumstances of Horrour. The Shout of Armies, the Rattling of Brazen Chariots, the Hurling of Rocks and Mountains, the Earthquake, the Fire, the Thunder, are all of them employ'd to lift up the Reader's Imagination, and give him a suitable Idea of so great an Action. With what Art has the Poet represented the whole Body of the Earth trembling, even before it was created.

> *All Heaven resounded, and had Earth been then,*
> *All Earth had to its Center shook.* . . .

In how sublime and just a Manner does he afterwards describe the whole Heaven shaking under the Wheels of the Messiah's Chariot, with that exception to the Throne of God?

> *. . . Under his burning Wheels*
> *The steadfast* Empyrean *shook throughout,*
> *All but the Throne it self of God.* . . .

Notwithstanding the Messiah appears cloathed with so much Terrour and Majesty, the Poet has still found Means to make his Readers conceive an Idea of him beyond what he himself was able to describe.

> *Yet half his strength he put not forth, but checkt*
> *His thunder in mid Volly, for he meant*
> *Not to destroy, but root them out of Heaven.*

In a Word, *Milton*'s Genius, which was so great in it self, and so strengthened by all the Helps of Learning, appears in this Book every way equal to his Subject, which was the most sublime that could enter into the Thoughts of a Poet.   As he knew all the Arts of Affecting the Mind, he knew it was necessary to give it certain Resting-places and Opportunities of recovering it self from Time to Time: He has therefore with great Address interspersed several Speeches, Reflections, Similitudes, and the like Reliefs, to diversifie his Narration, and ease the Attention of the Reader, that he might come fresh to his great Action, and by such a Contrast of Ideas, have a more lively Taste of the noble Parts of his Description.   L

No. 334.

STEELE.]   Monday, March 24.

Voluisti enim in suo genere unumquemque nostrum quasi quendam esse Roscium, dixistique non tam ea quae recta essent probari, quam quae prava sunt fastidiis adhaerescere.—Cicero de Gestu.

IT is very natural to take for our whole Lives a light Impression of a Thing which at first fell into Contempt with us for want of Consideration.   The real Use of a certain Qualification (which the wiser Part of Mankind look upon us at best an indifferent thing, and generally a frivolous Circumstance) shews the ill Consequence of such Prepossessions.   What I mean is the Art, Skill, Accomplishment, or whatever you will call it, of Dancing. I knew a Gentleman of great Abilities, who bewailed the Want of this Part of his Education to the End of a very honourable Life.   He observed that there was not Occasion for the common Use of great Talents; that they are but seldom in Demand; and that these very great Talents were often render'd useless to a Man for want of small Attainments.   A good Mein (a becoming Motion, Gesture, and Aspect) is natural to some Men, but even these would be highly more graceful in their Carriage, if what they do from the Force of Nature were confirm'd and heighten'd from the Force of Reason.   To one who has not at all consider'd it, to mention the Force of Reason on such a Subject, will appear fantastical; but when you have a little attended to it, an Assembly of Men will have quite another View; and they will tell you, it is evident from plain and infallible Rules, why this Man with those beautiful Features, and well-fashion'd Person, is not so agreeable as he who sits by him without any of those Advantages. When we read we do it without any exerted Act of Memory that presents the Shape of the Letters; but Habit makes us do it mechanically, without staying, like Children, to recollect and join those Letters. A Man who has not the Regard of his Gesture in any Part of his Education, will find himself unable to act with Freedom before new Company, as a Child that is but now learning would be to read without Hesitation. It is for the Advancement of the Pleasure we receive in being agreeable to each other in ordinary Life, that one would wish Dancing were generally understood as conducive as it really is, to a proper Deportment in Matters that appear the most remote from it. A Man of Learning and Sense is distinguished from others as he is such, though he never runs upon Points too difficult for the rest of the World; in like manner the reaching out of the Arm, and the most ordinary Motion, discovers whether a Man ever learnt to know what is the true Harmony and Composure of his Limbs and Countenance. Whoever has seen *Booth* in the Character of *Pyrrhus* march to his Throne to receive *Orestes*, is convinced that majestick and great Conceptions are expressed in the very Step, but perhaps, though no other Man could perform that Incident as well as he does, he himself would do it with a yet greater Elevation, were he a Dancer. This is so dangerous a Subject to treat with Gravity, that I shall not at present enter into it any further; but the Author of the following Letter has treated it in the Essay he speaks of in such a Manner, that I am beholden to him for a Resolution, that I will never hereafter think meanly of any Thing, till I have heard what they who have another Opinion of it have to say in its Defence.

'*Mr.* Spectator,

Since there are scarce any of the Arts or Sciences that have not been recommended to the World by the Pens of some of the Professors, Masters, or Lovers of them, whereby the Usefulness, Excellence, and Benefit arising from them, both as to the speculative and practical Part, have been made publick, to the great Advantage and Improvement of such Arts and Sciences; why should Dancing, an Art celebrated by the Ancients in so extraordinary a Manner, be totally neglected by the Moderns, and left destitute of any Pen to recommend its various Excellencies and substantial Merit to Mankind?

The low Ebb to which Dancing is now fallen, is altogether

owing to this Silence. The Art is esteemed only as an amusing Trifle; it lies altogether uncultivated, and is unhappily fallen under the Imputation of Illiterate and Mechanick: And as *Terence*, in one of his Prologues, complains of the Rope-dancers drawing all the Spectators from his Play, so may we well say, that Capering and Tumbling is now preferred to, and supplies the place of, just and regular Dancing, on our Theatres. It is therefore, in my Opinion, high time, that some one should come in to its Assistance, and relieve it from the many gross and growing Errors that have crept into it, and over-cast its real Beauties; and to set Dancing in its true Light, would shew the Usefulness and Elegancy of it, with the Pleasure and Instruction produced from it; and also lay down some fundamental Rules, that might so tend to the Improvement of its Professors, and Information of the Spectators, that the first might be the better enabled to perform, and the latter rendred more capable of judging, what is (if there be any thing) valuable in this Art.

To encourage therefore some ingenious Pen capable of so generous an Undertaking, and in some measure to relieve Dancing from the Disadvantages it at present lies under, I who teach to dance, have attempted a small Treatise as an Essay towards an History of Dancing; in which I have enquired into its Antiquity, Original, and Use, and shewn what Esteem the Ancients had for it: I have likewise considered the Nature and Perfection of all its several Parts, and how beneficial and delightful it is, both as a Qualification and an Exercise; and endeavour'd to answer all Objections that have been maliciously rais'd against it. I have proceeded to give an Account of the particular Dances of the *Greeks* and *Romans*, whether Religious, Warlike, or Civil; and taken particular Notice of that Part of Dancing relating to the ancient Stage, and in which the *Pantomimes* had so great a Share: Nor have I been wanting in giving an historical Account of some particular Masters excellent in that surprizing Art; after which I have advanced some Observations on the modern Dancing, both as to the Stage, and that Part of it so absolutely necessary for the Qualification of Gentlemen and Ladies, and have concluded with some short Remarks on the Origin and Progress of the Character by which Dances are writ down, and communicated to one Master from another. If some great Genius after this would arise, and advance this Art to that Perfection it seems capable of receiving, what might not be expected from it? For if we consider the Origin of Arts and Sciences, we shall find that some of them took Rise from Beginnings so mean and unpromising, that it is very wonderful to think that ever such surprizing Structures should have been raised upon such

ordinary Foundations. But what cannot a great Genius effect?
Who would have thought that the clangorous Noise of a
Smith's Hammer should have given the first Rise to Musick?
Yet *Macrobius* in his second Book relates, that *Pythagoras*, in
passing by a Smith's Shop, found, that the Sounds proceeding
from the Hammers were either more grave or acute, according
to the different Weights of the Hammers. The Philosopher,
to improve this Hint, suspends different Weights by Strings of
the same Bigness, and found in like manner that the Sounds
answered to the Weights. This being discovered, he finds out
those Numbers which produced Sounds that were Consonants:
As, that two Strings of the same Substance and Tension, the
one being double the Length of the other, give that Interval
which is called *Diapason*, or an Eighth; the same was also
effected from two Strings of the same Length and Size, the
one having four times the Tension of the other. By these
Steps, from so mean a Beginning, did this great Man reduce,
what was only before Noise, to one of the most delightful
Sciences, by marrying it to the Mathematicks; and by that
means caused it to be one of most abstract and demonstrative
of Sciences. Who knows therefore but Motion, whether De-
corous or Representative, may not (as it seems highly probable
it may) be taken into Consideration by some Person capable
of reducing it into a regular Science, though not so demonstrative as that proceeding from Sounds, yet sufficient to
entitle it a Place among the magnified Arts.

Now, *Mr.* SPECTATOR, as you have declared your self Visitor
of Dancing-Schools, and this being an Undertaking which more
immediately respects them, I think my self indispensibly
obliged, before I proceed to the Publication of this my Essay,
to ask your Advice; and hold it absolutely necessary to have
your Approbation; and in order to recommend my Treatise to
the Perusal of the Parents of such as learn to dance, as well as
to the Young Ladies to whom, as Visitor, you ought to be
Guardian.

Salop, March 19. *I am, Sir,*
    1711–12. *Your most humble Servant.'*

                                                   T

No. 335.
[ADDISON.] Tuesday, March 25.

> *Respicere exemplar vitae morumque jubebo*
> *Doctum imitatorem, & vivas hinc ducere voces.*—Hor.

MY Friend Sir ROGER DE COVERLY, when we last met together
at the Club, told me, that he had a great Mind to see the new

Tragedy with me, assuring me at the same Time, that he had
not been at a Play these twenty Years. The last I saw, says
Sir ROGER, was the *Committee*, which I should not have gone
to neither, had not I been told before-hand that it was a good
Church of *England* Comedy. He then proceeded to enquire
of me who this Distress'd Mother was, and upon hearing that
she was *Hector*'s Widow, he told me, that her Husband was a
brave Man, and that when he was a School-boy, he had read
his Life at the end of the Dictionary. My Friend asked me, in
the next Place, if there would not be some Danger in coming
home late, in case the *Mohocks* should be abroad. I assure
you, says he, I thought I had fallen into their Hands last Night,
for I observ'd two or three lusty black Men that followed me
half way up *Fleet-street*, and mended their Pace behind me, in
Proportion as I put on to get away from them. You must
know, continued the Knight with a Smile, I fancied they had a
mind to *hunt* me; for I remember an honest Gentleman in my
Neighbourhood, who was serv'd such a Trick in King *Charles*
the Second's Time; for which Reason he has not ventured himself in Town ever since. I might have shown them very good
Sport, had this been their Design, for as I am an old Fox-
hunter, I should have turned and dodged, and have play'd
them a thousand Tricks they had never seen in their Lives
before. Sir ROGER added, that if these Gentlemen had any
such Intention, they did not succeed very well in it; for I threw
them out, says he, at the End of *Norfolk-street*, where I doubled
the Corner, and got Shelter in my Lodgings before they could
imagine what was become of me. However, says the Knight,
if Captain SENTRY will make one with us to Morrow Night,
and if you will both of you call upon me about Four a-Clock,
that we may be at the House before it is full, I will have my
own Coach in Readiness to attend you, for *John* tells me he has
got the Fore-Wheels mended.

The Captain, who did not fail to meet me there at the
appointed Hour, bid Sir ROGER fear nothing, for that he had
put on the same Sword which he made use of at the Battel of
Steenkirk. Sir ROGER's Servants, and among the rest my old
Friend the Butler, had, I found, provided themselves with good
Oaken Plants, to attend their Master upon this Occasion.
When we had plac'd him in his Coach, with my self at his Left
Hand, the Captain before him, and his Butler at the Head of
his Footmen in the Rear, we convoy'd him in Safety to the
Play-house; where, after having march'd up the Entry in good
Order, the Captain and I went in with him, and seated him
betwixt us in the Pit. As soon as the House was full, and the
Candles lighted, my old Friend stood up and looked about him

with that Pleasure, which a Mind seasoned with Humanity naturally feels in it self, at the Sight of a Multitude of People who seem pleased with one another, and partake of the same common Entertainment. I could not but fancy to my self, as the old Man stood up in the Middle of the Pit, that he made a very proper Center to a Tragick Audience. Upon the Entring of *Pyrrhus*, the Knight told me, that he did not believe the King of *France* himself had a better Strut. I was indeed very attentive to my old Friend's Remarks, because I looked upon them as a Piece of Natural Criticism, and was well pleased to hear him at the Conclusion of almost every Scene, telling me that he could not imagine how the Play would end. One while he appear'd much concerned for *Andromache*; and a little while after as much for *Hermione*; and was extremely puzzled to think what would become of *Pyrrhus*.

When Sir ROGER saw *Andromache*'s obstinate Refusal to her Lover's Importunities, he whispered me in the Ear, that he was sure she would never have him; to which he added, with a more than ordinary Vehemence, You can't imagine, Sir, what 'tis to have to do with a Widow. Upon *Pyrrhus* his threatning afterwards to leave her, the Knight shook his Head, and muttered to himself, Ay, do if you can. This Part dwelt so much upon my Friend's Imagination, that at the Close of the Third Act, as I was thinking of something else, he whispered in my Ear, These Widows, Sir, are the most perverse Creatures in the World. But pray, says he, you that are a Critick, is the Play according to your Dramatick Rules, as you call them? Should your People in Tragedy always talk to be understood? Why, there is not a single Sentence in this Play that I do not know the Meaning of.

The Fourth Act very luckily begun before I had Time to give the old Gentleman an Answer; Well, says the Knight, sitting down with great Satisfaction, I suppose we are now to see *Hector*'s Ghost. He then renewed his Attention, and, from Time to Time, fell a praising the Widow. He made, indeed, a little Mistake as to one of her Pages, whom, at his first Entring, he took for *Astyanax*; but he quickly set himself right in that Particular, though, at the same time, he owned he should have been very glad to have seen the little Boy, who, says he, must needs be a very fine Child by the Account that is given of him. Upon *Hermione*'s going off with a Menace to *Pyrrhus*, the Audience gave a loud Clap, to which Sir ROGER added, On my Word, a notable young Baggage.

As there was a very remarkable Silence and Stillness in the Audience during the whole Action, it was natural for them to take the Opportunity of these Intervals between the Acts, to express their Opinion of the Players, and of their respective Parts. Sir ROGER hearing a Cluster of them praise *Orestes*, struck in with them, and told them, that he thought his Friend *Pylades* was a very sensible Man; As they were afterwards applauding *Pyrrhus*, Sir ROGER put in a second time. And let me tell you, says he, though he speaks but little, I like the old Fellow in Whiskers as well as any of them. Captain SENTRY, seeing two or three Waggs who sat near us lean with an attentive Ear towards Sir ROGER, and fearing lest they should smoak the Knight, pluck'd him by the Elbow, and whispered something in his Ear, that lasted till the Opening of the Fifth Act. The Knight was wonderfully attentive to the Account which *Orestes* gives of *Pyrrhus* his Death, and at the Conclusion of it, told me it was such a bloody Piece of Work, that he was glad it was not done upon the Stage. Seeing afterwards *Orestes* in his raving Fit, he grew more than ordinary serious, and took Occasion to moralize (in his Way) upon an evil Conscience, adding, that *Orestes, in his Madness, looked as if he saw something*.

As we were the first that came into the House, so we were the last that went out of it; being resolved to have a clear Passage for our old Friend, whom we did not care to venture among the Justling of the Crowd. Sir ROGER went out fully satisfy'd with his Entertainment, and we guarded him to his Lodgings in the same manner that we brought him to the Playhouse; being highly pleased, for my own Part, not only with the Performance of the excellent Piece which had been presented, but with the Satisfaction which it had given to the good old Man. L

No. 336.
[STEELE.] Wednesday, March 26.

> . . . *Clament periisse pudorem*
> *Cuncti paene patres; ea cum reprehendere coner,*
> *Quae gravis Aesopus, quae doctus Roscius egit;*
> *Vel, quia nil rectum, nisi quod placuit sibi, ducunt;*
> *Vel, quia turpe putant parere minoribus, & quae*
> *Imberbes didicere, senes perdenda fateri.*
>
> —Hor. lib. 2, Ep. 1. v. 80.

'*Mr.* SPECTATOR,

As you are the daily Endeavourer to promote Learning and good Sense, I think my self obliged to suggest to your Consideration whatever may promote or prejudice them. There is an Evil which has prevailed from Generation to Generation

which grey Hairs and tyrannical Custom continue to support;
I hope your Spectatorial Authority will give a seasonable
Check to the Spread of the Infection; I mean old Men's over-
bearing the strongest Sense of their Juniors by the meer Force
of Seniority; so that for a young Man in the Bloom of Life and
Vigour of Age to give a reasonable Contradiction to his Elders,
is esteemed an unpardonable Insolence, and regarded as a
reversing the Decrees of Nature. I am a young Man I confess,
yet I honour the grey Head as much as any one; however, when
in Company with old Men I hear them speak obscurely, or
reason preposterously (into which Absurdities, Prejudice,
Pride, or Interest will sometimes throw the wisest) I count it
no Crime to rectify their Reasonings, unless Conscience must
truckle to Ceremony, and Truth fall a Sacrifice to Complaisance.
The strongest Arguments are enervated, and the brightest
Evidence disappears, before those tremendous Reasonings and
dazzling Discoveries of venerable old Age: You are young
giddy-headed Fellows, you have not yet had Experience of the
World. Thus we young Folks find our Ambition cramp'd, and
our Laziness indulged, since, while young, we have little Room
to display our selves; and, when old, the Weakness of Nature
must pass for Strength of Sense, and we hope that hoary Heads
will raise us above the Attacks of Contradiction. Now, Sir, as
you would enliven our Activity in the pursuit of Learning,
take our Case into Consideration; and, with a Gloss on brave
Elihu's Sentiments, assert the Rights of Youth, and prevent
the pernicious Encroachments of Age. The generous Reasonings of that gallant Youth would adorn your Paper; and I beg
you would insert them, not doubting but that they will give
good Entertainment to the most intelligent of your Readers.

So these three Men ceased to answer Job, *because he was
righteous in his own Eyes. Then was kindled the Wrath of*
Elihu *the Son of* Barachel *the* Buzite, *of the Kindred of* Ram:
Against Job *was his Wrath kindled, because he justified himself
rather than God. Also against his three Friends was his Wrath
kindled, because they had found no Answer, and yet had condemned* Job. *Now* Elihu *had waited till* Job *had spoken, because
they were elder than he. When* Elihu *saw there was no Answer
in the Mouth of these three Men, then his Wrath was kindled.
And* Elihu *the Son of* Barachel *the* Buzite *answered and said, I
am young, and ye are very old, wherefore I was afraid, and durst
not shew you mine Opinion. I said, Days would speak, and
Multitude of Years should teach Wisdom. But there is a Spirit
in Man: and the Inspiration of the Almighty giveth them Understanding. Great Men are not always wise: Neither do the aged*

understand Judgment. Therefore I said, hearken to me, I also will shew mine Opinion. Behold I waited for your Words; I gave ear to your Reasons, whilst you searched out what to say. Yea, I attended unto you: And behold there was none of you that convinced Job, *or that answered his Words: Lest ye should say, we have found out Wisdom: God thrusteth him down, not Man. Now he hath not directed his Words against me: Neither will I answer him with your Speeches. They were amazed, they answered no more: They left off speaking. When I had waited, (for they spake not, but stood still and answered no more,) I said, I will answer also my Part, I also will shew mine Opinion. For I am full of Matter, the Spirit within me constraineth me. Behold, my Belly is as Wine which hath no Vent, it is ready to burst like new Bottles. I will speak that I may be refreshed: I will open my Lips, and answer. Let me not, I pray you, accept any Man's Person, neither let me give flattering Titles unto Man. For I know not to give flattering Titles, in so doing my Maker would soon take me away.'*

'Mr. SPECTATOR,

I have formerly read with great Satisfaction your Papers about Idols, and the Behaviour of Gentlemen in those Coffeehouses where Women officiate, and impatiently waited to see you take India and China Shops into Consideration: But since you have pass'd us over in Silence, either that you have not as yet thought us worth your Notice, or that the Grievances we lie under have escaped your discerning Eye, I must make my Complaints to you, and am encouraged to do it because you seem a little at Leisure at this present Writing. I am, dear Sir, one of the top China-Women about Town; and though I say it, keep as good Things, and receive as fine Company as any o' this End of the Town, let the other be who she will: In short, I am in a fair way to be easy, were it not for a Club of Female Rakes, who, under Pretence of taking their innocent Rambles, forsooth, and diverting the Spleen, seldom fail to plague me twice or thrice a Day, to cheapen Tea, or buy a Screen; *what else should they mean?* as they often repeat it. These Rakes are your idle Ladies of Fashion, who having nothing to do, employ themselves in tumbling over my Ware One of these No-Customers (for by the way they seldom or never buy any thing) calls for a Set of Tea-Dishes, another for a Bason, a third for my best Green-Tea; and even to the Punch-Bowl there 's scarce a Piece in my Shop but must be displaced, and the whole agreeable Architecture disordered, so that I can compare 'em to nothing but to the Night-Goblins that take a Pleasure to over-turn the Disposition of Plates and

Dishes in the Kitchins of your housewifely Maids. Well, after all this Racket and Clutter, this is too dear, that is their Aversion; another thing is charming, but not wanted: The Ladies are cured of the Spleen, but I am not a Shilling the better for it. Lord! what signifies one poor Pot of Tea, considering the Trouble they put me to? Vapours, Mr. SPECTATOR, are terrible Things; for though I am not possess'd by them my self, I suffer more from 'em than if I were. Now I must beg you to admonish all such Day-Goblins to make fewer Visits, or to be less troublesome when they come to one's Shop; and to convince 'em, that we honest Shop-keepers have Something better to do, than to cure Folks of the Vapours *gratis*. A young Son of mine, a School-Boy, is my Secretary, so I hope you 'll make Allowances. I am, Sir,

Your constant Reader,

and very humble Servant,

March the 22d.

T   Rebecca *the Distress'd.'*

No. 337.

[BUDGELL.]   Thursday, March 27.

> *Fingit equum tenera docilem cervice magister*
> *Ire viam qua monstret eques* . . .—Hor.

I HAVE lately received a third Letter from the Gentleman, who has already given the Publick two Essays upon Education. As his Thoughts seem to be very just and new upon this Subject, I shall communcate them to the Reader.

'*Sir,*

If I had not been hindred by some extraordinary Business, I should have sent you sooner my further Thoughts upon Education. You may please to remember, that in my last Letter I endeavoured to give the best Reasons that could be urged in favour of a private or publick Education. Upon the whole it may perhaps be thought that I seemed rather enclined to the latter, though at the same time I confess'd that Vertue which ought to be our first and principal Care, was more usually acquired in the former.

I intend therefore, in this Letter, to offer at Methods, by which I conceive Boys might be made to improve in Virtue, as they advance in Letters.

I know that in most of our publick Schools Vice is punished and discouraged whenever it is found out; but this is far from being sufficient, unless our Youth are at the same time taught to form a right Judgment of Things, and to know what is properly Virtue.

To this End, whenever they read the Lives and Actions of such Men as have been famous in their Generation, it should not be thought enough to make them barely understand so many *Greek* or *Latin* Sentences, but they should be asked their Opinion of such an Action or Saying, and obliged to give their Reasons why they take it to be good or bad. By this means they would insensibly arrive at proper Notions of Courage, Temperance, Honour and Justice.

There must be great Care taken how the Example of any particular Person is recommended to them in gross; instead of which they ought to be taught wherein such a Man, tho' great in some Respects, was weak and faulty in others. For want of this Caution, a Boy is often so dazzled with the Lustre of a great Character, that he confounds its Beauties with its Blemishes, and looks even upon the faulty Parts of it with an Eye of Admiration.

I have often wondered how *Alexander*, who was naturally of a generous and merciful Disposition, came to be guilty of so barbarous an Action as that of dragging the Governour of a Town after his Chariot. I know this is generally ascribed to his Passion for *Homer*; but I lately met with a Passage in *Plutarch*, which, if I am not very much mistaken, still gives us a clearer Light into the Motives of this Action. *Plutarch* tells us, that *Alexander* in his Youth had a Master named *Lysimachus*, who though he was a Man destitute of all Politeness, ingratiated himself both with *Philip* and his Pupil, and became the second man at Court, by calling the King *Peleus*, the Prince *Achilles*, and himself *Phoenix*. It is no Wonder if *Alexander*, having been thus used not only to admire, but to personate *Achilles*, should think it glorious to imitate him in this Piece of Cruelty and Extravagance.

To carry this Thought yet further, I shall submit it to your Consideration, whether instead of a Theme or Copy of Verses, which are the usual Exercises, as they are called in the School-phrase, it would not be more proper that a Boy should be tasked once or twice a Week to write down his Opinion of such Persons and Things as occur to him in his Reading; that he should descant upon the Actions of *Turnus* or *Aeneas*, shew wherein they excelled or were defective, censure or approve any particular Action, observe how it might have been carried to a greater Degree of Perfection, and how it exceeded or fell short of another. He might at the same Time mark what was moral in any Speech, and how far it agreed with the Character of the Person speaking. This Exercise would soon Strengthen his Judgment in what is blameable or praise-worthy, and give him an early seasoning of Morality.

Next to those Examples which may be met with in Books, I very much approve *Horace's* Way of setting before Youth the infamous or honourable Characters of their Contemporaries; that Poet tells us this was the Method his Father made use of to incline him to any particular Virtue, or give him an Aversion to any particular Vice. If, says *Horace*, my Father advised me to live within Bounds, and be contented with the Fortune he should leave me; Do not you see (says he) the miserable Condition of *Burrus*, and the Son of *Albus*? Let the Misfortunes of those two Wretches teach you to avoid Luxury and Extravagance. If he would inspire me with an Abhorrence to Debauchery, Do not (says he) make your self like *Sectanus*, when you may be happy in the Enjoyment of lawful Pleasures. How scandalous (says he) is the Character of *Trebonius*, who was lately caught in Bed with another Man's Wife? To illustrate the Force of this Method, the Poet adds, That as a headstrong Patient, who will not at first follow his Physician's Prescriptions, grows orderly when he hears that his Neighbours die all about him; so Youth is often frighted from Vice, by hearing the ill Report it brings upon others.

Xenophon's Schools of Equity, in his Life of *Cyrus* the Great, are sufficiently famous: He tells us that the *Persian* Children went to School, and employed their Time as diligently in learning the Principles of Justice and Sobriety, as the Youth in other Countries did to acquire the most difficult Arts and Sciences; their Governours spent most Part of the Day in hearing their mutual Accusations one against the other, whether for Violence, Cheating, Slander, or Ingratitude, and taught them how to give Judgment against those who were found to be any ways guilty of these Crimes. I omit the Story of the long and short Coat, for which *Cyrus* himself was punished, as a Case equally known with any in *Littleton*.

The Method, which *Apuleius* tells us the *Indian Gymnosophists* took to educate their Disciples, is still more curious and remarkable. His Words are as follow. When their Dinner is ready, before it is served up, the Masters enquire of every particular Scholar how he has employed his Time since Sunrising; some of them answer, that having been chosen as Arbiters between two Persons, they have composed their Differences, and made them Friends; some, that they have been executing the Orders of their Parents; and others, that they have either found out something new by their own Application, or learnt it from the Instructions of their Fellows: But if there happens to be any one among them, who cannot make it appear that he has employed the Morning to Advantage, he is immediately excluded from the Company, and obliged to work while the rest are at Dinner.

It is not impossible, that from these several Ways of producing Virtue in the Minds of Boys, some general Method might be invented. What I would endeavour to inculcate is, That our Youth cannot be too soon taught the Principles of Virtue, seeing the first Impressions which are made on the Mind are always the strongest.

The Archbishop of *Cambray* makes *Telemachus* say, that tho' he was young in Years he was old in the Art of knowing how to keep both his own and his Friend's Secrets. When my Father, says the Prince, went to the Siege of *Troy*, he took me on his Knees, and after having embraced and blessed me, as he was surrounded by the Nobles of *Ithaca*, O my Friends, says he, into your Hands I commit the Education of my Son; if ever you lov'd his Father, shew it in your Care towards him; but above all, do not omit to form him just, sincere, and faithful in keeping a Secret. These Words of my Father, says *Telemachus*, were continually repeated to me by his Friends in his Absence; who made no Scruple of communicating to me their Uneasiness to see my Mother surrounded with Lovers, and the Measures they designed to take on that Occasion. He adds, that he was so ravished at being thus treated like a Man, and at the Confidence reposed in him, that he never once abused it; nor could all the Insinuations of his Father's Rivals ever get him to betray what was committed to him under the Seal of Secrecy.

There is hardly any Virtue which a Lad might not thus learn by Practice and Example.

I have heard of a good Man, who used at certain Times to give his Scholars Six Pence apiece, that they might tell him the next Day how they had employ'd it. The third Part was always to be laid out in Charity, and every Boy was blamed or commended as he could make it appear that he had chosen a fit Object.

In short, nothing is more wanting to our publick Schools, than that the Masters of them should use the same Care in fashioning the Manners of their Scholars, as in forming their Tongues to the Learned Languages. Where ever the former is omitted, I cannot help agreeing with Mr. *Lock*, That a Man must have a very strange Value for Words, when preferring the Languages of the *Greeks* and *Romans* to that which made them such brave Men, he can think it worth while to hazard the Innocence and Virtue of his Son for a little *Greek* and *Latin*.

As the Subject of this Essay is of the highest Importance, and what I do not remember to have yet seen treated by any Author, I have sent you what occurr'd to me on it from my own Observation or Reading, and which you may either suppress or publish as you think fit.

X   *I am, Sir, Yours, &c.'*

No. 338.   Friday, March 28.

> . . . *Nil fuit unquam*
> *Sic impar sibi* . . .—Hor.

I FIND the Tragedy of the *Distrest Mother* is publish'd to Day: The Author of the Prologue, I suppose, pleads an old Excuse I have read somewhere, of being *dull with Design*; and the Gentleman who writ the Epilogue, has, to my Knowledge, so much of greater Moment to value himself upon, that he will easily forgive me for publishing the Exceptions made against Gayety at the End of serious Entertainments, in the following letter: I should be more unwilling to pardon him than any Body, a Practice which cannot have any ill Consequence, but from the Abilities of the Person who is guilty of it.

'*Mr.* SPECTATOR,

I had the Happiness the other Night of sitting very near you, and your worthy Friend Sir ROGER, at the acting of the new Tragedy, which you have in a late Paper or two so justly recommended. I was highly pleas'd with the advantageous Situation Fortune had given me, in placing me so near two Gentlemen, from one of which I was sure to hear such Reflections on the several Incidents of the Play as pure Nature suggested, and from the other such as flow'd from the exactest Art and Judgment: Tho' I must confess that my Curiosity led me so much to observe the Knight's Reflections, that I was not so well at Leisure to improve my self by yours. Nature, I found, play'd her Part in the Knight pretty well, 'till at the last concluding Lines she entirely forsook him. You must know, Sir, that it is always my Custom, when I have been well entertain'd at a new Tragedy, to make my Retreat before the facetious Epilogue enters; not but that those Pieces are often very well writ, but having paid down my Half-Crown, and made a fair Purchase of as much of the pleasing Melancholy as the Poet's Art can afford me, or my own Nature admit of, I am willing to carry some of it Home with me; and can't endure to be at once trick'd out of all, tho' by the wittiest Dexterity in the World. However, I kept my Seat t'other Night, in Hopes of finding my own Sentiments of this Matter favour'd by your Friend's; when, to my great Surprize, I found the Knight entering with equal Pleasure into both Parts, and as much satisfied with Mrs. *Oldfield*'s Gayety, as he had been before with *Andromache*'s Greatness. Whether this were no other than an Effect of the Knight's peculiar Humanity, pleas'd to find at last, that after all the tragical Doings, every thing was safe and well, I don't know. But for my own Part, I must confess, I was so dissatisfied, that I was sorry the Poet had sav'd *Andromache*, and could heartily have wish'd that he had left her stone-dead upon the Stage. For you cannot imagine, Mr. Spectator, the Mischief she was reserv'd to do me. I found my Soul, during the Action, gradually work'd up to the highest Pitch; and felt the exalted Passion which all generous Minds conceive at the Sight of Virtue in Distress. The Impression, believe me, Sir, was so strong upon me, that I am perswaded, if I had been let alone in it, I could at an Extremity have ventured to defend your self and Sir Roger against half a Score of the fiercest *Mohocks*: But the ludicrous Epilogue in the Close exstinguish'd all my Ardour, and made me look upon all such noble Atchievements as downright silly and romantick. What the rest of the Audience felt, I can't so well tell: For my self, I must declare, that at the End of the Play I found my Soul uniform, and all of a Piece; but at the End of the Epilogue it was so jumbled together, and divided between Jest and Earnest, that if you will forgive me an extravagant Fancy, I will here set it down. I could not but fancy, if my Soul had at that Moment quitted my Body, and descended to the Poetical Shades in the Posture it was then in, what a strange Figure it would have made among them. They would not have known what to have made of my mottley Spectre, half Comic and half Tragic, all over resembling a ridiculous Face, that at the same Time laughs on one Side and cries o' t'other. The only Defence, I think, I have ever heard made for this, as it seems to me, the most unnatural Tack of the Comic Tail to the Tragic Head, is this, that the Minds of the Audience must be refreshed, and Gentlemen and Ladies not sent away in their own Homes with too dismal and melancholy Thoughts about them: For who knows the Consequence of this? We are much obliged indeed to the Poets for the great Tenderness they express for the Safety of our Persons, and heartily thank them for it. But if that be all, pray, good Sir, assure them, that we are none of us like to come to any great Harm; and that, let them do their best, we shall in all Probability live out the Length of our Days, and frequent the Theatres more than ever.

What makes me more desirous to have some Reformation of this Matter, is because of an ill Consequence or two attending it: For a great many of our Church-Musicians being related to the Theatre, they have, in Imitation of these Epilogues, introduc'd in their farewell Voluntaries a sort of Musick quite foreign to the Design of Church-Services, to the great Prejudice of well-dispos'd People. Those fingering Gentlemen should be inform'd, that they ought to suit their Airs to the Place and Business; and that the Musician is oblig'd to keep to the Text as much as the Preacher. For want of this, I have found by Experience a great deal of Mischief: For when the Preacher has often, with great Piety and Art enough, handled his Subject, and the judicious Clark has with utmost Diligence cull'd out two Staves proper to the Discourse, and I have found in my self, and in the rest of the Pew, good Thoughts and Dispositions, they have been all in a Moment dissipated by a merry Jigg from the Organ-Loft. One knows not what further ill Effects the Epilogues I have been speaking of may in Time produce: But this I am credibly inform'd of, that *Paul Lorrain* has resolv'd upon a very suddain Reformation in his tragical Dramas; and that at the next Monthly Performance, he designs, instead of a Penitential Psalm, to dismiss his Audience with an excellent new Ballad of his own composing. Pray, Sir, do what you can to put a Stop to these growing Evils, and you will very much oblige

Your humble Servant,
Physibulus.'

No. 339.
[ADDISON.]   Saturday, March 29.

> . . . *Ut his exordia primis*
> *Omnia, & ipse tener mundi concreverit orbis,*
> *Tum durare solum, & discludere Nerea ponto*
> *Coeperit, & rerum paullatim sumere formas.*—Virg.

Longinus has observed, that there may be a Loftiness in Sentiments, where there is no Passion, and brings Instances out of ancient Authors to support this his Opinion. The Pathetick, as that great Critick observes, may animate and inflame the Sublime, but is not essential to it. Accordingly, as he further remarks, we very often find that those who excel most in stirring up the Passions very often want the Talent of writing in the great and sublime Manner; and so on the contrary. *Milton* has shewn himself a Master in both these Ways of

Writing. The seventh Book, which we are now entering upon, is an Instance of that Sublime which is not mixt and work'd up with Passion. The Author appears in a kind of composed and sedate Majesty; and tho' the Sentiments do not give so great an Emotion as those in the former Book, they abound with as magnificent Ideas. The sixth Book, like a troubled Ocean, represents Greatness in Confusion; the seventh affects the Imagination like the Ocean in a Calm, and fills the Mind of the Reader, without producing in it any thing like Tumult or Agitation.

The Critick above-mentioned, among the Rules which he lays down for succeeding in the sublime way of writing, proposes to his Reader, that he should imitate the most celebrated Authors who have gone before him, and have been engaged in Works of the same Nature; as in particular that if he writes on a poetical Subject, he should consider how *Homer* would have spoken on such an Occasion. By this Means one great Genius often catches the Flame from another, and writes in his Spirit without copying servilely after him. There are a thousand shining Passages in *Virgil*, which have been lighted up by *Homer*.

Milton, tho' his own natural Strength of Genius was capable of furnishing out a perfect Work, has doubtless very much raised and enobled his conceptions, by such an Imitation as that which *Longinus* has recommended.

In this Book, which gives us an Account of the Six Days Works, the Poet received but very few Assistances from Heathen Writers, who were Strangers to the Wonders of Creation. But as there are many glorious Stroaks of Poetry upon this Subject in Holy Writ, the Author has numberless Allusions to them through the whole Course of this Book. The great Critick I have before mentioned, though an Heathen, has taken Notice of the sublime Manner in which the Law-giver of the *Jews* has described the Creation in the First Chapter of *Genesis*; and there are many other Passages in Scripture, which rise up to the same Majesty, where this Subject is touched upon. *Milton* has shewn his Judgment very remarkably, in making use of such of these as were proper for his Poem, and in duly qualifying those high Strains of Eastern Poetry, which were suited to Readers whose Imaginations were set to an higher Pitch than those of colder Climates.

Adam's Speech to the Angel, wherein he desires an Account of what had passed within the Regions of Nature before the Creation, is very great and solemn. The following Lines, in which he tells him, that the Day is not too far spent for him to enter upon such a Subject, are exquisite in their Kind.

> *And the Great Light of Day yet wants to run*
> *Much of his race, though steep; suspens in Heav'n*
> *Held by thy voice, thy potent voice he hears,*
> *And longer will delay, to hear thee tell*
> *His Generation, &c.* . . .

The Angel's encouraging our First Parents in a modest Pursuit after Knowledge, with the Causes which he assigns for the Creation of the World, are very just and beautiful. The Messiah, by whom, as we are told in Scripture, the Heavens were made, comes forth in the Power of his Father, surrounded with an Host of Angels, and cloathed with such a Majesty as becomes his entering upon a Work, which, according to our Conceptions, appears the utmost Exertion of Omnipotence. What a beautiful Description has our Author raised upon that Hint in one of the Prophets. *And behold there came four Chariots out from between two Mountains, and the Mountains were Mountains of Brass.*

> *About his Chariot numberless were pour'd*
> Cherub *and* Seraph, *Potentates and Thrones,*
> *And Virtues, winged Spirits, and Chariots wing'd*
> *From the Armoury of God, where stand of old*
> *Myriads between two brazen Mountains lodg'd*
> *Against a solemn day, harnest at hand,*
> *Celestial Equipage; and now came forth*
> *Spontaneous, for within them Spirit liv'd,*
> *Attendant on their Lord; Heav'n open'd wide*
> *Her ever during Gates, Harmonious sound*
> *On golden Hinges moving* . . .

I have before taken Notice of these Chariots of God, and of these Gates of Heaven, and shall here only add, that *Homer* gives us the same Idea of the latter as opening of themselves, tho' he afterwards takes off from it, by telling us, that the Hours first of all removed those prodigious Heaps of Clouds which lay as a Barrier before them.

I do not know any thing in the whole Poem more sublime than the Description which follows, where the Messiah is represented at the Head of his Angels, as looking down into the *Chaos*, calming its Confusion, riding into the midst of it, and drawing the first Out Line of the Creation.

> *On Heav'nly ground they stood, and from the shore*
> *They view'd the vast immeasurable Abyss*
> *Outragious as a Sea, dark, wasteful, wild,*
> *Up from the bottom turn'd by furious winds*
> *And surging waves, as Mountains to assault*
> *Heav'ns height, and with the Center mix the Pole.*
>   *Silence ye troubled waves, and thou Deep, Peace,*

> *Said then th' Omnific word, your Discord end:*
> *Nor staid, but on the wings of Cherubim*
> *Up-lifted, in Paternal Glory rode*
> *Far into Chaos, and the world unborn;*
> *For Chaos heard his voice; him all his train*
> *Follow'd in bright Procession to behold*
> *Creation, and the wonders of his might.*
> *Then staid the fervid Wheels, and in his hand*
> *He took the golden Compasses, prepared*
> *In God's eternal Store, to circumscribe*
> *This Universe, and all created things:*
> *One foot he Center'd, and the other turn'd*
> *Round through the vast profundity obscure,*
> *And said, thus far extend, thus far thy bounds,*
> *This be thy just Circumference, O World.*

The Thought of the Golden Compasses is conceiv'd altogether in *Homer's* Spirit, and is a very noble Incident in this wonderful Description. *Homer*, when he speaks of the Gods, ascribes to them several Arms and Instruments with the same Greatness of Imagination. Let the Reader only peruse the Description of *Minerva's Aegis*, or Buckler, in the Fifth Book, with her Spear which would overturn whole Squadrons, and her Helmet, that was sufficient to cover an Army drawn out of an Hundred Cities: The Golden Compasses in the above-mentioned Passage appear a very natural Instrument in the Hand of him, whom *Plato* somewhere calls the Divine Geometrician. As Poetry delights in cloathing abstracted Ideas in Allegories and sensible Images, we find a magnificent Description of the Creation form'd after the same manner in one of the Prophets, wherein he describes the Almighty Architect as measuring the Waters in the Hollow of his Hand, meeting out the Heavens with his Span, comprehending the Dust of the Earth in a Measure, weighing the Mountains in Scales, and the Hills in a Ballance. Another of them describing the Supreme Being in this great Work of Creation, represents him as laying the Foundations of the Earth, and stretching a Line upon it. And in another Place as garnishing the Heavens, stretching out the North over the empty Place, and hanging the Earth upon nothing. This last noble Thought *Milton* has express'd in the following Verse.

> *And Earth self-ballanc'd on her Center hung,*

The Beauties of Description in this Book lie so very thick, that it is impossible to enumerate them in this Paper. The Poet has employ'd on them the whole Energy of our Tongue. The several great Scenes of the Creation rise up to view one after another, in such a Manner that the Reader seems present at this wonderful Work, and to assist among the Choirs of

Angels, who are the Spectators of it. How glorious is the Conclusion of the first Day.

> . . . *Thus was the first day Ev'n and Morn.*
> *Nor past uncelebrated, nor unsung*
> *By the Celestial Quires, when Orient light*
> *Exhaling first from Darkness they beheld;*
> *Birth-day of Heav'n and Earth; with joy and shout*
> *The hollow universal Orb they fill'd.*

We have the same Elevation of Thought in the third Day, when the Mountains were brought forth, and the Deep was made.

> *Immediately the Mountains huge appear*
> *Emergent, and their broad bare backs up heave*
> *Into the Clouds; their tops ascend the Sky;*
> *So high as heav'd the tumid hills, so low*
> *Down sunk a hollow bottom broad and deep,*
> *Capacious bed of Waters.*

We have also the Rising of the whole vegetable World describ'd in this Day's Work, which is fill'd with all the Graces that other Poets have lavished on their Description of the Spring, and leads the Reader's Imagination into a Theatre equally surprizing and beautiful.

The several Glories of the Heav'ns make their Appearance on the fourth Day.

> *First in his East the glorious lamp was seen,*
> *Regent of day, and all the Horizon round*
> *Invested with bright rays, jocund to run*
> *His Longitude thro' Heav'n's high rode: the Gray*
> *Dawn, and the* Pleiades *before him danced*
> *Shedding sweet influence; less bright the Moon.*
> *But opposite in levell'd West was set,*
> *His Mirror, with full face borrowing her light*
> *From him, for other light she needed none*
> *In that aspect, and still that distance keeps*
> *Till night; then in the East her turn she shines*
> *Revolv'd on Heaven's great Axle, and her reign*
> *With thousand lesser lights dividual holds,*
> *With thousand thousand stars that then appear'd*
> *Spangling the Hemisphere.*

One would wonder how the Poet could be so concise in his Description of the Six Days' Works, as to comprehend them within the Bounds of an Episode, and at the same Time so particular, as to give us a lively Idea of them. This is still more remarkable in his Account of the fifth and sixth Days, in which he has drawn out to our View the whole Animal Creation, from the Reptil to the Behemoth. As the Lion and the

Leviathan are two of the noblest Productions in the World of living Creatures, the Reader will find a most exquisite Spirit of Poetry in the Account which our Author gives us of them. The Sixth Day concludes with the Formation of Man, upon which the Angel takes Occasion, as he did after the Battle in Heaven, to remind *Adam* of his Obedience, which was the principal Design of this his Visit.

The Poet afterwards represents the Messiah, returning into Heaven, and taking a Survey of his great Work. There is something inexpressibly sublime in this Part of the Poem, where the Author describes that great Period of Time, filled with so many glorious Circumstances; when the Heavens and Earth were finished; when the Messiah ascended up in Triumph through the Everlasting Gates; when he looked down with Pleasure upon his new Creation; when every Part of Nature seem'd to rejoice in its Existence; when the Morning Stars sang together, and all the Sons of God shouted for Joy.

> *So Ev'n and Morn accomplish'd the Sixth day:*
> *Yet not till the Creator from his Work*
> *Desisting, tho' unwearied, up return'd,*
> *Up to the Heav'n of Heav'ns his high abode,*
> *Thence to behold this new created World*
> *Th' addition of his Empire; how it shew'd*
> *In prospect from his throne, how good, how fair,*
> *Answering his great Idea. Up he rode*
> *Follow'd with acclamation and the Sound*
> *Symphonious of ten thousand harps that tuned*
> *Angelic Harmonies: the earth, the air*
> *Resounding, (thou remember'st, for thou heard'st)*
> *The Heavens and all the Constellations rung,*
> *The Planets in their Stations list'ning stood,*
> *While the bright pomp ascended jubilant.*
> *Open ye everlasting gates, they sung,*
> *Open ye Heav'ns, your living doors, let in*
> *The great Creator from his work return'd*
> *Magnificent, his six days' work, a World.*

I cannot conclude this Book upon the Creation, without mentioning a Poem which has lately appear'd under that Title. The Work was undertaken with so good an Intention, and is executed with so great a Mastery, that it deserves to be looked upon as one of the most useful and noble Productions in our *English* Verse. The Reader cannot but be pleased to find the Depths of Philosophy enlivened with all the Charms of Poetry, and to see so great a Strength of Reason, amidst so beautiful a Redundancy of the Imagination. The Author has shewn us that Design in all the Works of Nature, which necessarily leads us to the Knowledge of its first Cause. In short, he has illustrated, by numberless and incontestible Instances, that Divine Wisdom, which the Son of *Sirach* has so nobly ascribed to the Supreme Being in his Formation of the World, when he tells us, that *He created her, and saw her, and numbered her, and poured her out upon all his Works.* L

No. 340.
[STEELE.]   Monday, March 31.

> *Quis novus hic nostris successit sedibus hospes!*
> *Quem sese ore ferens! quam forti pectore & armis!*
> —Virg.

I TAKE it to be the highest Instance of a noble Mind to bear great Qualities without discovering in a Man's Behaviour any Consciousness that he is superior to the rest of the World: Or, to say it otherwise, it is the Duty of a great Person so to demean himself, as that whatever Endowments he may have, he may appear to value himself upon no Qualities but such as any Man may arrive at: He ought to think no Man valuable but for his publick Spirit, Justice and Integrity; and all other Endowments to be esteemed only as they contribute to the exerting those Virtues. Such a Man, if he is wise or valiant, knows it is of no Consideration to other Men that he is so, but as he employs those high Talents for their Use and Service. He who affects the Applause and Addresses of a Multitude, or assumes to himself a Pre-eminence upon any other Consideration, must soon turn Admiration into Contempt. It is certain that there can be no Merit in any Man who is not conscious of it; but the Sense that it is valuable only according to the Application of it, makes that Superiority amiable, which would otherwise be invidious. In this Light it is considered as a Thing in which every Man bears a Share: It annexes the Ideas of Dignity, Power, and Fame, in an agreeable and familiar manner to him who is Possessor of it; and all Men who were Strangers to him are naturally incited to indulge a Curiosity in beholding the Person, Behaviour, Feature, and Shape of him, in whose Character, perhaps, each Man had formed something in common with himself. Whether such, or any other, are the Causes, all Men have a yearning Curiosity to behold a Man of heroick Worth; and I have had many Letters from all Parts of this Kingdom, that request I would give them an exact Account of the Stature, the Mein, the Aspect of the Prince who lately visited *England*, and has done such Wonders for the Liberty of *Europe*. It would puzzle the most Curious to form to himself the Sort of Man my several Correspondents expect to hear of, by the Action mentioned when they desire a Description of him: There is always something that concerns themselves, and growing out of their own Circumstances, in all their Enquiries. A Friend of mine in *Wales* beseeches me to be very exact in my Account of that wonderful Man, who had marched an Army and all its Baggage over the *Alps*; and, if possible, to learn whether the Peasant who shew'd him the Way, and is drawn in the Map, be yet living. A Gentleman from the University, who is deeply intent on the Study of Humanity, desires me to be as particular, if I had Opportunity in observing the whole Interview between his Highness and our late General. Thus do Men's Fancies work according to their several Educations and Circumstances; but all pay a Respect, mixed with Admiration, to this illustrious Character. I have waited for his Arrival in *Holland*, before I would let my Correspondents know, that I have not been so uncurious a Spectator, as not to have seen Prince *Eugene*. It would be very difficult, as I said just now, to answer every Expectation of those who have writ to me on that Head; nor is it possible for me to find Words to let one know what an artful Glance there is in his Countenance who surprized *Cremona*; how daring he appears who forced the Trenches of *Turin*: But in general can say, that he who beholds him, will easily expect from him any thing that is to be imagined or executed by the Wit or Force of Man. The Prince is of that Stature which makes a Man most easily become all Parts of Exercise, has Height to be graceful on Occasions of State and Ceremony, and no less adapted for Agility and Dispatch: His Aspect is erect and compos'd; his Eye lively and thoughtful, yet rather vigilant than sparkling; his Action and Address the most easie imaginable, and his Behaviour in an Assembly peculiarly graceful in a certain Art of mixing insensibly with the rest, and becoming one of the Company, instead of receiving the Courtship of it. The Shape of his Person, and Composure of his Limbs, are remarkably exact and beautiful. There is in his Look something sublime, which does not seem to arise from his Quality or Character, but the innate Disposition of his Mind. It is apparent that he suffers the Presence of much Company, instead of taking Delight in it; and he appear'd in Publick while with us, rather to return Good-will, or satisfie Curiosity, than to gratifie any Taste he himself had of being popular. As his Thoughts are never tumultuous in Danger, they are as little discomposed on Occasions of Pomp and Magnificence: A great Soul is affected in either Case, no further than in considering the properest Methods to extricate it self from them. If this Hero has the strong Incentives to uncommon Enterprizes that were remarkable in *Alexander*, he prosecutes and enjoys the Fame of them with the Justness, Propriety, and good Sense of *Caesar*. It is easie to observe in him a Mind as capable of being entertained with Contemplation as Enterprize; a Mind ready for great Exploits, but not impatient for Occasions to exert it self. The Prince has Wisdom and Valour in as high Perfection as Man can enjoy it; which noble Faculties in Conjunction, banish all Vain-glory, Ostentation, Ambition, and all other Vices which might intrude upon his Mind to make it unequal. These Habits and Qualities of Soul and Body render this Personage so extraordinary, that he appears to have nothing in him but what every Man should have in him, the Exertion of his very self, abstracted from the Circumstances in which Fortune has placed him. Thus were you to see Prince *Eugene*, and were told he was a private Gentleman, you would say he is a Man of Modesty and Merit: Should you be told that was Prince *Eugene*, he would be diminished no otherwise, than that part of your distant Admiration would turn into familiar Goodwill. This I thought fit to entertain my Reader with, concerning an Hero who never was equalled but by one Man; over whom also he has this Advantage, that he has had an Opportunity to manifest an Esteem for him in his Adversity.   T

No. 341.
[BUDGELL.]   Tuesday, April 1.

> . . . *Revocate animos maestumque timorem*
> *Mittite.* . . .—Virg.

HAVING, to oblige my Correspondent *Physibulus*, printed his Letter last *Friday*, in relation to the new Epilogue, he cannot take it amiss, if I now publish another, which I have just received from a Gentleman, who does not agree with him in his Sentiments upon that Matter.

'*Sir*,

I am amazed to find an Epilogue attacked in your last *Friday's* Paper, which has been so generally applauded by the Town, and received such Honours as were never before given to any in an *English* Theatre.

The Audience would not permit Mrs. *Oldfield* to go off the Stage the first Night till she had repeated it twice: the second Night the Noise of *Ancoras* was as loud as before, and she was again obliged to speak it twice: the third Night it was still called for a second time; and, in short, contrary to all other Epilogues, which are drop'd after the third Representation of the Play, this has already been repeated nine times.

I must own, I am the more surprized to find this Censure in Opposition to the whole Town, in a Paper which has hitherto been famous for the Candour of its Criticisms.

I can by no Means allow your melancholy Correspondent, that the new Epilogue is unnatural because it is gay. If I had a Mind to be learned, I could tell him that the Prologue and Epilogue were real Parts of the ancient Tragedy; but every one knows that on the *British* Stage they are distinct Performances by themselves, Pieces intirely detached from the Play, and no way essential to it.

The Moment the Play ends, Mrs. *Oldfield* is no more *Andromache*, but Mrs. *Oldfield*; and tho' the Poet had left *Andromache stone-dead upon the Stage*, as your ingenious Correspondent phrases it, Mrs. *Oldfield* might still have spoke a merry Epilogue. We have an Instance of this in a Tragedy where there is not only a Death but a Martyrdom. St. *Catherine* was there personated by *Nell Gwin*; she lies *stone-dead upon the Stage*, but upon those Gentlemen's offering to remove her Body, whose Business it is to carry off the Slain in our *English* Tragedies, she breaks out into that abrupt Beginning, of what was a very ludicrous, but at the same Time thought a very good Epilogue.

> *Hold, are you mad? you damn'd confounded Dog,*
> *I am to rise and speak the Epilogue.*

This diverting Manner was always practised by Mr. *Dryden*, who, if he was not the best Writer of Tragedies in his Time, was allowed by every one to have the happiest Turn for a Prologue or an Epilogue. The Epilogues to *Cleomenes, Don Sebastian, The Duke of Guise, Aureng-zebe*, and *Love Triumphant*, are all Precedents of this Nature.

I might further justify this Practice by that excellent Epilogue which was spoken a few Years since, after the Tragedy of *Phaedra* and *Hippolitus*; with a great many others, in which the Authors have endeavour'd to make the Audience merry. If they have not all succeeded so well as the Writer of this, they have, however, shewn that it was not for want of Goodwill.

I must further observe, that the Gayety of it may be still the more proper, as it is at the End of a *French* Play; since every one knows that Nation, who are generally esteemed to have as polite a Taste as any in *Europe*, always close their Tragic Entertainments with what they call a *Petite Pièce*, which is purposely design'd to raise Mirth, and send away the Audience well pleased. The same Person who has supported the chief Character in the Tragedy, very often plays the principal

Part in the *Petite Pièce*; so tnat I have my self seen at *Paris*, *Orestes* and *Lubin* acted the same Night by the same Man.

Tragi-Comedy, indeed, you have your self in a former Speculation found Fault with very justly, because it breaks the Tide of the Passions while they are yet flowing; but this is nothing at all to the present Case, where they have already had their full Course.

As the new Epilogue is written conformably to the Practice of our best Poets, so it is not such an one which, as the Duke of *Buckingham* says in his *Rehearsal*, might serve for any other Play, but wholly rises out of the Occurrences of the Piece it was composed for.

The only Reason your mournful Correspondent gives against this *facetious Epilogue*, as he calls it, is, that he has a Mind to go home *Melancholy*.   I wish the Gentleman may not be more grave than wise.   For my own Part, I must confess I think it very sufficient to have the Anguish of a fictitious Piece remain upon me while it is representing, but I love to be sent home to Bed in a good Humour.   If *Physibulus* is however resolved to be inconsolable, and not to have his Tears dried up, he need only continue his old Custom, and when he has had his Half Crown's Worth of Sorrow, slink out before the Epilogue begins.

It is pleasant enough to hear this Tragical Genius complaining of the *great Mischief Andromache* had done him: What was that?   Why, she made him laugh.   The poor Gentleman's Sufferings put me in Mind of *Harlequin*'s Case, who was tickled to Death.   He tells us soon after, thro' a small Mistake of Sorrow for Rage, that during the whole Action he was so very sorry, that he thinks he could have attack'd *half a Score of the fiercest Mohocks* in the Excess of his Grief.   I cannot but look upon it as an happy Accident, that a Man who is so bloodyminded in his Affliction, was diverted from this Fit of outragious Melancholy.   The Valour of this Gentleman in his Distress, brings to one's Memory the *Knight of the Sorrowful Countenance*, who lays about him at such an unmerciful Rate in an old Romance.   I shall readily grant him, that his Soul, as he himself says, *would have made a very ridiculous Figure, had it quitted the Body, and descended to the Poetical Shades* in such an Encounter.

As to his Conceit of tacking a *Tragic Head* with a *Comic Tail*, in order to *refresh the Audience*, it is such a piece of *Jargon* that I don't know what to make of it.

The Elegant Writer makes a very sudden Transition from the Play-house to the Church, and from thence to the Gallows.

As for what relates to the Church, he is of Opinion that these Epilogues have given Occasion to those *merry Jiggs from the*

Organ-Loft, which have dissipated those good Thoughts and Dispositions he has found in himself, and the rest of the Pew, upon the singing of two Staves cull'd out by the judicious and diligent Clark.

He fetches his next Thought from *Tyburn*; and seems very apprehensive lest there should happen any Innovations in the Tragedies of his Friend *Paul Lorrain*.

In the mean Time, Sir, this gloomy Writer, who is so mightily scandalized at a gay Epilogue after a serious Play, speaking of the Fate of those unhappy Wretches who are condemned to suffer an ignominious Death by the Justice of our Laws, endeavours to make the Reader merry on so improper an Occasion, by those poor Burlesque Expressions of *Tragical Dramas and Monthly Performances.*

> *I am, Sir, with great Respect,*
>
> *Your most obedient, most humble Servant,*

X   Philomeides.'

No. 342.

[STEELE.]   Wednesday, April 2.

> *Justitiae partes sunt non violare homines: Verecundiae non offendere.*—Tull.

As Regard to Decency is a great Rule of Life in general, but more especially to be consulted by the Female World, I cannot overlook the following Letter, which describes an egregious Offender.

'*Mr.* SPECTATOR,

I was this Day looking over your Papers, and reading in that of *December* the 6th with great Delight the amiable Grief of *Asteria* for the Absence of her Husband, it threw me into a great deal of Reflection. I cannot say but this arose very much from the Circumstances of my own Life, who am a Soldier, and expect every Day to receive Orders, which will oblige me to leave behind me a Wife that is very dear to me, and that very deservedly. She is, at present, I am sure, no way below your *Asteria* for Conjugal Affection: But I see the Behaviour of some Women so little suited to the Circumstances wherein my Wife and I shall soon be, that it is with a Reluctance I never knew before, I am going to my Duty. What puts me to present Pain, is the Example of a young Lady, whose Story you shall have as well as I can give it you. *Hortensius*, an Officer of good Rank in her Majesty's Service, happened in a certain Part of *England* to be brought to a Country-Gentleman's House, where he was received with that more than ordinary Welcome, with which Men of domestick Lives entertain such few Soldiers whom a military Life, from the Variety of Adventures, has not rendered over-bearing but humane, easy, and agreeable. *Hortensius* stay'd here some Time, and had easy Access at all Hours, as well as unavoidable Conversation at some Parts of the Day with the beautiful *Sylvana*, the Gentleman's Daughter. People who live in Cities are wonderfully struck with every little Country Abode they see when they take the Air; and 'tis natural to fancy they could live in every neat Cottage (by which they pass) much happier than in their present Circumstances. The turbulent way of Life which *Hortensius* was us'd to, made him reflect with much Satisfaction on all the Advantages of a sweet Retreat one Day; and among the rest, you 'll think it not improbable, it might enter into his Thought, that such a Woman as *Sylvana* would consummate the Happiness. The World is so debauched with mean Considerations, that *Hortensius* knew it would be received as an Act of Generosity, if he asked for a Woman of the highest Merit, without further Questions of a Parent who had nothing to add to her personal Qualifications. The Wedding was celebrated at her Father's House: When that was over, the generous Husband did not proportion his Provision for her to the Circumstances of her Fortune, but considered his Wife as his Darling, his Pride, and his Vanity, or rather that it was in the Woman he had chosen that a Man of Sense could shew Pride or Vanity with an Excuse, and therefore adorned her with rich Habits and valuable Jewels. He did not however omit to admonish her that he did his very utmost in this; that it was an Ostentation he could not but be guilty of to a Woman he had so much Pleasure in, desiring her to consider it as such; and begged of her also to take these Matters rightly, and believe the Gems, the Gowns, the Laces, would still become her better, if her Air and Behaviour was such, that it might appear she dressed thus rather in Compliance to his Humour that way, than out of any Value she her self had for the Trifles. To this Lesson, too hard for a Woman, *Hortensius* added, that she must be sure to stay with her Friends in the Country till his Return. As soon as *Hortensius* departed, *Sylvana* saw in her Looking-glass that the Love he conceived for her was wholly owing to the Accident of seeing her; and she is convinced it was only her Misfortune the rest of Mankind had not beheld her, or Men of much greater Quality and Merit had contended for one so genteel, tho' bred in Obscurity; so very witty, tho' never acquainted with Court or Town. She therefore resolved not to hide so much Excellence from the World, but without any Regard to the Absence of the most generous Man alive, she is now the gayest Lady about this Town, and has shut out the Thoughts of her Husband by a constant Retinue of the vainest young Fellows this Age has produced; to entertain whom she squanders away all *Hortensius* is able to supply her with, tho' that Supply is purchased with no less Difficulty than the Hazard of his Life.

Now, *Mr.* SPECTATOR, would it not be a Work becoming your Office to treat this Criminal as she deserves? You should give it the severest Reflections you can: You should tell Women, that they are more accountable for Behaviour in Absence than after Death. The Dead are not dishonoured by their Levities; the Living may return, and be laughed at by empty Fops, who will not fail to turn into Ridicule the good Man, who is so unseasonable as to be still alive, and come and spoil good Company.

I am, Sir, your most obedient humble Servant.'

All Strictness of Behaviour is so unmercifully laughed at in our Age, that the other much worse Extreme is the more common Folly. But let any Woman consider which of the two Offences an Husband would the more easily forgive, that of being less entertaining than she could to please Company, or raising the Desires of the whole Room to his Disadvantage; and she will easily be able to form her Conduct. We have indeed carried Women's Characters too much into publick Life, and you shall see them now-a-Days affect a sort of Fame; but I cannot help venturing to disoblige them for their Service, by telling them, that the utmost of a Woman's Character is contained in domestick Life; she is Blameable or Praiseworthy according as her Carriage affects the House of her Father or her Husband. All she has to do in this World, is contained within the Duties of a Daughter, a Sister, a Wife, and a Mother: All these may be well performed, tho' a Lady should not be the very finest Woman at an Opera or an Assembly. They are likewise consistent with a moderate Share of Wit, a plain Dress, and a modest Air. But when the very Brains of the Sex are turned, and they place their Ambition on Circumstances wherein to excel, it 's no Addition to what is truly commendable. Where can this end but, as it frequently does, in their placing all their Industry, Pleasure, and Ambition on things, which will naturally make the Gratifications of Life last, at best, no longer than Youth and good Fortune? And when we consider the least ill Consequence, it can be no less than looking, on their own Condition as Years advance, with a

Disrelish of Life, and falling into Contempt of their own Persons, or being the Derision of others.   But when they consider themselves as they ought, no other than an additional Part of the Species, (for their own Happiness and Comfort, as well as that of those for whom they were born) their Ambition to excel will be directed accordingly; and they will in no Part of their Lives want Opportunities of being shining Ornaments to their Fathers, Husbands, Brothers, or Children.

No. 343.
[ADDISON.]   Thursday, April 3.

Errat, & illinc
Huc venit, hinc illuc, & quoslibet occupat artus
Spiritus; eque feris humana in corpora transit,
Inque feras noster. . . . Pythag. ap. Ov.

WILL. HONEYCOMB, who loves to shew upon Occasion all the little Learning he has picked up, told us Yesterday at the Club, that he thought there might be a great deal said for the Transmigration of Souls, and that the Eastern Parts of the World believed in that Doctrine to this Day.   Sir *Paul Rycaut*, says he, gives us an Account of several well-disposed Mahometans that purchase the Freedom of any little Bird they see confined to a Cage, and think they merit as much by it, as we should do here by ransoming any of our Country men from their Captivity at *Algiers*.   You must know, says WILL, the Reason is, because they consider every Animal as a Brother or a Sister in Disguise, and therefore think themselves obliged to extend their Charity to them, tho' under such mean Circumstances. They 'll tell you, says WILL, that the Soul of a Man, when he dies, immediately passes into the Body of another Man, or of some Brute, which he resembled in his Humour, or his Fortune, when he was one of *us*.

As I was wondering what this Profusion of Learning would end in, WILL told us that *Jack Freelove*, who was a Fellow of Whim, made Love to one of those Ladies, who throw away all their Fondness on Parrots, Monkeys, and Lap-dogs.   Upon going to pay her a Visit one Morning, he writ a very pretty Epistle upon this Hint.   *Jack*, says he, was conducted into the Parlour, where he diverted himself for some Time with her Favourite Monkey, which was chained in one of the Windows; till at length observing a Pen and Ink lie by him, he writ the following Letter to his Mistress, in the Person of the Monkey; and upon her not coming down so soon as he expected, left it in the Window; and went about his Business.

The Lady soon after coming into the Parlour, and seeing

her Monkey look upon a Paper with great Earnestness, took it up, and to this Day is in some Doubt, says WILL, whether it was written by *Jack* or the Monkey.

' *Madam,*

Not having the Gift of Speech, I have a long Time waited in vain for an Opportunity of making my self known to you; and having at present the Conveniencies of Pen, Ink, and Paper by me, I gladly take the Occasion of giving you my History in Writing, which I could not do by Word of Mouth. You must know, Madam, that about a thousand Years ago I was an *Indian* Brachman, and versed in all those mysterious Secrets which your *European* Philosopher, called *Pythagoras*, is said to have learned from our Fraternity. I had so ingratiated my self by my great Skill in the Occult Sciences with a Daemon whom I used to converse with, that he promised to grant me whatever I should ask of him. I desired that my Soul might never pass into the Body of a Brute Creature; but this he told me was not in his Power to grant me. I then begg'd that into whatever Creature I should chance to transmigrate, I might still retain my Memory, and be conscious that I was the same Person who lived in different Animals. This he told me was within his Power, and accordingly promised on the Word of a Daemon that he would grant me what I desired. From that Time forth I lived so very unblameably, that I was made President of a College of Brachmans, an Office which I discharged with great Integrity till the Day of my Death.

I was then shuffled into another human Body, and acted my Part so very well in it, that I became first Minister to a Prince who reigned upon the Banks of the *Ganges*. I here lived in great Honour for several Years, but by Degrees lost all the Innocence of the Brachman, being obliged to rifle and oppress the People to enrich my Sovereign; till at length I became so odious, that my Master, to recover his Credit with his Subjects, shot me through the Heart with an Arrow, as I was one Day addressing my self to him at the Head of his Army.

Upon my next remove I found my self in the Woods under the Shape of a Jack-call, and soon listed my self in the Service of a Lion. I used to yelp near his Den about Midnight, which was his Time of rouzing and seeking after his Prey. He always followed me in the Rear, and when I had run down a fat Buck, a wild Goat, or an Hare, after he had feasted very plentifully upon it himself, would now and then throw me a Bone that was but half picked for my Encouragement; but upon my being unsuccessful in two or three Chaces, he gave me such a confounded Gripe in his Anger that I died of it.

In my next Transmigration I was again set upon two Legs, and became an *Indian* Tax-gatherer; but having been guilty of great Extravagancies, and being married to an expensive Jade of a Wife, I ran so cursedly in Debt that I durst not shew my Head. I could no sooner step out of my House, but I was arrested by some Body or other that lay in wait for me. As I ventured abroad one Night in the Dusk of the Evening, I was taken up and hurried into a Dungeon, where I died a few Months after.

My Soul then entered into a Flying-Fish, and in that State led a most melancholy Life for the Space of six Years. Several Fishes of Prey pursued me when I was in the Water, and if I betook my self to my Wings, it was ten to one but I had a Flock of Birds aiming at me. As I was one Day flying amidst a Fleet of *English* Ships, I observed an huge Sea-Gull whetting his Bill and hovering just over my Head: Upon my dipping into the Water to avoid him, I fell into the Mouth of a monstrous Shark that swallow'd me down in an Instant.

I was some Years afterwards, to my great Surprize, an eminent Banker in *Lombard-street*; and remembring how I had formerly suffered for want of Money, became so very sordid and avaritious that the whole Town cried Shame of me. I was a miserable little old Fellow to look upon, for I had in a Manner starved my self, and was nothing but Skin and Bone when I died.

I was afterwards very much troubled and amazed to find my self dwindled into an Emmet. I was heartily concerned to make so insignificant a Figure, and did not know but, some Time or other, I might be reduced to a Mite if I did not mend my Manners. I therefore applied my self with great Diligence to the Offices that were allotted me, and was generally looked upon as the notablest Ant in the whole Molehill. I was at last picked up, as I was groaning under a Burden, by an unlucky Cock-Sparrow that lived in the Neighbourhood, and had before made great Depredations upon our Common-wealth.

I then bettered my Condition a little, and lived a whole Summer in the Shape of a Bee; but being tired with the painful and penurious Life I had undergone in my two last Transmigrations, I fell into the other Extream, and turned Drone. As I one Day headed a Party to plunder an Hive, we were received so warmly by the Swarm which defended it, that we were most of us left dead upon the Spot.

I might tell you of many other Transmigrations which I went through; how I was a Town-Rake, and afterwards did Penance in a Bay Gelding for ten Years; as also how I was a Taylor, a Shrimp, and a Tom-Tit. In the last of these my

Shapes I was shot in the *Christmas* Holydays by a young Jack-a-napes, who would needs try his new Gun upon me.

But I shall pass over these and several other Stages of Life, to remind you of the young Beau who made Love to you about Six Years since. You may remember, Madam, how he masked, and danced, and sung, and played a thousand Tricks to gain you; and how he was at last carried off by a Cold that he got under your Window one Night in a Serenade. I was that unfortunate young Fellow, whom you were then so cruel to. Not long after my shifting that unlucky Body, I found my self upon a Hill in *Aethiopia*, where I lived in my present Grotesque Shape, till I was caught by a Servant of the *English* Factory, and sent over into *Great-Britain*: I need not inform you how I came into your Hands. You see, Madam, this is not the first Time that you have had me in a Chain; I am, however, very happy in this my Captivity, as you often bestow on me those Kisses and Caresses which I would have given the World for when I was a Man. I hope this Discovery of my Person will not tend to my Disadvantage, but that you will still continue your accustomed Favours to

Your most devoted humble Servant,

Pugg.

P. S. I would advise your little Shock-dog to keep out of my Way; for as I look upon him to be the most formidable of my Rivals, I may chance one Time or other to give him such a Snap as he won't like.' L

No. 344.
[STEELE.]   Friday, April 4.

. . . *In solo vivendi causa palato est.*—Juv.

'*Mr.* Spectator,

I think it has not yet fallen into your Way to discourse on little Ambition, or the many whimsical Ways Men fall into, to distinguish themselves among their Acquaintance: Such Observations, well pursued, would make a pretty History of low Life. I my self am got into a great Reputation, which arose (as most extraordinary Occurrences in a Man's Life seem to do) from a meer Accident. I was some Days ago unfortunately engaged among a Set of Gentlemen, who esteem a Man according to the Quantity of Food he throws down at a Meal. Now I, who am ever for distinguishing my self according to the Notions of Superiority which the rest of the Company entertain, eat so immoderately for their Applause, as had like to have cost me my Life. What added to my Misfortune was, that having naturally a good Stomach, and having lived soberly for some Time, my Body was as well prepared for this Contention as if it had been by Appointment. I had quickly vanquished every Glutton in Company but one, who was such a Prodigy in his Way, and withall so very merry during the whole Entertainment, that he insensibly betrayed me to continue his Competitor, which in a little Time concluded in a compleat Victory over my Rival; after which, by way of Insult, I eat a considerable Proportion beyond what the Spectators thought me obliged in Honour to do. The Effect, however, of this Engagement, has made me resolve never to eat more for Renown; and I have, pursuant to this Resolution, compounded three Wagers I had depending on the Strength of my Stomach; which happened very luckily, because it was stipulated in our Articles either to play or pay. How a Man of common Sense could be thus engaged, is hard to determine; but the Occasion of this is to desire you, to inform several Gluttons of my Acquaintance, who look on me with Envy, that they had best moderate their Ambition in Time, lest Infamy or Death attend their Success. I forgot to tell you, Sir, with what unspeakable Pleasure I received the Acclamations and Applause of the whole Board, when I had almost eat my Antagonist into Convulsions: It was then that I returned his Mirth upon him, with such Success as he was hardly able to swallow, though prompted by a Desire of Fame, and a passionate Fondness for Distinction: I had not endeavoured to excell so far, had not the Company been so loud in their Approbation of my Victory. I don't question but the same Thirst after Glory has often caused a Man to drink Quarts without taking Breath, and prompted Men to many other as difficult Enterprizes; though, if otherwise pursued, might turn very much to a Man's Advantage. This Ambition of mine was indeed extravagantly pursued: However I can't help observing, that you hardly ever see a Man commended for a good Stomach, but he immediately falls to eating more (though he had before dined) as well to confirm the Person that commended him in his good Opinion of him, as to convince any other at the Table, who may have been unattentive enough not to have done Justice to his Character.

I am, Sir,

Your most humble Servant,

Epicure Mammon.'

'*Mr.* Spectator,

I have writ to you three or four times, to desire you would take Notice of an impertinent Custom the Women, the fine

Women have lately fallen into, of taking Snuff. This silly Trick is attended with such a Coquet Air in some Ladies, and such a sedate Masculine one in others, that I cannot tell which most to complain of; but they are to me equally disagreeable. Mrs. *Saunter* is so impatient of being without it, that she takes it as often as she does Salt at Meals; and as she affects a wonderful Ease and Negligence in all her Manner, an upper Lip mixed with Snuff and the Sauce, is what is presented to the Observation of all who have the Honour to eat with her. The pretty Creature her Neice does all she can to be as disagreeable as her Aunt; and if she is not as offensive to the Eye, she is quite as much to the Ear, and makes up all she wants in a confident Air, by a nauseous Rattle of the Nose when the Snuff is delivered, and the Fingers make the Stops and Closes on the Nostrils. This, perhaps, is not a very courtly Image in speaking of Ladies; that is very true, but where arises the Offence? Is it in those who commit, or those who observe it? As for my Part, I have been so extreamly disgusted with this filthy Physick hanging on the Lip, that the most agreeable Conversation, or Person, has not been able to make up for it. As to those who take it for no other End but to give themselves Occasion for pretty Action, or to fill up little Intervals of Discourse, I can bear with them; but then they must not use it when another is speaking, who ought to be heard with too much Respect, to admit of offering at that Time from Hand to Hand the Snuff-Box. But *Flavilla* is so far taken with her Behaviour in this kind, that she pulls out her Box (which is indeed full of good *Brazile*) in the Middle of the Sermon; and to shew she has the Audacity of a well bred Woman, she offers it to the Men as well as the Women who sit near her: But since by this Time all the World knows she has a fine Hand, I am in Hopes she may give her self no further Trouble in this Matter. On *Sunday* was Sevennight, when they came about for the Offering, she gave her Charity with a very good Air, but at the same Time asked the Church-warden if he would take a Pinch. Pray, Sir, think of these things in Time, and you will oblige,

T   *Sir, your most humble Servant.'*

No. 345.
[ADDISON.]   Saturday, April 5.

> *Sanctius his animal, mentisque capacius altae*
> *Deerat adhuc, et quod dominari in cetera posset.*
> *Natus homo est. . . . Ov. Met.*

THE Accounts which *Raphael* gives of the Battle of Angels, and the Creation of the World, have in them those Qualifications which the Criticks judge requisite to an Episode. They are nearly related to the principal Action, and have a just Connection with the Fable.

The Eighth Book opens with a beautiful Description of the Impression which this Discourse of the Archangel made on our first Parent. *Adam* afterwards, by a very natural Curiosity, enquires concerning the Motions of those Celestial Bodies which make the most glorious Appearance among the six Days Works. The Poet here, with a great deal of Art, represents *Eve* as withdrawing from this Part of their Conversation to Amusements more suitable for her Sex. He well knew, that the Episode in this Book, which is filled with *Adam's* Account of his Passion and Esteem for *Eve*, would have been improper for her Hearing, and has therefore devised very just and beautiful Reasons for her retiring.

> *So spake our Sire, and by his Count'nance seem'd*
> *Entring on studious Thoughts abstruse; which* Eve
> *Perceiving where she sat retired in sight,*
> *With Lowliness majestick from her Seat,*
> *And Grace that won who saw to wish her Stay,*
> *Rose, and went forth among her Fruits and Flowers,*
> *To visit how they prosper'd, Bud and Bloom,*
> *Her Nursery: they at her Coming sprung,*
> *And toucht by her fair Tendance gladlier grew.*
> *Yet went she not, as not with such Discourse*
> *Delighted, or not capable her Ear*
> *Of what was high: Such Pleasure she reserv'd,*
> Adam *relating, she sole Auditress:*
> *Her Husband the Relater she preferr'd*
> *Before the Angel, and of him to ask*
> *Chose rather: he, she knew, would intermix*
> *Grateful Digressions, and solve high Dispute*
> *With Conjugal Caresses; from his Lip*
> *Not Words alone pleased her. O when meet now*
> *Such Pairs in Love, and mutual Honour joyn'd!*

The Angel's returning a doubtful Answer to *Adam's* Enquiries, was not only proper for the moral Reason which the Poet assigns, but because it would have been highly absurd to have given the Sanction of an Archangel to any particular System of Philosophy. The chief Points in the *Ptolomaick* and *Copernican* Hypothesis are described with great Conciseness and Perspicuity, and at the same Time dressed in very pleasing and poetical Images.

Adam, to detain the Angel, enters afterwards upon his own History, and relates to him the Circumstances in which he found himself upon his Creation; as also his Conversation with his Maker, and his first meeting with *Eve*. There is no Part of the Poem more apt to raise the Attention of the Reader, than this Discourse of our great Ancestor; as nothing can be more surprizing and delightful to us, than to hear the Sentiments that arose in the first Man while he was yet new and fresh from the Hands of his Creator. The Poet has interwoven every thing which is delivered upon this Subject in Holy Writ with so many beautiful Imaginations of his own, that nothing can be conceived more just and natural than this whole Episode. As our Author knew this Subject could not but be agreeable to his Reader, he would not throw it into the Relation of the six Days Works, but reserved it for a distinct Episode, that he might have an Opportunity of expatiating upon it more at large. Before I enter on this Part of the Poem, I cannot but take Notice of two shining Passages in the Dialogue between *Adam* and the Angel. The first is that wherein our Ancestor gives an Account of the Pleasure he took in conversing with him, which contains a very noble Moral.

> *For while I sit with thee, I seem in Heav'n;*
> *And sweeter thy Discourse is to my Ear*
> *Than Fruits of Palm-tree, pleasantest to thirst*
> *And Hunger both, from Labour, at the Hour*
> *Of sweet Repast; they satiate, and soon fill,*
> *Tho' pleasant; but thy Words, with Grace divine*
> *Imbu'd, bring to their Sweetnes no Satiety.*

The other I shall mention is that in which the Angel gives a Reason why he should be glad to hear the story *Adam* was about to relate.

> *For I that Day was absent, as befell,*
> *Bound on a Voyage uncouth and obscure,*
> *Far on Excursion towards the Gates of Hell,*
> *Squared in full Legion (such command we had)*
> *To see that none thence issued forth a Spy,*
> *Or Enemy, while God was in his Work,*
> *Lest he incenst at such Eruption bold,*
> *Destruction with Creation might have mix'd.*

There is no Question but our Poet drew the Image in what follows from that in *Virgil*'s Sixth Book, where *Aeneas* and the Sybil stand before the Adamantine Gates, which are there describ'd as shut upon the Place of Torments, and listen to the Groans, the Clank of Chains, and the Noise of Iron Whips, that were heard in those Regions of Pain and Sorrow.

> *. . . Fast we found, fast shut,*
> *The dismal Gates, and barricadoed strong;*
> *But long e'er our approaching heard within*
> *Noise, other than the Sound of Dance or Song,*
> *Torment, and loud Lament, and furious Rage.*

Adam then proceeds to give an Account of his condition and Sentiments immediately after his Creation. How agreeably does he represent the Posture in which he found himself, the beautiful Landskip that surrounded him, and the Gladness of Heart which grew up in him on that Occasion?

> . . . *As new waked from soundest Sleep,*
> *Soft on the flowry Herb I found me laid*
> *In balmy Sweat, which with his Beams the Sun*
> *Soon dried, and on the reaking Moisture fed.*
> *Straight toward Heav'n my wondering Eyes I turn'd,*
> *And gaz'd a while the ample Sky, till rais'd*
> *By quick instinctive Motion up I sprung,*
> *As thitherward endeavouring, and upright*
> *Stood on my Feet; About me round I saw*
> *Hill, Dale, and shady Woods, and sunny Plains,*
> *And liquid Lapse of murmuring Streams: by these*
> *Creatures that liv'd, and mov'd, and walk'd, or flew,*
> *Birds on the Branches warbling; all things smil'd,*
> *With Fragrance and with Joy my heart o'erflow'd.*

Adam is afterwards describ'd as surpriz'd at his own Existence, and taking a Survey of himself, and of all the Works of Nature. He likewise is represented as discovering by the Light of Reason, that he and every thing about him must have been the Effect of some Being infinitely good and powerful, and that this Being had a Right to his Worship and Adoration. His first Address to the Sun, and to those Parts of the Creation which made the most distinguished Figure, is very natural and amusing to the Imagination.

> . . . *Thou Sun, said I, fair Light,*
> *And thou enlight'ned Earth, so fresh and gay,*
> *Ye Hills and Dales, ye Rivers, Woods, and Plains,*
> *And ye that live and move, fair Creatures, tell,*
> *Tell if ye saw, how came I thus, how here!*

His next Sentiment, when upon his first going to sleep he fancies himself losing his Existence, and falling away into nothing, can never be sufficiently admired. His Dream, in which he still preserves the Consciousness of his Existence, together with his Removal into the Garden which was prepared for his Reception, are also Circumstances finely imagined, and grounded upon what is delivered in sacred Story.

These and the like wonderful Incidents in this Part of the Work, have in them all the Beauties of Novelty, at the same Time that they have all the Graces of Nature. They are such as none but a great Genius could have thought of, though, upon the Perusal of them, they seem to rise of themselves from the Subject of which he treats. In a Word, though they are natural they are not obvious, which is the true Character of all fine Writing.

The Impression which the Interdiction of the Tree of Life left in the Mind of our first Parent, is described with great Strength and Judgment; as the Image of the several Beasts and Birds passing in Review before him is very beautiful and lively.

> . . . *Each Bird and Beast behold*
> *Approaching two and two, these cowring low*
> *With Blandishment; each Bird stoop'd on his Wing:*
> *I nam'd them as they pass'd* . . .

Adam, in the next Place, describes a Conference which he held with his Maker upon the Subject of Solitude. The Poet here represents the supreme Being, as making an Essay of his own Work, and putting to the Trial that reasoning Faculty with which he had endued his Creature. *Adam* urges, in this divine Colloquy the Impossibility of his being happy, tho' he was the Inhabitant of *Paradise*, and Lord of the whole Creation, without the Conversation and Society of some rational Creature, who should partake those Blessings with him. This Dialogue, which is supported chiefly by the Beauty of the Thoughts, without other poetical Ornaments, is as fine a Part as any in the whole Poem: The more the Reader examines the Justness and Delicacy of its Sentiments, the more he will find himself pleased with it. The Poet has wonderfully preserved the Character of Majesty and Condescension in the Creator, and at the same Time that of Humility and Adoration in the Creature, as particularly in those beautiful Lines,

> *Thus I presumptuous; and the Vision bright,*
> *As with a Smile more brightened, thus reply'd, &c.*
> *. . . I, with leave of Speech implor'd*
> *And humble Deprecation, thus reply'd,*
> *Let not my Words offend thee, heavenly Power;*
> *My Maker, be propitious while I speak, &c.*

Adam then proceeds to give an Account of his second Sleep, and of the Dream in which he beheld the Formation of *Eve*. The new Passion that was awakened in him at the Sight of her is touched very finely.

> *Under his forming Hands a Creature grew,*
> *Manlike, but different Sex; so lovely fair,*
> *That what seem'd fair in all the World seem'd now*
> *Mean, or in her summ'd up, in her contain'd,*
> *And in her Looks, which from that time infus'd*
> *Sweetness into my Heart, unfelt before,*
> *And into all things from her Air inspir'd*
> *The Spirit of Love and amorous Delight.*

Adam's Distress upon losing Sight of this beautiful Phantom, with his Exclamations of Joy and Gratitude at the Discovery of a real Creature, who resembled the Apparition which had been presented to him in his Dream; the Approaches he makes to her, and his Manner of Courtship, are all laid together in a most exquisite Propriety of Sentiments.

Tho' this Part of the Poem is work'd up with great Warmth and Spirit, the Love which is described in it is every way suitable to a State of Innocence. If the Reader compares the Description which *Adam* here gives of his leading *Eve* to the Nuptial Bower, with that which Mr. *Dryden* has made on the same Occasion in a Scene of his *Fall of Man,* he will be sensible of the great Care which *Milton* took to avoid all Thoughts on so delicate a Subject, that might be offensive to Religion or good Manners. The Sentiments are chaste, but not cold, and convey to the Mind Ideas of the most transporting Passion, and of the greatest Purity. What a Noble Mixture of Rapture and Innocence has the Author joined together, in the Reflection which *Adam* makes on the Pleasures of Love, compared to those of Sense.

> *Thus have I told thee all my State, and brought*
> *My Story to the Sum of earthly Bliss*
> *Which I enjoy, and must confess to find*
> *In all things else delight indeed, but such*
> *As, us'd or not, works in the mind no change,*
> *Nor vehement desire, these delicacies*
> *I mean of taste, sight, smell, herbs, fruits, & flowers,*
> *Walks, and the melody of Birds; but here*
> *Far otherwise, transported I behold,*
> *Transported touch, here Passion first I felt,*
> *Commotion strange; in all enjoyments else*
> *Superiour and unmov'd, here only weak*
> *Against the Charm of Beauty's powerful glance,*
> *Or Nature fail'd in me, and left some part*
> *Not proof enough such object to sustain,*
> *Or from my side subduing, took perhaps*
> *More than enough; at least on her bestow'd*
> *Too much of ornament, in outward shew*
> *Elaborate, of inward less exact.*
> *. . . When I approach*
> *Her loveliness, so absolute she seems*
> *And in her self compleat, so well to know*
> *Her own, that what she wills to do or say*
> *Seems wisest, vertuousest, discreetest, best;*
> *All higher knowledge in her presence falls*
> *Degraded: Wisdom in discourse with her*
> *Loses discountenanc'd, and like folly shews;*
> *Authority and reason on her wait,*
> *As one intended first, not after made*

> *Occasionally; and to consummate all,*
> *Greatness of Mind, and Nobleness their Seat*
> *Build in her loveliest, and create an awe*
> *About her, as a Guard angelick plac'd.*

These Sentiments of Love, in our first Parent, gave the
Angel such an Insight into humane Nature, that he seems
apprehensive of the Evils which might befal the Species in
general, as well as *Adam* in particular, from the Excess of
this Passion.   He therefore fortifies him against it by timely
Admonitions; which very artfully prepare the Mind of the
Reader for the Occurrences of the next Book, where the Weakness of which *Adam* here gives such distant Discoveries brings
about that fatal Event which is the Subject of the Poem.   His
Discourse, which follows the gentle Rebuke he receiv'd from
the Angel, shews that his Love, however violent it might
appear, was still founded in Reason, and consequently not
improper for *Paradise.*

> *Neither her outside form so fair, nor aught*
> *In procreation common to all kinds*
> *(Though higher of the genial bed by far,*
> *And with mysterious reverence I deem)*
> *So much delights me as those graceful acts,*
> *Those thousand decencies that daily flow*
> *From all her words and actions mixt with love*
> *And sweet compliance, which declare unfeign'd*
> *Union of Mind, or in us both one Soul;*
> *Harmony to behold in wedded pair.*

Adam's Speech, at parting with the Angel, has in it a
Deference and Gratitude agreeable to an inferior Nature, and
at the same Time a certain Dignity and Greatness suitable to
the Father of Mankind in his State of Innocence.   L

No. 346.
[STEELE.]   Monday, April 7.

Consuetudinem benignitatis largitioni munerum longe antepono.
Haec est gravium hominum atque magnorum; illa quasi assenta-
torum populi, multitudinis levitatem voluptate quasi titillantium.
    —Tull.

WHEN we consider the offices of humane Life, there is, methinks, something in what we ordinarily call Generosity, which
when carefully examined, seems to flow rather from a loose
and unguarded Temper, than an honest and liberal Mind.
For this Reason it is absolutely necessary that all Liberality
should have for its Basis and Support Frugality.   By this

means the beneficent Spirit works in a Man from the Convictions of Reason, not from the Impulses of Passion. The generous Man, in the ordinary Acceptation, without respect of the Demands of his own Family, will soon find, upon the Foot of his Account, that he has sacrificed to Fools, Knaves, Flatterers, or the deservedly unhappy, all the Opportunities of affording any future Assistance where it ought to be. Let him therefore reflect, that if to bestow be in it self laudable, should not a Man take Care to secure an Ability to do Things praise-worthy as long as he lives? or could there be a more cruel Piece of Railery upon a Man who should have reduced his Fortune below the Capacity of acting according to his natural Temper, than to say of him, *That Gentleman was generous*. My beloved Author therefore has, in the Sentence on the Top of my Paper, turned his Eye with a certain Satiety from beholding the Addresses to the People by Largesses and publick Entertainments, which he asserts to be in general vitious, and are always to be regulated according to the Circumstances of Time and a Man's own Fortune. A constant Benignity in Commerce with the rest of the World, which ought to run through all a Man's Actions, has Effects more useful to those whom you oblige, and less ostentatious in your self. He turns his Recommendation of this Virtue in Commercial Life; and according to him, a Citizen who is frank in his Kindnesses, and abhors Severity in his Demands; he who in buying, selling, lending, doing Acts of good Neighbourhood, is just and easy; he who appears naturally averse to Disputes, and above the Sense of little Sufferings; bears a nobler Character, and does much more good to Mankind than any other Man's Fortune without Commerce can possibly support. For the Citizen above all other Men has Opportunities of arriving at *that highest Fruit of Wealth, to be liberal without the least Expence of a Man's own Fortune*. It is not to be denied but such a Practice is liable to Hazard; but this therefore adds to the Obligation, that, among Traders, he who obliges is as much concerned to keep the Favour a Secret, as he who receives it. The unhappy Distinctions among us in *England* are so great, that to celebrate the Intercourse of commercial Friendship (with which I am daily made acquainted) would be to raise the virtuous Man so many Enemies of the contrary Party. I am obliged to conceal all I know of *Tom the Bounteous*, who lends at the ordinary Interest, to give Men of less Fortune Opportunities of making greater Advantages. He conceals, under a rough Air and distant Behaviour, a bleeding Compassion and womanish Tenderness. This is governed by the most exact Circumspection, that there is no Industry wanting in the Person whom he is to serve, and that he is guilty of no improper Expences. This I know of *Tom*, but who dares say it of so known a Tory? The same Care I was forced to use some Time ago in the Report of another's Virtue, and said Fifty instead of an Hundred, because the Man I pointed at was a Whigg. Actions of this Kind are popular without being invidious, for every Man of ordinary Circumstances looks upon a Man who has this known Benignity in his Nature, as a Person ready to be his Friend upon such Terms as he ought to expect it; and the Wealthy, who may envy such a Character, can do no Injury to its Interests but by the Imitation of it, in which the good Citizens will rejoice to be rivalled. I know not how to form to my self a greater Idea of humane Life, than in what is the Practice of some wealthy Men whom I could name, that make no Step to the Improvement of their own Fortunes, wherein they do not also advance those of other Men, who would languish in Poverty without that Munificence. In a Nation where there are so many publick Funds to be supported, I know not whether he can be called a good Subject, who does not imbark some Part of his Fortune with the State to whose Vigilance he owes the Security of the whole. This certainly is an immediate Way of laying an Obligation upon many, and extending your Benignity the furthest a Man can possibly, who is not engaged in Commerce. But he who Trades, besides giving the State some Part of this sort of Credit he gives his Banker, may in all the Occurrences of his Life have his Eye upon removing Want from the Door of the Industrious, and defending the unhappy upright Man from Bankrupcy. Without this Benignity, Pride or Vengeance will precipitate a Man to chuse the Receipt of half his Demands from one whom he has undone, rather than the Whole from whom he has shewn Mercy. This Benignity is essential to the Character of a fair Trader, and any Man who designs to enjoy his Wealth with Honour and Self-Satisfaction: Nay it would not be hard to maintain, that the Practice of supporting good and industrious Men, would carry a Man further, even to his Profit, than indulging the Propensity of serving and obliging the Fortunate. My Author argues on this Subject, in order to incline Men's Minds to those who want them most, after this Manner, *We must always consider the Nature of Things, and govern our selves accordingly. The wealthy Man, when he has repaid you, is upon a Balance with you; but the Person whom you favoured with a Loan, if he be a good Man, will think himself in your Debt after he has paid you. The Wealthy and the Conspicuous are not obliged by the Benefits you do them, they think they conferred a Benefit when they receive one. Your good Offices are always suspected, and it is with them the same thing to expect their Favour as to receive it. But the Man below you, who knows, in the good you have done him, you respected himself more than his Circumstances, does not act like an obliged Man only to him from whom he has received a Benefit, but also to all who are capable of doing him one. And whatever little Offices he can do for you, he is so far from magnifying it, that he will labour to extenuate it in all his Actions and Expressions. Moreover the Regard to what you do to a great Man, at best is taken Notice of no further than by himself or his Family; but what you do to a Man of an humble Fortune, (provided always that he is a good and a modest Man) raises the Affections towards you of all Men of that Character (of which there are many) in the whole City.*

There is nothing gains a Reputation to a Preacher so much as his own Practice; I am therefore casting about what Act of Benignity is in the Power of a SPECTATOR. Alas, that lies but in a very narrow Compass, and I think the most immediately under my Patronage, are either Players, or such whose Circumstances bear an Affinity with theirs: All therefore I am able to do at this Time of this Kind, is to tell the Town, that on *Friday* the 11th of this Instant *April*, there will be perform'd in *York-Buildings* a Consort of Vocal and Instrumental Musick, for the Benefit of Mr. *Edward Keen*, the Father of Twenty Children; and that this Day the haughty *George Powell* hopes all the good natured Part of the Town will favour him, whom they applauded in *Alexander*, *Timon*, *Lear* and *Orestes*, with their Company this Night, when he hazards all his Heroic Glory for their Approbation in the humbler Condition of honest *Jack Falstaffe*.   T

No. 347.
[BUDGELL.]   Tuesday, April 8.

Quis furor, o cives, quae tanta licentia ferri.—Luc.

I DO not question but my Country Readers have been very much surprized at the several Accounts they have met with in our publick Papers of that Species of Men among us, lately known by the Name of *Mohocks*. I find the Opinions of the Learned, as to their Origin and Designs, are altogether various, insomuch that very many begin to doubt whether indeed there were ever any such Society of Men. The Terror which spread it self over the whole Nation some Years since, on account of the *Irish*, is still fresh in most People's Memories, tho' it afterwards appeared there was not the least Ground for that general Consternation.

The late Pannick Fear was, in the Opinion of many deep and penetrating Persons, of the same Nature.   These will have it, that the *Mohocks* are like those Spectres and Apparitions which frighten several Towns and Villages in Her Majesty's Dominions, tho' they were never seen by any of the Inhabitants. Others are apt to think that these *Mohocks* are a kind of Bull-Beggars, first invented by prudent married Men, and Masters of Families, in order to deter their Wives and Daughters from taking the Air at unseasonable Hours; and that when they tell them *the* Mohocks *will catch them*, it is a Caution of the same Nature with that of our Fore-fathers, when they bid their Children have a care of *Raw-head* and *Bloody-bones*.

For my own Part I am afraid there was too much Reason for that great Alarm the whole City has been in upon this Occasion; tho' at the same Time I must own that I am in some Doubt whether the following Pieces are Genuine and Authentic, and the more so, because I am not fully satisfied that the Name by which the Emperor subscribes himself, is altogether conformable to the *Indian* Orthography.

I shall only further inform my Readers, that it was some time since I received the following Letter and Manifesto, tho' for particular Reasons I did not think fit to publish them till now.

'*To the* SPECTATOR,

Sir,

Finding that our earnest Endeavours for the Good of Mankind have been basely and maliciously represented to the World, we send you enclosed our Imperial Manifesto, which it is our Will and Pleasure that you forthwith communicate to the Publick, by inserting it in your next daily Paper.   We do not doubt of your ready Compliance in this Particular, and therefore bid you heartily Farewell.

Sign'd,
Taw Waw Eben Zan Kaladar,
Emperor of the Mohocks.

'*The Manifesto of* Taw Waw Eben Zan Kaladar,
Emperor of the Mohocks.

Whereas we have received Information from sundry Quarters of this great and populous City, of several Outrages committed on the Legs, Arms, Noses, and other Parts of the good People of *England*, by such as have stiled themselves our Subjects; in order to vindicate our Imperial Dignity from those false Aspersions which have been cast on it, as if we our selves might have encouraged or abetted any such Practices; We have, by these Presents, thought fit to signifie our utmost Abhorrence and Detestation of all such tumultuous and irregular Proceedings; and do hereby further give Notice, that if any Person or Persons has or have suffered any Wound, Hurt, Damage or Detriment in his or their Limb or Limbs, otherwise than shall be hereafter specified, the said Person or Persons, upon applying themselves to such as we shall appoint for the Inspection and Redress of the Grievances aforesaid, shall be forthwith committed to the Care of our principal Surgeon, and be cured at our own Expence, in some one or other of those Hospitals which we are now erecting for that purpose.

And to that end that no one may, either through Ignorance or Inadvertency incur those Penalties which we have thought fit to inflict on Persons of loose and dissolute Lives, we do hereby notifie to the Publick, that if any Man be knock'd down or assaulted while he is employed in his lawful Business, at proper Hours, that it is not done by our Order; and we do hereby permit and allow any such Person so knocked down or assaulted, to rise again, and defend himself in the best Manner that he is able.

We do also command all and every our good Subjects, that they do not presume, upon any Pretext whatsoever, to issue and sally forth from their respective Quarters till between the Hours of Eleven and Twelve. That they never *Tip the Lion* upon Man, Woman, or Child till the Clock at St. *Dunstan's* shall have struck One.

That the *Sweat* be never given but between the Hours of One and Two; always provided, that our *Hunters* may begin to *Hunt* a little after the Close of the Evening, any thing to the contrary herein notwithstanding. Provided also that if ever they are reduced to the Necessity of *Pinking*, it shall always be in the most fleshy Parts, and such as are least exposed to View.

It is also our Imperial Will and Pleasure, that our good Subjects the *Sweaters* do establish their *Hummums* in such close Places, Alleys, Nooks and Corners, that the Patient or Patients may not be in Danger of catching Cold.

That the *Tumblers*, to whose Care we chiefly commit the Female Sex, confine themselves to *Drurylane* and the Purlieus of the *Temple*; and that every other Party and Division of our Subjects do each of them keep within the respective Quarters we have allotted to them. Provided nevertheless, that nothing herein contained shall in any wise be construed to extend to the *Hunters*, who have our full Licence and Permission to enter into any Part of the Town where ever their Game shall lead them.

And whereas we have nothing more at our Imperial Heart than the Reformation of the Cities of *London* and *Westminster*, which to our unspeakable Satisfaction we have in some measure already effected, we do hereby earnestly pray and exhort all Husbands, Fathers, House-keepers, and Masters of Families, in either of the aforesaid Cities, not only to repair themselves to their respective Habitations at early and seasonable Hours; but also to keep their Wives and Daughters, Sons, Servants and Apprentices, from appearing in the Streets at those Times and Seasons which may expose them to Military Discipline, as it is practised by our good Subjects the *Mohocks*; and we do further promise, on our Imperial Word, that as soon as the Reformation aforesaid shall be brought about, we will forthwith cause all Hostilities to cease.

*Given from our Court at the Devil-
    Tavern, March 15, 1712.'*   X

No. 348.
[STEELE.]   Wednesday, April 9.

Invidiam placare paras virtute relicta?—Hor.

    '*Mr.* SPECTATOR,

I HAVE not seen you lately at any of the Places where I visit, so that I am afraid you are wholly unacquainted with what passes among my Part of the World, who are, though I say it, without Controversie, the most accomplished and best bred of the Town. Give me Leave to tell you, that I am extreamly discomposed when I hear Scandal, and am an utter Enemy to all manner of Detraction, and think it the greatest Meanness that People of Distinction can be guilty of: However, it is hardly possible to come into Company, where you do not find them pulling one another to Pieces, and that from no other Provocation but that of hearing any one commended. Merit, both as to Wit and Beauty, is become no other than the Possession of a few trifling People's Favour, which you cannot possibly arrive at, if you have really any thing in you that is deserving. What they would bring to pass, is, to make all Good and Evil consist in Report, and with Whispers, Calumnies and Impertinencies, to have the Conduct of those Reports. By this means Innocents are blasted upon their first appearance in Town; and there is nothing more required to make a young Woman the Object of Envy and Hatred, than to deserve Love and Admiration. This abominable Endeavour to suppress or lessen every thing that is praise-worthy, is as frequent among

the Men as the Women. If I can remember what pass'd at a
Visit last Night, it will serve as an Instance that the Sexes are
equally enclined to Defamation, with equal Malice, with equal
Impotence. *Jack Triplett* came into my Lady *Airy's* about
Eight of the Clock: You know the Manner we sit at a Visit, and
I need not describe the Circle; but Mr. *Triplett* came in, introduced by two Tapers supported by a spruce Servant, whose
Hair is under a Cap till my Lady's Candles are all lighted up,
and the Hour of Ceremony begins: I say, *Jack Triplett* came
in, and singing (for he is really good Company) *Every Feature,
charming Creature,*—he went on, *It is a most unreasonable
Thing that People cannot go peaceably to see their Friends, but
these Murderers are let loose. Such a Shape! such an Air! what
a Glance was that as her Chariot passed by mine*—— My Lady
her self interrupted him; *Pray who is this fine Thing?—I
warrant,* says another, *'tis the Creature I was telling your
Ladyship of just now.—You were telling of?* says *Jack; I wish I
had been so happy as to have come in and heard you, for I have
not Words to say what she is:* But if an agreeable Height, a
modest Air, a Virgin Shame, and Impatience of being beheld,
amidst a Blaze of ten thousand Charms—— The whole
Room flew out.—Oh—Mr. *Triplett!*—When Mrs. *Lofty,* a
known Prude, said she believed she knew whom the Gentleman
meant; but she was indeed, as he civilly represented her, impatient of being beheld.—Then turning to the Lady next
to her.—*The most unbred Creature you ever saw.* Another
pursued the Discourse: As unbred, Madam, as you may think
her, she is extreamly bely'd if she is the Novice she appears;
she was last Week at a Ball till Two in the Morning; Mr.
*Triplett knows whether he was the happy Man that took Care
of her home; but*—— This was followed by some particular
Exception that each Woman in the Room made to some
peculiar Grace, or Advantage; so that Mr. *Triplett* was beaten
from one Limb and Feature to another, till he was forced to
resign the whole Woman. In the End, I took Notice *Triplett*
recorded all this Malice in his Heart; and saw in his Countenance, and a certain waggish Shrug, that he designed to repeat
the Conversation; I therefore let the Discourse die, and soon
after took an Occasion to commend a certain Gentleman of
my Acquaintance for a Person of singular Modesty, Courage,
Integrity, and withal as a Man of an entertaining Conversation,
to which Advantages he had a Shape and Manner peculiarly
graceful. Mr. *Triplett,* who is a Woman's Man, seemed to hear
me with Patience enough commend the Qualities of his Mind:
He never heard indeed but that he was a very honest Man, and
no Fool; but for a fine Gentleman he must ask Pardon. Upon

no other Foundation than this, Mr. *Triplett* took Occasion to give the Gentleman's Pedigree, by what Methods some part of the Estate was acquired, how much it was beholden to a Marriage for the present Circumstances of it: After all, he could see nothing but a common Man in his Person, his Breeding, or Understanding.

Thus, Mr. SPECTATOR, this impertinent Humour of diminishing every one who is produced in Conversation to their Advantage, runs through the World; and I am, I confess, so fearful of the Force of ill Tongues, that I have begged of all those who are my Well-wishers never to commend me, for it will but bring my Frailties into Examination, and I had rather be unobserved than conspicuous for disputed Perfections. I an confident a thousand young People, who would have been Ornaments to Society, have, from Fear of Scandal, never dared to exert themselves in the polite Arts of Life. Their Lives have passed away in an odious Rusticity, in spite of great Advantages of Person, Genius, and Fortune. There is a vicious Terrour of being blamed in some well-inclined People, and a wicked Pleasure in suppressing them in others; both which I recommend to your Spectatorial Wisdom to animadvert upon; and if you can be successful in it, I need not say how much you will deserve of the Town, but new Toasts will owe to you their Beauty, and new Wits their Fame. I am,

> *Sir,*
>
> *Your most obedient humble Servant*

T   Mary.'

No. 349.
[ADDISON.]   Thursday, April 10.

> . . . *Quos ille timorum*
> *Maximus haud urget leti metus; inde ruendi*
> *In ferrum mens prona viris animaeque capaces*
> *Mortis* . . .—Lucan.

I AM very much pleased with a Consolatary Letter of *Phalaris*, to one who had lost a Son that was a young Man of great Merit. The Thought with which he comforts the afflicted Father, is, to the best of my Memory as follows; That he should consider Death had set a kind of Seal upon his Son's Character, and placed him out of the Reach of Vice and Infamy: That while he lived he was still within the Possibility of falling away from Virtue, and losing the Fame of which he was possessed. Death only closes a Man's Reputation, and determines it as good or bad.

This, among other Motives, may be one Reason why we are naturally averse to the launching out into a Man's Praise till his Head is laid in the Dust. Whilst he is capable of changing we may be forced to retract our Opinions. He may forfeit the Esteem we have conceived of him, and some time or other appear to us under a different Light from what he does at present. In short, as the Life of any Man cannot be called happy or unhappy, so neither can it be pronounced vicious or virtuous, before the Conclusion of it.

It was upon this Consideration that *Epaminondas*, being asked, whether *Chabrias*, *Iphicrates*, or he himself, deserved most to be esteemed? You must first see us die, said he, before that Question can be answered.

As there is not a more melancholy Consideration to a good Man than his being obnoxious to such a change, so there is nothing more glorious than to keep up an Uniformity in his Actions, and preserve the Beauty of his Character to the last.

The End of a Man's Life is often compared to the winding up of a well-written Play, where the principal Persons still act in Character, whatever the Fate is which they undergo. There is scarce a great Person in the *Graecian* or *Roman* History whose Death has not been remarked upon by some Writer or other, and censured or applauded according to the Genius or Principles of the Person who has descanted on it. Monsieur *de St. Evremont* is very particular in setting forth the Constancy and Courage of *Petronius Arbiter* during his last Moments, and thinks he discovers in them a greater Firmness of Mind and Resolution than in the Death of *Seneca, Cato*, or *Socrates*. There is no Question but this polite Author's Affectation of appearing singular in his Remarks, and making Discoveries which had escaped the Observation of others, threw him into this Course of Reflection. It was *Petronius* his Merit that he died in the same Gaiety of Temper in which he lived; but as his Life was altogether loose and dissolute, the Indifference which he shewed at the Close of it, is to be looked upon as a Piece of natural Carelessness and Levity, rather than Fortitude. The Resolution of *Socrates* proceeded from very different Motives, the Consciousness of a well-spent Life, and the Prospect of a happy Eternity. If the ingenious Author above-mentioned was so pleased with Gayety of Humour in a dying Man, he might have found a much nobler Instance of it in our Countryman Sir *Thomas More*.

This great and learned Man was famous for enlivening his ordinary Discourses with Wit and Pleasantry, and, as *Erasmus* tells him in an Epistle Dedicatory, acted in all Parts of Life like a second *Democritus*.

He died upon a Point of Religion, and is respected as a Martyr by that Side for which he suffered. That innocent Mirth which had been so conspicuous in his Life, did not forsake him to the last: He maintain'd the same Chearfulness of Heart upon the Scaffold, which he used to shew at his Table; and upon laying his Head on the Block, gave Instances of that good Humour with which he had always entertained his Friends in the most ordinary Occurrences. His Death was of a Piece with his Life. There was nothing in it new, forced or affected. He did not look upon the severing of his Head from his Body as a Circumstance that ought to produce any Change in the Disposition of his Mind; and as he died under a fixed and settled Hope of Immortality, he thought any unusual Degree of Sorrow and Concern improper on such an Occasion as had nothing in it which could deject or terrifie him.

There is no great Danger of Imitation from this Example. Men's natural Fears will be a sufficient Guard against it. I shall only observe, that what was Philosophy in this extraordinary Man, would be Frenzy in one who does not resemble him as well in the Chearfulness of his Temper, as in the Sanctity of his Life and Manners.

I shall conclude this Paper with the Instance of a Person who seems to me to have shewn more Intrepidity and Greatness of Soul in his dying Moments, than what we meet with among any of the most celebrated *Greeks* and *Romans*. I met with this Instance in the History of the Revolutions in *Portugal*, written by the Abbot de *Vertot*.

When Don *Sebastian*, king of *Portugal*, had invaded the Territories of *Muly Moluc*, Emperor of *Morocco*, in order to dethrone him, and set his Crown upon the Head of his Nephew, *Moluc* was wearing away with a Distemper which he himself knew was incurable. However, he prepared for the Reception of so formidable an Enemy. He was indeed so far spent with his Sickness, that he did not expect to live out the whole Day, when the last decisive Battle was given; but knowing the fatal Consequences that would happen to his Children and People in case he should die before he put an End to that War, he commanded his principal Officers that if he died during the Engagement they should conceal his Death from the Army, and that they should ride up to the Litter in which his Corps was carried, under Pretence of receiving Orders from him as usual. Before the Battel begun he was carried through all the Ranks of his Army in an open Litter, as they stood drawn up in Array, encouraging them to fight valiantly in Defence of their Religion and Country, Finding afterwards the Battel to go against him, though he was very near his last Agonies, he threw him-

self out of his Litter, rallied his Army, and led them on to
the Charge, which afterwards ended in a compleat Victory on the
Side of the *Moors*.   He had no sooner brought his Men to the
Engagement, but finding himself utterly spent, he was again
replaced in his Litter, where laying his Finger on his Mouth,
to enjoin Secrecy to his Officers, who stood about him, he died
a few Moments after in that Posture.   L

No. 350.
[STEELE.]   Friday, April 11.

*Ea animi elatio, quae cernitur in periculis . . . , si justitia vacat
 pugnatque . . . pro suis commodis, in vitio est.*—Tull.

CAPTAIN SENTREY was last Night at the Club, and produced a
Letter from *Ipswich*, which his Correspondent desired him to
communicate to his Friend the SPECTATOR.   It contained an
Account of an Engagement between a *French* Privateer, commanded by one *Dominick Pottiere*, and a little Vessel of that
Place laden with Corn, the Master whereof, as I remember, was
one *Goodwin*.   The *English* Man defended himself with incredible Bravery, and beat off the *French*, after having been
boarded three or four times.   The Enemy still came on with
greater Fury, and hoped by his Number of Men to carry the
Prize; till at last the *English* Man, finding himself sink apace,
and ready to Perish, struck: But the Effect which this singular
Gallantry had upon the Captain of the Privateer, was no other
than an unmanly Desire of Vengeance for the Loss he had
sustained in his several Attacks.   He told the *Ipswich* Man in
a Speaking-Trumpet, that he would not take him aboard; and
that he stay'd to see him sink.   The *English* Man at the same
time observed a Disorder in the Vessel, which he rightly judged
to proceed from the Disdain which the Ship's Crew had of
their Captain's Inhumanity: With this Hope he went into his
Boat, and approached the Enemy.   He was taken in by the
Sailors in spite of their Commander; but though they received
him against his Command, they treated him when he was in
the Ship in the Manner he directed.   *Pottiere* caused his Men
to hold *Goodwin* while he beat him with a Stick till he fainted
with Loss of Blood, and Rage of Heart; after which he ordered
him into Irons, without allowing him any Food, but such as
one or two of the Men stole to him under Peril of the like
Usage: After having kept him several Days overwhelmed with
the Misery of Stench, Hunger, and Soreness, he brought him
into *Calais*.   The Governour of the Place was soon acquainted
with all that had passed, dismissed *Pottiere* from his Charge

with Ignominy, and gave *Goodwin* all the Relief which a Man of Honour would bestow upon an Enemy barbarously treated, to recover the Imputation of Cruelty upon his Prince and Country.

When Mr. SENTREY had read his Letter, full of many other Circumstances which aggravate the Barbarity, he fell into a sort of Criticism upon Magnanimity and Courage, and argued, that they were inseparable; and that Courage, without Regard to Justice and Humanity, was no other than the Fierceness of a wild Beast. A good and truly bold Spirit, continued he, is ever actuated by Reason and a Sense of Honour and Duty: The Affectation of such a Spirit exerts it self in an impudent Aspect, an over-bearing Confidence, and a certain Negligence of giving Offence. This is visible in all the cocking Youths you see about this Town, who are noisy in Assemblies, unawed by the Presence of wise and virtuous Men; in a Word, insensible of all the Honours and Decencies of humane Life. A shameless Fellow takes Advantage of Merit cloathed with Modesty and Magnanimity, and in the Eyes of little People appears sprightly and agreeable; while the Man of Resolution and true Gallantry is over-looked and disregarded, if not despised. There is a Propriety in all things; and I believe what you Scholars call just and sublime, in Opposition to turgid and bombast Expression, may give you an Idea of what I mean, when I say Modesty is the certain Indication of a great Spirit, and Impudence the Affectation of it. He that writes with Judgment, and never rises into improper Warmths, manifests the true Force of Genius; in like manner, he who is quiet and equal in all his Behaviour, is supported in that Deportment by what we may call true Courage. Alas, it is not so easy a thing to be a brave Man as the unthinking Part of Mankind imagine: To dare is not all that there is in it. The Privateer we were just now talking of, had Boldness enough to attack his Enemy, but not Greatness of Mind enough to admire the same Quality exerted by that Enemy in defending himself. Thus his base and little Mind was wholly taken up in the sordid Regard to the Prize, of which he failed, and the Damage done to his own Vessel; and therefore he used an honest Man, who defended his own from him, in the Manner as he would a Thief that should rob him.

He was equally disappointed, and had not Spirit enough to consider that one Case would be laudable, and the other criminal. Malice, Rancour, Hatred, Vengeance, are what tear the Breasts of mean Men in Fight; but Fame, Glory, Conquests, Desires of Opportunities to pardon and oblige their Opposers, are what glow in the Minds of the Gallant. The Captain ended his Discourse with a Specimen of his Book-Learning; and gave us to understand that he had read a *French* Author on the Subject of Justness in point of Gallantry. I love, said Mr. SENTREY, a Critick who mixes the Rules of Life with Annotations upon Writers. My Author, added he, in his Discourse upon Epick Poem, takes Occasion to speak of the same Quality of Courage drawn in the two different Characters of *Turnus* and *Aeneas*: He makes Courage the chief and greatest Ornament of *Turnus*; but in *Aeneas* there are many others which out-shine it, among the rest that of Piety. *Turnus* is therefore all along painted by the Poet full of Ostentation, his Language haughty and vain-glorious, as placing his Honour in the Manifestation of his Valour; *Aeneas* speaks little, is slow to Action, and shews only a Sort of defensive Courage. If Equipage and Address makes *Turnus* appear more couragious than *Aeneas*, Conduct and Success prove *Aeneas* more valiant than *Turnus*.

No. 351.
[ADDISON.]   Saturday, April 12.

. . . *In te omnis domus inclinata recumbit.*—Virg.

IF we look into the three great Heroic Poems which have appear'd in the World, we may observe that they are built upon very slight Foundations. *Homer* lived near 300 Years after the *Trojan* War, and, as the Writing of History was not then in use among the *Greeks*, we may very well suppose, that the Tradition of *Achilles* and *Ulysses* had brought down but very few Particulars to his Knowledge, tho' there is no Question but he has wrought into his two Poems such of their remarkable Adventures as were still talked of among his Contemporaries.

The story of *Aeneas*, on which *Virgil* founded his Poem, was likewise very bare of Circumstances, and by that Means afforded him an Opportunity of embellishing it with Fiction, and giving a full Range to his own Invention. We find, however, that he has interwoven, in the Course of his Fable, the principal Particulars, which were generally believed among the *Romans*, of *Aeneas* his Voyage and Settlement in *Italy*.

The Reader may find an Abridgment of the whole Story as collected out of the ancient Historians, and as it was received among the *Romans*, in *Dionysius Halicarnasseus*.

Since none of the Criticks have considered *Virgil*'s Fable, with relation to this History of *Aeneas*, it may not, perhaps, be amiss to examine it in this Light, so far as regards my present

Purpose. Whoever looks into the Abridgment above-mentioned, will find that the Character of *Aeneas* is filled with Piety to the Gods, and a superstitious Observation of Prodigies, Oracles, and Predictions. *Virgil* has not only preserved this Character in the Person of *Aeneas*, but has given a Place in his Poem to those particular Prophecies which he found recorded of him in History and Tradition. The Poet took the Matters of Fact as they came down to him, and circumstanced them after his own Manner, to make them appear the more natural, agreeable, or surprizing. I believe very many Readers have been shocked at that ludicrous Prophecy, which one of the *Harpyes* pronounces to the *Trojans* in the Third Book, namely, that, before they had built their intended City, they should be reduced by Hunger to eat their very Tables. But, when they hear that this was one of the Circumstances that had been transmitted to the *Romans* in the History of *Aeneas*, they will think the Poet did very well in taking Notice of it. The Historian above-mentioned acquaints us, a Prophetess had foretold *Aeneas*, that he should take his Voyage Westward, till his Companions should eat their Tables; and that accordingly, upon his landing in *Italy*, as they were eating their Flesh upon Cakes of Bread, for want of other Conveniencies, they afterwards fed on the Cakes themselves; upon which one of the Company said merrily, *We are eating our Tables*. They immediately took the Hint, says the Historian, and concluded the Prophecy to be fulfilled. As *Virgil* did not think it proper to omit so material a Particular in the History of *Aeneas*, it may be worth while to consider with how much Judgment he has qualified it, and taken off every thing that might have appeared improper for a Passage in an Heroic Poem. The Prophetess who foretells it is an hungry *Harpy*, as the Person who discovers it is young *Ascanius*.

Heus etiam mensas consumimus! inquit Iulus.

Such an Observation, which is beautiful in the Mouth of a Boy, would have been ridiculous from any other of the Company. I am apt to think that the changing of the *Trojan* Fleet into Water-Nymphs, which is the most violent Machine in the whole *Aeneid*, and has given Offence to several Criticks, may be accounted for the same way. *Virgil* himself, before he begins that Relation, premises that what he was going to tell appeared incredible, but that it was justified by Tradition. What further confirms me that this Change of the Fleet was a celebrated Circumstance in the History of *Æneas*, is, that *Ovid* has given a Place to the same *Metamorphosis* in his Account of the heathen Mythology.

None of the Criticks I have met with having considered the
Fable of the *Aeneid* in this Light, and taken Notice how the
Tradition, on which it was founded, authorizes those Parts in it
which appear the most exceptionable; I hope the Length of
this Reflection will not make it unacceptable to the curious
Part of my Readers.

The History, which was the Basis of *Milton*'s Poem, is still
shorter than either that of the *Iliad* or *Aeneid*, The Poet has
likewise taken Care to insert every Circumstance of it in the
Body of his Fable.   The Ninth Book, which we are here to
consider, is raised upon that brief Account in Scripture, wherein we are told that the Serpent was more subtle than any Beast
of the Field, that he tempted the Woman to eat of the forbidden Fruit, that she was overcome by this Temptation, and
that *Adam* followed her Example.   From these Few Particulars
Milton has formed one of the most entertaining Fables that
Invention ever produced.   He has disposed of these several
Circumstances among so many beautiful and natural Fictions
of his own, that his whole Story looks only like a comment
upon sacred Writ, or rather seems to be a full and compleat
Relation of what the other is only an Epitome.   I have insisted the longer on this consideration, as I look upon the
Disposition and Contrivance of the Fable to be the principal
Beauty of the Ninth Book, which has more *Story* in it, and is
fuller of Incidents, than any other in the whole Poem.   *Satan*'s
traversing the Globe, and still keeping within the Shadow of the
Night, as fearing to be discovered by the Angel of the Sun, who
had before detected him, is one of those beautiful Imaginations
with which he introduces this his second Series of Adventures.
Having examined the Nature of every Creature, and found out
one which was the most proper for his Purpose, he again returns
to Paradise; and, to avoid Discovery, sinks by Night with a
River that ran under the Garden, and rises up again through a
Fountain that issued from it by the Tree of Life.   The Poet,
who, as we have before taken Notice, speaks as little as possible
in his own Person, and, after the Example of *Homer*, fills every
Part of his Work with Manners and Characters, introduces a
Soliloquy of this infernal Agent, who was thus restless in the
Destruction of Man.   He is then describ'd as gliding through
the Garden under the Resemblance of a Mist, in order to
find out that Creature in which he design'd to tempt our first
Parents.   This Description has something in it very poetical
and surprizing.

> *So saying, through each Thicket dank or dry*
> *Like a black Mist, low creeping, he held on*
> *His midnight Search, where soonest he might find*

> *The Serpent; him fast sleeping soon he found*
> *In Labyrinth of many a round self-roll'd,*
> *His head the midst, well stor'd with subtle wiles.*

The Author afterwards gives us a Description of the Morning, which is wonderfully suitable to a Divine Poem, and peculiar to that first Season of Nature: He represents the Earth before it was curst as a great Altar breathing out its Incense from all Parts, and sending up a pleasant Savour to the Nostrils of its Creator; to which he adds a noble Idea of *Adam* and *Eve*, as offering their Morning Worship, and filling up the Universal Consort of Praise and Adoration.

> *Now when as sacred Light began to dawn*
> *In* Eden *on the humid Flowers, that breathed*
> *Their Morning Incense, when all things that breathe*
> *From th' Earth's great Altar send up silent Praise*
> *To the Creator, and his Nostrils fill*
> *With grateful Smell; forth came the human Pair.*
> *And joyn'd their vocal Worship to the Choir*
> *Of Creatures wanting Voice. . . .*

The Dispute which follows between our two first Parents is represented with great Art: It proceeds from a Difference of Judgment, not of Passion, and is managed with Reason, not with Heat: It is such a Dispute as we may suppose might have happened in *Paradise*, had Man continued happy and innocent. There is a great Delicacy in the Moralities which are interspersed in *Adam*'s Discourse, and which the most ordinary Reader cannot but take Notice of.   That Force of Love which the Father of Mankind so finely describes in the Eighth Book, and which I inserted in my last *Saturday*'s Paper, shews it self here in many beautiful Instances: As in those fond Regards he casts towards *Eve* at her parting from him.

> *Her long with ardent look his Eye pursued*
> *Delighted, but desiring more her stay.*
> *Oft he to her his Charge of quick Return*
> *Repeated; she to him as oft engaged*
> *To be return'd by Noon amid the Bowre.*

In his Impatience and Amusement during her Absence.

> .   Adam *the while*
> *Waiting desirous her Return, had wove*
> *Of choicest Flowers a Garland to adorn*
> *Her Tresses, and her Rural Labours crown,*
> *As Reapers oft are wont their Harvest Queen.*
> *Great Joy he promised to his Thoughts, and new*
> *Solace in her Return, so long delay'd.*

But particularly in that passionate Speech, where seeing her irrecoverably lost, he resolves to perish with her rather than to live without her.

> . . . *Some cursed Fraud*
> *Or Enemy hath beguil'd thee, yet unknown,*
> *And me with thee hath ruin'd, for with thee*
> *Certain my Resolution is to die;*
> *How can I live without thee, how forego*
> *Thy sweet Converse, and Love so dearly joyn'd*
> *To live again in these wild Woods forlorn?*
> *Should God create another* Eve, *and I*
> *Another Rib afford, yet loss of thee*
> *Would never from my Heart; no, no, I feel*
> *The link of Nature draw me: Flesh of Flesh,*
> *Bone of my Bone thou art, and from thy State*
> *Mine never shall be parted, Bliss or Woe.*

The Beginning of this Speech, and the Preparation to it are animated with the same Spirit as the Conclusion, which I have here quoted.

The several Wiles which are put in Practice by the Tempter, when he found *Eve* separated from her Husband, the many pleasing Images of Nature which are intermixt in this Part of the Story, with its gradual and regular Progress to the fatal Catastrophe, are so very remarkable, that it would be superfluous to point out their respective Beauties.

I have avoided mentioning any particular Similitudes in my Remarks on this great Work, because I have given a general Account of them in my Paper on the First Book. There is one, however, in this Part of the Poem which I shall here quote, as it is not only very beautiful, but the closest of any in the whole Poem; I mean that where the Serpent is describ'd as rolling forward in all his Pride, animated by the evil Spirit, and conducting *Eve* to her Destruction, while *Adam* was at too great a Distance from her to give her his Assistance. These several Particulars are all of them wrought into the following Similitude.

> . . . *Hope elevates, and Joy*
> *Brightens his Crest; as when a wand'ring Fire*
> *Compact of unctuous Vapour, which the Night*
> *Condenses, and the Cold invirons round,*
> *Kindled through agitation to a Flame,*
> *(Which oft, they say, some evil Spirit attends)*
> *Hovering and blazing with delusive Light,*
> *Misleads the amaz'd Night-wanderer from his way*
> *To Bogs and Mires, and oft thro' Pond or Pool,*
> *There swallow'd up and lost, from Succour far.*

That secret Intoxication of Pleasure, with all those transient Flushings of Guilt and Joy which the Poet represents in our first Parents upon their eating the forbidden Fruit, to those Flaggings of Spirit, Damps of Sorrow, and mutual Accusations which succeed it, are conceiv'd with a wonderful Imagination, and described in very natural Sentiments.

When *Dido* in the Fourth *Aeneid* yielded to that fatal Temptation which ruin'd her, *Virgil* tells us the Earth trembled, the Heavens were filled with Flashes of Lightning, and the Nymphs howled upon the Mountain Tops. *Milton*, in the same poetical Spirit, has described all Nature as disturbed upon *Eve*'s eating the forbidden Fruit.

> *So saying, her rash Hand in evil Hour*
> *Forth reaching to the Fruit, she pluckt, she eat;*
> *Earth felt the Wound, and Nature from her Seat*
> *Sighing thro' all her Works gave Signs of Woe*
> *That all was lost. . . .*

Upon *Adam*'s falling into the same Guilt, the whole Creation appears a second time in Convulsions.

> *. . . He scrupled not to eat*
> *Against his better Knowledge; not deceiv'd,*
> *But fondly overcome with Female Charm.*
> *Earth trembled from her Entrails, as again*
> *In Pangs, and Nature gave a second Groan,*
> *Sky lowred, and muttering Thunder, some sad Drops*
> *Wept at compleating of the mortal Sin . . .*

As all Nature suffer'd by the Guilt of our first Parents, these Symptoms of Trouble and Consternation are wonderfully imagined, not only as Prodigies, but as Marks of her sympathizing in the Fall of Man.

Adam's Converse with *Eve*, after having eaten the forbidden Fruit, is an exact Copy of that between *Jupiter* and *Juno* in the Fourteenth *Iliad*. *Juno* there approaches *Jupiter* with the Girdle which she had received from *Venus*; upon which he tells her, that she appeared more charming and desirable than she had ever done before, even when their Loves were at the highest. The Poet afterwards describes them as reposing on a Summet of Mount *Ida*, which produced under them a Bed of Flowers, the *Lotos*, the *Crocus*, and the *Hyacinth*; and concludes his Description with their falling asleep.

Let the Reader compare this with the following Passage in *Milton*, which begins with *Adam*'s Speech to *Eve*.

> *For never did thy Beauty since the Day*
> *I saw thee first and wedded thee, adorn'd*
> *With all Perfections, so inflame my Sense*

> *With Ardor to enjoy thee, fairer now*
> *Than ever, bounty of this virtuous Tree.*
> *So said he, and forbore not glance or toy*
> *Of amorous Intent, well understood*
> *Of* Eve, *whose Eye darted contagious fire.*
> *Her hand he seised, and to a shady bank*
> *Thick over-head with verdant roof embowr'd,*
> *He led her nothing loath: Flow'rs were the Couch,*
> *Pansies, and Violets, and Asphodel,*
> *And Hyacinth, Earth's freshest softest Lap.*
> *There they their fill of Love and Love's disport*
> *Took largely, of their mutual guilt the Seal,*
> *The Solace of their Sin, till dewy Sleep*
> *Oppress'd them.* . . .

As no Poet seems ever to have studied *Homer* more, or to have more resembled him in the Greatness of Genius than *Milton*, I think I should have given but a very imperfect Account of his Beauties, if I had not observed the most remarkable Passages which look like Parallels in these two great Authors. I might, in the Course of these Criticisms, have taken Notice of many particular Lines and Expressions which are translated from the *Greek* Poet; but as I thought this would have appeared too minute and over-curious, I have purposely omitted them. The greater Incidents, however, are not only set off by being shown in the same Light with several of the same Nature in *Homer*, but by that Means may be also guarded against the Cavils of the Tasteless or Ignorant. L

No. 352.

[STEELE.] Monday, April 14.

. . . *Si ad honestatem nati sumus, eaque aut sola expetenda est* . . .
aut certe omni pondere gravior habenda quam reliqua omnia.
—Tull.

WILL. HONEYCOMB was complaining to me Yesterday, that the Conversation of the Town is so altered of late Years, that a fine Gentleman is at a Loss for Matter to start Discourse, as well as unable to fall in with the Talk he generally meets with. WILL. takes Notice, that there is now an Evil under the Sun which he supposes to be entirely new, because not mentioned by any Satyrist or Moralist in any Age: Men, said he, grow Knaves sooner than they ever did since the Creation of the World before. If you read the Tragedies of the last Age, you find the artful Men, and Persons of Intrigue are advanced very far in Years, and beyond the Pleasures and Sallies of Youth; but now WILL. observes, that the Young have taken in the

Vices of the Aged; and you shall have a Man of five and twenty crafty, false, and intriguing, not ashamed to over-reach, cousen, and beguile. My Friend adds, that till about the latter End of King *Charles*'s Reign, there was not a Rascal of any Eminence under forty: In the Places of Resort for Conversation, you now hear nothing but what relates to the improving Men's Fortunes, without regard to the Methods toward it. This is so fashionable, that young Men form themselves upon a certain Neglect of every thing that is candid, simple, and worthy of true Esteem; and affect being yet worse than they are, by acknowledging in their general Turn of Mind and Discourse, that they have not any remaining Value for true Honour and Honesty; preferring the Capacity of being artful to gain their Ends, to the Merit of despising those Ends when they come in competition with their Honesty. All this is due to the very silly Pride that generally prevails, of being valued for the Ability of carrying their Point; In a Word, from the Opinion that shallow and unexperienced People entertain of the short-liv'd Force of Cunning. But I shall, before I enter upon the various Faces which Folly covered with Artifice puts on to impose upon the Unthinking, produce a great Authority for asserting, that nothing but Truth and Ingenuity has any lasting good Effect even upon a Man's Fortune and Interest.

'Truth and Reality have all the Advantages of Appearance, and many more. If the Shew of any thing be good for any thing, I am sure Sincerity is better: For why does any Man dissemble, or seem to be that which he is not, but because he thinks it good to have such a Quality as he pretends to? for to counterfeit and dissemble, is to put on the Appearance of some real Excellency. Now the best way in the World for a Man to seem to be any thing, is really to be what he would seem to be. Besides that, it is many times as troublesome to make good the Pretence of a good Quality, as to have it; and if a Man have it not, it is ten to one but he is discovered to want it, and then all his Pains and Labour to seem to have it is lost. There is something unnatural in Painting, which a skilful Eye will easily discern from native Beauty and Complexion.

It is hard to personate and act a Part long; for where Truth is not at the Bottom, Nature will always be endeavouring to return, and will peep out and betray her self one time or other. Therefore if any Man think it convenient to seem good, let him be so indeed, and then his Goodness will appear to every Body's Satisfaction; so that upon all Accounts Sincerity is true Wisdom. Particularly as to the Affairs of this World, Integrity hath many Advantages over all the fine and artificial ways of Dissimulation and Deceit; it is much the plainer and easier, much the safer and more secure way of dealing in the World; it has less of Trouble and Difficulty, of Entanglement and Perplexity, of Danger and Hazard in it; it is the shortest and nearest way to our End, carrying us thither in a streight Line, and will hold out and last longest. The Arts of Deceit and Cunning do continually grow weaker and less effectual and serviceable to them that use them; whereas Integrity gains Strength by use, and the more and longer any Man practiseth it, the greater Service it does him, by confirming his Reputation, and encouraging those with whom he hath to do, to repose the greatest Trust and Confidence in him, which is an unspeakable Advantage in the Business and Affairs of Life.

Truth is always consistent with it self, and needs nothing to help it out; it is always near at Hand, and sits upon our Lips, and is ready to drop out before we are aware; whereas a Lie is troublesome, and sets a Man's Invention upon the Rack, and one Trick needs a great many more to make it good. It is like building upon a false Foundation, which continually stands in need of Props to shoar it up, and proves at last more chargeable, than to have raised a substantial Building at first upon a true and solid Foundation; for Sincerity is firm and substantial, and there is nothing hollow and unsound in it, and because it is plain and open, fears no Discovery; of which the crafty Man is always in danger, and when he thinks he walks in the Dark, all his Pretences are so transparent, that he that runs may read them; he is the last Man that finds himself to be found out, and whilst he takes it for granted that he makes Fools of others, he renders himself ridiculous.

Add to all this, that Sincerity is the most compendious Wisdom, and an excellent Instrument for the speedy Dispatch of Business; it creates Confidence in those we have to deal with, saves the Labour of many Enquiries, and brings things to an Issue in few Words: It is like travelling in a plain beaten Road, which commonly brings a Man sooner to his Journey's End than By-ways, in which Men often lose themselves. In a Word, whatsoever Conveniences may be thought to be in Falsehood and Dissimulation, it is soon over; but the Inconvenience of it is perpetual, because it brings a Man under an everlasting Jealousie and Suspicion, so that he is not believed when he speaks Truth, nor trusted when perhaps he means honestly: When a Man has once forfeited the Reputation of his Integrity, he is set fast, and nothing will then serve his Turn, neither Truth nor Falsehood.

And I have often thought, that God hath in his great Wisdom hid from Men of false and dishonest Minds the wonderful

Advantages of Truth and Integrity to the Prosperity even of our worldly Affairs; these Men are so blinded by their Covetousness and Ambition, that they cannot look beyond a present Advantage, nor forbear to seize upon it, though by ways never so indirect; they cannot see so far, as to the remote Consequences of a steady Integrity, and the vast Benefit and Advantages which it will bring a Man at last. Were but this sort of Men wise and clear-sighted enough to discern this, they would be honest out of very Knavery, not out of any Love to Honesty and Virtue, but with a crafty Design to promote and advance more effectually their own Interests; and therefore the Justice of the Divine Providence hath hid this truest Point of Wisdom from their Eyes, that bad Men might not be upon equal Terms with the Just and Upright, and serve their own wicked Designs by honest and lawful Means.

Indeed, if a Man were only to deal in the World for a Day, and should never have Occasion to converse more with Mankind, never more need their good Opinion or good Word, it were then no great Matter (speaking as to the Concernments of this World) if a Man spent his Reputation all at once, and ventured it at one Throw: But if he be to continue in the World, and would have the Advantage of Conversation whilst he is in it, let him make use of Truth and Sincerity in all his Words and Actions; for nothing but this will last and hold out to the End; all other Arts will fail, but Truth and Integrity will carry a Man through, and bear him out to the last.' T

No. 353.
[BUDGELL.]   Tuesday, April 15.

In tenui labor . . .—Virg.

THE Gentleman who obliges the World in general, and me in particular, with his Thoughts upon Education, has just sent me the following Letter.

'*Sir*,

I take the Liberty to send you a Fourth Letter upon the Education of Youth: In my last I gave you my Thoughts about some particular Tasks which I conceived it might not be amiss to mix with their usual Exercises, in order to give them an early Seasoning of Virtue; I shall in this propose some others which I fancy might contribute to give them a right Turn for the World, and enable them to make their Way in it.

The Design of Learning is, as I take it, either to render a Man an agreeable Companion to himself, and teach him to

support Solitude with Pleasure; or, if he is not born to an
Estate, to supply that Defect, and furnish him with the Means
of acquiring one. A Person who applies himself to Learning
with the first of these Views, may be said to study for Ornament, as he who proposes to himself the second properly
studies for Use. The one does it to raise himself a Fortune,
the other to set off that which he is already possessed of: But
as far as the greater part of Mankind are included in the latter
Class, I shall only propose some Methods at present for the
Service of such who expect to advance themselves in the World
by their Learning: In order to which, I shall premise, that
many more Estates have been acquired by little Accomplishments than by extraordinary ones; those Qualities which make
the greatest Figure in the Eye of the World, not being always
the most useful in themselves, or the most advantageous to
their Owners.

The Posts which require Men of shining and uncommon
Parts to discharge them, are so very few, that many a great
Genius goes out of the World without ever having an opportunity to exert it self; whereas Persons of ordinary Endowments meet with Occasions fitted to their Parts and Capacities
every Day in the common Occurrences of Life.

I am acquainted with two Persons who were formerly
School-fellows, and have been good Friends ever since: One of
them was not only thought an impenetrable Block-head at
School, but still maintained his Reputation at the University;
the other was the Pride of his Master, and the most celebrated
Person in the College of which he was a Member. The Man of
Genius is at present buried in a Country Parsonage of Eight-
score Pounds a Year; while the other, with the bare Abilities
of a common Scrivener, has got an Estate of above an hundred
thousand Pounds.

I fancy from what I have said it will almost appear a doubtful Case to many a wealthy Citizen, whether or no he ought to
wish his Son should be a great Genius; but this I am sure of,
that nothing is more absurd than to give a Lad the Education
of one, whom Nature has not favoured with any particular
Marks of Distinction.

The Fault therefore of our Grammar-Schools is, that every
Boy is pushed on to Works of Genius; whereas it would be far
more advantageous for the greatest part of them to be taught
such little practical Arts and Sciences as do not require any
great Share of Parts to be Master of them, and yet may come
often into Play during the course of a Man's Life.

Such are all the Parts of Practical Geometry. I have
known a Man contract a Friendship with a Minister of State,

upon cutting a Dial in his Window; and remember a Clergy-man who got one of the best Benefices in the West of *England*, by setting a Country Gentleman's Affairs in some Method, and giving him an exact Survey of his Estate.

While I am upon this Subject, I cannot forbear mentioning a Particular which is of use in every Station of Life, and which methinks every Master should teach his Scholars, I mean the writing of *English* Letters. To this End, instead of perplexing them with *Latin* Epistles, Themes and Verses, there might be a punctual Correspondence established between two Boys, who might act in any imaginary Parts of Business, or be allowed sometimes to give a Range to their own Fancies, and communicate to each other whatever Trifles they thought fit, provided neither of them ever failed at the appointed Time to answer his Correspondent's Letter.

I believe I may venture to affirm, that the generality of Boys would find themselves more advantaged by this Custom, when they come to be Men, than by all the *Greek* and *Latin* their Masters can teach them in seven or eight Years.

The Want of it is very visible in many Learned Persons, who while they are admiring the Stiles of *Demosthenes* or *Cicero*, want Phrases to express themselves on the most common Occasions. I have seen a Letter from one of these *Latin* Orators, which would have been deservedly laughed at by a common Attorney.

Under this Head of Writing I cannot omit Accounts and Short-hand, which are learned with little Pains, and very properly come into the Number of such Arts as I have been here recommending.

You must, doubtless, Sir, observe, that I have hitherto chiefly insisted upon these things for such Boys as do not appear to have any thing extraordinary in their natural Talents, and consequently are not qualified for the finer Parts of Learning; yet I believe I might carry this Matter still further, and venture to assert that a Lad of Genius has sometimes Occasion for these little Acquirements, to be as it were the Fore-runners of his Parts, and to introduce him into the World.

History is full of Examples of Persons, who though they have had the largest Abilities, have been obliged to insinuate themselves into the Favour of great Men by these trivial Accomplishments; as the compleat Gentleman, in some of our Modern Comedies, makes his first Advances to his Mistress under the Disguise of a Painter or a Dancing-Master.

The Difference is, that in a Lad of Genius these are only so many Accomplishments, which in another are Essentials; the one diverts himself with them, the other works at them. In short, I look upon a great Genius, with these little Additions, in the same Light as I regard the Grand Signior, who is obliged by an Express Command in the Alcoran, to learn and practice some Handy-craft Trade: Tho' I need not to have gone for my Instance further than *Germany*, where several Emperors have voluntarily done the same Thing. *Leopold* the last worked in Wood, and I have heard there are several Handy-craft Works of his Making to be seen at *Vienna*, so neatly turned, that the best Joyner in *Europe* might safely own them, without any Disgrace to his Profession.

I would not be thought, by any thing I have said, to be against improving a Boy's Genius to the utmost Pitch it can be carried. What I would endeavour to shew in this Essay is, that there may be Methods taken to make Learning advantageous even to the meanest Capacities.

I am, Sir,

Yours, &c.'

X

No. 354.
[STEELE.]   Wednesday, April 16.

. . . *Cum magnis virtutibus affers*
Grande supercilium.—Juv.

'*Mr.* SPECTATOR,

You have in some of your Discourses described most sort of Women in their distinct and proper Classes, as the *Ape*, the *Coquet*, and many others; but I think you have never yet said any thing of a *Devotée*. A *Devotée* is one of those who disparage Religion by their indiscreet and unseasonable introduction of the Mention of Virtue on all Occasions: She professes she is what no Body ought to doubt she is; and betrays the Labour she is put to, to be what she ought to be with Chearfulness and Alacrity. She lives in the World, and denies herself none of the Diversions of it, with a constant Declaration how insipid all things in it are to her. She is never herself but at Church; there she displays her Virtue, and is so fervent in her Devotions, that I have frequently seen her pray herself out of Breath. While other young Ladies in the House are Dancing, or playing at Questions and Commands, she reads aloud in her Closet. She says all Love is ridiculous, except it be Celestial; but she speaks of the Passion of one Mortal to another with too much Bitterness, for one that had no jealousy mixed with her Contempt of it. If at any time she sees a Man warm in his Addresses to his Mistress, she will lift up her Eyes to Heaven and cry, What Nonsense is that Fool talking? Will the Bell never ring for Prayers? We have an eminent Lady of this Stamp in our Country, who pretends to Amusements very much above the rest of her Sex. She never carries a white Shock Dog with Bells under her Arm, nor a Squirrel or Dormouse in her Pocket, but always an abridg'd Piece of Morality to steal out when she is sure of being observed. When she went to the famous Ass-Race (which I must confess was but an odd Diversion to be encouraged by People of Rank and Figure) it was not, like other Ladies, to hear those poor Animals Bray, nor to see Fellows run naked, or to hear Country Squires in Bob Wigs and white Girdles make Love at the side of a Coach, and cry, Madam this is dainty Weather. Thus she described the Diversion; for she went only to pray heartily that no body might be hurt in the Crowd, and to see if the poor Fellow's Face, which was distorted with Grinning, might any way be brought to it self again. She never chats over her Tea, but covers her Face, and is supposed in an Ejaculation before she tastes a Sup. This ostentatious Behaviour is such an Offence to true Sanctity, that it disparages it, and makes Virtue not only unamiable, but also ridiculous. The Sacred Writings are full of Reflections which abhor this kind of Conduct; and a *Devotée* is so far from promoting Goodness, that she deters others by her Example. Folly and Vanity in one of these Ladies, is like Vice in a Clergyman; it does not only debase him, but makes the inconsiderate part of the World think the worse of Religion.

> *I am, Sir,*
>
> > *Your humble Servant,*
> >
> > > Hotspur.'

'*Mr.* SPECTATOR,

Xenophon in his short Account of the *Spartan* Commonwealth, speaking of the Behaviour of their young Men in the Streets, says, There was so much Modesty in their Looks, that you might as soon have turned the Eyes of a Marble Statue upon you as theirs; and that in all their Behaviour they were more modest than a Bride when put to Bed upon her Wedding-Night: This Virtue, which is always joyn'd to Magnanimity, had such an Influence upon their Courage, that in Battel an Enemy could not look them in the Face; and they durst not but Die for their Country.

Whenever I walk into the Streets of *London* and *West-minster*, the Countenances of all the young Fellows that pass by me, make me wish my self in *Sparta*: I meet with such blustering Airs, big Looks, and bold Fronts, that to a super-ficial Observer would bespeak a Courage above those *Grecians*. I am arrived to that Perfection in Speculation, that I under-stand the Language of the Eyes, which would be a great Mis-fortune to me, had I not corrected the Testiness of old Age by Philosophy. There is scarce a Man in a red Coat who does not tell me, with a full Stare, he's a bold Man: I see several Swear inwardly at me, without any Offence of mine, but the Oddness of my Person: I meet Contempt in every Street, ex-press'd in different Manners, by the scornful Look, the elevated Eye-brow, and the swelling Nostrils of the Proud and Pros-perous. The Prentice speaks his Disrespect by an extended Finger, and the Porter by stealing out his Tongue. If a Country Gentleman appears a little curious in observing the Edifices, Signs, Clocks, Coaches and Dials, it is not to be imagined how the polite Rabble of this Town, who are acquainted with these Objects, ridicule his Rusticity. I have known a Fellow with a Burden on his Head steal a Hand down from his Load, and slily twirl the Cock of a Squire's Hat behind him; while the offended Person is swearing, or out of Countenance, all the Wagg-Wits in the High-way are grinning in Applause of the ingenious Rogue that gave him the Tip; and the Folly of him who had not Eyes all round his Head to prevent receiving it. These Things arise from a general Affectation of Smartness, Wit, and Courage: *Wicherly* somewhere rallies the Pretensions this way, by making a Fellow say, Red Breeches are a certain Sign of Valour; and *Otway* makes a Man, to boast his Agility, trip up a Beggar on Crutches. From such Hints I beg a Speculation on this Subject; in the mean time I shall do all in the Power of a weak old Fellow in my own Defence: for as *Diogenes*, being in quest of an honest Man, sought for him when it was broad Day-light with a Lanthorn and Candle, so I intend for the future to walk the Streets with a dark Lanthorn, which has a convex Chrystal in it; and if any Man stares at me, I give fair Warning that I'll direct the Light full into his Eyes; thus despairing to find Men modest, I hope by this Means to evade their Impudence.

> *I am,*
>> *Sir,*
>>> *Your most humble Servant,*
>>>> Sophrosunius.'

T

No. 355.
[ADDISON.]   Thursday, April 17.

Non ego mordaci distrinxi carmine quenquam.—Ovid.

I HAVE been very often tempted to write Invectives upon those
who have detracted from my Works, or spoken in Derogation
of my Person; but I look upon it as a particular Happiness
that I have always hinder'd my Resentments from proceeding
to this Extremity. I once had gone through half a Satyr, but
found so many Motions of Humanity rising in me towards the
Persons whom I had severely treated, that I threw it into the
Fire without ever finishing it. I have been angry enough to
make several little Epigrams and Lampoons, and after having
admired them a Day or two, have likewise committed them to
the Flames. These I look upon as so many Sacrifices to
Humanity, and have received much greater Satisfaction from
the suppressing such Performances, than I could have done
from any Reputation they might have procured me, or from
any Mortification they might have given my Enemies, in case
I had made them publick. If a Man has any Talent in Writing,
it shews a good Mind to forbear answering Calumnies and
Reproaches in the same Spirit of Bitterness with which they
are offered: But when a Man has been at some Pains in making
suitable Returns to an Enemy, and has the Instruments of
Revenge in his Hands, to let drop his Wrath, and stifle his
Resentments, seems to have something in it Great and Heroical.
There is a particular Merit in such a way of forgiving an
Enemy, and the more violent and unprovoked the Offence has
been, the greater still is the Merit of him who thus forgives it.

I never met with a Consideration that is more finely spun,
and what has better pleased me, than one in *Epictetus*, which
places an Enemy in a new Light, and gives us a View of him
altogether different from that in which we are used to regard
him. The Sense of it is as follows: Does a Man reproach
thee for being Proud or Ill-natured, Envious or Conceited,
Ignorant or Detracting? Consider with thy self whether his
Reproaches are true, if they are not, consider that thou art not
the Person whom he reproaches, but that he reviles an imaginary Being, and perhaps loves what thou really art, though
he hates what thou appearest to be. If his Reproaches are
true, if thou art the envious ill-natur'd Man he takes thee for,
give thy self another Turn, become mild, affable and obliging,
and his Reproaches of thee naturally cease: His Reproaches
may indeed continue, but thou art no longer the Person whom
he reproaches.

I often apply this Rule to my self, and, when I hear of a

Satyrical Speech or Writing that is aimed at me, I examine my own Heart, whether I deserve it or not. If I bring in a Verdict against my self, I endeavour to rectify my Conduct for the future in those Particulars which have drawn the Censure upon me; but if the whole Invective be grounded upon a Falshood, I trouble my self no further about it, and look upon my Name at the Head of it to signifie no more than one of those fictitious Names made use of by an Author to introduce an imaginary Character. Why should a Man be sensible of the Sting of a Reproach who is a Stranger to the Guilt that is implied in it? or subject himself to the Penalty when he knows he has never committed the Crime? This is a Piece of Fortitude which every one owes to his own Innocence, and without which it is impossible for a Man of any Merit or Figure to live at Peace with himself in a Country that abounds with Wit and Liberty.

The famous Monsieur *Balzac*, in a Letter to the Chancellor of *France*, who had prevented the Publication of a Book against him, has the following Words, which are a lively Picture of the Greatness of Mind so visible in the Works of that Author. *If it was a new Thing, it may be I should not be displeased with the Suppression of the first Libel that should abuse me; but since there are enough of 'em to make a small Library, I am secretly pleased to see the Number encreased, and take Delight in raising a Heap of Stones that Envy has cast at me without doing me any Harm.*

The Author here alludes to those Monuments of the Eastern Nations, which were Mountains of Stones raised upon the dead Body by Travellers, that used to cast every one his Stone upon it as they passed by. It is certain that no Monument is so glorious as one which is thus raised by the Hands of Envy. For my Part, I admire an Author for such a Temper of Mind, as enables him to bear an undeserved Reproach without Resentment, more than for all the Wit of any the finest Satyrical Reply.

Thus far I thought necessary to explain my self in relation to those who have animadverted on this Paper, and to shew the Reasons why I have not thought fit to return them any formal Answer. I must further add, that the Work would have been of very little use to the Publick, had it been filled with personal Reflections and Debates; for which Reason I have never once turned out of my Way to observe those little Cavils which have been made against it by Envy or Ignorance. The common Fry of Scribblers, who have no other Way of being taken Notice of but by attacking what has gain'd some reputation in the World, would have furnished me with Business enough, had they found me disposed to enter the Lists with 'em

I shall conclude with the Fable of *Boccalini*'s Traveller, who was so pestered with the Noise of Grashoppers in his Ears, that he alighted from his Horse in great Wrath to kill them all. This, says the Author, was troubling himself to no manner of Purpose: Had he pursued his Journey without taking Notice of them, the troublesome Insects would have died of themselves in a very few Weeks, and he would have suffered nothing from them.

L

No. 356.

[STEELE.]   Friday, April 18.

> . . . *Aptissima quaeque dabunt di,*
> *Carior est illis homo quam sibi* . . .—Juv.

It is owing to Pride, and a secret Affectation of a certain Self-Existence, that the noblest Motive for Action that ever was proposed to Man, is not acknowledged the Glory and Happiness of their Being.   The Heart is treacherous to it self, and we do not let our Reflections go deep enough to receive Religion as the most honourable Incentive to good and worthy Actions. It is our natural Weakness to flatter our selves into a Belief, that if we search into our inmost Thoughts, we find our selves wholly disinterested, and divested of any Views arising from Self-Love and Vain-Glory.   But however Spirits of superficial Greatness may disdain at first Sight to do any thing, but from a noble Impulse in themselves, without any future Regards in this or another Being; upon stricter Enquiry they will find, to act worthily and expect to be rewarded only in another World, is as heroick a Pitch of Virtue as humane Nature can arrive at. If the Tenour of our Actions have any other Motive than the Desire to be pleasing in the Eye of the Deity, it will necessarily follow that we must be more than Men, if we are not too much exalted in Prosperity and depressed in Adversity: But the Christian World has a Leader, the Contemplation of whose Life and Sufferings must administer Comfort in Affliction, while the Sense of his Power and Omnipotence must give them Humiliation in Prosperity.

It is owing to the forbidding and unlovely Constraint with which Men of low Conceptions act when they think they conform themselves to Religion, as well as to the more odious Conduct of Hypocrites, that the Word *Christian* does not carry with it at first View all that is Great, Worthy, Friendly, Generous, and Heroick.   The Man who suspends his Hopes of the Reward of worthy Actions till after Death, who can bestow unseen, who can overlook Hatred, do Good to his Slanderer, who can never be angry at his Friend, never revengeful to his Enemy, is certainly formed for the Benefit of Society: Yet these are so far from heroick Virtues, that they are but the ordinary Duties of a Christian.

When a Man with a steddy Faith looks back on the great Catastrophe of this Day, with what bleeding Emotions of Heart must he contemplate the Life and Sufferings of his Deliverer? When his Agonies occur to him, how will he weep to reflect that he has often forgot them for the Glance of a Wanton, for the Applause of a vain World, for an Heap of fleeting past Pleasures, which are at present aking Sorrows?

How pleasing is the Contemplation of the lowly Steps our Almighty Leader took in conducting us to his heavenly Mansions! In plain and apt Parable, Similitude, and Allegory, our great Master enforced the Doctrine of our Salvation; but they of his Acquaintance, instead of receiving what they could not oppose, were offended at the Presumption of being wiser than they: They could not raise their little Ideas above the Consideration of him, in those Circumstances familiar to them, or conceive that he who appeared not more terrible or pompous, should have any thing more exalted than themselves; he in that Place therefore would not longer ineffectually exert a Power which was incapable of conquering the Prepossession of their narrow and mean Conceptions.

Multitudes follow'd him, and brought him the Dumb, the Blind, the Sick, and Maim'd; whom when their Creator had touch'd, with a second Life they saw, spoke, leap'd, and ran. In Affection to him, and Admiration of his Actions, the Crowd could not leave him, but waited near him till they were almost as faint and helpless as others they brought for Succour. He had Compassion on them, and by a Miracle supplyed their Necessities. Oh, the Extatick Entertainment, when they could behold their food immediately encrease to the Distributer's Hand, and see their God in Person feeding and refreshing his Creatures! Oh envied Happiness! But why do I say envied, as if our God did not still preside over our temperate Meals, chearful Hours, and innocent Conversations.

But tho' the sacred Story is every where full of Miracles not inferior to this, and tho' in the Midst of those Acts of Divinity he never gave the least Hint of a Design to become a secular Prince; yet had not hitherto the Apostles themselves any other than Hopes of worldly Power, Preferment, Riches and Pomp; for *Peter*, upon an Accident of Ambition among the Apostles, hearing his Master explain that his Kingdom was not of this World, was so scandaliz'd that he whom he had so long follow'd should suffer the Ignominy, Shame, and Death which he foretold, that he took him aside and said, *Be it far from thee, Lord, this shall not be unto thee:* For which he suffer'd a severe Reprehension from his Master, as having in his View the Glory of Man rather than that of God.

The great Change of things began to draw near, when the Lord of Nature thought fit as a Saviour and Deliverer to make his publick entry into *Jerusalem* with more than the Power and Joy, but none of the Ostentation and Pomp of a Triumph: He came humble, meek, and lowly; with an unfelt new Extasie Multitudes strow'd his Way with Garments and Olive-branches, crying with loud Gladness and Acclamation, *Hosannah to the Son of* David, *blessed is he that cometh in the Name of the Lord!* At this great King's Accession to his Throne Men were not ennobled but sav'd: Crimes were not remitted, but Sins forgiven; he did not bestow Medals, Honours, Favours, but Health, Joy, Sight, Speech. The first Object the Blind ever saw, was the Author of Sight; while the Lame ran before, and the Dumb repeated the *Hosannah.* Thus attended, he entered into his own House, the sacred Temple, and by his Divine Authority expelled Traders and Worldlings that prophaned it; and thus did he, for a Time, use a great and despotick Power, to let Unbelievers understand, that 'twas not want of, but Superiority to all worldly Dominion, that made him not exert it. But is this then the Saviour? is this the Deliverer? Shall this obscure *Nazarene* command *Israel*, and sit in the Throne of *David?* Their proud and disdainful Hearts, which were petrified with the Love and Pride of this World, were impregnable to the Reception of so mean a Benefactor, and were now enough exasperated with Benefits to conspire his Death. Our Lord was sensible of their Design, and prepar'd his Disciples for it, by recounting to 'em more distinctly what should befall him; but *Peter* with an ungrounded Resolution, and in a Flush of Temper, made a sanguine Protestation, that tho' all Men were offended in him, yet would not he be offended. It was a great Article of our Saviour's Business in the World, to bring us to a Sense of our Inability, without God's Assistance, to do any thing great or good; he therefore told *Peter*, who thought so well of his Courage and Fidelity, that they would both fail him, and even he should deny him thrice that very Night.

But what Heart can conceive, what Tongue utter the Sequel? Who is that yonder buffeted, mock'd, and spurn'd? Whom do they drag like a Felon? Whither do they carry my Lord, my King, my Saviour, and my God? And will he die to expiate those very Injuries? See where they have nail'd the Lord and

Giver of Life! How his Wounds blacken, his Body writhes, and Heart heaves with Pity and with Agony! Oh Almighty Sufferer, look down, look down from thy triumphant Infamy: Lo he inclines his Head to his sacred Bosom! Hark, he groans; see, he expires! The Earth trembles, the Temple rends, the Rocks burst, the Dead arise: Which are the Quick? which are the Dead? Sure Nature, all Nature is departing with her Creator.

T

No. 357.
[ADDISON.]   Saturday, April 19.

. . . *Quis talia fando*

.   .   .   .   .

Temperet a lacrimis? . . .—Virg.

THE tenth Book of *Paradise Lost* has a greater Variety of Persons in it than any other in the whole Poem. The Author upon the winding up of his Action introduces all those who had any Concern in it, and shews with great Beauty the Influence which it had upon each of them. It is like the last Act of a well written Tragedy, in which all who had a Part in it are generally drawn up before the Audience, and represented under those Circumstances in which the Determination of the Action places them.

I shall therefore consider this Book under four Heads, in relation to the Celestial, the Infernal, the Human, and the Imaginary Persons, who have their respective Parts allotted in it.

To begin with the Celestial Persons: The Guardian Angels of *Paradise* are described as returning to Heaven upon the Fall of Man, in order to approve their Vigilance; their Arrival, their Manner of Reception, with the Sorrow which appeared in themselves, and in those Spirits who are said to Rejoice at the Conversion of a Sinner, are very finely laid together in the following Lines.

> *Up into Heav'n from Paradise in haste*
> *Th' angelick guards ascended, mute and sad*
> *For Man, for of his state by this they knew,*
> *Much wond'ring how the subtle Fiend had stoln*
> *Entrance unseen. Soon as th' unwelcome news*
> *From Earth arriv'd at Heaven Gate displeas'd*
> *All were who heard; dim Sadness did not spare*
> *That time Celestial visages, yet mixt*
> *With pity, violated not their Bliss.*
> *About the new-arriv'd. in multitudes*

> *Th' Aethereal People ran, to hear and know*
> *How all befell; They tow'rds the Throne supreame*
> *Accountable made haste to make appear*
> *With righteous plea, their utmost vigilance,*
> *And easily approv'd; when the most High*
> *Eternal Father from his secret Cloud*
> *Amidst in thunder utter'd thus his Voice.*

The same Divine Person, who in the foregoing Parts of this Poem interceded for our first Parents before their Fall, overthrew the Rebel Angels, and created the World, is now represented as descending to *Paradise*, and pronouncing Sentence upon the three Offenders. The cool of the Evening, being a Circumstance with which Holy Writ introduces this great Scene, it is Poetically described by our Author, who has also kept religiously to the Form of Words, in which the three several Sentences were passed upon *Adam, Eve,* and the Serpent. He has rather chosen to neglect the Numerousness of his Verse, than to deviate from those Speeches which are recorded on this great Occasion. The Guilt and Confusion of our first Parents standing naked before their Judge, is touched with great Beauty. Upon the Arrival of *Sin* and *Death* into the Works of the Creation, the Almighty is again introduced as speaking to his Angels that surrounded him.

> *So with what heat these Dogs of Hell advance*
> *To waste and havock yonder World, which I*
> *So fair and good created, &c.*

The following Passage is formed upon that glorious Image in Holy Writ, which compares the Voice of an innumerable Host of Angels, uttering Hallelujahs, to the Voice of mighty Thunderings, or of many Waters.

> *He ended, and the Heav'nly Audience loud*
> *Sung Hallelujah, as the sound of Seas,*
> *Through multitude that sung: Just are thy ways,*
> *Righteous are thy Decrees in all thy Works,*
> *Who can extenuate thee? . . .*

Though the Author in the whole Course of his Poem, and particularly in the Book we are now examining, has infinite Allusions to Places of Scripture, I have only taken Notice in my Remarks of such as are of a Poetical Nature, and which are woven with great Beauty into the Body of the Fable. Of this kind is that Passage in the present Book, where describing *Sin* and *Death* as marching through the Works of Nature, he adds,

> . . . *Behind her Death*
> *Close following pace for pace, not mounted yet*
> *On his pale Horse:* . . .

Which alludes to that Passage in Scripture so wonderfully
Poetical, and terrifying to the Imagination. *And I looked, and
behold a pale Horse, and his Name that sat on him was* Death,
and Hell *followed with him: and Power was given unto them over
the fourth Part of the Earth, to kill with sword, and with Hunger,
and with Sickness, and with the Beasts of the Earth.* Under this
first Head of Celestial Persons we must likewise take Notice of
the Command which the Angels received, to produce the several
Changes in Nature, and sully the Beauty of the Creation.
Accordingly they are represented as infecting the Stars and
Planets with malignant Influences, weakning the Light of the
Sun, bringing down the Winter into the milder Regions of
Nature, planting Winds and Storms in several Quarters of the
Sky, storing the Clouds with Thunder, and in short, perverting
the whole Frame of the Universe to the Condition of its
Criminal Inhabitants. As this is a noble Incident in the
Poem, the Following Lines, in which we see the Angels heaving
up the Earth, and placing it in a different Posture to the Sun
from what it had before the Fall of Man, is conceived with
that sublime Imagination which was so peculiar to this great
Author.

> *Some say he bid his Angels turn ascance*
> *The Poles of earth twice ten degrees and more*
> *From the Sun's Axle; they with labour push'd*
> *Oblique the Centrick Globe:* . . .

We are in the second Place, to consider the Infernal Agents
under the View which *Milton* has given us of them in this
Book. It is observed by those who would set forth the Greatness of *Virgil*'s Plan, that he conducts his Reader thro' all the
Parts of the Earth which were discovered in his Time. *Asia,
Africk,* and *Europe* are the several Scenes of his Fable. The
Plan of *Milton*'s Poem is of an infinitely greater Extent, and
fills the Mind with many more astonishing Circumstances.
Satan, having surrounded the Earth seven times, departs at
length from *Paradise.* We then see him steering his Course
among the Constellations, and after having traversed the
whole Creation, pursuing his Voyage thro' the *Chaos,* and
entering into his own infernal Dominions.

His first Appearance in the Assembly of Fallen Angels, is
work'd up with Circumstances which give a delightful Surprize
to the Reader; but there is no Incident in the whole Poem
which does this more than the Transformation of the whole

Audience, that follows the Account their Leader gives them of his Expedition. The gradual Change of *Satan* himself is described after *Ovid*'s Manner, and may vie with any of those celebrated Transformations which are looked upon as the most Beautiful Parts in that Poet's Works. *Milton* never fails of improving his own Hints, and bestowing the last finishing Touches to every Incident which is admitted into his Poem. The unexpected Hiss which rises in this Episode, the Dimensions and Bulk of *Satan* so much superior to those of the Infernal Spirits who lay under the same Transformation, with the annual Change which they are supposed to suffer, are Instances of this Kind. The Beauty of the Diction is very remarkable in this whole Episode, as I have observed in the Sixth Paper of these my Remarks the great Judgment with which it was contrived.

The Parts of *Adam* and *Eve*, or the Humane Persons, come next under our Consideration. *Milton*'s Art is no where more shewn than in his conducting the Parts of these our first Parents. The Representation he gives of them, without falsifying the Story, is wonderfully contrived to influence the Reader with Pity and Compassion towards them. Though *Adam* involves the whole Species in Misery, his Crime proceeds from a Weakness which every Man is inclined to pardon and commiserate, as it seems rather the Frailty of Humane Nature, than of the Person who offended. Every one is apt to excuse a Fault which he himself might have fallen into. It was the Excess of Love for *Eve* that ruin'd *Adam* and his Posterity. I need not add, that the Author is Justify'd in this Particular by many of the Fathers, and the most Orthodox Writers. *Milton* has by this means filled a great part of his Poem with that kind of Writing which the *French* Criticks call the *Tender*, and which is in a particular manner engaging to all sorts of Readers.

Adam and *Eve*, in the Book we are now considering, are likewise drawn with such Sentiments as do not only interest the Reader in their Afflictions, but raise in him the most melting Passions of Humanity and Commiseration. When *Adam* sees the several Changes in Nature produced about him, he appears in a Disorder of Mind suitable to one who had forfeited both his Innocence and his Happiness: he is filled with Horror, Remorse, Despair; in the Anguish of his Heart he expostulates with his Creator for having given him an unasked Existence.

> *Did I request thee, Maker, from my Clay*
> *To mould me Man; did I solicit thee*
> *From darkness to promote me, or here place*

> *In this delicious Garden ? as my will*
> *Concurr'd not to my being, 'twere but right*
> *And equal to reduce me to my dust,*
> *Desirous to resign, and render back*
> *All I receiv'd . . .*

He immediately after recovers from his Presumption, owns
his Doom to be just, and begs that the Death which is threatned
him may be inflicted on him.

> *. . . Why delays*
> *His Hand to execute what his decree*
> *Fix'd on this day ?   Why do I overlive,*
> *Why am I mock'd with Death, and lengthen'd out*
> *To Deathless pain ? how gladly would I meet*
> *Mortality, my Sentence, and be Earth*
> *Insensible, how glad would lay me down*
> *As in my Mother's lap ? there should I rest*
> *And sleep secure; his dreadful Voice no more*
> *Would thunder in my ears; no fear of worse*
> *To me and to my Off-spring, would torment me*
> *With cruel expectation. . . .*

This whole Speech is full of the like Emotion, and varied
with all those Sentiments which we may suppose natural to a
Mind so broken and disturb'd.   I must not omit that generous
Concern which our first Father shews in it for his Posterity,
and which is so proper to affect the Reader.

> *. . . Hide me from the Face*
> *Of God, whom to behold was then my height*
> *Of Happiness; yet well if here would end*
> *The Misery; I deserv'd it, and would bear*
> *My own deservings; but this will not serve;*
> *All that I eat, or drink, or shall beget,*
> *Is propagated Curse.   O voice once heard*
> *Delightfully, encrease and multiply;*
> *Now Death to hear! . . .*
> *. . . In me all*
> *Posterity stands curst: Fair Patrimony*
> *That I must leave you, Sons: O were I able*
> *To waste it all my self, and leave you none!*
> *So disinherited how would you bless*
> *Me now your curse!   Ah, why should all Mankind*
> *For one Man's fault thus guiltless be condemned*
> *If guiltless ?   But from me what can proceed*
> *But all corrupt . . .*

Who can afterwards behold the Father of Mankind extended
upon the Earth, uttering his Midnight Complaints, bewailing
his Existence, and wishing for Death, without sympathizing
with him in his Distress?

> *Thus* Adam *to himself lamented loud*
> *Through the still night, not now, as e'er Man fell,*
> *Wholesome and cool and mild, but with black Air*
> *Accompanied, with damps and dreadful gloom;*
> *Which to his evil Conscience represented*
> *All things with double terrour; on the Ground*
> *Outstretch'd he lay, on the cold Ground, and oft*
> *Curs'd his Creation; Death as oft accus'd*
> *Of tardy execution. . . .*

The Part of *Eve* in this Book is no less passionate, and apt to sway the Reader in her Favour. She is represented with great Tenderness as approaching *Adam*, but is spurn'd from him with a Spirit of Upbraiding and Indignation conformable to the Nature of Man, whose Passions had now gained the Dominion over him. The following Passage wherein she is described as renewing her Addresses to him, with the whole Speech that follows it, have something in them exquisitely moving and pathetick.

> *He added not, and from her turn'd; but* Eve
> *Not so repulst, with Tears that ceas'd not flowing,*
> *And Tresses all disorder'd, at his Feet*
> *Fell humble, and embracing them besought*
> *His peace, and thus proceeding in her plaint.*
> *Forsake me not thus* Adam: *witness Heav'n*
> *What love sincere and reverence in my heart*
> *I bear thee, and unweeting have offended,*
> *Unhappily deceiv'd; thy Suppliant*
> *I beg, and clasp thy knees; bereave me not,*
> *Whereon I live, thy gentle looks, thy aid,*
> *Thy Counsel in this uttermost distress,*
> *My only strength and stay: Forlorn of thee*
> *Whither shall I betake me, where subsist?*
> *While yet we live, scarce one short hour perhaps,*
> *Between us two let there be peace, &c.*

Adam's Reconcilement to her is work'd up in the same Spirit of Tenderness. *Eve* afterwards proposes to her Husband, in the Blindness of her despair, that to prevent their Guilt from descending upon Posterity they should resolve to live Childless; or, if that could not be done, they should seek their own Deaths by violent Methods. As those Sentiments naturally engage the Reader to regard the Mother of Mankind with more than ordinary Commiseration, they likewise contain a very fine Moral. The Resolution of dying to end our Miseries, does not shew such a degree of Magnanimity as a Resolution to bear them, and submit to the Dispensations of Providence. Our Author has therefore, with great Delicacy, represented *Eve* as entertaining this Thought, and *Adam* as disapproving it.

We are, in the last Place, to consider the Imaginary Persons, or *Death* and *Sin*, who act a large Part in this Book. Such beautiful extended Allegories are certainly some of the finest Compositions of Genius; but, as I have before observed, are not agreeable to the Nature of an Heroic Poem. This of *Sin* and *Death* is very exquisite in its Kind, if not considered as a Part of such a Work. The Truths contained in it are so clear and open, that I shall not lose Time in explaining them; but shall only observe, that a Reader who knows the Strength of the *English* Tongue, will be amazed to think how the Poet could find such apt Words and Phrases to describe the Actions of those two imaginary Persons, and particularly in that Part where *Death* is exhibited as forming a Bridge over the *Chaos*; a Work suitable to the Genius of *Milton*.

Since the Subject I am upon gives me an Opportunity of speaking more at large of such Shadowy and Imaginary Persons as may be introduced into Heroic Poems, I shall beg Leave to explain my self in a Matter which is curious in its Kind, and which none of the Criticks have treated of. It is certain *Homer* and *Virgil* are full of imaginary Persons, who are very beautiful in Poetry when they are just shewn without being engaged in any Series of Action. *Homer* indeed represents *Sleep* as a Person, and ascribes a short Part to him in his *Iliad*; but we must consider that tho' we now regard such a Person as entirely shadowy and unsubstantial, the Heathens made Statues of him, placed him in their Temples, and looked upon him as a real Deity. When *Homer* makes use of other such Allegorical Persons, it is only in short Expressions, which convey an ordinary Thought to the Mind in the most pleasing Manner, and may rather be looked upon as Poetical Phrases than Allegorical Descriptions. Instead of telling us that Men naturally fly when they are terrified, he introduces the Persons of *Flight* and *Fear*, who, he tells us, are inseparable Companions. Instead of saying that the Time was come when *Apollo* ought to have received his Recompence, he tells us that the *Hours* brought him his Reward. Instead of describing the Effects which *Minerva's Aegis* produced in Battel, he tells us that the Brims of it were encompassed by *Terrour, Rout, Discord, Fury, Pursuit, Massacre,* and *Death*. In the same Figure of speaking, he represents *Victory* as following *Diomedes*; *Discord* as the Mother of Funerals and Mourning; *Venus* as dressed by the *Graces*; *Bellona* as wearing Terrour and Consternation like a Garment. I might give several other Instances out of *Homer*, as well as a great many out of *Virgil*. *Milton* has likewise very often made use of the same way of Speaking, as where he tells us, that *Victory* sat on the Right

Hand of the Messiah when he marched forth against the Rebel Angels; that at the rising of the Sun the *Hours* unbarr'd the Gates of Light; that *Discord* was the Daughter of *Sin*. Of the same Nature are those Expressions, where describing the Singing of the Nightingale, he adds, *Silence was pleased;* and upon the Messiah's bidding Peace to the *Chaos, Confusion heard his Voice.* I might add innumerable Instances of our Poet's writing in this beautiful Figure. It is plain that these I have mentioned, in which Persons of an imaginary Nature are introduced, are such short Allegories as are not designed to be taken in the literal Sense, but only to convey particular Circumstances to the Reader after an unusual and entertaining Manner. But when such Persons are introduced as principal Actors, and engaged in a Series of Adventures, they take too much upon them, and are by no means proper for an Heroic Poem, which ought to appear credible in its principal Parts. I cannot forbear therefore thinking that *Sin* and *Death* are as improper Agents in a Work of this Nature, as *Strength* and *Necessity* in one of the Tragedies of *Eschylus*, who represented those two Persons nailing down *Prometheus* to a Rock, for which he has been justly censured by the greatest Criticks. I do not know any imaginary Person made use of in a more sublime manner of Thinking than that in one of the Prophets, who describing God as descending from Heaven, and visiting the Sins of Mankind, adds that dreadful Circumstance, *Before him went the Pestilence.* It is certain this imaginary Person might have been described in all her purple Spots. The *Fever* might have marched before her, *Pain* might have stood at her Right Hand, *Phrenzy* on her Left, and *Death* in her Rear. She might have been introduced as gliding down from the Tail of a Comet, or darted upon the Earth in a Flash of Lightning: She might have tainted the Atmosphere with her Breath; the very Glaring of her Eyes might have scattered Infection. But I believe every Reader will think, that in such sublime Writings the mentioning of her as it is done in Scripture, has something in it more just, as well as great, than all that the most fanciful Poet could have bestowed upon her in the Richnesss of his Imagination. L

No. 358.
[STEELE.]   Monday, April 21.

Desipere in loco.—Hor.

Charles Lillie attended me the other Day, and made me a Present of a large Sheet of Paper, on which is delineated a Pavement in Mosaick Work, lately discovered at *Stunsfield* near *Woodstock*. A Person who has so much the Gift of Speech as Mr. *Lillie*, and can carry on a Discourse without Reply, had great Opportunity on that Occasion to expatiate upon so fine a Piece of Antiquity. Among other things, I remember he gave me his Opinion, which he drew from the Ornaments of the Work, That this was the Floor of a Room dedicated to Mirth and Concord. Viewing this Work, made my Fancy run over the many gay Expressions I had read in ancient Authors, which contained Invitations to lay aside Care and Anxiety, and give a Loose to that pleasing Forgetfulness wherein Men put off their Characters of Business, and enjoy their very Selves. These Hours were usually passed in Rooms adorned for that Purpose, and set out in such a Manner, as the Objects all around the Company gladdened their Hearts; which joined to the cheerful Looks of well-chosen and agreeable Friends, gave new Vigour to the Airy, produced the latent Fire of the Modest, and gave Grace to the slow Humour of the Reserved. A judicious Mixture of such Company, crowned with Chaplets of Flowers, and the whole Apartment glittering with gay Lights, cheared with a Profusion of Roses, artificial Falls of Water, and Intervals of soft Notes to Songs of Love and Wine, suspended the Cares of humane Life, and made a Festival of mutual Kindness. Such Parties of Pleasure as these, and the Reports of the agreeable Passages in their Jollities, have in all Ages awakened the dull Part of Mankind to pretend to Mirth and good Humour without Capacity for such Entertainments; for if I may be allowed to say so, there are an hundred Men fit for any Employment, to one who is capable of passing a Night in the Company of the first Taste, without shocking any Member of the Society, over-rating his own Part of the Conversation, but equally receiving and contributing to the Pleasure of the whole Company. When one considers such Collections of Companions in past Times, and such as one might name in the present Age, with how much Spleen must a Man needs reflect upon the awkard Gayety of those who affect the Frolick with an ill Grace? I have a Letter from a Correspondent of mine, who desires me to admonish all loud, mischievous, airy, dull Companions, that they are mistaken in what they call a Frolick. Irregularity in it self is not what creates Pleasure and Mirth; but to see a Man who knows what Rule and Decency are, descend from them agreeably in our Company, is what denominates him a pleasant Companion. Instead of that, you find many whose Mirth consists only in doing things which do not become them, with a secret Consciousness that all the World know they know better: To this is always added something mischievous to themselves or others.

I have heard of some very merry Fellows, among whom the Frolick was started, and passed by a great Majority, that every Man should immediately draw a Tooth; after which they have gone in a Body and smoked a Cobler. The same Company, at another Night, has each Man burned his Cravat; and one perhaps, whose Estate would bear it, has thrown a long Wigg and laced Hat into the same Fire. Thus they have jested themselves stark naked, and ran into the Streets, and frighted Women very successfully. There is no Inhabitant of any standing in *Covent-Garden*, but can tell you a hundred good Humours, where People have come off with little Blood-shed, and yet scowred all the witty Hours of the Night. I know a Gentleman that has several Wounds in the Head by Watch-Poles, and has been thrice run through the Body to carry on a good Jest: He is very old for a Man of so much good Humour; but to this Day he is seldom merry, but he has Occasion to be valiant at the same time. But by the Favour of these Gentlemen, I am humbly of Opinion, that a Man may be a very witty Man, and never offend one Statute of this Kingdom, not excepting even that of Stabbing.

The Writers of Plays have what they call Unity of Time and Place to give a Justness to their Representation; and it would not be amiss if all who pretend to be Companions, would confine their Action to the Place of Meeting: For a Frolick carried further may be better performed by other Animals than Men. It is not to rid much Ground, or do much Mischief, that should denominate a pleasant Fellow; but that is truly Frolick which is the Play of the Mind, and consists of various and unforced Sallies of Imagination. Festivity of Spirit is a very uncommon Talent, and must proceed from an Assemblage of agreeable Qualities in the same Person: There are some few whom I think peculiarly happy in it; but it is a Talent one cannot name in a Man, especially when one considers that it is never very graceful but where it is regarded by him who possesses it in the second Place. The best Man that I know of for heightning the Revel-Gayety of a Company, is *Estcourt*, whose jovial Humour diffuses it self from the highest Person at an Entertainment to the meanest Waiter. Merry Tales, accompanied with apt Gestures and lively Representations of Circumstances and Persons, beguile the gravest Mind into a Consent to be as humourous as himself. Add to this, that when a Man is in his good Graces, he has a Mimickry that does not debase the Person he represents: but which, taking from the Gravity of the Character, adds to the Agreeableness of it. This pleasant Fellow gives one some Idea of the ancient *Pantomime*, who is said to have given the Audience, in Dumb-show, an exact Idea of any Character or Passion, or an intelligible Relation of any publick Occurrence, with no other Expression than that of his Looks and Gestures. If all who have been obliged to these Talents in *Estcourt*, will be at *Love for Love* to Morrow Night, they will but pay him what they owe him; at so easie a Rate as being present at a Play which no Body would omit seeing that had, or had not ever seen it before.

No. 359.
BUDGELL.]   Tuesday, April 22.

Torva leaena lupum sequitur ; lupus ipse capellam :
Florentem cytisum sequitur lasciva capella.—Virg.

As we were at the Club last Night, I observ'd that my Friend Sir ROGER, contrary to his usual Custom, sat very silent, and instead of minding what was said by the Company, was whistling to himself in a very thoughtful Mood, and playing with a Cork. I jogg'd Sir ANDREW FREEPORT who sat between us; and as we were both observing him, we saw the Knight shake his Head, and heard him say to himself, *A foolish Woman! I can't believe it.* Sir ANDREW gave him a gentle Pat upon the Shoulder, and offer'd to lay him a Bottle of Wine that he was thinking of the Widow. My old Friend started, and recovering out of his brown Study, told Sir ANDREW that once in his Life he had been in the Right. In short, after some little Hesitation, Sir ROGER told us in the Fulness of his Heart that he had just receiv'd a Letter from his Steward, which acquainted him that his old Rival and Antagonist in the Country, Sir *David Dundrum*, had been making a Visit to the Widow. However, says Sir ROGER, I can never think that she 'll have a Man that 's half a Year older than I am, and a noted Republican into the Bargain.

WILL. HONEYCOMB, who looks upon Love as his particular Province, interrupting our Friend with a jainty Laugh, I thought, Knight, says he, thou hadst lived long enough in the World, not to pin thy Happiness upon one that is a Woman and a Widow. I think that without Vanity I may pretend to know as much of the Female World, as any Man in *Great Britain*, though the chief of my Knowledge consists in this, that they are not to be known. WILL. immediately, with his usual Fluency, rambled into an Account of his own Amours. I am now, says he, upon the Verge of Fifty, though by the way we all knew he was turn'd of Threescore. You may easily guess, continued WILL, that I have not lived so long in the

World without having had some Thoughts of *settling* in it, as the Phrase is. To tell you truly, I have several times tried my Fortune that way, though I can't much boast of my Success.

I made my first Addresses to a young Lady in the Country, but when I thought things were pretty well drawing to a Conclusion, her Father happening to hear that I had formerly boarded with a Surgeon, the old Put forbid me his House, and within a Fortnight after married his Daughter to a Fox-hunter in the Neighbourhood.

I made my next Applications to a Widow, and attacked her so briskly, that I thought my self within a Fortnight of her. As I waited upon her one Morning, she told me that she intended to keep her Ready-Money and Jointure in her own Hand, and desired me to call upon her Attorney in *Lyons-Inn,* who would adjust with me what it was proper for me to add to it. I was so rebuffed by this Overture, that I never enquired either for her or her Attorney afterwards.

A few Months after I addressed my self to a young Lady, who was an only Daughter, and of a good Family. I danced with her at several Balls, squeezed her by the Hand, said soft things, and, in short, made no doubt of her Heart; and though my Fortune was not equal to hers, I was in Hopes that her fond Father would not deny her the Man she had fixed her Affections upon. But as I went one Day to the House in order to break the Matter to him, I found the whole Family in Confusion, and heard, to my unspeakable Surprize, that Miss *Jenny* was that very Morning run away with the Butler.

I then courted a second Widow, and am at a Loss to this Day how I came to miss her, for she had often commended my Person and Behaviour. Her Maid indeed told me one Day, that her Mistress had said she never saw a Gentleman with such a Spindle Pair of Legs as Mr. HONEYCOMB.

After this I laid Siege to four Heiresses successively, and being a handsome young Dog in those Days, quickly made a Breach in their Hearts; but I don't know how it came to pass, though I seldom failed of getting the Daughter's Consent, I could never in my Life get the old People on my Side.

I could give you an Account of a thousand other unsuccessful Attempts, particularly of one which I made some Years since upon an old Woman, whom I had certainly born away with flying Colours, if her Relations had not come pouring in to her Assistance from all Parts of *England*; nay, I believe I should have got her at last, had not she been carried off by an hard Frost.

As WILL's Transitions are extreamly quick, he turned from

Sir ROGER, and applying himself to me, told me there was a Passage in the Book I had considered last *Saturday* which deserved to be writ in Letters of Gold; and taking out a Pocket *Milton* read the following Lines, which are Part of one of *Adam's* Speeches to *Eve* after the Fall.

> *. . . O why did our*
> *Creator wise, that peopled highest heaven*
> *With Spirits masculine, create at last*
> *This Novelty on Earth, this fair Defect*
> *Of nature, and not fill the world at once*
> *With Men as Angels, without feminine?*
> *Or find some other way to generate*
> *Mankind? This Mischief had not then befall'n,*
> *And more that shall befall, innumerable*
> *Disturbances on earth through female Snares,*
> *And strait conjunction with this Sex; for either*
> *He never shall find out fit mate, but such*
> *As some misfortune brings him, or mistake;*
> *Or whom he wishes most shall seldom gain*
> *Through her perverseness, but shall see her gain'd*
> *By a far worse, or if she love, withheld*
> *By parents; or his happiest Choice too late*
> *Shall meet already link'd and Wedlock-bound*
> *To a fell adversary, his hate or shame;*
> *Which infinite calamity shall cause*
> *To humane Life, and houshold peace confound.*

Sir ROGER listned to this Passage with great Attention, and desiring Mr. HONEYCOMB to fold down a Leaf at the Place, and lend him his Book, the Knight put it up in his Pocket, and told us that he would read over those Verses again before he went to Bed.　　　　　　　　　　　　　　　　　　　　　　X

No. 360.

[STEELE.]　　　　　　　　　　　　　　　　Wednesday, April 23.

> *. . . De paupertate tacentes*
> *Plus poscente ferent.*—Hor.

I HAVE nothing to do with the Business of this Day, any further than affixing the Piece of Latin on the Head of my Paper; which I think a Motto not unsuitable, since if Silence of our Poverty is a Recommendation, still more commendable is his Modesty who conceals it by a decent Dress.

　'*Mr.* SPECTATOR,

There is an Evil under the Sun which has not yet come within your Speculation, and is, the Censure, Disesteem, and Contempt which some young Fellows meet with from particular

Persons, for the reasonable Methods they take to avoid them in general. This is by appearing in a better Dress, than may seem to a Relation regularly consistent with a small Fortune; and therefore may occasion a Judgment of a suitable Extravagance in other Particulars: But the Disadvantage with which the Man of narrow Circumstances acts and speaks, is so feelingly set forth in a little Book called the *Christian Hero*, that the appearing to be otherwise is not only pardonable but necessary. Every one knows the Hurry of Conclusions that are made in Contempt of a Person that appears to be Calamitous, which makes it very excusable to prepare one's self for the Company of those that are of a Superior Quality and Fortune, by appearing to be in a better Condition than one is, so far as such Appearance shall not make us really of worse.

It is a Justice due to the Character of one who suffers hard Reflections from any particular Person upon this Account, that such Persons would enquire into his Manner of spending his Time; of which, tho' no further Information can be had than that he remains so many Hours in his Chamber, yet if this is clear'd, to Imagine that a reasonable Creature wrung with a narrow Fortune does not make the best use of this Retirement, would be a Conclusion extreamly uncharitable. From what has, or will be said, I hope no Consequence can be extorted, implying, that I would have any young Fellow spend more Time than the common Leisure which his Studies require, or more Money than his Fortune or Allowance may admit of, in the Pursuit of an Acquaintance with his Betters: For as to his Time, the Gross of that ought to be sacred to more substantial Acquisitions; for each irrevocable Moment of which he ought to believe he stands religiously accountable. And as to his Dress, I shall engage my self no further than in the modest defence of two plain Suits a Year: For being perfectly satisfied in *Eutrapelus*'s Contrivance of making a *Mohock* of a Man by presenting him with lac'd and embroider'd Suits, I would by no Means be thought to controvert that Conceit by insinuating the Advantages of Foppery. It is an Assertion which admits of much Proof, that a Stranger of tolerable Sense dress'd like a Gentleman, will be better received by those of Quality above him, than one of much better Parts, whose Dress is regulated by the rigid Notions of Frugality. A Man's Appearance falls within the Censure of every one that sees him; his Parts and Learning very few are Judges of; and even upon these few, they can't at first be well intruded; for Policy and good Breeding will counsel him to be reserv'd among Strangers, and to support himself only by the common Spirit of Conversation. Indeed, among the Injudicious, the Words

Delicacy, Idiom, fine Images, Structure of Periods, Genius, Fire, and the rest, made use of with a frugal and comely Gravity, will maintain the Figure of immense Reading and the Depth of Criticism.

All Gentlemen of Fortune, at least the young and middle aged, are apt to Pride themselves a little too much upon their Dress, and consequently to value others in some Measure upon the same Consideration. With what Confusion is a Man of Figure obliged to return the Civilities of a Hat to a Person whose Air and Attire hardly entitle him to it? For whom nevertheless the other has particular Esteem, tho' he is ashamed to have it challenged in so publick a Manner. It must be allowed, that any young Fellow that affects to dress and appear genteely, might by artificial Management save ten Pound a Year; as instead of fine Holland he might mourn in Sack-cloath, and in other particulars be proportionably shabby: But of what great Service would this Sum be to avert any Misfortune, whilst it would leave him deserted by the little good Acquaintance he has, and prevent his gaining any other? As the appearance of an easy Fortune is necessary towards making one, I don't know but it might be of Advantage sometimes to throw into one's Discourse certain Exclamations upon Bank-stock and to shew a marvellous Surprize upon its Fall, as well as the most affected Triumph upon its Rise. The Veneration and Respect which the Practice of all Ages has preserved to Appearances, without Doubt suggested to our Tradesmen that wise and politick Custom, to apply and recommend themselves to the Publick by all those Decorations upon their Sign-posts and Houses, which the most eminent Hands in the Neighbourhood can furnish them with. What can be more attractive to a Man of Letters, than that immense Erudition of all Ages and Languages, which a skilful Bookseller, in Conjunction with a Painter, shall image upon his Column and the Extremities of his Shop? The same Spirit of maintaining a handsome Appearance reigns among the grave and solid Apprentices of the Law (here I could be particularly dull in proving the Word Apprentice to be significant of a Barrister) and you may easily distinguish who has most lately made his Pretensions to Business, by the whitest and most ornamental Frame of his Window: If indeed the Chamber is a Ground-Room, and has Rails before it, the Finery is of necessity more extended, and the Pomp of Business better maintained. And what can be a greater Indication of the Dignity of Dress, than that burthensome Finery which is the regular Habit of our Judges, Nobles, and Bishops, with which upon certain Days we see them incumbered? And though it may be said this is awful and necessary for the Dignity of the State, yet the wisest of them have been remarkable before they arrived at their present Stations, for being *very well dressed Persons.* As to my own part, I am near Thirty; and since I left School have not been idle, which is a modern Phrase for having studied hard. I brought off a clean System of Moral Philosophy, and a tolerable Jargon of Metaphysicks from the University; since that, I have been engaged in the clearing part of the perplex'd Style and Matter of the Law, which so hereditarily descends to all its Professors: To all which severe Studies I have thrown in, at proper Interims, the pretty Learning of the Classicks. Notwithstanding which I am what *Shakespear* calls *A Fellow of no Mark or Likelihood*; which makes me understand the more fully, that since the regular Methods of making Friends and a Fortune by the meer Force of a Profession is so very slow and uncertain, a Man should take all reasonable Opportunities by enlarging a good Acquaintance, to court that Time and Chance which is said to happen to every Man.'   T

No. 361.

[ADDISON.]   Thursday, April 24.

> *Tartaream intendit vocem, qua protinus omne*
> *Contremuit nemus. . . .*—Virg.

I HAVE lately received the following Letter from a Country Gentleman.

'*Mr.* SPECTATOR,

The Night before I left *London* I went to see a Play, called *The Humourous Lieutenant.* Upon the Rising of the Curtain I was very much surprized with the great Consort of Cat-calls which was exhibited that Evening, and began to think with my self that I had made a Mistake, and gone to a Musick Meeting instead of the Play house. It appeared indeed a little odd to me to see so many Persons of Quality of both Sexes assembled together at a kind of Catterwawling; for I cannot look upon that Performance to have been any thing better, whatever the Musicians themselves might think of it. As I had no Acquaintance in the House to ask Questions of, and was forced to go out of Town early the next Morning, I could not learn the Secret of this Matter. What I would therefore desire of you is, to give some Account of this strange Instrument, which I found the Company called a Cat-call; and particularly to let me know whether it be a piece of Musick lately come from *Italy*. For my own part, to be free with you, I would rather hear an *English* Fiddle; though I durst not shew my Dislike whilst I was in the Play-house, it being my Chance to sit the very next Man to one of the Performers.

> *I am, Sir,*
> *Your most affectionate Friend and Servant,*
> John Shallow, *Esq.*'

In Compliance with Squire *Shallow*'s Requests, I design this Paper as a Dissertation upon the Cat-call. In order to make my self a Master of the Subject, I purchased one the Beginning of last Week, though not without great Difficulty, being informed at two or three Toy-shops that the Players had lately bought them all up. I have since consulted many learned Antiquaries in relation to its Original, and find them very much divided among themselves upon that Particular. A Fellow of the Royal Society, who is my good Friend, and a great Proficient in the Mathematical Part of Musick, concludes from the Simplicity of its Make, and the Uniformity of its Sound, that the Cat-call is older than any of the Inventions of *Jubal*. He observes very well, that Musical Instruments took their first Rise from the Notes of Birds, and other Melodious Animals; and what, says he, was more natural than for the first Ages of Mankind to imitate the Voice of a Cat that lived under the same Roof with them? He added, that the Cat had contributed more to Harmony than any other Animal; as we are not only beholden to her for this Wind Instrument, but for our String-Musick in general.

Another Virtuoso of my Acquaintance will not allow the Cat-call to be older than *Thespis*, and is apt to think it appeared in the World soon after the Ancient Comedy; for which Reason it has still a Place in our Dramatick Entertainments: Nor must I here omit what a very curious Gentleman, who is lately return'd from his Travels, has more than once assured me, namely, that there was lately dug up at *Rome* the Statue of a *Momus*, who holds an Instrument in his Right-Hand very much resembling our modern Cat-call.

There are others who ascribe this Invention to *Orpheus*, and look upon the Cat-call to be one of those Instruments which that famous Musician made use of to draw the Beasts about him. It is certain, that the Roasting of a Cat does not call together a greater Audience of that Species, than this Instrument, if dexterously play'd upon in proper Time and Place.

But notwithstanding these various and learned Conjectures, I cannot forbear thinking that the Cat-call is originally a Piece of *English* Musick. Its Resemblance to the Voice of some of our *British* Songsters, as well as the Use of it, which is peculiar to our Nation, confirms me in this Opinion. It has at least received great Improvements among us, whether we consider the Instrument it self, or those several Quavers and Graces which are thrown into the Playing of it. Every one might be sensible of this, who heard that remarkable over-grown Cat-call which was placed in the Center of the Pit, and presided over all the rest at the celebrated Performance lately exhibited in *Drury-Lane.*

Having said thus much concerning the Original of the Cat-call, we are in the next Place to consider the Use of it. The Cat-call exerts it self to most Advantage in the *British* Theatre: It very much improves the Sound of Nonsense, and often goes along with the Voice of the Actor who pronounces it, as the Violin or Harpsicord accompanies the *Italian* Recitativo.

It has often supplied the Place of the ancient *Chorus,* in the Words of Mr. * * *. In short, a bad Poet has as great an Antipathy to a Cat-call as many People have to a real Cat.

Mr. *Collier,* in his ingenious Essay upon Musick, has the following Passage:

I believe 'tis possible to invent an Instrument *that shall have a quite contrary effect to those Martial ones now in Use. An* Instrument *that shall sink the Spirits, and shake the Nerves, and curdle the Blood, and inspire Despair, and Cowardize and Consternation, at a surprizing rate. 'Tis probable the Roaring of Lions, the Warbling of Cats and Scritch-Owls, together with a Mixture of the Howling of Dogs, judiciously imitated and compounded, might go a great way in this Invention. Whether such Anti-Musick as this might not be of Service in a Camp, I shall leave to the Military Men to consider.*

What this learned Gentleman supposes in Speculation, I have known actually verified in Practice. The Cat-call has struck a Damp into Generals, and frighted Heroes off the Stage. At the first Sound of it I have seen a Crowned Head Tremble, and a Princess fall into Fits. The *Humourous Lieutenant* himself could not stand it; nay, I am told that even *Almanzor* looked like a Mouse, and trembled at the Voice of this terrifying Instrument.

As it is of a Drammatick Nature, and peculiarly appropriated to the Stage, I can by no means approve the Thought of that angry Lover, who, after an unsuccessful Pursuit of some Years, took Leave of his Mistress in a Serenade of Cat-calls.

I must conclude this Paper with the Account I have lately received of an ingenious Artist, who has long studied this Instrument, and is very well versed in all the Rules of the

Drama. He teaches to play on it by Book, and to express by
it the whole Art of Criticism. He has his Base and his Treble
Cat-call; the former for Tragedy, the latter for Comedy; only
in Tragy-Comedies they may both play together in Consort.
He has a particular Squeak to denote the Violation of each of
the Unities, and has different Sounds to shew whether he aims
at the Poet or the Player. In short, he teaches the Smut-note,
the Fustian-note, the Stupid-note, and has composed a kind
of Air that may serve as an Act-tune to an incorrigible Play,
and which takes in the whole Compass of the Cat-call.   L

No. 362.

[STEELE.]   Friday, April 25.

Laudibus arguitur vini vinosus.—Hor.

'*Mr.* SPECTATOR.   *Temple, Apr.* 24.

SEVERAL of my Friends were this Morning got together over a
Dish of Tea in very good Health, though we had celebrated
Yesterday with more Glasses than we could have dispensed
with, had we not been beholden to *Brooke* and *Hellier.* In
Gratitude therefore to those good Citizens, I am, in the Name
of the Company, to accuse you of great Negligence in over-
looking their Merit who have imported true and generous
Wine, and taken Care that it should not be adulterated by the
Retailers before it comes to the Tables of private Families or
the Clubs of honest Fellows. I cannot imagine how a SPEC-
TATOR can be supposed to do his Duty, without frequent Re-
sumption of such Subjects as concern our Health, the first
thing to be regarded if we have a Mind to relish any thing else.
It would therefore very well become your spectatorial Vigilance to give it in Orders to your Officer for inspecting Signs,
that in his Match he would look into the Itinerants who deal
in Provisions, and enquire where they buy their several Wares.
Ever since the Decease of *Cully Mully Puff* of agreeable and
noisy Memory, I cannot say I have observed any thing sold in
Carts, or carried by Horse or Ass, or in fine, in any moving
Market, which is not perished or putrified; witness the Wheel-
barrows of rotten Raisins, Almonds, Figs, and Currants, which
you see vended by a Merchant dressed in a second-hand Suit
of a Foot Soldier. You should consider that a Child may be
poisoned for the Worth of a Farthing; but except his poor
Parents send to one certain Doctor in Town, they can have no
Advice for him under a Guinea. When Poisons are thus cheap

and Medicines thus dear, how can you be negligent in inspecting what we eat and drink, or take no Notice of such as the above-mentioned Citizens who have been so serviceable to us of late in that Particular? It was a Custom among the old *Romans*, to do him particular Honours who had saved the Life of a Citizen; how much more does the World owe to those who prevent the Death of Multitudes? As these Men deserve well of your Office, so such as act to the Detriment of our Health, you ought to represent to themselves and their Fellow-Subjects in the Colours which they deserve to wear. I think it would be for the publick Good, that all who vend Wines should be under Oaths in that Behalf. The Chairman at a Quarter Sessions should inform the Country, that the Vintner who mixes Wine to his Customers, shall (upon Proof that the Drinker thereof died within a Year and a Day after taking it) be deemed guilty of wilful Murder; and the Jury shall be instructed to enquire and prevent such Delinquents accordingly. It is no Mitigation of the Crime, nor will it be conceived that it can be brought in Chance-Medley or Man Slaughter, upon Proof that it shall appear Wine joined to Wine, or right *Herefordshire* poured into *Port O Port*; but his selling it for one thing knowing it to be another, must justly bear the foresaid Guilt of wilful Murder: For that he, the said Vintner, did an unlawful Act willingly in the false Mixture; and is therefore with Equity liable to all the Pains to which a Man would be, if it were proved he designed only to run a Man through the Arm whom he whipped through the Lungs. This is my third Year at the *Temple*, and this is or should be Law. An ill Intention well proved should meet with no Alleviation, because it out-ran it self. There cannot be too great Severity used against the Injustice as well as Cruelty of those who play with Men's Lives, by preparing Liquors whose Nature, for ought they know, may be noxious when mixed, tho' innocent when apart: And *Brooke* and *Hellier*, who have ensured our Safety at our Meals, and driven Jealousy from our Cups in Conversation, deserve the Custom and Thanks of the whole Town; and it is your Duty to remind them of the Obligation.

> *I am, Sir,*
>> *Your humble Servant,*
>>> Tom Pottle.'

'*Mr.* SPECTATOR,

I am a Person who was long immured in a College, read much, saw little; so that I knew no more of the World than what a Lecture or a View of the Map taught me. By this Means I improved in my Study, but became unpleasant in

Conversation. By conversing generally with the Dead, I grew almost unfit for the Society of the Living; so by a long Confinement I contracted an ungainly Aversion to Conversation, and ever discoursed with Pain to my self, and little Entertainment to others. At last I was in some Measure made sensible of my Failing, and the Mortification of never being spoke to, or speaking, unless the Discourse ran upon Books, put me upon forcing my self amongst Men. I immediately affected the politest Company, by the frequent use of which I hoped to wear off the Rust I had contracted; but by an uncouth Imitation of Men used to act in Publick, I got no further than to discover I had a Mind to appear a finer thing than I really was.

Such I was, and such was my Condition, when I became an ardent Lover, and passionate Admirer of the beauteous *Belinda*: Then it was that I really began to improve. This Passion changed all my Fears and Diffidences in my general Behaviour, to the sole Concern of pleasing her. I had now to study the Action of a Gentleman, but Love possessing all my Thoughts, made me truly be the thing I had a Mind to appear. My Thoughts grew free and generous, and the Ambition to be agreeable to her I admired, produced in my Carriage a feint Similitude of that disengaged Manner of my *Belinda*. The Way we are in at present is, that she sees my Passion, and sees I at present forbear speaking of it through prudential Regards. This Respect to her she returns with much Civility, and makes my Value for her as little a Misfortune to me as is consistent with Discretion. She sings very charmingly, and is readier to do so at my Request, because she knows I love her: She will dance with me rather than another for the same Reason. My Fortune must alter from what it is before I can speak my Heart to her, and her Circumstances are not considerable enough to make up for the Narrowness of mine. But I write to you now only to give you the Character of *Belinda*, as a Woman that has Address enough to demonstrate a Gratitude to her Lover, without giving him Hopes of Success in his Passion. *Belinda* has from a great Wit, governed by as great Prudence, and both adorned with Innocence, the Happiness of always being ready to discover her real Thoughts. She has many of us, who now are her Admirers; but her Treatment of us is so just and proportioned to our Merit towards her, and what we are in our selves, that I protest to you I have neither Jealousie nor Hatred towards my Rivals. Such is her Goodness, and the Acknowledgement of every Man who admires her, that he thinks he ought to believe she will take him who best deserves her. I will not say that this Peace among us is not owing to Self-Love, which prompts each to think himself

the best Deserver, I think there is something uncommon and
worthy of Imitation in this Lady's Character.   If you will
please to print my Letter, you will oblige the little Fraternity
of happy Rivals, and in a more particular Manner,

Sir,

Your most humble Servant,

T   Will. Cymon.'

No. 363.

[ADDISON.]   Saturday, April 26.

. . . *Crudelis ubique*
Luctus, ubique pavor, & plurima mortis imago.—Virg.

Milton has shewn a wonderful Art in describing that Variety
of Passions which arise in our first Parents upon the Breach
of the Commandment that had been given them.   We see them
gradually passing from the Triumph of their Guilt thro' Remorse, Shame, Despair, Contrition, Prayer, and Hope, to a
perfect and compleat Repentance.   At the End of the Tenth
Book they are represented as prostrating themselves upon the
Ground, and watering the Earth with their Tears: To which
the Poet joins this beautiful Circumstance, that they offer'd up
their penitential Prayers on the very Place where their Judge
appeared to them when he pronounced their Sentence.

> . . . *They forthwith to the place*
> *Repairing where he judg'd them, prostrate fell*
> *Before him reverent, and both confess'd*
> *Humbly their faults, and pardon begg'd, with tears*
> *Watering the Ground* . . .

There is a Beauty of the same kind in a Tragedy of *Sophocles*,
where *Oedipus*, after having put out his own Eyes, instead of
breaking his Neck from the Palace Battlements (which furnishes so elegant an Entertainment for our *English* Audience)
desires that he may be conducted to Mount *Cithaeron*, in order
to end his Life in that very Place where he was exposed in his
Infancy, and where he should then have died, had the Will of
his Parents been executed.

As the Author never fails to give a poetical Turn to his
Sentiments, he describes in the Beginning of this Book the
Acceptance which these their Prayers met with, in a short
Allegory form'd upon that beautiful Passage in Holy Writ;
*And another Angel came and stood at the Altar, having a golden
Censer; and there was given unto him much incense, that he*

*should offer it with the Prayers of all Saints upon the Golden
Altar, which was before the Throne: And the smoak of the incense
which came with the Prayers of the Saints ascended up before God.*

> . . . *To Heav'n their prayers*
> *Flew up nor miss'd the way, by envious winds*
> *Blown vagabond or frustrate: in they pass'd*
> *Dimentionless thro' heav'nly Doors; then clad*
> *With incense, where the Golden Altar fumed,*
> *By their great intercessor, came in sight*
> *Before the Father's throne* . . .

We have the same Thought expressed a second Time in the
Intercession of the Messiah, which is conceived in very em-
phatick Sentiments and Expressions.

Among the poetical Parts of Scripture which *Milton* has so
finely wrought into this Part of his Narration, I must not omit
that wherein *Ezekiel* speaking of the Angels who appeared to
him in a Vision, adds, that *every one had four faces,* and that
*their whole bodies, and their backs, and their hands, and their
wings were full of eyes round about.*

> . . . *The Cohort bright*
> *Of watchful Cherubim; four faces each*
> *Had, like a double* Janus; *all their Shape*
> *Spangled with Eyes* . . .

The assembling of all the Angels of Heaven to hear the
solemn Decree passed upon Man, is represented in very lively
Ideas.   The Almighty is here describ'd as remembring Mercy
in the Midst of Judgment, and commanding *Michael* to deliver
his Message in the mildest Terms, lest the Spirit of Man, which
was already broken with the Sense of his Guilt and Misery,
should fail before him.

> . . . *Yet lest they faint*
> *At the sad Sentence rigorously urg'd,*
> *For I behold them softened and with tears*
> *Bewailing their excess, all terror hide.*

The Conference of *Adam* and *Eve* is full of moving Sentiments.   Upon their going abroad after the melancholy Night
which they had passed together, they discover the Lion and
the Eagle pursuing each of them their Prey towards the
Eastern Gates of *Paradise.*   There is a double Beauty in this
Incident, not only as it presents great and just Omens, which
are always agreeable in Poetry, but as it expresses that Enmity
which was now produced in the Animal Creation.   The Poet,
to shew the like Changes in Nature, as well as to grace his
Fable with a noble Prodigy, represents the Sun in an Eclipse.

This particular Incident has likewise a fine Effect upon the
Imagination of the Reader, in regard to what follows; for at
the same Time that the Sun is under an Eclipse, a bright Cloud
descends in the western Quarter of the Heavens, filled with a
Host of Angels, and more luminous than the Sun it self.   The
whole Theatre of Nature is darkned, that this glorious Machine
may appear in all its Lustre and Magnificence.

> . . . *Why in the East*
> *Darkness ere day's mid-course, and morning light*
> *More orient in that western Cloud that draws*
> *O'er the blue firmament a radiant white,*
> *And slow descends, with something heav'nly fraught?*
> *He err'd not, for by this the heav'nly bands*
> *Down from a Sky of Jasper lighted now*
> *In Paradise, and on a Hill made halt;*
> *A glorious apparition* . . .

I need not observe how properly this Author, who always
suits his Parts to the Actors whom he introduces, has employed
Michael in the Expulsion of our first Parents from *Paradise*.
The Archangel on this Occasion neither appears in his proper
Shape, nor in that familiar Manner with which *Raphael* the
sociable Spirit entertained the Father of Mankind before the
Fall.   His Person, his Port, and Behaviour are suitable to a
Spirit of the highest Rank, and exquisitely describ'd in the
following Passage.

> . . . *Th' Archangel soon drew nigh,*
> *Not in his shape Celestial, but as Man*
> *Clad to meet Man; over his lucid Arms*
> *A military Vest of Purple flow'd*
> *Livelier than* Meliboean, *or the grain*
> *Of* Sarra, *worn by Kings and Heroes old*
> *In time of truce;* Iris *had dipt the Wooff:*
> *His starry Helm, unbuckled, shew'd him prime*
> *In Manhood where Youth ended; by his side*
> *As in a glistring Zodiack hung the Sword,*
> Satan's *dire dread, and in his Hand the Spear.*
> Adam *bow'd low; he kingly from his State*
> *Inclined not, but his coming thus declared.*

Eve's Complaint upon hearing that she was to be removed
from the Garden of *Paradise* is wonderfully Beautiful: The
Sentiments are not only proper to the Subject, but have something in them particularly soft and Womanish.

> *Must I then leave thee, Paradise? thus leave*
> *Thee, native Soil, these happy walks and shades,*
> *Fit haunt of Gods?   Where I had hope to spend*
> *Quiet, though sad, the respite of that day*

> *That must be mortal to us both. O flow'rs*
> *That never will in other Climate grow,*
> *My early visitation and my last*
> *At Even, which I bred up with tender hand*
> *From the first opening bud, and gave you names;*
> *Who now shall rear you to the Sun, or rank*
> *Your Tribes, and Water from th' ambrosial Fount ?*
> *Thee, lastly, nuptial Bowre, by me adorn'd*
> *With what to sight or smell was sweet; from thee*
> *How shall I part, and whither wander down*
> *Into a lower World, to this obscure*
> *And wild ? how shall we breath in other Air*
> *Less pure, accustom'd to immortal Fruits ?*

Adam's Speech abounds with Thoughts which are equally moving, but of a more masculine and elevated Turn. Nothing can be conceived more sublime and poetical than the following Passage in it.

> *This most afflicts me, that departing hence*
> *As from his Face I shall be hid, deprived*
> *His blessed Count'nance; here I could frequent,*
> *With worship, place by place where he vouchsafed*
> *Presence divine, and to my Sons relate,*
> *On this Mount he appear'd; under this Tree*
> *Stood visible; among these Pines his Voice*
> *I heard; here with him at this Fountain talk'd:*
> *So many grateful Altars I would rear*
> *Of grassy Turf, and pile up every Stone*
> *Of lustre from the Brook, in memory*
> *Or Monument to Ages, and thereon*
> *Offer sweet smelling Gums and Fruits and Flowers.*
> *In yonder nether World where shall I seek*
> *His bright Appearances, or Footsteps trace ?*
> *For though I fled him angry, yet recall'd*
> *To life prolong'd and promised race I now*
> *Gladly behold though but his utmost Skirts*
> *Of Glory, and far off his Steps adore.*

The Angel afterwards leads *Adam* to the highest Mount of *Paradise*, and lays before him a whole Hemisphere, as a proper Stage for those Visions which were to be represented on it. I have before observed how the Plan of *Milton*'s Poem is in many particulars greater than that of the *Iliad* or *Aeneid*. *Virgil*'s Hero, in the last of these Poems, is entertained with a sight of all those who are to descend from him; but tho' that Episode is justly admired as one of the noblest Designs in the whole *Aeneid*, every one must allow that this of *Milton* is of a much higher Nature. *Adam*'s Vision is not confined to any particular Tribe of Mankind, but extends to the whole Species.

In this great Review which *Adam* takes of all his Sons and

Daughters, the first Objects he is presented with exhibit to him the Story of *Cain* and *Abel*, which is drawn together with much Closeness and Propriety of Expression. That Curiosity and natural Horror which arises in *Adam* at the Sight of the first dying Man, is touched with great Beauty.

> *But have I now seen death, is this the way*
> *I must return to native dust? O Sight*
> *Of terrour, foul and ugly to behold,*
> *Horrid to think, how horrible to feel!*

The second Vision sets before him the Image of Death in a great Variety of Appearances. The Angel, to give him a general Idea of those Effects which his Guilt had brought upon his Posterity, places before him a large Hospital or Lazer-House, fill'd with Persons lying under all kinds of mortal Diseases. How finely has the Poet told us that the sick Persons languished under lingring and incurable Distempers, by an apt and judicious use of such imaginary Beings as those I mentioned in my last *Saturday*'s Paper.

> *Dire was the tossing, deep the Groans;* Despair
> *Tended the Sick, busy from Couch to Couch:*
> *And over them triumphant* Death *his dart*
> *Shook, but delay'd to strike, though oft invoked*
> *With Vows as their chief good and final hope.*

The Passion which likewise rises in *Adam* on this occasion is very natural.

> *Sight so deform what Heart of rock could long*
> *Dry-eyed behold?* Adam *could not, but wept,*
> *Tho' not of Woman born; Compassion quell'd*
> *His best of Man, and gave him up to tears.*

The Discourse between the Angel and *Adam* which follows, abounds with noble Morals.

As there is nothing more delightful in Poetry than a Contrast and Opposition of Incidents, the Author, after this melancholy Prospect of Death and Sickness, raises up a Scene of Mirth, Love and Jollity. The secret Pleasure that steals into *Adam*'s Heart as he is intent upon this Vision, is imagined with great Delicacy. I must not omit the Description of the loose female Troupe, who seduced the Sons of God as they are called in Scripture.

> *For that fair female troupe thou saw'st, that seem'd*
> *Of Goddesses, so blithe, so smooth, so gay,*
> *Yet empty of all good wherein consists*
> *Woman's domestick honour and chief praise;*
> *Bred only and compleated to the taste*

> *Of lustful appetence, to sing, to dance,*
> *To dress and troule the Tongue, and roul the Eye ;*
> *To these that sober race of Men, whose lives*
> *Religious titled them the Sons of God,*
> *Shall yield up all their Virtue, all their Fame,*
> *Ignobly to the Trains and to the smiles*
> *Of those fair Atheists . . .*

The next Vision is of a quite contrary Nature, and filled with the Horrors of War. *Adam* at the Sight of it melts into Tears, and breaks out in that passionate Speech.

> *. . . O what are these ?*
> *Death's ministers, not Men, who thus deal death*
> *Inhumanly to Men, and multiply*
> *Ten thousand fold the Sin of him who slew*
> *His Brother : for of whom such Massacre*
> *Make they but of their Brethren, Men of Men ?*

Milton, to keep up an agreeable Variety in his Visions, after having raised in the Mind of his Reader the several Ideas of Terror which are conformable to the Description of War, passes on to those softer Images of Triumphs and Festivals, in that Vision of Lewdness and Luxury which ushers in the Flood.

As it is Visible that the Poet had his Eye upon *Ovid's* Account of the universal Deluge, the Reader may observe with how much Judgment he has avoided every thing that is redundant or puerile in the *Latin* Poet. We do not here see the Wolf swimming among the Sheep, nor any of those wanton Imaginations which *Seneca* found fault with, as unbecoming the great Catastrophe of Nature. If our Poet has imitated that Verse in which *Ovid* tells us that there was nothing but Sea, and that this Sea had no Shoar to it, he has not set the Thought in such a Light as to incur the Censure which Criticks have passed upon it. The latter part of that Verse in *Ovid* is idle and superfluous, but just and beautiful in *Milton.*

> *Jamque mare & tellus nullum discrimen habebant.*
> *Nil nisi pontus erat : deerant quoque littora ponto.*
> —Ovid

> *. . . Sea cover'd Sea,*
> *Sea without Shore . . .*
> —Milton.

In *Milton* the former part of the Description does not forestall the latter. How much more great and solemn on this Occasion is that which follows in our *English* Poet,

> *. . . And in their Palaces*
> *Where luxury late reign'd, Sea Monsters whelp'd*
> *And stabl'd . . .*

than that in *Ovid*, where we are told that the Sea-Calfs lay in those Places where the Goats were used to browze? The Reader may find several other parallel Passages in the *Latin* and *English* Description of the Deluge, wherein our Poet has visibly the Advantage. The Sky's being over-charged with Clouds, the descending of the Rains, the rising of the Seas, and the appearance of the Rainbow, are such Descriptions as every one must take Notice of. The Circumstance relating to *Paradise* is so finely imagined and suitable to the Opinions of many learned Authors, that I cannot forbear giving it a Place in this Paper.

> . . . *Then shall this mount*
> *Of Paradise by might of waves be mov'd*
> *Out of his place, push'd by the horned flood,*
> *With all his verdure spoil'd, and trees adrift*
> *Down the great River to the op'ning Gulf,*
> *And there take root, an Island salt and bare,*
> *The haunt of Seals and Orcs and Sea-Mews' clang.*

The Transition which the Poet makes from the Vision of the Deluge, to the Concern it occasioned in *Adam*, is exquisitely graceful, and copied after *Virgil*, though the first Thought it introduces is rather in the Spirit of *Ovid*.

> *How didst thou grieve then,* Adam, *to behold*
> *The end of all thy Off-spring, end so sad,*
> *Depopulation; thee another floud,*
> *Of tears and sorrow, a floud thee also drown'd,*
> *And sunk thee as thy Sons; till gently rear'd*
> *By th' Angel, on thy feet thou stoodst at last,*
> *Though comfortless, as when a father mourns*
> *His Children, all in view destroy'd at once.*

I have been the more particular in my Quotations out of the Eleventh Book of *Paradise Lost*, because it is not generally reckoned among the most shining Books of this Poem; for which Reason the Reader might be apt to overlook those many Passages in it which deserve our Admiration. The Eleventh and Twelfth are indeed built upon that single Circumstance of the Removal of our first Parents from *Paradise*; but though this is not in it self so great a Subject as that in most of the foregoing Books, it is extended and diversified with so many surprizing Incidents and pleasing Episodes, that these two last Books can by no means be looked upon as unequal Parts of this Divine Poem. I must further add, that had not *Milton* represented our first Parents as driven out of *Paradise*, his Fall of Man would not have been compleat, and consequently his Action would have been imperfect.   L

No. 364.

[STEELE.] Monday, April 28.

> . . . *Navibus atque*
> *Quadrigis petimus bene vivere.*—Hor.

'*Mr.* SPECTATOR,

A LADY of my Acquaintance, for whom I have too much Respect to be easie while she is doing an indiscreet Action, has given Occasion to this Trouble: She is a Widow, to whom the Indulgence of a tender Husband has entrusted the Management of a very great Fortune, and a Son about Sixteen, both which she is extreamly fond of. The Boy has Parts of the middle Size, neither shining nor despicable, and has passed the common Exercises of his Years with tolerable Advantage; but is withal what you would call a forward Youth: By the Help of this last Qualification, which serves as a Varnish to all the rest, he is enabled to make the best Use of his Learning, and display it at full Length upon all Occasions. Last Summer he distinguished himself two or three times very remarkably, by puzzling the Vicar before an Assembly of most of the Ladies in the Neighbourhood; and from such weighty Considerations as these, as it too often unfortunately falls out, the Mother is become invincibly perswaded that her Son is a great Scholar; and that to chain him down to the ordinary Methods of Education with others of his Age, would be to cramp his Faculties, and do an irreparable Injury to his wonderful Capacity.

I happened to visit at the House last Week, and missing the young Gentleman at the Tea-Table, where he seldom fails to officiate, could not upon so extraordinary a Circumstance avoid enquiring after him. My Lady told me, He was gone out with her Woman, in order to make some Preparations for their Equipage; for that she intended very speedily to carry him to travel. The Oddness of the Expression shock'd me a little; however, I soon recovered my self enough to let her know, that all I was willing to understand by it was, that she designed this Summer to shew her Son his Estate in a distant County, in which he has never yet been: But she soon took Care to rob me of that agreeable Mistake, and let me into the whole Affair. She enlarged upon young Master's prodigious Improvements, and his comprehensive Knowledge of all Book-learning; concluding, that it was now high time he should be made acquainted with Men and Things: That she had resolved he should make the Tour of *France* and *Italy*, but could not bear to have him out of her Sight, and therefore intended to go along with him.

I was going to rally her for so extravagant a Resolution, but found my self not in fit Humour to meddle with a Subject that demanded the most soft and delicate Touch imaginable. I was afraid of dropping something that might seem to bear hard either upon the Son's Abilities, or the Mother's Discretion; being sensible that in both these Cases, though supported with all the Powers of Reason, I should, instead of gaining her Ladyship over to my Opinion, only expose my self to her Disesteem: I therefore immediately determined to refer the whole Matter to the SPECTATOR.

When I came to reflect at Night, as my Custom is, upon the Occurrences of the Day, I could not but believe that this Humour of carrying a Boy to travel in his Mother's Lap, and that upon Pretence of learning Men and Things, is a Case of an extraordinary Nature, and carries on it a particular Stamp of Folly. I did not remember to have met with its Parallel within the Compass of my Observation, though I could call to mind some not extreamly unlike it: From hence my Thoughts took Occasion to ramble into the general Notion of Travelling, as it is now made a Part of Education. Nothing is more frequent than to take a Lad from Grammar and Taw, and under the Tuition of some poor Scholar, who is willing to be banished for Thirty Pounds a Year and a little Victuals, send him crying and snivelling into Foreign Countries. Thus he spends his Time as Children do at Puppet-Shows, and with much the same Advantage, in staring and gaping at an amazing Variety of strange Things; strange indeed to one that is not prepared to comprehend the Reasons and Meaning of them; whilst he should be laying the solid Foundations of Knowledge in his Mind, and furnishing it with just Rules to direct his future Progress in Life under some skilful Master of the Art of Instruction.

Can there be a more astonishing Thought in Nature, than to consider how Men should fall into so palpable a Mistake? It is a large Field, and may very well exercise a sprightly Genius; but I don't remember you have yet taken a Turn in it. I wish, Sir, you would make People understand, that *Travel* is really the last Step to be taken in the Institution of Youth; and that to set out with it, is to begin where they should end.

Certainly the true End of visiting Foreign Parts, is to look into their Customs and Policies, and observe in what Particulars they excel or come short of our own; to unlearn some odd Peculiarities in our Manners, and wear off such awkard Stiffnesses and Affectations in our Behaviour, as may possibly have been contracted from constantly associating with one Nation of Men, by a more free, general, and mixed Conversation. But how can any of these Advantages be attained by one who is a meer Stranger to the Customs and Policies of his native Country, and has not yet fixed in his Mind the first Principles of Manners and Behaviour? To endeavour it, is to build a gawdy structure without any Foundation; or, if I may be allowed the Expression, to work a rich Embroidery upon a Cobweb.

Another End of Travelling, which deserves to be considered, is the Improving our Taste of the best Authors of Antiquity, by seeing the Places where they lived, and of which they wrote; to compare the natural Face of the Country with the Descriptions they have given us, and observe how well the Picture agrees with the Original. This must certainly be a most charming Exercise to the Mind that is rightly turn'd for it; besides, that it may in a good measure be made subservient to Morality, if the Person is capable of drawing just Conclusions concerning the Uncertainty of humane Things, from the ruinous Alterations Time and Barbarity have brought upon so many Palaces, Cities, and whole Countries, which make the most illustrious Figures in History. And this Hint may be not a little improved by examining every Spot of Ground that we find celebrated as the Scene of some famous Action, or retaining any Footsteps of a *Cato, Cicero,* or *Brutus,* or some such great vertuous Man. A nearer View of any such Particular, tho' really little and trifling in its self, may serve the more powerfully to warm a generous Mind to an Emulation of their Virtues, and a greater Ardency of Ambition to imitate their bright Examples, if it comes duly tempered and prepared for the Impression. But this I believe you 'll hardly think those to be, who are so far from entring into the Sense and Spirit of the Ancients, that they don't yet understand their Language with any Exactness.

But I have wandered from my Purpose, which was only to desire you to save, if possible, a fond *English* Mother, and Mother's *own* Son, from being shewn a ridiculous Spectacle through the most polite Part of *Europe.* Pray tell them, that though to be Sea-sick, or jumbled in an outlandish Stage-Coach, may perhaps be healthful for the Constitution of the Body, yet it is apt to cause such a Dizziness in young empty Heads, as too often lasts their Life-time.

> *I am,*
>> *Sir,*
>>> *Your most humble Servant,*
>>>> Philip Homebred.'

'*Sir*,   *Birchin-Lane.*

I was married on *Sunday* last, and went peaceably to Bed; but, to my Surprize, was awakened the next Morning by the Thunder of a Set of Drums. These warlike Sounds (methinks) are very improper in a Marriage-Consort, and give great Offence; they seem to insinuate, that the Joys of this State are short, and that Jars and Discord soon ensue. I fear they have been ominous to many Matches, and sometimes proved a Prelude to a Battle in the Honey-Moon. A Nod from you may hush them; therefore pray Sir, let them be silenced, that for the future none but soft Airs may usher in the Morning of a Bridal Night, which will be a favour not only to those who come after, but to me, who can still subscribe my self,

> *Your most humble,*
> *and most obedient Servant,*
> Robin Bridegroom.'

'*Mr.* SPECTATOR,

I am one of that Sort of Women whom the gayer part of our Sex are apt to call a Prude. But to shew them that I have very little regard to their Railery, I shall be glad to see them all at the *Amorous Widow*, or, *the Wanton Wife*; which is to be acted, for the Benefit of Mrs. *Porter*, on *Monday* the 28th Instant. I assure you I can laugh at an Amorous Widow, or Wanton Wife, with as little Temptation to imitate them, as I could at any other vitious Character. Mrs. *Porter* obliged me so very much in the exquisite Sense she seemed to have of the honourable Sentiments and noble Passions in the Character of *Hermione*, that I shall appear in her Behalf at a Comedy, though I have no great Relish for any Entertainments where the Mirth is not seasoned with a certain Severity, which ought to recommend it to People who pretend to keep Reason and Authority over all their Actions.

> *I am, Sir,*
> *Your frequent Reader,*
> T   Altamira.'

No. 365.
[BUDGELL.]   Tuesday, April 29.

Vere magis, quia vere calor redit ossibus . . .—Virg.

THE Author of the *Menagiana* acquaints us, that discoursing one Day with several Ladies of Quality about the Effects of the Month of *May*, which infuses a kindly Warmth into the Earth, and all its Inhabitants; the Marchioness of *S*——, who was one of the Company, told him, *That though she would promise to be chaste in every Month besides, she could not engage for herself in May*. As the Beginning therefore of this Month is now very near, I design this Paper for a Caveat to the Fair Sex, and publish it before *April* is quite out, that if any of them should be caught tripping, they may not pretend they had not timely Notice.

I am induced to this, being perswaded the above-mentioned Observation is as well calculated for our Climate as for that of *France*, and that some of our *British* Ladies are of the same Constitution with the *French* Marchioness.

I shall leave it among Physicians to determine what may be the Cause of such an anniversary Inclination; whether or no it is that the Spirits after having been as it were frozen and congealed by Winter, are now turned loose, and set a rambling; or that the gay Prospects of Fields and Meadows, with the Courtship of the Birds in every Bush, naturally unbend the Mind, and soften it to Pleasure; or that, as some have imagined, a Woman is prompted by a kind of Instinct to throw her self on a Bed of Flowers, and not to let those beautiful Couches which Nature has provided lie useless. However it be, the Effects of this Month on the lower part of the Sex, who act without Disguise, is very visible. It is at this Time that we see the young Wenches in a Country Parish dancing round a *May-Pole*, which one of our learned Antiquaries supposes to be a Relique of a certain Pagan Worship that I do not think fit to mention.

It is likewise on the first Day of this Month that we see the ruddy Milk-Maid exerting herself in a most sprightly manner under a Pyramid of Silver-Tankards, and like the Virgin *Tarpeia*, oppress'd by the costly Ornaments which her Benefactors lay upon her.

I need not mention the Ceremony of the Green Gown, which is also peculiar to this gay Season.

The same periodical Love-Fit spreads through the whole Sex, as Mr. *Dryden* well observes in his Description of this merry Month.

> *For thee, sweet Month, the Groves green Liv'ries wear,*
> *If not the first, the fairest of the Year;*
> *For thee the Graces lead the dancing Hours,*
> *And Nature's ready Pencil paints the Flow'rs.*
> *The sprightly* May *commands our Youth to keep*
> *The Vigils of her Night, and breaks their Sleep;*
> *Each gentle Breast with kindly Warmth she moves,*
> *Inspires new Flames, revives extinguish'd Loves.*

Accordingly among the Works of the great Masters in Painting, who have drawn this genial Season of the Year, we often observe *Cupids* confused with *Zephirs*, flying up and down promiscuously in several Parts of the Picture. I cannot but add from my own Experience, that about this Time of the Year Love-Letters come up to me in great Numbers from all Quarters of the Nation.

I receiv'd an Epistle in particular by the last Post from a *Yorkshire* Gentleman, who makes heavy Complaints of one *Zelinda*, whom it seems he has courted unsuccessfully these three Years past. He tells me that he designs to try her this *May*, and if he does not carry his Point, he will never think of her more.

Having thus fairly admonished the female Sex, and laid before them the Dangers they are exposed to in this Critical Month, I shall in the next Place lay down some Rules and Directions for their better avoiding those Calentures which are so very frequent in this Season.

In the first Place I would advise them never to venture abroad in the Fields, but in the Company of a Parent, a Guardian, or some other sober discreet Person. I have before shewn how apt they are to trip in a flowery Meadow, and shall further observe to them, that *Proserpine* was out a Maying, when she met with that fatal Adventure to which *Milton* alludes when he mentions

> . . . *That fair Field*
> *Of* Enna, *where* Proserpine *gathering Flowers,*
> *Her self a fairer Flower, by gloomy* Dis
> *Was gathered . . .*

Since I am got into Quotations, I shall conclude this Head with *Virgil*'s Advice to young People, while they are gathering wild Strawberies and Nosegays, that they should have a care of the *Snake in the Grass.*

In the second Place I cannot but approve those Prescriptions, which our Astrological Physicians give in their Almanacks for this Month; such as are a *spare and simple Diet, with the moderate use of Phlebotomy.*

Under this Head of Abstinence I shall also advise my fair Readers to be in a particular Manner careful how they meddle with Romances, Chocolate, Novels, and the like Inflamers, which I look upon as very dangerous to be made use of during this great Carnival of Nature.

As I have often declared, that I have nothing more at Heart than the Honour of my dear Country-Women, I would beg them to consider, whenever their Resolutions begin to fail them, that there are but one and thirty Days of this soft Season, and that if they can but weather out this one Month, the rest of the Year will be easy to them. As for that Part of the fair Sex who stay in town, I would advise them to be particularly cautious how they give themselves up to their most innocent Entertainments. If they cannot forbear the Playhouse, I would recommend *Tragedy* to them, rather than *Comedy*; and should think the *Puppet-show* much safer for them than the *Opera* all the while the Sun is in *Gemini*.

The Reader will observe, that this Paper is written for the use of those Ladies who think it worth while to war against Nature in the Cause of Honour. As for that abandoned Crew, who do not think Virtue worth contending for, but give up their Reputation at the first Summons, such Warnings and Premonitions are thrown away upon them. A Prostitute is the same easy Creature in all Months of the Year, and makes no Difference between *May* and *December*.   X

No. 366.
[STEELE.]   Wednesday, April 30.

> *Pone me pigris ubi nulla campis*
> *Arbor aestiva recreatur aura,*
>
> .   .   .   .   .   .
>
> *Dulce ridentem Lalagen amabo,*
> *Dulce loquentem.*—Hor.

THERE are such wild Inconsistencies in the Thoughts of a Man in Love, that I have often reflected there can be no Reason for allowing him more Liberty than others possessed with Phrenzy; but that his Distemper has no Malevolence in it to any Mortal. That Devotion to his Mistress kindles in his Mind a general Tenderness, which exerts it self towards every Object as well as his fair one. When this Passion is represented by Writers, it is common with them to endeavour at certain Quaintnesses and Turns of Imagination, which are apparently the Work of a Mind at Ease; but the Men of true Taste can easily distinguish the Exertion of a Mind which overflows with tender Sentiments, and the Labour of one which is only describing Distress. In Performances of this Kind, the most absurd of all things is to be witty; every Sentiment must grow out of the Occasion, and be suitable to the Circumstances of the Character. Where this Rule is transgressed, the humble Servant, in all the fine things he says, is but shewing his Mistress how well he can dress, instead of saying how well he loves. Lace and Drapery is as much a Man, as Wit and Turn is Passion.

'*Mr.* SPECTATOR,

The following Verses are a Translation of a *Lapland* Love-Song, which I met with in *Scheffer's* History of that Country. I was agreeably surpriz'd to find a Spirit of Tenderness and Poetry in a Region which I never suspected for Delicacy.   In hotter Climates, though altogether uncivilized, I had not wondered if I had found some sweet wild Notes among the Natives, where they live in Groves of Oranges, and hear the Melody of Birds about them: But a *Lapland* Lyric, breathing Sentiments of Love and Poetry not unworthy old *Greece* or *Rome*; a regular Ode from a Climate pinched with Frost, and cursed with Darkness so great a Part of the Year; where 'tis amazing that the poor Natives shou'd get Food, or be tempted to propagate their Species; this, I confess, seemed a greater Miracle to me, than the famous Stories of their Drums, their Winds, and Inchantments.

I am the bolder in commending this Northern Song, because I have faithfully kept to the Sentiments, without adding or diminishing; and pretend to no greater Praise from my Translation, than they who smooth and clean the Furrs of that Country which have suffered by Carriage.   The Numbers in the Original are as loose and unequal, as those in which the *British* Ladies sport their *Pindariques*; and perhaps the fairest of them might not think it a disagreeable Present from a Lover: But I have ventured to bind it in stricter Measures, as being more proper for our Tongue, though perhaps wilder Graces may better suit the Genius of the *Laponian* Language.

It will be necessary to imagine, that the Author of this Song, not having the Liberty of visiting his Mistress at her Father's House, was in Hopes of spying her at a Distance in the Fields.

I.

Thou rising Sun, whose gladsome Ray
Invites my Fair to rural Play,
Dispel the Mist, and clear the Skies,
And bring my Orra *to my Eyes.*

II.

Oh! were I sure my Dear to view,
I 'd climb that Pine-Tree's topmost Bough
Aloft in Air that quivering plays,
And round and round for ever gaze.

III.

My Orra Moor, *where art thou laid?*
What Wood conceals my sleeping Maid?
Fast by the Roots enrag'd I 'll tear
The Trees that hide my promis'd Fair.

IV.

Oh! I cou'd ride the Clouds and Skies,
Or on the Raven's Pinions rise:
Ye Storks, ye Swans, a Moment stay,
And waft a Lover on his Way.

V.

My Bliss too long my Bride denies,
Apace the wasting Summer flies:
Nor yet the wintry Blasts I fear,
Not Storms or Night shall keep me here.

VI.

What may for Strength with Steel compare?
Oh! Love has Fetters stronger far:
By Bolts of Steel are Limbs confin'd,
But cruel Love enchains the Mind.

VII.

No longer then perplex thy Breast,
When Thoughts torment the first are best;
'Tis mad to go, 'tis Death to stay,
Away to Orra, *hast away.'*

'*Mr.* SPECTATOR, *April* the 10*th.*

I am one of those despicable Creatures called a Chamber-Maid, and have lived with a Mistress for some Time, whom I love as my Life, which has made my Duty and Pleasure inseparable. My greatest Delight has been in being imployed about her Person; and indeed she is very seldom out of Humour, for a Woman of her Quality: But here lies my Complaint, Sir, To bear with me is all the Encouragement she is pleased to bestow upon me; for she gives her cast-off Cloaths from me to others; some she is pleased to bestow in the House to those that neither wants nor wears them, and some to Hangers-on that frequents the House daily, who comes dressed out in them. This, Sir, is a very mortifying Sight to me, who am a little necessitous for Cloaths, and loves to appear what I am, and causes an Uneasiness, so that I can't serve with that Chearfulness as formerly; which my Mistress takes Notice of, and calls Envy and ill Temper at seeing others preferred before me. My Mistress has a younger Sister lives in the House with her that is some Thousands below her in Estate, who is continually heaping her Favours on her Maid; so that she can appear every *Sunday,* for the first Quarter, in a fresh Suit of Cloaths of her Mistress's giving, with all other things suitable: All this I see without envying, but not without wishing my

Mistress would a little consider what a Discouragement it is to me to have my Perquisites divided between Fawners and Jobbers, which others enjoy entire to themselves. I have spoke to my Mistress, but to little Purpose; I have desired to be discharged (for indeed I fret my self to nothing), but that she answers with Silence. I beg, Sir, your Direction what to do, for I am fully resolved to follow your Counsel; who am

> *Your Admirer,*
> *and humble Servant,*
>> Constantia Comb-brush.

I beg that you would put it in a better Dress, and let it come abroad, that my Mistress, who is an Admirer of your Speculations, may see it.'   T

No. 367.
[ADDISON.]   Thursday, May 1.

. . . *Periturae parcere chartae.*—Juv.

I HAVE often pleas'd my self with considering the two kinds of Benefits which accrue to the Publick from these my Speculations, and which, were I to speak after the Manner of Logicians, I would distinguish into the *Material* and the *Formal*. By the latter I understand those Advantages which my Readers receive, as their Minds are either improved or delighted by these my daily Labours; but having already several times descanted on my Endeavours in this Light, I shall at present wholly confine my self to the Consideration of the former. By the Word *Material* I mean those Benefits which arise to the Publick from these my Speculations, as they consume a considerable Quantity of our Paper Manufacture, employ our Artisans in Printing, and find Business for great Numbers of indigent Persons.

Our Paper Manufacture takes into it several mean Materials which could be put to no other use, and affords Work for several Hands in the collecting of them, which are incapable of any other Employment. Those poor Retailers, whom we see so busie in every Street, deliver in their respective Gleanings to the Merchant. The Merchant carries them in Loads to the Paper-Mill, where they pass through a fresh Set of Hands, and give Life to another Trade. Those who have Mills on their Estates by this Means considerably raise their Rents, and the whole Nation is in a great Measure supplied with a Manufacture, for which formerly she was obliged to her Neighbours.

The Materials are no sooner wrought into Paper, but they are distributed among the Presses, where they again set innumerable Artists at work, and furnish Business to another Mystery. From hence, accordingly as they are stained with News or Politicks, they fly thro' the Town in *Post-Men*, *Post-boys*, *Daily-Courants*, *Reviews*, *Medleys*, and *Examiners*. Men, Women, and Children contend who shall be the first Bearers of them, and get their daily Sustenance by spreading them. In short, when I trace in my Mind a Bundle of Rags to a Quire of *Spectators*, I find so many Hands employ'd in every Step they take through their whole Progress, that while I am writing a *Spectator*, I fancy my self providing Bread for a Multitude.

If I do not take care to obviate some of my witty Readers, they will be apt to tell me, that my Paper, after it is thus printed and published, is still beneficial to the Publick on several Occasions. I must confess I have lighted my Pipe with my own Works for this Twelve-month past: My Landlady often sends up her little Daughter to desire some of my old *Spectators*, and has frequently told me, that the Paper they are printed on is the best in the World to wrap Spice in. They likewise make a good Foundation for a Mutton-pye, as I have more than once experienced, and were very much sought for last *Christmas* by the whole Neighbourhood.

It is pleasant enough to consider the Changes that a Linnen Fragment undergoes by passing through the several Hands above-mentioned. The finest Pieces of Holland, when worn to Tatters, assume a new Whiteness more beautiful than their first, and often return in the Shape of Letters to their Native Country. A Lady's Shift may be metamorphosed into Billets doux, and come into her Possession a second time. A Beau may peruse his Cravat after it is worn out, with greater Pleasure and Advantage than ever he did in a Glass. In a Word, a Piece of Cloth, after having officiated for some Years as a Towel or a Napkin, may by this Means be raised from a Dunghill, and become the most valuable Piece of Furniture in a Prince's Cabinet.

The politest Nations of *Europe* have endeavoured to vie with one another for the Reputation of the finest Printing: Absolute Governments, as well as Republicks, have encouraged an Art which seems to be the noblest and most beneficial that was ever invented among the Sons of Men. The present King of *France*, in his Pursuits after Glory, has particularly distinguished himself by the promoting of this useful Art, insomuch that several Books have been printed in the *Louvre* at his own Expence, upon which he sets so great a Value, that he considers them as the noblest Presents he can make to foreign

Princes and Ambassadors. If we look into the Commonwealths of *Holland* and *Venice*, we shall find that in this Particular they have made themselves the Envy of the greatest Monarchies. *Elzever* and *Aldus* are more frequently mentioned than any Pensioner of the one or Doge of the other.

The several Presses which are now in *England*, and the great Encouragement which has been given to Learning for some Years last past, has made our own Nation as glorious upon this Account, as for its late Triumphs and Conquests. The new Edition which is given us of *Caesar's* Commentaries, has already been taken Notice of in foreign *Gazettes*, and is a Work that does Honour to the *English* Press. It is no wonder that an Edition should be very correct, which has passed through the Hands of one of the most accurate, learned, and judicious Writers this Age has produced. The Beauty of the Paper, of the Character, and of the several Cuts with which this noble Work is Illustrated, makes it the finest Book that I have ever seen; and is a true Instance of the *English* Genius, which, though it does not come the first into any Art, generally carries it to greater Heights than any other Country in the World. I am particularly glad that this Author comes from a *British* Printing-house in so great a Magnificence, as he is the first who has given us any tolerable Account of our Country.

My illiterate Readers, if any such there are, will be surprized to hear me talk of Learning as the Glory of a Nation, and of Printing as an Art that gains a Reputation to a People among whom it flourishes. When Men's Thoughts are taken up with Avarice and Ambition, they cannot look upon any thing as great or valuable, which does not bring with it an extraordinary Power or Interest to the Person who is concerned in it. But as I shall never sink this Paper so far as to engage with *Goths* and *Vandals*, I shall only regard such kind of Reasoners with that Pity which is due to so deplorable a Degree of Stupidity and Ignorance.   L

No. 368.
[STEELE.]   Friday, May 2.

> . . . *Nos decebat* . . .
> *Lugere, ubi esset aliquis in lucem editus,*
> *Humanae vitae varia reputantes mala;*
> *At, qui labores morte finisset graves,*
> *Omnes amicos laude & laetitia exequi.*
> —Eurip. apud Tull.

As the *Spectator* is in a kind a Paper of News from the Natural World, as others are from the busie and politick Part of Man-

kind, I shall translate the following Letter written to an
eminent *French* Gentleman in this Town from *Paris,* which
gives us the Exit of an Heroine who is a Pattern of Patience
and Generosity.

'*Sir,*   *Paris, April* 18, 1712.

It is so many Years since you left your native Country, that
I am to tell you the Characters of your nearest Relations as
much as if you were an utter Stranger to them.   The Occasion
of this is to give you an Account of the Death of Madam *de
Villacerfe,* whose Departure out of this Life I know not whether
a Man of your Philosophy will call unfortunate or not, since it
was attended with some Circumstances as much to be desired
as to be lamented.   She was her whole Life happy in an uninterrupted Health, and was always honoured for an Evenness
of Temper and Greatness of Mind.   On the 10th Instant that
Lady was taken with an Indisposition which confined her to
her Chamber, but was such as was too slight to make her take
a sick Bed, and yet too grievous to admit of any Satisfaction
in being out of it.   It is notoriously known, that some Years
ago Monsieur *Festeau,* one of the most considerable Surgeons
in *Paris,* was desperately in Love with this Lady: Her Quality
placed her above any Application to her on the Account of
his Passion; but as a Woman always has some Regard to the
Person whom she believes to be her real Admirer, she now
took it in her Head (upon Advice of her Physicians to lose
some of her Blood) to send for Monsieur *Festeau* on that
Occasion.   I happened to be there at that Time, and my near
Relation gave me the Privilege to be present.   As soon as her
Arm was stripped bare, and he began to press it in order to
raise the Vein, his Colour changed, and I observed him seized
with a sudden Tremor, which made me take the Liberty to
speak of it to my Cousin with some Apprehension: She smiled,
and said she knew Mr. *Festeau* had no Inclination to do her
Injury.   He seemed to recover himself, and smiling also, proceeded in his Work.   Immediately after the Operation he
cried out, that he was the most unfortunate of all Men, for that
he had opened an Artery instead of a Vein.   It is as impossible
to express the Artist's Distraction as the Patient's Composure.
I will not dwell on little Circumstances, but go on to inform
you, that within three Days Time it was thought necessary to
take off her Arm.   She was so far from using *Festeau* as it
would be natural to one of a lower Spirit to treat him, that she
would not let him be absent from any Consultation about her
present Condition, and on every Occasion asked whether he
was satisfied in the Measures that were taken about her.

Before this last Operation she ordered her Will to be drawn, and after having been about a Quarter of an Hour alone, she bid the Surgeons, of whom poor *Festeau* was one, go on in their Work. I know not how to give you the Terms of Art, but there appeared such Symptoms after the Amputation of her Arm, that it was visible she could not live four and twenty Hours. Her Behaviour was so magnanimous throughout this whole Affair, that I was particularly curious in taking Notice of what passed as her Fate approached nearer and nearer, and took Notes of what she said to all about her, particularly Word for Word what she spoke to Mr. *Festeau*, which was as follows.

"Sir, you give me inexpressible Sorrow for the Anguish with which I see you overwhelmed. I am removed to all Intents and Purposes from the Interests of human Life, therefore I am to begin to think like one wholly unconcerned in it. I do not consider you as one by whose Error I have lost my Life; no, you are my Benefactor, as you have hastened my Entrance into a happy Immortality. This is my Sense of this Accident; but the World in which you live may have Thoughts of it to your Disadvantage: I have therefore taken Care to provide for you in my Will, and have placed you above what you have to fear from their ill Nature."

While this excellent Woman spoke these Words, *Festeau* looked as if he received a Condemnation to die instead of a Pension for his Life. Madam *de Villacerfe* lived till Eight of the Clock the next Night; and tho' she must have laboured under the most exquisite Torments, she possessed her Mind with so wonderful a Patience, that one may rather say she ceased to breathe than she died at that Hour. You who had not the Happiness to be personally known to this Lady, have nothing but to rejoyce in the Honour you had of being related to so great Merit; but we who have lost her Conversation, cannot so easily resign our own Happiness by Reflection upon hers.

> *I am, Sir, your affectionate Kinsman,*
>
> *And most obedient humble Servant,*
>
> Paul Regnaud.'

There hardly can be a greater Instance of an Heroick Mind, than the unprejudiced manner in which this Lady weighed this Misfortune. The Regard of Life it self could not make her overlook the Contrition of the unhappy Man, whose more than ordinary Concern for her was all his Guilt. It would certainly be of singular Use to humane Society to have an exact Account of this Lady's ordinary Conduct, which was crowned by so uncommon Magnanimity. Such Greatness was not to be acquired in her last Article, nor is it to be doubted but it was a constant Practice of all that is praiseworthy, which made her capable of beholding Death, not as the Dissolution, but Consummation of her Life.   T

No. 369.
[ADDISON.]   Saturday, May 3.

> *Segnius irritant animos demissa per aurem*
> *Quam quae sunt oculis subjecta fidelibus . . .*—Hor.

Milton, after having represented in Vision the History of Mankind to the first great Period of Nature, dispatches the remaining Part of it in Narration. He has devised a very handsome Reason for the Angel's proceeding with *Adam* after this manner; though doubtless the true Reason was the Difficulty which the Poet would have found to have shadowed out so mix'd and complicated a Story in visible Objects. I could wish, however, that the Author had done it, whatever Pains it might have cost him. To give my Opinion freely, I think that the exhibiting part of the History of Mankind in Vision, and part in Narrative, is as if an History-Painter should put in Colours one Half of his Subject, and write down the remaining part of it. If *Milton*'s Poem flags any where, it is in this Narration, where in some Places the Author has been so attentive to his Divinity, that he has neglected his Poetry. The Narration, however, rises very happily on several Occasions, where the Subject is capable of Poetical Ornaments, as particularly in the Confusion which he describes among the Builders of Babel, and in his short Sketch of the Plagues of *Aegypt.* The Storm of Hail and Fire, with the Darkness that overspread the Land for three Days, are described with great Strength. The beautiful Passage which follows, is raised upon noble Hints in Scripture.

> *. . . Thus with ten wounds*
> *The River-Dragon tamed at length submits*
> *To let his Sojourners depart, and oft*
> *Humbles his stubborn Heart, but still as Ice*
> *More harden'd after thaw, till in his rage*
> *Pursuing whom he late dismiss'd, the Sea*
> *Swallows him with his host, but them lets pass*
> *As on dry land between two Chrystal walls,*
> *Aw'd by the rod of* Moses, *so to stand*
> *Divided . . .*

The *River-Dragon* is an Allusion to the Crocodile, which inhabits the *Nile*, from whence *Aegypt* derives her Plenty. This Allusion is taken from that sublime Passage in *Ezekiel*; *Thus saith the Lord God, behold I am against thee* Pharaoh *King of* Egypt, *the great Dragon that lieth in the midst of his Rivers, which hath said, My River is mine own, and I have made it for my self.* *Milton* has given us another very noble and poetical Image in the same Description, which is copied almost Word for Word out of the History of *Moses*.

> *All night he will pursue, but his approach*
> *Darkness defends between till morning watch;*
> Then thro' the fiery pillar and the cloud
> God looking forth will trouble all his host,
> And craze their Chariot Wheels: *when by command*
> Moses *once more his potent rod extends*
> *Over the Sea; the Sea his Rod obeys;*
> *On their Embattelled ranks the waves return*
> *And overwhelm their War:* . . .

As the principal Design of this *Episode* was to give *Adam* an Idea of the Holy Person, who was to reinstate Humane Nature in that Happiness and Perfection from which it had fallen, the Poet confines himself to the Line of *Abraham*, from whence the *Messiah* was to descend. The Angel is described as seeing the Patriarch actually travelling towards the *Land of Promise*, which gives a particular Liveliness to this Part of the Narration.

> *I see him, but thou canst not, with what Faith*
> *He leaves his Gods, his Friends, his native Soil*
> Ur *of* Chaldaea, *passing now the Ford*
> *Of* Haran, *after him a cumbrous train*
> *Of Herds and Flocks and numerous servitude;*
> *Not wand'ring poor, but trusting all his wealth*
> *With God who call'd him, in a Land unknown.*
> Canaan *he now attains; I see his Tents*
> *Pitcht about* Sechem, *and the neighbouring Plain*
> *Of* Moreh: *there by promise he receives*
> *Gift to his progeny of all that Land,*
> *From* Hamath *Northward to the desert South,*
> *(Things by their names I call, though yet unnamed).*

As *Virgil*'s Vision in the sixth *Aeneid* probably gave *Milton* the Hint of this whole *Episode*, the last Line is a Translation of that Verse, where *Anchises* mentions the Names of Places, which they were to bear hereafter.

> *Haec tum nomina erunt, nunc sunt sine nomine terrae.*

The Poet has very finely represented the Joy and Gladness of Heart which rises in *Adam* upon his Discovery of the *Messiah*.

As he sees his Day at a Distance through Types and Shadows, he rejoices in it; but when he finds the Redemption of Man compleated, and *Paradise* again renewed, he breaks forth in Rapture and Transport,

> *O goodness infinite, Goodness immense!*
> *That all this good of evil shall produce, &c.*

I have hinted in my Sixth Paper on *Milton*, that an Heroick Poem, according to the Opinion of the best Criticks, ought to end happily, and leave the Mind of the Reader, after having conducted it through many Doubts and Fears, Sorrows and Disquietudes, in a state of Tranquility and Satisfaction. *Milton's* Fable, which had so many other Qualifications to recommend it, was deficient in this Particular. It is here therefore, that the Poet has shewn a most exquisite Judgment, as well as the finest Invention, by finding out a Method to supply the natural Defect in his Subject. Accordingly he leaves the Adversary of Mankind, in the last View which he gives us of him, under the lowest State of Mortification and Disappointment. We see him chewing Ashes, grovelling in the Dust, and loaden with supernumerary Pains and Torments. On the contrary, our two first Parents are comforted by Dreams and Visions, cheared with promises of Salvation, and, in a manner, raised to a greater Happiness than that which they had forfeited: In short, *Satan* is represented miserable in the Height of his Triumphs, and *Adam* Triumphant in the Height of Misery.

Milton's Poem ends very nobly. The last Speeches of *Adam* and the Arch-Angel are full of Moral and Instructive Sentiments. The Sleep that fell upon *Eve*, and the Effects it had in quieting the Disorders of her Mind, produces the same kind of Consolation in the Reader, who cannot peruse the last beautiful Speech which is ascribed to the Mother of Mankind, without a secret Pleasure and Satisfaction.

> *Whence thou return'st, and whither went'st, I know;*
> *For God is also in Sleep, and Dreams advise,*
> *Which he hath sent propitious, some great good*
> *Presaging, since with Sorrow and Heart's distress*
> *Wearied I fell asleep: but now lead on;*
> *In me is no delay: with thee to go*
> *Is to stay here; without thee here to stay*
> *Is to go hence unwilling; thou to me*
> *Art all things under Heav'n, all Places thou,*
> *Who for my wilful Crime art banish'd hence.*
> *This farther Consolation yet secure*
> *I carry hence; though all by me is lost,*
> *Such Favour, I unworthy, am vouchsaf'd,*
> *By me the promised Seed shall all restore.*

The following Lines, which conclude the Poem, rise in a most glorious Blaze of Poetical Images and Expressions.

Heliodorus in his *Aethiopicks* acquaints us, that the Motion of the Gods differs from that of Mortals, as the former do not stir their Feet, nor proceed Step by Step, but slide o'er the Surface of the Earth by an uniform Swimming of the whole Body. The Reader may observe with how Poetical a Description *Milton* has attributed the same kind of Motion to the Angels who were to take possession of *Paradise*.

> *So spake our Mother* Eve, *and* Adam *heard*
> *Well pleas'd, but answer'd not; for now too nigh*
> *Th' Arch-Angel stood, and from the other Hill*
> *To their fix'd station, all in bright array*
> *The Cherubim descended; on the Ground*
> *Gliding meteorous, as ev'ning mist*
> *Ris'n from a River, o'er the marish glides,*
> *And gathers ground fast at the lab'rer's heel*
> *Homeward returning. High in Front advanc'd,*
> *The brandish'd Sword of God before them blaz'd*
> *Fierce as a Comet . . .*

The Author helped his Invention in the following Passage, by reflecting on the Behaviour of the Angel, who, in Holy Writ, has the Conduct of *Lot* and his Family. The Circumstances drawn from that Relation are very gracefully made use of on this Occasion.

> *In either hand the hastning Angel caught*
> *Our ling'ring Parents, and to the Eastern gate*
> *Led them direct; and down the Cliff as fast*
> *To the subjected plain; then disappear'd.*
> *They looking back, &c. . . .*

The Scene which our first Parents are surprized with upon their looking back on *Paradise*, wonderfully strikes the Reader's Imagination, as nothing can be more natural than the Tears they shed on that Occasion.

> *They looking back, all th' Eastern side beheld*
> *Of* Paradise, *so late their happy Seat,*
> *Wav'd over by that flaming brand, the gate*
> *With dreadful faces throng'd and fiery Arms:*
> *Some natural tears they dropp'd, but wiped them soon:*
> *The world was all before them, where to chuse*
> *Their place of rest, and Providence their Guide.*

If I might presume to offer at the smallest Alteration in this Divine Work, I should think the Poem would end better with the Passage here quoted, than with the two Verses which follow.

> *They hand in hand with wandering steps and slow,*
> *Through* Eden *took their solitary way.*

These two Verses, though they have their Beauty, fall very much below the foregoing Passage, and renew in the Mind of the Reader that Anguish which was pretty well laid by that Consideration.

> *The World was all before them, where to chuse*
> *Their place of rest, and Providence their Guide.*

The Number of Books in *Paradise Lost* is equal to those of the *Aeneid.* Our Author in his First Edition had divided his Poem into ten Books, but afterwards broke the Seventh and the Eleventh each of them into two different Books, by the Help of some small Additions. This second Division was made with great Judgment, as any one may see who will be at the pains of examining it. It was not done for the sake of such a Chimerical Beauty as that of resembling *Virgil* in this Particular, but for the more just and regular Disposition of this great Work.

Those who have read *Bossu,* and many of the Criticks who have written since his Time, will not pardon me if I do not find out the particular Moral which is inculcated in *Paradise Lost.* Though I can by no means think with the last-mentioned *French* Author, that an Epic Writer first of all pitches upon a certain Moral, as the Ground-Work and Foundation of his Poem, and afterwards finds out a Story to it: I am, however, of Opinion, that no just Heroic Poem ever was, or can be made from whence one great Moral may not be deduced. That which reigns in *Milton* is the most universal and most useful that can be imagined: it is in short this, that *Obedience to the Will of God makes Men happy, and that Disobedience makes them miserable.* This is visibly the Moral of the principal Fable which turns upon *Adam* and *Eve,* who continued in *Paradise* while they kept the Command that was given them, and were driven out of it as soon as they had transgressed. This is likewise the Moral of the principal Episode, which shews us how an innumerable Multitude of Angels fell from their State of Bliss, and were cast into Hell upon their Disobedience. Besides this great Moral, which may be looked upon as the Soul of the Fable, there are an Infinity of Under Morals which are to be drawn from the several Parts of the Poem, and which makes this Work more useful and instructive than any other Poem in any Language.

Those who have Criticised on the *Odissey,* the *Iliad,* and *Aeneid,* have taken a great deal of Pains to fix the Number of Months or Days contained in the Action of each of those

Poems. If any one thinks it worth his while to examine this Particular in *Milton*, he will find that from *Adam's* first Appearance in the Fourth Book, to his Expulsion from *Paradise* in the Twelfth, the Author reckons ten Days. As for that Part of the Action which is described in the three first Books, as it does not pass within the Regions of Nature, I have before observed that it is not subject to any Calculations of Time.

I have now finished my Observations on a Work which does an Honour to the *English* Nation. I have taken a general View of it under those four Heads, the Fable, the Characters, the Sentiments, and the Language, and made each of them the Subject of a particular Paper. I have in the next place spoken of the Censures which our Author may incur under each of these Heads, which I have confined to two Papers, though I might have enlarged the Number, if I had been disposed to dwell on so ungrateful a Subject. I believe, however, that the severest Reader will not find any little Fault in Heroic Poetry, which this Author has fallen into, that does not come under one of those Heads among which I have distributed his several Blemishes. After having thus treated at large of *Paradise Lost*, I could not think it sufficient to have celebrated this Poem in the whole, without descending to Particulars. I have therefore bestowed a Paper upon each Book, and endeavoured not only to prove that the Poem is beautiful in general, but to point out its particular Beauties, and to determine wherein they consist. I have endeavoured to shew how some Passages are beautifull by being Sublime, others by being Soft, others by being Natural; which of them are recommended by the Passion, which by the Moral, which by the Sentiment, and which by the Expression. I have likewise endeavoured to shew how the Genius of the Poet shines by a happy Invention, a distant Allusion, or a judicious Imitation; how he has copied or improved *Homer* or *Virgil*, and raised his own Imaginations by the Use which he has made of several Poetical Passages in Scripture. I might have inserted also several Passages of *Tasso*, which our Author has imitated; but as I do not look upon *Tasso* to be a sufficient Voucher, I would not perplex my Reader with such Quotations, as might do more Honour to the *Italian* than the *English* Poet. In short, I have endeavoured to particularize those innumerable Kinds of Beauty, which it would be tedious to recapitulate, but which are essential to Poetry, and which may be met with in the Works of this great Author. Had I thought, at my first engaging in this Design, that it would have led me to so great a Length, I believe I should never have entred upon it; but the kind Reception which it has met with among those whose

Judgments I have a Value for, as well as the uncommon Demand which my Bookseller tells me has been made for these particular Discourses, give me no Reason to repent of the pains I have been at in composing them.   L

No. 370.
[STEELE.]   Monday, May 5.

Totus mundus agit histrionem.

MANY of my fair Readers, as well as very gay and well-received Persons of the other Sex, are extreamly perplexed at the *Latin* Sentences at the Head of my Speculations; I do not know whether I ought not to indulge them with Translations of each of them: However, I have to Day taken down from the Top of the Stage in *Drury-Lane* a Bit of *Latin* which often stands in their View, and signifies that *the whole World acts the Player.* It is certain that if we look all round us and behold the different Employments of Mankind, you hardly see one who is not, as the Player is, in an assumed Character. The Lawyer, who is vehement and loud in a Cause wherein he knows he has not the Truth of the Question on his Side, is a Player as to the personated Part, but incomparably meaner than he as to the Prostitution of himself for Hire; because the Pleader's Falshood introduces Injustice, the Player feigns for no other End but to divert or instruct you. The Divine, whose Passions transport him to say any thing with any View but promoting the Interests of true Piety and Religion, is a Player with a still greater Imputation of Guilt in Proportion to his depreciating a Character more sacred. Consider all the different Pursuits and Employments of Men, and you will find half their Actions tend to nothing else but Disguise and Imposture; and all that is done which proceeds not from a Man's very self is the Action of a Player. For this Reason it is that I make so frequent Mention of the Stage: It is, with me, a Matter of the highest Consideration what Parts are well or ill performed, what Passions or Sentiments are indulged or cultivated, and consequently what Manners and Customs are transfused from the Stage to the World, which reciprocally imitate each other. As the Writers of Epick Poems introduce shadowy Persons and represent Vices and Virtues under the Characters of Men and Women; so I, who am a SPECTATOR in the World, may perhaps sometimes make use of the Names of the Actors on the Stage, to represent or admonish those who transact Affairs in the World. When I am commending *Wilks* for representing the Tenderness of a Husband and a Father in *Mackbeth*, the

Contrition of a reformed Prodigal in *Harry* the Fourth, the winning Emptiness of a young Man of Good-nature and Wealth in *the Trip to the Jubilee*, the Officiousness of an artful Servant in *the Fox*: When thus I celebrate *Wilks*, I talk to all the World who are engaged in any of those Circumstances. If I were to speak of Merit neglected, misapplied, or misunderstood, might not I say *Eastcourt* has a great Capacity? but it is not the Interest of others who bear a Figure on the Stage that his Talents were understood; it is their Business to impose upon him what cannot become him, or keep out of his Hands any thing in which he would shine. Were one to raise a Suspicion of himself in a Man who passes upon the World for a fine Thing, in order to alarm him, one might say, if Lord *Foppington* were not on the Stage (*Cibber* acts the false Pretentions to a genteel Behaviour so very justly), he would have in the generality of Mankind more that would admire than deride him. When we come to characters directly comical, it is not to be imagined what Effect a well regulated Stage would have upon Men's Manners. The Craft of an Usurer, the Absurdity of a rich Fool, the awkard Roughness of a Fellow of half Courage, the ungraceful Mirth of a Creature of half Wit, might be for ever put out of Countenance by proper parts for *Dogget*. *Johnson* by acting *Corbacchio* the other Night, must have given all who saw him a through Detestation of aged Avarice. The petulancy of a peevish old Fellow, who loves and hates he knows not why, is very excellently performed by the Ingenious Mr. *William Penkethman* in the *Fop's Fortune*; where, in the Character of *Don Cholerick Snap Shorto de Testy*, he answers no Questions but to those whom he likes, and wants no Account of any thing from those he approves. Mr. *Penkethman* is also Master of as many Faces in the Dumb-Scene, as can be expected from a Man in the Circumstances of being ready to perish out of Fear and Hunger: He wonders throughout the whole Scene very masterly, without neglecting his Victuals. If it be, as I have heard it sometimes mentioned, a great Qualification for the World to follow Business and Pleasure too, what is it in the ingenious Mr. *Penkethman* to represent a Sense of Pleasure and Pain at the same time; as you may see him do this Evening?

As it is certain that a Stage ought to be wholly suppressed, or judiciously encouraged, while there is one in the Nation, Men turned for regular Pleasure cannot employ their Thoughts more usefully for the Diversion of Mankind, than by convincing them that it is in themselves to raise this Entertainment to the greatest Height. It would be a great Improvement, as well as Embellishment to the Theatre, if Dancing were more regarded, and taught to all the Actors. One who has the Advantage of such an agreeable girlish Person as Mrs. *Bicknell*, joyned with her Capacity of Imitation, could in proper Gesture and Motion represent all the decent Characters of Female Life. An amiable Modesty in one Aspect of a Dancer, an assumed Confidence in another, a sudden Joy in another, a falling off with an Impatience of being beheld, a Return towards the Audience with an unsteady Resolution to approach them, and a well-acted Solicitude to please, would revive in the Company all the fine Touches of Mind raised in observing all the Objects of Affection or Passion they had before beheld. Such elegant Entertainments as these, would polish the Town into Judgment in their Gratifications; and Delicacy in Pleasure is the first Step People of Condition take in Reformation from Vice. Mrs. *Bicknell* has the only Capacity for this sort of Dancing of any on the Stage; and I dare say all who see her Performance to Morrow Night, when sure the Romp will do her best for her own Benefit, will be of my Mind.   T

No. 371.
[ADDISON.]   Tuesday, May 6.

> *Jamne igitur laudas quod de sapientibus alter*
> *Ridebat?* . . .—Juv.

I SHALL communicate to my Reader the following Letter for the Entertainment of this Day.

'*Sir*,

You know very well that our Nation is more famous for that sort of Men who are called *Whims* and *Humourists*, than any other Country in the World, for which Reason it is observed that our *English* Comedy excells that of all other Nations in the Novelty and Variety of its Characters.

Among those innumerable Sets of *Whims* which our Country produces, there are none whom I have regarded with more Curiosity than those who have invented any particular Kind of Diversion, for the Entertainment of themselves or their Friends. My Letter shall single out those who take Delight in sorting a Company that has something of Burlesque and Ridicule in its Appearance. I shall make my self understood by the following Example. One of the Wits of the last Age, who was a Man of a good Estate, thought he never laid out his Money better than in a Jest. As he was one Year at the *Bath*, observing that in the great Confluence of fine People, there were several among them with long Chins, a Part of the Visage by which he himself was very much distinguished, he invited to Dinner half a Score of these remarkable Persons who had their Mouths in the Middle of their Faces. They had no sooner placed themselves about the Table, but they began to stare upon one another, not being able to imagine what had brought them together. Our *English* Proverb says,

> *'Tis merry in the Hall,*
> *When Beards wag all.*

It proved so in an Assembly I am now speaking of, who seeing so many Peaks of Faces agitated with Eating, Drinking, and Discourse, and observing all the Chins that were present meeting together very often over the Center of the Table, every one grew sensible of the Jest, and came into it with so much good Humour, that they lived in strict Friendship and Alliance from that Day forward.

The same Gentleman some time after packed together a Set of Oglers, as he called them, consisting of such as had an unlucky Cast in their Eyes. His Diversion on this Occasion was to see the cross Bows, mistaken Signs, and wrong Connivances that passed amidst so many broken and refracted Rays of Sight.

The third Feast which this merry Gentleman exhibited was to the Stammerers, whom he got together in a sufficient Body to fill his Table. He had order'd one of his Servants, who was placed behind a skreen, to write down their Table-Talk, which was very easie to be done without the Help of Short-hand. It appears by the Notes which were taken, that though their Conversation never fell, there were not above twenty Words spoken during the first Course; that upon serving up the second, one of the Company was a Quarter of an Hour in telling them, that the Ducklins and Sparrow-grass were very good; and that another took up the same Time in declaring himself of the same Opinion. This Jest did not, however, go off so well as either of the former; for one of the Guests being a brave Man, and fuller of Resentment than he knew how to express, went out of the Room, and sent the facetious Inviter a Challenge in Writing, which though it was afterwards dropp'd by the Interposition of Friends, put a Stop to these ludicrous Entertainments.

Now, Sir, I dare say you will agree with me, that as there is no Moral in these Jests, they ought to be discouraged, and looked upon rather as Pieces of Unluckiness than Wit. However, as it is natural for one Man to refine upon the Thought of another, and impossible for any single Person, how great soever his Parts may be, to invent an Art, and bring it to its utmost Perfection, I shall here give you an Account of an

honest Gentleman of my Acquaintance, who upon hearing the
Character of the Wit abovementioned, has himself assumed it,
and endeavoured to convert it to the Benefit of Mankind.
He invited half a Dozen of his Friends one Day to Dinner, who
were each of them famous for inserting several redundant
Phrases in their Discourse, as, *d' y' hear me, d' y' see, that is, and
so Sir*. Each of the Guests making frequent use of his particular Elegance, appeared so ridiculous to his Neighbour, that
he could not but reflect upon himself as appearing equally
ridiculous to the rest of the Company; By this Means, before
they had sat long together, every one talking with the greatest
Circumspection, and carefully avoiding his favourite Expletive,
the Conversation was cleared of its Redundancies, and had a
greater Quantity of Sense, though less of Sound in it.

The same well-meaning Gentleman took Occasion, at another
Time, to bring together such of his Friends as were addicted
to a foolish habitual Custom of Swearing. In order to shew
them the Absurdity of the Practice, he had Recourse to the
Invention above-mentioned, having placed an *Amanuensis* in
a private Part of the Room. After the second Bottle, when
Men open their Minds without Reserve, my honest Friend
began to take Notice of the many sonorous but unnecessary
Words that had passed in his House since their sitting down at
Table, and how much good Conversation they had lost by
giving way to such superfluous Phrases. What a Tax, says he,
would they have raised for the Poor, had we put the Laws in
Execution upon one another? Every one of them took this
gentle Reproof in good Part: Upon which he told them, that
knowing their Conversation would have no Secrets in it, he had
ordered it to be taken down in Writing, and for the Humour
sake would read it to them if they pleased. There were ten
Sheets of it, which might have been reduced to two, had
there not been those abominable Interpolations I have beforementioned. Upon the reading of it in cold Blood, it looked
rather like a Conference of Fiends than of Men. In short,
every one trembled at himself upon hearing calmly what he
had pronounced amidst the Heat and Inadvertency of Discourse.

I shall only mention another Occasion wherein he made use
of the same Invention to cure a different kind of Men, who are
the Pests of all polite Conversation, and murder Time as much
as either of the two former, though they do it more innocently;
I mean that dull Generation of Story-tellers. My Friend got
together about half a Dozen of his Acquaintance, who were
infected with this strange Malady. The first Day one of them
sitting down, enter'd upon the Siege of *Namur*, which lasted

till four a Clock, their Time of parting. The second Day a *North-Briton* took Possession of the Discourse, which it was impossible to get out of his Hands so long as the Company staid together. The third Day was engrossed after the same Manner by a Story of the same Length. They at last began to reflect upon this barbarous way of treating one another, and by this means awaken'd out of that Lethargy with which each of them had been seized for several Years.

As you have somewhere declared, that extraordinary and uncommon Characters of Mankind are the Game which you delight in, and as I look upon you to be the greatest Sportsman, or, if you please, the *Nimrod* among this Species of Writers, I thought this Discovery would not be unacceptable to you.

> *I am,*
>
> *Sir, &c.'*

No. 372.

[STEELE.] Wednesday, May 7.

> . . . *Pudet haec opprobria nobis*
> *Et dici potuisse & non potuisse referri.*—Ovid.

'Mr. Spectator, *May 6,* 1712.

I AM Sexton of the Parish of *Covent-Garden,* and complained to you some Time ago, that as I was tolling in to Prayers at Eleven in the Morning, Crowds of People of Quality hastened to assemble at a Puppet-Show on the other Side of the Garden. I had at the same Time a very great Disesteem for Mr. *Powell* and his little thoughtless Common-wealth, as if they had enticed the Gentry into those Wandrings: But let that be as it will, I now am convinced of the honest Intentions of the said Mr. *Powell* and Company; and send this to acquaint you, that he has given all the Profits which shall arise to Morrow Night by his Play to the use of the poor Charity Children of this Parish. I have been inform'd, Sir, that in *Holland* all Persons who set up any Show, or act any Stage-Play, be the Actors either of Wood and Wire, or Flesh and Blood, are obliged to pay out of their Gain such a Proportion to the honest and industrious Poor in the Neighbourhood: By this Means they make Diversion and Pleasure pay a Tax to Labour and Industry. I have been told also, that all the Time of *Lent,* in Roman-Catholick Countries, the Persons of Condition administred to the Necessities of the Poor, and attended the Beds of Lazars and diseased Persons. Our Protestant Ladies and Gentlemen are much to seek for proper ways of passing Time, that they are obliged to *Punchinello* for knowing what to do

with themselves.   Since the Case is so, I desire only you would
entreat our People of Quality, who are not to be interrupted
in their Pleasure to think of the Practice of any Moral Duty,
that they would at least fine for their Sins, and give something
to these poor Children; a little out of their Luxury and Super-
fluity, would attone, in some Measure, for the wanton use of
the rest of their Fortunes.   It would not, methinks, be amiss,
if the Ladies who haunt the Cloysters and Passages of the
Play-house, were upon every Offence obliged to pay to this
excellent Institution of Schools of Charity: This Method would
make Offenders themselves do Service to the Publick.   But in
the mean Time I desire you would publish this voluntary
Reparation which Mr. _Powell_ does our Parish, for the Noise he
has made in it by the constant rattling of Coaches, Drums,
Trumpets, Triumphs, and Battles.   The Destruction of _Troy_,
adorned with Highland Dances, are to make up the Entertainment of all who are so well disposed as not to forbear a light
Entertainment, for no other Reason but that it is to do a
good Action.

> _I am,_
>> _Sir,_
>>> _Your most humble Servant,_
>>>> Ralph Bellfry.

I am credibly informed, that all the Insinuations which a
certain Writer made against Mr. _Powell_ at the _Bath_, are false
and groundless.'

'_Mr._ SPECTATOR,

My Employment, which is that of a Broker, leading me often
into Taverns about the _Exchange_, has given me Occasion to
observe a certain Enormity, which I shall here submit to your
Animadversion.   In three or four of these Taverns, I have, at
different Times, taken Notice of a precise Set of People with
grave Countenances, short Wiggs, black Cloaths, or dark
Camlet trimm'd with Black, and mourning Gloves and Hat-
bands, who meet on certain Days at each Tavern successively,
and keep a sort of moving Club.   Having often met with their
Faces, and observ'd a certain slinking way in their dropping
in one after another, I had the Curiosity to enquire into their
Characters, being the rather mov'd to it by their agreeing in
the Singularity of their Dress; and I find upon due Examination they are a Knot of Parish-Clarks, who have taken a Fancy
to one another, and perhaps settle the Bills of Mortality over
their Half-Pints.   I have so great a Value and Veneration for
any who have but even an assenting _Amen_ in the Service of

Religion, that I am afraid lest these Persons should incur some Scandal by this Practice; and wou'd therefore have them, without Raillery advis'd to send the Florence and Pullets home to their own Houses, and not pretend to live as well as the Overseers of the Poor.

> *I am,*
>> *Sir,*
>>> *Your humble Servant,*
>>>> Humphry Transfer.'

'*Mr.* SPECTATOR,   *May* 6.

I was last *Wednesday* Night at a Tavern in the City, among a Set of Men who call themselves the *Lawyer's Club.* You must know, Sir, this Club consists only of Attorneys; and at this Meeting every one proposes the Cause he has then in Hand to the Board, upon which each Member gives his Judgment according to the Experience he has met with. If it happens that any one puts a Case of which they have had no Precedent, it is noted down by their Clerk *Will. Goosequill* (who registers all their Proceedings), that one of them may go the next Day with it to a Council. This indeed is commendable, and ought to be the principal End of their Meeting; but had you been there to have heard them relate their Methods of managing a Cause, their Manner of drawing out their Bills, and, in short, their Arguments upon the several ways of abusing their Clients, with the Applause that is given to him who has done it most artfully, you would before now have given your Remarks on them. They are so conscious that their Discourses ought to be kept secret, that they are very cautious of admitting any Person who is not of their Profession. When any who are not of the Law are let in, the Person who introduces him says he is a very honest Gentleman, and he is taken in, as their Cant is, to pay Costs. I am admitted upon the Recommendation of one of their Principals, as *a very honest good-natur'd Fellow* that will never be in a Plot, and only desires to drink his Bottle and smoke his Pipe. You have formerly remarked upon several sorts of Clubs; and as the Tendency of this is only to increase Fraud and Deceit, I hope you will please to take Notice of it.

> *I am* (*with respect*)
>> *Your humble Servant,*

T   H. R.'

No. 373.

[BUDGELL.]   Thursday, May 8.

Fallit enim vitium specie virtutis & umbra.—Juv.

MR. *Lock*, in his Treatise of Human Understanding, has spent two Chapters upon the Abuse of Words. The first and most palpable Abuse of Words, he says, is, when they are used without clear and distinct Ideas: The second, when we are so inconstant and unsteady in the Application of them, that we sometimes use them to signify one Idea, sometimes another. He adds, that the Result of our Contemplations and Reasonings, while we have no precise Ideas fixed to our Words, must needs be very confused and absurd. To avoid this Inconvenience, more especially in moral Discourses, where the same Word should constantly be used in the same Sense, he earnestly recommends the use of Definitions. *A Definition*, says he, *is the only way whereby the precise Meaning of moral Words can be known.* He therefore accuses those of great Negligence, who discourse of moral things with the least Obscurity in the Terms they make use of, since upon the fore-mention'd Ground he does not scruple to say, that he thinks *Morality is capable of Demonstration as well as the Mathematicks.*

I know no two Words that have been more abused by the different and wrong Interpretations which are put upon them, than those two, *Modesty* and *Assurance.* To say such an one is a *modest Man*, sometimes indeed passes for a good Character; but at present is very often used to signify a sheepish awkard Fellow, who has neither Good-breeding, Politeness, nor any Knowledge of the World.

Again, *A Man of Assurance*, tho' at first it only denoted a Person of a free and open Carriage, is now very usually applied to a profligate Wretch, who can break through all the Rules of Decency and Morality without a Blush.

I shall endeavour therefore in this Essay to restore these Words to their true Meaning, to prevent the Idea of *Modesty* from being confounded with that of *Sheepishness*, and to hinder *Impudence* from passing for *Assurance.*

If I was put to define *Modesty*, I would call it, *The Reflection of an ingenious Mind, either when a Man has committed an Action for which he censures himself, or fancies that he is exposed to the Censure of others.*

For this Reason a Man truly modest is as much so when he is alone as in Company, and as subject to a Blush in his Closet, as when the Eyes of Multitudes are upon him.

I do not remember to have met with any Instance of Modesty with which I am so well pleased, as that celebrated one of the young Prince, whose Father being a tributary King to the *Romans*, had several Complaints laid against him before the Senate, as a Tyrant and Oppressor of his Subjects. The Prince went to *Rome* to defend his Father; but coming into the Senate, and hearing a Multitude of Crimes proved upon him, was so oppressed when it came to his Turn to speak, that he was unable to utter a Word. The Story tells us, that the Fathers were more moved at this Instance of Modesty and Ingenuity, than they could have been by the most pathetick Oration; and, in short, pardoned the guilty Father for this early Promise of Virtue in the Son.

I take *Assurance* to be *the Faculty of possessing a Man's self,* or *of saying and doing indifferent things without any Uneasiness or Emotion in the Mind.* That which generally gives a Man Assurance is a moderate Knowledge of the World, but above all a Mind fixed and determined in it self to do nothing against the Rules of Honour and Decency. An open and assured Behaviour is the natural Consequence of such a Resolution. A Man thus armed, if his Words or Actions are at any Time misinterpreted, retires within himself, and from a Consciousness of his own Integrity, assumes Force enough to despise the little Censures of Ignorance or Malice.

Every one ought to cherish and encourage in himself the Modesty and Assurance I have here mentioned.

A man without Assurance is liable to be made uneasy by the Folly or Ill-nature of every one he converses with. A Man without Modesty is lost to all Sense of Honour and Virtue.

It is more than probable, that the Prince above-mentioned possessed both these Qualifications in a very eminent Degree. Without Assurance he would never have undertaken to speak before the most august Assembly in the World; without Modesty he would have pleaded the Cause he had taken upon him, tho' it had appeared never so scandalous.

From what has been said it is plain, that Modesty and Assurance are both amiable, and may very well meet in the same Person. When they are thus mixed and blended together, they compose what we endeavour to express when we say *a modest Assurance*; by which we understand the just Mean between Bashfulness and Impudence.

I shall conclude with observing, that as the same Man may be both modest and assured, so it is also possible for the same Person to be both impudent and bashful.

We have frequent Instances of this odd kind of Mixture in People of depraved Minds and mean Education; who tho' they are not able to meet a Man's Eyes, or pronounce a Sentence without Confusion, can voluntarily commit the greatest Villanies, or most indecent Action.

Such a Person seems to have made a Resolution to do ill even in spite of himself, and in Defiance of all those Checks and Restraints his Temper and Complection seem to have laid in his way.

Upon the Whole, I would endeavour to establish this Maxim, That the Practice of *Virtue* is the most proper Method to give a Man a becoming Assurance in his Words and Actions. *Guilt* always seeks to shelter it self in one of the Extreams, and is sometimes attended with both.   X

No. 374.
[STEELE.]   Friday, May 9.

Nil actum reputans si quid superesset agendum.—Luc.

THERE is a Fault, which, tho' common, wants a Name. It is the very contrary to Procrastination: As we lose the present Hour by delaying from Day to Day to execute what we ought to do immediately; so most of us take Occasion to sit still and throw away the Time in our Possession, by Retrospect on what is past, imagining we have already acquitted our selves, and established our Characters in the Sight of Mankind. But when we thus put a Value upon our selves for what we have already done, any further than to explain our selves in order to assist our future Conduct, that will give us an over-weaning Opinion of our Merit to the Prejudice of our present Industry. The great Rule, methinks, should be to manage the Instant in which we stand with Fortitude, Aequanimity, and Moderation, according to Men's respective Circumstances. If our past Actions reproach us, they cannot be attoned for by our own severe Reflections so effectually as by a contrary Behaviour. If they are praise-worthy, the Memory of them is of no Use but to act suitably to them. Thus a good present Behaviour is an implicit Repentance for any Miscarriage in what is past; but present Slackness will not make up for past Activity. Time has swallowed up all that we Contemporaries did Yesterday, as irrevocably as it has the Actions of the Antediluvians: But we are again awake, and what shall we do to Day, to Day which passes while we are yet speaking? Shall we remember the Folly of last Night, or resolve upon the Exercise of Virtue to Morrow? Last Night is certainly gone, and to Morrow may never arrive: This Instant make use of. Can you oblige any Man of Honour and Virtue? Do it immediately. Can you visit a sick Friend? Will it revive him to see you enter, and suspend your own Ease and Pleasure to comfort his Weakness, and hear the Impertinencies of a Wretch in Pain? Don't stay to take Coach, but be gone. Your Mistress will bring Sorrow, and your Bottle Madness: Go to neither.—Such Virtues and Diversions as these are mentioned because they occur to all Men. But every Man is sufficiently convinced, that to suspend the Use of the present Moment, and resolve better for the future only, is an unpardonable Folly; what I attempted to consider, was the Mischief of setting such a Value upon what is past, as to think we have done enough. Let a Man have filled all the Offices of Life with the highest Dignity till Yesterday, and begin to live only to himself to Day, he must expect he will in the Effects upon his Reputation be considered as the Man who died Yesterday. The Man who distinguishes himself from the rest, stands in a Press of People; those before him intercept his Progress, and those behind him, if he does not urge on, will tread him down. *Caesar*, of whom it was said, *that he thought nothing done while there was any thing left for him to do*, went on in performing the greatest Exploits, without assuming to himself a Privilege of taking Rest upon the Foundation of the Merit of his former Actions. It was the Manner of that glorious Captain to write down what Scenes he passed through, but it was rather to keep his Affairs in Method, and capable of a clear Review in case they should be examined by others, than that he built a Renown upon any thing which was past. I shall produce two Fragments of his to demonstrate, that it was his Rule of Life to support himself rather by what he should perform, than what he had done already. In the Tablet which he wore about him the same Year in which he obtained the Battle of *Pharsalia*, there were found these loose Notes for his own Conduct. It is supposed by the Circumstances they alluded to, that they might be set down the Evening of the same Night.

'My Part is now but begun, and my Glory must be sustained by the Use I make of this Victory; otherwise my Loss will be greater than that of *Pompey*. Our personal Reputation will rise or fall as we bear our respective Fortunes. All my private Enemies among the Prisoners shall be spared. I will forget this, in order to obtain such another Day. *Trebutius* is ashamed to see me: I will go to his Tent, and be reconciled in private. Give all the Men of Honour, who take part with me, the Terms I offered before the Battle: Let them owe this to their Friends who have been long in my Interest. Power is weakened by the full use of it, but extended by Moderation. *Galbinius* is Proud, and will be servile in his present Fortune;

let him wait.   Send for *Stertinius*: He is modest, and his Virtue is worth gaining.   I have cooled my Heart with Reflection; and am fit to rejoice with the Army to Morrow.   He is a popular General who can expose himself like a private Man during a Battle; but he is more popular who can rejoice but like a private Man after a Victory.'

What is particularly proper for the Example of all who pretend to Industry in the Pursuit of Honour and Virtue, is, that this Hero was more than ordinarily sollicitous about his Reputation, when a Common Mind would have thought it self in Security, and given it self a Loose to Joy and Triumph.   But though this is a very great Instance of his Temper, I must confess I am more taken with his Reflections when he retired to his Closet in some Disturbance upon the Repeated ill Omens of *Calphurnia*'s Dream the Night before his Death. The literal Translation of that Fragment shall conclude this Paper.

'Be it so then.   If I am to die to Morrow, that is what I am to do to Morrow: It will not be then, because I am willing it should be then; nor shall I escape it, because I am unwilling. It is in the Gods when, but in my self how I shall die.   If *Calphurnia*'s Dreams are Fumes of Indigestion, how shall I behold the Day after to Morrow?   If they are from the Gods, their Admonition is not to prepare me to escape from their Decree, but to meet it.   I have lived to a Fulness of Days and of Glory; what is there that *Caesar* has not done with as much Honour as ancient Heroes?   *Caesar* has not yet died: *Caesar* is prepared to die.'   T

No. 375.
[HUGHES.]   Saturday, May 10.

> *Non possidentem multa vocaveris*
> *Recte beatum: rectius occupat*
> *   Nomen beati, qui deorum*
> *   Muneribus sapienter uti,*
> *Duramque callet pauperiem pati,*
> *Pejusque letho flagitium timet.*—Hor.

I HAVE more than once had Occasion to mention a noble Saying of *Seneca* the Philosopher, that a Virtuous Person strugling with Misfortunes, and rising above them, is an Object on which the Gods themselves may look down with Delight.   I shall therefore set before my Reader a Scene of this kind of Distress in private Life, for the Speculation of this Day.

An eminent Citizen, who had lived in good Fashion and

Credit, was by a Train of Accidents, and by an unavoidable Perplexity in his Affairs, reduced to a low Condition. There is a Modesty usually attending faultless Poverty, which made him rather chuse to reduce his Manner of Living to his present Circumstances, than solicit his Friends in order to support the shew of an Estate when the Substance was gone. His Wife, who was a Woman of Sense and Virtue, behaved herself on this Occasion with uncommon Decency, and never appeared so amiable in his Eyes as now. Instead of upbraiding him with the ample Fortune she had brought, or the many great offers she had refused for his sake, she redoubled all the Instances of her Affection, while her Husband was continually pouring out his Heart to her in Complaints that he had ruined the best Woman in the World. He sometimes came home at a Time when she did not expect him, and surprized her in Tears, which she endeavoured to conceal, and always put on an Air of Chearfulness to receive him. To lessen their Expence, their eldest Daughter (whom I shall call *Amanda*) was sent into the Country, to the House of an honest Farmer, who had married a Servant of the Family. This young Woman was apprehensive of the Ruin which was approaching, and had privately engaged a Friend in the Neighbourhood to give her an Account of what passed from time to time in her Father's Affairs. *Amanda* was in the Bloom of her Youth and Beauty, when the Lord of the Manor, who often called in at the Farmer's House as he followed his Country Sports, fell passionately in Love with her. He was a Man of great Generosity, but from a loose Education had contracted a hearty Aversion to Marriage. He therefore entertained a Design upon *Amanda*'s Virtue, which at present he thought fit to keep Private. The innocent Creature, who never suspected his Intentions, was pleased with his Person, and having observed his growing Passion for her, hoped by so advantageous a Match she might quickly be in a Capacity of supporting her impoverished Relations. One Day as he called to see her, he found her in Tears over a Letter she had just received from her Friend, which gave an Account that her Father had lately been stripped of every thing by an Execution. The Lover, who with some Difficulty found out the Cause of her Grief, took this Occasion to make her a Proposal. It is impossible to express *Amanda*'s Confusion when she found his Pretensions were not honourable. She was now deserted of all her Hopes, and had no Power to speak; but rushing from him in the utmost Disturbance, locked her self up in her Chamber. He immediately dispatched a Messenger to her Father with the following Letter.

' *Sir,*

I have heard of your Misfortune, and have offered your Daughter, if she will live with me, to settle on her four hundred Pounds a Year, and to lay down the Sum for which you are now distressed. I will be so ingenious as to tell you that I do not intend Marriage: But if you are wise, you will use your Authority with her not to be too nice, when she has an Opportunity of saving you and your Family, and of making her self happy.

I am, &c.'

This Letter came to the Hands of *Amanda*'s Mother; she opened and read it with great Surprize and Concern. She did not think it proper to explain herself to the Messenger, but desiring him to call again the next Morning, she wrote to her Daughter as follows.

' *Dearest Child,*

Your Father and I have just now received a Letter from a Gentleman who pretends Love to you, with a Proposal that insults our Misfortunes, and would throw us to a lower Degree of Misery than any thing which is come upon us. How could this barbarous Man think, that the tenderest of Parents would be tempted to supply their Want by giving up the best of Children to Infamy and Ruin? It is a mean and cruel Artifice to make this Proposal at a Time when he thinks our Necessities must compel us to any thing; but we will not eat the Bread of Shame; and therefore we charge thee not to think of us, but to avoid the Snare which is laid for thy Virtue. Beware of pitying us: It is not so bad as you have perhaps been told. All things will yet be well, and I shall write my Child better News.

I have been interrupted. I know not how I was moved to say Things would mend. As I was going on, I was startled by a Noise of one that knocked at the Door, and hath brought us an unexpected Supply of a Debt which had long been owing. Oh I will now tell thee all. It is some Days I have lived almost without Support, having conveyed what little Money I could raise to your poor Father.—Thou wilt weep to think where he is, yet be assured he will be soon at Liberty. That cruel Letter would have broke his Heart, but I have concealed it from him. I have no Companion at present besides little *Fanny*, who stands watching my Looks as I write, and is crying for her Sister. She says she is sure you are not well, having discovered that my present Trouble is about you. But do not think I would thus repeat my Sorrows, to grieve thee; No, it is to entreat thee not to make them insupportable, by adding what would be worse than all. Let us bear chearfully an Affliction, which we have not brought on our selves, and remember there is a Power who can better deliver us out of it than by the Loss of thy Innocence. Heaven preserve my dear Child.

Thy Affectionate Mother ——'

The Messenger, notwithstanding he promised to deliver this Letter to *Amanda*, carry'd it first to his Master, who he imagined would be glad to have an Opportunity of giving it into her Hands himself. His Master was impatient to know the Success of his Proposal, and therefore broke open the Letter privately to see the Contents. He was not a little moved at so true a Picture of Virtue in Distress: But at the same time was infinitely surprised to find his Offers rejected. However, he resolved not to suppress the Letter, but carefully sealed it up again, and carried it to *Amanda*. All his Endeavours to see her were in vain, till she was assured he brought a Letter from her Mother. He would not part with it, but upon Condition that she should read it without leaving the Room. While she was perusing it, he fixed his Eyes on her Face with the deepest Attention: Her Concern gave a new Softness to her Beauty, and when she burst into Tears, he could no longer refrain from bearing a Part in her Sorrow, and telling her, that he too had read the Letter, and was resolved to make Reparation for having been the Occasion of it. My Reader will not be displeased to see the second Epistle, which he now wrote to *Amanda*'s Mother.

'*Madam*,

I am full of Shame, and will never forgive my self, if I have not your Pardon for what I lately wrote. It was far from my Intention to add Trouble to the Afflicted; nor could any thing, but my being a Stranger to you, have betrayed me into a Fault, for which, if I live, I shall endeavour to make you Amends, as a Son. You cannot be unhappy while *Amanda* is your Daughter; nor shall be, if any thing can prevent it, which is in the Power of,

Madam,

Your most obedient

Humble Servant ——'

This Letter he sent by his Steward, and soon after went up to Town himself, to compleat the generous Act he had now resolved on. By his Friendship and Assistance *Amanda*'s Father was quickly in a Condition of retrieving his perplex'd Affairs. To conclude, he marry'd *Amanda*, and enjoyed the double Satisfaction of having restored a worthy Family to their Former Prosperity, and of making himself happy by an Alliance to their Virtues.

No. 376.

[STEELE.] Monday, May 12.

. . . *Pavone ex Pythagoreo.*—Persius.

'Mr. SPECTATOR,

I HAVE not observed that the Officer you some time ago appointed as Inspector of Signs, has done his duty so well as to give you an Account of very many strange Occurrences in the publick Streets, which are worthy of, but have escaped your Notice. Among all the Oddnesses which I have ever met with, that which I am now telling you gave me most Delight. You must have observed that all the Criers in the Street attract the Attention of the Passengers, and of the Inhabitants in the several Parts, by something very particular in their Tone it self, in the dwelling upon a Note, or else making themselves wholly unintelligible by a Stream. The Person I am so delighted with has nothing to sell, but very gravely receives the Bounty of the People, for no other Merit but the Homage they pay to his Manner of signifying to them that he wants a Subsidy. You must, sure, have heard speak of an old Man who walks about the City, and that part of the Suburbs which lies beyond the *Tower*, performing the Office of a *Day-Watchman*, followed by a Goose, which bears the Bob of his Ditty, and confirms what he says with a Quack, Quack. I gave little Heed to the Mention of this known Circumstance, till, being the other Day in those Quarters, I passed by a decrepid old Fellow with a Pole in his Hand, who just then was bawling out, Half an Hour after One a Clock, and immediately a dirty Goose behind him made her Response, Quack, Quack. I could not forbear attending this grave Procession for the Length of half a Street, with no small Amazement to find the whole Place so familiarly acquainted with a melancholy Mid-night Voice at Noon day, giving them the Hour, and exhorting them of the Departure of Time, with a Bounce at their Doors. While I was full of this Novelty, I went into a Friend's House, and told him how I was diverted with their whimsical Monitor and his Equipage. My Friend gave me the History; and interrupted my Commendation of the Man, by telling me the Livelihood of these two Animals is purchased rather by the good Parts of the Goose than of the Leader: For it seems the Peripatetick who walked before her was a Watchman in that Neighbourhood; and the Goose of herself by frequent hearing his Tone, out of her natural Vigilance, not only observed but answered it very regularly from Time to Time. The Watchman was so affected with it, that he bought

her, and has taken her in Partner, only altering their Hours of
Duty from Night to Day. The Town has come into it, and
they live very comfortably. This is the Matter of fact: Now I
desire you, who are a profound Philosopher to consider this
Alliance of Instinct and Reason; your Speculation may turn
very naturally upon the Force the superior Part of Mankind
may have upon the Spirits of such as like this Watchman, may
be very near the Standard of Geese. And you may add to
this practical Observation, how in all Ages and Times the
World has been carried away by odd unaccountable Things,
which one would think would pass upon no Creature which
had Reason; and, under the Symbol of this Goose, you may
enter into the Manner and Method of leading Creatures, with
their Eyes open, through thick and thin, for they know not
what they know not why.

All which is humbly submitted to your Spectatorial Wisdom,
by,

Sir,

Your most humble Servant,

Michael Gander.'

' *Mr.* Spectator,

I have for several Years had under my Care the Government
and Education of young Ladies, which Trust I have endeavoured to discharge with due Regard to their several Capacities
and Fortunes: I have left nothing undone to imprint in every
one of them an humble courteous Mind, accompanied with a
graceful becoming Mein, and have made them pretty much
acquainted with the Houshold Part of Family Affairs; but
still I find there is something very wanting in the Air of my
Ladies, different from what I observe in those that are esteemed
your fine bred Women. Now, Sir, I must own to you, I never
suffered my Girls to learn to Dance; but since I have read your
Discourse of Dancing, where you have described the Beauty
and Spirit there is in regular Motion, I own my self your Convert, and resolve for the future to give my young Ladies that
Accomplishment. But upon imparting my Design to their
Parents, I have been made very uneasy for some time, because
several of them have declared, that if I did not make use
of the Master they recommended, they would take away their
Children. There was Colonel *Jumper*'s Lady, a Collonel of the
Train-Bands, that has a great Interest in her Parish; she recommends Mr. *Trot* for the prettiest Master in Town, that no
Man teaches a Jigg like him, that she has seen him rise six or
seven Capers together with the greatest Ease imaginable, and
that his Scholars twist themselves more Ways than the Scholars

of any Master in Town; besides, there is Madam *Prim*, an Alderman's Lady, recommends a Master of her own Name, but she declares he is not of their Family, yet a very extraordinary Man in his Way; for, besides a very soft Air he has in Dancing, he gives them a particular Behaviour at a Tea-Table, and in presenting their Snuff Box, to Twerl, Slip, or Flirt a Fan, and how to place patches to the best Advantage, either for Fat or Lean, Long or Oval Faces; for my Lady says there is more in these Things than the world imagines: But I must confess the major part of those I am concerned with leave it to me. I desire therefore, according to the inclosed Direction, you would send your Correspondent who has writ to you on that Subject to my House. If proper Application this way can give Innocence new Charms, and make Virtue legible in the Countenance, I shall spare no Charge to make my Scholars in their very Features and Limbs bear witness how careful I have been in the other Parts of their Education.

> *I am, Sir,*
>
> *Your most humble Servant,*

T   Rachael Watchfull.'

No. 377.
[ADDISON.]   Tuesday, May 13.

> *Quid quisque vitet, nunquam homini satis*
> *Cautum est in horas* . . .—Hor.

LOVE was the Mother of Poetry, and still produces, among the most Ignorant and Barbarous, a thousand imaginary Distresses and Poetical Complaints. It makes a Footman talk like *Oroondates*, and converts a brutal Rustick into a gentle Swain. The most ordinary Plebeian or Mechanick in Love, bleeds and pines away with a certain Elegance and Tenderness of Sentiments which this Passion naturally inspires.

These inward Languishings of a Mind infected with this Softness, have given Birth to a Phrase which is made use of by all the melting Tribe, from the highest to the lowest, I mean that of *dying for Love.*

Romances, which owe their very Being to this Passion, are full of these metaphorical Deaths. Heroes and Heroines, Knights, Squires, and Damsels, are all of them in a dying Condition. There is the same kind of Mortality in our Modern Tragedies, where every one gasps, faints, bleeds and dies. Many of the Poets, to describe the Execution which is done by this Passion, represent the fair Sex as *Basilisks* that destroy

with their Eyes; but I think Mr. *Cowley* has with great Justness of Thought compared a beautiful Woman to a *Porcupine*,
that sends an Arrow from every Part.

I have often thought, that there is no way so effectual for
the Cure of this general Infirmity, as a Man's reflecting upon
the Motives that produce it. When the Passion proceeds
from the Sense of any Virtue or Perfection in the Person
beloved, I would by no Means discourage it; but if a Man considers that all his heavy Complaints of Wounds and Deaths
rise from some little Affectations of Coquettry, which are improved into Charms by his own fond Imagination, the very
laying before himself the Cause of his Distemper, may be
sufficient to effect the Cure of it.

It is in this View that I have looked over the several Bundles
of Letters which I have received from dying People, and composed out of them the following Bill of Mortality, which I shall
lay before my Reader without any further Preface, as hoping
that it may be useful to him in discovering those several Places
where there is most Danger, and those fatal Arts which are
made use of to destroy the Heedless and Unwary.

Lysander, slain at a Puppet-show on the 3d of *September*.

Thyrsis, shot from a Casement in *Pickadilly*.

T. S., wounded by *Zelinda's* Scarlet Stocking, as she was
stepping out of a Coach.

Will. Simple, smitten at the Opera by the Glance of an Eye
that was aimed at one who stood by him.

Tho. Vainlove, lost his Life at a Ball.

Tim. Tattle, killed by the Tap of a Fan on his left Shoulder
by *Coquetilla*, as he was talking carelessly with her in a Bow-
window.

Sir *Simon Softly*, murder'd at the Play-house in *Drury-lane*
by a Frown.

Philander, mortally wounded by *Cleora*, as she was adjusting
her Tucker.

Ralph Gapely, Esq., hit by a random Shot at the Ring.

F. R. caught his Death upon the Water, *April* the 31st.

W. W., killed by an unknown Hand, that was playing with
the Glove off upon the side of the front Box in *Drury-lane*.

Sir *Christopher Crazy*, Bar., hurt by the Brush of a Whale-
bone Petticoat.

Sylvius, shot through the Sticks of a Fan at St. *James's*
Church.

Damon, struck thro' the Heart by a Diamond Necklace.

*Thomas Trusty, Francis Goosequill, William Meanwell,
Edward Callow*, Esqrs., standing in a Row, fell all four at the
same Time by an Ogle of the Widow *Trapland*.

Tom Rattle, chancing to tread upon a Lady's Tail as he came out of the Play-house, she turned full upon him, and laid him dead upon the Spot.

Dick Tastewell, slain by a Blush from the Queen's Box in the third Act of the *Trip to the Jubilee*.

Samuel Felt, Haberdasher, wounded in his Walk to *Islington* by Mrs. *Susannah Crossstitch*, as she was clambring over a Stile.

R, F. T, W. S, I. M, P. &c. put to Death in the last Birth-Day Massacre.

Roger Blinko, cut off in the twenty first Year of his Age by a White-wash.

Musidorus, slain by an Arrow that flew out of a Dimple in *Belinda*'s left Cheek.

Ned Courtly, presenting *Flavia* with her Glove (which she had dropped on Purpose) she received it, and took away his Life with a Curtsy.

John Gosselin having received a slight Hurt from a Pair of blue Eyes, as he was making his Escape was dispatch'd by a Smile.

Strephon, kill'd by *Clarinda* as she looked down into the Pit.

Charles Careless, shot flying by a Girl of fifteen, who unexpectedly popped her Head upon him out of a Coach.

Josiah Wither, aged Threescore and three, sent to his long home by *Elizabeth Jett-well*, Spinster.

Jack Freelove, murder'd by *Melissa* in her Hair.

William Wiseaker, Gent, drowned in a Flood of Tears by *Moll Common*.

John Pleadwell, Esq., of the *Middle Temple*, Barrister at Law, assassinated in his Chambers the sixth Instant by *Kitty Sly*, who pretended to come to him for his Advice.   I

No. 378.
[STEELE.]   Wednesday, May 14.

Aggredere, O magnos, aderit jam tempus, honores.—Virg.

I WILL make no Apology for entertaining the Reader with the following Poem, which is written by a great Genius, a Friend of mine, in the Country, who is not ashamed to employ his Wit in the Praise of his Maker.

MESSIAH.

A sacred Eclogue, compos'd of several Passages
of *Isaiah* the Prophet.

Written in Imitation of Virgil's POLLIO.

Ye Nymphs of Solyma! *begin the Song:*
To heav'nly Themes sublimer Strains belong.

The Mossie Fountains and the Sylvan Shades,
The Dreams of Pindus *and th' Aonian Maids,*
Delight no more.—O thou my Voice inspire
Who touch'd Isaiah's hallow'd Lips with Fire!
   RAPT into future Times, the Bard begun:
A Virgin *shall conceive, a* Virgin *bear a Son!*

Isaiae, Cap. *From* Jesse's *Root behold a Branch arise,*
11. v. 1. *Whose sacred Flow'r with Fragrance fills the Skies.*
   Th' Aethereal Spirit o'er its Leaves shall move,
   And on its Top descends the Mystic Dove,

Cap. 45. *Ye Heav'ns! from high the dewy Nectar pour,*
v. 8. *And in soft Silence shed the kindly Show'r!*

Cap. 25. *The Sick and Weak the healing Plant shall aid,*
v. 4. *From Storms a Shelter, and from Heat a Shade.*
   All Crimes shall cease, and ancient Fraud shall fail;

Cap. 9. *Returning Justice lift aloft her Scale;*
v. 7. *Peace o'er the World her Olive Wand extend,*
   And white-rob'd Innocence from Heav'n descend.
   Swift fly the Years, and rise th' expected Morn!
   Oh spring to Light, auspicious Babe be born!
   See Nature hastes her earliest Wreaths to bring,
   With all the Incense of the breathing Spring:
   See lofty Lebanon *his Head advance,*
   See nodding Forrests on the Mountains dance;
   See spicy Clouds from lowly Saron *rise,*
   And Carmel's *flowry Top perfumes the Skies!*

Cap. 40. *Hark! a glad Voice the lonely Desart chears;*
v. 3, 4. *Prepare the Way! a God, a God appears;*
   A God, a God! the vocal Hills reply,
   The Rocks proclaim the approaching Deity.
   Lo Earth receives him from the bending Skies!
   Sink down ye Mountains, and ye Vallies rise.
   With Heads declin'd, ye Cedars, Homage pay;
   Be smooth ye Rocks, ye rapid Floods give Way!
   The SAVIOUR comes! by ancient Bards foretold;

C. 42. v. 18. *Hear him ye Deaf, and all ye Blind behold!*
Cap. 35. *He from thick Films shall purge the visual Ray,*
v. 5, 6. *And on the sightless Eye-ball pour the Day,*
   'Tis he th' obstructed Paths of Sound shall clear,
   And bid new Musick charm th' unfolding Ear.
   The Dumb shall sing, the Lame his Crutch foregoe,
   And leap exulting like the bounding Roe.
   No Sigh, no Murmur the wide World shall hear,

Cap. 25. *From ev'ry Face he wipes off ev'ry Tear.*
v. 8. *In Adamantine Chains shall Death be bound,*
   And Hell's grim Tyrant feel th' eternal Wound.

As the good Shepherd tends his fleecy Care, Cap. 40.
Seeks freshest Pastures and the purest Air, v. 11.
Explores the lost, the wandring Sheep directs,
By Day o'ersees them, and by Night protects;
The tender Lambs he raises in his Arms,
Feeds from his Hand, and in his Bosom warms:
Mankind shall thus his Guardian Care engage,
The promis'd Father of the future Age. C. 9. v. 6.
No more shall Nation against Nation rise, C. 2. v. 4.
Nor ardent Warriors meet with hateful Eyes,
Nor Fields with gleaming Steel be cover'd o'er,
The Brazen Trumpets kindle Rage no more;
But useless Lances into Scythes shall bend,
And the broad Faulcion in a Plow-share end.
Then Palaces shall rise; the joyful Son Cap. 65.
Shall finish what his short-liv'd Sire begun; v. 21, 22.
Their Vines a Shadow to their Race shall yield,
And the same Hand that sow'd shall reap the Field.
The Swain in barren Deserts with Surprize Cap. 35.
Sees Lillies spring, and sudden Verdure rise, v. 1, 7.
And starts amidst the thirsty wilds to hear
New Falls of Water murmuring in his Ear:
On rifted Rocks, the Dragon's late Abodes,
The green Reed trembles, and the Bulrush nods.
Waste sandy Vallies, once perplex'd with Thorn, Cap. 41. v.
The spiry Firr and shapely Box adorn; 19, and C.
To leafless Shrubs the flow'ring Palm succeed, 55. v. 13.
And od'rous Myrtle to the noisome Weed.
The Lambs with Wolves shall graze the verdant Mead, Cap. 11.
And Boys in flow'ry Bands the Tyger lead: v. 6, 7, 8.
The Steer and Lion at one Crib shall meet,
And harmless Serpents lick the Pilgrim's Feet.
The smiling Infant in his Hand shall take
The crested Basilisk and speckled Snake;
Pleas'd the green Lustre of the Scales survey,
And with their forky Tongue and pointless Sting shall
    play.
Rise, crown'd with Light, imperial Salem *rise!* C. 60. v. 1.
Exalt thy tow'ry Head, and lift thy Eyes!
See, a long Race thy spacious Courts adorn; C. 60. v. 4.
See future Sons and Daughters yet unborn
In crowding Ranks on ev'ry Side arise,
Demanding Life, impatient for the Skies!
See barb'rous Nations at thy Gates attend,
Walk in thy Light, and in thy Temple bend; C. 60. v. 3.
See thy bright Altars throng'd with prostrate Kings,

C. 60. v. 6. *And heap'd with Products of* Sabaean *Springs!*
For thee Idume's *spicy Forests blow,*
And Seeds of Gold in Ophyr's *Mountains glow.*
See Heav'n its sparkling Portals wide display,
And break upon thee in a Flood of Day!

Cap. 60. *No more the rising* Sun *shall gild the Morn,*
v. 19, 20. *Nor Evening* Cynthia *fill her Silver Horn,*
But lost, dissolv'd in thy superior Rays,
One Tide of Glory, one unclouded Blaze
O'erflow thy Courts: The LIGHT HIMSELF *shall shine*
Reveal'd, and God's *eternal Day be thine!*

Cap. 51. v. *The Seas shall waste, the Skies in Smoke decay,*
6, and C. *Rocks fall to Dust, and Mountains melt away;*
54. v. 10. *But fix'd* His *Word,* His *saving Pow'r remains,*
Thy Realm *for ever lasts, thy own* Messiah *reigns.*

T

No. 379.
[BUDGELL.]   Thursday, May 15.

Scire tuum nihil est, nisi te scire hoc sciat alter.—Pers.

I HAVE often wonder'd at that ill-natur'd Position which has
been sometimes maintained in the Schools, and is comprised
in an old *Latin* Verse, namely, that *A Man's Knowledge is
worth nothing, if he communicates what he knows to any one
besides.* There is certainly no more sensible Pleasure to a
good-natured Man, than if he can by any Means gratify or
inform the Mind of another. I might add, that this Virtue
naturally carries its own Reward along with it, since it is
almost impossible it should be exercised without the improvement of the Person who Practices it. The reading of Books,
and the daily Occurrences of Life, are continually furnishing
us with Matter for Thought and Reflection. It is extreamly
natural for us to desire to see such our Thoughts put into the
Dress of Words, without which indeed we can scarce have a
clear and distinct Idea of them our selves: When they are thus
cloathed in Expressions, nothing so truly shews us whether
they are just or false, as those Effects which they produce in
the Minds of others.

I am apt to flatter my self, that in the Course of these my
Speculations, I have treated of several Subjects, and laid down
many such Rules for the Conduct of a Man's Life, which my
Readers were either wholly ignorant of before, or which at
least those few who were acquainted with them, looked upon
as so many Secrets they have found out for the Conduct of
themselves, but were resolved never to have made publick.

I am the more confirmed in this Opinion from my having received several Letters, wherein I am censured for having prostituted Learning to the Embraces of the Vulgar, and made her, as one of my Correspondents phrases it, a common Strumpet; I am charged by another with laying open the *Arcana*, or Secrets of Prudence, to the Eyes of every Reader.

The narrow Spirit which appears in the Letters of these my Correspondents is the less surprising, as it has shewn it self in all ages. There is still extant an Epistle written by *Alexander* the Great to his Tutor *Aristotle*, upon that Philosopher's publishing some part of his Writings; in which the Prince complains of his having made known to all the World, those Secrets in Learning which he had before communicated to him in private Lectures; concluding, *that he had rather excell the rest of Mankind in Knowledge than in Power.*

Luisa de Padilla, a Lady of great Learning, and Countess of *Aranda*, was in like Manner angry with the famous *Gratian*, upon his publishing his Treatise of the *Discreto*; wherein she fancied that he had laid open those Maxims to common Readers, which ought only to have been reserved for the Knowledge of the Great.

These Objections are thought by many of so much Weight, that they often defend the above-mentioned Authors, by affirming they have affected such an Obscurity in their Stile and Manner of Writing, that tho' every one may read their Works, there will be but very few who can comprehend their Meaning.

Persius, the *Latin* Satyrist, affected Obscurity for another Reason; with which however Mr. *Cowley* is so offended, that Writing to one of his Friends, You, says he, tell me, that you do not know whether *Persius* be a good Poet or no, because you cannot understand him; for which very Reason I affirm that he is not so.

However, this Art of *writing unintelligibly* has been very much improved, and followed by several of the Moderns, who observing the general Inclination of Mankind to dive into a Secret, and the Reputation many have acquired by concealing their Meaning under obscure Terms and Phrases, resolve, that they may be still more abstruse, to write without any Meaning at all. This Art, as it is at present practised by many eminent Authors, consists in throwing so many Words at a Venture into different Periods, and leaving the curious Reader to find the Meaning of them.

The *Egyptians*, who made use of Hieroglyphicks to signify several things, expressed a Man who confined his Knowledge and Discoveries altogether within himself, by the Figure of a

Dark Lanthorn closed on all Sides, which tho' it was illuminated within, afforded no Manner of Light or Advantage to such as stood by it.   For my own Part, as I shall from Time to Time communicate to the Publick whatever Discoveries I happen to make, I should much rather be compared to an ordinary Lamp, which consumes and wastes it self for the Benefit of every Passenger.

I shall conclude this Paper with the Story of *Rosicrucius*'s Sepulchre.   I suppose I need not inform my Readers that this Man was the Founder of the *Rosicrucian* Sect, and that his Disciples still pretend to new Discoveries, which they are never to communicate to the rest of Mankind.

A certain Person having Occasion to dig somewhat deep in the Ground where this Philosopher lay interr'd, met with a small Door having a Wall on each side of it.   His Curiosity, and the hopes of finding some hidden Treasure, soon prompted him to force open the Door.   He was immediately surprized by a sudden Blaze of Light, and discovered a very fair Vault: At the upper end of it was a Statue of a Man in Armour sitting by a Table, and leaning on his Left Arm.   He held a Truncheon in his Right-Hand, and had a Lamp burning before him.   The Man had no sooner set one Foot within the Vault, than the Statue erecting it self from its leaning Posture, stood bolt upright; and upon the Fellow's advancing another Step, lifted up the Truncheon in its Right Hand.   The Man still ventured a third Step, when the Statue with a furious Blow broke the Lamp into a thousand Pieces, and left his Guest in a sudden Darkness.

Upon the Report of this Adventure the Country People soon came with Lights to the Sepulchre, and discovered that the Statue, which was made of Brass, was nothing more than a Piece of Clock-work; that the Floor of the Vault was all loose, and underlaid with several Springs, which, upon any Man's entring, naturally produced that which had happened.

Rosicrucius, say his Disciples, made use of this Method, to shew the World that he had re-invented the ever-burning Lamps of the Ancients, tho' he was resolved no one should reap any Advantage from the Discovery.   X

No. 380.
[STEELE.]   Friday, May 16.

Rivalem patienter habe.—Ovid.

'*Sir*,   *Thursday, May* 8, 1712.
THE Character you have in the World of being the Lady's Philosopher, and the pretty Advice I have seen you give to

others in your Papers, make me address my self to you in this abrupt Manner, and to desire your Opinion what in this Age a Woman may call a Lover.   I have lately had a Gentleman that I thought made Pretensions to me, insomuch that most of my Friends took Notice of it and thought we were really Married; which I did not take much Pains to undeceive them, and especially a young Gentlewoman of my particular Acquaintance which was then in the Country.   She coming to Town, and seeing our Intimacy so great, she gave her self the Liberty of taking me to task concerning it: I ingeniously told her we were not married, but I did not know what might be the Event.   She soon got acquainted with the Gentleman, and was pleased to take upon her to examine him about it.   Now whether a new Face had made a greater Conquest than the old, I 'll leave you to judge: But I am informed that he utterly denied all Pretensions to Courtship, but withal profess'd a sincere Friendship for me; but whether Marriages are proposed by way of Friendship or not, is what I desire to know, and what I may really call a Lover.   There are so many who talk in a Language fit only for that Character, and yet guard themselves against speaking in direct Terms to the Point, that it is impossible to distinguish between Courtship and Conversation. I hope you will do me Justice both upon my Lover and my Friend if they provoke me further; in the mean Time I carry it with so equal a Behaviour, that the Nymph and the Swain too are mightily at a Loss; each believes I, who know them both well, think my self revenged in their Love to one another, which creates an Irreconcileable Jealousy.   If all comes right again, you shall hear further from,

> *Sir,*
>> *Your most obedient Servant,*
>>> Mirtilla.'

'*Mr.* SPECTATOR,   *April* 28, 1712.

Your Observations on Persons that have behaved themselves irreverently at Church, I doubt not have had a good Effect on some that have read them: But there is another Fault which has hitherto escaped your Notice, I mean of such Persons as are very zealous and punctual to perform an Ejaculation that is only preparatory to the Service of the Church, and yet neglect to join in the Service it self.   There is an instance of this in a Friend of WILL. HONEYCOMB'S, who sits opposite to me: He seldom comes in till the Prayers are about half over, and when he has entered his Seat (instead of joyning with the Congregation) he devoutly holds his Hat before his Face for three or four Moments, then bows to all his Acquaintance, sits down, takes a Pinch of Snuff, (if it be Evening Service perhaps a Nap) and spends the remaining Time in surveying the Congregation. Now, Sir, what I would desire is, that you will animadvert a little on this Gentleman's Practice. In my Opinion, this Gentleman's Devotion, Cap in Hand, is only a Compliance to the Custom of the Place, and goes no further than a little Ecclesiastical good Breeding. If you will not pretend to tell us the Motives that bring such Triflers to solemn Assemblies, yet let me desire that you will give this Letter a Place in your Paper, and I shall remain,

> *Sir,*
>
> *Your obliged humble Servant,*
>
> J. S.'

'*Mr.* Spectator,   *May the* 5th

The Conversation at a Club of which I am a Member, last Night falling upon Vanity and the Desire of being admired, put me in Mind of relating how agreeably I was entertained at my own Door last *Thursday* by a clean fresh-coloured Girl, under the most elegant and the best furnished Milk-Pail I had ever observed. I was glad of such an Opportunity of seeing the Behaviour of a Coquet in Low Life, and how she received the extraordinary Notice that was taken of her; which I found had effected every Muscle of her Face in the same Manner as it does the Feature of a first Rate Toast at a Play, or in an Assembly. This Hint of mine made the Discourse turn upon the Sense of Pleasure; which ended in a general Resolution, that the Milk-Maid enjoys her Vanity as exquisitly as the Woman of Quality. I think it would not be an improper Subject for you to examine this Frailty, and trace it to all Conditions of Life; which is recommended to you as an Occasion of obliging many of your Readers, among the rest,

> *Your most humble Servant,*
>
> T. B.'

'*Sir,*

Coming last Week into a Coffee-house not far from the *Exchange* with my Basket under my Arm, a *Jew* of considerable Note, as I am informed, takes half a Dozen Oranges of me, and at the same Time slides a Guinea into my Hand. I made him a Courtesy and went my Way: He followed me, and finding I was going about my Business, he came up with me, and told me plainly, that he gave me the Guinea with no other Intent but to purchase my Person for an Hour. Did you so, Sir? says I: You gave it me then to make me be wicked, I'll keep it to make me honest.   However, not to be in the least un-grateful, I promise you I 'll lay it out in a Couple of Rings, and wear them for your Sake.   I am so just, Sir, besides, as to give every Body that asks how I came by my Rings this Account of my Benefactor: but to save me the Trouble of telling my Tale over and over again, I humbly beg the Favour of you so to tell it once for all, and you will extreamly oblige,

May 12,   *Your humble Servant,*
1712.   Betty Lemon.'

'*Sir,*   *St. Bride's, May* 15, 1712.

'Tis a great deal of Pleasure to me, and, I daresay, will be no less Satisfaction to you, that I have an Opportunity of in-forming you, that the Gentlemen and others of the Parish of St. *Bride's,* have raised a Charity-School of fifty Girls, as before of fifty Boys.   You were so kind to recommend the Boys to the charitable World, and the other Sex hope you will do them the same Favour in *Friday's Spectator* for *Sunday* next, when they are to appear with their humble Airs at the Parish-Church of St. *Bride's.*   Sir, the Mention of this may possibly be serviceable to the Children; and sure no one will omit a good Action attended with no Expence.

> *I am, Sir,*
>> *Your very humble Servant,*

T   The Sexton.'

No. 381.
[ADDISON.]   Saturday, May 17.

> *Aequam memento rebus in arduis*
> *Servare mentem, non secus in bonis*
> *Ab insolenti temperatam*
> *Laetitia, moriture Deli.*—Hor.

I HAVE always preferred Chearfulness to Mirth.   The latter I consider as an Act, the former as an Habit of the Mind.   Mirth is short and transient, Chearfulness fix'd and permanent. Those are often raised into the greatest Transports of Mirth who are subject to the greatest Depressions of Melancholy: On the contrary, Chearfulness, tho' it does not give the Mind such an exquisite Gladness, prevents us from falling into any Depths of Sorrow.   Mirth is like a Flash of Lightning, that breaks thro' a Gloom of Clouds, and glitters for a Moment; Chearfulness keeps up a kind of Day-light in the Mind, and fills it with a steady and perpetual Serenity.

Men of austere Principles look upon Mirth as too wanton and dissolute for a State of Probation, and as fill'd with a certain Triumph and Insolence of Heart, that is inconsistent with a Life which is every Moment obnoxious to the greatest Dangers. Writers of this Complexion have observed, that the sacred Person who was the great Pattern of Perfection was never seen to laugh.

Chearfulness of Mind is not liable to any of these Exceptions; it is of a serious and composed Nature, it does not throw the Mind into a Condition improper for the present State of Humanity, and is very conspicuous in the Characters of those who are looked upon as the greatest Philosophers among the Heathens, as well as among those who have been deservedly esteemed as Saints and holy Men among Christians.

If we consider Chearfulness in three Lights, with regard to our selves, to those we converse with, and to the great Author of our Being, it will not a little recommend it self on each of these Accounts. The Man who is possessed of this excellent Frame of Mind, is not only easy in his Thoughts, but a perfect Master of all the Powers and Faculties of his Soul: His Imagination is always clear, and his Judgment undisturbed: His Temper is even and unruffled, whether in Action or in Solitude. He comes with a Relish to all those Goods which Nature has provided for him, tastes all the Pleasures of the Creation which are poured about him, and does not feel the full Weight of those accidental Evils which may befall him.

If we consider him in relation to the Persons whom he converses with, it naturally produces Love and Good-will towards him. A chearful Mind is not only disposed to be affable and obliging, but raises the same good Humour in those who come within its Influence. A Man finds himself pleased, he does not know why, with the Chearfulness of his Companion: It is like a sudden Sun-shine that awakens a secret Delight in the Mind, without her attending to it. The Heart rejoices of its own Accord, and naturally flows out into Friendship and Benevolence towards the Person who has so kindly an Effect upon it.

When I consider this chearful State of Mind in its third Relation, I cannot but look upon it as a constant habitual Gratitude to the great Author of Nature. An inward Chearfulness is an implicit Praise and Thanksgiving to Providence under all its Dispensations. It is a kind of Acquiescence in the State wherein we are placed, and a secret Approbation of the Divine Will in his Conduct towards Man.

There are but two things which, in my Opinion, can reasonably deprive us of this Chearfulness of Heart. The first of these is the Sense of Guilt. A Man who lives in a State of Vice and Impenitence, can have no Title to that Evenness and Tranquility of Mind which is the Health of the Soul, and the natural Effect of Virtue and Innocence. Chearfulness in an ill Man deserves a harder Name than Language can furnish us with, and is many Degrees beyond what we commonly call Folly or Madness.

Atheism, by which I mean a Disbelief of a Supreme Being, and consequently of a future State, under whatsoever Titles it shelters itself, may likewise very reasonably deprive a Man of this Chearfulness of Temper. There is something so particularly gloomy and offensive to human Nature in the Prospect of Non-Existence, that I cannot but wonder, with many excellent Writers, how it is possible for a Man to out-live the Expectation of it. For my own Part, I think the Being of a God is so little to be doubted, that it is almost the only Truth we are sure of, and such a Truth as we meet with in every Object, in every Occurrence, and in every Thought. If we look into the Characters of this Tribe of Infidels, we generally find they are made up of Pride, Spleen and Cavil: It is indeed no Wonder, that Men, who are uneasy to themselves, should be so to the rest of the World; and how is it possible for a Man to be otherwise than uneasy in himself, who is in Danger every Moment of losing his entire Existence, and dropping into Nothing?

The vicious Man and Atheist have therefore no Pretence to Chearfulness, and would act very unreasonably, should they endeavour after it. It is impossible for any one to live in good Humour, and enjoy his present Existence, who is apprehensive either of Torment or of Annihilation; of being miserable, or of not being at all.

After having mentioned these two great Principles, which are destructive of Chearfulness in their own Nature, as well as in right Reason, I cannot think of any other than ought to banish this happy Temper from a virtuous Mind. Pain and Sickness, Shame and Reproach, Poverty and old Age, nay Death it self, considering the Shortness of their Duration, and the Advantage we may reap from them, do not deserve the Name of Evils. A good Mind may bear up under them with Fortitude, with Indolence, and with Chearfulness of Heart. The Tossing of a Tempest does not discompose him, which he is sure will bring him to a joyful Harbour.

A Man who uses his best Endeavours to live according to the Dictates of Virtue and right Reason, has two perpetual Sources of Chearfulness; in the Consideration of his own Nature, and of that Being on whom he has a Dependance. If he looks into himself, he cannot but rejoice in that Existence,

which is so lately bestowed upon him, and which, after Millions
of Ages, will be still new, and still in its Beginning. How
many Self-Congratulations naturally arise in the Mind, when
it reflects on this its Entrance into Eternity, when it takes a
View of those improveable Faculties, which in a few Years, and
e en at its first setting out, have made so considerable a Progress, and which will be still receiving an Increase of Perfection,
and consequently an Increase of Happiness. The Consciousness
of such a Being spreads a perpetual Diffusion of Joy through
the Soul of a virtuous Man, and makes him look upon himself
every Moment as more happy than he knows how to conceive.

The second Source of Chearfulness to a good Mind, is its
Consideration of that Being on whom we have our Dependance,
and in whom, though we behold him as yet but in the first
faint Discoveries of his Perfections, we see every thing that
we can imagine as great, glorious, or amiable. We find our
selves every where upheld by his Goodness, and surrounded
with an Immensity of Love and Mercy. In short, we depend
upon a Being, whose Power qualifies him to make us happy by
an Infinity of Means, whose Goodness and Truth engage him to
make those happy who desire it of him, and whose Unchange-
ableness will secure us in this Happiness to all Eternity.

Such Considerations, which every one should perpetually
cherish in his Thoughts, will banish from us all that secret
Heaviness of Heart which unthinking Men are subject to when
they lie under no real Affliction, all that Anguish which we
may feel from any Evil that actually oppresses us, to which I
may likewise add those little Cracklings of Mirth and Folly
that are apter to betray Virtue than support it; and establish
in us such an even and chearful Temper, as makes us pleasing
to our selves, to those with whom we converse, and to him
whom we were made to please.   I

No. 382.

[STEELE.]   Monday, May 19.

Habes confitentem reum.—Tull.

I ought not to have neglected a Request of one of my Correspondents so long as I have; but I dare say I have given him
Time to add Practice to Profession. He sent me sometime
ago a Bottle or two of excellent Wine to drink the Health of a
Gentleman, who had by the Penny-Post advertised him of an
egregious Error in his Conduct. My Correspondent received
the Obligation from an unknown Hand with the Candour
which is natural to an ingenious Mind; and promises a contrary

Behaviour in that Point for the future: He will offend his
Monitor with no more Errors of that kind, but thanks him for
his Benevolence.   This frank Carriage makes me reflect upon
the amiable Atonement a Man makes in an ingenious Acknowledgement of a Fault: All such Miscarriages as flow from Inadvertency are more than repaid by it; for Reason, though not
concerned in the Injury, employs all its Force in the Atonement.   He that says he did not design to disoblige you in
such an Action, does as much as if he should tell you, that
though the Circumstance which displeased was never in his
Thoughts, he has that Respect for you, that he is unsatisfied
till it is wholly out of yours.   It must be confessed, that when
an Acknowledgment of an Offence is made out of Poorness of
Spirit, and not Conviction of Heart, the Circumstance is quite
different: But in the Case of my Correspondent, where both the
Notice is taken and the Return made in private, the Affair
begins and ends with the highest Grace on each Side.   To make
the Acknowledgment of a Fault in the highest manner graceful,
it is lucky when the Circumstances of the Offender place him
above any ill Consequences from the Resentment of the Person
offended.   A Dauphin of *France*, upon a Review of the Army,
and a Command of the King to alter the Posture of it by a
March of one of the Wings, gave an improper Order to an
Officer at the Head of a Brigade, who told his Highness, he
presumed he had not received the last Orders, which were to
move a contrary Way.   The Prince, instead of taking the
Admonition which was delivered in a Manner that accounted
for his Errour with Safety to his Understanding, shaked a Cane
at the Officer; and with the Return of Opprobrious Language
persisted in his own Orders.   The whole Matter came necessarily before the King, who commanded his Son, on Foot, to
lay his Right-Hand on the Gentleman's Stirrup as he sat or
Horse-back in Sight of the whole Army, and ask his Pardon.
When the Prince touched his Stirrup, and was going to speak,
the Officer, with an incredible Agility, threw himself on the
Earth, and kissed his Feet.

The Body is very little concerned in the Pleasures or Sufferings of Souls truly great; and the Reparation, when an Honour
was designed this Soldier, appeared as much too great to be
born by his Gratitude, as the injury was intolerable to his
Resentment.

When we turn our Thoughts from these extraordinary
Occurrences into common Life, we see an ingenious kind of
Behaviour not only make up for Faults committed, but in a
manner expiate them in the very Commission.   Thus many
Things wherein a Man has pressed too far, he implicitly excuses,

by owning, *This is a Trespass; You'll pardon my Confidence; I am sensible I have no Pretension to this Favour;* and the like. But commend me to those gay Fellows about Town who are directly impudent, and make up for it no otherwise than by calling themselves such, and exulting in it. But this sort of Carriage, which prompts a Man against Rules to urge what he has a mind to, is pardonable only when you sue for another. When you are confident in Preference of your self to others of equal Merit, every Man that loves Virtue and Modesty ought in Defence of those Qualities, to oppose you: But, without considering the Morality of the Thing, let us at this Time behold only the natural Consequence of Candour when we speak of our selves.

The SPECTATOR writes often in an Elegant, often in an Argumentative, and often in a Sublime Stile, with equal Success; but how would it hurt the reputed Author of that Paper to own, that of the most beautiful Pieces under his Title, he is barely the Publisher? There is nothing but what a Man really performs can be an Honour to him; what he takes more than he ought in the Eye of the World, he loses in the Conviction of his own Heart; and a Man must lose his Consciousness, that is, his very self, before he can rejoice in any Falshood without inward Mortification.

Who has not seen a very Criminal at the Bar, when his Council and Friends have done all that they could for him in vain, prevail upon the whole Assembly to pity him, and his Judge to recommend his Case to the Mercy of the Throne, without offering any thing new in his Defence, but that he, whom before we wished Convicted, became so out of his own Mouth, and took upon himself all the Shame and Sorrow we were just before preparing for him? The great Opposition to this kind of Candour, arises from the unjust Idea People ordinarily have of what we call an high Spirit. It is far from Greatness of Spirit to persist in the Wrong in any thing, nor is it a Diminution of Greatness of Spirit to have been in the Wrong: Perfection is not the Attribute of Man, therefore he is not degraded by the Acknowledgment of an Imperfection: But it is the Work of little Minds to imitate the Fortitude of great Spirits on worthy Occasions, by Obstinacy in the Wrong. This Obstinacy prevails so far upon them, that they make it extend to the Defence of Faults in their very Servants. It would swell this Paper to too great a Length, should I insert all the Quarrels and Debates which are now on Foot in this Town; where one Party, and in some Cases both, is sensible of being on the faulty Side, and have not Spirit enough to acknowledge it. Among the Ladies the Case is very common, for there are very few of them who know that it is to maintain a true and high Spirit, to throw away from it all which it self disapproves, and to scorn so pitiful a Shame, as that which disables the Heart from acquiring a Liberality of Affections and Sentiments. The candid Mind, by acknowledging and discarding its Faults, has Reason and Truth for the Foundation of all its Passions and Desires, and consequently is happy and simple; the disingenuous Spirit by Indulgence of one unacknowledged Errour, is entangled with an After-Life of Guilt, Sorrow, and Perplexity. T

No. 383.
[ADDISON.]   Tuesday, May 20.

Criminibus debent hortos . . .—Juv.

As I was sitting in my Chamber, and thinking on a Subject for my next *Spectator*, I heard two or three irregular Bounces at my Landlady's Door, and upon the opening of it, a loud chearful Voice enquiring whether the Philosopher was at Home. The Child who went to the Door answered very Innocently, that he did not lodge there. I immediately recollected that it was my good Friend Sir ROGER's Voice: and that I had promised to go with him on the Water to *Spring-Garden*, in case it proved a good Evening. The Knight put me in mind of my Promise from the Bottom of the Stair-Case, but told me that if I was Speculating he would stay below till I had done. Upon my coming down I found all the Children of the Family got about my old Friend, and my Landlady herself, who is a notable prating Gossip, engaged in a Conference with him, being mightily pleased with his stroaking her little Boy upon the Head, and bidding him be a good Child, and mind his Book.

We were no sooner come to the *Temple* Stairs, but we were surrounded with a crowd of Water-men, offering us their respective Services. Sir ROGER, after having looked about him very attentively, spied one with a Wooden-Leg, and immediately gave him Orders to get his Boat ready. As we were walking towards it, *You must know*, says Sir ROGER, *I never make use of any Body to row me that has not either lost a Leg or an Arm. I wou'd rather bate him a few Strokes of his Oar, than not employ an honest Man that has been wounded in the Queen's Service. If I was a Lord or a Bishop, and kept a Barge, I would not put a Fellow in my Livery that had not a Wooden-Leg.*

My old Friend, after having seated himself, and trimmed the Boat with his Coachman, who, being a very sober Man, always serves for Ballast on these Occasions, we made the best of our

way for *Fox-Hall*. Sir ROGER obliged the Waterman to give
us the History of his Right Leg, and hearing that he had left
it at *La Hogue*, with many Particulars which passed in that
glorious Action, the Knight in the Triumph of his Heart made
several Reflections on the Greatness of the *British* Nation; as,
that one *Englishman* could beat three *Frenchmen*; that we cou'd
never be in Danger of Popery so long as we took care of
our Fleet; that the *Thames* was the noblest River in *Europe*;
that *London-Bridge* was a greater Piece of Work than any of
the Seven Wonders of the World; with many other honest
Prejudices which naturally cleave to the Heart of a true
Englishman.

After some short Pause, the old Knight turning about his
Head twice or thrice, to take a Survey of this great Metropolis,
bid me observe how thick the City was set with Churches, and
that there was scarce a single Steeple on this side *Temple-Bar*.
A most Heathenish Sight! says Sir ROGER: *There is no Religion
at this End of the Town. The Fifty new Churches will very much
mend the Prospect; but Church-work is slow, Church-work is slow!*

I do not remember I have any where mentioned, in Sir
ROGER's Character, his Custom of saluting every Body that
passes by him with a Good-morrow, or a Good-night. This
the old Man does out of the Overflowings of his Humanity,
though at the same time it renders him so popular among all
his Country Neighbours, that it is thought to have gone a good
way in making him once or twice Knight of the Shire. He
cannot forbear this Exercise of Benevolence even in Town,
when he meets with any one in his Morning or Evening Walk.
It broke from him to several Boats that passed by us upon the
Water; but, to the Knight's great Surprize, as he gave the
Good-night to two or three young Fellows a little before our
Landing, one of them, instead of returning the Civility, asked
us what queer old Putt we had in the Boat; and whether he
was not ashamed to go a Wenching at his Years? with a great
deal of the like *Thames*-Ribaldry. Sir ROGER seemed a little
shocked at first, but at length assuming a Face of Magistracy,
told us, *That if he were a* Middlesex *Justice, he would make such
Vagrants know that her Majesty's Subjects were no more to be
abused by Water than by Land.*

We were now arrived at *Spring-Garden*, which is exquisitely
pleasant at this Time of the Year. When I considered the
Fragrancy of the Walks and Bowers, with the Choirs of Birds
that sung upon the Trees, and the loose Tribe of People that
walk'd under their Shades, I could not but look upon the
Place as a kind of *Mahometan* Paradise. Sir ROGER told me
it put him in mind of a little Coppice by his House in the

Country, which his Chaplain us'd to call an Aviary of Nightingales. *You must understand,* says the Knight, *there is nothing in the World that pleases a Man in Love so much as your Nightingale. Ah, Mr.* SPECTATOR! *The many Moonlight Nights that I have walked by my self, and thought on the Widow by the Musick of the Nightingale!* Here he fetch'd a deep Sigh, and was falling into a Fit of musing, when a Mask, who came behind him, gave him a gentle Tap upon the Shoulder, and asked him if he would drink a Bottle of Mead with her? But the Knight being startled at so unexpected a Familiarity, and displeased to be interrupted in his Thoughts of the Widow, told her, *She was a wanton Baggage,* and bid her go about her Business.

We concluded our Walk with a Glass of *Burton-Ale,* and a Slice of Hung-Beef. When we had done eating our selves, the Knight called a Waiter to him, and bid him carry the Remainder to the Waterman that had but one Leg. I perceived the Fellow stared upon him at the Oddness of the Message, and was going to be saucy; upon which I ratified the Knight's Commands with a peremptory Look.

As we were going out of the Garden, my old Friend thinking himself obliged, as a Member of the *Quorum,* to animadvert upon the Morals of the Place, told the Mistress of the House, who sat at the Bar, That he should be a better Customer to her Garden, if there were more Nightingales, and fewer Strumpets.   I

No. 384.
[STEELE.]   **Wednes**day, May 21.

Hague, May 24. N. S. *The same Republican Hands, who have so often since the Chevalier* de St. George's *Recovery, killed him in our publick Prints, have now reduced the young Dauphin of* France *to that desperate Condition of Weakness, and Death it self, that it is hard to conjecture what Method they will take to bring him to Life again. Mean time we are assured by a very good Hand from* Paris, *That on the* 20th *Instant this young Prince was as well as ever he was known to be since the Day of his Birth. As for the other, they are now sending his Ghost, we suppose, (for they never had the Modesty to contradict their Assertions of his Death) to* Commerci *in* Lorrain, *attended only by four Gentlemen, and a few Domesticks of little Consideration.* The Baron *de Bothmar* having delivered in his Credentials, to qualify him as an Ambassador to this State (an *Office* to which his greatest Enemies will acknowledge him to be *equal*) is gone to *Utrecht,* whence he will proceed to *Hanover,* but not stay long at that Court, for fear the Peace should be made during his *lamented* Absence.   *Post-Boy,* May 20.

I should be thought not able to read, should I overlook some excellent Pieces lately come out. My Lord Bishop of St. Asaph has just now published some Sermons, the Preface to which seems to me to determine a great Point. He has, like a good Man and a good Christian, in Opposition to all the Flattery and base Submission of false Friends to Princes, asserted, That Christianity left us where it found us as to our Civil Rights. The present Entertainment shall consist only of a Sentence out of the Post-Boy, *and the said Preface of the Lord of* St. Asaph. *I should think it a little odd if the Author of the* Post-Boy *should with impunity call Men Republicans for a Gladness on Report of the Death of the* Pretender; *and treat Baron Bothmar, the Minister of* Hanover, *in such a manner as you see in my Motto. I must own, I think every Man in* England *concerned to support the Succession of that Family.*

'The publishing a few Sermons, whilst I live, the latest of which was preached about eight Years since, and the first above seventeen, will make it very natural for People to enquire into the occasion of doing so: And to such I do very willingly assign these following Reasons.

First, From the Observations I have been able to make, for these many Years last past, upon our publick Affairs; and from the natural Tendency of several Principles and Practices, that have of late been studiously revived; and from what has followed thereupon, I could not help both fearing and presaging, that these Nations would some time or other, if ever we should have an Enterprizing Prince upon the Throne, of more Ambition than Virtue, Justice and true Honour, fall into the Way of all other Nations, and lose their *Liberty*.

Nor could I help foreseeing to whose Charge a great deal of this dreadful Mischief, whenever it should happen, would be laid, whether justly or unjustly was not my Business to determine; but I resolved, for my own particular Part, to deliver my self, as well as I could, from the Reproaches and the Curses of Posterity, by publickly declaring to all the World, that although in the constant Course of my Ministry, I have never failed, on proper Occasions, to recommend, urge, and insist upon the loving, honouring, and the reverencing the Prince's Person, and holding it, according to the Laws, inviolable and sacred, and paying all Obedience and Submission to the Laws, tho' never so hard and inconvenient to private People: Yet did I never think my self at Liberty, or authorized to tell the People, that either *Christ*, St. *Peter*, or St. *Paul*, or any other Holy Writer, had, by any Doctrine delivered by them, subverted the *Laws* and *Constitutions* of the Country in which they lived, or put them in a worse Condition, with respect to their Civil Liberties, than they would have been had they not been Christians. I ever thought it a most impious Blasphemy against that Holy Religion, to father any thing upon it that might encourage Tyranny, Oppression, or Injustice in a Prince, or that easily tended to make a free and happy People *Slaves* and *miserable*. No: People may make themselves as wretched as they will, but let not God be called into that wicked Party. When Force, and Violence, and hard Necessity have brought the Yoak of Servitude upon a People's Neck, Religion will supply them with a patient and submissive Spirit under it till they can innocently shake it off; but certainly Religion never puts it on. This always was, and this at present is, my Judgment of these Matters: And I would be transmitted to Posterity (for the little Share of Time such Names as mine can live) under the Character of one who lov'd his Country, and would be thought a *good Englishman* as well as a *good Clergyman*.

This Character I thought would be transmitted by the following Sermons, which were made for, and preached in a private Audience, when I could think of nothing else but doing my Duty on the Occasions that were then offered by God's Providence, without any manner of Design of making them publick: And for that Reason I give them now as they were then delivered; by which I hope to satisfie those People who have objected a Change of Principles to me, as if I were not now the same Man I formerly was. I never had but one Opinion of these Matters; and that I think is so reasonable and well-grounded, that I believe I never can have any other.

Another Reason of my publishing these Sermons at this Time, is, that I have a mind to do my self some Honour, by doing what Honour I could to the Memory of two most excellent Princes, and who have very highly deserved at the Hands of all the People of these Dominions, who have any true Value for the *Protestant Religion*, and the *Constitution* of the *English Government*, of which they were the great *Deliverers* and *Defenders*. I have lived to see their illustrious Names very rudely handled, and the great Benefits they did this Nation treated slightly and contemptuously. I have lived to see our Deliverance from *Arbitrary Power* and *Popery* traduced and villified by some who formerly thought it was their greatest Merit, and made it part of their Boast and Glory to have had a little Hand and Share in bringing it about; and others who, without it, must have lived in Exile, Poverty, and Misery, meanly disclaiming it, and using ill the *glorious Instruments* thereof. Who could expect such a Requital of such Merit? I have, I own it, an Ambition of exempting my self from the Number of *unthankful* People: And as I loved and honoured those great Princes living, and lamented over them when dead, so I would gladly raise them up a Monument of Praise as lasting as any thing of mine can be; and I choose to do it at this Time, when it is so unfashionable a Thing to speak honourably of them.

The Sermon that was preached upon the Duke of *Gloucester's* Death was printed quickly after, and is now, because the Subject was so suitable, join'd to the others. The Loss of that most promising and hopeful Prince was, at that Time, I saw, unspeakably great; and many Accidents since have convinced us, that it could not have been over-valued. That precious Life, had it pleased God to have prolonged it the usual Space, had saved us many Fears, and Jealousies, and dark Distrusts, and prevented many Alarms, that have long kept us, and will keep us still, waking and uneasy. Nothing remained to comfort and support us under this heavy Stroke, but the Necessity it brought the King and Nation under, of settling the *Succession* in the House of HANOVER, and giving it an *Hereditary Right*, by *Act* of *Parliament*, as long as it continues *Protestant*. So much Good did God, in his merciful Providence, produce from a Misfortune, which we could never otherwise have sufficiently deplored.

The fourth Sermon was preached upon the Queen's *Accession* to the Throne, and the first Year in which that Day was solemnly observed (for, by some Accident or other, it had been over-looked the Year before); and every one will see, without the Date of it, that it was preached very early in this Reign, since I was able only to *promise* and *presage* its future Glories and Successes, from the good Appearances of Things, and the happy Turn our Affairs began to take; and could not then count up the Victories and Triumphs that, for seven Years after, made it in the Prophet's Language, *a Name and a Praise among all the People of the Earth*. Never did seven such Years together pass over the Head of any *English Monarch*, nor cover it with so much Honour: The Crown and Sceptre seemed to be the *Queen's* least Ornaments; those other Princes wore in common with Her, and her great personal Virtues were the same before and since; but such was the Fame of Her Administration of Affairs at home, such was the Reputation of Her Wisdom and Felicity in choosing Ministers, and such was then esteemed their Faithfulness and Zeal, their Diligence and great Abilities in executing Her Commands; to such a Height of military Glory did Her Great *General* and Her *Armies* carry the *British* Name abroad; such was the Harmony and Concord betwixt Her and Her *Allies*, and such was the Blessing of God upon all Her Counsels and Undertakings, that I am as sure as

History can make me, no Prince of ours was ever yet so Prosperous and Successful, so loved, esteemed, and honoured by their Subjects and their Friends, nor near so formidable to their Enemies. We were, as all the World imagined then, just entring on the Ways that promised to lead to such a Peace, as would have answered all the Prayers of our Religious Queen, the Care and Vigilance of a most able Ministry, the Payments of a willing and obedient People, as well as all the glorious Toils and Hazards of the Soldiery; when God, for our Sins, permitted *the Spirit of Discord* to go forth, and, by troubling sore the Camp, the City, and the Country, (and oh that it had altogether spared the Places sacred to his Worship!) to spoil for a Time, this beautiful and pleasing Prospect, and give us in its Stead, I know not what.—Our Enemies will tell the rest with Pleasure. It will become me better to pray to God to restore us to the Power of obtaining such a Peace, as will be to his Glory, the Safety, Honour, and the Welfare of the Queen and Her Dominions, and the general Satisfaction of all Her High and Mighty Allies.

May 2, 1712.' T

No. 385.
[BUDGELL.] Thursday, May 22.
. . . *Thesea pectora juncta fide.*—Ovid.

I INTEND the Paper for this Day as a loose Essay upon *Friendship,* in which I shall throw my Observations together without any set Form, that I may avoid repeating what has been often said on this Subject.

Friendship is *a strong and habitual Inclination in two Persons to Promote the Good and Happiness of one another.* Tho' the Pleasures and Advantages of Friendship have been largely celebrated by the best moral Writers, and are considered by all as great Ingredients of human Happiness, we very rarely meet with the Practice of this Virtue in the World.

Every Man is ready to give in a long Catalogue of those Virtues and good Qualities he expects to find in the Person of a Friend, but very few of us are careful to cultivate them in ourselves.

Love and Esteem are the first Principles of Friendship, which always is imperfect where either of these two is wanting.

As, on the one Hand, we are soon ashamed of loving a Man whom we cannot esteem; so, on the other, tho' we are truly sensible of a Man's Abilities, we can never raise ourselves to the Warmths of Friendship, without an affectionate Good-Will towards his Person.

Friendship immediately banishes Envy under all its Disguises. A Man who can once doubt whether he should rejoice in his Friend's being happier than himself, may depend upon it that he is an utter Stranger to this Virtue.

There is something in Friendship so very great and noble, that in those fictitious Stories which are invented to the Honour of any particular Person, the Authors have thought it as necessary to make their Hero a Friend as a Lover. *Achilles* has his *Patroclus*, and *Aeneas* his *Achates*. In the first of these Instances we may observe, for the Reputation of the Subject I am treating of, that *Greece* was almost ruin'd by the Heroe's Love, but was preserved by his Friendship.

The Character of *Achates* suggests to us an Observation we may often make on the Intimacies of great Men, who frequently chose their Companions rather for the Qualities of the Heart than those of the Head, and prefer Fidelity in an easy inoffensive complying Temper to those Endowments which make a much greater Figure among Mankind. I do not remember that *Achates*, who is represented as the first Favourite, either gives his Advice, or strikes a Blow, thro' the whole *Aeneid*.

A Friendship which makes the least Noise is very often most useful, for which Reason I should prefer a prudent Friend to a zealous one.

Atticus, one of the best Men of ancient Rome, was a very remarkable instance of what I am here speaking. This extraordinary Person, amidst the Civil Wars of his Country, when he saw the Designs of all Parties equally tended to the Subversion of Liberty, by constantly preserving the Esteem and Affection of both the Competitors, found Means to serve his Friends on either Side; and while he sent Money to young *Marius*, whose Father was declared an Enemy of the Commonwealth, he was himself one of *Sylla*'s chief Favourites, and always near that General.

During the War between *Caesar* and *Pompey*, he still maintained the same Conduct. After the Death of *Caesar* he sent Money to *Brutus* in his Troubles, and did a Thousand good Offices to *Anthony*'s Wife and Friends when that Party seemed ruined. Lastly, even in that bloody War between *Anthony* and *Augustus*, *Atticus* still kept his Place in both their Friendships; insomuch that the first, says *Cornelius Nepos*, whenever he was absent from *Rome* in any Part of the Empire, writ punctually to him what he was doing, what he read, and whither he intended to go; and the latter gave him constantly an exact Account of all his Affairs.

A Likeness of Inclinations in every Particular is so far from being requisite to form a Benevolence in two Minds towards

each other, as it is generally imagined, that I believe we shall
find some of the firmest Friendships to have been contracted
between Persons of different Humours; the Mind being often
pleased with those Perfections which are new to it, and which
it does not find among its own Accomplishments. Besides that
a Man in some Measure supplies his own Defects, and fancies
himself at second hand possessed of those good Qualities and
Endowments which are in the Possession of him who in the
Eye of the World is looked on as his *other self*.

The most difficult Province in Friendship is the letting a
Man see his Faults and Errors; which should, if possible, be
so contrived, that he may perceive our Advice is given him not
so much to please our selves as for his own Advantage. The
Reproaches therefore of a Friend should always be strictly
just, and not too frequent.

The violent Desire of pleasing in the Person reproved, may
otherwise change into a Despair of doing it, while he finds
himself censur'd for Faults he is not conscious of. A mind that
is softened and humanised by Friendship, cannot bear frequent Reproaches; either it must quite sink under the
Oppression, or abate considerably of the Value and Esteem it
had for him who bestows them.

The proper Business of Friendship is to inspire Life and
Courage; and a Soul thus supported outdoes it self; whereas if
it be unexpectedly deprived of these Succours, it droops and
languishes.

We are in some Measure more inexcusable if we violate our
Duties to a Friend, than to a Relation; since the former arise
from a voluntary Choice, the latter from a Necessity to which
we could not give our own Consent.

As it has been said on one Side, that a Man ought not to
break with a faulty Friend, that he may not expose the Weakness of his Choice; it will doubtless hold much stronger with
respect to a worthy one, that he may never be upbraided for having lost so valuable a Treasure which was once in his possession.

X

No. 386.
[STEELE.]   Friday, May 23.

*Cum tristibus severe, cum remissis jucunde, cum senibus graviter,
cum juventute comiter . . . vivere.*—Tull.

THE Piece of *Latin* on the Head of this Paper is part of a
Character extreamly vitious, but I have set down no more than
may fall in with the Rules of Justice and Honour. *Cicero*
spoke it of *Cataline*, who, he said, lived with the Sad severely,

with the Cheerful agreeably, with the Old gravely, with the Young pleasantly; he added, with the Wicked boldly, with the Wanton lasciviously The two last Instances of his Complaisance I forbear to consider, having it in my Thoughts at present only to speak of obsequious Behaviour as it sits upon a Companion in Pleasure, not a Man of Design and Intrigue. To vary with every Humour in this Manner cannot be agreeable, except it comes from a Man's own Temper and natural Complexion; to do it out of an Ambition to excel that Way, is the most Fruitless and unbecoming Prostitution imaginable. To put on an artful Part to obtain no other End but an unjust Praise from the Undiscerning, is of all Endeavours the most despicable. A Man must be sincerely pleased to become Pleasure, or not to interrupt that of others: For this Reason it is a most Calamitous Circumstance, that many People who want to be alone, or should be so, will come into Conversation. It is certain, that all Men who are the least given to Reflection, are seized with an Inclination that Way; when, perhaps, they had rather be inclined to Company; but indeed they had better go home, and be tired with themselves, than force themselves upon others to recover their good Humour. In all this the Case of communicating to a Friend a sad Thought or Difficulty, in order to relieve an heavy Heart, stands excepted; but what is here meant, is, that a Man should always go with Inclination to the Turn of the Company he is going into, or not pretend to be of the Party. It is certainly a very happy Temper to be able to live with all kinds of Dispositions, because it argues a Mind that lies open to receive what is pleasing to others, and not obstinately bent on any Particularity of its own.

This is it which makes me pleased with the Character of my good acquaintance *Acasto*. You meet him at the Tables and Conversations of the Wise, the Impertinent, the Grave, the Frolick, and the Witty; and yet his own Character has nothing in it that can make him particularly agreeable to any one Sect of Men; but *Acasto* has natural good Sense, good Nature, and Discretion, so that every Man enjoys himself in his Company; and tho' *Acasto* contributes nothing to the Entertainment, he never was at a Place where he was not welcome a second time. Without these subordinate good Qualities of *Acasto*, a Man of Wit and Learning would be painful to the Generality of Mankind instead of being pleasing. Witty Men are apt to imagine they are agreeable as such, and by that Means grow the worst Companions imaginable; they deride the Absent or rally the Present in a wrong Manner, not knowing that if you pinch or tickle a Man till he is uneasy in his Seat, or ungracefully distinguished from the rest of the Company, you equally hurt him.

I was going to say, the true Art of being agreeable in Company (but there can be no such thing as Art in it) is to appear well pleased with those you are engaged with, and rather to seem well Entertained, than to bring Entertainment to others. A Man thus disposed is not indeed what we ordinarily call a good Companion, but essentially is such, and in all the Parts of his Conversation has something Friendly in his Behaviour, which conciliates Men's Minds more than the highest Sallies of Wit or Starts of Humour can possibly do. The Feebleness of Age in a Man of this Turn, has something which should be treated with Respect even in a Man no otherwise Venerable. The Forwardness of Youth, when it proceeds from Alacrity and not Insolence, has also its Allowances. The Companion who is formed for such by Nature, gives to every Character of Life its due Regards, and is ready to account for their Imperfections, and receive their Accomplishments as if they were his own. It must appear that you receive Law from, and not give it to your Company, to make you agreeable.

I remember *Tully*, speaking, I think of *Anthony*, says, That *in eo facetiae erant quae nulla arte tradi possunt. He had a witty Mirth which could be acquired by no Art.* This Quality must be of the kind of which I am now speaking; for all Sorts of Behaviour which depend upon Observation and Knowledge of Life is to be acquired; but that which no one can describe, and is apparently the Act of Nature, must be every where prevalent, because every thing it meets is a fit Occasion to exert it; for he who follows Nature, can never be improper or unseasonable.

How unaccountable then must their Behaviour be, who without any Manner of Consideration of what the Company they have just now entered are upon, give themselves the Air of a Messenger, and make as distinct Relations of the Occurrences they last met with, as if they had been dispatched from those they talk to, to be punctually exact in a Report of those Circumstances? It is unpardonable to those who are met to enjoy one another, that a fresh Man shall pop in, and give us only the last Part of his own Life, and put a Stop to ours during the History. If such a Man comes from *Change*, whether you will or not, you must hear how the Stocks go; and tho' you are never so intently employed on a graver Subject, a young Fellow of the other End of the Town will take his Place, and tell you, Mrs. such a one is charmingly handsome, because he just now saw her. But I think I need not dwell on this Subject, since I have acknowledged there can be no Rules made for excelling this Way; and Precepts of this kind fare like Rules for writing Poetry, which, 'tis said, may have prevented ill Poets, but never made good ones.   T

No. 387.
[ADDISON.]   Saturday, May 24.

Quid pure tranquillet . . .—Hor.

IN my last *Saturday's* Paper I spoke of Chearfulness as it is a
Moral Habit of the Mind, and accordingly mentioned such
moral Motives as are apt to cherish and keep alive this happy
Temper in the Soul of Man: I shall now consider Chearfulness
in its *Natural* State, and reflect on those Motives to it, which
are indifferent either as to Virtue or Vice.

Chearfulness is, in the first Place, the best Promoter of
Health. Repinings and secret Murmurs of Heart give imperceptible Strokes to those delicate Fibres of which the vital
Parts are composed, and wear out the Machine insensibly; not
to mention those violent Ferments which they stir up in the
Blood, and those irregular disturbed Motions, which they raise
in the animal Spirits. I scarce remember, in my own Observation, to have met with many old Men, or with such, who (to
use our *English* Phrase) *wear well*, that had not at least a certain
Indolence in their Humour, if not a more than ordinary Gaiety
and Chearfulness of Heart. The Truth of it is, Health and
Chearfulness mutually beget each other, with this Difference,
that we seldom meet with a great Degree of Health which is
not attended with a certain Chearfulness, but very often see
Chearfulness where there is no great Degree of Health.

Chearfulness bears the same friendly Regard to the Mind
as to the Body: It banishes all anxious Care and Discontent,
sooths and composes the Passions, and keeps the Soul in a
perpetual Calm. But having already touched on this last
Consideration, I shall here take Notice that the World, in which
we are placed, is filled with innumerable Objects that are proper
to raise and keep alive this happy Temper of Mind.

If we consider the World in its Subserviency to Man, one
would think it was made for our Use; but if we consider it in
its Natural Beauty and Harmony, one would be apt to conclude it was made for our Pleasure. The Sun, which is as
the great Soul of the Universe, and produces all the Necessaries
of Life, has a particular Influence in chearing the Mind of
Man, and making the Heart glad.

Those several living Creatures which are made for our Service
or Sustenance, at the same Time either fill the Woods with
their Musick, furnish us with Game, or raise pleasing Ideas
in us by the Delightfulness of their Appearance. Fountains,
Lakes, and Rivers are as refreshing to the Imagination, as the
Soil through which they pass.

There are Writers of great Distinction, who have made it an

Argument for Providence that the whole Earth is covered with
Green, rather than with any other Colour, as being such a right
Mixture of Light and Shade, that it comforts and strengthens
the Eye instead of weakning or grieving it.   For this Reason
several Painters have a green Cloth hanging near them, to ease
the Eye upon after too great an Application to their Colouring.
A famous modern Philosopher accounts for it in the following
Manner: All Colours that are more luminous, overpower and
dissipate the animal Spirits which are employed in Sight; on
the contrary, those that are more obscure do not give the
animal Spirits a sufficient Exercise; whereas the Rays that
produce in us the Idea of Green fall upon the Eye in such a
due Proportion, that they give the animal Spirits their proper
Play, and by keeping up the Struggle in a just Balance, excite
a very pleasing and agreeable Sensation.   Let the Cause be
what it will, the Effect is certain, for which Reason the Poets
ascribe to this particular Colour the Epithet of *Chearful.*

To consider further this double End in the Works of Nature,
and how they are at the same Time both useful and entertaining, we find that the most important Parts in the vegetable
World are those which are the most beautiful.   These are the
Seeds by which the several Races of Plants are propagated and
continued, and which are always lodged in Flowers or Blossoms.   Nature seems to hide her principal Design, and to be
industrious in making the Earth gay and delightful, while she
is carrying on her great Work, and intent upon her own Preservation.   The Husband-man after the same manner is employed in laying out the whole Country into a kind of Garden
or Landskip, and making every thing smile about him, whilst
in Reality he thinks of nothing but of the Harvest, and Encrease which is to arise from it.

We may further observe how Providence has taken Care to
keep up this Chearfulness in the Mind of Man, by having
formed it after such a Manner, as to make it capable of con-
ceiving Delight from several Objects which seem to have very
little Use in them, as from the Wildness of Rocks and Desarts,
and the like grotesque Parts of Nature.   Those who are versed
in Philosophy may still carry this Consideration higher, by
observing that if Matter had appeared to us endow'd only with
those real Qualities which it actually possesses, it would have
made but a very joyless and uncomfortable Figure; and why
has Providence given it a Power of producing in us such
imaginary Qualities as Tastes and Colours, Sounds and Smells,
Heat and Cold, but that Man, while he is conversant in the
lower Stations of Nature, might have his Mind cheared and
delighted with agreeable Sensations?   In short, the whole

Universe is a kind of Theatre filled with Objects that either raise in us Pleasure, Amusement, or Admiration.

The Reader's own Thoughts will suggest to him the Vicissitude of Day and Night, the Change of Seasons, with all that Variety of Scenes which diversify the Face of Nature, and fill the Mind with a perpetual Succession of beautiful and pleasing Images.

I shall not here mention the several Entertainments of Art, with the Pleasures of Friendship, Books, Conversation, and other accidental Diversions of Life, because I would only take Notice of such Incitements to a chearful Temper, as offer themselves to Persons of all Ranks and Conditions, and which may sufficiently shew us that Providence did not design this World should be filled with Murmurs and Repinings, or that the Heart of Man should be involved in Gloom and Melancholy.

I the more inculcate this Chearfulness of Temper, as it is a Virtue in which our Countrymen are observed to be more deficient than any other Nation. Melancholy is a kind of Demon that haunts our Island, and often conveys her self to us in an easterly Wind. A celebrated *French* Novelist, in Opposition to those who begin their Romances with the flowry Season of the Year, enters on his Story thus, *In the gloomy Month of* November, *when the People of* England *hang and drown themselves, a disconsolate Lover walked out into the Fields, &c.*

Every one ought to fence against the Temper of his Climate or Constitution, and frequently to indulge in himself those Considerations which may give him a Serenity of Mind, and enable him to bear up chearfully against those little Evils and Misfortunes which are common to human Nature, and which by a right Improvement of them will produce a Satiety of Joy, and an uninterrupted Happiness.

At the same time that I would engage my Reader to consider the World in its most agreeable Lights, I must own there are many Evils which naturally spring up amidst the Entertainments that are provided for us; but these, if rightly consider'd, should be far from overcasting the Mind with Sorrow, or destroying that Chearfulness of Temper which I have been recommending. This Interspersion of Evil with Good, and Pain with Pleasure in the Works of Nature, is very truly ascrib'd by Mr. *Lock* in his Essay on human Understanding to a moral Reason, in the following Words:

Beyond all this, we may find another Reason why God hath scattered up and down several Degrees of Pleasure and Pain, in all the things that environ and affect us, and blended them together, in almost all that our Thoughts and Senses have to do

*with; that we finding Imperfection, Dissatisfaction, and want of
compleat Happiness, in all the Enjoyments which the Creatures
can afford us, might be led to seek it in the Enjoyment of him,* with
whom there is Fulness of Joy, and at whose Right Hand are
Pleasures for evermore. L

No. 388.
[STEELE] Monday, May 26.

> . . . *Tibi res antiquae laudis & artis*
> *Ingredior, sanctos ausus recludere fontes.*—Virg.

'*Mr.* SPECTATOR,

IT is my Custom when I read your Papers, to read over the
Quotations in the Authors from whence you take them: As
you mentioned a Passage lately out of the second Chapter of
Solomon's Song, it occasioned my looking into it; and upon
reading it I thought the Ideas so exquisitely soft and tender,
that I could not help making this Paraphrase of it, which, now
it is done, I can as little forbear sending to you. Some Marks
of your Approbation, which I have already received, have given
me so sensible a Taste of them, that I cannot forbear endeavouring after them as often as I can with any Appearance of Success.

> *I am, Sir,*
>
> *Your most obedient humble Servant.*'

The Second Chapter of *Solomon's Song.*

I.

As when in Sharon's *Field the Blushing Rose
Does its chaste Bosom to the Morn disclose,
Whilst all around the* Zephyrs *bear
The fragrant Odours thro' the Air,
Or as the Lilly in the shady Vale,
Does o'er each Flow'r with beauteous Pride prevail.
And stands with Dews and kindest Sun-shine blest,
In fair Pre-eminence, superiour to the rest;
So if my Love with happy Influence shed
His Eyes' bright Sunshine on his Lover's Head,
Then shall the Rose of* Sharon's *Field,
And whitest Lillies to my Beauties yield.
Then fairest Flow'rs with studious Art combine,*
The Roses with the Lillies join,
And their united Charms are less than mine.

II.

As much as fairest Lillies can surpass
A Thorn in Beauty, or in Height the Grass;
So does my Love among the Virgins shine,
Adorn'd with Graces more than half Divine.
Or as a Tree, that, glorious to behold,
Is hung with Apples all of ruddy Gold,
Hesperian *Fruit! and Beautifully high*
Extends its Branches to the Sky;
So does my Love the Virgin's Eye invite:
'Tis he alone can fix their wand'ring Sight,
Among ten thousand eminently bright.

III.

Beneath his pleasing Shade
My wearied Limbs at Ease I laid,
And on his fragrant Boughs reclin'd my Head.
I pull'd the Golden Fruit with eager Haste,
Sweet was the Fruit, and pleasing to the Taste;
With sparkling Wine he crown'd the Bowl,
With gentle Extasies he fill'd my Soul;
Joyous we sat beneath the shady Grove,
And o'er my Head he hung the Banners of his Love.

IV.

I faint! I die! my labouring Breast
Is with the mighty Weight of Love opprest,
I feel the Fire possess my Heart,
And Pain convey'd to every Part.
Thro' all my Veins the Passion flies,
My feeble Soul forsakes its Place,
A trembling Faintness seals my Eyes,
And Paleness dwells upon my Face:

V.

Oh! let my Love with pow'rful Odours stay
My fainting love-sick Soul, that dies away;
One Hand beneath me let him place,
With t'other press me in a chaste Embrace.
I charge you, Nymphs of Sion, *as you go*
Arm'd with the sounding Quiver and the Bow,
Whilst thro' the Lonesome Woods you rove,
You ne'er disturb my sleeping Love.
Be only gentle Zephyrs *there,*
With downy Wings to fan the Air;

Let sacred Silence dwell around,
To keep off each intruding Sound:
And when the balmy Slumber leaves his Eyes,
May he to Joys unknown till then, arise.

VI.

But see! he comes! with what majestick Gate
He onward bears his lovely State.
Now thro' the Lattice he appears,
With softest Words dispels my Fears;
Arise, my Fair one, and receive
All the Pleasures Love can give.
For now the sullen Winter's past,
No more we fear the Northern Blast:
No Storms nor threat'ning Clouds appear,
No falling Rains deform the Year.
My Love admits of no Delay,
Arise, my Fair, and come away.

VII.

Already, see! the teeming Earth
Brings forth the Flow'rs, her beauteous Birth,
The Dews, and soft-descending Show'rs,
Nurse the new-born tender Flow'rs.
Hark! the Birds melodious sing,
And sweetly usher in the Spring.
Close by his Fellow sits the Dove,
And billing, whispers her his Love.
The spreading Vines with Blossoms swell,
Diffusing round a grateful Smell.
Arise, my Fair One, and receive
All the Blessings Love can give:
For Love admits of no Delay,
Arise, my Fair, and come away.

VIII.

As to its Mate the constant Dove
Flies through the Covert of the Spicy Grove,
So let us hasten to some lonesome Shade.
There let me safe in thy lov'd Arms be laid,
Where no intruding hateful Noise
Shall damp the Sound of thy Melodious Voice;
Where I may gaze and mark each beauteous Grace,
For sweet thy Voice, and lovely is thy Face.

IX.

As all of Me, my Love, is Thine,
Let all of Thee be ever Mine.
Among the Lillies we will play,
Fairer, my Love thou art than they;
Till the Purple Morn arise,
And balmy Sleep forsake thine Eyes;
Till the gladsome Beams of Day
Remove the Shades of Night away;
Then when soft Sleep shall from thy Eyes depart,
Rise like the bounding Roe, or lusty Hart,
Glad to behold the Light again
From Bether's *Mountains darting o'er the Plain.*

T

No. 389.
[BUDGELL.]   Tuesday, May 27.

. . . *Meliora pii docuere parentes.*—Hor.

NOTHING has more surprized the Learned in *England*, than the
Price which a small Book, entitled *Spaccio della Bestia trium-*
fante, bore in a late Auction.   This Book was sold for thirty
Pound.   As it was written by one *Jordanus Brunus*, a professed Atheist, with a Design to depreciate Religion, every one
was apt to fancy, from the extravagant Price it bore, that there
must be something in it very formidable.

I must confess, that happening to get a Sight of one of them
my self, I could not forbear perusing it with this Apprehension;
but found there was so very little Danger in it, that I shall
venture to give my Readers a fair Account of the whole Plan
upon which this wonderful Treatise is built.

The Author pretends that *Jupiter* once upon a time resolved
on a Reformation of the Constellations; for which purpose
having summoned the Stars together, he complains to them
of the great Decay of the Worship of the Gods, which he
thought so much the harder, having called several of those
Celestial Bodies by the Names of the Heathen Deities, and by
that means made the Heavens as it were a Book of the Pagan
Theology.   *Momus* tells him, that this is not to be wondered
at, since there were so many scandalous Stories of the Deities,
upon which the Author takes Occasion to cast Reflections upon
all other Religions, concluding that *Jupiter*, after a full Hearing, discarded the Deities out of Heaven, and called the Stars
by the Names of the Moral Virtues.

This short Fable, which has no Pretence in it to Reason or

Argument, and but a very small Share of Wit, has however recommended it self wholly by its Impiety, to those weak Men, who would distinguish themselves by the Singularity of their Opinions.

There are two Considerations which have been often urged against Atheists, and which they never yet could get over. The first is, that the greatest and most eminent Persons of all Ages have been against them, and always complied with the publick Forms of Worship established in their respective Countries, when there was nothing in them either derogatory to the Honour of the Supream Being, or prejudicial to the Good of Mankind.

The *Platos* and *Ciceros* among the Ancients; the *Bacons*, the *Boyles*, and the *Locks* among our own Countrymen, are all Instances of what I have been saying, not to mention any of the Divines however celebrated, since our Adversaries challenge all those as Men who have too much Interest in this Case to be impartial Evidences.

But what has been often urged as a Consideration of much more Weight, is not only the Opinion of the better sort, but the general Consent of Mankind to this great Truth; which I think could not possibly have come to pass but from one of the three following Reasons; either that the Idea of a God is innate and co-existent with the Mind it self; or that this Truth is so very obvious, that it is discovered by the first Exertion of Reason in Persons of the most ordinary Capacities; or, lastly, that it has been delivered down to us thro' all Ages by a Tradition from the first Man.

The Atheists are equally confounded, to which ever of these three Causes we assign it; they have been so pressed by this last Argument from the general Consent of Mankind, that after great Search and Pains they pretend to have found out a Nation of Atheists, I mean that polite People the *Hottentots*.

I dare not shock my Readers with a Description of the Customs and Manners of these Barbarians, who are in every respect scarce one Degree above Brutes, having no Language among them but a confused *Gabble*, which is neither well understood by themselves or others.

It is not however to be imagined how much the Atheists have gloried in these their good Friends and Allies.

If we boast of a *Socrates*, or a *Seneca*, they may now confront them with these great Philosophers the *Hottentots*.

Tho' even this Point has, not without Reason, been several times controverted, I see no manner of Harm it could do Religion, if we should entirely give them up this elegant Part of Mankind.

Methinks nothing more shews the Weakness of their Cause, than that no Division of their Fellow-Creatures join with them, but those among whom they themselves own Reason is almost defaced, and who have little else but their Shape, which can entitle them to any Place in the Species.

Besides these poor Creatures, there have now and then been Instances of a few crazed People in several Nations, who have denied the Existence of a Deity.

The Catalogue of these is, however, very short; even *Vanini*, the most celebrated Champion for the Cause, professed before his Judges that he believed the Existence of a God, and taking up a Straw which lay before him on the Ground, assured them, that alone was sufficient to convince him of it; alledging several Arguments to prove that 'twas impossible Nature alone could create any thing.

I was the other Day reading an Account of *Casimir Liszynski*, a Gentleman of *Poland*, who was convicted and executed for this Crime. The manner of his Punishment was very particular. As soon as his Body was burnt, his Ashes were put into a Cannon, and shot into the Air towards *Tartary*.

I am apt to believe, that if something like this Method of Punishment should prevail in *England*, such is the natural good Sense of the *British* Nation, that whether we ramm'd an Atheist whole into a great Gun, or pulverized our Infidels, as they do in *Poland*, we should not have many Charges.

I should, however, propose, while our Ammunition lasted, that instead of *Tartary*, we should always keep two or three Cannons ready pointed towards the Cape of *Good-Hope*, in order to shoot our Unbelievers into the Country of the *Hottentots*.

In my Opinion, a solemn, judicial Death is too great an Honour for an Atheist, tho' I must allow the Method of exploding him, as it is practised in this ludicrous kind of Martyrdom, has something in it proper enough to the Nature of his Offence.

There is indeed a great Objection against this manner of treating them. Zeal for Religion is of so affective a Nature, that it seldom knows where to rest; for which Reason I am afraid, after having discharged our Atheists, we might possibly think of shooting off our Sectaries; and, as one does not foresee the Vicissitude of Humane Affairs, it might one time or other come to a Man's own Turn to fly out of the Mouth of a Demi-Culverin.

If any of my Readers imagine that I have treated these Gentlemen in too ludicrous a manner, I must confess, for my own Part, I think Reasoning against such Unbelievers upon a

Point that shocks the common Sense of Mankind, is doing them too great an Honour, giving them a Figure in the Eye of the World, and making People fancy that they have more in them than they really have.

As for those Persons who have any Scheme of Religious Worship, I am for treating such with the utmost Tenderness, and should endeavour to shew them their Errors with the greatest Temper and Humanity; but as these Miscreants are for throwing down Religion in general, for stripping Mankind of what themselves own is of excellent Use in all great Societies, without once offering to establish any thing in the Room of it, I think the best way of dealing with them, is to retort their own Weapons upon them, which are those of Scorn and Mockery.   X

No. 390.
[STEELE.]   Wednesday, May 28.

Non pudendo sed non faciendo id quod non decet impudentiae nomen effugere debemus.—Tull.

MANY are the Epistles I receive from Ladies extremely afflicted that they lie under the Observation of scandalous People, who love to defame their Neighbours, and make the unjustest Interpretation of innocent and indifferent Actions. They describe their own Behaviour so unhappily, that there indeed lies some Cause of Suspicion upon them. It is certain, that there is no Authority for Persons who have nothing else to do, to pass away Hours of Conversation upon the Miscarriages of other People; but since they will do so, they who value their Reputation should be cautious of Appearances to their Disadvantage. But very often our young Women, as well as the middle-aged and the gay Part of those growing old, without entring into a formal League for that Purpose, to a Woman, agree upon a short Way to preserve their Characters, and go on in a Way that at best is only not vicious. The Method is, when an ill-natur'd or talkative Girl has said any thing that bears hard upon some Part of another's Carriage, this Creature, if not in any of their little Cabals, is run down for the most censorious dangerous Body in the World. Thus they guard their Reputation rather than their Modesty; as if Guilt lay in being under the Imputation of a Fault, and not in a Commission of it. *Orbicilla* is the kindest poor Thing in the Town, but the most blushing Creature living: It is true she has not lost the Sense of Shame, but she has lost the Sense of Innocence. If she had more Confidence, and never did any thing which ought to stain her Cheeks, would she not be much more modest without that ambiguous Suffusion, which is the Livery both of Guilt and Innocence? Modesty consists in being conscious of no Ill, and not in being ashamed of having done it. When People go upon any other Foundation than the Truth of their own Hearts for the Conduct of their Actions, it lies in the Power of scandalous Tongues to carry the World before them, and make the rest of Mankind fall in with the Ill for fear of Reproach. On the other Hand, to do what you ought, is the ready way to make Calumny either silent, or ineffectually malicious. *Spencer*, in his *Fairy Queen*, says admirably to young Ladies under the Distress of being defamed:

> *The best, said he, that I can you advise,*
> *Is to avoid th' Occasion of the Ill;*
> *For when the Cause, whence Evil doth arise,*
> *Removed is, th' Effect surceaseth still.*
> *Abstain from Pleasure, and restrain your Will;*
> *Subdue Desire, and bridle loose Delight;*
> *Use scanted Diet, and forbear your Fill;*
> *Shun Secrecy, and talk in open Sight;*
> *So shall you soon repair your present evil Plight.*

Instead of this Care over their Words and Actions, recommended by a Poet in old Queen *Bess*'s Days, the modern Way is to do and say what you please, and yet be the *prettiest sort of Woman in the World*. If Fathers and Brothers will defend a Lady's Honour, she is quite as safe as in her own Innocence. Many of the Distressed, who suffer under the Malice of evil Tongues, are so harmless that they are every Day they live asleep till Twelve at Noon; concern themselves with nothing but their own Persons till Two; take their necessary Food between that Time and Four; visit, go to the Play, and sit up at Cards till towards the ensuing Morn; and the malicious World shall draw Conclusions from innocent Glances, short Whispers, or pretty familiar Railleries with fashionable Men, that these Fair Ones are not as rigid as Vestals. It is certain, say these goodest Creatures very well, that Virtue does not consist in constrained Behaviour and wry Faces,—that must be allowed; but there is a Decency in the Aspect and Manner of Ladies contracted from an Habit of Virtue, and from general Reflections that regard a modest Conduct, all which may be understood though they cannot be described. A young Woman of this sort claims an Esteem mixed with Affection and Honour, and meets with no Defamation; or if she does, the wild Malice is overcome with an undisturbed Perseverance in her Innocence. To speak freely, there are such Coveys of Coquets about this Town, that if the Peace were not kept by some impertinent Tongues of their own Sex, which keep them under some Restraint, we should have no manner of Engagement upon them to keep them in any tolerable Order.

As I am a SPECTATOR, and behold how plainly one part of Womankind ballance the Behaviour of the other, whatever I may think of Talebearers or Slanderers, I cannot wholly suppress them no more than a General would discourage Spies. The Enemy would easily surprize him whom they knew had no Intelligence of their Motions. It is so far otherwise with me, that I acknowledge I permit a She-Slanderer or two in every Quarter of the Town, to live in the Characters of Coquets, and take all the innocent Freedoms of the rest, in order to send me Information of the Behaviour of their respective Sisterhoods.

But as the Matter of Respect to the World, which looks on, is carried on, methinks it is so very easy to be what is in the general called Virtuous, that it need not cost one Hour's Reflection in a Month to preserve that Appellation. It is pleasant to hear the pretty Rogues talk of Virtue and Vice among each other: She is the lazyest Creature in the World, but I must confess, strictly Virtuous: The peevishest Hussy breathing, but as to her Virtue she is without Blemish: She has not the least Charity for any of her Acquaintance, but I must allow her rigidly Virtuous. As the unthinking Part of the Male World call every Man a Man of Honour who is not a Coward; so the Crowd of the other Sex terms every Woman who will not be a Wench Virtuous.   T

No. 391.
[ADDISON.]   Thursday, May 29.

> . . . *Non tu prece poscis emaci,*
> *Quae nisi seductis nequeas committere divis.*
> *At bona pars procerum tacita libabit acerra.*
> *Haud cuivis promptum est murmurque humilesque susurros*
> *Tollere de templis & aperto vivere voto.*
> *Mens bona, fama, fides, haec clare & ut audiat hospes.*
> *Illa sibi introrsum & sub lingua murmurat: O si*
> *Ebulliat patruus, praeclarum funus! Et O si*
> *Sub rastro crepet argenti mihi seria dextro*
> *Hercule! pupillumve utinam, quem proximus heres*
> *Impello, expungam! . . .*—Pers.

WHERE *Homer* represents *Phoenix*, the Tutor of *Achilles*, as perswading his Pupil to lay aside his Resentments, and give himself up to the Entreaties of his Countrymen, the Poet, in order to make him speak in Character, ascribes to him a

Speech full of those Fables and Allegories which old Men take Delight in relating, and which are very proper for Instruction. *The Gods*, says he, *suffer themselves to be prevailed upon by Entreaties. When Mortals have offended them by their Transgressions, they appease them by Vows and Sacrifices. You must know*, Achilles, *that PRAYERS are the Daughters of* Jupiter. *They are crippled by frequent Kneeling, have their Faces full of Cares and Wrinkles, and their Eyes always cast towards Heaven. They are constant Attendants on the Goddess* ATE, *and march behind her. This Goddess walks forward with a bold and haughty Air, and being very light of Foot, runs thro' the whole Earth, grieving and afflicting the Sons of Men. She gets the Start of PRAYERS, who always follow her, in order to heal those Persons whom she Wounds. He who honours these Daughters of* Jupiter, *when they draw near to him, receives great Benefit from them; but as for him who rejects them, they intreat their Father to give his Orders to the Goddess* ATE *to punish him for his Hardness of Heart.* This noble Allegory needs but little Explanation; for whether the Goddess *ATE* signifies Injury, as some have explained it, or Guilt in general, as others, or Divine Justice, as I am the more apt to think, the interpretation is obvious enough.

I shall produce another Heathen Fable relating to Prayers, which is of a more diverting kind. One would think by some Passages in it, that it was composed by *Lucian*, or at least by some Author who has endeavoured to imitate his Way of Writing; but as Dissertations of this Nature are more curious than useful, I shall give my Reader the Fable without any further Enquiries after the Author.

Menippus *the Philosopher was a second time taken up into Heaven by* Jupiter, *when for his Entertainment he lifted up a Trap-Door that was placed by his Footstool. At its rising there issued through it such a Din of Cries as astonished the Philosopher. Upon his asking what they meant,* Jupiter *told him they were the Prayers that were sent up to him from the Earth.* Menippus, *amidst the Confusion of Voices, which was so great, that nothing less than the Ear of* Jove *could distinguish them, heard the Words,* Riches, Honour, *and* Long-Life *repeated in several different Tones and Languages. When the first Hubbub of Sounds was over, the Trap-Door being left open, the Voices came up more separate and distinct. The first Prayer was a very odd one, it came from* Athens, *and desired* Jupiter *to encrease the Wisdom and the Beard of his humble Supplicant.* Menippus *knew it by the Voice to be the Prayer of his Friend* Licander *the Philosopher. This was succeeded by the Petition of one who had just laden a Ship, and promised* Jupiter, *if he took care of it,*

*and Returned it home again full of Riches, he would make him
an offering of a Silver Cup.* Jupiter *thanked him for nothing;
and bending down his Ear more attentively than Ordinary, heard
a Voice complaining to him of the Cruelty of an* Ephesian *Widow,
and begging him to breed Compassion in her Heart. This,* says
Jupiter, *is a very honest fellow; I have received a great deal of
Incense from him; I will not be so cruel to him as not to hear his
Prayers. He was then interrupted with a whole Volly of Vows
which were made for the Health of a Tyrannical Prince by his
Subjects who prayed for him in his Presence.* Menippus *was
surprized, after having listned to Prayers offered up with so
much Ardour and Devotion, to hear low Whispers from the same
Assembly expostulating with* Jove *for suffering such a Tyrant to
live, and asking him how his Thunder could lie idle?* Jupiter
*was so offended at these prevaricating Rascals, that he took down
the first Vows, and puffed away the last. The Philosopher seeing
a great Cloud mounting upwards, and making its Way directly
to the Trap-Door, enquired of* Jupiter *what it meant. This,* says
Jupiter, *is the Smoak of a whole Hecatomb that is offered me by
the General of an Army, who is very importunate with me to let
him cut off an hundred thousand Men that are drawn up in
Array against him: What does the impudent Wretch think I see
in him, to believe that I will make a Sacrifice of so many Mortals
as good as himself, and all this to his Glory, forsooth? But hark,*
says Jupiter, *there is a Voice I never heard but in time of Danger;
'tis a Rogue that is shipwreck'd in the* Ionian *Sea: I saved him
on a Plank but three Days ago, upon his promise to mend his
Manners; the Scoundrel is not worth a Groat, and yet has the
Impudence to offer me a Temple if I will keep him from sinking.
—But yonder,* says he, *is a special Youth for you, he desires
me to take his Father, who keeps a great Estate from him, out of
the Miseries of Human Life. The old Fellow shall live till he
makes his Heart ake, I can tell him that for his Pains. This was
followed by the soft Voice of a pious Lady, desiring* Jupiter *that
she might appear amiable and charming in the Sight of her
Emperor. As the Philosopher was reflecting on this extraordinary Petition, there blew a gentle Wind through the Trap-Door,
which he at first mistook for a Gale of* Zephirs, *but afterwards found it to be a Breeze of Sighs: They smelt strong of
Flowers and Incense, and were succeeded by most passionate
Complaints of Wounds and Torments, Fires and Arrows,
Cruelty, Despair, and Death.* Menippus *fancied that such
lamentable Cries arose from some general Execution, or from
Wretches lying under the Torture; but* Jupiter *told him that they
came up to him from the Isle of* Paphos, *and that he every Day
received Complaints of the same Nature from that whimsical*

*Tribe of Mortals who are called Lovers. I am so trifled with,
says he, by this Generation of both Sexes, and find it so impossible
to please them, whether I grant or refuse their Petitions, that I
shall order a Western Wind for the Future to intercept them in
their Passage, and blow them at Random upon the Earth. The
last Petition I heard was from a very aged Man of near an hundred Years old, begging but for one Year more of Life, and then
promising to die Contented. This is the rarest old Fellow! says*
Jupiter. *He has made this Prayer to me for above Twenty
Years together. When he was but Fifty Years old, he desired
only that he might live to see his Son settled in the World; I
granted it. He then begged the same Favour for his Daughter,
and afterwards that he might see the Education of a Grandson:
When all this was brought about, he puts up a Petition that he
might live to finish a house he was building. In short, he is an
unreasonable old Cur, and never wants an Excuse; I will hear
no more of him. Upon which he flung down the Trap-Door in a
Passion, and was resolved to give no more Audiences that Day.*

Notwithstanding the Levity of this Fable, the Moral of it
very well deserves our Attention, and is the same with that
which has been inculcated by *Socrates* and *Plato*, not to mention *Juvenal* and *Persius*, who have each of them made the
finest Satyr in their whole Works upon this Subject. The
Vanity of Men's Wishes, which are the natural Prayers of the
Mind, as well as many of those Secret Devotions which they
offer to the Supreme Being, are sufficiently exposed by it.
Among other Reasons for Set Forms of Prayer, I have often
thought it a very good one, that by this means the Folly and
Extravagance of Men's Desires may be kept within due Bounds,
and not break out in absurd and ridiculous Petitions on so
great and solemn an Occasion.   I

No. 392.
[STEELE.]   Friday, May 30.

*Per ambages & ministeria deorum
Praecipitandus est liber spiritus.*—Pet.

'*To the* SPECTATOR.

The Transformation of Fidelio *into a Looking-Glass.*

I WAS lately at a Tea-Table, where some young Ladies entertained the Company with a Relation of a Coquet in the Neighbourhood, who had been discovered practising before her Glass.
To turn the Discourse, which, from being witty grew to be
malicious, the Matron of the Family took Occasion, from the

Subject, to wish that there were to be found amongst Men such faithful Monitors to dress the Mind by, as we consult to adorn the Body. She added, that if a sincere Friend were miraculously changed into a Looking-Glass, she should not be ashamed to ask its Advice very often. This whimsical Thought worked so much upon my Fancy the whole Evening, that it produced a very odd Dream.

Methought, that as I stood before my Glass, the Image of a Youth, of an open ingenuous Aspect, appeared in it; who with a small Shrill Voice spoke in the following Manner.

The Looking-Glass, you see, was heretofore a Man, even I, the unfortunate *Fidelio*. I had two Brothers whose Deformity in Shape was made up by the Clearness of their Understanding. It must be owned however, that (as it generally happens) they had each a Perverseness of Humour suitable to their Distortion of Body. The eldest, whose Belly sunk in monstrously, was a great Coward; and tho' his splenetick contracted Temper made him take Fire immediately, he made Objects that beset him appear greater than they were. The second, whose Breast swelled into a bold Relievo, on the contrary, took great Pleasure in lessening every thing, and was perfectly the Reverse of his Brother. These Oddnesses pleased Company once or twice, but disgusted when often seen: for which Reason the young Gentlemen were sent from Court, to study Mathematicks at the University.

I need not acquaint you, that I was very well made, and reckoned a bright, polite Gentleman. I was the Confident and Darling of all the Fair; and if the Old and Ugly spoke Ill of me, all the World knew it was because I scorned to flatter them. No Ball, no Assembly was attended till I had been consulted. *Flavia* colour'd her Hair before me, *Celia* shewed me her Teeth, *Panthea* heaved her Bosom, *Cleora* brandished her Diamond; I have seen *Cloe*'s Foot, and tied artificially the Garters of *Rhodope*.

'Tis a general Maxim, that those who doat upon themselves, can have no violent Affection for another: But on the contrary, I found that the Women's Passion for me rose in Proportion to the Love they bore to themselves. This was verified in my Amour with *Narcissa*, who was so constant to me, that it was pleasantly said, Had I been little enough, she would have hung me at her Girdle. The most dangerous Rival I had, was a gay empty Fellow, who by the Strength of a long Intercourse with *Narcissa*, joined to his natural Endowments, had formed himself into a perfect Resemblance with her. I had been discarded, had she not observed that he frequently asked my Opinion about Matters of the last Consequence: This made me still more considerable in her Eye.

Though I was eternally caressed by the Ladies such was their Opinion of my Honour, that I was never envied by the Men. A jealous Lover of *Narcissa* one Day thought he had caught her in an amorous Conversation; for though he was at such a Distance that he could hear nothing, he imagined strange things from her Airs and Gestures Sometimes with a serene Look she stepp'd back in a listening Posture, and brightened into an innocent Smile. Quickly after she swelled into an Air of Majesty and Disdain, then kept her Eyes half shut after a languishing manner, then covered her Blushes with her Hand, breathed a Sigh, and seemed ready to sink down. In rushed the furious Lover; but how great was his Surprize to see no one there but the innocent *Fidelio*, with his Back against the Wall betwixt two Windows.

It were endless to recount all my Adventures. Let me hasten to that which cost me my Life, and *Narcissa* her Happiness.

She had the Misfortune to have the Small-Pox, upon which I was expresly forbid her Sight; it being apprehended that it would encrease her Distemper, and that I should infallibly catch it at the first Look. As soon as she was suffered to leave her Bed, she stole out of her Chamber, and found me all alone in an adjoining Apartment. She ran with Transport to her Darling, and without Mixture of Fear, lest I should dislike her. But, oh me; What was her Fury when she heard me say, I was afraid and shock'd at so loathsome a Spectacle. She stepp'd back, swollen with Rage, to see if I had the Insolence to repeat it. I did with this Addition, that her ill-timed Passion had increased her Ugliness. Enraged, Inflamed, distracted, she snatched a Bodkin, and with all her Force stabb'd me to the Heart. Dying I preserved my Sincerity, and express'd the Truth, tho' in broken Words; and by reproachful Grimaces to the last I mimick'd the Deformity of my Murderess.

Cupid, who always attends the Fair, and pity'd the Fate of so useful a Servant as I was, obtained of the *Destinies*, that my Body should be made incorruptible, and retain the Qualities my Mind had possessed. I immediately lost the Figure of Man, and became smooth, polished and bright, and to this Day am the first Favourite of the Ladies.' T

No. 393.
[ADDISON.] Saturday, May 31.

Nescio qua praeter solitum dulcedine laeti.—Virg.

LOOKING over the Letters that have been sent me, I chanced to find the following one, which I received about two Years ago from an ingenious Friend, who was then in *Denmark*.

'*Dear Sir*,   *Copenhagen, May* 1, 1710.

The Spring with you has already taken Possession of the
Fields and Woods: Now is the Season of Solitude, and of
moving Complaints upon trivial Sufferings: Now the Griefs of
Lovers begin to flow, and their Wounds to bleed afresh. I
too, at this distance from the softer Climates, am not without
my Discontents at present. You, perhaps, may laugh at me
for a most Romantick Wretch, when I have disclosed to you
the Occasion of my Uneasiness; and yet I cannot help thinking
my Unhappiness real, in being confined to a Region, which is
the very Reverse of *Paradise*. The Seasons here are all of
them unpleasant, and the Country quite destitute of Rural
Charms. I have not heard a Bird sing, nor a Brook murmur,
nor a Breeze whisper, neither have I been blest with the Sight
of a flow'ry Meadow these two Years. Every Wind here is a
Tempest, and every Water a turbulent Ocean. I hope, when
you reflect a little, you will not think the Grounds of my Complaint in the least frivolous and unbecoming a Man of serious
Thought; since the Love of Woods, of Fields and Flowers, of
Rivers and Fountains, seems to be a Passion implanted in our
Natures the most early of any, even before the fair Sex had a
Being.

I am, Sir, &c.'

Could I transport my self with a wish from one Country to
another, I should chuse to pass my Winter in *Spain*, my Spring
in *Italy*, my Summer in *England*, and my Autumn in *France*.
Of all these Seasons there is none that can vie with the Spring
for Beauty and Delightfulness. It bears the same Figure
among the Seasons of the Year, that the Morning does among
the Divisions of the Day, or Youth among the Stages of Life.
The *English* Summer is pleasanter than that of any other
Country in *Europe*, on no other Account but because it has a
greater Mixture of Spring in it. The Mildness of our Climate,
with those frequent Refreshments of Dews and Rains that fall
among us, keep up a perpetual Chearfulness in our Fields, and
fill the hottest Months of the Year with a lively Verdure.

In the opening of the Spring, when all Nature begins to
recover her self, the same animal Pleasure which makes the
Birds sing, and the whole brute Creation rejoyce, rises very
sensibly in the Heart of Man. I know none of the Poets who
have observed so well as *Milton* those secret Overflowings of
Gladness which diffuse themselves through the Mind of the
Beholder, upon surveying the gay Scenes of Nature; he has
touch'd upon it twice or thrice in his *Paradise Lost*, and describes it very beautifully under the Name of Vernal Delight,

in that Passage where he represents the Devil himself as almost
sensible of it.

> *Blossoms and Fruits at once of golden hue*
> *Appear'd, with gay enamel'd colours mixt;*
> *On which the Sun more glad impress'd his Beams*
> *Than in fair evening Cloud, or humid Bow,*
> *When God hath shower'd the Earth; so lovely seem'd*
> *That Landskip: And of pure now purer Air*
> *Meets his approach, and to the Heart inspires*
> *Vernal delight, and Joy able to drive*
> *All sadness but despair, &c.*

Many Authors have written on the Vanity of the Creature,
and represented the Barrenness of every thing in this World,
and its Incapacity of producing any solid or substantial Happiness. As Discourses of this Nature are very useful to the
Sensual and Voluptuous, those Speculations which shew the
bright Side of things, and lay forth those innocent Entertainments which are to be met with among the several Objects
that encompass us, are no less beneficial to Men of dark and
melancholy Tempers. It was for this Reason that I endeavoured to recommend a Chearfulness of Mind in my two last
Saturday's Papers, and which I would still inculcate, not only
from the Consideration of our selves, and of that Being on
whom we depend, nor from the general Survey of that Universe
in which we are placed at present, but from Reflections on the
particular Season in which this Paper is written. The Creation
is a perpetual Feast to the Mind of a good Man, every thing
he sees chears and delights him; Providence has imprinted so
many Smiles on Nature, that it is impossible for a Mind which
is not sunk in more gross and sensual Delights to take a Survey
of them without several secret Sensations of Pleasure. The
Psalmist has in several of his divine Poems celebrated those
beautiful and agreeable Scenes which make the Heart glad,
and produce in it that vernal Delight which I have before
taken Notice of.

Natural Philosophy quickens this Taste of the Creation, and
renders it not only pleasing to the Imagination, but to the
Understanding. It does not rest in the Murmur of Brooks,
and the Melody of Birds, in the Shade of Groves and Woods,
or in the Embroidery of Fields and Meadows, but considers
the several Ends of Providence which are served by them, and
the Wonders of Divine Wisdom which appear in them. It
heightens the Pleasures of the Eye, and raises such a rational
Admiration in the Soul as is little inferior to Devotion.

It is not in the Power of every one to offer up this kind of
Worship to the great Author of Nature, and to indulge these

more refined Meditations of Heart, which are doubtless highly acceptable in his Sight; I shall therefore conclude this short Essay on that Pleasure which the Mind naturally conceives from the present Season of the Year, by the recommending of a Practice for which every one has sufficient Abilities.

I would have my Readers endeavour to moralize this natural Pleasure of the Soul, and to improve this vernal Delight, as *Milton* calls it, into a Christian Virtue. When we find our selves inspired with this pleasing Instinct, this secret Satisfaction and Complacency, arising from the Beauties of the Creation, let us consider to whom we stand indebted for all these Entertainments of Sense, and who it is that thus opens his Hand and fills the World with Good. The Apostle instructs us to take Advantage of our present Temper of Mind, to graft upon it such a religious Exercise as is particularly conformable to it, by that Precept which advises those who are sad to pray, and those who are merry to sing Psalms. The Chearfulness of Heart which springs up in us from the Survey of Nature's Works, is an admirable Preparation for gratitude. The Mind has gone a great way towards Praise and Thanksgiving that is filled with a secret Gladness: A grateful Reflection on the supreme Cause who produces it, sanctifies it in the Soul, and gives it its proper Value. Such an habitual Disposition of Mind consecrates every Field and Wood, turns an ordinary Walk into a morning or evening Sacrifice, and will improve those transient Gleams of Joy, which naturally brighten up and refresh the Soul on such Occasions, into an inviolable and perpetual State of Bliss and Happiness.   I

No. 394.

[STEELE.]   Monday, June 2.

Bene colligitur haec pueris & mulierculis & servis & servorum simillimis liberis esse grata. Gravi vero homini & ea quae fiunt judicio certo ponderanti probari posse nullo modo.—Tull.

I HAVE been considering the little and frivolous things which give Men Accesses to one another, and Power with each other, not only in the common and indifferent Accidents of Life, but also in Matters of greater Importance. You see in Elections for Members to sit in Parliament, how far saluting Rows of old Women, drinking with Clowns, and being upon a Level with the lowest Part of Mankind in that wherein they themselves are lowest, their Diversions, will carry a Candidate. A Capacity for prostituting a Man's self in his Behaviour, and descending to the present Humour of the Vulgar, is perhaps as good an Ingredient as any other for making a considerable Figure in the World; and if a Man has nothing else, or better, to think of, he could not make his way to Wealth and Distinction by properer Methods, than studying the particular Bent or Inclination of People with whom he converses, and working from the Observation of such their Biass in all Matters wherein he has any Intercourse with them: For his Ease and Comfort he may assure himself, he need not be at the Expence of any great Talent or Virtue to please even those who are possessed of the highest Qualifications. Pride in some particular Disguise or other, (often a secret to the Proud Man himself) is the most ordinary Spring of Action among Men. You need no more than to discover what a Man values himself for; then of all things admire that Quality, but be sure to be failing in it your self in Comparison of the Man whom you court. I have heard, or read, of a Secretary of State in *Spain*, who served a Prince who was happy in an elegant use of the *Latin* Tongue, and often writ Dispatches in it with his own Hand. The King shewed his Secretary a Letter he had written to a foreign Prince, and under the Colour of asking his Advice, laid a Trap for his Applause. The honest Man read it as a faithful Counsellor, and not only excepted against his tying himself down too much by some Expressions, but mended the Phrase in others. You may guess the Dispatches that Evening did not take much longer Time. Mr. Secretary, as soon as he came to his own House, sent for his eldest Son, and communicated to him that the Family must retire out of *Spain* as soon as possible; for, said he, the King knows I understand *Latin* better than he does.

This egregious Fault in a Man of the World should be a Lesson to all who would make their Fortunes; But a Regard must be carefully had to the Person with whom you have to do; for it is not to be doubted but a great Man of common Sense must look with secret Indignation, or bridled Laughter, on all the Slaves who stand round him with ready Faces to approve and smile at all he says in the Gross. It is good Comedy enough to observe a Superior talking half Sentences, and playing an humble Admirer's Countenance from one thing to another, with such Perplexity that he knows not what to sneer in Approbation of. But this kind of Complaisance is peculiarly the Manner of Courts; in all other Places you must constantly go farther in Compliance with the Persons you have to do with, than a meer Conformity of Looks and Gestures. If you are in a Country-Life, and would be a leading Man, a good Stomach, a loud Voice, and a rustick Chearfulness will go a great way, provided you are able to drink, and drink any thing.

But I was just now going to draw the Manner of Behaviour I would advise People to practise under some Maxim, and intimated, that every one almost was governed by his Pride. There was an old Fellow about forty Years ago so peevish and fretful, tho' a Man of Business, that no one could come at him: But he frequented a particular little Coffee-house, where he triumphed over every Body at Trick-track and Baggammon. The way to pass his Office well, was first to be insulted by him at one of those Games in his leisure Hours; for his Vanity was to shew, that he was a Man of Pleasure as well as Business. Next to this sort of Insinuation, which is called in all Places (from its taking its Birth in the Housholds of Princes) making one's Court, the most prevailing way is, by what better bred People call a Present, the Vulgar a Bribe.   I humbly conceive that such a thing is conveyed with more Gallantry in a *Billet-doux* that should be understood at the *Bank*, than in gross Money: But as to stubborn People, who are so surly as to accept of Neither Note or Cash, having formerly dabbled in Chymistry, I can only say that one Part of Matter asks one thing, and another another, to make it fluent; but there is nothing but may be dissolved by a proper Mean: Thus the Virtue which is too obdurate for Gold or Paper, shall melt away very kindly in a Liquid.   The Island of *Barbadoes* (a shrewd People) manage all their Appeals to *Great Britain*, by a skilful Distribution of Citron-Water among the Whisperers about Men in Power.   Generous Wines do every Day prevail, and that in great Points where ten thousand times their Value would have been rejected with Indignation.

But to wave the Enumeration of the sundry ways of applying by Presents, Bribes, Management of People's Passions and Affections, in such a Manner as it shall appear that the Virtue of the best Man is by one Method or other corruptible; let us look out for some Expedient to turn those Passions and Affections on the Side of Truth and Honour.   When a Man has laid it down for a Position, that parting with his Integrity, in the minutest Circumstance, is losing so much of his very Self, Self-Love will become a Virtue.   By this means Good and Evil will be the only Objects of Dislike and Approbation; and he that injures any Man, has effectually wounded the Man of this Turn as much as if the Harm had been to himself.   This seems to be the only Expedient to arrive at an Impartiality; and a Man who follows the Dictates of Truth and right Reason, may by Artifice be led into Error, but never can into Guilt.
T

The End of the Fifth Volume.

TO THE RIGHT HONOURABLE

CHARLES EARL OF *SUNDERLAND.*

My LORD,

VERY many Favours and Civilities (received from You in a private Capacity) which I have no other Way to acknowledge, will, I hope, excuse this Presumption; but the Justice I, as a *Spectator*, owe your Character, places me above the want of an Excuse. Candor and Openness of Heart, which shine in all your Words and Actions, exact the highest Esteem from all who have the Honour to know You, and a winning Condescension to all subordinate to You, made Business a Pleasure to those who executed it under You, at the same time that it heightened Her Majesty's Favour to all who had the Happiness of having it convey'd through your Hands: A Secretary of State, in the Interests of Mankind, joined with that of his Fellow-Subjects, accomplish'd with a great Facility and Elegance in all the Modern as well as Ancient Languages, was a happy and proper Member of a Ministry, by whose Services your Sovereign and Country are in so high and flourishing a Condition, as makes all other Princes and Potentates powerful or inconsiderable in *Europe*, as they are Friends or Enemies to *Great-Britain*. The Importance of those great Events which happened during that Administration, in which Your Lordship bore so important a Charge, will be acknowledg'd as long as Time shall endure; I shall not therefore attempt to rehearse those Illustrious Passages, but give this Application a more private and particular Turn, in desiring your Lordship would continue your Favour and Patronage to me, as You are a Gentleman of the most polite Literature, and perfectly accomplished in the Knowledge of Books and Men, which makes it necessary to beseech your Indulgence to the following Leaves, and the Author of them: Who is, with the greatest Truth and Respect.

> *My Lord,*
>
> > *Your Lordship's*
> >
> > > *Oblig'd, Obedient, and*
> > >
> > > > *Humble Servant,*
> > > >
> > > > > *THE SPECTATOR.*

THE SPECTATOR.

VOL. VI.

No. 395.

[BUDGELL.] Tuesday, June 3, 1712.

> . . . *Quod nunc ratio est, impetus ante fuit.*—Ovid.

Beware of the Ides of March, said the *Roman* Augur to *Julius Caesar: Beware of the Month of* May, says the *British Spectator* to his fair Countrywomen. The Caution of the first was unhappily neglected, and *Caesar's* Confidence cost him his Life: I am apt to flatter my self that my pretty Readers had much more Regard to the Advice I gave them, since I have yet received very few Accounts of any notorious Trips made in the last Month.

But tho' I hope for the best, I shall not pronounce too positively on this Point, 'till I have seen forty Weeks well over, at which Period of Time, as my good Friend Sir ROGER has often told me, he has more Business as a Justice of Peace, among the dissolute young People in the Country, than at any other Season of the Year.

Neither must I forget a Letter which I received near a fortnight since from a Lady, who, it seems, could hold out no longer, telling me she looked upon the Month as then out, for that she had all along reckoned by the New Stile.

On the other hand, I have great Reason to believe, from several angry Letters which have been sent to me by disappointed Lovers, that my Advice has been of very signal Service to the fair Sex, who, according to the old Proverb, were *Forewarn'd forearm'd*.

One of these Gentlemen tells me, that he would have given me an hundred Pounds, rather than I should have publish'd that Paper; for that his Mistress, who had promised to explain her self to him about the beginning of *May*, upon reading that Discourse told him that *she would give him her Answer in* June.

Thyrsis acquaints me, that when he desir'd *Sylvia* to take a Walk in the Fields, she told him *the* Spectator *had forbidden her*.

Another of my Correspondents, who writes himself *Mat. Meager*, complains, that whereas he constantly used to Breakfast with his Mistress upon Chocolate, going to wait upon her the first of *May* he found his usual Treat very much changed for the worse, and has been forced to feed ever since upon Green Tea.

As I begun this Critical Season with a Caveat to the Ladies, I shall conclude it with a Congratulation, and do most heartily wish them Joy of their happy Deliverance.

They may now reflect with Pleasure on the Dangers they have escaped, and look back with as much Satisfaction on the Perils that threatned them, as their Great grandmothers did formerly on the burning Ploughshares, after having passed through the Ordeal Tryal. The Instigations of the Spring are now abated. The Nightingale gives over her *Love-labour'd Song*, as *Milton* phrases it, the Blossoms are fallen, and the Beds of Flowers swept away by the Scythe of the Mower.

I shall now allow my Fair Readers to return to their Romances and Chocolate, provided they make use of them with Moderation, 'till about the middle of the Month, when the Sun shall have made some Progress in the *Crab*. Nothing is more dangerous, than too much Confidence and Security. The *Trojans*, who stood upon their Guard all the while the *Grecians* lay before their City, when they fancied the Siege was raised, and the Danger past, were the very next Night burnt in their Beds. I must also observe, that as in some Climates there is a perpetual *Spring*, so in some Female Constitutions there is a perpetual *May*: These are a kind of *Valetudinarians* in Chastity, whom I would continue in a constant Diet. I cannot think these wholly out of Danger, 'till they have looked upon the other Sex at least Five Years through a Pair of Spectacles. WILL. HONEYCOMB has often assured me, that 'tis much easier to steal one of this Species, when she is passed her grand Climacterick, than to carry off an *icy* Girl on this side Five and Twenty; and that a Rake of his Acquaintance, who had in vain endeavoured to gain the Affections of a young Lady of Fifteen, had at last made his Fortune by running away with her Grandmother.

But as I do not design this Speculation for the *Evergreens* of the Sex, I shall again apply my self to those who would willingly listen to the Dictates of Reason and Virtue, and can now hear me in cold Blood. If there are any who have forfeited their Innocence, they must now consider themselves under that Melancholy View, in which *Chamont* regards his Sister, in those beautiful Lines,

> . . . *Long she flourish'd,*
> *Grew sweet to Sense, and lovely to the Eye,*
> *'Till at the last a cruel Spoiler came,*
> *Cropt this fair Rose, and rifled all its Sweetness,*
> *Then cast it like a loathsome Weed away.*

On the contrary, she who has observed the timely Cautions I gave her, and lived up to the Rules of Modesty, will now Flourish like *a Rose in* June, with all her Virgin Blushes and Sweetness about her: I must, however, desire these last to consider, how shameful it would be for a General, who has made a successful Campaign, to be surprised in his Winter-Quarters: It would be no less dishonourable for a Lady to lose, in any other Month of the Year, what she has been at the Pains to preserve in *May*.

There is no Charm in the Female Sex, that can supply the Place of Virtue. Without Innocence Beauty is unlovely, and Quality contemptible, Good breeding degenerates into Wantonness, and Wit into Impudence. It is observed, that all the Virtues are represented by both Painters and Statuaries, under Female Shapes; but if any one of them has a more particular Title to that Sex, it is Modesty. I shall leave it to the Divines to guard them against the opposite Vice, as they may be overpowered by Temptations; It is sufficient for me to have warned them against it, as they may be led astray by Instinct.

I desire this Paper may be read with more than ordinary Attention, at all Tea-tables within the Cities of London *and* Westminster.   X

No. 396.
[STEELE.]   Wednesday, June 4.

Barbara, Celarent, Darii, Ferio, Baralipton.

HAVING a great deal of Business upon my Hands at present, I shall beg the Reader's Leave to present him with a Letter that I received about half a Year ago from a Gentleman of *Cambridge*, who stiles himself *Peter de Quir*. I have kept it by me some Months, and though I did not know at first what to make of it, upon my reading it over very frequently I have at last discovered several Conceits in it: I would not therefore have my Reader discouraged if he does not take them at the first Perusal.

              '*To Mr.* SPECTATOR.

From St. John's *College*, Cambridge, *Feb.* 3, **1712**.

    Sir,

The Monopoly of Punns in this University has been an immemorial Privilege of the *Johnians*; and we can't help resenting the late Invasion of our ancient Right as to that Particular, by a little Pretender to Clenching in a neighbouring

College, who in an Application to you by way of Letter, awhile
ago, stiled himself *Philobrune.* Dear Sir, as you are by
Character a profest Well-wisher to Speculation, you will excuse
a Remark which this Gentleman's Passion for the *Brunette*
has suggested to a Brother Theorist; 'tis an Offer towards a
mechanical Account of his Lapse to Punning, for he belongs
to a Set of Mortals, who value themselves upon an uncommon
Mastery in the more humane and polite Part of Letters. A
Conquest by one of this Species of Females gives a very odd
Turn to the Intellectuals of the captivated Person, and very
different from that Way of thinking which a Triumph from the
Eyes of another more emphatically of the fair Sex, does
generally occasion. It fills the Imagination with an Assemblage of such Ideas and Pictures as are hardly any thing but
Shade, such as Night, the Devil, &c. These Portraitures very
near over-power the Light of the Understanding, almost be-
night the Faculties, and give that melancholy Tincture to the
most sanguine Complexion, which this Gentleman calls an
Inclination to be in a Brown-study, and is usually attended
with worse Consequences, in case of a Repulse. During this
Twilight of Intellects, the Patient is extremely apt, as Love is
the most witty Passion in Nature, to offer at some pert Sallies
now and then, by way of Flourish, upon the amiable Enchant-
ress, and unfortunately stumbles upon that Mongrel mis-
created (to speak in *Miltonic*) kind of Wit, vulgarly termed,
the Punn. It would not be much amiss to consult Dr. *T——
W——* (who is certainly a very able Projector, and whose
System of Divinity and Spiritual Mechanicks obtains very
much among the better Part of our Under-Graduates) whether
a general Inter-marriage, enjoined by Parliament, between
this Sisterhood of the Olive Beauties, and the Fraternity of
the People called Quakers, would not be a very serviceable
Expedient, and abate that Overflow of Light which shines
within them so powerfully, that it dazzles their Eyes, and
dances them into a thousand Vagaries of Error and Enthusiasm. These Reflexions may impart some Light towards a
Discovery of the Origin of Punning among us, and the Foundation of its prevailing so long in this famous Body. 'Tis
notorious from the Instance under Consideration, that it must
be owing chiefly to the use of brown Juggs, muddy Belch, and
the Fumes of a certain memorable Place of Rendezvous with
us at Meals, known by the Name of *Staincoat Hole.* For the
Atmosphere of the Kitchen, like the Tail of a Comet, pre-
dominates least about the Fire, but resides behind, and
fills the fragrant Receptacle above-mentioned. Besides, 'tis
farther observable, that the delicate Spirits among us, who

declare against these nauseous Proceedings, sip Tea, and put up for Critic and Amour, profess likewise an equal Abhorrence for Punning, the ancient innocent Diversion of this Society. After all, Sir, tho' it may appear something absurd, that I seem to approach you with the Air of an Advocate for Punning, (you who have justified your Censures of the Practice in a set Dissertation upon that Subject) yet, I 'm confident, you 'll think it abundantly attoned for by observing, that this humbler Exercise may be as instrumental in diverting us from any innovating Schemes and Hypothesis in Wit, as dwelling upon honest Orthodox Logic would be in securing us from Heresie in Religion. Had Mr. *W——n*'s Researches been confin'd within the Bounds of *Ramus* or *Crackanthorp*, that learned Newsmonger might have acquiesc'd in what the holy Oracles pronounced upon the Deluge like other Christians; and had the surprising Mr. *L——y* been content with the Employment of refining upon *Shakespear*'s Points and Quibbles, (for which he must be allowed to have a superlative Genius) and now and then penning a Catch or a Ditty, instead of inditing Odes, and Sonnets, the Gentlemen of the *Bon Goust* in the Pit would never have been put to all that Grimace in damning the Frippery of State, the Poverty and Languor of Thought, the unnatural Wit, and inartificial Structure of his Dramas.

> *I am, Sir,*
> *Your very humble Servant,*
> Peter de Quir.'

No. 397.

[ADDISON.]   Thursday, June 5.

> . . . *Dolor ipse disertum*
> *Fecerat* . . .—Ovid.

As the *Stoick* Philosophers discard all Passions in general, they will not allow a Wise Man so much as to pity the Afflictions of another. If thou seest thy Friend in Trouble, says *Epictetus*, thou may'st put on a Look of Sorrow, and condole with him, but take care that thy Sorrow be not real. The more rigid of this Sect would not comply so far as to shew even such an outward Appearance of Grief; but when one told them of any Calamity that had befallen even the nearest of their Acquaintance, would immediately reply, What is that to me? If you aggravated the Circumstances of the Affliction, and shewed how one Misfortune was follow'd by another, the Answer was still, All this may be true, but what is it to me?

For my own part, I am of Opinion, Compassion does not only refine and civilize Human Nature, but has something in it more pleasing and agreeable than what can be met with in such an indolent Happiness, such an Indifference to Mankind as that in which the *Stoicks* placed their Wisdom.   As Love is the most delightful Passion, Pity is nothing else but Love softned by a degree of Sorrow: in short, it is a kind of pleasing Anguish, as well as generous Sympathy, that knits Mankind together, and blends them in the same common Lot.

Those who have laid down Rules for Rhetorick or Poetry, advise the Writer to work himself up, if possible, to the pitch of Sorrow which he endeavours to produce in others.   There are none therefore who stir up Pity so much as those who indite their own Sufferings.   Grief has a natural Eloquence belonging to it, and breaks out in more moving Sentiments than can be supplied by the finest Imagination.   Nature on this Occasion dictates a thousand Passionate things which cannot be supplied by Art.

It is for this Reason that the short Speeches or Sentences which we often meet with in Histories, make a deeper Impression on the Mind of the Reader, than the most laboured Strokes in a well written Tragedy.   Truth and Matter of Fact sets the Person actually before us in the one, whom Faction places at a greater Distance from us in the other.   I do not remember to have seen any Ancient or Modern Story more affecting than a Letter of *Ann* of *Bologne*, Wife to King *Henry* the Eighth, and Mother to Queen *Elizabeth*, which is still extant in the *Cotton* Library, as written by her own Hand.

Shakespear himself could not have made her talk in a Strain so suitable to her Condition and Character.   One sees in it the Expostulations of a slighted Lover, the Resentments of an injured Woman, and the Sorrows of an imprisoned Queen.   I need not acquaint my Reader that this Princess was then under Prosecution for Disloyalty to the King's Bed, and that she was afterwards publickly beheaded upon the same Account, though this Prosecution was believed by many to proceed, as she herself intimates, rather from the King's Love to *Jane Seymour*, than from any actual Crime in *Ann* of *Bologne*.

　　　'*Queen* Ann Boleyn*'s last Letter to King* Henry.
　　　　Sir,

Cotton Lib.　　Your Grace's Displeasure, and my Imprison-
Otho C. 10.　　ment, are things so strange unto me, as what to write, or what to excuse, I am altogether ignorant.   Whereas you send unto me (willing me to confess a Truth, and so obtain your Favour) by such an one, whom you know to be mine ancient professed Enemy, I no sooner receiv'd this Message by him, than I rightly conceived your Meaning; and if, as you

say, confessing a Truth indeed may procure my Safety, I shall with all Willingness and Duty perform your Command.

But let not your Grace ever imagine, that your poor Wife will ever be brought to acknowledge a Fault, where not so much as a Thought thereof preceded. And to speak a Truth, never Prince had Wife more Loyal in all Duty, and in all true Affection, than you have ever found in *Anne Boleyn*; with which Name and Place I could willingly have contented my self, if God and your Grace's Pleasure had been so pleased. Neither did I at any time so far forget my self in my Exaltation, or received Queenship, but that I always looked for such an Alteration as now I find; for the Ground of my Preferment being on no surer Foundation than your Grace's Fancy, the least Alteration I knew was fit and sufficient to draw that Fancy to some other Subject. You have chosen me, from a low Estate, to be your Queen and Companion, far beyond my Desert or Desire. If then you found me worthy of such Honour, good your Grace let not any light Fancy, or bad Counsel of mine Enemies, withdraw your Princely Favour from me; neither let that Stain, that unworthy Stain, of a Disloyal Heart towards your good Grace, ever cast so foul a Blot on your most Dutiful Wife, and the Infant-Princess your Daughter. Try me, good King, but let me have a lawful Tryal, and let not my sworn Enemies sit as my Accusers and Judges; Yea let me receive an open Tryal, for my Truth shall fear no open Shame; then shall you see either mine Innocency cleared, your Suspicion and Conscience satisfied, the Ignominy and Slander of the World stopped, or my Guilt openly declared. So that whatsoever God or you may determine of me, your Grace may be freed from an open Censure, and mine Offence being so lawfully proved, your Grace is at Liberty, both before God and Man, not only to execute worthy Punishment on me as an unlawful Wife, but to follow your Affection, already settled on that Party, for whose sake I am now as I am, whose Name I could some good while since have pointed unto, your Grace being not ignorant of my Suspicion therein.

But if you have already determined of me, and that not only my Death, but an Infamous Slander must bring you the enjoying of your desired Happiness; then I desire of God, that he will pardon your great Sin therein, and likewise mine Enemies, the Instruments thereof; and that he will not call you to a strict Account for your unprincely and cruel Usage of me, at his general Judgment Seat, where both you and myself must shortly appear, and in whose Judgment I doubt not (whatsoever the World may think of me) mine Innocence shall be openly known, and sufficiently cleared.

My last and only Request shall be, that my self may only bear the Burthen of your Grace's Displeasure, and that it may not touch the innocent Souls of those poor Gentlemen, who (as I understand) are likewise in strait Imprisonment for my sake. If ever I have found Favour in your Sight, if ever the Name of *Ann Boleyn* hath been pleasing in your Eyes, then let me obtain this Request, and I will so leave to trouble your Grace any further, with mine earnest Prayers to the Trinity to have your Grace in his good Keeping, and to direct you in all your Actions. From my doleful Prison in the *Tower*, this sixth of *May*;

> *Your most Loyal*
> *and ever Faithful Wife,*

L   Ann Boleyn.'

No. 398.
[STEELE.]   Friday, **June 6**.

Insanire paret certa ratione modoque.—Hor.

Cynthio and *Flavia* are Persons of Distinction in this Town, who have been Lovers these ten Months last past, and writ to each other for Gallantry sake, under those feigned Names; Mr. Such a one and Mrs. Such a one not being capable of raising the Soul out of the ordinary Tracts and Passages of Life, up to that Elevation which makes the Life of the En-amoured so much superior to that of the rest of the World. But ever since the beauteous *Cecilia* has made such a Figure as she now does in the Circle of charming Women, *Cynthio* has been secretly one of her Adorers. *Laetitia* has been the finest Woman in Town these three Months, and so long *Cynthio* has acted the Part of a Lover very aukwardly in the Presence of *Flavia*. *Flavia* has been too blind towards him, and has too sincere an Heart of her own to observe a thousand things which would have discovered this Change of Mind to any one less engaged than she was. *Cynthio* was musing Yesterday in the Piazza in *Covent Garden*, and was saying to himself that he was a very ill Man to go on in visiting and professing Love to *Flavia*, when his Heart was enthralled to another. It is an Infirmity that I am not constant to *Flavia*; but it would be still a greater Crime, since I cannot continue to love her, to profess that I do. To marry a Woman with the Coldness that usually indeed comes on after Marriage, is ruining one's self with one's Eyes open; besides it is really doing her an Injury. This last Consideration, forsooth, of injuring her in persisting, made him resolve to break off upon the first favourable

Opportunity of making her angry. When he was in this Thought, he saw *Robin* the Porter, who waits at *Will*'s Coffeehouse, passing by. *Robin,* you must know, is the best Man in Town for carrying a Billet; the Fellow has a thin Body, swift Step, demure Looks, sufficient Sense, and knows the Town. This Man carry'd *Cynthio*'s first Letter to *Flavia,* and by frequent Errands ever since, is well known to her. The Fellow covers his Knowledge of the Nature of his Messages with the most exquisite low Humour imaginable: The first he obliged *Flavia* to take, was by complaining to her that he had a Wife and three Children, and if she did not take that Letter, which, he was sure, there was no Harm in, but rather Love, his Family must go supperless to Bed, for the Gentleman would pay him according as he did his Business. *Robin* therefore *Cynthio* now thought fit to make use of, and gave him Orders to wait before *Flavia*'s Door, and if she called him to her, and asked whether it was *Cynthio* who passed by, he should at first be loth to own it was, but upon Importunity confess it. There needed not much Search into that Part of the Town to find a well-dressed Hussey fit for the Purpose *Cynthio* designed her. As soon as he believed *Robin* was posted, he drove by *Flavia*'s Lodgings in an Hackney-Coach and a Woman in it. *Robin* was at the Door talking with *Flavia*'s Maid, and *Cynthio* pull'd up the Glass as surprized, and hid his Associate. The Report of this Circumstance soon flew up Stairs, and *Robin* could not deny but the Gentleman favoured his Master; yet if it was he, he was sure the Lady was but his Cousin whom he had seen ask for him; adding that he believed she was a poor Relation, because they made her wait one Morning till he was awake. *Flavia* immediately writ the following Epistle, which *Robin* brought to *Will*'s.

'*Sir,*   *June* 4, 1712.

It is in vain to deny it, basest, falsest of Mankind; my maid, as well as the Bearer, saw you.

The injured Flavia.'

After *Cynthio* had read the Letter, he asked *Robin* how she looked, and what she said at the Delivery of it. *Robin* said she spoke short to him, and called him back again, and had nothing to say to him, and bid him and all the Men in the World go out of her Sight; but the Maid followed, and bid him bring an Answer.

Cynthio returned as follows.

'*Madam,*   *June* 4, *Three Afternoon,* 1712.

That your Maid and the Bearer has seen me very often is

very certain; but I desire to know, being engaged at Picket, what your Letter means by *'tis in vain to deny it.* I shall stay here all the Evening.

Your amazed Cynthio.'

As soon as *Robin* arrived with this, *Flavia* answered:

'*Dear* Cynthio,

I have walked a Turn or two in my Anti-chamber since I writ to you, and have recovered my self from an impertinent Fit which you ought to forgive me; and desire you would come to me immediately to laugh off a Jealousie that you and a Creature of the Town went by in a Hackney-Coach an Hour ago.

I am your most humble Servant,

FLAVIA.

I will not open the Letter which my *Cynthio* writ, upon the Misapprehension you must have been under when you writ for want of hearing the whole Circumstance.'

Robin came back in an Instant, and *Cynthio* answered;

Half an Hour, six Minutes after Three,

'*Madam,*   June 4, Will's *Coffee-House.*

It is certain I went by your Lodging with a Gentlewoman to whom I have the Honour to be known; she is indeed my Relation, and a pretty sort of Woman. But your starting Manner of Writing, and owning you have not done me the Honour so much as to open my Letter, has in it something very unaccountable, and alarms one that has had Thoughts of passing his Days with you. But I am born to admire you with all your little Imperfections.

CYNTHIO.'

Robin run back, and brought for Answer;

'Exact Sir, that are at *Will's* Coffee-House six Minutes after Three, *June* 4; one that has had Thoughts, and all my little Imperfections. Sir, come to me immediately, or I shall determine what may perhaps not be very pleasing to you.

FLAVIA.'

Robin gave an Account that she looked excessive angry when she gave him the Letter; and that he told her, for she asked, that *Cynthio* only looked at the Clock, taking Snuff, and writ two or three Words to the Top of the Letter when he gave him his.

Now the Plot thickened so well, as that *Cynthio* saw he had not much more to do to accomplish being irreconcileably banished, he writ,

'*Madam,*

I have that Prejudice in Favour of all you do, that it is not possible for you to determine upon what will not be very pleasing to,

Your Obedient Servant,
CYNTHIO.'

This was delivered, and the Answer returned, in a little more than two Seconds.

'*Sir,*

Is it come to this? You never loved me; and the Creature you were with is the properest Person for your Associate. I despise you, and hope I shall soon hate you as a Villain to

The Credulous Flavia.'

Robin ran back, with

'*Madam,*

Your Credulity when you are to gain your Point, and Suspicion when you fear to lose it, make it a very hard Part to behave as becomes

Your humble Slave,
CYNTHIO.'

Robin whipt away, and returned with,

'Mr. *Wellford,*

Flavia and *Cynthio* are no more. I relieve you from the hard Part of which you complain, and banish you from my Sight for ever.

Ann Heart.'

Robin had a Crown for his Afternoon's Work; and this is published to admonish *Cecilia* to avenge the Injury done to *Flavia.*   T

No. 399.
[ADDISON.]   Saturday, June 7.

Ut nemo in sese tentat descendere!—Pers.

HYPOCRISIE at the fashionable End of the Town, is very different from Hypocrisie in the City. The modish Hypocrite endeavours to appear more Vicious than he really is, the other kind of Hypocrite more Virtuous. The former is afraid of every thing that has the Shew of Religion in it, and would be thought engaged in many Criminal Gallantries and Amours, which he is not guilty of. The latter assumes a Face of Sanctity, and covers a Multitude of Vices under a seeming Religious Deportment.

But there is another kind of Hypocrisie, which differs from both these, and which I intend to make the Subject of this Paper: I mean that Hypocrisie, by which a Man does not only deceive the World, but very often imposes on himself; That Hypocrisie, which conceals his own Heart from him, and makes him believe he is more virtuous than he really is, and either not attend to his Vices, or mistake even his Vices for Virtues. It is this fatal Hypocrisie and Self-deceit, which is taken notice of in those Words, *Who can understand his Errours? cleanse thou me from secret Faults.*

If the open Professors of Impiety deserve the utmost Application and Endeavours of Moral Writers to recover them from Vice and Folly, how much more may those lay a Claim to their Care and Compassion, who are walking in the Paths of Death, while they fancy themselves engaged in a Course of Virtue! I shall endeavour, therefore, to lay down some Rules for the Discovery of those Vices that lurk in the secret Corners of the Soul, and to shew my Reader those Methods by which he may arrive at a true and impartial Knowledge of himself. The usual Means prescribed for this Purpose, are to examine our selves by the Rules which are laid down for our Direction in Sacred Writ, and to compare our Lives with the Life of that Person who acted up to the Perfection of Human Nature, and is the standing Example, as well as the great Guide and Instructor, of those who receive his Doctrines. Though these two Heads cannot be too much insisted upon, I shall but just mention them, since they have been handled by many Great and Eminent Writers.

I would therefore propose the following Methods to the Consideration of such as would find out their secret Faults, and make a true Estimate of themselves.

In the first Place, let them consider well what are the Characters which they bear among their Enemies. Our Friends very often flatter us, as much as our own Hearts. They either do not see our Faults, or conceal them from us, or soften them by their Representations, after such a manner, that we think them too trivial to be taken notice of. An Adversary, on the contrary, makes a stricter Search into us, discovers every Flaw and Imperfection in our Tempers, and though his Malice may set them in too strong a Light, it has generally some Ground for what it advances. A Friend exaggerates a Man's Virtues, an Enemy inflames his Crimes. A Wise Man should give a just Attention to both of them, so far as they may tend to the Improvement of the one, and the Diminution of the other. *Plutarch* has written an Essay on the Benefits which a Man may receive from his Enemies, and, among the good Fruits of Enmity, mentions this in particular, that by the Reproaches which it casts upon us we see the worst side of our selves, and open our Eyes to several Blemishes and Defects in our Lives and Conversations, which we should not have observed, without the help of such ill-natured Monitors.

In order likewise to come at a true Knowledge of our selves, we should consider, on the other hand, how far we may deserve the Praises and Approbations which the World bestow upon us; whether the Actions they celebrate proceed from laudable and worthy Motives, and how far we are really possessed of the Virtues which gain us Applause among those with whom we converse. Such a Reflection is absolutely necessary, if we consider how apt we are either to value or condemn our selves by the Opinions of others, and to sacrifice the Report of our own Hearts to the Judgment of the World.

In the next place, that we may not deceive our selves in a Point of so much Importance, we should not lay too great a Stress on any supposed Virtues we possess that are of a doubtful Nature: And such we may esteem all those in which Multitudes of Men dissent from us, who are as good and wise as our selves. We should always act with great Cautiousness and Circumspection in Points where it is not impossible that we may be deceived. Intemperate Zeal, Bigotry and Persecution for any Party or Opinion, how praise-worthy soever they may appear to weak Men of our own Principles, produce infinite Calamities among Mankind, and are highly Criminal in their own Nature; and yet how many Persons eminent for Piety suffer such monstrous and absurd Principles of Action to take Root in their minds under the Colour of Virtues? For my own part, I must own I never yet knew any Party so just and reasonable, that a Man could follow it in its Height and Violence, and at the same time be innocent.

We should likewise be very apprehensive of those Actions which proceed from natural Constitution, favourite Passions, particular Education, or whatever promotes our worldly Interest or Advantage. In these and the like Cases, a Man's Judgment is easily perverted, and a wrong Bias hung upon his Mind. These are the Inlets of Prejudice, the unguarded Avenues of the Mind, by which a thousand Errors and secret Faults find Admission, without being observed or taken Notice of. A wise Man will suspect those Actions to which he is directed by something besides Reason, and always apprehend some concealed Evil in every Resolution that is of a disputable Nature, when it is conformable to his particular Temper, his Age, or Way of Life, or when it favours his Pleasure or his Profit.

There is nothing of greater Importance to us than thus diligently to fit our Thoughts, and examine all these dark Recesses of the Mind, if we would establish our Souls in such a solid and substantial Virtue, as will turn to Account in that great Day, when it must stand the Test of infinite Wisdom and Justice.

I shall conclude this Essay with observing, that the two kinds of Hypocrisie I have here spoken of, namely that of deceiving the World, and that of imposing on our selves, are touched with wonderful Beauty in the hundred and thirty ninth Psalm. The Folly of the first kind of Hypocrisie is there set forth by Reflections on God's Omniscience and Omnipresence, which are celebrated in as noble Strains of Poetry as any other I ever met with, either Sacred or Prophane. The other kind of Hypocrisie, whereby a Man deceives himself, is intimated in the two last Verses, where the Psalmist addresses himself to the great Searcher of Hearts in that emphatical Petition; *Try me, O God, and seek the ground of my Heart: prove me, and examine my Thoughts. Look well if there be any way of wickedness in me, and lead me in the way everlasting.*

L

No. 400.
[STEELE.]   Monday, June 9.

. . . *Latet anguis in herba.*—Virg.

It should, methinks, preserve Modesty and its Interests in the World, that the Transgression of it always creates Offence; and the very Purposes of Wantonness are defeated by a Carriage which has in it so much Boldness, as to intimate that Fear and Reluctance are quite extinguished in an Object which would be otherwise desirable. It was said of a Wit of the last Age,

> Sidley *has that prevailing gentle Art,*
> *Which can with a resistless Charm impart*
> *The loosest Wishes to the chastest Heart;*
> *Raise such a Conflict, kindle such a Fire,*
> *Between declining Virtue and Desire,*
> *That the poor vanquish'd Maid dissolves away*
> *In Dreams all Night, in Sighs and Tears all Day.*

This prevailing gentle Art was made up of Complaisance, Courtship, and artful Conformity to the Modesty of a Woman's Manners. Rusticity, broad Expression, and forward Obtrusion, offend those of Education, and make the Transgressors odious to all who have Merit enough to attract Regard. It is in this Taste that the Scenary is so beautifully ordered in the

Description which *Antony* makes, in the Dialogue between him
and *Dolabella*, of *Cleopatra* in her Barge.

> *Her Galley down the Silver* Cydnos *row'd;*
> *The Tackling Silk, the Streamers wav'd with Gold;*
> *The Gentle Winds were lodg'd in purple Sails;*
> *Her Nymphs, like Nereids, round her Couch were **plac'd**,*
> *Where she, another Sea-born Venus, lay.*
> *She lay, and lean'd her Cheek upon her Hand,*
> *And cast a Look so languishingly sweet,*
> *As if, secure of all Beholders' Hearts,*
> *Neglecting she could take them.　Boys like* Cupids
> *Stood fanning with their painted Wings the Winds*
> *That play'd about her Face; but if she smil'd,*
> *A darting Glory seem'd to blaze abroad,*
> *That Men's desiring Eyes were never weary'd,*
> *But hung upon the Object.　To soft Flutes*
> *The silver Oars kept Time; and while they **play'd**,*
> *The Hearing gave new Pleasure to the Sight,*
> *And both to Thought.　. . .*

Here the Imagination is warmed with all the Objects pre-
sented, and yet there is nothing that is luscious, or what raises
any Idea more loose than that of a beautiful Woman set off to
Advantage.　The like, or a more delicate and careful Spirit of
Modesty, appears in the following Passage in one of Mr.
Philips's Pastorals.

> *Breathe soft ye Winds, ye Waters gently flow,*
> *Shield her ye Trees, ye Flowers around her grow,*
> *Ye Swains, I beg you, pass in Silence by,*
> *My Love in yonder Vale asleep does lie.*

Desire is corrected when there is a Tenderness or Admiration
expressed which partakes the Passion.　Licentious Language
has something brutal in it, which disgraces Humanity, and
leaves us in the Condition of the Savages in the Field.　But it
may be asked to what good Use can tend a Discourse of this
Kind at all?　It is to alarm chaste Ears against such as have
what is above called the prevailing gentle Art.　Masters of
that Talent are capable of cloathing their Thoughts in so soft
a Dress, and something so Distant from the secret Purpose of
their Heart, that the Imagination of the Unguarded is touched
with a Fondness which grows too insensibly to be resisted.
Much Care and Concern for the Lady's Welfare, to seem afraid
lest she should be annoyed by the very Air which surrounds
her, and this uttered rather with kind Looks, and expressed
by an Interjection, an Ah, or an Oh, at some little Hazard in
moving or making a Step, than in any direct Profession of
Love, are the Methods of skilful Admirers.　They are honest

Arts when their Purpose is such, but infamous when misapplied. It is certain that many a young Woman in this Town has had her Heart irrecoverably won, by Men who have not made one Advance which ties their Admirers, tho' the Females languish with the utmost Anxiety. I have often, by way of Admonition to my female Readers, given them Warning against agreeable Company of the other Sex, except they are well acquainted with their Characters. Women may disguise it if they think fit, and the more to do it, they may be angry at me for saying it; but I say it is natural to them, that they have no Manner of Approbation of Men, without some Degree of Love: For this Reason he is dangerous to be entertained as a Friend or Visitant, who is capable of gaining any eminent Esteem or Observation, though it be never so remote from Pretentions as a Lover. If a Man's Heart has not the Abhorrence of any treacherous Design, he may easily improve Approbation into Kindness, and Kindness into Passion. There may possibly be no Manner of Love between them in the Eyes of all their Acquaintance; no, it is all Friendship; and yet they may be as fond as Shepherd and Shepherdess in a Pastoral, but still the Nymph and the Swain may be to each other no other, I warrant you, than *Pylades* and *Orestes*.

> *When* Lucy *decks with Flowers her swelling **Breast**,*
> *And on her Elbow leans, dissembling Rest;*
> *Unable to refrain my madding Mind,*
> *Nor Sleep nor Pasture worth my Care I find.*
> *Once* Delia *slept, on easie Moss reclin'd,*
> *Her lovely Limbs half bare, and rude the **Wind**;*
> *I smooth'd her Coats, and stole a silent Kiss:*
> *Condemn me, Shepherds, if I did amiss.*

Such good Offices as these, and such friendly Thoughts and Concerns for one another, are what make up the Amity, as they call it, between Man and Woman.

It is the Permission of such Intercourse, that makes a young Woman come to the Arms of her Husband, after the Disappointment of four or five Passions which she has successfully had for different Men, before she is prudentially given to him for whom she has neither Love nor Friendship: For what should a poor Creature do that has lost all her Friends? There 's *Marinet* the Agreeable, has, to my Knowledge, had a Friendship for Lord *Welford*, which had like to break her Heart; then she had so great a Friendship for Collonel *Hardy*, that she could not endure any Woman else should do any thing but rail at him. Many and fatal have been Disasters between Friends who have fallen out, and their Resentments are more keen than ever those of other Men can possibly be: But in this it happens unfortunately, that as there ought to be nothing concealed from one Friend to another, the Friends of different Sexes very often find fatal Effects from their Unanimity.

For my part, who study to pass Life in as much Innocence and Tranquillity as I can, I shun the Company of agreeable Women as much as possible; and must confess that I have, though a tolerable good Philosopher, but a low Opinion of Platonick Love: for which Reason I thought it necessary to give my fair Readers a Caution against it, having, to my great Concern, observed the Waste of a Platonist lately swell to a Roundness which is inconsistent with that Philosophy.   T

No. 401.

[BUDGELL.]   Tuesday, June 10.

> *In amore haec omnia insunt vitia: injuriae,*
> *Suspiciones, inimicitiae, induciae,*
> *Bellum, pax rursum. . . .*—Ter.

I SHALL publish for the Entertainment of this Day, an odd sort of a Packet, which I have just received from one of my Female Correspondents.

' *Mr.* SPECTATOR,

Since you have often confess'd that you are not displeased your Paper should sometimes convey the Complaints of distressed Lovers to each other, I am in Hopes you will favour one who gives you an undoubted Instance of her Reformation, and at the same time a Convincing Proof of the happy Influence your Labours have had over the most Incorrigible Part of the most Incorrigible Sex.   You must know, Sir, I am one of that Species of Women, whom you have often Characteriz'd under the Name of *Jilts,* and that I send you these Lines as well to do publick Penance for having so long continued in a known Error, as to beg Pardon of the Party offended.   I the rather chuse this way, because it in some measure answers the Terms on which he intimated the Breach between us might possibly be made up, as you will see by the Letter he sent me the next Day after I had discarded him; which I thought fit to send you a Copy of, that you might the better know the whole Case.

I must further acquaint you, that before I Jilted him, there had been the greatest Intimacy between us for a Year and half together, during all which time I cherished his Hopes, and indulged his Flame.   I leave you to guess after this what must be his Surprise, when upon his pressing for my full Consent one Day, I told him I wondered what could make him fancy he had ever any Place in my Affections.   His own Sex allow him

Sense, and all ours Good-breeding. His Person is such as might, without Vanity, make him believe himself not incapable to be beloved. Our Fortunes indeed, weighed in the nice Scale of Interest, are not exactly equal, which by the way was the true Cause of my Jilting him, and I had the Assurance to acquaint him with the following Maxim, That I should always believe that Man's Passion to be the most Violent, who could offer me the largest Settlement. I have since changed my Opinion, and have endeavoured to let him know so much by several Letters, but the barbarous Man has refused them all; so that I have no way left of writing to him but by your Assistance. If we can bring him about once more, I promise to send you all Gloves and Favours, and shall desire the Favour of Sir ROGER and your self to stand as God-fathers to my first Boy.

> *I am, Sir,*
>> *Your most Obedient most Humble Servant,*
>>> *AMORET.*

"Philander *to* Amoret.

Madam,

I am so surprised at the Question you were pleased to ask me Yesterday, that I am still at loss what to say to it. At least my Answer would be too long to trouble you with, as it would come from a Person, who, it seems, is so very indifferent to you. Instead of it, I shall only recommend to your Consideration the Opinion of one whose Sentiments on these matters I have often heard you say are extremely just. *A generous and constant Passion,* says your favourite Author, *in an agreeable Lover, where there is not too great a Disparity in their Circumstances, is the greatest Blessing that can befal a Person beloved; and if over-look'd in one, may perhaps never be found in another.*

I do not, however, at all despair of being very shortly much better beloved by you than *Antenor* is at present; since whenever my Fortune shall exceed his, you were pleased to intimate your Passion would increase accordingly.

The World has seen me shamefully lose that Time to please a fickle Woman, which might have been employed much more to my Credit and Advantage in other Pursuits. I shall therefore take the Liberty to acquaint you, however harsh it may be found in a Lady's Ears, that tho' your Love-Fit should happen to return, unless you could contrive a way to make your Recantation as well known to the Publick, as they are already apprised of the manner with which you have treated me, you shall never more see

> *PHILANDER.*"

"Amoret *to* Philander.

Sir,

Upon Reflection, I find the Injury I have done both to you and my self to be so great, that though the Part I now act may appear contrary to that Decorum usually observed by our Sex, yet I purposely break through all Rules, that my Repentance may in some measure equal my Crime. I assure you that in my present Hopes of recovering you, I look upon *Antenor*'s Estate with Contempt. The Fop was here Yesterday in a gilt Chariot and new Liveries, but I refused to see him. Tho' I dread to meet your Eyes after what has pass'd, I flatter my self, that amidst all their Confusion you will discover such a Tenderness in mine, as none can imitate but those who Love. I shall be all this month at Lady *D*——'s in the Country; but the Woods, the Fields and Gardens, without *Philander*, afford no Pleasures to the unhappy

AMORET."

I must desire you, dear Mr. *Spectator*, to publish this my Letter to *Philander* as soon as possible, and to assure him that I know nothing at all of the Death of his rich Uncle in *Gloucestershire.'*   X

No. 402.
[STEELE.]   Wednesday, June 11.

. . . *quae*
. . . *sibi tradit spectator.* . . .—Hor.

WERE I to publish all the Advertisements I receive from different Hands, and Persons of different Circumstances and Quality, the very Mention of them, without Reflexions on the several Subjects, would raise all the Passions which can be felt by human Mind. As Instances of this, I shall give you two or three Letters; the Writers of which can have no Recourse to any legal Power for Redress, and seem to have written rather to vent their Sorrow than to receive Consolation.

'*Mr.* SPECTATOR,

I am a young Woman of Beauty and Quality, and suitably married to a Gentleman who doates on me: But this Person of mine is the Object of an unjust Passion in a Nobleman who is very intimate with my Husband. This Friendship gives him very easie Access, and frequent Opportunities of entertaining me apart. My Heart is in the utmost Anguish, and my Face is covered over with Confusion, when I impart to you another Circumstance, which is, that my Mother, the most mercenary of all Women, is gained by this false Friend of my Husband to solicit me for him. I am frequently chid by the poor believing Man my Husband, for shewing an Impatience of his Friend's Company; and I am never alone with my Mother, but she tells me Stories of the discretionary Part of the World, and such a one, and such a one who are guilty of as much as she advises me to. She laughs at my Astonishment; and seems to hint to me, that as virtuous as she has always appeared, I am not the Daughter of her Husband. It is possible that printing this Letter may relieve me from the unnatural Importunity of my Mother, and the perfidious Courtship of my Husband's Friend. I have an unfeigned Love of Virtue, and am resolved to preserve my Innocence. The only Way I can think of to avoid the fatal Consequences of the Discovery of this Matter, is to fly away for ever; which I must do to avoid my Husband's fatal Resentment against the Man who attempts to abuse him, and the Shame of exposing a Parent to Infamy. The Persons concerned will know these Circumstances relate to 'em; and though the Regard to Virtue is dead in them, I have some Hopes from their Fear of Shame upon reading this in your Paper; which I conjure you to do if you have any Compassion for injured Virtue.

SYLVIA.'

'*Mr.* Spectator,

I am the Husband of a Woman of Merit, but am fallen in Love, as they call it, with a Lady of her Acquaintance, who is going to be married to a Gentleman who deserves her. I am in a Trust relating to this Lady's Fortune, which makes my Concurrence in this Matter necessary; but I have so irresistible a Rage and Envy rise in me when I consider his future Happiness, that against all Reason, Equity, and common Justice, I am ever playing mean Tricks to suspend the Nuptials. I have no manner of Hopes for my self; *Emilia*, for so I'll call her, is a Woman of the most strict Virtue; her Lover is a Gentleman who of all others I could wish my Friend; but Envy and Jealousie, though placed so unjustly, waste my very Being, and with the Torment and Sense of a Demon, I am ever cursing what I cannot but approve. I wish it were the Beginning of Repentance, that I sit down and describe my present Disposition with so hellish an Aspect; but at present the Destruction of these two excellent Persons would be more welcome to me than their Happiness. Mr. Spectator, pray let me have a Paper on these terrible groundless Sufferings, and do all you can to exorcise Crowds who are in some Degree possessed as I am.

Canniball.'

'*Mr.* SPECTATOR,

I have no other Means but this to express my Thanks to one Man, and my Resentment against another. My Circumstances are as follows. I have been for five Years last past courted by a Gentleman of greater Fortune than I ought to expect, as the Market for Women goes. You must to be sure have observed People who live in that sort of Way, as all their Friends reckon it will be a Match, and are marked out by all the World for each other. In this View we have been regarded for some Time, and I have above these three Years loved him tenderly. As he is very careful of his Fortune, I always thought he lived in a near Manner to lay up what he thought was wanting in my Fortune to make up what he might expect in another. Within few Months I have observed his Carriage very much altered, and he has affected a certain Art of getting me alone, and talking with a mighty Profusion of passionate Words, How I am not to be resisted longer, how irresistible his Wishes are, and the like. As long as I have been acquainted with him, I could not on such Occasions say downright to him, You know you may make me yours when you please. But the other Night he with great Frankness and Impudence explained to me, that he thought of me only as a Mistress. I answered this Declaration as it deserv'd; upon which he only doubled the Terms on which he proposed my Yielding. When my Anger heightned upon him, he told me he was sorry he had made so little Use of the unguarded Hours we had been together so remote from Company, as indeed, continued he, so we are at present. I flew from him to a neighbouring Gentlewoman's House, and tho' her Husband was in the Room, threw my self on a Couch, and burst into a Passion of Tears. My Friend desired her Husband to leave the Room: but, said he, there is something so extraordinary in this, that I will partake in the Affliction; and be it what it will, she is so much your Friend, that she knows she may command what Services I can do her. The Man sate down by me, and spoke so like a Brother, that I told him my whole Affliction. He spoke of the Injury done me with so much Indignation, and animated me against the Love he said he saw I had for the Wretch who would have betrayed me, with so much Reason and Humanity to my Weakness, that I doubt not of my Perseverance. His Wife and he are my Comforters, and I am under no more Restraint in their Company than if I were alone;

and I doubt not but in a small time Contempt and Hatred will take place of the Remains of Affection to a Rascal.

> *I am, Sir,*
>
> *Your affectionate Reader,*
>
> DORINDA.'

'*Mr.* SPECTATOR,

I had the Misfortune to be an Uncle before I knew my Nephews from my Nieces, and now we are grown up to better Acquaintance they deny me the Respect they owe. One upbraids me with being their Familiar, another will hardly be perswaded that I am an Uncle, a third calls me Little Uncle, and a fourth tells me there is no Duty at all to an Uncle. I have a Brother-in-law whose Son will win all my Affection, unless you shall think this worthy of our Cognizance, and will be pleased to prescribe some Rules for our future reciprocal Behaviour. It will be worthy the Particularity of your Genius to lay down Rules for his Conduct who was as it were born an old Man, in which you will much oblige,

> *Sir,*
>
> *Your most obedient Servant,*
>
> Cornelius Nepos.'

No. 403.

[ADDISON.]   Thursday, June 12.

Qui mores hominum multorum vidit . . .—Hor.

WHEN I consider this great City in its several Quarters and Divisions, I look upon it as an Aggregate of various Nations distinguished from each other by their respective Customs, Manners and Interests. The Courts of two Countries do not so much differ from one another, as the Court and City in their peculiar ways of Life and Conversation. In short, the Inhabitants of St *James's*, notwithstanding they live under the same Laws, and speak the same Language, are a distinct People from those of *Cheapside*, who are likewise removed from those of the *Temple* on the one side, and those of *Smithfield* on the other, by several Climates and Degrees in their way of Thinking and Conversing together.

For this Reason, when any publick Affair is upon the Anvil, I love to hear the Reflections that arise upon it in the several Districts and Parishes of *London* and *Westminster*, and to ramble up and down a whole Day together, in order to make my self acquainted with the Opinions of my ingenious Countrymen. By this means I know the Faces of all the principal

Politicians within the Bills of Mortality; and as every Coffee-house has some particular Statesman belonging to it, who is the Mouth of the Street where he lives, I always take care to place my self near him, in order to know his Judgment on the present Posture of Affairs. The last Progress that I made with this Intention, was about three Months ago, when we had a Current Report of the King of *France*'s Death. As I foresaw this would produce a new Face of things in *Europe*, and many curious Speculations in our *British* Coffee-houses, I was very desirous to learn the Thoughts of our most eminent Politicians on this Occasion.

That I might begin as near the Fountain-head as possible, I first of all called in at St. *James*'s, where I found the whole outward Room in a Buzz of Politics. The Speculations were but very indifferent towards the Door, but grew finer as you advanced to the upper end of the Room, and were so very much improved by a Knot of Theorists, who sate in the inner Room, within the Steams of the Coffee-Pot, that I there heard the whole *Spanish* Monarchy disposed of, and all the Line of *Bourbon* provided for in less than a Quarter of an Hour.

I afterwards called in at *Giles*'s, where I saw a Board of *French* Gentlemen sitting upon the Life and Death of their *Grand Monarque*. Those among them who had espoused the Wigg Interest, very positively affirmed, that he departed this Life about a Week since, and therefore proceeded without any further Delay to the Release of their Friends on the Gallies, and to their own Re-establishment; but finding they could not agree among themselves, I proceeded on my intended Progress.

Upon my Arrival at *Jenny Man*'s, I saw an *alerte* young Fellow that cocked his Hat upon a Friend of his who entered just at the same time with my self, and accosted him after the following manner. Well *Jack*, the old Prig is dead at last. Sharp 's the Word. Now or never Boy. Up to the Walls of *Paris* directly. With several other deep Reflections of the same Nature.

I met with very little variation in the Politics between *Charing-Cross* and *Covent-Garden*. And upon my going into *Will*'s I found their Discourse was gone off from the Death of the *French* King to that of Monsieur *Boileau, Racine, Corneille*, and several other Poets, whom they regretted on this Occasion, as Persons who would have obliged the World with very noble Elegies on the Death of so great a Prince, and so eminent a Patron of Learning.

At a Coffee-house near the *Temple*, I found a couple of young Gentlemen engaged very smartly in a Dispute on the Succession to the *Spanish* Monarchy. One of them seemed to have been

retained as Advocate for the Duke of *Anjou*, the other for his
Imperial Majesty. They were both for regulating the Title to
that Kingdom by the Statute Laws of *England*; but finding
them going out of my Depth I passed forward to *Paul's*
Church-yard, where I listned with great Attention to a learned
Man, who gave the Company an Account of the deplorable
State of *France* during the Minority of the *deceased* King.

I then turned on my right Hand into *Fish-street*, where the
chief Politician of that Quarter, upon hearing the News, (after
having taken a Pipe of Tobacco, and ruminated for some time)
If, says he, the King of *France* is certainly dead, we shall have
plenty of Mackerel this Season; our Fishery will not be disturbed by Privateers, as it has been for these ten Years past.
He afterwards considered how the Death of this great Man
would affect our Pilchards, and by several other Remarks
infused a general Joy into his whole Audience.

I afterwards entered a By-Coffee-house that stood at the
upper End of a narrow Lane, where I met with a Nonjuror,
engaged very warmly with a Laceman who was the great
Support of a neighbouring Conventicle. The Matter in Debate
was, whether the *late French* King was most like *Augustus
Caesar*, or *Nero*. The Controversie was carried on with great
Heat on both sides, and as each of them looked upon me very
frequently during the Course of their Debate, I was under some
Apprehension that they would appeal to me, and therefore laid
down my Penny at the Barr, and made the best of my way to
Cheapside.

I here gazed upon the Signs for some time before I found one
to my Purpose. The first Object I met in the Coffee-room was
a Person who expressed a great Grief for the Death of the
French King; but upon his explaining himself, I found his
Sorrow did not arise from the Loss of the Monarch, but for his
having sold out of the Bank about three Days before he heard
the News of it: Upon which a Haberdasher, who was the Oracle
of the Coffee-house, and had his Circle of Admirers about him,
called several to witness that he had declared his Opinion above
a Week before, that the *French* King was certainly dead; to
which he added, that considering the late Advices we had
received from *France*, it was impossible that it could be otherwise. As he was laying these together, and dictating to his
Hearers with great Authority, there came in a Gentleman from
Garraway's, who told us that there were several Letters from
France just come in, with Advice that the King was in good
Health, and was gone out a Hunting the very Morning the Post
came away: Upon which the Haberdasher stole off his Hat that
hung upon a Wooden Pegg by him, and retired to his Shop

with great Confusion. This Intelligence put a Stop to my Travels, which I had prosecuted with much Satisfaction; not being a little pleased to hear so many different Opinions upon so great an Event, and to observe how naturally upon such a Piece of News every one is apt to consider it with a regard to his particular Interest and Advantage.   L

No. 404.
                                        Friday, June 13.

>   . . . *Non omnia possumus omnes.*—Virg.

NATURE does nothing in vain; the Creator of the Universe has appointed every thing to a certain Use and Purpose, and determin'd it to a settled Course and Sphere of Action, from which, if it in the least deviates, it becomes unfit to answer those Ends for which it was design'd. In like Manner it is in the Dispositions of Society, the civil Oeconomy is formed in a Chain as well as the natural; and in either Case the Breach but of one Link puts the whole in some Disorder. It is, I think, pretty plain, that most of the Absurdity and Ridicule we meet with in the World, is generally owing to the impertinent Affectation of excelling in Characters Men are not fit for, and for which Nature never designed them.

Every Man has one or more Qualities which may make him useful both to himself and others: Nature never fails of pointing them out, and while the Infant continues under her Guardianship, she brings him on in his Way, and then offers herself for a Guide in what remains of the Journey; if he proceeds in that Course, he can hardly miscarry: Nature makes good her Engagements; for as she never promises what she is not able to perform, so she never fails of performing what she promises. But the Misfortune is, Men despise what they may be Masters of, and affect what they are not fit for; they reckon themselves already possessed of what their Genius inclined them to, and so bend all their Ambition to excell in what is out of their Reach: Thus they destroy the Use of their natural Talents, in the same Manner as covetous Men do their Quiet and Repose; they can enjoy no Satisfaction in what they have, because of the absurd Inclination they are possessed with for what they have not.

Cleanthes had good Sense, a great Memory, and a Constitution capable of the closest Application: In a Word, there was no Profession in which *Cleanthes* might not have made a very good Figure; but this won't satisfy him, he takes up an unaccountable Fondness for the Character of a fine Gentleman; all his Thoughts are bent upon this, instead of attending a Dissection, frequenting the Courts of Justice, or studying the

Fathers. *Cleanthes* reads Plays, dances, dresses and spends his Time in Drawing-rooms, instead of being a good Lawyer, Divine, or Physician; *Cleanthes* is a downright Coxcomb, and will remain to all that knew him a contemptible Example of Talents misapplied. It is to this Affectation the World owes its whole Race of Coxcombs: Nature in her whole Drama never drew such a Part; she has sometimes made a Fool, but a Coxcomb is always of a Man's own making, by applying his Talents otherwise than Nature designed, who ever bears an high Resentment for being put out of her Course, and never fails of taking her Revenge on those that do so. Opposing her Tendency in the Application of a Man's Parts, has the same Success as declining from her Course in the Production of Vegetables, by the Assistance of Art and an hot Bed: We may possibly extort an unwilling Plant, or an untimely Sallad; but how weak, how tasteless and insipid? Just as insipid as the Poetry of *Valerio*: *Valerio* had an universal Character, was genteel, had Learning, thought justly, spoke correctly; 'twas believed there was nothing in which *Valerio* did not excell; and 'twas so far true, that there was but one; *Valerio* had no Genius for Poetry, yet he's resolved to be a Poet; he writes Verses, and takes great Pains to convince the Town, that *Valerio* is not that extraordinary Person he was taken for.

If Men would be content to graft upon Nature, and assist her Operations, what mighty Effects might we expect? *Tully* would not stand so much alone in Oratory, *Virgil* in Poetry, or *Caesar* in War. To build upon Nature, is laying the Foundation upon a Rock; every thing disposes it self into Order as it were of Course, and the whole Work is half done as soon as undertaken. *Cicero*'s Genius inclined him to Oratory, *Virgil*'s to follow the Train of the Muses; they piously obey'd the Admonition, and were rewarded. Had *Virgil* attended the Bar, his modest and ingenious Virtue would surely have made but a very indifferent Figure; and *Tully*'s declamatory Inclination would have been as useless in Poetry. Nature, if left to her self, leads us on in the best Course, but will do nothing by Compulsion and Constraint; and if we are not satisfied to go her Way, we are always the greatest Sufferers by it.

Wherever Nature designs a Production, she always disposes Seeds proper for it, which are as absolutely necessary to the Formation of any moral or intellectual Excellence, as they are to the Being and Growth of Plants; and I know not by what Fate and Folly it is, that Men are taught not to reckon him equally absurd that will write Verses in Spite of Nature, with that Gardiner that should undertake to raise a Junquil or Tulip without the Help of their respective Seeds.

As there is no good or bad Quality that does not affect both Sexes, so it is not to be imagined but the fair Sex must have suffered by an Affectation of this Nature, at least as much as the other: The ill Effect of it is in none so conspicuous as in the two opposite Characters of *Caelia* and *Iras*; *Caelia* has all the Charms of Person, together with an abundant Sweetness of Nature, but wants Wit, and has a very ill Voice; *Iras* is ugly and ungenteel, but has Wit and good Sense: If *Caelia* would be silent, her Beholders would adore her; if *Iras* would talk, her Hearers would admire her; but *Caelia*'s Tongue runs incessantly, while *Iras* gives her self silent Airs and soft Languors; so that 'tis Difficult to persuade ones self that *Caelia* has Beauty and *Iras* Wit: Each neglects her own Excellence, and is ambitious of the other's Character; *Iras* would be thought to have as much Beauty as *Caelia*, and *Caelia* as much Wit as *Iras*.

The great Misfortune of this Affectation is, that Men not only lose a good Quality, but also contract a bad one: They not only are unfit for what they were designed, but they assign themselves to what they are not fit for; and instead of making a very good Figure one Way, make a very ridiculous one another. If *Semanthe* would have been satisfied with her natural Complexion, she might still have been celebrated by the Name of the Olive Beauty; but *Semanthe* has taken up an Affectation to White and Red, and is now distinguished by the Character of the Lady that paints so well.   In a Word, could the World be reformed to the Obedience of that famed Dictate, *Follow Nature*, which the Oracle of *Delphos* pronounced to *Cicero* when he consulted what Course of Studies he should pursue, we should see almost every Man as eminent in his proper Sphere as *Tully* was in his, and should in a very short Time find Impertinence and Affectation banish'd from among the Women, and Coxcombs and false Characters from among the Men.   For my Part, I could never consider this preposterous Repugnancy to Nature any otherwise, than not only as the greatest Folly, but also one of the most heinous Crimes, since it is a direct Opposition to the Disposition of Providence, and (as *Tully* expresses it) like the Sin of the Giants, an actual Rebellion against Heaven.   Z

No. 405.
[ADDISON.]   Saturday, June 14.

Οἱ δὲ πανημέριοι μολπῇ θεὸν ἱλάσκοντο
Καλὸν ἀείδοντες παιήονα κοῦροι Ἀχαιῶν,
Μέλποντες ἑκάεργον· ὁ δὲ φρένα τέρπετ' ἀκούων.—Hom.

I AM very sorry to find, by the Opera Bills for this Day, that
we are likely to lose the greatest Performer in Dramatick
Musick that is now living, or that perhaps ever appeared upon
a Stage.   I need not acquaint my Reader, that I am speaking
of *Signior Nicolini*.   The Town is highly obliged to that Excellent Artist, for having shewn us the *Italian* Musick in its
Perfection, as well as for that generous Approbation he lately
gave to an Opera of our own Country, in which the Composer
endeavoured to do Justice to the Beauty of the Words, by
following that Noble Example, which has been set him by the
greatest Foreign Masters in that Art.

I could heartily wish there was the same Applications and
Endeavours to cultivate and improve our Church-Musick, as
have been lately bestowed on that of the Stage.   Our Composers have one very great Incitement to it: They are sure to
meet with Excellent Words, and at the same time, a wonderful
Variety of them.   There is no Passion that is not finely expressed in those parts of the inspired Writing, which are proper
for Divine Songs and Anthems.

There is a certain Coldness and Indifference in the Phrases
of our *European* Languages, when they are compared with the
Oriental Forms of Speech; and it happens very luckily, that
the *Hebrew* Idioms run into the *English* Tongue with a particular Grace and Beauty.   Our Language has received innumerable Elegancies and Improvements, from that Infusion of
Hebraism, which are derived to it out of the Poetical Passages
in Holy Writ.   They give a Force and Energy to our Expressions, warm and animate our Language, and convey our
Thoughts in more ardent and intense Phrases, than any that
are to be met with in our own Tongue.   There is something so
pathetick in this kind of Diction, that it often sets the Mind in
a Flame, and makes our Hearts burn within us.   How cold
and dead does a Prayer appear, that is composed in the most
Elegant and Polite Forms of Speech, which are natural to our
Tongue, when it is not heightned by that Solemnity of Phrase,
which may be drawn from the Sacred Writings.   It has been
said by some of the Ancients, that if the Gods were to talk with
Men, they would certainly speak in *Plato*'s Stile; but I think
we may say, with Justice, that when Mortals converse with

their Creator, they cannot do it in so proper a Stile as in that of the Holy Scriptures.

If any one wou'd judge of the Beauties of Poetry that are to be met with in the Divine Writings, and examine how kindly the *Hebrew* Manners of Speech mix and incorporate with the *English* Language; after having perused the Book of Psalms, let him read a literal Translation of *Horace* or *Pindar*. He will find in these two last such an Absurdity and Confusion of Stile with such a Comparative Poverty of Imagination, as will make him very sensible of what I have been here advancing.

Since we have therefore such a Treasury of Words, so beautiful in themselves, and so proper for the Airs of Musick, I cannot but wonder that Persons of Distinction should give so little Attention and Encouragement to that kind of Musick which would have its Foundation in Reason, and which would improve our Virtue in proportion as it raised our Delight. The Passions that are excited by ordinary Compositions generally flow from such silly and absurd Occasions, that a Man is ashamed to reflect upon them seriously; but the Fear, the Love, the Sorrow, the Indignation that are awakened in the Mind by Hymns and Anthems, make the Heart better, and proceed from such Causes as are altogether reasonable and praise-worthy. Pleasure and Duty go hand in hand, and the greater our Satisfaction is, the greater is our Religion.

Musick among those who were stiled the chosen People was a Religious Art. The Songs of *Sion*, which we have reason to believe were in high repute among the Courts of the Eastern Monarchs, were nothing else but Psalms and Pieces of Poetry that adored or celebrated the Supreme Being. The greatest Conqueror in this Holy Nation, after the manner of the old *Grecian* Lyricks, did not only compose the Words of his Divine Odes, but generally set them to Musick himself. After which, his Works, tho' they were consecrated to the Tabernacle, became the National Entertainment, as well as the Devotion of his People.

The first Original of the Drama was a Religious Worship consisting only of a Chorus, which was nothing else but an Hymn to a Deity. As Luxury and Voluptuousness prevailed over Innocence and Religion, this form of Worship degenerated into Tragedies; in which however the Chorus so far remembered its first Office, as to brand every thing that was vicious, and recommend every thing that was laudable, to intercede with Heaven for the Innocent, and to implore its Vengeance on the Criminal.

Homer and *Hesiod* intimate to us how this Art should be applied, when they represent the Muses as surrounding *Jupiter*, and warbling their Hymns about his Throne. I might shew, from innumerable Passages in Ancient Writers, not only that Vocal and Instrumental Musick were made use of in their Religious Worship, but that their most favourite Diversions were filled with Songs and Hymns to their respective Deities. Had we frequent Entertainments of this Nature among us, they would not a little purifie and exalt our Passions, give our Thoughts a proper Turn, and cherish those Divine Impulses in the Soul, which every one feels that has not stifled them by sensual and immoderate Pleasures.

Musick, when thus applied, raises noble Hints in the Mind of the Hearer, and fills it with great Conceptions. It strengthens Devotion, and advances Praise into Rapture. It lengthens out every act of Worship, and produces more lasting and permanent Impressions in the Mind, than those which accompany any transient Form of Words that are uttered in the ordinary Method of Religious Worship.   O

No. 406.

[STEELE.]   Monday, June 16.

Haec studia adolescentiam alunt, senectutem oblectant, secundas res ornant, adversis perfugium & solatium praebent, delectant domi, non impediunt foris, pernoctant nobiscum, peregrinantur, rusticantur.—Tull.

THE following Letters bear a pleasing Image of the Joys and Satisfactions of a private Life. The first is from a Gentleman to a Friend, for whom he has a very great Respect, and to whom he communicates the Satisfaction he takes in Retirement; the other is a Letter to me, occasioned by an Ode written by my *Lapland* Lover; this Correspondent is so kind as to translate another of *Scheffer's* Songs in a very agreeable Manner. I publish them together, that the Young and Old may find something in the same Paper which may be suitable to their respective Taste in Solitude; for I know no Fault in the Description of ardent Desires, provided they are honourable.

   '*Dear Sir*,

You have obliged me with a very kind Letter; by which I find you shift the Scene of your Life from the Town to the Country, and enjoy that mixt State which wise Men both delight in, and are qualified for. Methinks most of the Philosophers and Moralists have run too much into Extreams in praising entirely either Solitude or publick Life; in the former Men generally grow useless by too much Rest, and in the latter are destroyed by too much Precipitation: As Waters, lying

still, putrifie and are good for nothing; and running violently
on, do but the more Mischief in their Passage to others, and are
swallowed up and lost the sooner themselves.   Those who,
like you, make themselves useful to all States, should be like
gentle Streams, that not only glide through lonely Vales and
Forests amidst the Flocks and Shepherds, but visit populous
Towns in their Course, and are at once of Ornament and
Service to them.   But there is another sort of People who seem
designed for Solitude, those I mean who have more to hide
than to shew: As for my own Part, I am one of those of whom
Seneca says, *Tam umbratiles sunt, ut putent in turbido esse
quicquid in luce est.*   Some Men, like Pictures, are fitter for a
Corner than a full Light; and I believe such as have a natural
Bent to Solitude, are like Waters which may be forced into
Fountains, and exalted to a great Height, may make a much
nobler Figure, and a much louder Noise, but after all run more
smoothly, equally and plentifully, in their own natural Course
upon the Ground.   The Consideration of this would make me
very well contented with the Possession only of that Quiet
which *Cowley* calls the Companion of Obscurity; but who ever
has the Muses too for his Companions, can never be idle enough
to be uneasie.   Thus, Sir, you see I would flatter my self into a
good Opinion of my own Way of Living: *Plutarch* just now told
me, that 'tis in human Life as in a Game at Tables, one may
wish he had the highest Cast, but if his Chance be otherwise
he is even to play it as well as he can, and make the best of it.

> *I am,* Sir,
>> *Your most obliged*
>>> *and most humble Servant.'*

'Mr. SPECTATOR,

The Town being so well pleased with the fine Picture of
artless Love, which Nature inspired the *Laplander* to paint in
the Ode you lately printed; we were in Hopes that the ingenious Translator would have obliged it with the other also
which *Scheffer* has given us; but since he has not, a much
inferior Hand has ventured to send you this.

It is a Custom with the Northern Lovers to divert themselves with a Song, whilst they journey through the fenny
Moors to pay a Visit to their Mistresses.   This is addressed by
the Lover to his Rain-Deer, which is the Creature that in that
Country supplies the Want of Horses.   The Circumstances
which successively present themselves to him in his Way, are,
I believe you will think, naturally interwoven.   The Anxiety
of Absence, the Gloominess of the Roads, and his Resolution
of frequenting only those, since those only can carry him to

the Object of his Desires; the Dissatisfaction he expresses even at the greatest Swiftness with which he is carryed, and his joyful Surprize at an unexpected Sight of his Mistress as she is bathing, seem beautifully described in the Original.

If all those pretty Images of Rural Nature are lost in the Imitation, yet possibly you may think fit to let this supply the Place of a long Letter, when want of Leisure or Indisposition for Writing will not permit our being entertained by your own Hand. I propose such a Time, because tho' it is natural to have a Fondness for what one does one's self, yet I assure you I would not have any thing of mine displace a single Line of yours.

I.

Haste my Rain-Deer, and let us nimbly go
   Our am'rous Journey through this dreery Waste;
Haste, my Rain-Deer, still still thou art too slow,
   Impetuous Love demands the Lightning's Haste.

II.

Around us far the Rushy Moors are spread;
   Soon will the Sun withdraw his chearful Ray;
Darkling and tir'd we shall the Marshes tread,
   No Lay unsung to cheat the tedious Way.

III.

The wat'ry Length of these unjoyous Moors
   Does all the flow'ry Meadows' Pride excel;
Through these I fly to her my Soul adores;
   Ye flow'ry Meadows, empty Pride, Farewel.

IV.

Each Moment from the Charmer I 'm confin'd,
   My Breast is tortur'd with impatient Fires;
Fly my Rain-Deer, fly swifter than the Wind,
   Thy tardy Feet wing with my fierce Desires.

V.

Our pleasing Toil will then be soon o'erpaid,
   And thou, in Wonder lost, shalt view my Fair,
Admire each Feature of the lovely Maid,
   Her artless Charms, her Bloom, her sprightly Air.

VI.

But lo! with graceful Motion there she swims,
   Gently removing each ambitious Wave;
The crowding Waves transported clasp her Limbs:
   When, when, oh when, shall I such Freedoms have!

VII.

In vain, you envious Streams, so fast you flow,
To hide her from a Lover's ardent Gaze:
From every Touch ye more transparent grow,
And all reveal'd the beauteous Wanton plays.

T

No. 407.
[ADDISON.]   Tuesday, June 17.

. . . *abest facundis gratia dictis.*—Ov.

MOST Foreign Writers who have given any Character of the *English* Nation, whatever Vices they ascribe to it, allow in general, that the People are naturally Modest. It proceeds perhaps from this our National Virtue, that our Orators are observed to make use of less Gesture or Action than those of other Countries. Our Preachers stand stock-still in the Pulpit, and will not so much as move a Finger to set off the best Sermons in the World. We meet with the same speaking Statues at our Bars, and in all publick Places of Debate. Our Words flow from us in a smooth continued Stream, without those Strainings of the Voice, Motions of the Body, and Majesty of the Hand which are so much celebrated in the Orators of *Greece* and *Rome*. We can talk of Life and Death in cold Blood, and keep our Temper in a Discourse which turns upon every thing that is dear to us. Though our Zeal breaks out in the finest Tropes and Figures, it is not able to stir a Limb about us. I have heard it observed more than once by those who have seen *Italy*, that an untravelled *Englishman* cannot relish all the Beauties of *Italian* Pictures, because the Postures which are expressed in them are often such as are peculiar to that Country. One who has not seen an *Italian* in the Pulpit, will not know what to make of that noble Gesture in *Raphael's* Picture of St. *Paul* preaching at *Athens*, where the Apostle is represented as lifting up both his Arms, and pouring out the Thunder of his Rhetorick amidst an Audience of Pagan Philosophers.

It is certain that proper Gestures and vehement Exertions of the Voice cannot be too much studied by a publick Orator. They are a kind of Comment to what he utters, and enforce every thing he says, with weak Hearers, better than the strongest Argument he can make use of. They keep the Audience awake, and fix their Attention to what is delivered to them, at the same time that they shew the Speaker is in earnest, and affected himself with what he so passionately recommends to others. Violent Gesture and Vociferation naturally shake the Hearts of the Ignorant, and fill them with a kind of Religious Horror. Nothing is more frequent than to see Women weep and tremble at the Sight of a moving Preacher, though he is placed quite out of their Hearing; as in *England* we very frequently see People lulled Asleep with solid and elaborate Discourses of Piety, who would be warmed and transported out of themselves by the Bellowings and Distortions of Enthusiasm.

If Nonsense, when accompanied with such an Emotion of Voice and Body, has such an Influence on Men's Minds, what might we not expect from many of those admirable Discourses which are printed in our Tongue, were they delivered with a becoming Fervour, and with the most agreeable Graces of Voice and Gesture?

We are told, that the great *Latin* Orator very much impaired his Health by this *laterum contentio,* this Vehemence of Action, with which he used to deliver himself. The *Greek* Orator was likewise so very Famous for this Particular in Rhetorick, that one of his Antagonists, whom he had banished from *Athens,* reading over the Oration which had procured his Banishment, and seeing his friends admire it, could not forbear asking them, if they were so much affected by the bare reading of it, how much more they would have been alarmed, had they heard him actually throwing out such a Storm of Eloquence?

How cold and dead a Figure, in Comparison of these two Great Men, does an Orator often make at the *British* Bar, holding up his Head, with the most insipid Serenity, and stroking the sides of a long Wigg that reaches down to his Middle? The Truth of it is, there is often nothing more ridiculous than the Gestures of an *English* Speaker; you see some of them running their Hands into their Pockets as far as ever they can thrust them, and others looking with great Attention on a piece of Paper that has nothing written in it; you may see many a smart Rhetorician turning his Hat in his Hands, moulding it into several different Cocks, examining sometimes the Lining of it, and sometimes the Button, during the whole course of his Harangue. A deaf Man would think he was Cheapning a Beaver, when perhaps he is talking of the Fate of the *British* Nation. I remember when I was a young Man, and used to frequent *Westminster-Hall,* there was a Counsellor who never pleaded without a Piece of Pack-thread in his Hand, which he used to twist about a Thumb or a Finger, all the while he was speaking: The Waggs of those Days used to call it the Thread of his Discourse, for he was not able to utter a Word without it. One of his Clients, who was more merry than wise, stole it from him one Day in the midst of his Pleading, but he had better have let it alone, for he lost his Cause by his Jest.

I have all along acknowledged my self to be a dumb Man, and therefore may be thought a very improper Person to give Rules for Oratory; but I believe every one will agree with me in this, that we ought either to lay aside all kinds of Gesture (which seems to be very suitable to the Genius of our Nation) or at least to make use of such only as are graceful and expressive.   O

No. 408.

Wednesday, June 18.

Decet affectus animi neque se nimium erigere, nec subjacere serviliter,
  —Tull. *de Finibus.*

'Mr. SPECTATOR,

I HAVE always been a very great Lover of your Speculations, as well in Regard to the Subject, as to your Manner of Treating it. Human Nature I always thought the most useful Object of human Reason, and to make the Consideration of it pleasant and entertaining, I always thought the best Employment of human Wit: Other Parts of Philosophy may perhaps make us wiser, but this not only answers that End, but makes us better too. Hence it was that the Oracle pronounced *Socrates* the wisest of all Men living, because he judiciously made Choice of human Nature for the Object of his Thoughts; an Enquiry into which as much exceeds all other Learning, as it is of more Consequence to adjust the true Nature and Measures of Right and Wrong, than to settle the Distance of the Planets, and compute the Times of their Circumvolutions.

One good Effect that will immediately arise from a near Observation of human Nature, is, that we shall cease to wonder at those Actions which Men are used to reckon wholly unaccountable; for as nothing is produced without a Cause, so by observing the Nature and Course of the Passions, we shall be able to trace every Action from its first Conception to its Death. We shall no more admire at the Proceedings of *Cataline* or *Tiberius*, when we know the one was actuated by a cruel Jealousie, the other by a furious Ambition; for the Actions of Men follow their Passions as naturally as Light does Heat, or as any other Effect flows from its Cause; Reason must be employed in adjusting the Passions, but they must ever remain the Principles of Action.

The strange and absurd Variety that is so apparent in Men's Actions. shews plainly they can never proceed immediately from Reason; so pure a Fountain emits no such troubled Waters: They must necessarily arise from the Passions, which are to the Mind as the Winds to a Ship; they only can move it, and they too often destroy it; if fair and gentle they guide it into the Harbour; if contrary and furious they overset it in the Waves: In the same Manner is the Mind assisted or endangered by the Passions; Reason must then take the Place of Pilot, and can never fail of securing her Charge if she be not wanting to her self: The Strength of the Passions will never be accepted as an Excuse for complying with them; they were designed for Subjection, and if a Man suffers them to get the upper Hand, he then betrays the Liberty of his own Soul.

As Nature has framed the several Species of Beings as it were in a Chain, so Man seems to be placed as the middle Link between Angels and Brutes: Hence he participates both of Flesh and Spirit by an admirable Tie, which in him occasions perpetual War of Passions; and as a Man inclines to the angelick or brute Part of his Constitution, he is then denominated good or bad, virtuous, or wicked; if Love, Mercy, and Good-nature prevail, they speak him of the Angel; if Hatred, Cruelty, and Envy predominate, they declare his Kindred to the Brute. Hence it was that some of the Ancients imagined, that as Men in this Life inclined more to the Angel or the Brute, so after their Death they should transmigrate into the one or the other; and it would be no unpleasant Notion to consider the several Species of Brutes, into which we may imagine that Tyrants, Misers, the Proud, Malicious, and Ill-natured might be changed.

As a Consequence of this Original, all Passions are in all Men, but appear not in all; Constitution, Education, Custom of the Country, Reason, and the like Causes, may improve or abate the Strength of them, but still the Seeds remain, which are ever ready to sprout forth upon the least Encouragement. I have heard a Story of a good religious Man, who, having been bred with the Milk of a Goat, was very modest in Publick by a careful Reflection he made on his Actions, but he frequently had an Hour in Secret, wherein he had his Frisks and Capers; and if we had an Opportunity of examining the Retirement of the strictest Philosophers, no Doubt but we should find perpetual Returns of those Passions they so artfully conceal from the Publick. I remember *Machiavel* observes, that every State should entertain a perpetual Jealousie of its Neighbours, that so it should never be unprovided when an Emergency happens; in like Manner should the Reason be perpetually on its Guard against the Passions, and never suffer them to carry on any Design that may be destructive of its Security; yet at the same Time it must be careful, that it don't so far break their Strength as to render them contemptible, and consequently it self unguarded.

The Understanding being of its self too slow and lazy to exert it self into Action, it 's necessary it should be put in Motion by the gentle Gales of the Passions, which may preserve it from stagnating and Corruption; for they are necessary to the Health of the Mind, as the Circulation of the animal Spirits is to the Health of the Body; they keep it in Life, and Strength, and Vigour; nor is it possible for the Mind to perform its Offices without their Assistance: These Motions are given us with our Being, they are little Spirits that are born and dye with us; to some they are mild, easie, and gentle, to others wayward and unruly, yet never too strong for the Reins of Reason and the Guidance of Judgment.

We may generally observe a pretty nice Proportion between the Strength of Reason and Passion; the greatest Geniuses have commonly the strongest Affections, as, on the other hand, the weaker Understandings have generally the weaker Passions; and 'tis fit the Fury of the Coursers should not be too great for the Strength of the Charioteer.   Young Men whose Passions are not a little unruly, give small Hopes of their ever being considerable; the Fire of Youth will of Course abate, and is a Fault, if it be a Fault, that mends every Day; but surely, unless a Man has Fire in Youth, he can hardly have Warmth in Old Age.   We must therefore be very cautious, lest while we think to regulate the Passions, we should quite extinguish them, which is putting out the Light of the Soul; for to be without Passion, or to be hurried away with it, makes a Man equally blind.   The extraordinary Severity used in most of our Schools has this fatal Effect, it breaks the Spring of the Mind, and most certainly destroys more good Geniuses than it can possibly improve.   And surely 'tis a mighty Mistake that the Passions should be so intirely subdued; for little Irregularities are sometimes not only to be bore with but to be cultivated too, since they are frequently attended with the greatest Perfections.   All great Geniuses have Faults mixed with their Virtues, and resemble the flaming Bush which has Thorns amongst Lights.

Since therefore the Passions are the Principles of human Actions, we must endeavour to manage them so as to retain their Vigour, yet keep them under strict Command; we must govern them rather like free Subjects than Slaves, lest, while we intend to make them obedient, they become abject, and unfit for those great Purposes to which they were designed. For my Part I must confess I could never have any Regard to that Sect of Philosophers, who so much insisted upon an absolute Indifference and Vacancy from all Passion; for it seems to me a thing very inconsistent for a Man to divest himself of Humanity, in order to acquire Tranquillity of Mind, and to eradicate the very Principles of Action, because it 's possible they may produce ill Effects.

>   *I am, Sir,*
>   *Your affectionate Admirer,*

Z   T. B.'

No. 409.
[ADDISON.]   Thursday, June 19.

>   . . . *Musaeo contingens cuncta lepore.*—Lucr.

Gratian very often recommends *the fine Taste,* as the utmost Perfection of an accomplished Man.   As this Word arises very often in Conversation, I shall endeavour to give some Account of it, and to lay down Rules how we may know whether we are possessed of it, and how we may acquire that fine Taste of Writing, which is so much talked of among the Polite World.

Most Languages make use of this Metaphor, to express that Faculty of the Mind, which distinguishes all the most concealed Faults and nicest Perfections in Writing.   We may be sure this Metaphor would not have been so general in all Tongues, had there not been a very great Conformity between that Mental Taste, which is the Subject of this Paper, and that Sensitive Taste which gives us a Relish of every different Flavour that affects the Palate.   Accordingly we find, there are as many Degrees of Refinement in the intellectual Faculty, as in the Sense, which is marked out by this common Denomination.

I knew a Person who possessed the one in so great a Perfection, that after having tasted ten different Kinds of Tea, he would distinguish, without seeing the Colour of it, the particular Sort which was offered him; and not only so, but any two Sorts of them that were mixt together in an equal Proportion; nay, he has carried the Experiment so far, as upon tasting the Composition of three different Sorts, to name the Parcels from whence the three several Ingredients were taken.   A man of a fine Taste in Writing will discern after the same manner, not only the general Beauties and Imperfections of an Author, but discover the several Ways of thinking and expressing himself, which diversify him from all other Authors, with the several Foreign Infusions of Thought and Language, and the particular Authors from whom they were borrowed.

After having thus far explained what is generally meant by a fine Taste in Writing, and shewn the Propriety of the Metaphor which is used on this Occasion, I think I may define it to be *that Faculty of the Soul, which discerns the Beauties of an Author with Pleasure, and the Imperfections with Dislike.* If a Man would know whether he is possessed of this Faculty, I would have him read over the celebrated Works of Antiquity, which have stood the Test of so many different Ages and Countries; or those Works among the Moderns, which have the Sanction of the Politer Part of our Contemporaries. If upon the Perusal of such Writings he does not find himself delighted in an extraordinary Manner, or if, upon reading the admired Passages in such Authors, he finds a Coldness and Indifference in his Thoughts, he ought to conclude, not (as is too usual among tasteless Readers) that the Author wants those Perfections which have been admired in him, but that he himself wants the Faculty of discovering them.

He should, in the second Place, be very careful to observe, whether he tastes the distinguishing Perfections, or, if I may be allowed to call them so, the Specifick Qualities of the Author whom he peruses; whether he is particularly pleased with *Livy* for his Manner of telling a Story, with *Sallust* for his entring into those internal Principles of Action which arise from the Characters and Manners of the Persons he describes, or with *Tacitus* for his displaying those outward Motives of Safety and Interest, which give birth to the whole Series of Transactions which he relates.

He may likewise consider, how differently he is affected by the same Thought, which presents it self in a great Writer, from what he is when he finds it delivered by a Person of an ordinary Genius. For there is as much difference in apprehending a Thought cloathed in *Cicero*'s Language, and that of a common Author, as in seeing an Object by the Light of a Taper, or by the Light of the Sun.

It is very difficult to lay down Rules for the Acquirement of such a Taste as that I am here speaking of. The Faculty must in some degree be born with us, and it very often happens, that those who have other Qualities in Perfection are wholly void of this. One of the most eminent Mathematicians of the Age has assured me, that the greatest Pleasure he took in reading *Virgil*, was in examining *Aeneas* his Voyage by the Map; as I question not but many a Modern Compiler of History would be delighted with little more in that Divine Author, than the bare Matters of Fact.

But notwithstanding this Faculty must in some measure be born with us, there are several Methods for Cultivating and

Improving it, and without which it will be very uncertain, and of little use to the Person that possesses it. The most natural Method for this Purpose is to be conversant among the Writings of the most Polite Authors. A Man who has any Relish for fine Writing, either discovers new Beauties, or receives stronger Impressions from the Masterly Stroaks of a great Author every time he peruses him: Besides that he naturally wears himself into the same manner of Speaking and Thinking.

Conversation with Men of a Polite Genius is another Method for improving our Natural Taste. It is impossible for a Man of the greatest Parts to consider any thing in its whole Extent, and in all its variety of Lights. Every Man, besides those general Observations which are to be made upon an Author, forms several Reflections that are peculiar to his own manner of Thinking; so that Conversation will naturally furnish us with Hints which we did not attend to, and make us enjoy other Men's Parts and Reflections as well as our own. This is the best Reason I can give for the Observation which several have made, that Men of great Genius in the same way of Writing, seldom rise up singly, but at certain Periods of Time appear together, and in a Body; as they did at *Rome* in the Reign of *Augustus*, and in *Greece* about the Age of *Socrates*. I cannot think that *Corneille, Racine, Moliere, Boileau, la Fontaine, Bruyere, Bossu,* or the *Daciers,* would have written so well as they have done, had they not been Friends and Contemporaries.

It is likewise necessary for a Man who would form to himself a finished Taste of good Writing, to be well versed in the Works of the best *Criticks* both Ancient and Modern. I must confess that I could wish there were Authors of this Kind, who beside the Mechanical Rules which a Man of very little Taste may discourse upon, would enter into the very Spirit and Soul of fine Writing, and shew us the several Sources of that Pleasure which rises in the Mind upon the Perusal of a noble Work. Thus altho' in Poetry it be absolutely necessary that the Unities of Time, Place and Action, with other Points of the same Nature, should be thoroughly explained and understood; there is still something more essential to the Art, something that elevates and astonishes the Fancy, and gives a Greatness of Mind to the Reader, which few of the Criticks besides *Longinus* have considered.

Our general Taste in *England* is for Epigram, turns of Wit, and forced Conceits, which have no manner of Influence, either for the bettering or enlarging the Mind of him who reads them, and have been carefully avoided by the greatest Writers, both among the Ancients and Moderns. I have endeavoured in several of my Speculations to banish this *Gothic* Taste, which has taken Possession among us. I entertained the Town for a Week together with an Essay upon Wit, in which I endeavoured to detect several of those false Kinds which have been admired in the different Ages of the World; and at the same time to shew wherein the Nature of true Wit consists. I afterwards gave an Instance of the great Force which lyes in a natural Simplicity of Thought to affect the Mind of the Reader, from such vulgar Pieces as have little else besides this single Qualification to recommend them. I have likewise examined the Works of the greatest Poet which our Nation or perhaps any other has produced, and particularized most of those rational and manly Beauties which give a Value to that Divine Work. I shall next *Saturday* enter upon an Essay *on the Pleasures of the Imagination*, which, though it shall consider that Subject at large, will perhaps suggest to the Reader what it is that gives a Beauty to many Passages of the finest Writers both in Prose and Verse. As an Undertaking of this Nature is intirely new, I question not but it will be received with Candour.

O

No. 410.

Friday, June 20.

. . . *Dum foris sunt, nihil videtur mundius,*
Nec magis compositum quidquam, nec magis elegans:
Quae, cum amatore suo cum coenant, liguriunt,
Harum videre ingluviem, sordes, inopiam:
Quam inhonestae solae sint domi atque avidae cibi,
Quo pacto ex jure hesterno panem atrum vorent.
Nosse omnia haec salus est adolescentulis.—Ter.

WILL. HONEYCOMB, who disguises his present Decay by visiting the Wenches of the Town only by Way of Humour, told us, that the last rainy Night he with Sir ROGER DE COVERLY was driven into the *Temple* Cloister, whither had escaped also a Lady most exactly dressed from Head to Foot. WILL. made no Scruple to acquaint us, that she saluted him very familiarly by his Name, and turning immediately to the Knight, she said, she supposed that was his good Friend Sir ROGER DE COVERLY: Upon which nothing less could follow than Sir ROGER's Approach to Salutation, with, Madam, the same at your Service. She was dressed in a black Tabby Mantua and Petticoat, without Ribbonds; her Linnen striped Muslin, and in the whole in an agreeable Second-Mourning; decent Dresses being often affected by the Creatures of the Town, at once consulting Cheapness and the Pretension to Modesty. She went on with a familiar easie Air. Your Friend, Mr. HONEYCOMB, is a little surprised to see a Woman here alone and unattended; but I dismissed my Coach at the Gate, and tripped it down to my Council's Chambers, for Lawyers' Fees take up too much of a small disputed Joynture to admit any other Expences but meer Necessaries. Mr. HONEYCOMB begged they might have the Honour of setting her down, for Sir ROGER'S Servant was gone to call a Coach. In the Interim the Footman returned, with no Coach to be had; and there appeared nothing to be done but trusting her self with Mr. HONEYCOMB and his Friend to wait at the Tavern at the Gate for a Coach, or to be subjected to all the Impertinence she must meet with in that publick Place. Mr. HONEYCOMB being a Man of Honour determined the Choice of the first, and Sir ROGER, as the better Man, took the Lady by the Hand, leading through all the Shower, covering her with his Hat, and gallanting a familiar Acquaintance through Rows of young Fellows, who winked at *Sukey* in the State she marched off, WILL. HONEYCOMB bringing up the Rear.

Much Importunity prevailed upon the Fair one to admit of a Collation, where, after declaring she had no Stomach, and eaten a Couple of Chickens, devoured a Trusse of Sallet, and drunk a full Bottle to her Share, she sung the old Man's Wish to Sir ROGER. The Knight left the Room for some Time after Supper, and writ the following Billet, which he conveyed to *Sukey*, and *Sukey* to her Friend WILL. HONEYCOMB. WILL. has given it to Sir ANDREW FREEPORT, who read it last Night to the Club.

'*Madam,*

I am not so meer a Country-Gentleman, but I can guess at the Law-Business you had at the *Temple.* If you would go down to the Country and leave off all your Vanities but your Singing, let me know at my Lodgings in *Bow-street, Covent-Garden,* and you shall be encouraged by

Your humble Servant,

ROGER DE COVERLY.'

My good Friend could not well stand the Raillery which was rising upon him; but to put a Stop to it I delivered WILL. HONEYCOMB the following Letter, and desired him to read it to the Board.

'*Mr.* SPECTATOR,

Having seen a Translation of one of the Chapters in the *Canticles* into *English* Verse inserted among your late Papers, I have ventured to send you the 7th Chapter of the *Proverbs* in a poetical Dress. If you think it worthy appearing among your Speculations, it will be a sufficient Reward for the Trouble of

Your constant Reader,

A. B.'

My Son, th' Instruction that my Words impart,
Grave on the living Tablet of thy Heart:
And all the wholsome Precepts that I give,
Observe with strictest Reverence, and live.
    Let all thy Homage be to Wisdom paid,
Seek her Protection and implore her Aid;
That she may keep thy Soul from Harm secure,
And turn thy Footsteps from the Harlot's Door,
Who with curs'd Charms lures th' Unwary in,
And sooths with Flattery their Souls to Sin.
    Once from my Window as I cast mine Eye
On those that pass'd in giddy Numbers by,
A Youth among the foolish Youths I spy'd,
Who took not sacred Wisdom for his Guide.
    Just as the Sun withdrew his cooler Light,
And Evening soft led on the Shades of Night,
He stole in covert Twilight to his Fate,
And pass'd the Corner near the Harlot's Gate;
When, lo, a Woman comes! . . .
Loose her Attire, and such her glaring Dress,
As aptly did the Harlot's Mind express:
Subtle she is, and practis'd in the Arts,
By which the Wanton conquer heedless Hearts:
Stubborn and loud she is; she hates her Home;
Varying her Place and Form, she loves to roam;
Now she 's within, now in the Street do 's stray,
Now at each Corner stands, and waits her Prey.
The Youth she seiz'd, and laying now aside
All Modesty, the Female's justest Pride,
She said, with an Embrace, Here at my House,
Peace-offerings are, this Day I paid my Vows.
I therefore came abroad to meet my Dear,
And Lo, in happy Hour I find thee here.
    My Chamber I 've adorn'd, and o'er my Bed
Are Cov'rings of the richest Tap'stry spread;
With Linnen it is deck'd from Egypt *brought,*
And Carvings by the Curious Artist wrought;
It wants no Glad Perfume Arabia *yields*
In all her Citron Groves, and spicy Fields;
Here all her Store of richest Odours meets,

> *I 'll lay thee in a Wilderness of Sweets,*
> *Whatever to the Sense can grateful be*
> *I have collected there.—I want but Thee.*
> *My Husband's gone a Journey far away,*)
> *Much Gold he took abroad and long will stay,* }
> *He nam'd for his Return a distant Day.*)
>   *Upon her Tongue did such smooth Mischief dwell,*
> *And from her Lips such welcome Flatt'ry fell,*
> *Th' unguarded Youth, in Silken Fetters ty'd,*
> *Resign'd his Reason, and with Ease comply'd.*
> *Thus does the Ox to his own Slaughter go,*
> *And thus is senseless of th' impending Blow.*
> *Thus flies the simple Bird into the Snare,*
> *That skilful Fowlers for his Life prepare.*
> *But let my Sons attend, Attend may they*
> *Whom Youthful Vigour may to Sin betray;*
> *Let them false Charmers fly, and guard their Hearts*
> *Against the wily Wanton's pleasing Arts.*
> *With Care direct their Steps, nor turn astray*
> *To tread the Paths of her deceitful Way;*
> *Lest they too late of Her fell Power complain,*
> *And fall, where many mightier have been slain.*

T

No. 411.
[ADDISON.]
Saturday, June 21.

> *Avia Pieridum peragro loca, nullius ante*
> *Trita solo; juvat integros accedere fontes,*
> *Atque haurire* . . . Lucr.

OUR Sight is the most perfect and most delightful of all our Senses. It fills the Mind with the largest Variety of Ideas, converses with its Objects at the greatest Distance, and continues the longest in Action without being tired or satiated with its proper Enjoyments. The Sense of Feeling can indeed give us a Notion of Extension, Shape, and all other Ideas that enter at the Eye, except Colours; but at the same time it is very much streightned and confined in its Operations, to the Number, Bulk, and Distance of its particular Objects. Our Sight seems designed to supply all these Defects, and may be considered as a more delicate and diffusive kind of Touch, that spreads its self over an infinite Multitude of Bodies, comprehends the largest Figures, and brings into our reach some of the most remote Parts of the Universe.

It is this Sense which furnishes the Imagination with its

Ideas; so that by the Pleasures of the Imagination or Fancy (which I shall use promiscuously) I here mean such as arise from visible Objects, either when we have them actually in our View, or when we call up their Ideas into our Minds by Paintings, Statues, Descriptions, or any the like Occasion. We cannot indeed have a single Image in the Fancy that did not make its first Entrance through the Sight; but we have the Power of retaining, altering and compounding those Images, which we have once received, into all the Varieties of Picture and Vision that are most agreeable to the Imagination; for by this Faculty a Man in a Dungeon is capable of entertaining himself with Scenes and Landskips more beautiful than any that can be found in the whole Compass of Nature.

There are few Words in the *English* Language which are employed in a more loose and uncircumscribed Sense than those of the *Fancy* and the *Imagination*. I therefore thought it necessary to fix and determine the Notion of these two Words, as I intend to make use of them in the Thread of my following Speculations, that the Reader may conceive rightly what is the Subject which I proceed upon. I must therefore desire him to remember, that by the Pleasures of the Imagination, I mean only such Pleasures as arise originally from Sight, and that I divide these Pleasures into two Kinds: My Design being first of all to discourse of those Primary Pleasures of the Imagination, which entirely proceed from such Objects as are before our Eyes; and in the next place to speak of those Secondary Pleasures of the Imagination which flow from the Ideas of visible Objects, when the Objects are not actually before the Eye, but are called up into our Memories, or formed into agreeable Visions of Things that are either Absent or Fictitious.

The Pleasures of the Imagination, taken in the full Extent, are not so gross as those of Sense, nor so refined as those of the Understanding. The last are, indeed, more preferable, because they are founded on some new Knowledge or Improvement in the Mind of Man; yet it must be confest, that those of the Imagination are as great and as transporting as the other. A beautiful Prospect delights the Soul, as much as a Demonstration; and a Description in *Homer* has charm'd more Readers than a Chapter in *Aristotle*. Besides, the Pleasures of the Imagination have this Advantage, above those of the Understanding, that they are more obvious, and more easie to be acquired. It is but opening the Eye, and the Scene enters. The Colours paint themselves on the Fancy, with very little Attention of Thought or Application of Mind in the Beholder. We are struck, we know not how, with the Symmetry of any thing we see, and immediately assent to the Beauty of an Object, without enquiring into the particular Causes and Occasions of it.

A Man of a Polite Imagination is let into a great many Pleasures, that the Vulgar are not capable of receiving. He can converse with a Picture, and find an agreeable Companion in a Statue. He meets with a secret Refreshment in a Description, and often feels a greater Satisfaction in the Prospect of Fields and Meadows, than another does in the Possession. It gives him, indeed, a kind of Property in every thing he sees, and makes the most rude uncultivated Parts of Nature administer to his Pleasures: So that he looks upon the World, as it were, in another Light, and discovers in it a Multitude of Charms, that conceal themselves from the generality of Mankind.

There are, indeed, but very few who know how to be idle and innocent, or have a Relish of any Pleasures that are not Criminal; every Diversion they take is at the Expence of some one Virtue or another, and their very first Step out of Business is into Vice or Folly. A Man should endeavour, therefore, to make the Sphere of his innocent Pleasures as wide as possible, that he may retire into them with Safety, and find in them such a Satisfaction as a wise Man would not blush to take. Of this Nature are those of the Imagination, which do not require such a Bent of Thought as is necessary to our more serious Employments, nor, at the same Time, suffer the Mind to sink into that Negligence and Remissness, which are apt to accompany our more sensual Delights, but, like a gentle Exercise to the Faculties, awaken them from Sloth and Idleness, without putting them upon any Labour or Difficulty.

We might here add, that the Pleasures of the Fancy are more conducive to Health, than those of the Understanding, which are worked out by Dint of Thinking, and attended with too violent a Labour of the Brain. Delightful Scenes, whether in Nature, Painting, or Poetry, have a kindly Influence on the Body, as well as the Mind, and not only serve to clear and brighten the Imagination, but are able to disperse Grief and Melancholy, and to set the Animal Spirits in pleasing and agreeable Motions. For this Reason Sir *Francis Bacon*, in his Essay upon Health, has not thought it improper to prescribe to his Reader a Poem or a Prospect, where he particularly dissuades him from knotty and subtile Disquisitions, and advises him to pursue Studies that fill the Mind with splendid and illustrious Objects, as Histories, Fables, and Contemplations of Nature.

I have in this Paper, by way of Introduction, settled the

Notion of those Pleasures of the Imagination which are the
Subject of my present Undertaking, and endeavoured, by
several Considerations, to recommend to my Reader the Pursuit of those Pleasures. I shall, in my next Paper, examine
the several Sources from whence these Pleasures are derived.

O

No. 412.
[ADDISON.]   Monday, June 23.

> . . . *Divisum sic breve fiet opus.*—Mart.

I SHALL first consider those Pleasures of the Imagination,
which arise from the actual View and Survey of outward
Objects: And these, I think, all proceed from the Sight of what
is *Great, Uncommon,* or *Beautiful.* There may, indeed, be
something so terrible or offensive, that the Horrour or Loath-
someness of an Object may over-bear the Pleasure which results
from its *Greatness, Novelty* or *Beauty*; but still there will be
such a Mixture of Delight in the very Disgust it gives us, as
any of these three Qualifications are most conspicuous and
prevailing.

By *Greatness,* I do not only mean the Bulk of any single
Object, but the Largeness of a whole View, considered as one
entire Piece. Such are the Prospects of an open Champain
Country, a vast uncultivated Desart, of huge Heaps of Mountains, high Rocks and Precipices, or a wide Expanse of Waters,
where we are not struck with the Novelty or Beauty of the
Sight, but with that rude kind of Magnificence which appears
in many of these stupendous Works of Nature. Our Imagination loves to be filled with an Object, or to grasp at any
thing that is too big for its Capacity. We are flung into a
pleasing Astonishment at such unbounded Views, and feel a
delightful Stilness and Amazement in the Soul at the Apprehension of them. The Mind of Man naturally hates every thing
that looks like a Restraint upon it, and is apt to fancy it self
under a sort of Confinement, when the Sight is pent up in a
narrow Compass, and shortned on every side by the Neighbourhood of Walls or Mountains. On the contrary, a spacious
Horizon is an Image of Liberty, where the Eye has Room to
range abroad, to expatiate at large on the Immensity of its
Views, and to lose it self amidst the Variety of Objects that
offer themselves to its Observation. Such wide and undetermined Prospects are as pleasing to the Fancy, as the Speculations of Eternity or Infinitude are to the Understanding. But
if there be a Beauty or Uncommonness joined with this

Grandeur, as in a troubled Ocean, a Heaven adorned with Stars and Meteors, or a spacious Landskip cut out into Rivers, Woods, Rocks, and Meadows, the Pleasure still grows upon us, as it arises from more than a single Principle.

Every thing that is *new* or *uncommon* raises a Pleasure in the Imagination, because it fills the Soul with an agreeable Surprise, gratifies its Curiosity, and gives it an Idea of which it was not before possest. We are indeed so often conversant with one Sett of Objects, and tired out with so many repeated Shows of the same Things, that whatever is *new* or *uncommon* contributes a little to vary human Life, and to divert our Minds, for a while, with the Strangeness of its Appearance: It serves us for a Kind of Refreshment, and takes off from that Satiety we are apt to complain of in our usual and Ordinary Entertainments. It is this that bestows Charms on a Monster, and makes even the Imperfections of Nature please us. It is this that recommends Variety, where the Mind is every Instant called off to something new, and the Attention not suffered to dwell too long, and waste it self on any particular Object. It is this, likewise, that improves what is great or beautiful, and makes it afford the Mind a double Entertainment. Groves, Fields, and Meadows, are at any Season of the Year pleasant to look upon, but never so much as in the opening of the Spring, when they are all new and fresh, with their first Gloss upon them, and not yet too much accustomed and familiar to the Eye. For this Reason there is nothing that more enlivens a Prospect than Rivers, Jetteaus, or Falls of Water, where the Scene is perpetually shifting, and entertaining the Sight every Moment with something that is new. We are quickly tired with looking upon Hills and Vallies, where every thing continues fixt and settled in the same Place and Posture, but find our Thoughts a little agitated and relieved at the Sight of such Objects as are ever in Motion, and sliding away from beneath the Eye of the Beholder.

But there is nothing that makes its way more directly to the Soul than *Beauty*, which immediately diffuses a secret Satisfaction and Complacency through the Imagination, and gives a Finishing to any thing that is Great or Uncommon. The very first Discovery of it strikes the Mind with an inward Joy, and spreads a Chearfulness and Delight through all its Faculties. There is not perhaps any real Beauty or Deformity more in one piece of Matter than another, because we might have been so made, that whatsoever now appears loathsom to us, might have shewn it self agreeable; but we find by Experience, that there are several Modifications of Matter which the Mind, without any previous Consideration, pronounces at first sight

Beautiful or Deformed. Thus we see that every different Species of sensible Creatures has its different Notions of Beauty, and that each of them is most affected with the Beauties of its own Kind. This is no where more remarkable than in Birds of the same Shape and Proportion, where we often see the Male determined in his Courtship by the single Grain or Tincture of a Feather, and never discovering any Charms but in the Colour of its Species.

> *Scit thalamo servare fidem, sanctasque veretur*
> *Connubii leges; non illum in pectore candor*
> *Sollicitat niveus; neque pravum accendit amorem*
> *Splendida lanugo, vel honesta in vertice crista,*
> *Purpureusve nitor pennarum; ast agmina late*
> *Foeminea explorat cautus, maculasque requirit*
> *Cognatas, paribusque interlita corpora guttis:*
> *Ni faceret, pictis sylvam circum undique monstris*
> *Confusam aspiceres vulgo, partusque biformes,*
> *Et genus ambiguum, & veneris monumenta nefandae,*
> *Hinc merula in nigro se oblectat nigra marito,*
> *Hinc socium lasciva petit philomela canorum,*
> *Agnoscitque pares sonitus, hinc noctua tetram*
> *Canitiem alarum, & glaucos miratur ocellos.*
> *Nempe sibi semper constat, crescitque quotannis*
> *Lucida progenies, castos confessa parentes;*
> *Dum virides inter saltus lucosque sonoros*
> *Vere novo exultat, plumasque decora juventus*
> *Explicat ad solem, patriisque coloribus ardet.*

There is a second Kind of *Beauty* that we find in the several Products of Art and Nature, which does not work in the Imagination with that Warmth and Violence as the Beauty that appears in our proper Species, but is apt however to raise in us a secret Delight, and a kind of Fondness for the Places or Objects in which we discover it. This consists either in the Gaiety or Variety of Colours, in the Symmetry and Proportion of Parts, in the Arrangement and Disposition of Bodies, or in a just Mixture and Concurrence of all together. Among these several Kinds of Beauty the Eye takes most Delight in Colours. We no where meet with a more glorious or pleasing Show in Nature, than what appears in the Heavens at the rising and setting of the Sun, which is wholly made up of those different Stains of Light that shew themselves in Clouds of a different Situation. For this Reason we find the Poets, who are always addressing themselves to the Imagination, borrowing more of their Epithets from Colours than from any other Topic.

As the Fancy delights in every thing that is Great, Strange, or Beautiful, and is still more pleased the more it finds of these Perfections in the same Object, so it is capable of receiving a

new Satisfaction by the Assistance of another Sense.   Thus any
continued Sound, as the Musick of Birds, or a Fall of Water,
awakens every moment the Mind of the Beholder, and makes
him more attentive to the several Beauties of the Place that lye
before him.   Thus if there arises a Fragrancy of Smells or
Perfumes, they heighten the Pleasures of the Imagination, and
make even the Colours and Verdure of the Landskip appear
more agreeable; for the Ideas of both Senses recommend each
other, and are pleasanter together, than when they enter the
Mind separately: As the different Colours of a Picture, when
they are well disposed, set off one another, and receive an
additional Beauty from the Advantage of their Situation.   O

No. 413.
[ADDISON.]   Tuesday, June 24.

. . . *Causa latet; vis est notissima* . . .—Ovid.

THOUGH in Yesterday's Paper we consider'd how every thing
that is *Great, New,* or *Beautiful,* is apt to affect the Imagination
with Pleasure, we must own that it is impossible for us to
assign the necessary Cause of this Pleasure, because we know
neither the Nature of an Idea, nor the Substance of a Human
Soul, which might help us to discover the Conformity or Disagreeableness of the one to the other; and therefore, for want
of such a Light, all that we can do in Speculations of this kind,
is to reflect on those Operations of the Soul that are most
agreeable, and to range, under their proper Heads, what is
pleasing or displeasing to the Mind, without being able to trace
out the several necessary and efficient Causes from whence the
Pleasure or Displeasure arises.

Final Causes lie more bare and open to our Observation, as
there are often a greater Variety that belong to the same
Effect; and these, tho' they are not altogether so satisfactory,
are generally more useful than the other, as they give us greater
Occasion of admiring the Goodness and Wisdom of the first
Contriver.

One of the Final Causes of our Delight, in any thing that is
great, may be this.   The Supreme Author of our Being has so
formed the Soul of Man, that nothing but himself can be its
last, adequate, and proper Happiness.   Because, therefore, a
great Part of our Happiness must arise from the Contemplation
of his Being, that he might give our Souls a just Relish of such
a Contemplation, he has made them naturally delight in the
Apprehension of what is Great or Unlimited.   Our Admiration,
which is a very pleasing Motion of the Mind, immediately rises

at the Consideration of any Object that takes up a great deal of room in the Fancy, and, by consequence, will improve into the highest pitch of Astonishment and Devotion when we contemplate his Nature, that is neither circumscribed by Time nor Place, nor to be comprehended by the largest Capacity of a Created Being.

He has annexed a secret Pleasure to the Idea of any thing that is *new* or *uncommon*, that he might encourage us in the Pursuit after Knowledge, and engage us to search into the Wonders of his Creation; for every new Idea brings such a Pleasure along with it, as rewards any Pains we have taken in its Acquisitions, and consequently serves as a Motive to put us upon fresh Discoveries.

He has made every thing that is *beautiful in our own Species* pleasant, that all Creatures might be tempted to multiply their Kind, and fill the World with Inhabitants; for 'tis very remarkable that where-ever Nature is crost in the Production of a Monster (the Result of any unnatural Mixture) the Breed is incapable of propagating its Likeness, and of founding a new Order of Creatures; so that unless all Animals were allured by the Beauty of their own Species, Generation would be at an end, and the Earth unpeopled.

In the last Place, he has made every thing that is beautiful in all other Objects pleasant, or rather has made so many Objects appear beautiful, that he might render the whole Creation more gay and delightful. He has given almost every thing about us the Power of raising an agreeable Idea in the Imagination: So that it is impossible for us to behold his Works with Coldness or Indifference, and to survey so many Beauties without a secret Satisfaction and Complacency. Things would make but a poor Appearance to the Eye, if we saw them only in their proper Figures and Motions: And what Reason can we assign for their exciting in us many of those Ideas which are different from any thing that exists in the Objects themselves, (for such are Light and Colours) were it not to add Supernumerary Ornaments to the Universe, and make it more agreeable to the Imagination? We are every where entertained with pleasing Shows and Apparitions, we discover imaginary Glories in the Heavens, and in the Earth, and see some of this Visionary Beauty poured out upon the whole Creation; but what a rough unsightly Sketch of Nature should we be entertained with, did all her Colouring disappear, and the several Distinctions of Light and Shade vanish? In short, our Souls are at present delightfully lost and bewildered in a pleasing Delusion, and we walk about like the Enchanted Hero in a Romance, who sees beautiful Castles, Woods and Meadows;

and at the same time hears the warbling of Birds, and the purling of Streams; but upon the finishing of some secret Spell, the fantastick Scene breaks up, and the disconsolate Knight finds himself on a barren Heath, or in a solitary Desart. It is not improbable that something like this may be the State of the Soul after its first Separation, in respect of the Images it will receive from Matter; tho' indeed the Ideas of Colours are so pleasing and beautiful in the Imagination, that it is possible the Soul will not be deprived of them, but perhaps find them excited by some other Occasional Cause, as they are at present by the different Impressions of the subtle Matter on the Organ of Sight.

I have here supposed that my Reader is acquainted with that great Modern Discovery, which is at present universally acknowledged by all the Enquirers into Natural Philosophy: Namely, that Light and Colours, as apprehended by the Imagination, are only Ideas in the Mind, and not Qualities that have any Existence in Matter. As this is a Truth which has been proved incontestably by many Modern Philosophers, and is indeed one of the finest Speculations in that Science, if the *English* Reader would see the Notion explained at large, he may find it in the Eighth Chapter of the second Book of Mr. *Lock*'s Essay on Human Understanding.   O

No. 414.
[ADDISON.]   Wednesday, June 25.

. . . *Alterius sic*
Altera poscit opem res & conjurat amice.—Hor.

IF we consider the Works of *Nature* and *Art*, as they are qualified to entertain the Imagination, we shall find the last very defective, in Comparison of the former; for though they may sometimes appear as Beautiful or Strange, they can have nothing in them of that Vastness and Immensity, which afford so great an Entertainment to the Mind of the Beholder. The one may be as Polite and Delicate as the other, but can never shew herself so August and Magnificent in the Design. There is something more bold and masterly in the rough careless Strokes of Nature, than in the nice Touches and Embellishments of Art. The Beauties of the most stately Garden or Palace lie in a narrow Compass, the Imagination immediately runs them over, and requires something else to gratify her; but, in the wide Fields of Nature, the Sight wanders up and down without Confinement, and is fed with an infinite variety of Images, without any certain Stint or Number. For this

Reason we always find the Poet in Love with a Country-Life, where Nature appears in the greatest Perfection, and furnishes out all those Scenes that are most apt to delight the Imagination.

Scriptorum chorus omnis amat nemus & fugit urbes.—Hor.

Hic secura quies, & nescia fallere vita,
Dives opum variarum, hic latis otia fundis,
Speluncae, vivique lacus, hic frigida Tempe,
Mugitusque boum, mollesque sub arbore somni.—Virg.

But tho' there are several of these wild Scenes, that are more delightful than any artificial Shows; yet we find the Works of Nature still more pleasant, the more they resemble those of Art: For in this case our Pleasure rises from a double Principle; from the Agreeableness of the Objects to the Eye, and from their Similitude to other Objects: We are pleased as well with comparing their Beauties, as with surveying them, and can represent them to our Minds, either as Copies or Originals. Hence it is that we take Delight in a Prospect which is well laid out, and diversified with Fields and Meadows, Woods and Rivers; in those accidental Landskips of Trees, Clouds and Cities, that are sometimes found in the Veins of Marble; in the curious Fret-work of Rocks and Grottos; and, in a Word, in any thing that hath such a Variety or Regularity as may seem the Effect of Design in what we call the Works of Chance.

If the Products of Nature rise in Value, according as they more or less resemble those of Art, we may be sure that artificial Works receive a greater Advantage from their Resemblance of such as are natural; because here the Similitude is not only pleasant, but the Pattern more perfect. The prettiest Landskip I ever saw, was one drawn on the Walls of a dark Room, which stood opposite on one side to a navigable River, and on the other to a Park. The Experiment is very common in Opticks. Here you might discover the Waves and Fluctuations of the Water in strong and proper Colours, with the Picture of a Ship entring at one end, and sailing by Degrees through the whole Piece. On another there appeared the Green Shadows of Trees, waving to and fro with the Wind, and Herds of Deer among them in Miniature, leaping about upon the Wall. I must confess, the Novelty of such a Sight may be one occasion of its Pleasantness to the Imagination, but certainly the chief Reason is its near Resemblance to Nature, as it does not only, like other Pictures, give the Colour and Figure, but the Motion of the Things it represents.

We have before observed, that there is generally in Nature something more Grand and August, than what we meet with in the Curiosities of Art. When, therefore, we see this imitated in any measure, it gives us a nobler and more exalted kind of Pleasure than what we receive from the nicer and more accurate Productions of Art. On this Account our *English* Gardens are not so entertaining to the Fancy as those in *France* and *Italy*, where we see a large Extent of Ground covered over with an agreeable Mixture of Garden and Forest, which represent every where an artificial Rudeness, much more charming than that Neatness and Elegancy which we meet with in those of our own Country. It might, indeed, be of ill Consequence to the Publick, as well as unprofitable to private Persons, to alienate so much Ground from Pasturage, and the Plow, in many Parts of a Country that is so well peopled, and cultivated to a far greater Advantage. But why may not a whole Estate be thrown into a kind of Garden by frequent Plantations, that may turn as much to the Profit, as the Pleasure of the Owner? A Marsh overgrown with Willows, or a Mountain shaded with Oaks, are not only more beautiful, but more beneficial, than when they lie bare and unadorned. Fields of Corn make a pleasant Prospect, and if the Walks were a little taken care of that lie between them, if the natural Embroidery of the Meadows were helpt and improved by some small Additions of Art, and the several Rows of Hedges set off by Trees and Flowers, that the soil was capable of receiving, a Man might make a pretty Landskip of his own Possessions.

Writers, who have given us an Account of *China*, tell us the Inhabitants of that Country laugh at the Plantations of our *Europeans*, which are laid out by the Rule and Line; because, they say, any one may place Trees in equal Rows and uniform Figures. They chuse rather to shew a Genius in Works of this Nature, and therefore always conceal the Art by which they direct themselves. They have a Word it seems in their Language, by which they express the particular Beauty of a Plantation that thus strikes the Imagination at first Sight, without discovering what it is that has so agreeable an Effect. Our *British* Gardeners, on the contrary, instead of humouring Nature, love to deviate from it as much as possible. Our Trees rise in Cones, Globes, and Pyramids. We see the Marks of the Scissars upon every Plant and Bush. I do not know whether I am singular in my Opinion, but, for my own part, I would rather look upon a Tree in all its Luxuriancy and Diffusion of Boughs and Branches, than when it is thus cut and trimmed into a Mathematical Figure; and cannot but fancy that an Orchard in Flower looks infinitely more delightful than all the little Labyrinths of the most finished Parterre. But as our great Modellers of Gardens have their Magazines of Plants to dispose of, it is very natural for them to tear up all the

Beautiful Plantations of Fruit Trees, and contrive a Plan that may most turn to their own Profit, in taking off their Evergreens, and the like Moveable Plants, with which their Shops are plentifully stocked.   O

No. 415.
[ADDISON.]   Thursday, June 26.

Adde tot egregias urbes, operumque laborem.—Virg.

HAVING already shewn how the Fancy is affected by the Works of Nature, and afterwards considered in general both the Works of Nature and of Art, how they mutually assist and compleat each other, in forming such Scenes and Prospects as are most apt to delight the Mind of the Beholder, I shall in this Paper throw together some Reflections on that Particular Art, which has a more immediate Tendency, than any other, to produce those primary Pleasures of the Imagination, which have hitherto been the Subject of this Discourse. The Art I mean is that of Architecture, which I shall consider only with regard to the Light in which the forgoing Speculations have placed it, without entring into those Rules and Maxims which the great Masters of Architecture have laid down, and explained at large in numberless Treatises upon that Subject.

Greatness, in the Works of Architecture, may be considered as relating to the Bulk and Body of the Structure, or to the *Manner* in which it is built. As for the first, we find the Antients, especially among the Eastern Nations of the World, infinitely superior to the Moderns.

Not to mention the Tower of *Babel*, of which an old Author says, there were the Foundations to be seen in his time, which looked like a Spacious Mountain; what could be more noble than the Walls of *Babylon*, its hanging Gardens, and its Temple to *Jupiter Belus*, that rose a Mile high by Eight several Stories, each Story a Furlong in Height, and on the Top of which was the *Babylonian* Observatory? I might here, likewise, take Notice of the huge Rock that was cut into the Figure of *Semiramis*, with the smaller Rocks that lay by it in the Shape of Tributary Kings; the prodigious Basin, or artificial Lake, which took in the whole *Euphrates*, 'till such time as a new Canal was formed for its Reception, with the several Trenches through which that River was conveyed. I know there are Persons who look upon some of these Wonders of Art as fabulous, but I cannot find any Grounds for such a Suspicion, unless it be that we have no such Works among us at present. There were indeed many greater Advantages for Building in

those Times, and in that Part of the World, than have been
met with ever since.   The Earth was extremely fruitful, Men
lived generally on Pasturage, which requires a much smaller
number of Hands than Agriculture: There were few Trades to
employ the busie Part of Mankind, and fewer Arts and Sciences
to give Work to Men of Speculative Tempers; and what is more
than all the rest, the Prince was absolute; so that when he
went to War, he put himself at the Head of a whole People:
As we find *Semiramis* leading her three Millions to the Field,
and yet overpowered by the Number of her Enemies.   'Tis no
wonder, therefore, when she was at Peace, and turned her
Thoughts on Building, that she could accomplish so great
Works, with such a prodigious Multitude of Labourers: Besides
that, in her Climate, there was small Interruption of Frosts
and Winters, which make the Northern Workmen lye half the
Year idle.   I might mention too, among the Benefits of the
Climate, what Historians say of the Earth, that it sweated out
a Bitumen or natural kind of Mortar, which is doubtless the
same with that mentioned in Holy Writ, as contributing to the
Structure of *Babel*.   *Slime they used instead of Mortar*.

In *Egypt* we still see their Pyramids, which answer to the
Descriptions that have been made of them; and I question
not but a Traveller might find out some Remains of the Laby-
rinth that covered a whole Province, and had a hundred
Temples disposed among its several Quarters and Divisions.

The Wall of *China* is one of these Eastern Pieces of Magnificence, which makes a Figure even in the Map of the World,
altho' an Account of it would have been thought Fabulous,
were not the Wall it self still extant.

We are obliged to Devotion for the noblest Buildings that
have adorned the several Countries of the World.   It is this
which has set Men at work on Temples and Publick Places of
Worship, not only that they might, by the Magnificence of the
Building, invite the Deity to reside within it, but that such
stupendous Works might, at the same time, open the Mind to
vast Conceptions, and fit it to converse with the Divinity of
the Place.   For every thing that is Majestick imprints an
Awfulness and Reverence on the Mind of the Beholder, and
strikes in with the Natural Greatness of the Soul.

In the second place we are to consider *Greatness of Manner*
in Architecture, which has such force upon the Imagination,
that a small Building, where *it* appears, shall give the Mind
nobler Ideas than one of twenty times the Bulk, where the
Manner is ordinary or little.   Thus, perhaps, a Man would
have been more astonished with the Majestick Air that
appeared in one of *Lysippus*'s Statues of *Alexander*, tho' no

bigger than the Life, than he might have been with Mount *Athos*, had it been cut into the Figure of the Heroe, according to the Proposal of *Phidias*, with a River in one Hand, and a City in the other.

Let any one reflect on the Disposition of Mind he finds in himself, at his first Entrance into the *Pantheon* at *Rome*, and how his Imagination is filled with something Great and Amazing; and, at the same time, consider how little, in proportion, he is affected with the Inside of a *Gothick* Cathedral, tho' it be five times larger than the other; which can arise from nothing else but the Greatness of the Manner in the one, and the Meanness in the other.

I have seen an Observation upon this Subject in a *French* Author, which very much pleased me. It is in Monsieur *Freart*'s Parallel of the Ancient and Modern Architecture. I shall give it the Reader with the same Terms of Art which he has made use of. *I am observing* (says he) *a thing, which, in my Opinion, is very curious, whence it proceeds, that in the same quantity of Superficies, the one* Manner *seems great and magnificent, and the other poor and trifling; the Reason is fine and uncommon. I say then, that to introduce into Architecture this Grandeur of Manner, we ought so to proceed, that the Division of the Principal Members of the Order may consist but of few Parts, that they be all great and of a bold and ample Relievo, and Swelling; and that the Eye beholding nothing little and mean, the Imagination may be more vigorously touched and affected with the Work that stands before it. For Example; In a Cornice, if the Gola or Cymatium of the Corona, the Coping, the Modillions or Dentelli, make a noble Show by their graceful Projections, if we see none of that ordinary Confusion which is the Result of those little Cavities, Quarter Rounds of the Astragal, and I know not how many other intermingled Particulars, which produce no effect in great and massy Works, and which very unprofitably take up place to the prejudice of the Principal Member, it is most certain that this Manner will appear Solemn and Great; as on the contrary, that will have but a poor and mean Effect, where there is a Redundancy of those smaller Ornaments, which divide and scatter the Angles of the Sight into such a multitude of Rays, so pressed together that the whole will appear but a Confusion.*

Among all the Figures in Architecture, there are none that have a greater Air than the Concave and the Convex, and we find in all the Ancient and Modern Architecture, as well in the remote Parts of *China*, as in Countries nearer home, that round Pillars and Vaulted Roofs make a great Part of those Buildings which are designed for Pomp and Magnificence. The Reason I take to be, because in these Figures we generally see more of the Body, than in those of other Kinds. There are, indeed, Figures of Bodies, where the Eye may take in two Thirds of the Surface; but as in such Bodies the Sight must split upon several Angles, it does not take in one uniform Idea, but several Ideas of the same kind. Look upon the Outside of a Dome, your Eye half surrounds it; look up into the Inside, and at one Glance you have all the Prospect of it; the intire Concavity falls into your Eye at once, the Sight being as the Center that collects and gathers into it the Lines of the whole Circumference: In a Square Pillar, the Sight often takes in but a fourth Part of the Surface, and, in a Square Concave, must move up and down to the different Sides, before it is Master of all the inward Surface. For this Reason, the Fancy is infinitely more struck with the view of the open Air, and Skies, that passes through an Arch, tban what comes through a Square, or any other Figure. The Figure of the Rainbow does not contribute less to its Magnificence, than the Colours to its Beauty, as it is very Poetically described by the Son of *Sirach*: *Look upon the Rainbow, and praise him that made it; very beautiful it is in its Brightness; it encompasses the Heavens with a glorious Circle, and the Hands of the most High have bended it.*

Having thus spoken of that Greatness which affects the Mind in Architecture, I might next shew the Pleasure that rises in the Imagination from what appears new and beautiful in this Art; but as every Beholder has naturally a greater Taste of these two Perfections in every Building which offers it self to his View, than of that which I have hitherto considered, I shall not trouble my Reader with any Reflections upon it. It is sufficient for my present Purpose, to observe, that there is nothing in this whole Art which pleases the Imagination, but as it is Great, Uncommon, or Beautiful.   O

No. 416.
[ADDISON.]   Friday, June 27.

Quatenus hoc simile est oculis, quod mente videmus.—Lucr.

I AT first divided the Pleasures of the Imagination, into such as arise from Objects that are actually before our Eyes, or that once entered in at our Eyes, and are afterwards called up into the Mind either barely by its own Operations, or on occasion of something without us, as Statues, or Descriptions. We have already considered the first Division, and shall therefore enter on the other, which, for Distinction sake, I have called the Secondary Pleasures of the Imagination. When I say the Ideas we receive from Statues, Descriptions, or such like

Occasions, are the same that were once actually in our View, it must not be understood that we had once seen the very Place, Action, or Person which are carved or described. It is sufficient, that we have seen Places, Persons, or Actions in general, which bear a Resemblance, or at least some remote Analogy with what we find represented. Since it is in the Power of the Imagination, when it is once Stocked with particular Ideas, to enlarge, compound, and vary them at her own Pleasure.

Among the different Kinds of Representation, *Statuary* is the most natural, and shews us something *likest* the Object that is represented. To make use of a common Instance, let one who is born Blind take an Image in his Hands, and trace out with his Fingers the different Furrows and Impressions of the Chissel, and he will easily conceive how the Shape of a Man, or Beast, may be represented by it; but should he draw his Hand over a *Picture*, where all is smooth and uniform, he would never be able to imagine how the several Prominencies and Depressions of a human Body could be shewn on a plain Piece of Canvas, that has in it no Unevenness or Irregularity. *Description* runs yet further from the things it represents than Painting; for a Picture bears a real Resemblance to its Original, which Letters and Syllables are wholly void of. Colours speak all Languages, but Words are understood only by such a People or Nation. For this reason, tho' Men's Necessities quickly put them on finding out Speech, Writing is probably of a later Invention than Painting; particularly we are told, that in *America* when the *Spaniards* first arrived there, Expresses were sent to the Emperor of *Mexico* in Paint, and the News of his Country delineated by the Strokes of a Pencil, which was a more natural Way than that of Writing, tho' at the same time much more imperfect, because it is impossible to draw the little connexions of Speech, or to give the Picture of a Conjunction or an Adverb. It would be yet more strange, to represent visible Objects by Sounds that have no Ideas annexed to them, and to make something like Description in *Musick*. Yet it is certain, there may be confused, imperfect Notions of this Nature raised in the Imagination by an Artificial Composition of Notes; and we find that great Masters in the Art are able, sometimes to set their Hearers in the heat and hurry of a Battel, to overcast their Minds with melancholy Scenes and Apprehensions of Deaths and Funerals, or to lull them into pleasing Dreams of Groves and Elisiums.

In all these Instances, this Secondary Pleasure of the Imagination proceeds from that Action of the Mind, which compares the Ideas arising from the Original Objects, with the Ideas we receive from the Statue, Picture, Description, or

Sound that represents them. It is impossible for us to give the necessary Reason, why this Operation of the Mind is attended with so much Pleasure, as I have before observed on the same Occasion; but we find a great variety of Entertainments derived from this single Principle: For it is this that not only gives us a relish of Statuary, Painting and Description, but makes us delight in all the Actions and Arts of Mimickry. It is this that makes the several kinds of Wit pleasant, which consists, as I have formerly shewn, in the Affinity of Ideas: And we may add, it is this also that raises the little Satisfaction we sometimes find in the different Sorts of false Wit; whether it consist in the Affinity of Letters, as an Anagram, Acrostick; or of Syllables, as in Doggerel Rhimes, Ecchos; or of Words, as in Puns, Quibbles; or of a whole Sentence or Poem, to Wings, and Altars. The *final Cause*, probably, of annexing Pleasure to this Operation of the Mind, was to quicken and encourage us in our Searches after Truth, since the distinguishing one thing from another, and the right discerning betwixt our Ideas, depends wholly upon our comparing them together, and observing the Congruity or Disagreement that appears among the several Works of Nature.

But I shall here confine my self to those Pleasures of the Imagination, which proceed from Ideas raised by *Words*, because most of the Observations that agree with Descriptions, are equally Applicable to Painting and Statuary.

Words, when well chosen, have so great a Force in them, that a Description often gives us more lively Ideas than the Sight of Things themselves. The Reader finds a Scene drawn in Stronger Colours, and painted more to the Life in his Imagination, by the help of Words, than by an actual Survey of the Scene which they describe. In this Case the Poet seems to get the better of Nature; he takes, indeed, the Landskip after her, but gives it more vigorous Touches, heightens its Beauty, and so enlivens the whole Piece, that the Images which flow from the Objects themselves appear weak and faint, in Comparison of those that come from the Expressions. The Reason, probably, may be, because in the Survey of any Object, we have only so much of it painted on the Imagination, as comes in at the Eye; but in its Description, the Poet gives us as free a View of it as he pleases, and discovers to us several Parts, that either we did not attend to, or that lay out of our Sight when we first beheld it. As we look on any Object, our Idea of it is, perhaps, made up of two or three simple Ideas; but when the Poet represents it, he may either give us a more complex Idea of it, or only raise in us such Ideas as are most apt to affect the Imagination.

It may be here worth our while to examine, how it comes to pass that several Readers, who are all acquainted with the same Language, and know the Meaning of the Words they read, should nevertheless have a different Relish of the same Descriptions. We find one transported with a Passage, which another runs over with Coldness and Indifference, or finding the Representation extremely natural, where another can perceive nothing of Likeness and Conformity. This different Taste must proceed either from the *Perfection of Imagination* in one more than in another, or from the *different Ideas* that several Readers affix to the same Words. For, to have a true Relish, and form a right Judgment of a Description, a Man should be born with a good Imagination, and must have well weighed the Force and Energy that lye in the several Words of a Language, so as to be able to distinguish which are most significant and expressive of their proper Ideas, and what additional Strength and Beauty they are capable of receiving from Conjunction with others. The Fancy must be warm, to retain the Print of those Images it hath received from outward Objects; and the Judgment discerning, to know what Expressions are most proper to cloath and adorn them to the best Advantage. A Man who is deficient in either of these Respects, tho' he may receive the general Notion of a Description, can never see distinctly all its particular Beauties: As a Person with a weak Sight may have the confused Prospect of a Place that lyes before him, without entering into its several Parts, or discerning the variety of its Colours in their full Glory and Perfection.   O

No. 417.
[ADDISON.]   Saturday, June 28.

> *Quem tu, Melpomene, semel*
> *Nascentem placido lumine videris,*
> *Illum non labor Isthmius*
> *Clarabit pugilem, non equus impiger, &c.*
>
> .   .   .   .   .
>
> *Sed quae Tibur aquae fertile perfluunt,*
> *Et spissae nemorum comae*
> *Fingent Aeolio carmine nobilem.*—Hor.

WE may observe, that any single Circumstance of what we have formerly seen often raises up a whole Scene of Imagery, and awakens numberless Ideas that before slept in the Imagination; such a particular Smell or Colour is able to fill the Mind, on a sudden, with the Picture of the Fields or Gardens where we first met with it, and to bring up into View all the

Variety of Images that once attended it. Our Imagination takes the Hint, and leads us unexpectedly into Cities or Theatres, Plains or Meadows. We may further observe, when the Fancy thus reflects on the Scenes that have past in it formerly, those, which were at first pleasant to behold, appear more so upon Reflection, and that the Memory heightens the Delightfulness of the Original. A *Cartesian* would account for both these Instances in the following Manner.

The Sett of Ideas which we received from such a Prospect or Garden, having entred the Mind at the same time, have a Sett of Traces belonging to them in the Brain, bordering very near upon one another; when, therefore, any one of these Ideas arises in the Imagination, and consequently dispatches a flow of Animal Spirits to its proper Trace, these Spirits, in the Violence of their Motion, run not only into the Trace, to which they were more particularly directed, but into several of those that lye about it: By this means they awaken other Ideas of the same Sett, which immediately determine a new Dispatch of Spirits, but in the same manner open other Neighbouring Traces, till at last the whole Sett of them is blown up, and the whole Prospect or Garden flourishes in the Imagination. But because the Pleasure we received from these Places far surmounted, and overcame the little Disagreeableness we found in them, for this Reason there was at first a wider Passage worn in the Pleasure Traces, and, on the contrary, so narrow a one in those which belonged to the disagreeable Ideas, that they were quickly stopt up, and rendered incapable of receiving any Animal Spirits, and consequently of exciting any unpleasant Ideas in the Memory.

It would be in vain to enquire, whether the Power of imagining Things strongly proceeds from any greater Perfection in the Soul, or from any nicer Texture in the Brain of one Man than of another. But this is certain, that a noble Writer should be born with this Faculty in its full Strength and Vigour, so as to be able to receive lively Ideas from outward Objects, to retain them long, and to range them together, upon occasion, in such Figures and Representations as are most likely to hit the Fancy of the Reader. A Poet should take as much Pains in forming his Imagination, as a Philosopher in cultivating his Understanding. He must gain a due Relish of the Works of Nature, and be thoroughly conversant in the various Scenery of a Country Life.

When he is stored with Country Images, if he would go beyond Pastoral, and the lower kinds of Poetry, he ought to acquaint himself with the Pomp and Magnificence of Courts. He should be very well versed in every thing that is noble and stately in the Productions of Art, whether it appear in Painting or Statuary, in the great Works of Architecture which are in their present Glory, or in the Ruins of those which flourished in former Ages.

Such Advantages as these help to open a Man's Thoughts, and to enlarge his Imagination, and will therefore have their Influence on all kinds of Writing, if the Author knows how to make right use of them. And among those of the learned Languages who excel in this Talent, the most perfect in their several kinds, are perhaps *Homer, Virgil,* and *Ovid.* The first strikes the Imagination wonderfully with what is Great, the seond with what is Beautiful, and the last with what is Strange. Reading the *Iliad* is like travelling through a Country un-inhabited, where the Fancy is entertained with a thousand Savage Prospects of vast Desarts, wide uncultivated Marshes, huge Forests, mishapen Rocks and Precipices. On the con-trary, the *Aeneid* is like a well ordered Garden, where it is impossible to find out any Part unadorned, or to cast our Eyes upon a single Spot, that does not produce some beautiful Plant or Flower. But when we are in the *Metamorphosis,* we are walking on inchanted Ground, and see nothing but Scenes of Magick lying round us.

Homer is in his Province, when he is describing a Battel or a Multitude, a Heroe or a God. *Virgil* is never better pleas'd, than when he is in his *Elysium,* or copying out an entertaining Picture. *Homer's* Epithets generally mark out what is great, *Virgil's* what is Agreeable. Nothing can be more Magnificent than the Figure *Jupiter* makes in the first *Iliad,* nor more charming than that of *Venus* in the first *Aeneid.*

> ῍Η καὶ κυανέῃσιν ἐπ' ὀφρύσι νεῦσε Κρονίων·
> ῍Αμβρόσιαι δ' ἄρα χαῖται ἐπερρώσαντο ἄνακτος
> Κρατὸς ἀπ' ἀθανάτοιο· μέγαν δ' ἐλέλιξεν ῾Ολυμπον.

> *Dixit, & avertens rosea cervice refulsit;*
> *Ambrosiaeque comae divinum vertice odorem*
> *Spiravere: pedes vestis defluxit ad imos;*
> *Et vera incessu patuit dea. . . .*

Homer's Persons are most of them God-like and Terrible: *Virgil* has scarce admitted any into his Poem, who are not beautiful, and has taken particular Care to make his Heroe so.

> *. . . lumenque juventae*
> *Purpureum, & laetos oculis afflavit honores.*

In a word, *Homer* fills his Readers with Sublime *Ideas,* and, I believe, has raised the Imagination of all the good Poets that have come after him. I shall only instance *Horace*, who immediately takes Fire at the first Hint of any Passage in the *Iliad* or *Odyssee* and always rises above himself, when he has *Homer* in his View. *Virgil* has drawn together, into his *Aeneid*, all the pleasing Scenes his Subject is capable of admitting, and in his *Georgics* has given us a Collection of the most delightful Landskips that can be made out of Fields and Woods, Herds of Cattle, and Swarms of Bees.

Ovid, in his *Metamorphosis*, has shewn us how the Imagination may be affected by what is Strange. He describes a Miracle in every Story, and always gives us the Sight of some new Creature at the end of it. His Art consists chiefly in well-timing his Description, before the first Shape is quite worn off, and the new one perfectly finished; so that he every where entertains us with something we never saw before, and shews Monster after Monster, to the end of the *Metamorphosis*.

If I were to name a Poet that is a perfect Master in all these Arts of working on the Imagination, I think *Milton* may pass for one: And if his *Paradise Lost* falls short of the *Aeneid* or *Iliad* in this respect, it proceeds rather from the Fault of the Language in which it is written, than from any Defect of Genius in the Author. So Divine a Poem in *English*, is like a stately Palace, built of Brick, where one may see Architecture in as great a Perfection as in one of Marble, tho' the Materials are of a coarser Nature. But to consider it only as it regards our present Subject: What can be conceived greater than the Battel of Angels, the Majesty of Messiah, the Stature and Behaviour of Satan and his Peers? What more beautiful than *Pandaemonium*, Paradise, Heaven, Angels, *Adam* and *Eve*? What more strange, than the Creation of the World, the several Metamorphoses of the fallen Angels, and the surprising Adventures their Leader meets with in his Search after Paradise? No other Subject could have furnished a Poet with Scenes so proper to strike the Imagination, as no other Poet could have painted those Scenes in more strong and lively Colours.   O

No. 418.
[ADDISON.]   Monday, June 30.

. . . *Ferat & rubus asper amomum.*—Virg.

THE Pleasures of these Secondary Views of the Imagination, are of a wider and more universal Nature than those it has when joined with Sight; for not only what is Great, Strange or Beautiful, but any Thing that is Disagreeable when looked upon, pleases us in an apt Description. Here, therefore, we must enquire after a new Principle of Pleasure, which is nothing else but the Action of the Mind, which *compares* the Ideas that arise from Words, with the Ideas that arise from the Objects themselves; and why this Operation of the Mind is attended with so much Pleasure, we have before considered. For this Reason therefore, the Description of a Dunghill is pleasing to the Imagination, if the Image be represented to our Minds by suitable Expressions; tho', perhaps, this may be more properly called the Pleasure of the Understanding than of the Fancy, because we are not so much delighted with the Image that is contained in the Description, as with the Aptness of the Description to excite the Image.

But if the Description of what is Little, Common or Deformed, be acceptable to the Imagination, the Description of what is Great, Surprising or Beautiful, is much more so; because here we are not only delighted with *comparing* the Representation with the Original, but are highly pleased with the Original it self. Most Readers, I believe, are more charmed with *Milton*'s Description of Paradise, than of Hell; they are both, perhaps, equally perfect in their Kind, but in the one the Brimstone and Sulphur are not so refreshing to the Imagination, as the Beds of Flowers and the Wilderness of Sweets in the other.

There is yet another Circumstance which recommends a Description more than all the rest, and that is, if it represents to us such Objects as are apt to raise a secret Ferment in the Mind of the Reader, and to work, with Violence, upon his Passions. For, in this Case, we are at once warmed and enlightened, so that the Pleasure becomes more Universal, and is several ways qualified to entertain us. Thus, in Painting, it is pleasant to look on the Picture of any Face, where the Resemblance is hit, but the Pleasure increases, if it be the Picture of a Face that is beautiful, and is still greater, if the Beauty be softened with an Air of Melancholy or Sorrow. The two leading Passions which the more serious Parts of Poetry endeavour to stir up in us, are Terror and Pity. And here, by the way, one would wonder how it comes to pass, that such Passions as are very unpleasant at all other times, are very agreeable when excited by proper Descriptions. It is not strange, that we should take Delight in such Passages as are apt to produce Hope, Joy, Admiration, Love, or the like Emotions in us, because they never rise in the Mind without an inward Pleasure which attends them. But how comes it to pass, that we should take delight in being terrified or dejected by a Description, when we find so much Uneasiness in the Fear or Grief which we receive from any other Occasion?

If we consider, therefore, the Nature of this Pleasure, we shall find that it does not arise so properly from the Description of what is Terrible, as from the Reflection we make on our selves at the time of reading it. When we look on such hideous Objects, we are not a little pleased to think we are in no Danger of them. We consider them at the same time, as Dreadful and Harmless; so that the more frightful Appearance they make, the greater is the Pleasure we receive from the Sense of our own Safety. In short, we look upon the Terrors of a Description, with the same Curiosity and Satisfaction that we survey a dead Monster.

> *. . . Informe cadaver*
> *Protrahitur: nequeunt expleri corda tuendo*
> *Terribiles oculos, vultum, villosaque setis*
> *Pectora semiferi, atque extinctos faucibus ignes.*—Virg.

It is for the same Reason that we are delighted with the reflecting upon Dangers that are past, or in looking on a Precipice at a distance, which would fill us with a different kind of Horrour, if we saw it hanging over our Heads.

In the like manner, when we read of Torments, Wounds, Deaths, and the like dismal Accidents, our Pleasure does not flow so properly from the Grief which such melancholy Descriptions give us, as from the secret Comparison which we make between our selves and the Person who suffers. Such Representations teach us to set a just Value upon our own Condition, and make us prize our good Fortune, which exempts us from the like Calamities. This is, however, such a kind of Pleasure as we are not capable of receiving, when we see a Person actually lying under the Tortures that we meet with in a Description; because, in this Case, the Object presses too close upon our Senses, and bears so hard upon us, that it does not give us Time or Leisure to reflect on our selves. Our Thoughts are so intent upon the Miseries of the Sufferer, that we cannot turn them upon our own Happiness. Whereas, on the contrary, we consider the Misfortunes we read in History or Poetry, either as past, or as fictitious, so that the Reflection upon our selves rises in us insensibly, and over-bears the Sorrow we conceive for the Sufferings of the Afflicted.

But because the Mind of Man requires something more perfect in Matter, than what it finds there, and can never meet with any Sight in Nature which sufficiently answers its highest Ideas of Pleasantness; or, in other Words, because the Imagination can fancy to it self Things more Great, Strange, or Beautiful, than the Eye ever saw, and is still sensible of some Defect in what it has seen; on this account it is the part of a

Poet to humour the Imagination in its own Notions, by mending and perfecting Nature where he describes a Reality, and by adding greater Beauties than are put together in Nature, where he describes a Fiction.

He is not obliged to attend her in the slow Advances which she makes from one Season to another, or to observe her Conduct in the successive Production of Plants and Flowers. He may draw into his Description all the Beauties of the Spring and Autumn, and make the whole Year contribute something to render it the more agreeable. His Rose-trees, Wood-bines and Jessamines may flower together, and his Beds be covered at the same time with Lilies, Violets, and Amaranths. His Soil is not restrained to any particular Sett of Plants, but is proper either for Oaks or Mirtles, and adapts it self to the Products of every Climate. Oranges may grow wild in it; Myrrh may be met with in every Hedge, and if he thinks it proper to have a Grove of Spices, he can quickly command Sun enough to raise it. If all this will not furnish out an agreeable Scene, he can make several new Species of Flowers, with richer Scents and higher Colours than any that grow in the Gardens of Nature. His Consorts of Birds may be as full and harmonious, and his Woods as thick and gloomy as he pleases. He is at no more Expence in a long Vista, than a short one, and can as easily throw his Cascades from a Precipice of half a Mile high, as from one of twenty Yards. He has his Choice of the Winds, and can turn the Course of his Rivers in all the variety of *Meanders*, that are most delightful to the Reader's Imagination. In a Word, he has the modelling of Nature in his own Hands, and may give her what Charms he pleases, provided he does not reform her too much, and run into Absurdities, by endeavouring to excel. O

No. 419.
[ADDISON.]   Tuesday, July 1.

. . . *Mentis gratissimus error.*—Hor.

THERE is a kind of Writing, wherein the Poet quite loses sight of Nature, and entertains his Reader's Imagination with the Characters and Actions of such Persons as have many of them no Existence, but what he bestows on them. Such are Fairies, Witches, Magicians, Demons, and departed Spirits. This Mr. *Dryden* calls *the Fairy Way of Writing*, which is, indeed, more difficult than any other that depends on the Poet's Fancy, because he has no Pattern to follow in it, and must work altogether out of his own Invention.

There is a very odd turn of Thought required for this sort of Writing, and it is impossible for a Poet to succeed in it, who has not a particular Cast of Fancy, and an Imagination naturally fruitful and superstitious. Besides this, he ought to be very well versed in Legends and Fables, antiquated Romances, and the Traditions of Nurses and old Women, that he may fall in with our natural Prejudices, and humour those Notions which we have imbibed in our Infancy. For, otherwise, he will be apt to make his Fairies talk like People of his own Species, and not like other Setts of Beings, who converse with different Objects, and think in a different manner from that of Mankind;

> *Sylvis deducti caveant, me judice, Fauni*
> *Ne velut innati triviis, ac pene forenses,*
> *Aut nimium teneris juvenentur versibus . . .*—Hor.

I do not say with Mr. *Bays* in the *Rehearsal*, that Spirits must not be confined to speak Sense, but it is certain their Sense ought to be a little discoloured, that it may seem particular, and proper to the Person and Condition of the Speaker.

These Descriptions raise a pleasing kind of Horrour in the Mind of the Reader, and amuse his Imagination with the Strangeness and Novelty of the Persons who are represented in them. They bring up into our Memory the Stories we have heard in our Childhood, and favour those secret Terrors and Apprehensions to which the Mind of Man is naturally subject. We are pleased with surveying the different Habits and Behaviours of Foreign Countries; how much more must we be delighted and surprised when we are led, as it were, into a new Creation, and see the Persons and Manners of another Species? Men of cold Fancies, and Philosophical Dispositions, object to this kind of Poetry, that it has not Probability enough to affect the Imagination. But to this it may be answered, that we are sure, in general, there are many intellectual Beings in the World besides our selves, and several Species of Spirits, who are subject to different Laws and Oeconomies from those of Mankind; when we see, therefore, any of these represented naturally, we cannot look upon the Representation as altogether impossible; nay, many are prepossest with such false Opinions, as dispose them to believe these particular Delusions; at least, we have all heard so many pleasing Relations in favour of them, that we do not care for seeing through the Falshood, and willingly give our selves up to so agreeable an Imposture. The Ancients have not much of this Poetry among them, for, indeed, almost the whole Substance of it owes its Original to the Darkness and Superstition of later Ages, when pious Frauds were made use of to amuse Mankind, and frighten them into a Sense of their Duty. Our Forefathers looked upon Nature with more Reverence and Horrour, before the World was enlightened by Learning and Philosophy, and loved to astonish themselves with the Apprehensions of Witchcraft, Prodigies, Charms and Enchantments. There was not a Village in *England* that had not a Ghost in it, the Church-yards were all haunted, every large Common had a Circle of Fairies belonging to it, and there was scarce a Shepherd to be met with who had not seen a Spirit.

Among all the Poets of this Kind our *English* are much the best, by what I have yet seen, whether it be that we abound with more Stories of this Nature, or that the Genius of our Country is fitter for this sort of Poetry. For the *English* are naturally Fanciful, and very often disposed by that Gloominess and Melancholy of Temper, which is so frequent in our Nation, to many wild Notions and Visions, to which others are not so liable.

Among the *English*, *Shakespear* has incomparably excelled all others. That noble Extravagance of Fancy, which he had in so great Perfection, thoroughly qualified him to touch this weak superstitious Part of his Reader's Imagination; and made him capable of succeeding, where he had nothing to support him besides the Strength of his own Genius. There is something so wild and yet so solemn in the Speeches of his Ghosts, Fairies, Witches and the like Imaginary Persons, that we cannot forbear thinking them natural, tho' we have no Rule by which to judge of them, and must confess, if there are such Beings in the World, it looks highly probable they should talk and act as he has represented them.

There is another sort of Imaginary Beings, that we sometimes meet with among the Poets, when the Author represents any Passion, Appetite, Virtue or Vice, under a visible Shape, and makes it a Person or an Actor in his Poem. Of this Nature are the Descriptions of Hunger and Envy in *Ovid*, of Fame in *Virgil*, and of Sin and Death in *Milton*. We find a whole Creation of the like shadowy Persons in *Spencer*, who had an admirable Talent in Representations of this kind. I have discoursed of these Emblematical Persons in former Papers, and shall therefore only mention them in this Place. Thus we see how many ways Poetry addresses it self to the Imagination, as it has not only the whole Circle of Nature for its Province, but makes new Worlds of its own, shews us Persons who are not to be found in Being, and represents even the Faculties of the Soul, with her several Virtues and Vices, in a sensible Shape and Character.

I shall, in my two following Papers, consider in general, how other kinds of Writing are qualified to please the Imagination; with which I intend to conclude this Essay. O

No. 420.
[ADDISON.]   Wednesday, July 2.

. . . *Quocunque volent animum auditoris agunto.*—Hor.

As the Writers in Poetry and Fiction borrow their several Materials from outward Objects, and join them together at their own Pleasure, there are others who are obliged to follow Nature more closely, and to take entire Scenes out of her. Such are Historians, natural Philosophers, Travellers, Geographers, and, in a Word, all who describe visible Objects of a real Existence.

It is the most agreeable Talent of an Historian to be able to draw up his Armies and fight his Battels in proper Expressions, to set before our Eyes the Divisions, Cabals and Jealousies of Great Men, and to lead us Step by Step into the several Actions and Events of his History. We love to see the Subject unfolding it self by just Degrees, and breaking upon us insensibly, that so we may be kept in a pleasing Suspense, and have Time given us to raise our Expectations, and to side with one of the Parties concerned in the Relation. I confess this shews more the Art than the Veracity of the Historian, but I am only to speak of him as he is qualified to please the Imagination. And in this respect *Livy* has, perhaps, excelled all who went before him, or have written since his Time. He describes every thing in so lively a Manner, that his whole History is an admirable Picture, and touches on such proper Circumstances in every Story, that this Reader becomes a kind of Spectator, and feels in himself all the variety of Passions which are correspondent to the several Parts of the Relation.

But among this Sett of Writers, there are none who more gratifie and enlarge the Imagination, than the Authors of the new Philosophy, whether we consider their Theories of the Earth or Heavens, the Discoveries they have made by Glasses, or any other of their Contemplations on Nature. We are not a little pleased to find every green Leaf swarm with Millions of Animals, that at their largest Growth are not visible to the naked Eye. There is something very engaging to the Fancy, as well as to our Reason, in the Treatises of Metals, Minerals, Plants, and Meteors. But when we survey the whole Earth at

once, and the several Planets that lye within its Neighbourhood, we are filled with a pleasing Astonishment, to see so
many Worlds hanging one above another, and sliding round
their Axles in such an amazing Pomp and Solemnity.   If, after
this, we contemplate those wide Fields of *Ether*, that reach in
height as far as from *Saturn* to the fixt Stars, and run abroad
almost to an infinitude, our Imagination finds its Capacity
filled with so immense a Prospect, and puts it self upon the
Stretch to comprehend it.   But if we yet rise higher, and consider the fixt Stars as so many vast Oceans of Flame, that are
each of them attended with a different Sett of Planets, and
still discover new Firmaments and new Lights, that are sunk
farther in those unfathomable Depths of *Ether*, so as not to be
seen by the strongest of our Telescopes, we are lost in such a
Labarinth of Suns and Worlds, and confounded with the
Immensity and Magnificence of Nature.

Nothing is more pleasant to the Fancy, than to enlarge it
self, by Degrees, in its Contemplation of the various Propor-
tions which its several Objects bear to each other, when it
compares the Body of Man to the Bulk of the whole Earth,
the Earth to the Circle it describes round the Sun, that Circle
to the Sphere of the fixt Stars, the Sphere of the fixt Stars to
the Circuit of the whole Creation, the whole Creation it self
to the Infinite Space that is every where diffused about it; or
when the Imagination works downward, and considers the
Bulk of a Human Body, in respect of an Animal a hundred
times less than a Mite, the particular Limbs of such an Animal,
the different Springs which actuate the Limbs, the Spirits
which set these Springs a going, and the proportionable
Minuteness of these several Parts, before they have arrived at
their full Growth and Perfection.   But if, after all this, we
take the least Particle of these Animal Spirits, and consider its
Capacity of being wrought into a World, that shall contain
within those narrow Dimensions a Heaven and Earth, Stars
and Planets, and every different Species of living Creatures, in
the same Analogy and Proportion they bear to each other in
our own Universe; such a Speculation, by reason of its Nicety,
appears ridiculous to those who have not turned their Thoughts
that way, tho' at the same time it is founded on no less than
the Evidence of a Demonstration.   Nay, we might yet carry
it farther, and discover in the smallest Particle of this little
World a new inexhausted Fund of Matter, capable of being
spun out into another Universe.

I have dwelt the longer on this Subject, because I think it
may shew us the proper Limits, as well as the Defectiveness, of
our Imagination; how it is confined to a very small Quantity

of Space, and immediately stopt in its Operations, when it endeavours to take in any thing that is very great, or very little. Let a Man try to conceive the different Bulk of an Animal, which is twenty, from another which is a hundred times less than a Mite, or to compare, in his Thoughts, a length of a thousand Diameters of the Earth, with that of a Million, and he will quickly find that he has no different Measures in his Mind, adjusted to such extraordinary Degrees of Grandeur or Minuteness. The Understanding, indeed, opens an infinite Space on every side of us, but the Imagination, after a few faint Efforts, is immediately at a stand, and finds her self swallowed up in the Immensity of the Void that surrounds it: Our Reason can pursue a Particle of Matter through an infinite variety of Divisions, but the Fancy soon loses sight of it, and feels in it self a kind of Chasm, that wants to be filled with Matter of a more sensible Bulk. We can neither widen, nor contract the Faculty to the Dimensions of either Extreme: The Object is too big for our Capacity, when we would comprehend the Circumference of a World, and dwindles into nothing, when we endeavour after the Idea of an Atom.

It is possible this Defect of Imagination may not be in the Soul it self, but as it acts in Conjunction with the Body. Perhaps there may not be room in the Brain for such a variety of Impressions, or the Animal Spirits may be incapable of figuring them in such a manner, as is necessary to excite so very large or very minute Ideas. However it be, we may well suppose that Beings of a higher Nature very much excel us in this respect, as it is probable the Soul of Man will be infinitely more perfect hereafter in this Faculty, as well as in all the rest; insomuch that, perhaps, the Imagination will be able to keep Pace with the Understanding, and to form in it self distinct Ideas of all the different Modes and Quantities of Space.   O

No. 421.
[ADDISON.]   Thursday, July 3.

> *Ignotis errare locis, ignota videre*
> *Flumina gaudebat; studio minuente laborem.*—Ovid.

THE Pleasures of the Imagination are not wholly confined to such particular Authors as are conversant in material Objects, but are often to be met with among the Polite Masters of Morality, Criticism, and other Speculations abstracted from Matter, who, tho' they do not directly treat of the visible Parts of Nature, often draw from them their Similitudes, Metaphors, and Allegories. By these Allusions a Truth in the Understanding is as it were reflected by the Imagination; we are able to see something like Colour and Shape in a Notion, and to discover a Scheme of Thoughts traced out upon Matter. And here the Mind receives a great deal of Satisfaction, and has two of its Faculties gratified at the same time, while the Fancy is busie in copying after the Understanding, and transcribing Ideas out of the Intellectual World into the Material.

The Great Art of a Writer shews it self in the Choice of pleasing Allusions, which are generally to be taken from the *great* or *beautiful* Works of Art or Nature; for though whatever is New or Uncommon is apt to delight the Imagination, the chief Design of an Allusion being to illustrate and explain the Passages of an Author, it should be always borrowed from what is more known and common, than the Passages which are to be explained.

Allegories, when well chosen, are like so many Tracks of Light in a Discourse, that make every thing about them clear and beautiful. A noble Metaphor, when it is placed to an Advantage, casts a kind of Glory round it, and darts a Lustre through a whole Sentence; These different Kinds of Allusion are but so many different Manners of Similitude, and, that they may please the Imagination, the Likeness ought to be very exact, or very agreeable, as we love to see a Picture where the Resemblance is just, or the Posture and Air graceful. But we often find eminent Writers very faulty in this respect; great Scholars are apt to fetch their Comparisons and Allusions from the Sciences in which they are most conversant, so that a Man may see the Compass of their Learning in a Treatise on the most indifferent Subject. I have read a Discourse upon Love, which none but a profound Chymist could understand, and have heard many a Sermon that should only have been preached before a Congregation of *Cartesians*. On the contrary, your Men of Business usually have recourse to such Instances as are too mean and familiar. They are for drawing the Reader into a Game of Chess or Tennis, or for leading him from Shop to Shop, in the Cant of particular Trades and Employments. It is certain, there may be found an infinite Variety of very agreeable Allusions in both these kinds, but, for the generality, the most entertaining ones lie in the Works of Nature, which are obvious to all Capacities, and more delightful than what is to be found in Arts and Sciences.

It is this Talent of affecting the Imagination, that gives an Embellishment to good Sense, and makes one Man's Compositions more agreeable than another's. It setts off all Writings in general, but is the very Life and highest Perfection of Poetry. Where it shines in an Eminent Degree, it has preserved several Poems for many Ages, that have nothing else to recommend them; and where all the other Beauties are present, the Work appears dry and insipid, if this single one be wanting. It has something in it like Creation; It bestows a kind of Existence, and draws up to the Reader's View several Objects which are not to be found in Being. It makes Additions to Nature, and gives a greater Variety to God's Works. In a word, it is able to beautifie and adorn the most illustrious Scenes in the Universe, or to fill the Mind with more glorious Shows and Apparitions, than can be found in any Part of it.

We have now discovered the several Originals of those Pleasures that gratify the Fancy; and here, perhaps, it would not be very difficult to cast under their proper Heads those contrary Objects, which are apt to fill it with Distaste and Terrour; for the Imagination is as liable to Pain as Pleasure. When the Brain is hurt by any Accident, or the Mind disordered by Dreams or Sickness, the Fancy is over-run with wild dismal Ideas, and terrified with a thousand hideous Monsters of its own framing.

> *Eumenidum veluti demens videt agmina Pentheus,*
> *Et solem geminum, & duplices se ostendere Thebas.*
> *Aut Agamemnonius scenis agitatus Orestes,*
> *Armatam facibus matrem & serpentibus atris*
> *Cum fugit, ultricesque sedent in limine Dirae.*—Virg.

There is not a Sight in Nature so mortifying as that of a Distracted Person, when his Imagination is troubled, and his whole Soul disordered and confused. *Babylon* in Ruins is not so melancholy a Spectacle. But to quit so disagreeable a Subject, I shall only consider by way of Conclusion, what an infinite Advantage this Faculty gives an Almighty Being over the Soul of Man, and how great a measure of Happiness or Misery we are capable of receiving from the Imagination only.

We have already seen the Influence that one Man has over the Fancy of another, and with what Ease he conveys into it a Variety of Imagery; how great a Power then may we suppose lodged in him, who knows all the ways of affecting the Imagination, who can infuse what Ideas he pleases, and fill those Ideas with Terrour and Delight to what Degree he thinks fit? He can excite Images in the Mind without the help of Words, and make Scenes rise up before us and seem present to the Eye, without the Assistance of Bodies or Exterior Objects. He can transport the Imagination with such beautiful and glorious Visions, as cannot possibly enter into our present Conceptions, or haunt it with such ghastly Spectres and Apparitions, as would make us hope for Annihiliation, and think Existence no better than a Curse. In short, he can so exquisitely ravish or torture the Soul through this single Faculty, as might suffice to make the whole Heaven or Hell of any finite Being.

This Essay on the Pleasures of the Imagination having been published in separate Papers, I shall conclude it with a Table of the principal Contents of each Paper.

The CONTENTS.

PAPER I.

The Perfection of our Sight above our other Senses. The Pleasures of the Imagination *arise originally from Sight. The Pleasures of the Imagination divided under* two Heads. *The Pleasures of the* Imagination *in some Respects equal to those of the Understanding. The* Extent *of the Pleasures of the Imagination. The Advantages a Man receives from a* Relish of these Pleasures. *In what Respect they are preferable to those of the Understanding.*

PAPER II.

Three Sources *of all the Pleasures of the Imagination, in our Survey of outward Objects. How what is* Great *pleases the Imagination. How what is* New *pleases the Imagination. How what is* Beautiful *in our own Species, pleases the Imagination. How what is* Beautiful *in general pleases the Imagination. What other Accidental Causes may contribute to the* heightning *of these Pleasures.*

PAPER III.

Why the Necessary Cause *of our being pleased with what is Great, New, or Beautiful, unknown. Why the* Final Cause *more known and more useful. The Final Cause of our being pleased with what is* Great. *The Final Cause of our being pleased with what is* New. *The Final Cause of our being pleased with what is* Beautiful in our own Species. *The Final Cause of our being pleased with what is* Beautiful in general.

PAPER IV.

The Works of Nature *more pleasant to the Imagination than those of* Art. *The Works of Nature still more pleasant, the more they* resemble *those of Art. The Works of Art more pleasant, the more they* resemble *those of Nature. Our* English Plantations *and* Gardens *considered in the foregoing Light.*

PAPER V.

Of Architecture *as it affects the Imagination.* Greatness *in Architecture relates either to the* Bulk *or to the* Manner. *Greatness*

of Bulk in the Ancient Oriental Buildings. *The Ancient
Accounts of these Buildings confirm'd,* 1. *From the Advantages,
for raising such Works, in the first Ages of the World and in the
Eastern Climates:* 2. *From several of them which are still Extant.
Instances how* Greatness of Manner *affects the Imagination.
A* French *Author's Observation on this Subject. Why Concave
and Convex Figures give a Greatness of Manner to Works of
Architecture. Every thing that pleases the Imagination in
Architecture is either Great, Beautiful, or New.*

PAPER VI.

The Secondary *Pleasures of the Imagination. The several
Sources of these Pleasures,* (Statuary, Painting, Description *and*
Musick) *compared together. The* Final Cause *of our receiving
Pleasure from these several Sources. Of* Descriptions *in Parti-
cular. The Power of Words over the Imagination. Why one
Reader more pleased with Descriptions than another.*

PAPER VII.

How a whole Set of Ideas Hang together, *&c. A Natural
Cause assigned for it. How to* perfect *the Imagination of a
Writer. Who among the* Ancient Poets *had this Faculty in its
greatest Perfection.* Homer *excelled in Imagining what is
Great;* Virgil *in Imagining what is Beautiful;* Ovid *in Imagining
what is New. Our own Country-Man* Milton, *very perfect in
all three respects.*

PAPER VIII.

Why any thing that is unpleasant *to behold, pleases the
Imagination when well Described. Why the Imagination receives
a more Exquisite Pleasure from the Description of what is* Great,
New, *or* Beautiful. *The Pleasure still heightned, if what is
described raises* Passion *in the Mind.* Disagreeable *Passions
pleasing when raised by apt Descriptions. Why* Terrour *and*
Grief *are pleasing to the Mind when excited by Descriptions. A
particular Advantage the Writers in Poetry and Fiction have to
please the Imagination. What Liberties are allowed them.*

PAPER IX.

Of that kind of Poetry *which Mr.* Dryden *calls the* Fairy-Way
of Writing. *How a Poet should be* Qualified *for it. The*
Pleasures *of the Imagination that arise from it. In this respect,
why the* Moderns *excell the* Ancients. *Why the* English *excell the*
Moderns. *Who the Best among the* English. *Of* Emblematical
Persons.

PAPER X.

What Authors please the Imagination who have nothing to do
with Fiction. *How* History *pleases the Imagination. How
the* Authors of the new Philosophy *please the Imagination.
The* Bounds *and* Defects *of the Imagination. Whether these
Defects are* Essential *to the Imagination.*

PAPER XI.

How those please the Imagination, who treat of Subjects
abstracted from Matter, *by Allusions taken from it. What*
Allusions *most pleasing to the Imagination. Great Writers how*
Faulty *in this Respect. Of the Art of* Imagining *in General.
The Imagination capable of* Pain *as well as Pleasure.* In what
Degree *the Imagination is capable either of Pain or Pleasure.* O

No. 422.
[STEELE.]   Friday, July 4.

Haec . . . scripsi . . . non otii abundantia sed amoris erga te.—
Tull. Epis.

I DO not know any thing which gives greater Disturbance to
Conversation, than the false Notion some People have of
Raillery. It ought certainly to be the first Point to be aimed
at in Society, to gain the good Will of those with whom you
converse. The way to that, is to shew you are well inclined
towards them: What then can be more absurd, than to set up
for being extremely sharp and biting, as the Term is, in your
Expressions to your Familiars? A Man who has no good
Quality but Courage, is in a very ill way towards making an
agreeable Figure in the World, because that which he has
superior to other People cannot be exerted, without raising
himself an *Enemy.* Your Gentleman of a Satyrical Vein is in
the like Condition. To say a thing which perplexes the Heart
of him you speak to, or brings Blushes into his Face, is a degree
of Murder; and it is, I think, an unpardonable Offence to shew
a Man you do not care, whether he is pleased or displeased.
But won't you then take a Jest? Yes, but pray let it be a
Jest. It is no Jest to put me, who am so unhappy as to have
an utter Aversion to speaking to more than one Man at a time,
under a necessity to explain my self in much Company, and
reducing me to Shame and Derision, except I perform what
my Infirmity of Silence disables me to do.

Callisthenes has great Wit accompanied with that Quality
(without which a Man can have no Wit at all) a sound

Judgment. This gentleman raillies the best of any Man I know, for he forms his Ridicule upon a Circumstance which you are in your Heart not unwilling to grant him, to wit, that you are Guilty of an Excess in something which is in it self laudable. He very well understands what you would be, and needs not fear your Anger for declaring you are a little too much that thing. The Generous will bear being reproach'd as Lavish, and the Valiant, Rash, without being provoked to Resentment against their Monitor. What has been said to be a Mark of a good Writer will fall in with the Character of a good Companion. The good Writer makes his Reader better pleased with himself, and the agreeable Man makes his Friends enjoy themselves, rather than him, while he is in their Company. *Callisthenes* does this with inimitable Pleasantry. He whispered a Friend the other Day, so as to be overheard by a young Officer, who gave symptoms of Cocking upon the Company, That Gentleman has very much of the Air of a General Officer. The Youth immediately put on a Composed Behaviour, and behaved himself suitably to the Conceptions he believed the Company had of him. It is to be allowed that *Callisthenes* will make a Man run into impertinent Relations, to his own Advantage, and express the Satisfaction he has in his own dear self till he is very ridiculous, but in this case the Man is made a Fool by his own Consent, and not exposed as such whether he will or no. I take it therefore that, to make Raillery agreeable, a Man must either not know he is raillied, or think never the worse of himself if he sees he is.

Acetus is of a quite contrary Genius, and is more generally admired than *Callisthenes*, but not with Justice. *Acetus* has no regard to the Modesty or Weakness of the Person he raillies; but if his Quality or Humility gives him any Superiority to the Man he would fall upon, he has no Mercy in making the Onset. He can be pleased to see his best Friend out of Countenance, while the Laugh is loud in his own Applause: His Raillery always puts the Company into little Divisions and separate Interests, while that of *Callisthenes* cements it, and makes every Man not only better pleased with himself, but also with all the rest in the Conversation.

To railly well, it is absolutely necessary that Kindness must run thro' all you say, and you must ever preserve the Character of a Friend to support your Pretentions to be free with a Man. *Acetus* ought to be banished human Society, because he raises his Mirth upon giving Pain to the Person upon whom he is pleasant. Nothing but the Malevolence, which is too general towards those who excell, could make his Company tolerated; but they, with whom he converses, are sure to see some Man sacrificed wherever he is admitted, and all the Credit he has for Wit is owing to the Gratification it gives to other Men's Ill-nature.

Minutius has a Wit that conciliates a Man's Love, at the same time that it is exerted against his Faults.   He has an Art in keeping the Person he raillies in Countenance, by insinuating that he himself is guilty of the same Imperfection.   This he does with so much Address, that he seems rather to bewail himself, than fall upon his Friend.

It is really monstrous to see how unaccountably it prevails among Men, to take the Liberty of displeasing each other. One would think sometimes that the Contention is, who shall be most disagreeable.   Allusions to past Follies, Hints which revive what a Man has a mind to forget for ever, and deserves that all the rest of the World should, are commonly brought forth even in Company of Men of Distinction.   They do not thrust with the Skill of Fencers, but cut up with the Barbarity of Butchers.   It is, methinks, below the Character of Men of Humanity and Good-manners, to be capable of Mirth while there is any one of the Company in Pain and Disorder.   They who have the true Taste of Conversation, enjoy themselves in a Communication of each other's Excellencies, and not in a Triumph over their Imperfections.   *Fortius* would have been reckoned a Wit, if there had never been a Fool in the World. He wants not Foils to be a Beauty, but has that natural Pleasure in observing Perfection in others, that his own Faults are over-looked out of Gratitude by all his Acquaintance.

After these several Characters of Men who succeed or fail in Raillery, it may not be amiss to reflect a little further what one takes to be the most agreeable Kind of it; and that to me appears when the Satyr is directed against Vice, with an Air of Contempt of the Fault, but no Ill-will to the Criminal.   Mr. *Congreve*'s *Doris* is a Master-piece in this Kind.   It is the Character of a Woman utterly abandoned, but her Impudence by the finest Piece of Raillery is made only Generosity.

> *Peculiar therefore is her Way,*
>   *Whether by Nature taught,*
> *I shall not undertake to say,*
>   *Or by Experience bought.*
>
> *For who o'er Night obtain'd her Grace,*
>   *She can next Day disown,*
> *And stare upon the strange Man's Face,*
>   *As one she ne'er had known.*

> *So well she can the Truth disguise,*
> *Such artful Wonder frame,*
> *The Lover or distrusts his Eyes,*
> *Or thinks 'twas all a Dream.*

> *Some censure this as lewd or* **low,**
> *Who are to Bounty blind;*
> *But to forget what we bestow,*
> *Bespeaks a noble Mind.*

T

No. 423.
[STEELE.]   Saturday, July 5.

Nuper idoneus.—Hor.

I LOOK upon my self as a kind of Guardian to the Fair, and am always watchful to observe any thing which concerns their Interest.   The present Paper shall be employed in the Service of a very fine young Woman; and the Admonitions I give her, may not be unuseful to the rest of the Sex.   *Gloriana* shall be the Name of the Heroine in to Day's Entertainment; and when I have told you that she is rich, witty, young, and beautiful, you will believe she does not want Admirers.   She has had since she came to Town about twenty five of those Lovers, who make their Addresses by way of Jointure and Settlement. These come and go, with great Indifference on both Sides; and as beauteous as she is, a Line in a Deed has had Exception enough against it, to outweigh the Lustre of her Eyes, the Readiness of her Understanding, and the Merit of her general Character.   But among the Crowd of such cool Adorers, she has two who are very assiduous in their Attendance.   There is something so extraordinary and artful in their Manner of Application, that I think it but common Justice to alarm her in it.   I have done it in the following Letter.

'*Madam,*

I have for some Time taken Notice of two Gentlemen who attend you in all publick Places, both of whom have also easie Access to you at your own House: But the Matter is adjusted between them, and *Damon*, who so passionately addresses you, has no Design upon you; but *Strephon*, who seems to be indifferent to you, is the Man who is, as they have settled it, to have you.   The Plot was laid over a Bottle of Wine; and *Strephon*, when he first thought of you, proposed to *Damon* to be his Rival.   The Manner of his breaking of it to him, I was so placed at a Tavern, that I could not avoid hearing. *Damon*, said he, with a deep Sigh, I have long languished for

that Miracle of Beauty *Gloriana*; and if you will be very sted-
fastly my Rival, I shall certainly obtain her. Do not, continued he, be offended at this Overture; for I go upon the
Knowledge of the Temper of the Woman, rather than any
Vanity that I should profit by an Opposition of your Pretensions to those of your humble Servant. *Gloriana* has very
good Sense, a quick Relish of the Satisfactions of Life, and will
not give her self, as the Crowd of Women do, to the Arms of a
Man to whom she is indifferent. As she is a sensible Woman,
Expressions of Rapture and Adoration will not move her
neither; but he that has her must be the Object of her Desire,
not her Pity. The Way to this End I take to be, that a Man's
general Conduct should be agreeable, without addressing in
particular to the Woman he loves. Now, Sir, if you will be
so kind as to sigh and die for *Gloriana*, I will carry it with great
Respect towards her, but seem void of any Thoughts as a Lover.
By this Means I shall be in the most amiable Light of which I
am capable; I shall be received with Freedom, you with
Reserve. *Damon*, who has himself no Designs of Marriage at
all, easily fell into the Scheme; and you may observe, that
wherever you are *Damon* appears also. You see he carries
on an unaffecting Exactness in his Dress and Manners, and
strives always to be the very Contrary of *Strephon*. They have
already succeeded so far, that your Eyes are ever in Search of
Strephon, and turn themselves of Course from *Damon*. They
meet and compare Notes upon your Carriage; and the Letter
which was brought to you the other Day was a Contrivance
to remark your Resentment. When you saw the Billet sub-
scribed *Strephon*, and turned away with a scornful Air, and
cried Impertinence! you gave Hopes to him that shuns you,
without mortifying him that languishes for you.

What I am concerned for, Madam, is, that in the disposal of
your Heart, you should know what you are doing, and examine
it before it is lost. *Strephon* contradicts you in Discourse with
the Civility of one who has a value for you, but gives up
nothing like one that loves you. This seeming Unconcern
gives his Behaviour the advantage of Sincerity, and insensibly
obtains your good Opinion, by appearing disinterested in the
purchase of it. If you watch these Correspondents hereafter,
you will find that *Strephon* makes his Visit of Civility immediately after *Damon* has tired you with one of Love. Tho'
you are very discreet, you will find it no easie matter to escape
the Toils so well laid, as when one studies to be disagreeable
in Passion, the other to be pleasing without it. All the Turns
of your Temper are carefully watched, and their quick and
faithful Intelligence gives your Lovers irresistible Advantage.

You will please, Madam, to be upon your guard, and take all the necessary Precautions against one who is amiable to you before you know he is enamoured.

> *I am,*
>> *Madam,*
>>> *Your most Obedient Servant.*'

Strephon makes great Progress in this Lady's good Graces, for most Women being actuated by some little Spirit of Pride and Contradiction, he has the good effects of both those Motives by this Covert-Way of Courtship. He received a Message Yesterday from *Damon* in the following words, superscribed *With speed*.

'All goes well; she is very angry at me, and I dare say hates me in earnest. It is a good time to Visit.

>> *Yours.*'

The Comparison of *Strephon*'s Gayety to *Damon*'s Languishment, strikes her Imagination with a Prospect of very agreeable Hours with such a Man as the former, and Abhorrence of the insipid Prospect with one like the latter. To know when a Lady is displeased with another, is to know the best time of advancing your self. This method of two Persons playing in each other's Hand is so dangerous, that I cannot tell how a Woman could be able to withstand such a Siege. The Condition of *Gloriana*, I am afraid, is irretrievable, for *Strephon* has had so many Opportunities of pleasing without suspicion, that all which is left for her to do is to bring him, now she is advised, to an Explanation of his Passion, and beginning again, if she can conquer the kind Sentiments she has already conceived for him. When one shews himself a Creature to be avoided, the other proper to be fled to for Succour, they have the whole Woman between them, and can occasionally rebound her Love and Hatred from one to the other, in such a manner as to keep her at a distance from all the rest of the World, and cast Lots for the Conquest.

N.B. *I have many other Secrets which concern the Empire of Love, but I consider that while I alarm my Women, I instruct my Men.*   T

No. 424.
[STEELE.]   Monday, July 7.

Est Ulubris, animus si te non deficit . . .—Hor.

'*Mr.* SPECTATOR,   *London, June* 24.

A MAN who has it in his Power to chuse his own Company,
would certainly be much to blame should he not, to the best
of his Judgment, take such as are of a Temper most suitable
to his own; and where that Choice is wanting, or where a Man
is mistaken in his Choice, and yet under a Necessity of con-
tinuing in the same Company, it will certainly be his Interest
to carry himself as easily as possible.

In this I am sensible I do but repeat what has been said a
thousand times, at which however I think no Body has any
Title to take Exception, but they who never failed to put this
in Practice.—Not to use any longer Preface, this being the
Season of the Year in which great Numbers of all sorts of
People retire from this Place of Business and Pleasure to
Country Solitude, I think it not improper to advise them to
take with them as great a Stock of Good-humour as they can;
for tho' a Country-Life is described as the most pleasant of all
others, and though it may in truth be so, yet it is so only to
those who know how to enjoy Leisure and Retirement.

As for those who can't live without the constant Helps of
Business or Company, let them consider, that in the Country
there is no *Exchange*, there are no Play-houses, no Variety of
Coffee-houses, nor many of those other Amusements, which
serve here as so many Reliefs from the repeated Occurrences
in their own Families; but that there the greatest Part of their
Time must be spent within themselves, and consequently it
behoves them to consider how agreeable it will be to them
before they leave this dear Town.

I remember, Mr. SPECTATOR, we were very well entertained
last Year, with the Advices you gave us from Sir ROGER'S
Country-Seat; which I the rather mention, because 'tis almost
impossible not to live pleasantly, where the Master of a Family
is such a one as you there describe your Friend, who cannot
therefore (I mean as to his domestick Character) be too often
recommended to the Imitation of others.   How amiable is that
Affability and Benevolence with which he treats his Neighbours, and every one, even the meanest of his own Family!
And yet how seldom imitated! instead of which we commonly
meet with ill-natured Expostulations, Noise, and Chidings.—
And this I hinted, because the Humour and Disposition of the
Head, is what chiefly influences all the other Parts of a Family.

An Agreement and kind Correspondence between Friends and Acquaintance, is the greatest Pleasure of Life. This is an undoubted Truth, and yet any Man who judges from the Practice of the World will be almost perswaded to believe the contrary; for how can we suppose People should be so industrious to make themselves uneasie? what can engage them to entertain and foment Jealousies of one another upon every the least Occasion? Yet so it is, there are People who (as it should seem) delight in being troublesome and vexatious, who (as *Tully* speaks) *Mira sunt alacritate ad litigandum, Have a certain Chearfulness in wrangling.* And thus it happens, that there are very few Families in which there are not Feuds and Animosities, tho' 'tis every one's Interest, there more particularly to avoid 'em, because (as I would willingly hope) no one gives another Uneasiness, without feeling some Share of it— But I am gone beyond what I designed, and had almost forgot what I chiefly proposed; which was, barely to tell you how hardly we who pass most of our Time in Town dispence with a long Vacation in the Country, how uneasie we grow to our selves and to one another when our Conversation is confined, insomuch that by *Michaelmas*, 'tis odds but we come to downright squabbling, and make as free with one another to our Faces, as we do with the rest of the World behind their Backs. After I have told you this, I am to desire that you would now and then give us a Lesson of Good-humour, a Family-Piece; which, since we are all very fond of you, I hope may have some Influence upon us. . . .

After these plain Observations give me leave to give you an Hint of what a Set of Company of my Acquaintance, who are now gone into the Country, and have the Use of an absent Nobleman's Seat, have settled among themselves, to avoid the Inconveniencies above-mentioned. They are a Collection of ten or twelve, of the same good Inclination towards each other, but of very different Talents and Inclinations: From hence they hope, that the Variety of their Tempers will only create Variety of Pleasures. But as there always will arise, among the same People, either for want of Diversity of Objects, or the like Causes, a certain Satiety, which may grow into Ill-Humour or Discontent, there is a large Wing of the House which they design to employ in the Nature of an Infirmary. Whoever says a peevish thing, or acts any thing which betrays a Sowerness or Indisposition to Company, is immediately to be conveyed to his Chambers in the Infirmary, from whence he is not to be relieved, 'till by his Manner of Submission, and the Sentiments expressed in his Petition for that Purpose, he appears to the Majority of the Company to be again fit for

Society. You are to understand, that all ill-natured Words or uneasie Gestures are sufficient Cause for Banishment; speaking impatiently to Servants, making a Man repeat what he says, or any thing that betrays Inattention or Dishumour, are also criminal without Reprieve: But it is provided, that whoever observes the ill-natured Fit coming upon himself, and voluntarily retires, shall be received at his Return from the Infirmary with the highest Marks of Esteem. By these and other wholsom Methods it is expected that if they cannot cure one another, yet at least they have taken care that the ill Humour of one shall not be troublesome to the rest of the Company. There are many other Rules which the Society have established for the Preservation of their Ease and Tranquility, the Effects of which, with the Incidents that arise among them, shall be communicated to you from Time to Time for the publick Good, by,

Sir,

Your most humble Servant,

T   R. O.'

No. 425.   Tuesday, July 8.

Frigora mitescunt Zephyris, ver proterit aestas
Interitura, simul
Pomifer autumnus fruges effuderit, & mox
Bruma recurrit iners.—Hor

'*Mr.* SPECTATOR,

THERE is hardly any thing gives me a more sensible Delight, than the Enjoyment of a cool still Evening after the Uneasiness of a hot sultry Day. Such a one I passed not long ago, which made me rejoyce, when the Hour was come for the Sun to set, that I might enjoy the Freshness of the Evening in my Garden, which then affords me the pleasantest Hours I pass in the whole Four and twenty. I immediately rose from my Couch, and went down into it. You descend at first by twelve Stone Steps into a large Square divided into four Grass-plots, in each of which is a Statue of white Marble. This is separated from a large Parterre by a low Wall, and from thence, thro' a Pair of Iron Gates, you are led into a long broad Walk of the finest Turf, set on each Side with tall Yews, and on either Hand border'd by a Canal, which on the Right divides the Walk from a Wilderness parted into Variety of Allies and Arbours, and on the Left from a kind of Amphitheatre, which is the Receptacle of a great Number of Oranges and Myrtles. The Moon shone bright, and seemed then most agreeably to supply the Place of the Sun, obliging me with as much Light as was necessary to discover a thousand pleasing Objects, and at the same Time divested of all Power of Heat. The Reflection of it in the Water, the fanning of the Wind rustling on the Leaves, the Singing of the Thrush and Nightingale, and the Coolness of the Walks, all conspired to make me lay aside all displeasing Thoughts, and brought me into such a Tranquility of Mind, as is I believe the next Happiness to that of hereafter. In this sweet Retirement I naturally fell into the Repetition of some Lines out of a Poem of *Milton*'s, which he entitles *Il Penseroso*, the Ideas of which were exquisitely suited to my present Wandrings of Thought.

> *Sweet Bird! that shun'st the Noise of Folly,*
> *Most musical! most melancholy!*
> *Thee, Chauntress, oft the Woods among,*
> *I wooe to hear thy Evening Song:*
> *And missing thee, I walk unseen*
> *On the dry smooth-shaven Green,*
> *To behold the wandring Moon,*
> *Riding near her highest Noon,*
> *Like one that hath been led astray,*
> *Thro' the Heav'n's wide pathless Way,*
> *And oft, as if her Head she bow'd,*
> *Stooping thro' a fleecy Cloud.*
>
> *Then let some strange mysterious Dream*
> *Wave with his Wings in airy Stream,*
> *Of lively Portraiture display'd,*
> *Softly on my Eyelids laid;*
> *And as I wake, sweet Musick breathe*
> *Above, about, or underneath,*
> *Sent by Spirits to Mortals Good,*
> *Or th' unseen Genius of the Wood.*

I reflected then upon the sweet Vicissitudes of Night and Day, on the charming Disposition of the Seasons, and their Return again in a perpetual Circle; and oh! said I, that I could from these my declining Years, return again to my first Spring of Youth and Vigour; but that, alas! is impossible: All that remains within my Power, is to soften the Inconveniencies I feel, with an easie contented Mind, and the Enjoyment of such Delights as this Solitude affords me. In this Thought I sate me down on a Bank of Flowers and dropt into a Slumber, which whether it were the Effect of Fumes and Vapours, or my present Thoughts, I know not; but methought the Genius of the Garden stood before me, and introduced into the Walk where I lay this Drama and different Scenes of the Revolution of the Year, which whilst I then saw, even in my Dream, I resolved to write down, and send to the SPECTATOR.

The first Person whom I saw advancing towards me, was a
Youth of a most beautiful Air and Shape, tho' he seemed not
yet arrived at that exact Proportion and Symmetry of Parts
which a little more Time would have given him; but however,
there was such a Bloom in his Countenance, such Satisfaction
and Joy, that I thought it the most desirable Form that I had
ever seen.   He was cloathed in a flowing Mantle of green Silk,
interwoven with Flowers: He had a Chaplet of Roses on his
Head, and a *Narcissus* in his Hand; Primroses and Violets
sprang up under his Feet, and all Nature was cheer'd at his
Approach.   *Flora* was on one Hand, and *Vertumnus* on the
other I this was surprised
to see the Moon-beams reflected with a sudden Glare from
Armour, and to see a Man compleatly armed advancing with
his Sword drawn.   I was soon informed by the Genius it was
Mars, who had long usurped a Place among the Attendants of
the *Spring*.   He made way for a softer Appearance; it was
Venus, without any Ornament but her own Beauties, not so
much as her own Cestus, with which she had incompass'd a
Globe, which she held in her right Hand, and in her left she
had a Sceptre of Gold.   After her followed the Graces with
their Arms intwined within one another, their Girdles were
loosed, and they moved to the Sound of soft Musick, striking
the Ground alternately with their Feet.   Then came up the
three Months which belong to this Season.   As *March* advanced towards me, there was methought in his Look a louring
Roughness, which ill befitted a Month which was ranked in so
soft a Season; but as he came forwards his Features became
insensibly more mild and gentle: He smooth'd his Brow, and
looked with so sweet a Countenance that I could not but
lament his Departure, though he made way for *April*.   He
appeared in the greatest Gayety imaginable, and had a
thousand Pleasures to attend him: His Look was frequently
clouded, but immediately return'd to its first Composure, and
remained fixed in a Smile.   Then came *May* attended by
Cupid, with his Bow strung, and in a Posture to let fly an
Arrow: As he passed by methought I heard a confused Noise
of soft Complaints, gentle Extasies, and tender Sighs of Lovers;
Vows of Constancy, and as many Complainings of Perfidious-
ness; all which the Winds wafted away as soon as they had
reached my Hearing.   After these I saw a Man advance in the
full Prime and Vigour of his Age, his Complexion was sanguine
and ruddy, his Hair black, and fell down in beautiful Ringlets
not beneath his Shoulders, a Mantle of hair-coloured Silk hung
loosely upon him: He advanced with a hasty Step after the
Spring, and sought out the Shade and cool Fountains which

plaid in the Garden. He was particularly well pleased when a
Troop of *Zephyrs* fanned him with their Wings; He had two
Companions who walked on each Side, that made him appear
the most agreeable; the one was *Aurora* with Fingers of Roses,
and her Feet dewy, attired in gray: The other was *Vesper* in a
Robe of Azure beset with Drops of Gold, whose Breath he
caught whilst it passed over a Bundle of Honey-suckles and
Tuberoses which he held in his Hand. *Pan* and *Ceres* followed
them with four Reapers, who danced a Morrice to the Sound
of Oaten Pipes and Cymbals. Then came the Attendant
Months. *June* retained still some small Likeness of the *Spring*;
but the other two seemed to step with a less vigorous Tread,
especially *August*, who seem'd almost to faint whilst for half
the Steps he took the Dog-Star levelled his Rays full at his
Head: They passed on and made Way for a Person that seemed
to bend a little under the Weight of Years; his Beard and Hair,
which were full grown, were composed of an equal Number of
black and grey; he wore a Robe which he had girt round him
of a yellowish Cast, not unlike the Colour of fallen Leaves
which he walked upon. I thought he hardly made Amends
for expelling the foregoing Scene by the large Quantity of
Fruits which he bore in his Hands. *Plenty* walked by his Side
with an healthy fresh Countenance, pouring out from an Horn
all the various Product of the Year. *Pomona* followed with a
Glass of Cyder in her Hand, with *Bacchus* in a Chariot drawn
by Tygers, accompanied by a whole Troop of Satyrs, Fauns,
and Sylvans. *September*, who came next, seemed in his Looks
to promise a new *Spring*, and wore the Livery of those Months.
The succeeding Month was all soiled with the Juice of Grapes,
as if he had just come from the Wine Press. *November*, though
he was in this Division, yet by the many Stops he made seemed
rather inclin'd to the *Winter*, which followed close at his Heels.
He advanced in the Shape of an old Man in the Extremity of
Age: The Hair he had was so very white it seem'd a real Snow;
his Eyes were red and piercing, and his Beard hung with a
great Quantity of Icicles. He was wrapt up in Furrs, but yet
so pinched with excess of Cold that his Limbs were all contracted and his Body bent to the Ground, so that he could not
have supported himself had it not been for *Comus* the God of
Revels, and *Necessity* the Mother of Fate, who sustained him
on each Side. The Shape and Mantle of *Comus* was one of the
things that most surprized me; as he advanced towards me his
Countenance seemed the most desirable I had ever seen: On
the fore Part of his Mantle was pictured Joy, Delight, and
Satisfaction, with a thousand Emblems of Merriment, and
Jests with Faces looking two Ways at once; but as he passed

from me I was amazed at a Shape so little correspondent to his Face: His Head was bald, and all the rest of his Limbs appeared old and deformed. On the hinder Part of his Mantel was represented Murder, with disheveled Hair and a Dagger all bloody, Anger in a Robe of Scarlet, and Suspicion squinting with both Eyes; but above all the most conspicuous was the Battel of the *Lapithae* and the *Centaurs.* I detested so hideous a Shape, and turned my Eyes upon *Saturn,* who was stealing away behind him with a Scythe in one Hand and an Hour-Glass in t'other unobserved. Behind *Necessity* was *Vesta* the Goddess of Fire with a Lamp which was perpetually supply'd with Oyl, and whose Flame was eternal. She cheered the rugged Brow of *Necessity,* and warmed her so far as almost to make her assume the Features and Likeness of *Choice. December, January,* and *February,* passed on after the rest all in Furrs; there was little Distinction to be made amongst them, and they were more or less displeasing as they discovered more or less Haste towards the grateful Return of *Spring.'*   Z

No. 426.
[STEELE.]   Wednesday, July 9.

> *. . . Quid non mortalia pectora cogis,*
> *Auri sacra fames?*—Virg.

A VERY agreeable Friend of mine, the other Day, carrying me in his Coach into the Country to Dinner, fell into Discourse concerning the Care of Parents due to their Children, and the Piety of Children towards their Parents. He was reflecting upon the Succession of particular Virtues and Qualities there might be preserved from one Generation to another, if these Regards were reciprocally held in Veneration: But as he never fails to mix an Air of Mirth and good Humour with his good Sense and Reasoning, he entered into the following Relation.

I will not be confident in what Century, or under what Reign it happened, that this Want of mutual Confidence and right Understanding between Father and Son was fatal to the Family of the *Valentines* in *Germany. Basilius Valentinus* was a Person who had arrived at the utmost Perfection in the Hermetick Art, and initiated his Son *Alexandrinus* in the same Mysteries: But as you know they are not to be attained but by the Painful, the Pious, the Chaste, and Pure of Heart, *Basilius* did not open to him, because of his Youth, and the Deviations too natural to it, the greatest Secrets of which he was Master, as well knowing that the Operation would fail in the Hands of a

Man so liable to Errors in Life as *Alexandrinus*. But believing, from a certain Indisposition of Mind as well as Body, his Dissolution was drawing nigh, he called *Alexandrinus* to him, and as he lay on a Couch, over-against which his Son was seated, and prepared by sending out Servants one after another, and Admonition to examine that no one over-heard them, he revealed the most important of his Secrets with the Solemnity and Language of an Adept. My Son, said he, many have been the Watchings, long the Lucubrations, constant the Labours of thy Father, not only to gain a great and plentiful Estate to his Posterity, but also to take Care that he should have no Posterity. Be not amazed, my Child; I do not mean that thou shalt be taken from me, but that I will never leave thee, and consequently cannot be said to have Posterity. Behold, my dearest *Alexandrinus*, the Effect of what was propagated in nine Months: We are not to contradict Nature, but to follow and to help her; just as long as an Infant is in the Womb of its Parent, so long are these Medicines of Revification in preparing. Observe this small Phial and this little Gallipot, in this an Unguent, in the other a Liquor. In these, my Child, are collected such Powers, as shall revive the Springs of Life when they are yet but just ceased, and give new Strength, new Spirits, and, in a word, wholly restore all the Organs and Senses of the human Body to as great a Duration, as it had before enjoyed from its Birth, to the Day of the Application of these my Medicines. But, my beloved Son, Care must be taken to apply them within ten Hours after the Breath is out of the Body, while yet the Clay is warm with its late Life, and yet capable of Resuscitation. I find my Frame grown crasie with perpetual Toil and Meditation; and I conjure you, as soon as I am dead, to anoint me with this Unguent; and when you see me begin to move, pour into my Lips this inestimable Liquor, else the Force of the Ointment will be ineffectual. By this means you will give me Life as I have you, and we will from that Hour mutually lay aside the Authority of having bestowed Life on each other, but live as Brethren, and prepare new Medicines against such another Period of Time as will demand another Application of the same Restoratives. In a few days after these wonderful Ingredients were delivered to *Alexandrinus*, *Basilius* departed this Life. But such was the pious Sorrow of the Son at the Loss of so excellent a Father, and the first Transports of Grief had so wholly disabled him from all manner of Business, that he never thought of the Medicines till the Time to which his Father had limited their Efficacy was expired. To tell the Truth, *Alexandrinus* was a Man of Wit and Pleasure, and considered his Father had lived out his natural Time, his Life was long and uniform, suitable to the Regularity of it; but that he himself, poor Sinner, wanted a new Life, to repent of a very bad one hitherto; and in the Examination of his Heart, resolved to go on as he did with this natural Being of his, but repent very faithfully, and spend very piously the Life to which he should be restored by Application of these Rarities, when Time should come, to his own Person.

It has been observed, that Providence frequently punishes the Self-Love of Men who would do immoderately for their own Offspring, with Children very much below their Characters and Qualifications, insomuch that they only transmit their Names to be born by those who give daily Proofs of the Vanity of the Labour and Ambition of their Progenitors.

It happened thus in the Family of *Basilius*; for *Alexandrinus* began to enjoy his ample Fortune in all the Extremities of Houshold Expence, Furniture, and insolent Equipage; and this he pursued till the Day of his own Departure began, as he grew sensible, to approach. As *Basilius* was punished with a Son very unlike him, *Alexandrinus* was visited with one of his own Disposition. It is natural that ill Men should be suspicious, and *Alexandrinus*, besides that Jealousie, had Proofs of the vitious Disposition of his Son *Renatus*, for that was his Name.

Alexandrinus, as I observed, having very good Reasons for thinking it unsafe to trust the real Secret of his Phial and Gally-pot to any Man living, projected to make sure Work, and Hope for his Success depending from the Avarice, not the Bounty of his Benefactor.

With this Thought he called *Renatus* to his Bedside, and bespoke him in the most pathetick Gesture and Accent. As much, my Son, as you have been addicted to Vanity and Pleasure, as I also have been before you, you nor I could escape the Fame, or the good Effects of the profound Knowledge of our Progenitor, the renowned *Basilius*. His Symbol is very well known in the Philosophick World, and I shall never forget the venerable Air of his Countenance, when he let me into the profound Mysteries of *the Smaragdine Table of* Hermes. *It is true*, said he, *and far removed from all Colour of Deceit, That which is Inferiour is like that which is Superiour, by which are acquired and perfected all the Miracles of a certain Work. The Father is the Sun, the Mother the Moon, the Wind is the Womb, the Earth is the Nurse of it, and Mother of all Perfection. All this must be received with Modesty and Wisdom.* The Chymical People carry in all their Jargon a whimsical Sort of Piety which is ordinary with great Lovers of Mony, and is no more but deceiving themselves, that their Regularity and Strictness of Manners for the Ends of this World, has some Affinity to the Innocence of Heart which must recommend them to the next. *Renatus* wondered to hear his Father talk like an Adept, and with such a Mixture of Piety; while *Alexandrinus* observing his Attention fixed, proceeded: This Phial, Child, and this little Earthen-Pot will add to thy Estate so much, as to make thee the richest Man in the *German* Empire. I am going to my Long Home, but shall not return to common Dust. Then he resumed a Countenance of Alacrity, and told him, That if within an Hour after his Death he anointed his whole Body, and poured down his Throat that Liquor which he had from old *Basilius*, the Corps would be converted into pure Gold. I will not pretend to express to you the unfeigned Tendernesses that passed between these two extraordinary Persons; but if the Father recommended the Care of his Remains with Vehemence and Affection, the Son was not behind-hand in professing that he would not cut the least Bit off him, but upon the utmost Extremity, or to provide for his younger Brothers and Sisters.

Well, *Alexandrinus* died, and the Heir of his Body (as our Term is) could not forbear in the Wantonnesses of his Heart, to measure the Length and Breadth of his beloved Father, and cast up the ensuing Value of him before he proceeded to Operation. When he knew the immense Reward of his Pains, he began the Work: But lo! when he had anointed the Corps all over, and began to apply the Liquor, the Body stirred, and *Renatus*, in a Fright, broke the Phial.   T

No. 427.
[STEELE.]   Thursday, July 10.

*Quantum a rerum turpitudine abes, tantum te a verborum libertate
    sejungas.*—Tull.

It is a certain Sign of an ill Heart to be inclined to Defamation. They who are harmless and innocent, can have no Gratification that way; but it ever arises from a Neglect of what is laudable in a Man's self, and an Impatience of seeing it in another. Else why should Virtue provoke? Why should Beauty displease in such a Degree, that a Man given to Scandal never lets the Mention of either pass by him without offering something to the Diminution of it? A Lady the other Day at a Visit being attacked somewhat rudely by one, whose own Character has been very roughly treated, answered a great deal of Heat and Intemperance very calmly, *Good Madam spare me, who*

am none of your Match; I speak Ill of no Body, and it is a new
Thing to me to be spoken Ill of. Little Minds think Fame consists in the Number of Votes they have on their Side among the
Multitude, whereas it is really the inseparable Follower of good
and worthy Actions. Fame is as natural a Follower of Merit,
as a Shadow is of a Body. It is true, when Crouds press upon
you, this Shadow cannot be seen, but when they separate from
around you, it will again appear. The Lazy, the Idle, and
the Froward, are the Persons who are most pleas'd with the
little Tales which pass about the Town to the Disadvantage of
the rest of the World. Were it not for the Pleasure of speaking
Ill, there are Numbers of People who are too Lazy to go out of
their own Houses, and too ill-natured to open their Lips in
Conversation. It was not a little diverting the other Day to
observe a Lady reading a Post-Letter, and at these Words,
After all her Airs, he has heard some Story or other, and the
Match is broke off, give Orders in the midst of her Reading, *Put*
to the Horses. That a young Woman of Merit had missed an
advantageous Settlement was News not to be delayed, lest
some Body else should have given her malicious Acquaintance
that Satisfaction before her. The Unwillingness to receive
good Tidings is a Quality as inseparable from a Scandal-
Bearer, as the Readiness to divulge bad. But, alas, how
wretchedly low and contemptible is that State of Mind, that
cannot be pleased but by what is the Subject of Lamentation.
This Temper has ever been in the highest Degree odious to
gallant Spirits. The *Persian* Soldier, who was heard reviling
Alexander the Great, was well admonished by his Officer; *Sir,*
You are paid to fight against Alexander, *and not to rail at him.*

Cicero in one of his Pleadings, defending his Client from
general Scandal, says very handsomly, and with much Reason,
There are many who have particular Engagements to the Prose-
cutor: There are many who are known to have Ill-will to him for
whom I appear; there are many who are naturally addicted to
Defamation, and envious of any Good to any Man, who may have
contributed to spread Reports of this kind: For nothing is so swift
as Scandal, nothing is more easie sent abroad, nothing received
with more Welcome, nothing diffuses it self so universally. I
shall not desire, that if any Report to our Disadvantage has any
Ground for it, you would overlook or extenuate it: But if there be
any thing advanced without a Person who can say whence he had
it, or which is attested by one who forgot who told him it, or who
had it from one of so little Consideration that he did not then think
it worth his Notice, all such Testimonies as these, I know, you
will think too slight to have any Credit against the Innocence and
Honour of your Fellow-Citizen. When an ill Report is traced,

it very often vanishes among such as the Orator has here recited. And how despicable a Creature must that be, who is in Pain for what passes among so frivolous a People? There is a Town in *Warwickshire* of good Note, and formerly pretty famous for much Animosity and Dissension, the chief Families of which have now turned all their Whispers, Backbitings, Envies, and private Malices, into Mirth and Entertainment, by means of a peevish old Gentlewoman, known by the Title of the Lady *Bluemantle*. This Heroine had for many Years together out-done the whole Sisterhood of Gossips in Invention, quick Utterance, and unprovoked Malice. This good Body is of a lasting Constitution, though extreamly decayed in her Eyes, and decrepid in her Feet. The two Circumstances of being always at Home from her Lameness, and very attentive from her Blindness, make her Lodgings the Receptacle of all that passes in Town, Good or Bad; but for the latter she seems to have the better Memory. There is another Thing to be noted of her, which is, That as it is usual with old People, she has a livelier Memory of Things which passed when she was very young, than of late Years. Add to all this, that she does not only not love any Body, but she hates every Body. The Statue in *Rome* does not serve to vent Malice half so well, as this old Lady does to disappoint it. She does not know the Author of any thing that is told her, but can readily repeat the Matter it self; therefore, though she exposes all the whole Town, she offends no one Body in it. She is so exquisitely restless and peevish, that she quarrels with all about her, and sometimes in a Freak will instantly change her Habitation. To indulge this Humour, she is led about the Grounds belonging to the same House she is in, and the Persons to whom she is to remove, being in the Plot, are ready to receive her at her own Chamber again. At stated Times, the Gentlewoman at whose House she supposes she is at the Time, is sent for to quarrel with, according to her common Custom: When they have a mind to drive the Jest, she is immediately urged to that Degree, that she will board in a Family with which she has never yet been; and away she will go this Instant, and tell them all that the rest have been saying of them. By this Means she has been an Inhabitant of every House in the Place without stirring from the same Habitation; and the many Stories which every Body furnishes her with to favour that Deceit, make her the general Intelligencer of the Town of all that can be said by one Woman against another. Thus groundless Stories die away, and sometimes Truths are smothered under the general Word: When they have a mind to discountenance a thing, Oh! that is in my Lady *Bluemantle's* Memoirs.

Whoever receives Impressions to the Disadvantage of others without Examination, is to be had in no other Credit for Intelligence than this good Lady *Bluemantle*, who is subjected to have her Ears imposed upon for want of other Helps to better Information. Add to this, that other Scandal-Bearers suspend the Use of these Faculties which she has lost, rather than apply them to do Justice to their Neighbours; and I think, for the Service of my fair Readers, to acquaint them, that there is a voluntary Lady *Bluemantle* at every Visit in Town. T

No. 428.
[STEELE.]   Friday, July 11.

Occupet extremum scabies.—Hor.

It is an impertinent and unreasonable Fault in Conversation, for one Man to take up all the Discourse. It may possibly be objected to me my self, that I am guilty in this kind, in entertaining the Town every Day, and not giving so many able Persons who have it more in their Power, and as much in their Inclination, an Opportunity to oblige Mankind with their Thoughts. Besides, said one whom I over-heard the other Day, why must this Paper turn altogether upon Topicks of Learning and Morality? Why should it pretend only to Wit, Humour, or the like? Things which are useful only to amuse Men of Literature and superior Education. I would have it consist also of all Things which may be necessary or useful to any Part of Society, and the mechanick Arts should have their Place as well as the Liberal. The Ways of Gain, Husbandry, and Thrift, will serve a greater Number of People, than Discourses upon what was well said or done by such a Philosopher, Heroe, General, or Poet. I no sooner heard this Critick talk of my Works, but I minuted what he had said; and from that Instant resolv'd to enlarge the Plan of my Speculations, by giving Notice to all Persons of all Orders, and each Sex, that if they are pleased to send me Discourses, with their Names and Places of Abode to them, so that I can be satisfied the Writings are authentick, such their Labours shall be faithfully inserted in this Paper. It will be of much more Consequence to a Youth in his Apprenticeship, to know by what Rules and Arts such a one became Sheriff of the City of *London*, than to see the Sign of one of his own Quality with a Lion's Heart in each Hand. The World indeed is enchanted with romantick and improbable Atchievements, when the plain Path to respective Greatness and Success in the Way of Life a Man is in, is wholly overlooked. Is it possible that a young Man at present could pass his Time better, than in reading the History of Stocks, and knowing by what secret Springs they have had such sudden Ascents and Falls in the same Day? Could he be better conducted in his Way to Wealth, which is the great Article of Life, than in a Treatise dated from *Change-Alley* by an able Proficient there? Nothing certainly could be more useful, than to be well instructed in his Hopes and Fears; to be diffident when others exult, and with a secret Joy buy when others think it their Interest to sell. I invite all Persons who have any thing to say for the profitable Information of the Publick, to take their Turns in my Paper: They are welcome, from the late noble Inventor of the Longitude, to the humble Author of Strops for Razors. If to carry Ships in Safety, to give Help to people lost in a troubled Sea, without knowing to what Shoar they bear, what Rocks to avoid, or what Coast to pray for in their Extremity, be a worthy Labour, and an Invention that deserves a Statue; at the same Time, he who has found a Means to let the Instrument which is to make your Visage less horrid and your Person more smug, easie in the Operation, is worthy of some kind of good Reception: If things of high Moment meet with Renown, those of little Consideration, since of any Consideration, are not to be despised. In order that no Merit may lye hid, and no Art unimprov'd, I repeat it, that I call Artificers, as well as Philosophers, to my Assistance in the Publick Service. It would be of great Use, if we had an exact History of the Successes of every great Shop within the City Walls, what Tracts of Land have been purchased by a constant Attendance within a Walk of thirty Foot. If it could also be noted in the Equipage of those who are ascended from the Successful Trade of their Ancestors into Figure and Equipage, such Accounts would quicken Industry in the Pursuit of such Acquisitions, and discountenance Luxury in the Enjoyment of them.

To diversifie these kind of Informations, the Industry of the Female World is not to be unobserved: She to whose Houshold-Virtues it is owing, that Men do Honour to her Husband, should be recorded with Veneration; she who has wasted his Labours, with Infamy. When we are come into Domestick Life in this manner, to awaken Caution and Attendance to the main Point, it would not be amiss to give now and then a Touch of Tragedy, and describe that most dreadful of all human Conditions, the Case of Bankruptcy; how Plenty, Credit, Chearfulness, full Hopes, and easie Possessions, are in an Instant turned into Penury, faint Aspects, Diffidence, Sorrow, and Misery; how the Man, who with an open Hand the Day before could administer to the Extremities of others, is shunned to Day by the Friend of his Bosom. It would be useful to shew how just this is on the Negligent, how lamentable on the Industrious. A Paper written by a Merchant, might give this Island a true Sense of the Worth and Importance of his Character: It might be visible from what he could say, That no Soldier entring a Breach adventures more for Honour, than the Trader does for Wealth to his Country. In both Cases the Adventurers have their own Advantage, but I know no Cases wherein every Body else is a Sharer in the Success.

It is objected by Readers of History, That the Battles in those Narrations are scarce ever to be understood. This Misfortune is to be ascribed to the Ignorance of Historians in the Methods of drawing up, changing the Forms of a Battalia, and the Enemy retreating from, as well as approaching to, the Charge. But in the Discourses from the Correspondents whom I now invite, the Danger will be of another kind; and it is necessary to caution them only against using Terms of Art, and describing Things that are familiar to them in Words unknown to their Reader. I promise my self a great Harvest of new Circumstances, Persons, and Things from this Proposal; and a World, which many think they are well acquainted with, discovered as wholly new. This Sort of Intelligence will give a lively Image of the Chain and Mutual Dependence of human Society, take off Impertinent Prejudices, enlarge the Minds of those, whose Views are confined to their own Circumstances; and, in short, if the Knowing in several Arts, Professions, and Trades will exert themselves, it cannot but produce a new Field of Diversion, an Instruction more agreeable than has yet appeared.   T

No. 429.

[STEELE.]   Saturday, July 12.

> *. . . Populumque falsis*
> *Dedocet uti*
> *Vocibus . . .*

'*Mr.* SPECTATOR,

SINCE I gave an Account of an agreeable Set of Company which were gone down into the Country, I have received Advices from thence, that the Institution of an Infirmary for those who should be out of Humour, has had very good Effects. My Letters mention particular Circumstances of two or three Persons, who had the good Sense to retire of their own Accord, and notified that they were withdrawn, with the Reasons of it, to the Company, in their respective Memorials.

"*The Memorial of Mrs.* Mary Dainty, *Spinster*,

Humbly sheweth,

That conscious of her own Want of Merit, accompanied with a Vanity of being admired, she had gone into Exile of her own accord.

She is sensible, that a vain Person is the most insufferable Creature living in a well-bred Assembly.

That she desired, before she appeared in publick again, she might have Assurances, that tho' she might be thought handsome, there might not more Address of Compliment be paid to her, than to the rest of the Company.

That she conceived it a Kind of Superiority, that one Person should take upon him to commend another.

Lastly, That she went into the Infirmary to avoid a particular Person who took upon him to profess an Admiration of her.

She therefore prayed, that to applaud out of due place, might be declared an Offence, and punished in the same Manner with Detraction, in that the latter did but report Persons defective, and the former made them so.

All which is submitted, &c."

There appeared a Delicacy and Sincerity in this Memorial very uncommon, but my Friend informs me, that the Allegations of it were groundless, insomuch that this Declaration of an Aversion to being praised, was understood to be no other than a secret Trap to purchase it, for which Reason it lyes still on the Table unanswered.

"*The humble Memorial of the Lady* Lydia Loller,

Sheweth,

That the Lady *Lydia* is a Woman of Quality married to a private Gentleman.

That she finds her self neither well nor ill.

That her Husband is a Clown.

That Lady *Lydia* cannot see Company.

That she desires the Infirmary may be her Apartment during her Stay in the Country.

That they would please to make merry with their Equals.

That Mr. *Loller* might stay with them if he thought fit."

It was immediately resolved, that Lady *Lydia* was still at *London*.

"*The humble Memorial of* Thomas Sudden, *Esq*; *of the* Inner-Temple.

Sheweth,

That Mr. *Sudden* is conscious that he is too much given to Argumentation.

That he talks loud.

That he is apt to think all Things Matter of Debate.

That he stayed behind in *Westminster-Hall*, when the late Shake of the Roof happened, only because a Council of the other Side asserted it was coming down.

That he cannot for his Life consent to any thing.

That he stays in the Infirmary to forget himself.

That as soon as he has forgot himself, he will wait on the Company."

His Indisposition was allowed to be sufficient to require a Cessation from Company.

"*The Memorial of* Frank Jolly,

Sheweth,

That he hath put himself into the Infirmary, in regard he is sensible of a certain rustick Mirth which renders him unfit for polite Conversation.

That he intends to prepare himself by Abstinence and thin Diet to be one of the Company.

That at present he comes into a Room as if he were an Express from Abroad.

That he has chosen an Apartment with a matted Anti-Chamber, to practise Motion without being heard.

That he bows, talks, drinks, eats, and helps himself before a Glass, to learn to act with Moderation.

That by reason of his luxuriant Health he is oppressive to Persons of composed Behaviour.

That he is endeavouring to forget the Word *Pshaw, Pshaw.*

That he is also weaning himself from his Cane.

That when he has learnt to live without his said Cane, he will wait on the Company, &c."

"*The Memorial of* John Rhubard, *Esq:*

Sheweth,

That your Petitioner has retired to the Infirmary, but that he is in perfect good Health, except that he has by long Use, and for want of Discourse, contracted an Habit of Complaint that he is sick.

That he wants for nothing under the Sun, but what to say, and therefore has fallen into this unhappy Malady of Complaining that he is sick.

That this Custom of his makes him, by his own Confession, fit only for the Infirmary, and therefore he has not waited for being sentenced to it.

That he is conscious there is nothing more improper than such a Complaint in good Company, in that they must pity, whether they think the Lamentor ill or not; and that the Complainant must make a silly Figure, whether he is pitied or not.

Your Petitioner humbly prays, that he may have Time to know how he does, and he will make his Appearance."

The *Valetudinarian* was likewise easily excused; and this Society being resolved not only to make it their Business to pass their Time agreeably for the present Season, but also to commence such Habits in themselves as may be of Use in their future Conduct in general, are very ready to give into a fancied or real Incapacity to join with their Measures, in order to have no Humorist, proud Man, impertinent or sufficient Fellow, break in upon their Happiness: Great Evils seldom happen to disturb Company; but Indulgence in Particularities of Humour is the Seed of making half our Time hang in Suspence, or waste away under real Discomposures.

Among other Things it is carefully provided that there may not be disagreeable Familiarities.   No one is to appear in the publick Rooms undressed, or enter abruptly into each other's Apartment without Intimation.   Every one has hitherto been so careful in his Behaviour, that there has but one offender in ten Days Time been sent into the Infirmary, and that was for throwing away his Cards at Whist.

" *The humble Petition of* Jeoffry Hotspur, *Esq;*

Sheweth,

Though the Petitioner swore, stamped, and threw down his Cards, he has all imaginable Respect for the Ladies, and the whole Company.

That he humbly desires it may be considered in the Case of Gaming, there are many Motives which provoke to Disorder.

That the Desire of Gain, and the Desire of Victory, are both thwarted in Losing.

That all Conversations in the World have indulged Human Infirmity in this Case.

Your Petitioner therefore most humbly prays, that he may be restored to the Company, and he hopes to bear ill Fortune with a good Grace for the future, and to demean himself so as to be no more than chearful when he wins, than grave when he loses." '   T

No. 430.

[STEELE.] Monday, July 14.

Quaere peregrinum vicinia rauca reclamat.—Hor.

'Sir,

As you are a Spectator-General you may with Authority censure whatsoever looks ill, and is offensive to the Sight; the
worst Nusance of which Kind methinks is the scandalous
Appearance of Poor in all Parts of this wealthy City. Such
miserable Objects affect the compassionate Beholder with
dismal Ideas, discompose the Chearfulness of his Mind, and
deprive him of the Pleasure that he might otherwise take in
surveying the Grandeur of our Metropolis. Who can without
Remorse see a disabled Sailor, the Purveyor of our Luxury,
destitute of Necessaries? Who can behold an honest Soldier
that bravely withstood the Enemy, prostrate and in Want
amongst his Friends? It were endless to mention all the
Variety of Wretchedness, and the Numberless Poor that not
only singly, but in Companies, implore your Charity. Spectacles of this Nature every where occur; and it is unaccountable, that amongst the many lamentable Cries that infest this
Town, your Comptroller-General should not take Notice of
the most shocking, *viz.* those of the Needy and Afflicted. I
can't but think he wav'd it meerly out of good Breeding,
chusing rather to stifle his Resentment, than upbraid his
Countrymen with Inhumanity; however, let not Charity be
sacrificed to Popularity, and if his Ears were deaf to their
Complaint, let not your Eyes overlook their Persons. There
are, I know, many Impostors among them. Lameness and
Blindness are certainly very often acted; but can those that
have their Sight and Limbs, employ them better than in
knowing whether they are counterfeited or not? I know not
which of the two misapplies his Senses most, he who pretends
himself blind to move Compassion, or he who beholds a
miserable Object without pitying it. But in order to remove
such Impediments, I wish, Mr. SPECTATOR, you would give us
a Discourse upon Beggars, that we may not pass by true
Objects of Charity, or give to Impostors. I looked out of my
Window the other Morning earlier than ordinary, and saw a
blind Beggar, an Hour before the Passage he stands in is
frequented, with a Needle and Thread, thriftily mending his
Stockings: My Astonishment was still greater when I beheld
a lame Fellow whose Legs were too big to walk within an
Hour after, bring him a Pot of Ale. I will not mention the
Shakings, Distortions and Convulsions which many of them
practise to gain an Alms; but sure I am, they ought to be taken

Care of in this Condition, either by the Beadle or the Magistrate. They, it seems, relieve their Posts according to their Talents; There is the Voice of an old Woman never begins to beg 'till nine in the Evening, and then she is destitute of Lodging, turned out for want of Rent, and has the same ill Fortune every Night in the Year. You should employ an Officer to hear the Distress of each Beggar that is constant at a particular Place, who is ever in the same Tone, and succeeds because his Audience is continually changing, tho' he does not alter his Lamentation. If we have nothing else for our Mony, let us have more Invention to be cheated with. All which is submitted to your Spectatorial Vigilance; and I am,

Sir,

Your most humble Servant.'

'*Sir,*

I was last *Sunday* highly transported at our Parish-Church; the Gentleman in the Pulpit pleaded movingly in Behalf of the poor Children, and they for themselves much more forcibly by singing an Hymn; and I had the Happiness to be a Contributor to this little religious Institution of Innocents, and am sure I never disposed of Mony more to my Satisfaction and Advantage. The inward Joy I find in my self, and the Goodwill I bear to Mankind, make me heartily wish those pious Works may be encouraged, that the present Promoters may reap the Delight, and Posterity the Benefit of them. But whilst we are building this beautiful Edifice, let not the old Ruins remain in View to sully the Prospect: Whilst we are cultivating and improving this young hopeful Offspring, let not the ancient and helpless Creatures be shamefully neglected. The Crowds of Poor, or pretended Poor, in every Place, are a great Reproach to us, and eclipse the Glory of all other Charity. It is the utmost Reproach to Society, that there should be a poor Man unrelieved, or a poor Rogue unpunished. I hope you will think no Part of Human Life out of your Consideration, but will, at your Leisure, give us the History of Plenty and Want, and the Natural Gradations towards them, calculated for the Cities of *London* and *Westminster.*

I am, Sir,

Your most humble Servant,

T. D.'

'*Mr.* Spectator,

I beg you would be pleas'd to take notice of a very great Indecency, which is extremely common, though, I think, never yet under your Censure. It is, Sir, the strange Freedoms some ill-bred married People take in Company: The unseasonable

Fondness of some Husbands, and the ill-timed Tenderness of some Wives. They talk and act, as if Modesty was only fit for Maids and Batchelors, and that too before both. I was once, Mr. SPECTATOR, where the Fault I speak of was so very flagrant, that, (being, you must know, a very bashful Fellow, and several young Ladies in the Room) I protest I was quite out of Countenance. *Lucina*, it seems, was breeding, and she did nothing but entertain the Company with a Discourse upon the Difficulty of Reckoning to a Day, and said, She knew those who were certain to an Hour; then fell a laughing at a silly unexperienced Creature, who was a Month above her Time. Upon her Husband's coming in, she put several Questions to him; which he not caring to resolve, Well, cries *Lucina*, I shall have 'em all at Night.—But, lest I should seem guilty of the very Fault I write against, I shall only intreat *Mr.* SPECTATOR to correct such Misdemeanors;

> *For higher of the Genial Bed by far,*
> *And with mysterious Reverence, I deem.*

> *I am, Sir,*

>> *Your humble Servant,*

T   T. Meanwell.'

No. 431.

[STEELE.]   Tuesday, July 15.

Quid dulcius hominum generi a natura datum est quam sui cuique liberi?—Tull.

I HAVE lately been casting in my Thoughts the several Unhappinesses of Life, and comparing the Infelicities of old Age to those of Infancy. The Calamities of Children are due to the Negligence and Misconduct of Parents, those of Age to the past Life which led to it. I have here the History of a Boy and Girl to their Wedding-Day, and think I cannot give the Reader a livelier Image of the insipid way which Time uncultivated passes, than by entertaining him with their authentick Epistles, expressing all that was remarkable in their Lives, 'till the Period of their Life above-mentioned. The Sentence at the Head of this Paper, which is only a warm Interrogation, *What is there in Nature so dear as a Man's own Children to him?* is all the Reflection I shall at present make on those who are negligent or cruel in the Education of them.

'*Mr.* SPECTATOR,

I am now entering into my One and Twentieth Year, and do not know that I had one Day's thorough Satisfaction since

I came to Years of any Reflection, 'till the Time they say others lose their Liberty, the Day of my Marriage. I am Son to a Gentleman of a very great Estate, who resolved to keep me out of the Vices of the Age; and in Order to it never let me see any Thing that he thought could give me the least Pleasure. At ten Years old I was put to a Grammar-School, where my Master received Orders every Post to use me very severely, and have no Regard to my having a great Estate. At Fifteen I was removed to the University, where I lived, out of my Father's great Discretion, in scandalous Poverty and Want, 'till I was big enough to be married, and I was sent for to see the Lady who sends you the Underwritten. When we were put together, we both considered that we could not be worse than we were in taking one another, and out of a Desire of Liberty entered into Wedlock. My Father says I am now a Man, and may speak to him like another Gentleman.

> *I am, Sir,*
>
> > *Your most humble Servant,*
> >
> > > Richard Rentfree.

Mr. SPEC,

I grew tall and wild at my Mother's, who is a gay Widow, and did not care for shewing me 'till about two Years and a half ago; at which Time my Guardian Uncle sent me to a Boarding-School, with Orders to contradict me in nothing, for I had been misused enough already. I had not been there above a Month, when, being in the Kitchen, I saw some Oat-meal on the Dresser; I put two or three Corns in my Mouth, liked it, stole a Handful, went into my Chamber, chewed it, and for two Months after never failed taking Toll of every Pennyworth of Oatmeal that came into the House: But one Day playing with a Tobacco-pipe between my Teeth, it happened to break in my Mouth, and the spitting out the Pieces left such a delicious Roughness on my Tongue, that I could not be satisfied 'till I had champed up the remaining Part of the Pipe. I forsook the Oatmeal, and stuck to the Pipes three Months, in which Time I had dispensed with 37 foul Pipes, all to the Boles: They belonged to an old Gentleman, Father to my Governess. . . . He locked up the clean ones. I left off eating of Pipes, and fell to licking of Chalk. I was soon tired of this; I then nibbled all the red Wax of our last Ball-Tickets, and three Weeks after, the black Wax from the Burying-Tickets of the old Gentleman. Two Months after this I lived upon Thunder-bolts, a certain long, round blueish Stone, which I found among the Gravel in our Garden. I was wonderfully delighted with this; but Thunder-bolts growing scarce, I fastned Tooth and Nail upon our Garden-Wall, which I stuck to almost a Twelve-month, and had in that Time peeled and devoured half a Foot toward our Neighbour's Yard. I now thought my self the happiest Creature in the World, but, I believe in my Conscience, I had eaten quite through, had I had it in my Chamber; but now I became lazy, and unwilling to stir, and was obliged to seek Food nearer Home. I then took a strange Hankering to Coals; I fell to scranching 'em, and had already consumed, I am certain, as much as would have dressed my Wedding-Dinner, when my Uncle came for me Home. He was in the Parlour with my Governess when I was called down. I went in, fell on my Knees, for he made me call him Father; and when I expected the Blessing I asked, the good Gentleman, in a Surprize, turns himself to my Governess, and asks, Whether this (pointing to me) was his Daughter? This (added he) is the very Picture of Death. My Child was a plump-fac'd, hale, fresh-coloured Girl; but this looks as if she were half-starved, a meer Skeleton. My Governess, who is really a good Woman, assured my Father I had wanted for nothing; and withal told him I was continually eating some Trash or other, and that I was almost eaten up with the Green-sickness, her Orders being never to cross me. But this magnified but little with my Father, who presently, in a kind of Pett, paying for my Board, took me Home with him. I had not been long at home, but one *Sunday* at Church (I shall never forget it) I saw a young neighbouring Gentleman that pleased me hugely; I liked him of all Men I ever saw in my Life; and began to wish I could be as pleasing to him. The very next Day he came, with his Father, a visiting to our House: We were left alone together, with Directions on both Sides to be in Love with one another, and in three Weeks Time we were married. I regained my former Health and Complexion, and am now as happy as the Day is long. Now, Mr. SPEC, I desire you would find out some Name for these craving Damsels, whether dignified or distinguished under some or all of the following Denominations, (to wit) *Trash - eaters, Oatmeal-chewers, Pipe - champers, Chalk - lickers, Wax niblers, Coal-Scranchers, Wall-peelers,* or *Gravel Diggers:* And, good Sir, do your utmost Endeavour to prevent (by exposing) this un-accountable Folly, so prevailing among the young ones of our Sex, who may not meet with such sudden good Luck as,

  Sir,

    Your constant Reader,
     and very Humble Servant,
       Sabina Green,
      Now Sabina Rentfree."'

No. 432.

[STEELE.] Wednesday, July 16.

> . . . *Inter strepit anser olores.*—Virg.

'Mr. SPECTATOR, *Oxford, July* 14.

ACCORDING to a late Invitation in one of your Papers to every Man who pleases to write, I have sent you the following short Dissertation against the Vice of being prejudiced.

Your most Humble Servant.

"Man is a sociable Creature, and a Lover of Glory; whence it is, that when several Persons are united in the same Society, they are studious to lessen the Reputation of others, in order to raise their own. The Wise are content to guide the Springs in Silence, and rejoice in Secret at their regular Progress: To prate and triumph is the Part allotted to the Trifling and Superficial: The Geese were providentially ordained to save the *Capitol*. Hence it is, that the Invention of Marks and Devices to distinguish Parties, is owing to the *Beaux* and *Belles* of this Island. Hats moulded into different Cocks and Pinches, have long bid mutual Defiance; Patches have been set against Patches in Battel-Array; Stocks have risen or fallen in Proportion to Head-Dresses; and Peace or War been expected, as the *White* or the *Red* Hood hath prevailed. These are the Standard-Bearers in our contending Armies, the Dwarfs and Squires who carry the Impresses of the Giants or Knights, not born to fight themselves, but to prepare the Way for the ensuing Combat.

It is Matter of Wonder to reflect how far Men of weak Understanding and strong Fancy are hurried by their Prejudices, even to the believing that the whole Body of the adverse Party are a Band of Villains and Daemons. Foreigners complain, that the *English* are the proudest Nation under Heaven. Perhaps they too have their Share; but be that as it will, general Charges against Bodies of Men is the Fault I am writing against. It must be own'd, to our Shame, that our common People, and most who have not travelled, have an irrational Contempt for the Language, Dress, Customs, and even the Shape and Minds of other Nations. Some Men, otherwise of Sense, have wondered that a great Genius should spring out of *Ireland*; and think you mad in affirming, that fine Odes have been written in *Lapland*.

This Spirit of Rivalship, which heretofore reigned in the two Universities, is extinct, and almost over betwixt College and College: In Parishes and schools the Thrift of Glory still obtains. At the Seasons of Football and Cock-fighting, these little Republicks reassume their National Hatred to each other. My Tenant in the Country is verily perswaded, that the Parish of the Enemy hath not one honest Man in it.

I always hated Satyrs against Woman, and Satyrs against Man; I am apt to suspect a Stranger who laughs at the Religion of *The Faculty*: My Spleen rises at a dull Rogue, who is severe upon Mayors and Aldermen; and was never better pleased than with a Piece of Justice executed upon the Body of a Templer, who was very arch upon Parsons.

The Necessities of Mankind require various Employments; and whoever excells in his Province is worthy of Praise. All Men are not educated after the same Manner, nor have all the same Talents. Those who are deficient deserve our Compassion, and have a Title to our Assistance. All cannot be bred in the same Place; but in all Places there arise, at different times, such Persons as do Honour to their Society, which may raise Envy in little Souls, but are admired and cherished by generous Spirits.

It is certainly a great Happiness to be educated in Societies of great and eminent Men. Their Instructions and Examples are of extraordinary Advantage. It is highly proper to instil such a Reverence of the governing Persons, and Concern for the Honour of the Place, as may spur the growing Members to worthy Pursuits and honest Emulation; but to swell young Minds with vain Thoughts of the Dignity of their own Brotherhood, by debasing and villifying all others, doth them a real Injury. By this means I have found that their Efforts have become languid, and their Prattle irksome, as thinking it sufficient Praise that they are Children of so illustrious and ample a Family. I should think it a surer, as well as more generous Method, to set before the Eyes of Youth such Persons as have made a noble Progress in Fraternities less talk'd of; which seems tacitly to reproach their Sloth, who loll so heavily in the Seats of mighty Improvement: Active Spirits hereby would enlarge their Notions, whereas by a servile Imitation of one, or perhaps two, admired Men in their own Body, they can only gain a secondary and derivative kind of Fame. These Copiers of Men, like those of Authors or Painters, run into Affectations of some Oddness, which perhaps was not disagreeable in the Original, but sits ungracefully on the narrow-soul'd Transcriber.

By such early Corrections of Vanity, while Boys are growing into Men, they will gradually learn not to censure superficially; but imbibe those Principles of general Kindness and Humanity, which alone can make them easie to themselves, and beloved by others.

Reflections of this Nature have expunged all Prejudices out of my Heart, insomuch that tho' I am a firm Protestant, I hope to see the Pope and Cardinals without violent Emotions; and tho' I am naturally grave, I expect to meet good Company at *Paris*.

I am, Sir,

Your Obedient Servant."'

'*Mr*. Spectator,

I find you are a general Undertaker, and have by your Correspondents or self an Insight into most things; which makes me apply myself to you at present in the sorest Calamity that ever befel Man. My Wife has taken something ill of me, and has not spoke one Word, good or bad, to me, or any Body in the Family, since *Friday* was Sevennight. What must a Man do in that Case? Your Advice would be a great Obligation to,

Sir,

Your most Humble Servant,

Ralph Thimbleton.'

'*Mr*. Spectator,

When you want a Trifle to fill up a Paper, in inserting this you will lay an Obligation on,

Your Humble Servant,

July 15*th*,
1712.   OLIVIA.

"Dear Olivia,

It is but this Moment I have had the Happiness of knowing to whom I am obliged for the Present I received the second of *April*. I am heartily sorry it did not come to Hand the Day before; for I can't but think it very hard upon People to lose their Jest, that offer at one but once a Year. I congratulate my self however upon the Earnest given me of something further intended in my Favour; for I am told, that the Man who is thought worthy by a Lady to make a Fool of, stands fair enough in her Opinion to become one Day her Husband. 'Till such time as I have the Honour of being sworn, I take Leave to subscribe my self,

Dear Olivia,

Your Fool Elect,

T   Nicodemuncio."'

No. 433.
[ADDISON.]   Thursday, July 17.

> *Perlege Maeonio cantatas carmine ranas,*
> *Et frontem nugis solvere disce meis.*—Mart.

THE Moral World, as consisting of Males and Females, is of a mixt Nature, and filled with several Customs, Fashions and Ceremonies, which would have no place in it, were there but *One* Sex. Had our Species no Females in it, Men would be quite different Creatures from what they are at present; their Endeavours to please the opposite Sex, polishes and refines them out of those Manners which are most Natural to them, and often sets them upon modelling themselves, not according to the Plans which they approve in their own Opinions, but according to those Plans which they think are most agreeable to the Female World. In a word, Man would not only be an unhappy, but a rude unfinished Creature, were he conversant with none but those of his own Make.

Women, on the other side, are apt to form themselves in every thing with regard to that other half of reasonable Creatures, with whom they are here blended and confused; their Thoughts are ever turned upon appearing amiable to the other Sex; they talk, and move, and smile, with a Design upon us; every Feature of their Faces, every part of their Dress is filled with Snares and Allurements. There would be no such Animals as Prudes or Coquets in the World, were there not such an Animal as Man. In short, it is the Male that gives Charms to Womankind, that produces an Air in their Faces, a Grace in their Motions, a Softness in their Voices, and a Delicacy in their Complections.

As this mutual Regard between the two Sexes tends to the Improvement of each of them, we may observe that Men are apt to degenerate into rough and brutal Natures, who live as if there were no such Things as Women in the World; as on the contrary, Women, who have an Indifference or Aversion for their Counter-parts in human Nature, are generally Sower and Unamiable, Sluttish and Censorious.

I am led into this Train of Thoughts by a little Manuscript which is lately fallen into my Hands, and which I shall communicate to the Reader, as I have done some other curious Pieces of the same Nature, without troubling him with any Enquiries about the Author of it. It contains a summary Account of two different States which bordered upon one another. The one was a Commonwealth of *Amazons*, or Women without Men; the other was a Republick of Males that had not a Woman in their whole Community. As these two

States bordered upon one another, it was their way, it seems, to meet upon their Frontiers at a certain Season of the Year, where those among the Men who had not made their Choice in any former Meeting, associated themselves with particular Women, whom they were afterwards obliged to look upon as their Wives in every one of these yearly Rencounters. The Children that sprung from this Alliance, if Males, were sent to their respective Fathers; if Females, continued with their Mothers. By means of this Anniversary Carnival, which lasted about a Week, the Commonwealths were recruited from time to time, and supplied with their respective Subjects.

These two States were engaged together in a perpetual League, Offensive and Defensive, so that if any Foreign Potentate offered to attack either of them, both the Sexes fell upon him at once, and quickly brought him to Reason. It was remarkable that for many Ages this Agreement continued inviolable between the two States, notwithstanding, as was said before, they were Husbands and Wives; but this will not appear so wonderful if we consider that they did not live together above a Week in a Year.

In the Account which my Author gives of the Male Republick, there were several Customs very remarkable. The Men never shaved their Beards, or pared their Nails above once in a Twelvemonth, which was probably about the time of the great annual Meeting upon their Frontiers. I find the Name of a Minister of State in one part of their History, who was fined for appearing too frequently in clean Linnen; and of a certain great General who was turned out of his Post for Effeminacy, it having been proved upon him by several credible Witnesses that he washed his Face every Morning. If any Member of the Commonwealth had a soft Voice, a smooth Face, or a supple Behaviour, he was banished into the Commonwealth of Females, where he was treated as a Slave, dressed in Petticoats and set a Spinning. They had no Titles of Honour among them, but such as denoted some bodily Strength or Perfection, as such an one *the Tall*, such an one *the Stocky*, such an one *the Gruff*. Their publick Debates were generally managed with Kicks and Cuffs, insomuch that they often came from the Council Table with broken Shins, black Eyes and bloody Noses. When they would reproach a Man in the most bitter Terms, they would tell him his Teeth were white, or that he had a fair Skin, and a soft Hand. The greatest Man I met with in their History, was one who could lift Five hundred Weight, and wore such a prodigious Pair of Whiskers as had never been seen in the Commonwealth before his Time. These Accomplishments it seems had rendred him so popular, that if he had not died very seasonably, it is thought he might have enslaved the Republick. Having made this short Extract out of the History of the Male Commonwealth, I shall look into the History of the neighbouring State which consisted of Females, and if I find any thing in it, will not fail to Communicate it to the Publick. C

No. 434.
[ADDISON.] Friday, July 18.

> *Quales Threiciae cum flumina Thermodoontis*
> *Pulsant, & pictis bellantur Amazones armis:*
> *Seu circum Hippolyten, seu cum se Martia curru*
> *Penthesilea refert, magnoque ululante tumultu*
> *Feminea exultant lunatis agmina peltis.*—Virg.

HAVING carefully perused the Manuscript I mentioned in my Yesterday's Paper, so far as it relates to the Republick of Women, I find in it several Particulars which may very well deserve the Reader's Attention.

The Girls of Quality, from six to twelve Years old, were put to publick Schools, where they learned to Box and play at Cudgels, with several other Accomplishments of the same Nature; so that nothing was more usual than to see a little Miss returning Home at Night with a broken Pate, or two or three Teeth knocked out of her Head. They were afterwards taught to ride the great Horse, to Shoot, Dart, or Sling, and listed into several Companies, in order to perfect themselves in Military Exercises. No Woman was to be married 'till she had killed her Man. The Ladies of Fashion used to play with young Lions instead of Lap-dogs, and when they made any Parties of Diversion, instead of entertaining themselves at Ombre or Piquet, they would Wrestle and pitch the Bar for a whole Afternoon together. There was never any such thing as a Blush seen, or a Sigh heard, in the Commonwealth. The Women never dressed but to look terrible, to which end they would sometimes after a Battel paint their Cheeks with the Blood of their Enemies. For this Reason likewise the Face which had the most Scars was looked upon as the most beautiful. If they found Lace, Jewels, Ribbons, or any Ornaments in Silver or Gold, among the Booty which they had taken, they used to dress their Horses with it, but never entertained a Thought of wearing it themselves. There were particular Rights and Privileges allowed to any Member of the Commonwealth, who was a Mother of three Daughters. The Senate was made up of old Women; for by the Laws of the Country none was to be a Councellor of State that was not past Child-bearing. They used to boast their Republick had continued Four thousand Years, which is altogether improbable, unless we may suppose, what I am very apt to think, that they measured their Time by *Lunar* Years.

There was a great Revolution brought about in this Female Republick, by means of a neighbouring King, who had made War upon them several Years with various Success, and at length overthrew them in a very great Battel. This Defeat they ascribe to several Causes; some say that the Secretary of State having been troubled with the Vapours had committed some fatal Mistakes in several Dispatches about that Time. Others pretend, that the first Minister being big with Child, could not attend the Publick Affairs, as so great an Exigency of State required; but this I can give no manner of Credit to, since it seems to contradict a Fundamental Maxim in their Government, which I have before mentioned. My Author gives the most probable Reason of this great Disaster; for he affirms, that the General was brought to Bed, or (as others say) Miscarried the very Night before the Battel: However it was, this signal Overthrow obliged them to call in the Male Republick to their Assistance; but notwithstanding their common Efforts to repulse the Victorious Enemy, the War continued for many Years before they could entirely bring it to a happy Conclusion.

The Campaigns which both Sexes passed together made them so well acquainted with one another, that at the End of the War they did not care for parting. In the beginning of it they lodged in separate Camps, but afterwards as they grew more familiar, they pitched their Tents promiscuously.

From this time the Armies being Chequered with both Sexes, they polished apace. The Men used to invite their Fellow-Soldiers into their Quarters, and would dress their Tents with Flowers and Boughs for their Reception. If they chanced to like one more than another, they would be cutting her Name in the Table, or Chalking out her Figure upon a Wall, or talking of her in a kind of rapturous Language, which by degrees improved into Verse and Sonnet. These were as the first Rudiments of Architecture, Painting and Poetry, among this Savage People. After any Advantage over the Enemy, both Sexes used to Jump together and make a Clattering with their Swords and Shields, for Joy, which in a few Years produced several Regular Tunes and Sett Dances.

As the two Armies romped on these Occasions, the Women complained of the thick bushy Beards and long Nails of their Confederates, who thereupon took care to prune themselves into such Figures as were most pleasing to their Female Friends and Allies.

When they had taken any Spoils from the Enemy, the Men would make a Present of every thing that was Rich and Showy to the Women whom they most admired, and would frequently dress the Necks, or Heads, or Arms of their Mistresses, with any thing which they thought appeared Gay or Pretty.   The Women observing that the Men took delight in looking upon 'em, when they were adorned with such Trappings and Gugaws, set their Heads at work to find out new Inventions, and to out-shine one another in all Councils of War or the like solemn Meetings.   On the other hand, the Men observing how the Women's Hearts were set upon Finery, begun to Embellish themselves and look as agreeable as they could in the Eyes of their Associates.   In short, after a few Years conversing together, the Women had learnt to Smile, and the Men to Ogle, the Women grew Soft, and the Men Lively.

When they had thus insensibly formed one another, upon finishing of the War, which concluded with an entire Conquest of their common Enemy, the Colonels in one Army married the Colonels in the other; the Captains in the same manner took the Captains to their Wives: The whole Body of common Soldiers were matched, after the Example of their Leaders. By this means the two Republicks incorporated with one another, and became the most Flourishing and Polite Government in the Part of the World which they Inhabited.   C

No. 435.
[ADDISON.]   Saturday, July 19.

Nec duo sunt at forma duplex, nec femina dici,
Nec puer ut possint; neutrumque & utrumque, videntur—Ovid.

MOST of the Papers I give the Publick are written on Subjects that never vary, but are for ever fixt and immutable.   Of this kind are all my more serious Essays and Discourses; but there is another Sort of Speculations, which I consider as Occasional Papers, that take their Rise from the Folly, Extravagance, and Caprice of the present Age.   For I look upon my self as one set to watch the Manners and Behaviour of my Countrymen and Contemporaries, and to mark down every absurd Fashion, ridiculous Custom, or affected Form of Speech that makes its appearance in the World, during the Course of these my Speculations.   The Petticoat no sooner begun to swell, but I observed its Motions.   The Party-patches had not time to muster themselves before I detected them.   I had Intelligence

of the Coloured Hood the very first time it appeared in a
Publick Assembly. I might here mention several other the
like Contingent Subjects, upon which I have bestowed distinct
Papers. By this means I have so effectually quashed those
Irregularities which gave Occasion to 'em, that I am afraid
Posterity will scarce have a sufficient Idea of them to Relish
those Discourses which were in no little Vogue at the time
when they were written. They will be apt to think that the
Fashions and Customs I attacked were some Fantastick Conceits of my own, and that their Great-Grandmothers could not
be so whimsical as I have represented them. For this Reason,
when I think on the Figure my several Volumes of Speculations will make about a Hundred Years hence, I consider them
as so many Pieces of old Plate, where the Weight will be
regarded, but the Fashion lost.

Among the several Female Extravagancies I have already
taken Notice of, there is one which still keeps its Ground. I
mean that of the Ladies who dress themselves in a Hat and
Feather, a Riding-coat and a Perriwig; or at least tie up their
Hair in a Bag or Ribbon, in imitation of the smart Part of the
opposite Sex. As in my Yesterday's Paper I gave an Account
of the Mixture of two Sexes in one Commonwealth, I shall here
take notice of this Mixture of two Sexes in one Person. I have
already shewn my Dislike of this Immodest Custom more than
once; but in Contempt of every thing I have hitherto said, I
am informed that the Highways about this great City are still
very much infested with these Female Cavaliers.

I remember when I was at my Friend Sir ROGER DE COVER-
LY's about this time Twelve-month, an Equestrian Lady of this
Order appeared upon the Plains which lay at a distance from
his House. I was at that time walking in the Fields with my
old Friend; and as his Tenants ran out on every side to see so
strange a Sight, Sir ROGER asked one of them who came by us
what it was? To which the Country Fellow reply'd, 'Tis a
Gentlewoman, saving your Worship's Presence, in a Coat and
Hat. This produced a great deal of Mirth at the Knight's
House, where we had a Story at the same time of another of his
Tenants, who meeting this Gentlemanlike Lady on the High-
way, was asked by her *whether that was* Coverly-Hall; the
Honest Man seeing only the Male Part of the Querist,
replied, *Yes, Sir*; but upon the second Question, *whether
Sir* ROGER DE COVERLY *was a Married Man*, having dropped
his Eye upon the Petticoat, he chang'd his Note into *No,
Madam*.

Had one of these Hermaphrodites appeared in *Juvenal's*
Days, with what an Indignation should we have seen her

described by that excellent Satyrist? He would have represented her in her Riding Habit, as a greater Monster than the Centaur. He would have called for Sacrifices, or Purifying Waters, to expiate the Appearance of such a Prodigy. He would have Invoked the Shades of *Portia* or *Lucretia*, to see into what the *Roman* Ladies had transformed themselves.

For my own part, I am for treating the Sex with greater Tenderness, and have all along made use of the most gentle Methods to bring them off from any little Extravagance into which they are sometimes unwarily fallen: I think it however absolutely necessary to keep up the Partition between the two Sexes, and to take Notice of the smallest Encroachments which the one makes upon the other. I hope therefore that I shall not hear any more Complaints on this Subject. I am sure my She-Disciples who peruse these my daily Lectures, have profited but little by them, if they are capable of giving into such an Amphibious Dress. This I should not have mentioned, had not I lately met one of these my Female Readers in *Hide Park*, who looked upon me with a masculine Assurance, and cocked her Hat full in my Face.

For my part, I have one general Key to the Behaviour of the Fair Sex. When I see them singular in any Part of their Dress, I conclude it is not without some Evil Intention; and therefore question not but the Design of this strange Fashion is to smite more effectually their Male Beholders. Now to set them right in this Particular, I would fain have them consider with themselves whether we are not more likely to be struck by a Figure entirely Female, than with such an one as we may see every Day in our Glasses: Or, if they please, let them reflect upon their own Hearts, and think how they would be affected should they meet a Man on Horseback, in his Breeches and Jackboots, and at the same time dressed up in a Commode and a Night-raile.

I must observe that this Fashion was first of all brought to us from *France*, a Country which has Infected all the Nations of *Europe* with its Levity. I speak not this in derogation of a whole People, having more than once found fault with those general Reflections which strike at Kingdoms or Commonwealths in the Gross: A piece of Cruelty, which an ingenious Writer of our own compares to that of *Caligula*, who wish'd the *Roman* People had all but one Neck, that he might behead them at a Blow. I shall therefore only Remark, that as Liveliness and Assurance are in a peculiar manner the Qualifications of the *French* Nation, the same Habits and Customs will not give the same Offence to that People, which they produce among those of our own Country. Modesty is our distinguishing Character, as Vivacity is theirs: And when this our National Virtue appears in that Female Beauty, for which our *British* Ladies are celebrated above all others in the Universe, it makes up the most amiable Object that the Eye of Man can possibly behold.   C

No. 436.
[STEELE.]   Monday, July 21.

> . . . *Verso pollice vulgus*
> *Quem jubet occidunt populariter.*—Juv.

BEING a Person of insatiable Curiosity, I could not forbear going on *Wednesday* last to a Place of no small Renown for the Gallantry of the lower Order of *Britons*, namely, to the Bear-Garden at *Hockley in the Hole;* where (as a whitish brown Paper, put into my Hands in the Street, inform'd me) there was to be a Tryal of Skill to be exhibited between two Masters of the Noble Science of Defence, at two of the Clock precisely. I was not a little charm'd with the Solemnity of the Challenge, which ran thus:

'*I* James Miller, *Serjeant, (lately come from the Frontiers of* Portugal) *Master of the Noble Science of Defence, hearing in most Places where I have been of the great Fame of* Timothy Buck *of* London, *Master of the said Science, do invite him to meet me, and exercise at the several Weapons following*, viz.

Back-Sword,	*Single Falchon,*
Sword and Dagger,	*Case of Falchons,*
Sword and Buckler,	*Quarter-Staff.*'

If the generous Ardour in *James Miller* to dispute the Reputation of *Timothy Buck*, had something resembling the old Heroes of Romance, *Timothy Buck* return'd Answer in the same Paper with the like Spirit, adding a little Indignation at being challenged, and seeming to condescend to fight *James Miller*, not in regard to *Miller* himself, but in that, as the Fame went out, he had fought *Parkes* of *Coventry*. The acceptance of the Combat ran in these Words:

'*I* Timothy Buck *of* Clare-Market, *Master of the Noble Science of Defence, hearing he did fight Mr.* Parkes *of* Coventry, *will not fail (God willing) to meet this fair Inviter at the Time and Place appointed, desiring a clear Stage and no Favour.*

Vivat Regina.'

I shall not here look back on the Spectacles of the *Greeks* and *Romans* of this Kind, but must believe this Custom took its Rise from the Ages of Knight-Errantry; from those who lov'd one Woman so well, that they hated all Men and Women else; from those who would fight you, whether you were or were not of their Mind; from those who demanded the Combat of their Contemporaries, both for admiring their Mistress or discommending her. I cannot therefore but lament, that the terrible Part of the ancient Fight is preserved, when the amorous Side of it is forgotten. We have retained the Barbarity, but lost the Gallantry of the old Combatants. I could wish, methinks, these Gentlemen had consulted me in the Promulgation of the Conflict. I was obliged by a fair young Maid whom I understood to be called *Elizabeth Preston,* Daughter of the Keeper of the Garden, with a Glass of Water; whom I imagined might have been, for Form's sake, the general Representative of the Lady fought for, and from her Beauty the proper *Amarillis* on these Occasions. It would have ran better in the Challenge; *I* James Miller, *Serjeant, who have travelled Parts abroad, and came last from the Frontiers of* Portugal, *for the Love of* Elizabeth Preston, *do assert, That the said* Elizabeth is the Fairest of Women. Then the Answer; *I* Timothy Buck, *who have stay'd in* Great Britain *during all the War in Foreign Parts for the Sake of* Susanna Page, *do deny that* Elizabeth Preston *is so fair as the said* Susanna Page. Let *Susanna Page* look on, and I desire of *James Miller* no Favour.

This would give the Battel quite another Turn; and a proper Station for the Ladies, whose Complexion was disputed by the Sword, would animate the Disputants with a more gallant Incentive than the Expectation of Mony from the Spectators; though I would not have that neglected, but thrown to that Fair One whose Lover was approved by the Donor.

Yet, considering the Thing wants such Amendments, it was carried with great Order. *James Miller* came on first; preceded by two disabled Drummers, to shew, I suppose, that the Prospect of maimed Bodies did not in the least deter him. There ascended with the daring *Miller* a Gentleman, whose Name I could not learn, with a dogged Air, as unsatisfied that he was not Principal. This Son of Anger lowred at the whole Assembly, and weighing himself as he march'd around from Side to Side, with a stiff Knee and Shoulder, he gave Intimations of the Purpose he smothered till he saw the Issue of this Encounter. *Miller* had a blue Ribbond tyed round the Sword Arm; which Ornament I conceive to be the Remain of that Custom of wearing a Mistress's Favour on such Occasions of old.

Miller is a Man of six Foot eight Inches Height, of a kind but bold Aspect, well-fashioned, and ready of his Limbs; and such Readiness as spoke his Ease in them, was obtained from a Habit of Motion in Military Exercise.

The Expectation of the Spectators was now almost at its Height, and the Crowd pressing in, several active Persons thought they were placed rather according to their Fortune than their Merit, and took it in their Heads to prefer themselves from the open Area, or Pit, to the Galleries. This Dispute between Desert and Property brought many to the Ground, and raised others in proportion to the highest Seats by Turns for the Space of ten Minutes, till *Timothy Buck* came on, and the whole Assembly giving up their Disputes, turned their Eyes upon the Champions. Then it was that every Man's Affection turned to one or the other irresistibly. A judicious Gentleman near me said, *I could, methinks, be* Miller's *Second, but I had rather have* Buck *for mine. Miller* had an audacious Look, that took the Eye; *Buck* a perfect Composure, that engaged the Judgment. *Buck* came on in a plain Coat, and kept all his Air till the Instant of Engaging; at which Time he undress'd to his Shirt, his Arm adorned with a Bandage of red Ribband. No one can describe the sudden Concern in the whole Assembly; the most tumultuous Crowd in Nature was as still and as much engaged, as if all their Lives depended on the first blow. The Combatants met in the Middle of the Stage, and shaking Hands as removing all Malice, they retired with much Grace to the Extremities of it; from whence they immediately faced about, and approached each other, *Miller* with an Heart full of Resolution, *Buck* with a watchful untroubled Countenance; *Buck* regarding principally his own Defence, *Miller* chiefly thoughtful of annoying his Opponent. It is not easie to describe the many Escapes and imperceptible Defences between two Men of quick Eyes and ready Limbs; but *Miller's* Heat laid him open to the Rebuke of the calm *Buck*, by a large Cut on the Forehead. Much Effusion of Blood covered his Eyes in a Moment and the Huzzas of the Crowd undoubtedly quickened the Anguish. The Assembly was divided into Parties upon their different ways of Fighting; while a poor Nymph in one of the Galleries apparently suffered for *Miller*, and burst into a Flood of Tears. As soon as his Wound was wrapped up, he came on again with a little Rage, which still disabled him further. But what brave Man can be wounded into more Patience and Caution? The next was a warm eager Onset which ended in a decisive Stroke on the left Leg of *Miller*. The Lady in the Gallery, during this second Strife, covered her Face; and for my Part, I could not keep my Thoughts from being mostly employed on the Consideration of her unhappy Circumstance that Moment, hearing the Clash of Swords, and apprehending Life or Victory concerned her Lover in every Blow, but not daring to satisfie herself on whom they fell. The Wound was exposed to the View of all who could delight in it, and sowed up on the Stage. The surly Second of *Miller* declared at this Time, that he would that Day Fortnight fight Mr. *Buck* at the same Weapons, declaring himself the Master of the renowned *Gorman*; but *Buck* denied him the Honour of that courageous Disciple, and asserting that he himself had taught that Champion, accepted the Challenge.

There is something in Nature very unaccountable on such Occasions, when we see the People take a certain painful Gratification in beholding these Encounters. Is it Cruelty that administers this Sort of Delight? or is it a Pleasure which is taken in the Exercise of Pity? It was methought pretty remarkable, that the Business of the Day being a Trial of Skill, the Popularity did not run so high as one would have expected on the Side of *Buck*. Is it that People's Passions have their Rise in Self-love, and thought themselves (in Spite of all the Courage they had) liable to the Fate of *Miller*, but could not so easily think themselves qualified like *Buck*?

Tully speaks of this Custom with less Horrour than one would expect, though he confesses it was much abused in his Time, and seems directly to approve of it under its first Regulations, when Criminals only fought before the People. *Crudele Gladiatorum spectaculum & inhumanum nonnullis videri solet; & haud scio annon ita sit ut nunc fit; cum vero sontes ferro depugnabant, auribus fortasse multa, oculis quidem nulla, poterat esse fortior contra dolorem & mortem disciplina. The Shows of Gladiators may be thought barbarous and inhumane, and I know not but it is so as it is now practised; but in those Times when only Criminals were Combatants, the Ear perhaps might receive many better Instructions, but it is impossible that any thing which affects our Eyes, should fortifie us so well against Pain and Death.*

T

No. 437.
[STEELE.]   Tuesday, July 22.

Tune impune haec facias? Tune hic homines adolescentulos Imperitos rerum, eductos libere, in fraudem illicis? Sollicitando & pollicitando eorum animos lactas? . . . Ac meretricios amores nuptiis conglutinas?—Ter. *And.*

THE other Day passed by me in her Chariot a Lady, with that pale and wan Complexion, which we sometimes see in young People, who are fallen into Sorrow, and private Anxiety of Mind, which antedate Age and Sickness. It is not three Years

ago since she was gay, airy, and a little towards Libertine in
her Carriage; but, methought, I easily forgave her that little
Insolence, which she so severely pays for in her present Condition. *Flavilla,* of whom I am speaking, is married to a sullen
Fool with Wealth: Her Beauty and Merit are lost upon the
Dolt, who is insensible of Perfection in any thing. Their
Hours together are either painful or insipid: The Minutes she
has to her self in his Absence are not sufficient to give Vent at
her Eyes to the Grief and Torment of his last Conversation.
This poor Creature was sacrificed with a Temper (which under
the Cultivation of a Man of Sense, would have made the most
agreeable Companion) into the Arms of this loathsome Yoke-
fellow by *Sempronia. Sempronia* is a good Lady, who supports her self in an affluent Condition, by contracting Friendship with rich young Widows, and Maids of plentiful Fortunes
at their own Disposal, and bestowing her Friends upon Worthless indigent Fellows; on the other Side, she ensnares inconsiderate and rash Youths of great Estates into the Arms of
vitious Women. For this Purpose, she is accomplished in all
the Arts which can make her acceptable at impertinent Visits;
she knows all that passes in every Quarter, and is well acquainted with all the favourite Servants, Busie-bodies, De-
pendants, and poor Relations of all Persons of Condition in the
whole Town. At the Price of a good Sum of Mony, *Sempronia,*
by the Instigation of *Flavilla*'s Mother brought about the
Match for the Daughter, and the Reputation of this which is
apparently, in point of Fortune, more than *Flavilla* could
expect, has gained her the Visits and frequent Attendance of
the Crowd of Mothers, who had rather see their Children
miserable in great Wealth, than the Happiest of the Race of
Mankind in a less conspicuous State of Life. When *Sempronia* is so well acquainted with a Woman's Temper and Circumstance, that she believes Marriage would be acceptable to
her, and advantageous to the Man who shall get her; her next
Step is to look out for some one, whose Condition has some
secret Wound in it, and wants a Sum, yet, in the Eye of the
World, not unsuitable to her. If such is not easily had, she
immediately adorns a worthless Fellow with what Estate she
thinks convenient, and adds as great a Share of good-humour
and Sobriety as is requisite: After this is settled, no Importunities, Arts, and Devices are omitted to hasten the Lady to
her Happiness. In the general indeed she is a Person of so
strict Justice, that she marries a poor Gallant to a rich Wench,
and a Monyless Girl to a Man of Fortune. But then she has
no manner of Conscience in the Disparity, when she has a mind
to impose a poor Rogue for one of an Estate; she has no Re-

morse in adding to it, that he is illiterate, ignorant, and un-fashioned; but makes those Imperfections Arguments of the Truth of his Wealth; and will, on such an Occasion, with a very grave Face, charge the People of Condition with Negligence in the Education of their Children. Exception being made t'other Day against an ignorant Booby of her own Cloathing, whom she was putting of for a rich Heir, *Madam*, said she, *you know there is no making Children who know they have Estates, attend their Books.*

Sempronia, by these Arts, is loaded with Presents, importuned for her Acquaintance, and admired by those who do not know the first Taste of Life, as a Woman of exemplary good Breeding. But sure, to murder and to rob are less Iniquities, than to raise Profit by Abuses, as irreparable as taking away Life; but more grievous, as making it lastingly unhappy. To rob a Lady at Play of half her Fortune, is not so ill, as giving the whole and herself to an unworthy Husband. But *Sempronia* can administer Consolation to an unhappy Fair at Home, by leading her to an agreeable Gallant elsewhere. She then can preach the general Condition of all the Married World, and tell an unexperienced young Woman the Methods of softning her Affliction, and laugh at her Simplicity and Want of Knowledge, with an *Oh! my Dear, you will know better.*

The Wickedness of *Sempronia*, one would think, should be superlative; but I cannot but esteem that of some Parents equal to it; I mean such as sacrifice the greatest Endowments and Qualifications to base Bargains. A Parent who forces a Child of a liberal and ingenuous Spirit into the Arms of a Clown or a Blockhead, obliges her to a Crime too odious for a Name. It is in a Degree the unnatural Conjunction of rational and brutal Beings. Yet what is there so common, as the bestowing an accomplished Woman with such a Disparity. And I could name Crowds who lead miserable Lives, for want of Knowledge in their Parents, of this Maxim, that good Sense and good Nature always go together. That which is attributed to Fools, and called good Nature, is only an Inability of observing what is faulty, which turns in Marriage, into a Suspicion of every thing as such, from a Consciousness of that Inability.

'*Mr.* SPECTATOR,

I am intirely of your Opinion with Relation to the Equestrian Females, who affect both the Masculine and Feminine Air at the same time; and cannot forbear making a Presentment against another Order of them who grow very numerous and powerful; and since our Language is not very capable of good compound Words, I must be contented to call them only the *Naked Shoulder'd.* These Beauties are not contented to make Lovers wherever they appear, but they must make Rivals at the same time. Were you to see *Gatty* walk the *Park* at high Mall, you would expect those who followed her and those who met her would immediately draw their Swords for her. I hope, Sir, you will provide for the future, that Women may stick to their Faces for doing any future Mischief, and not allow any but direct Traders in Beauty to expose more than the fore Part of the Neck, unless you please to allow this After-Game to those who are very defective in the Charms of the Countenance. I can say, to my Sorrow, the present Practice is very unfair, when to look back is Death; and it may be said of our Beauties, as a great Poet did of Bullets,

> *They kill and wound like* Parthians *as they fly.*

I submit this to your Animadversion; and am, for the little while I have left,

> *Your humble Servant,*
> *the languishing* PHILANTHUS.

P.S. *Suppose you mended my Letter, and made a Simile about the Porcupine, but I submit that also.'*

T

No. 438.
[STEELE.]   Wednesday, July 23.

> . . . *Animum rege, qui, nisi paret,*
> *Imperat* . . .—Hor.

IT is a very common Expression, That such a one is very good-natur'd, but very passionate. The Expression indeed is very good-natur'd, to allow passionate People so much Quarter: But I think a passionate Man deserves the least Indulgence imaginable. It is said, it is soon over; that is, all the Mischief he does is quickly dispatch'd, which, I think, is no great Recommendation to Favour. I have known one of those good-natur'd passionate Men say in a mix'd Company, even to his own Wife or Child, such Things as the most inveterate Enemy of his Family would not have spoke, even in Imagination. It is certain, that quick Sensibility is inseparable from a ready Understanding; but why should not that good Understanding call to it self all its Force on such Occasions, to master that sudden Inclination to Anger. One of the greatest Souls now in the World is the most subject by Nature to Anger, and yet so famous for a Conquest of himself this Way, that he is the known Example when you talk of Temper and Command of a Man's self. To contain the Spirit of Anger, is the worthiest Discipline we can put our selves to. When a Man has made any Progress this way, a frivolous Fellow in a Passion, is to him as contemptible as a froward Child. It ought to be the Study of every Man, for his own Quiet and Peace. When he stands combustible and ready to flame upon every thing that touches him, Life is as uneasie to himself as it is to all about him. *Syncropius* leads, of all Men living, the most ridiculous life; he is ever offending, and begging Pardon. If his Man enters the Room without what he sent for, *That Blockhead,* begins he—*Gentlemen, I ask your Pardon, but Servants now-a-days*—The wrong Plates are laid, they are thrown into the Middle of the Room; his Wife stands by in Pain for him, which he sees in her Face, and answers as if he had heard all she was thinking; *Why, what the Devil! Why don't you take care to give Orders in these Things?* His Friends sit down to a tasteless Plenty of every thing, every minute expecting new Insults from his Impertinent Passions. In a word, to eat with, or visit *Syncropius,* is no other than going to see him exercise his Family, exercise their Patience, and his own Anger.

It is monstrous that the Shame and Confusion in which this good-natured angry Man must needs behold his Friends while he thus lays about him, does not give him so much Reflection as to create an Amendment. This is the most scandalous Disuse of Reason imaginable; all the harmless Part of him is no more than that of a Bull-Dog, they are tame no longer than they are not offended. One of these good-natured angry Men shall, in an Instant, assemble together so many Allusions to secret Circumstances, as are enough to dissolve the Peace of all the Families and Friends he is acquainted with, in a Quarter of an Hour, and yet the next Moment be the best-natured Man in the whole World. If you would see Passion in its Purity, without Mixture of Reason, behold it represented in a mad Hero, drawn by a mad Poet. *Nat. Lee* makes his *Alexander* say thus:

> *Away, begon, and give a Whirlwind Room,*
> *Or I will blow you up like dust! Avaunt;*
> *Madness but meanly represents my Toil.*
> *Eternal Discord!*
> *Fury! Revenge! Disdain and Indignation!*
> *Tear my swoln Breast, make way for Fire and Tempest.*
> *My Brain is burst, Debate and Reason quench'd;*
> *The Storm is up, and my hot bleeding Heart*
> *Splits with the Rack, while Passions, like the Wind,*
> *Rise up to Heav'n, and put out all the Stars.*

Every passionate Fellow in Town talks half the Day with as little Consistency, and threatens Things as much out of his Power.

The next disagreeable Person to the outrageous Gentleman, is one of a much lower Order of Anger, and he is what we commonly call a peevish Fellow. A peevish Fellow is one who has some Reason in himself for being out of Humour, or has a natural Incapacity for Delight, and therefore disturbs all who are happier than himself with Pishes and Pshaws, or other well-bred Interjections, at every thing that is said or done in his Presence. There should be Physick mixed in the Food of all which these Fellows eat in good Company. This Degree of Anger passes, forsooth, for a Delicacy of Judgment, that won't admit of being easily pleas'd: But none above the Character of wearing a peevish Man's Livery, ought to bear with his ill Manners. All things among Men of Sense and Condition should pass the Censure, and have the Protection of the Eye of Reason.

No Man ought to be tolerated in an habitual Humour, Whim, or Particularity of Behaviour, by any who do not wait upon him for Bread. Next to the peevish Fellow is the Snarler. This Gentleman deals mightily in what we call the Irony, and as these sort of People exert themselves most against those below them, you see their Humour best, in their Talk to their Servants. That is so like you, you are a fine Fellow, thou art the quickest Head-piece, and the like. One would think the Hectoring, the Storming, the Sullen, and all the different Species and Subordinations of the Angry should be cured, by knowing they live only as pardoned Men, and how pityful is the Condition of being only suffered? But I am interrupted by the Pleasantest Scene of Anger and the Disappointment of it that I have ever known, which happened while I was yet Writing, and I over-heard as I sat in the Back-room at a French Bookseller's. There came into the Shop a very learned Man with an erect Solemn Air, and, tho' a Person of great Parts otherwise, slow in understanding any thing which makes against himself. The Composure of the faulty Man, and the whimsical Perplexity of him that was justly angry, is perfectly New: After turning over many Volumes, said the Seller to the Buyer, *Sir, you know I have long asked you to send me back the first Volume of French Sermons I formerly lent you;* Sir, said the Chapman, I have often looked for it but cannot find it; It is certainly lost, and I know not to whom I lent it, it is so many Years ago; *then, Sir, here is the other Volume, I'll send you home that, and please to pay for both.* My Friend, reply'd he, can'st thou be so Senseless as not to know that one Volume is as imperfect in my Library as in your Shop. *Yes, Sir, but it is you have lost the first Volume, and to be short I will be Paid.* Sir, answered the Chapman, you are a young Man, your Book is lost, and learn by this little Loss to bear much greater Adversities, which you must expect to meet with. *Yes, Sir, I 'll bear when I must, but I have not lost now, for I say you have it and shall Pay me.* Friend you grow Warm, I tell you the Book is lost, and I foresee in the Course even of a prosperous Life, that you will meet Afflictions to make you Mad, if you cannot bear this Trifle. *Sir, there is in this Case no need of bearing, for you have the Book.* I say, Sir, I have not the Book, but your Passion will not let you hear enough to be informed that I have it not. Learn Resignation of your self to the Distresses of this Life: Nay do not fret and fume, it is my Duty to tell you that you are of an impatient Spirit, and an impatient Spirit is never without Woe. *Was ever any thing like this?* Yes, Sir, there have been many things like this. The loss is but a Trifle, but your Temper is Wanton, and incapable of the least Pain; therefore let me advise you, be Patient, the Book is lost, but do not you for that Reason lose your self. T

No. 439.
[ADDISON.]   Thursday, July 24.

Hi narrata ferunt alio; mensuraque ficti
Crescit; & auditis aliquid novus adjicit auctor.—Ov.

Ovid describes the Palace of Fame as situated in the very Center of the Universe, and perforated with so many Windows and Avenues as gave her the Sight of every thing that was done in the Heavens, in the Earth, and in the Sea. The Structure of it was contrived in so admirable a manner, that it Eccho'd every Word which was spoken in the whole Compass of Nature; so that the Palace, says the Poet, was always filled with a confused Hubbub of low dying Sounds, the Voices being almost spent and worn out before they arrived at this General Rendezvous of Speeches and Whispers.

I consider Courts with the same regard to the Governments which they superintend, as *Ovid*'s Palace of Fame with regard to the Universe. The Eyes of a watchful Minister run through the whole People. There is scarce a Murmur or Complaint, that does not reach his Ears. They have News-Gatherers and Intelligencers distributed into their several Walks and Quarters, who bring in their respective Quotas, and make them acquainted with the Discourse and Conversation of the whole Kingdom or Common-wealth where they are employed. The

wisest of Kings, alluding to these Invisible and unsuspected
Spies, who are planted by Kings and Rulers over their Fellow-
Citizens, as well as to those Voluntary Informers that are
buzzing about the Ears of a great Man, and making their Court
by such secret Methods of Intelligence, has given us a very
prudent Caution: *Curse not the King, no not in thy Thought, and
Curse not the Rich in thy Bed-chamber: For a Bird of the Air
shall carry the Voice, and that which hath Wings shall tell the
matter.*

As it is absolutely necessary for Rulers to make use of other
People's Eyes and Ears, they should take particular Care to do
it in such a manner, that it may not bear too hard on the
Person whose Life and Conversation are enquired into. A
Man who is capable of so infamous a Calling as that of a Spy,
is not very much to be relied upon. He can have no great
Ties of Honour, or Checks of Conscience, to restrain him in
those covert Evidences, where the Person accused has no
Opportunity of vindicating himself. He will be more industrious to carry that which is grateful, than that which is
true. There will be no Occasion for him if he does not hear
and see things worth Discovery; so that he naturally inflames
every Word and Circumstance, aggravates what is faulty,
perverts what is good, and misrepresents what is indifferent.
Nor is it to be doubted but that such ignominious Wretches
let their private Passions into these their clandestine Informations, and often wreak their particular Spite or Malice against
the Person whom they are set to watch. It is a pleasant
Scene enough, which an *Italian* Author describes between a
Spy and a Cardinal who employed him. The Cardinal is represented as minuting down every thing that is told him. The
Spy begins with a low Voice, Such an one, the Advocate,
whispered to one of his Friends, within my Hearing, that your
Eminence was a very great Poultron; and after having given
his Patron time to take it down, adds, that another called him
a Mercenary Rascal in a Publick Conversation. The Cardinal
replies very well, and bids him go on. The Spy proceeds, and
loads him with Reports of the same Nature, till the Cardinal
rises in great Wrath, calls him an impudent Scoundrel, and
kicks him out of the Room.

It is observed of great and heroick Minds, that they have
not only shewn a particular Disregard to those unmerited
Reproaches which have been cast upon 'em, but have been
altogether free from that Impertinent Curiosity of Enquiring
after them, or the poor Revenge of resenting them. The
Histories of *Alexander* and *Caesar* are full of this kind of Instances. Vulgar Souls are of a quite contrary Character.

Dionysius, the Tyrant of *Sicily,* had a Dungeon which was a very curious Piece of Architecture; and of which, as I am informed, there are still to be seen some Remains in that Island. It was called *Dionysius*'s Ear, and built with several little Windings and Labyrinths in the form of a real Ear. The Structure of it made it a kind of whispering Place, but such a one as gathered the Voice of him who spoke into a Funnel, which was placed at the very Top of it. The Tyrant used to lodge all his State Criminals, or those whom he supposed to be engaged together in any Evil Designs upon him, in this Dungeon. He had at the same time an Apartment over it, where he used to apply himself to the Funnel, and by that means overheard every thing that was whispered in the Dungeon. I believe one may venture to affirm, that a *Caesar* or an *Alexander* would have rather died by the Treason, than having used so disingenuous a Means for the detecting it.

A Man, who in ordinary Life is very Inquisitive after every thing which is spoken ill of him, passes his Time but very indifferently. He is wounded by every Arrow that is shot at him, and puts it in the Power of every Insignificant Enemy to disquiet him. Nay, he will suffer from what has been said of him, when it is forgotten by those who said or heard it. For this Reason I could never bear one of those Officious Friends, that would be telling every malicious Report, every idle Censure that passed upon me. The Tongue of Man is so petulant, and his Thoughts so variable, that one should not lay too great a stress upon any present Speeches and Opinions. Praise and Obloquy proceed very frequently out of the same Mouth upon the same Person, and upon the same Occasion. A generous Enemy will sometimes bestow Commendations, as the dearest Friend cannot sometimes refrain from speaking Ill. The Man who is indifferent in either of these respects, gives his Opinion at random, and praises or disapproves as he finds himself in Humour.

I shall conclude this Essay with Part of a Character, which is finely drawn by the Earl of *Clarendon,* in the first Book of his History, and which gives us the lively Picture of a great Man teizing himself with an absurd Curiosity.

'He had not that Application and Submission, and Reverence for the Queen as might have been expected from his Wisdom and Breeding; and often crossed her Pretences and Desires with more Rudeness than was natural to him. Yet he was impertinently sollicitous to know what her Majesty said of him in private, and what Resentments she had towards him. And when by some Confidents, who had their Ends upon him from those Offices, he was inform'd of some bitter

Expressions fallen from her Majesty, he was so exceedingly afflicted and tormented with the Sense of it, that sometimes by passionate Complaints and Representations to the King; sometimes by more dutiful Addresses and Expostulations with the Queen in bewailing his Misfortune; he frequently exposed himself, and left his Condition worse than it was before, and the Eclaircisment commonly ended in the Discovery of the Persons from whom he had receiv'd his most secret Intelligence.'　　　　　　　　　　　　　　　　　　C

No. 440.
[ADDISON.]　　　　　　　　　　　　　　　Friday, July 25.

Vivere si recte nescis, decede peritis.—Hor.

I have already given my Reader an Account of a Sett of merry Fellows, who are passing their Summer together in the Country, being provided of a great House, where there is not only a convenient Apartment for every particular Person, but a large Infirmary for the Reception of such of them as are any way Indisposed, or out of Humour. Having lately receiv'd a Letter from the Secretary of this Society, by Order of the whole Fraternity, which acquaints me with their Behaviour during the last Week, I shall here make a Present of it to the Publick.

'*Mr.* Spectator,

We are glad to find that you approve the Establishment which we have here made for the retrieving of good Manners and agreeable Conversation, and shall use our best Endeavours so to improve ourselves in this our Summer Retirement, that we may next Winter serve as Patterns to the Town. But to the end that this our Institution may be no less Advantageous to the Publick than to our-selves, we shall communicate to you one Week of our Proceedings, desiring you at the same time, if you see any thing faulty in them, to favour us with your Admonitions. For you must know, Sir, that it has been proposed amongst us to chuse you for our Visitor, to which I must further add, that one of the College having declar'd last Week, he did not like the *Spectator* of the Day, and not being able to assign any just Reasons for such his Dislike, he was sent to the Infirmary, *Nemine contradicente*.

On *Monday* the Assembly was in very good Humour, having received some Recruits of *French* Claret that Morning; when unluckily, towards the middle of the Dinner, one of the Company swore at his Servant in a very rough manner, for having

put too much Water in his Wine.   Upon which the President
of the Day, who is always the Mouth of the Company, after
having convinced him of the Impertinence of his Passion, and
the Insult it had made upon the Company, ordered his Man
to take him from the Table, and convey him to the Infirmary.
There was but one more sent away that Day; this was a
Gentleman who is reckoned by some Persons one of the greatest
Wits, and by others one of the greatest Boobies about Town.
This you will say is a strange Character, but what makes it
stranger yet, is a very true one, for he is perpetually the
Reverse of himself, being always merry or dull to Excess.   We
brought him hither to divert us, which he did very well upon
the Road, having lavish'd away as much Wit and Laughter
upon the Hackney Coachman as might have served him during
his whole Stay here, had it been duly managed.   He had been
lumpish for two or three Days, but was so far connived at, in
hopes of Recovery, that we dispatched one of the briskest
Fellows among the Brotherhood into the Infirmary, for having
told him at Table he was not merry.   But our President
observing that he indulged himself in this long Fit of Stupidity,
and construing it as a Contempt of the College, ordered him
to retire into the Place prepared for such Companions.   He
was no sooner got into it, but his Wit and Mirth returned upon
him in so violent a manner, that he shook the whole Infirmary
with the Noise of it, and had so good an Effect upon the rest
of the Patients, that he brought them all out to Dinner with
him the next Day.

On *Tuesday* we were no sooner sat down, but one of the
Company complained that his Head aked; upon which another
asked him, in an insolent manner, what he did there then; this
insensibly grew into some warm Words; so that the President,
in order to keep the Peace, gave directions to take them both
from the Table, and lodge them in the Infirmary.   Not long
after, another of the Company telling us, he knew by a Pain in
his Shoulder that we should have some Rain, the President
ordered him to be removed, and placed as a Weather-glass in
the Apartment above-mentioned.

On *Wednesday* a Gentleman having received a Letter written
in a Woman's Hand, and changing Colour twice or thrice as
he read it, desired leave to retire into the Infirmary.   The
President consented, but denied him the Use of Pen, Ink and
Paper till such time as he had slept upon it.   One of the Company being seated at the lower end of the Table, and discovering
his secret Discontent by finding fault with every Dish that was
served up, and refusing to Laugh at any thing that was said,
the President told him, that he found he was in an uneasie

Seat, and desired him to accommodate himself better in the Infirmary. After Dinner a very honest Fellow chancing to let a Punn fall from him, his Neighbour cryed out, *to the Infirmary*; at the same time pretending to be Sick at it, as having the same Natural Antipathy to a Punn, which some have to a Cat. This produced a long Debate. Upon the whole the Punnster was Acquitted, and his Neighbour sent off.

On *Thursday* there was but one Delinquent. This was a Gentleman of strong Voice, but weak Understanding. He had unluckily engaged himself in a Dispute with a Man of excellent Sense, but of a modest Elocution. The Man of Heat replied to every Answer of his Antagonist with a louder Note than ordinary, and only raised his Voice when he should have enforced his Argument. Finding himself at length driven to an Absurdity, he still reasoned in a more clamorous and confused manner, and to make the greater Impression upon his Hearers, concluded with a loud Thump upon the Table. The President immediately ordered him to be carried off, and dieted with Water-gruel, till such time as he should be sufficiently weakened for Conversation.

On *Friday* there passed very little remarkable, saving only, that several Petitions were read of the Persons in Custody, desiring to be released from their Confinement, and vouching for one another's good Behaviour for the future.

On *Saturday* we received many Excuses from Persons who had found themselves in an unsociable Temper, and had voluntarily shut themselves up. The Infirmary was indeed never so full as on this Day, which I was at some loss to account for, till upon my going Abroad I observed that it was an Easterly Wind. The Retirement of most of my Friends has given me Opportunity and Leisure of writing you this Letter, which I must not conclude without assuring you, that all the Members of our College, as well those who are under Confinement, as those who are at Liberty, are your very humble Servants, tho' none more than, &c.'
C

No. 441.
[ADDISON.] Saturday, July 26.

> *Si fractus illabatur orbis,*
> *Impavidum ferient ruinae.*—Hor.

MAN, considered in himself, is a very helpless and a very wretched Being. He is subject every Moment to the greatest Calamities and Misfortunes. He is beset with Dangers on all sides, and may become unhappy by numberless Casualties, which he could not foresee, nor have prevented had he foreseen them.

It is our Comfort, while we are obnoxious to so many Accidents, that we are under the Care of one who directs Contingencies, and has in his Hands the Management of every Thing that is capable of annoying or offending us; who knows the Assistance we stand in need of, and is always ready to bestow it on those who ask it of him.

The natural Homage, which such a Creature bears to so infinitely Wise and Good a Being, is a firm Reliance on him for the Blessings and Conveniencies of Life, and an habitual Trust in him for Deliverance out of all such Dangers and Difficulties as may befal us.

The Man, who always lives in this Disposition of Mind, has not the same dark and melancholy Views of Human Nature, as he who considers himself abstractedly from this Relation to the Supreme Being. At the same time that he reflects upon his own Weakness and Imperfection, he comforts himself with the Contemplation of those Divine Attributes, which are employed for his Safety and his Welfare. He finds his want of Foresight made up by the Omniscience of him who is his Support. He is not sensible of his own want of Strength, when he knows that his Helper is Almighty. In short, the Person who has a firm Trust on the Supreme Being is Powerful in *his* Power, Wise by *his* Wisdom, Happy by *his* Happiness. He reaps the Benefit of every Divine Attribute, and loses his own Unsufficiency in the Fullness of infinite Perfection.

To make our Lives more easie to us, we are commanded to put our Trust in him, who is thus able to relieve and succour us; the Divine Goodness having made such a Reliance a Duty, notwithstanding we should have been miserable had it been forbidden us.

Among several Motives, which might be made use of to recommend this Duty to us, I shall only take notice of those that follow.

The first and strongest is, that we are promised, He will not fail those who put their Trust in him.

But without considering the Supernatural Blessing which accompanies this Duty, we may observe that it has a natural Tendency to its own Reward, or in other words, that this firm Trust and Confidence in the great Disposer of all Things, contributes very much to the getting clear of any Affliction, or to the bearing it manfully. A Person who believes he has his Succour at hand, and that he acts in the sight of his Friend, often exerts himself beyond his Abilities, and does Wonders that are not to be matched by one who is not animated with such a Confidence of Success. I could produce Instances from History, of Generals, who out of a Belief that they were under the Protection of some invisible Assistant, did not only encourage their Soldiers to do their utmost, but have acted themselves beyond what they would have done, had they not been inspired by such a Belief. I might in the same manner shew how such a Trust in the Assistance of an Almighty Being, naturally produces Patience, Hope, Chearfulness, and all other Dispositions of Mind that alleviate those Calamities which we are not able to remove.

The Practice of this Virtue administers great Comfort to the Mind of Man in times of Poverty and Affliction, but most of all in the Hour of Death. When the Soul is hovering in the last Moments of Separation, when it is just entring on another State of Existence, to converse with Scenes, and Objects, and Companions that are altogether new, what can support her under such tremblings of Thought, such Fear, such Anxiety, such Apprehensions, but the casting of all her Cares upon him who first gave her Being, who has conducted her through one stage of it, and will be always with her to Guide and Comfort her in her Progress thro' Eternity?

David has very beautifully represented this steady Reliance on God Almighty in his twenty third Psalm, which is a kind of *Pastoral* Hymn, and filled with those Allusions which are usual in that kind of Writing. As the Poetry is very exquisite, I shall present my Reader with the following Translation of it.

I.

The Lord my Pasture shall prepare,
And feed me with a Shepherd's Care:
His Presence shall my wants supply,
And guard me with a watchful Eye;
My Noon-day Walks he shall attend,
And all my midnight Hours defend.

II.

When in the sultry Glebe I faint,
Or on the thirsty Mountain pant;
To fertile Vales and dewy Meads
My weary wandr'ing Steps he leads;
Where peaceful Rivers, soft and slow,
Amid the verdant Landskip flow.

III.

Tho' in the Paths of Death I tread,
With gloomy Horrors over-spread;
My steadfast Heart shall fear no ill,
For thou, O Lord, art with me still;
Thy friendly Crook shall give me Aid,
And guide me through the dreadful Shade.

IV.

Tho' in a bare and rugged Way,
Through devious lonely Wilds I stray,
Thy Bounty shall my Pains beguile:
The barren Wilderness shall smile
With sudden Greens and Herbage crown'd,
And Streams shall murmur all around.

C

No. 442.
[STEELE.]   Monday, July 28.

Scribimus indocti doctique . . .—Hor.

I DO not know whether I enough explained my self to the
World, when I invited all Men to be assistant to me in this my
Work of Speculation; for I have not yet acquainted my
Readers, that besides the Letters and valuable Hints I have
from Time to Time received from my Correspondents, I have
by me several curious and extraordinary Papers sent with a
Design (as no one will doubt when they are published) that
they may be printed entire, and without any alteration, by
way of *Spectator.* I must acknowledge also, that I myself
being the first Projector of the Paper, thought I had a Right
to make them my own by dressing them in my own Stile, by
leaving out what would not appear like mine, and by adding
whatever might be proper to adapt them to the Character and
Genius of my Paper, with which it was almost impossible
these could exactly correspond, it being certain that hardly
two Men think alike, and therefore so many Men so many
Spectators. Besides, I must own my Weakness for Glory is
such, that if I consulted that only, I might be so far sway'd by
it, as almost to wish that no one could write a *Spectator* besides
my self; nor can I deny, but upon the first Perusal of those
Papers, I felt some secret Inclinations of Ill-will towards the
Persons who wrote them. This was the Impression I had
upon the first reading them; but upon a late Review (more

for the sake of Entertainment than Use) regarding them with
another Eye than I had done at first (for by converting them
as well as I could to my own Use, I thought I had utterly
disabled them from ever offending me again as *Spectators*),
I found my self moved by a Passion very different from that
of Envy; sensibly touched with Pity, the softest and most
generous of all Passions, when I reflected what a cruel Disappointment the neglect of those Papers must needs have been
to the Writers, who impatiently longed to see them appear in
Print, and who, no doubt, triumph'd to themselves in the
Hopes of having a Share with me in the Applause of the
Publick; a Pleasure so great, that none but those who have
experienced it can have a Sense of it. In this Manner of
viewing those Papers, I really found I had not done them
Justice, there being something so extreamly natural and
peculiarly good in some of them, that I will appeal to the
World whether it was possible to alter a Word in them without
doing them a manifest Hurt and Violence; and whether they
can ever appear rightly, and as they ought, but in their own
native Dress and Colours: And therefore I think I should not
only wrong them, but deprive the World of a considerable
Satisfaction, should I any longer delay the making them
publick.

After I have published a few of these *Spectators*, I doubt not
but I shall find the Success of them to equal, if not surpass,
that of the best of my own. An Author should take all
Methods to humble himself in the Opinion he has of his own
Performances. When these Papers appear to the World, I
doubt not but they will be followed by many others; and I shall
not repine, though I my self shall have left me but very few
Days to appear in Publick: But preferring the general Weal
and Advantage to any Considerations of my self, I am resolved
for the Future to publish any *Spectator* that deserves it, entire,
and without any Alteration; assuring the World (if there can
be Need of it) that it is none of mine; and if the Authors think
fit to subscribe their Names, I will add them.

I think the best way of promoting this generous and useful
Design, will be by giving out Subjects or Themes of all Kinds
whatsoever, on which (with a Preamble of the extraordinary
Benefit and Advantage that may accrue thereby to the
Publick) I will invite all manner of Persons, whether Scholars,
Citizens, Courtiers, Gentlemen, of the Town or Country, and
all Beaux, Rakes, Smarts, Prudes, Coquets, Housewives, and
all Sorts of Wits, whether Male or Female, and however distinguished, whether they be True-Wits, Whole, or Half-Wits,
or whether Arch, Dry, Natural, Acquired, Genuine, or De-

prav'd Wits; and Persons of all Sorts of Tempers and Complexions, whether the Severe, the Delightful, the Impertinent, the Agreeable, the Thoughtful, Busie, or Careless; the Serene or Cloudy, Jovial or Melancholly, Untowardly or Easie; the Cold, Temperate, or Sanguine; and of what Manners or Dispositions soever, whether the Ambitious or Humble-minded, the Proud or Pitiful, Ingenious or Base-minded, Good or Ill-natur'd, Publick-spirited or Selfish; and under what Fortune or Circumstance soever, whether the Contented or Miserable, Happy or Unfortunate, High or Low, Rich or Poor (whether so through Want of Money, or Desire of more) Healthy or Sickly, Married or Single; nay, whether Tall or Short, Fat or Lean; and of what Trade, Occupation, Profession, Station, Country, Faction, Party, Perswasion, Quality, Age or Condition soever, who have ever made Thinking a Part of their Business or Diversion, and have any thing worthy to impart on these Subjects to the World, according to these several and respective Talents or Geniuses, and as the Subject given out hits their Tempers, Humours, or Circumstances, or may be made profitable to the Publick by their particular Knowledge or Experience in the Matter proposed, to do their utmost on them by such a Time; to the End they may receive the inexpressible and irresistible Pleasure of seeing their Essay allowed of and relished by the rest of Mankind.

I will not prepossess the Reader with too great Expectation of the extraordinary Advantages which must redound to the Publick by these Essays, when the different Thoughts and Observations of all Sorts of Persons according to their Quality, Age, Sex, Education, Professions, Humours, Manners and Conditions, &c. shall be set out by themselves in the clearest and most genuine Light, and as they themselves would wish to have them appear to the World.

The Thesis *propos'd for the present Exercise of the Adventurers to write* Spectators, *is* MONY, *on which Subject all Persons are desired to send in their Thoughts within Ten Days after the Date hereof.* T

No. 443.
[STEELE.]   Tuesday, July 29.

Sublatam ex oculis quaerimus invidi.—Hor.

Camilla *to the* SPECTATOR.

'*Mr.* SPECTATOR.   *Venice, July* 10, N. S.

I TAKE it extreamly ill, that you do not reckon conspicuous Persons of your Nation are within your Cognizance, tho' out of the Dominions of *Great-Britain.* I little thought in the green Years of my Life, that I should ever call it an Happiness to be out of dear *England*; but as I grew to Woman, I found my self less acceptable in Proportion to the Encrease of my Merit. Their Ears in *Italy* are so differently formed from the Make of yours in *England*, that I never come upon the Stage, but a general Satisfaction appears in every Countenance of the whole People. When I dwell upon a Note, I behold all the Men accompanying me with Heads inclining and falling of their Persons on one Side, as dying away with me. The Women too do Justice to my Merit, and no ill-natured worthless Creature cries, *The vain Thing*, when I am wrapp'd up in the Performance of my Part, and sensibly touched with the Effect my Voice has upon all who hear me. I live here distinguished as one whom Nature has been liberal to in a graceful Person, an exalted Mien, and Heavenly Voice. These Particularities in this strange Country, are Arguments for Respect and Generosity to her who is possessed of them. The *Italians* see a thousand Beauties I am sensible I have no Pretence to, and abundantly make up to me the Injustice I received in my own Country, of disallowing me what I really had. The Humour of Hissing, which you have among you, I do not know any thing of; and their Applauses are uttered in Sighs, and bearing a Part at the Cadences of Voice with the Persons who are performing. I am often put in Mind of those complaisant Lines of my own Countryman, when he is calling all his Faculties together to hear *Arabella.*

> *Let all be hush'd, each softest Motion cease,*
> *Be ev'ry loud tumultuous Thought at Peace,*
> *And ev'ry ruder Gasp of Breath*
> *Be calm, as in the Arms of Death:*
> *And thou, most fickle, most uneasie Part,*
> *Thou restless Wanderer, my Heart,*
> *Be still; gently, ah! gently leave,*
> *Thou busie idle Thing, to heave.*
> *Stir not a Pulse; and let my Blood,*
> *That turbulent, unruly Flood,*
> *Be softly staid;*
> *Let me be all but my Attention dead.*

The whole City of *Venice* is as still when I am singing as this polite Hearer was to Mrs. *Hunt.* But when they break that Silence, did you know the Pleasure I am in, when every man utters his Applause, by calling me aloud the *Dear Creature,* the *Angel,* the *Venus*; *What Attitude she moves with!—Hush she sings again!* We have no boistrous Wits who dare disturb an Audience, and break the Publick Peace meerly to shew they dare. Mr. SPECTATOR, I write this to you thus in Haste, to tell you I am so very much at ease here, that I know nothing but Joy; and I will not return, but leave you in *England* to hiss all Merit of your own Growth off the Stage. I know, Sir, you were always my Admirer, and therefore I am yours,

CAMILLA.

P.S. I am ten times better dressed than ever I was in *England.*'

' *Mr.* SPECTATOR,

The Project in yours of the 11th Instant, of furthering the Correspondence and Knowledge of that considerable Part of Mankind, the Trading World, cannot but be highly commendable. Good Lectures to young Traders may have very good Effects on their Conduct: but beware you propagate no false Notions of Trade; let none of your Correspondents impose on the World, by putting forth base Methods in a good Light, and glazing them over with improper Terms. I would have no Means of Profit set for Copies to others, but such as are laudable in themselves. Let not Noise be called Industry, nor Impudence Courage. Let not good Fortune be imposed on the World for good Management, nor Poverty be called Folly; impute not always Bankruptcy to Extravagance, nor an Estate to Foresight: Niggardliness is not good Husbandry, nor Generosity Profusion.

Honestus is a well-meaning and judicious Trader, hath substantial Goods, and trades with his own Stock; husbands his Mony to the best Advantage, without taking all Advantages of the Necessities of his Workmen, or grinding the Face of the Poor. *Fortunatus* is stocked with Ignorance, and consequently with Self-Opinion; the Quality of his Goods cannot but be suitable to that of his Judgment. *Honestus* pleases discerning People, and keeps their Custom by good Usage; makes modest Profit by modest Means, to the decent Support of his Family: Whilst *Fortunatus* blustering always, pushes on, promising much, and performing little, with Obsequiousness offensive to People of Sense; strikes at all, catches much the greater Part; raises a considerable Fortune by Imposition on others, to the Disencouragement and Ruin of those who trade in the same Way.

I give here but loose Hints, and beg you to be very circumspect in the Province you have now undertaken: If you perform it successfully, it will be a very great Good; for nothing is more wanting, than that Mechanick Industry were set forth with the Freedom and Greatness of Mind which ought always to accompany a Man of a liberal Education.

From my Shop under the   *Your Humble Servant,*
Royal-Exchange, July 14.   R. C.'

' *Mr.* Spectator,   *July* 24, 1712.

Notwithstanding the repeated Censures that your Spectatorial Wisdom has passed upon People more remarkable for Impudence than Wit, there are yet some remaining, who pass with the giddy Part of Mankind for sufficient Sharers of the latter, who have nothing but the former Qualification to recommend them. Another timely Animadversion is absolutely necessary; be pleased therefore once for all to let these Gentlemen know, that there is neither Mirth nor good Humour in hooting a young Fellow out of Countenance; nor that it will ever constitute a Wit, to conclude a tart Piece of Buffoonry with a *what makes you blush?* Pray please to inform them again, That to speak what they know is shocking, proceeds from ill Nature, and a Sterility of Brain; especially when the Subject will not admit of Raillery, and their Discourse has no Pretension to Satyr but what is in their Design to disoblige. I should be very glad too if you would take Notice, that a daily Repetition of the same over-bearing Insolence is yet more insupportable, and a Confirmation of very extraordinary Dulness. The sudden Publication of this, may have an Effect upon a notorious Offender of this Kind, whose Reformation would redound very much to the Satisfaction and Quiet of

Your most humble Servant,

T   F. B.'

No. 444.
[STEELE.]   Wednesday, July 30.

Parturiunt montes.—Hor.

It gives me much Despair in the Design of reforming the World by my Speculations, when I find there always arise, from one Generation to another, successive Cheats and Bubbles, as naturally as Beasts of Prey and those which are to be their Food. There is hardly a Man in the World, one would think, so ignorant, as not to know that the ordinary quack Doctors, who publish their great Abilities in little brown Billets, distributed to all who pass by, are to a Man Impostors and Murderers; yet such is the Credulity of the Vulgar, and the

Impudence of these Professors, that the Affair still goes on, and new Promises of what was never done before are made every Day. What aggravates the Jest is, that even this Promise has been made as long as the Memory of Man can trace it, and yet nothing performed, and yet still prevails. As I was passing along to Day, a Paper given into my Hand by a Fellow without a Nose tells us as follows what good News is come to Town, to wit, that there is now a certain Cure for the *French* Disease, by a Gentleman just come from his travels.

In Russel-Court, *over-against the* Cannon-Ball, *at the* Surgeon's Arms *in* Drury-lane, *is lately come from his Travels a Surgeon who hath practised Surgery and Physick both by Sea and Land these twenty four Years. He (by the Blessing) cures the* Yellow Gandice, Green Sickness, Scurvey, Dropsie, Surfeits, long Sea Voyages, Campains, and Women's Miscarriages, Lying-In, *&c. as some People that has been lame these thirty Years can testifie; in short, he cureth all Diseases incident to Men, Women, or Children.*

If a Man could be so indolent as to look upon this Havock of the human Species which is made by Vice and Ignorance, it would be a good ridiculous Work to comment upon the Declaration of this accomplish'd Traveller. There is something unaccountably taking among the Vulgar in those who come from a great Way off. Ignorant People of Quality, as many there are of such, doat excessively this Way; many Instances of which every Man will suggest to himself without my Enumeration of them. The Ignorants of lower Order, who cannot, like the Upper Ones, be profuse of their Mony to those recommended by coming from a Distance, are no less complaisant than the others, for they venture their Lives from the same Admiration.

The Doctor is lately come from his Travels, and has practised both by Sea and Land, and therefore cures the *Green-Sickness, long Sea Voyages, Campains, and Lying-In.* Both by Sea and Land;—I will not answer for the Distempers called *Sea Voyages and Campains;* but I dare say, those of Green-Sickness and Lying-in might be as well taken Care of if the Doctor staid a-shoar. But the Art of managing Mankind, is only to make them stare a little, to keep up their Astonishment, to let nothing be familiar to them, but ever to have something in your Sleeve, in which they must think you are deeper than they are. There is an ingenious Fellow, a Barber, of my Acquaintance, who, besides his broken Fiddle and a dryed Sea-Monster, has a Twine-Cord, strained with two Nails at each End, over his Window, and the Words *Rainy, Dry, Wet,* and so forth, written to denote the Weather according to the Rising or Falling of the Cord. We very great Scholars are not apt to wonder at this: But I observed a very honest Fellow, a chance Customer, who sat in the Chair before me to be shaved, fix his Eye upon this miraculous Performance during the Operation upon his Chin and Face. When those and his Head also were cleared of all Incumbrances and Excrescences, he looked at the Fish, then at the Fiddle, still grubling in his Pockets, and casting his Eye again at the Twine, and the Words writ on each Side; then altered his Mind as to Farthings, and gave my Friend a Silver Sixpence. The Business, as I said, is to keep up the Amazement; and if my Friend had had only the Skeleton and Kitt, he must have been contented with a less Payment. But the Doctor we were talking of, adds to his long Voyages the Testimony of some People *that has been thirty Years lame*. When I received my Paper, a sagacious Fellow took one at the same time, and read till he came to the thirty Years Confinement of his Friends, and went off very well convinced of the Doctor's Sufficiency. You have many of these prodigious Persons, who have had some extraordinary Accident at their Birth, or a great Disaster in some part of their Lives. Any thing, however foreign from the Business the People want of you, will convince them of your Ability in that you profess. There is a Doctor in *Mouse Alley* near *Wapping*, who sets up for curing Cataracts upon the Credit of having, as his Bill sets forth, lost an Eye in the Emperor's Service. His Patients come in upon this, and he shews the Muster-Roll, which confirms that he was in his Imperial Majesty's Troops; and he puts out their Eyes with great Success. Who would believe that a Man should be a Doctor for the Cure of bursten Children, by declaring that his Father and Grandfather were born bursten? But *Charles Ingoltson*, next Door to the *Harp* in *Barbican*, has made a pretty Penny by that Asseveration. The Generality go upon their first Conception, and think no further; all the rest is granted. They take it, that there is something uncommon in you, and give you Credit for the rest. You may be sure it is upon that I go, when sometimes, let it be to the Purpose or not, I keep a *Latin* Sentence in my Front; and I was not a little pleased when I observ'd one of my Readers say, casting his Eye on my twentieth Paper, *More* Latin *still? What a prodigious Scholar is this Man!* But as I have here taken much Liberty with this learned Doctor, I must make up all I have said by repeating what he seems to be in Earnest in, and honestly promise to those who will not receive him as a great Man; to wit, *That from Eight to Twelve, and from Two till Six, he attends for the good of the Publick to bleed for Three Pence.* T

No. 445.
[ADDISON.]   Thursday, July 31.

Tanti non es ais. Sapis, Luperce.—Mart.

THIS is the Day on which many eminent Authors will probably
publish their Last Words.   I am afraid that few of our Weekly
Historians, who are Men that above all others delight in War,
will be able to subsist under the Weight of a Stamp, and an
approaching Peace.   A sheet of Blank Paper that must have
this new Imprimatur clapt upon it, before it is qualified to
Communicate any thing to the Publick, will make its way in
the World but very heavily.   In short, the Necessity of carrying a Stamp, and the Improbability of notifying a Bloody
Battel, will, I am afraid, both concur to the sinking of those
thin Folios, which have every other Day retailed to us the
History of *Europe* for several Years last past.   A Facetious
Friend of mine, who loves a Punn, calls this present Mortality
among Authors, *The Fall of the Leaf.*

I remember, upon Mr. *Baxter's* Death, there was published
a Sheet of very good Sayings, inscribed, *The Last Words of
Mr.* Baxter.   The Title sold so great a Number of these
Papers, that about a Week after, there came out a second
Sheet, inscribed, *More last Words of Mr.* Baxter.   In the same
Manner, I have reason to think, that several Ingenious Writers,
who have taken their Leave of the Publick, in farewel Papers,
will not give over so, but intend to appear again, tho' perhaps
under another Form, and with a different Title.   Be that as it
will, it is my Business, in this place, to give an Account of my
own Intentions, and to acquaint my Reader with the Motives
by which I Act, in this great Crisis of the Republick of Letters.

I have been long debating in my own Heart, whether I
should throw up my Pen, as an Author that is cashiered by the
Act of Parliament, which is to Operate within these Four and
Twenty Hours, or whether I should still persist in laying
my Speculations, from Day to Day, before the Publick.   The
Argument which prevails with me most on the first side of the
Question is, that I am informed by my Bookseller he must
raise the Price of every single Paper to Two-pence, or that he
shall not be able to pay the Duty of it.   Now as I am very
desirous my Readers should have their Learning as cheap as
possible, it is with great Difficulty that I comply with him in
this Particular.

However, upon laying my Reasons together in the Balance,
I find that those which plead for the Continuance of this Work,
have much the greater Weight.   For, in the first Place, in
Recompence for the Expence to which this will put my

Readers, it is to be hoped they may receive from every Paper so much Instruction, as will be a very good Equivalent. And in order to this, I would not advise any one to take it in, who, after the Perusal of it, does not find himself Twopence the wiser, or the better Man for it; or who, upon Examination, does not believe that he has had Two penny-worth of Mirth or Instruction for his Mony.

But I must confess there is another Motive which prevails with me more than the former. I consider that the Tax on Paper was given for the Support of the Government; and as I have Enemies, who are apt to pervert every thing I do or say, I fear they would ascribe the laying down my Paper, on such an occasion, to a Spirit of Malcontentedness, which I am resolved none shall ever justly upbraid me with. No, I shall glory in contributing my utmost to the Weal Publick; and if my Country receives Five or Six Pounds a-day by my Labours, I shall be very well pleased to find my self so useful a Member. It is a received Maxim, that no honest Man should enrich himself by Methods that are prejudicial to the Community in which he lives, and by the same Rule I think we may pronounce the Person to deserve very well of his Countrymen, whose Labours bring more into the Publick Coffers, than into his own Pocket.

Since I have mentioned the Word Enemies, I must explain my self so far as to acquaint my Reader, that I mean only the insignificant Party Zealots on both sides; Men of such poor narrow Souls, that they are not capable of thinking on any thing but with an Eye to Whig or Tory. During the Course of this Paper, I have been accused by these despicable Wretches of Trimming, Time-serving, Personal Reflection, secret Satire, and the like. Now, tho' in these my Compositions, it is visible to any Reader of Common Sense, that I consider nothing but my Subject, which is always of an Indifferent Nature; how is it possible for me to write so clear of Party, as not to lie open to the Censures of those who will be applying every Sentence, and finding out Persons and Things in it which it has no regard to?

Several Paltry Scribblers and Declaimers have done me the Honour to be dull upon me in Reflections of this Nature; but notwithstanding my Name has been sometimes traduced by this contemptible Tribe of Men, I have hitherto avoided all Animadversions upon 'em. The truth of it is, I am afraid of making them appear considerable by taking notice of them, for they are like those Imperceptible Insects which are discovered by the Microscope, and cannot be made the Subject of Observation without being magnified.

Having mentioned those few who have shewn themselves the Enemies of this Paper, I should be very ungrateful to the Publick, did not I at the same time testifie my Gratitude to those who are its Friends, in which number I may reckon many of the most distinguished Persons of all Conditions, Parties and Professions in the Isle of *Great Britain*. I am not so vain as to think this Approbation is so much due to the Performance as to the Design. There is, and ever will be, Justice enough in the World, to afford Patronage and Protection for those who endeavour to advance Truth and Virtue, without regard to the Passions and Prejudices of any particular Cause or Faction. If I have any other Merit in me, it is that I have new-pointed all the Batteries of Ridicule. They have been generally planted against Persons who have appeared Serious rather than Absurd; or at best, have aimed rather at what is Unfashionable than what is Vicious. For my own part, I have endeavoured to make nothing Ridiculous that is not in some measure Criminal. I have set up the immoral Man as the Object of Derision: In short, if I have not formed a new Weapon against Vice and Irreligion, I have at least shewn how that Weapon may be put to a right use, which has so often fought the Battels of Impiety and Profaneness.   C

No. 446.
[ADDISON.]   Friday, August, 1.

Quid deceat, quid non: quo virtus, quo ferat error.—Hor.

SINCE two or three Writers of Comedy who are now living have taken their Farewell of the Stage, those who succeed them finding themselves incapable of rising up to their Wit, Humour and good Sense, have only imitated them in some of those loose unguarded Strokes, in which they complied with the corrupt Taste of the more Vicious Part of their Audience. When Persons of a low Genius attempt this kind of Writing, they know no Difference between being Merry and being Lewd. It is with an Eye to some of these degenerate Compositions that I have written the following Discourse.

Were our *English* Stage but half so virtuous as that of the *Greeks* or *Romans*, we should quickly see the Influence of it in the Behaviour of all the Politer Part of Mankind. It would not be fashionable to ridicule Religion, or its Professors; the Man of Pleasure would not be the compleat Gentleman; Vanity would be out of Countenance, and every Quality which is Ornamental to Human Nature, would meet with that Esteem which is due to it.

If the *English* Stage were under the same Regulations the *Athenian* was formerly, it would have the same Effect that had, in recommending the Religion, the Government, and Publick Worship of its Country. Were our Plays subject to proper Inspections and Limitations, we might not only pass away several of our vacant Hours in the highest Entertainment; but should always rise from them wiser and better than we sat down to them.

It is one of the most unaccountable Things in our Age, that the Lewdness of our Theatre should be so much complained of, so well exposed, and so little redressed. It is to be hoped, that some time or other we may be at leisure to restrain the Licentiousness of the Theatre, and make it contribute its Assistance to the Advancement of Morality, and to the Reformation of the Age. As Matters stand at present, Multitudes are shut out from this noble Diversion, by reason of those Abuses and Corruptions that accompany it. A Father is often afraid that his Daughter should be ruined by those Entertainments, which were invented for the Accomplishment and Refining of Human Nature. The *Athenian* and *Roman* Plays were written with such a regard to Morality, that *Socrates* used to frequent the one, and *Cicero* the other.

It happened once indeed, that *Cato* dropped into the *Roman* Theatre, when the *Floralia* were to be represented; and as in that Performance, which was a kind of Religious Ceremony, there were several indecent Parts to be acted, the People refus'd to see them whilst *Cato* was present. *Martial* on this Hint made the following Epigram, which we must suppose was applied to some grave Friend of his, that had been accidentally present at some such Entertainment.

> *Nosses jocosae dulce cum sacrum Florae,*
> *Festosque lusus, & licentiam vulgi,*
> *Cur in theatrum, Cato severe, venisti?*
> *An ideo tantum veneras, ut exires?*

> *Why dost thou come, great Censor of thy Age,*
> *To see the loose Diversions of the Stage?*
> *With awful Countenance and Brow severe,*
> *What in the Name of Goodness dost thou here?*
> *See the mixt Crowd! how Giddy, Lewd and Vain!*
> *Didst thou come in but to go out again?*

An Accident of this Nature might happen once in an Age among the *Greeks* or *Romans*; but they were too wise and good to let the constant Nightly Entertainment be of such a Nature, that People of the most Sense and Virtue could not be at it. Whatever Vices are represented upon the Stage, they ought to be so marked and branded by the Poet, as not to appear either laudable or amiable in the Person who is tainted with them. But if we look into the *English* Comedies above-mentioned, we would think they were formed upon a quite contrary Maxim, and that this Rule, tho' it held good upon the Heathen Stage, was not to be regarded in Christian Theatres. There is another Rule likewise, which was observed by Authors of Antiquity, and which these modern Geniuses have no regard to, and that was never to chuse an improper Subject for Ridicule. Now a Subject is improper for Ridicule, if it is apt to stir up Horrour and Commiseration rather than Laughter. For this Reason, we do not find any Comedy in so polite an Author as *Terence*, raised upon the Violations of the Marriage-Bed. The Falshood of the Wife or Husband has given Occasion to Noble Tragedies, but a *Scipio* or *Lelius* would not have looked upon Incest or Murder to have been as proper Subjects for Comedy. On the contrary, Cuckoldom is the Basis of most of our Modern Plays. If an Alderman appears upon the Stage, you may be sure it is in order to be Cuckolded. An Husband that is a little grave or elderly, generally meets with the same Fate. Knights and Baronets, Country Squires, and Justices of the *Quorum*, come up to Town for no other Purpose. I have seen poor *Dogget* Cuckolded in all these Capacities. In short, our *English* Writers are as frequently severe upon this Innocent unhappy Creature, commonly known by the Name of a Cuckold, as the Ancient Comick Writers were upon an eating Parasite, or a vain-glorious Soldier.

At the same time the Poet so contrives Matters that the two Criminals are the Favourites of the Audience. We sit still, and wish well to them through the whole Play, are pleased when they meet with proper Opportunities, and out of humour when they are disappointed. The Truth of it is, the accomplished Gentleman upon the *English* Stage, is the Person that is familiar with other Men's Wives, and indifferent to his own; as the Fine Woman is generally a Composition of Sprightliness and Falshood. I do not know whether it proceeds from Barrenness of Invention, Depravation of Manners, or Ignorance of Mankind; but I have often wondered that our ordinary Poets cannot frame to themselves the Idea of a fine Man who is not a Whore-master, or of a Fine Woman that is not a Jilt.

I have sometimes thought of compiling a system of Ethics out of the Writings of these corrupt Poets, under the title of *Stage Morality*. But I have been diverted from this Thought, by a Project which has been executed by an Ingenious Gentleman of my Acquaintance. He has composed, it seems, the

History of a young Fellow, who has taken all his Notions of the World from the Stage, and who has directed himself, in every Circumstance of his Life, and Conversation, by the Maxims and Examples of the Fine Gentleman in *English* Comedies. If I can prevail upon him to give me a Copy of this new-fashioned Novel, I will bestow on it a Place in my Works, and question not but it may have as good an Effect upon the Drama, as *Don Quixote* had upon Romance.   C

No. 447.

[ADDISON.]   Saturday, August 2.

Φημὶ πολυχρονίην μελέτην ἔμεναι, φίλε · καὶ δὴ
Ταύτην ἀνθρώποισι τελευτῶσαν φύσιν εἶναι.

THERE is not a Common-Saying which has a better turn of Sense in it, than what we often hear in the Mouths of the Vulgar, that Custom is a second Nature. It is indeed able to form the Man anew, and to give him Inclinations and Capacities altogether different from those he was born with. Dr. *Plot*, in his History of *Staffordshire*, tells of an Ideot that chancing to live within the Sound of a Clock, and always amusing himself with counting the Hour of the Day whenever the Clock struck, the Clock being spoiled by some Accident, the Ideot continued to strike and count the Hour without the help of it, in the same manner as he had done when it was entire. Though I dare not vouch for the Truth of this Story, it is very certain that Custom has a Mechanical Effect upon the Body, at the same time that it has a very extraordinary Influence upon the Mind.

I shall in this Paper consider one very remarkable Effect which Custom has upon Human Nature; and which, if rightly observed, may lead us into very useful Rules of Life. What I shall here take notice of in Custom, is its wonderful Efficacy in making every thing pleasant to us. A Person who is addicted to Play or Gaming, tho' he took but little delight in it at first, by degrees contracts so strong an Inclination towards it, and gives himself up so intirely to it, that it seems the only End of his Being. The Love of a retired or busie Life will grow upon a Man insensibly, as he is conversant in the one or the other, 'till he is utterly unqualified for relishing that to which he has been for some time disused. Nay, a Man may Smoak, or Drink, or take Snuff, 'till he is unable to pass away his Time, without it; not to mention how our Delight in any particular Study, Art, or Science, rises and improves in Proportion to the Application which we bestow upon it. Thus what was at first an Exercise, becomes at length an Entertainment. Our Employments are changed into our Diversions. The Mind grows fond of those actions she is accustomed to, and is drawn with Reluctancy from those Paths in which she has been used to walk.

Not only such Actions as were at first Indifferent to us, but even such as were Painful, will by Custom and Practice become pleasant. Sir *Francis Bacon* observes in his Natural Philosophy, that our Taste is never pleased better than with those things which at first created a Disgust in it. He gives particular Instances of Claret, Coffee, and other Liquours, which the Palate seldom approves upon the first Taste; but when it has once got a Relish of them, generally retains it for Life. The Mind is constituted after the same manner, and after having habituated herself to any particular Exercise or Employment, not only loses her first Aversion towards it, but conceives a certain Fondness and Affection for it. I have heard one of the greatest Geniuses this Age has produced, who had been trained up in all the Polite Studies of Antiquity, assure me, upon his being obliged to search into several Rolls and Records, that notwithstanding such an Employment was at first very dry and irksome to him, he at last took an incredible Pleasure in it, and preferred it even to the reading of *Virgil* or *Cicero*. The Reader will observe, that I have not here considered Custom as it makes things easie, but as it renders them delightful; and though others have often made the same Reflections, it is possible they may not have drawn those Uses from it, with which I intend to fill the remaining Part of this Paper.

If we consider attentively this Property of Human Nature, it may instruct us in very fine Moralities. In the first place, I would have no Man discouraged with that kind of Life or Series of Action, in which the Choice of others, or his own Necessities, may have engaged him. It may perhaps be very disagreeable to him at first; but Use and Application will certainly render it not only less painful, but pleasing and satisfactory.

In the second place I would recommend to every one that admirable Precept which *Pythagoras* is said to have given to his Disciples, and which that Philosopher must have drawn from the Observation I have enlarged upon. *Optimum vitae genus eligito, nam consuetudo faciet jucundissimum*, Pitch upon that Course of Life which is the most Excellent, and Custom will render it the most Delightful. Men, whose Circumstances will permit them to chuse their own way of Life, are inexcusable if they do not pursue that which their Judgment tells them is the most laudable. The Voice of Reason is more to be regarded

than the Bent of any present Inclination, since by the Rule
above-mentioned, Inclination will at length come over to
Reason, though we can never force Reason to comply with
Inclination.

In the third place, this Observation may teach the most
sensual and irreligious Man, to overlook those Hardships and
Difficulties which are apt to discourage him from the Prosecution of a Virtuous Life. *The Gods, said Hesiod, have placed
Labour before Virtue; the way to her is at first rough and difficult,
but grows more smooth and easie the further you advance in it.*
The Man who proceeds in it, with Steadiness and Resolution,
will in a little time find, that *her Ways are Ways of Pleasantness, and that all her Paths are Peace.*

To enforce this Consideration, we may further observe, that
the Practice of Religion will not only be attended with that
Pleasure, which naturally accompanies those Actions to which
we are habituated, but with those Supernumerary Joys of
Heart, that rise from the Consciousness of such a Pleasure,
from the Satisfaction of acting up to the Dictates of Reason,
and from the Prospect of an happy Immortality.

In the fourth place, we may learn from this Observation
which we have made on the Mind of Man, to take particular
Care, when we are once setled in a regular Course of Life, how
we too frequently indulge ourselves in any the most innocent
Diversions and Entertainments, since the Mind may insensibly
fall off from the Relish of virtuous Actions, and, by degrees,
exchange that Pleasure which it takes in the Performance of its
Duty, for Delights of a much more inferior and unprofitable
Nature.

The last Use which I shall make of this remarkable Property
in Human Nature, of being delighted with those Actions to
which it is accustomed, is to shew how absolutely necessary it
is for us to gain Habits of Virtue in this Life, if we would enjoy
the Pleasures of the next. The State of Bliss we call Heaven
will not be capable of affecting those Minds, which are not thus
qualified for it; we must, in this World, gain a Relish of Truth
and Virtue, if we would be able to taste that Knowledge and
Perfection, which are to make us happy in the next. The
Seeds of those Spiritual Joys and Raptures, which are to rise
up and flourish in the Soul to all Eternity, must be planted in
her, during this her present State of Probation. In short,
Heaven is not to be look'd upon only as the Reward, but as the
natural Effect of a religious Life.

On the other Hand, those evil Spirits, who, by long Custom,
have contracted in the Body Habits of Lust and Sensuality,
Malice and Revenge, an Aversion to every thing that is good,

just or laudable, are naturally seasoned and prepared for Pain and Misery. Their Torments have already taken root in them, they cannot be happy when divested of the Body, unless we may suppose, that Providence will, in a manner, create them anew, and work a Miracle in the Rectification of their Faculties. They may, indeed, taste a kind of malignant Pleasure in those Actions to which they are accustomed, whilst in this Life; but when they are removed from all those Objects which are here apt to gratifie them, they will naturally become their own Tormentors, and cherish in themselves those painful Habits of Mind which are called, in Scripture Phrase, the Worm which never dies. This Notion of Heaven and Hell is so very conformable to the Light of Nature, that it was discovered by several of the most exalted Heathens. It has been finely improved by many eminent Divines of the last Age, as in particular by Arch-Bishop *Tillotson* and Dr. *Sherlock*, but there is none who has raised such noble Speculations upon it, as Dr. *Scott*, in the first Book of his Christian Life, which is one of the finest and most rational Schemes of Divinity, that is written in our Tongue, or in any other. That Excellent Author has shewn how every particular Custom and Habit of Virtue, will in its own Nature, produce the Heaven, or a State of Happiness, in him who shall hereafter practise it: As on the contrary, how every Custom or Habit of Vice will be the natural Hell of him in whom it subsists.   C

No. 448.
[STEELE.]   Monday, August 4.

Foedius hoc aliquid quandoque audebis . . .—Juv.

THE first Steps towards Ill are very carefully to be avoided, for Men insensibly go on when they are once entered, and do not keep up a lively Abhorrence of the least Unworthiness. There is a certain frivolous Falshood that People indulge themselves in, which ought to be had in greater Detestation than it commonly meets with: What I mean is a Neglect of Promises made on small and indifferent Occasions, such as Parties of Pleasure, Entertainments, and sometimes Meetings out of Curiosity in Men of like Faculties to be in each other's Company. There are many Causes to which one may assign this light Infidelity. *Jack Sippet* never keeps the Hour he has appointed to come to a Friend's to Dinner; but he is an insignificant Fellow who does it out of Vanity. He could never,

he knows, make any Figure in Company, but by giving a little
Disturbance at his Entry, and therefore takes Care to drop in
when he thinks you are just seated.   He takes his Place after
having discomposed every Body, and desires there may be no
Ceremony; then does he begin to call himself the saddest
Fellow in disappointing so many Places as he was invited to
elsewhere.   It is the Fop's Vanity to name Houses of better
Chear, and to acquaint you that he chose yours out of ten
Dinners which he was obliged to be at that Day.   The last
time I had the Fortune to eat with him, he was imagining how
very fat he should have been had he eaten all he had ever been
invited to.   But it is impertinent to dwell upon the Manners
of such a Wretch as obliges all whom he disappoints, tho' his
Circumstances constrain them to be civil to him.   But there
are those that every one would be glad to see, who fall into the
same detestable Habit.   It is a merciless thing that any one
can be at Ease, and suppose a Set of People who have a Kindness for him, at that Moment waiting out of Respect to him,
and refusing to taste their Food or Conversation with the
utmost Impatience.   One of these Promisers sometimes shall
make his Excuses for not coming at all, so late that half
the Company have only to lament, that they have neglected
Matters of Moment to meet him whom they find a Trifler.
They immediately repent for the Value they had for him; and
such Treatment repeated, makes Company never depend upon
his Promise any more; so that he often comes at the Middle of
a Meal, where he is secretly slighted by the Persons with
whom he eats, and cursed by the Servants, whose Dinner is
delayed by his prolonging their Master's Entertainment.   It
is wonderful, that Men guilty this Way, could never have
observed, that the whiling Time, and gathering together, and
waiting a little before Dinner, is the most awkwardly passed
away of any Part in the four and twenty Hours.   If they did
think at all, they would reflect upon their Guilt, in lengthening
such a Suspension of agreeable Life.   The constant offending
this Way, has, in a Degree, an Effect upon the Honesty of his
Mind who is guilty of it, as common Swearing is a kind of
habitual Perjury: It makes the Soul unattentive to what an
Oath is, even while it utters it at the Lips.   *Phocion* beholding
a wordy Orator while he was making a magnificent Speech to
the People full of vain Promises, *Methinks,* said he, *I am now
fixing my Eyes upon a Cypress Tree; it has all the Pomp and
Beauty imaginable in its Branches, Leaves, and Height, but
alas it bears no Fruit.*

Though the Expectation which is raised by impertinent
Promises is thus barren, their Confidence, even after Failures,

is so great, that they subsist by still promising on. I have heretofore discoursed of the insignificant Liar, the Boaster, and the Castle-builder, and treated them as no ill-designing Men (tho' they are to be placed among the frivolously false ones), but Persons who fall into that Way purely to recommend themselves by their Vivacities; but indeed I cannot let heedless Promisers, tho' in the most minute Circumstances, pass with so slight a Censure. If a Man should take a Resolution to pay only Sums above an hundred Pounds, and yet contract with different People Debts of five and ten, how long can we suppose he will keep his Credit? This Man will as long support his good Name in Business, as he will in Conversation, who without Difficulty makes Assignations which he is indifferent whether he keeps or not.

I am the more severe upon this Vice, because I have been so unfortunate as to be a very great Criminal my self. Sir ANDREW FREEPORT, and all my other Friends who are scrupulous to Promises of the meanest Consideration imaginable from an Habit of Virtue that way, have often upbraided me with it. I take Shame upon myself for this Crime, and more particularly for the greatest I ever committed of the Sort, that when as agreeable a Company of Gentlemen and Ladies as ever were got together, and I forsooth Mr. SPECTATOR, to be of the Party with Women of Merit, like a Booby as I was, mistook the Time of Meeting, and came the Night following. I wish every Fool who is negligent in this Kind, may have as great a Loss as I had in this; for the same Company will never meet more, but are dispersed into various Parts of the World, and I am left under the Compunction that I deserve, in so many different Places to be called a Trifler.

This fault is sometimes to be accounted for, when desirable People are fearful of appearing precious and reserved by Denials; but they will find the Apprehension of that Imputation will betray them into a childish Impotence of Mind, and make them promise all who are so kind to ask it of them. This leads such soft Creatures into the Misfortune of seeming to return Overtures of Good-will with Ingratitude. The first Steps in the Breach of a Man's Integrity are much more important than Men are aware of. The Man who scruples breaking his Word in little Things would not suffer in his own Conscience so great Pain for Failures of Consequence, as he who thinks every little Offence against Truth and Justice a Disparagement. We should not make any thing we our selves disapprove habitual to us, if we would be sure of our Integrity.

I remember a Falshood of the trivial Sort, tho' not in relation to Assignations, that exposed a Man to a very uneasie Adventure. *Will Trap* and *Jack Stint* were Chamber-fellows in the *Inner-Temple* about 25 Years ago. They one Night sat in the Pit together at a Comedy, where they both observed and liked the same young Woman in the Boxes. Their Kindness for her entered both Hearts deeper than they imagined. *Stint* had a good Faculty in writing Letters of Love, and made his Address privately that Way; while *Trap* proceeded in the ordinary Course, by Mony and her Waiting-Maid. The Lady gave them both Encouragement, receiving *Trap* into the utmost Favour, and answering at the same time *Stint's* Letters, and giving him Appointments at third Places. *Trap* began to suspect the Epistolary Correspondence of his Friend, and discovered also that *Stint* opened all his Letters which came to their common Lodgings, in order to form his own Assignations. After much Anxiety and Restlessness, *Trap* came to a Resolution, which he thought would break off their Commerce with one another without any hazardous Explanation. He therefore writ a Letter in a feign'd Hand to Mr. *Trap* at his Chambers in the *Temple*. *Stint*, according to Custom, seized and opened it, and was not a little surpriz'd to find the Inside directed to himself, when, with great Perturbation of Spirit, he read as follows.

'Mr. *Stint*,

You have gained a slight Satisfaction at the Expence of doing a very heinous Crime. At the Price of a faithful Friend you have obtained an inconstant Mistress. I rejoice in this Expedient I have thought of to break my Mind to you, and tell you, You are a base Fellow, by a Means which does not expose you to the Affront except you deserve it. I know, Sir, as criminal as you are, you have still Shame enough to avenge yourself against the Hardiness of any one that should publickly tell you of it. I therefore, who have received so many secret Hurts from you, shall take Satisfaction with Safety to my self. I call you Base, and you must bear it, or acknowledge it; I triumph over you that you cannot come at me; nor do I think it dishonourable to come in Armour to assault him, who was in Ambuscade when he wounded me.

What need more be said to convince you of being guilty of the basest Practice imaginable, than that it is such as has made you liable to be treated after this Manner, while you your self cannot in your own Conscience but allow the Justice of the Upbraidings of

Your Injur'd Friend,

Ralph Trap.'

T

No. 449.

[STEELE.]   Tuesday, August 5.

> . . . *Tibi scriptus, matrona, libellus.*—Mart.

WHEN I reflect upon my Labours for the Publick, I cannot but observe, that Part of the Species, of which I profess my self a Friend and Guardian, is sometimes treated with Severity; that is, there are in my Writings many Descriptions given of ill Persons, and not any direct Encomium made of those who are good. When I was convinced of this Error, I could not but immediately call to Mind several of the Fair Sex of my Acquaintance, whose Characters deserve to be transmitted to Posterity in Writings which will long outlive mine. But I do not think that a Reason why I should not give them their Place in my Diurnal as long as it will last. For the Service therefore of my Female Readers, I shall single out some Characters of Maids, Wives, and Widows, which deserve the Imitation of the Sex. She who shall lead this small illustrious Number of Heroines shall be the amiable *Fidelia*.

Before I enter upon the particular Parts of her Character, it is necessary to Preface, that she is the only Child of a decrepid Father, whose Life is bound up in hers. This Gentleman has used *Fidelia* from her Cradle with all the Tenderness imaginable, and has view'd her growing Perfections with the Partiality of a Parent, that soon thought her accomplished above the Children of all other Men, but never thought she was come to the utmost Improvement of which she her self was capable. This Fondness has had very happy Effects upon his own Happiness, for she reads, she dances, she sings, uses her Spinet and Lute to the utmost Perfection: And the Lady's Use of all these Excellencies, is to divert the old Man in his easie Chair, when he is out of the Pangs of a Chronical Distemper. *Fidelia* is now in the twenty third Year of her Age; but the Application of many Lovers, her vigorous Time of Life, her quick Sense of all that is truly gallant and elegant in the Enjoyment of a plentiful Fortune, are not able to draw her from the Side of her good old Father. Certain it is, that there is no Kind of Affection so pure and angelick as that of a Father to a Daughter. He beholds her both with, and without Regard to her Sex. In Love to our Wives there is Desire, to our Sons there is Ambition; but in that to our Daughters, there is something which there are no Words to express. Her Life is designed wholly domestick, and she is so ready a Friend and Companion, that every thing that passes about a Man, is accompanied with the Idea of her Presence. Her Sex also is

naturally so much exposed to Hazard both as to Fortune and
Innocence, that there is, perhaps, a new Cause of Fondness
arising from that Consideration also. None but Fathers can
have a true Sense of these Sort of Pleasures and Sensations;
but my Familiarity with the Father of *Fidelia*, makes me let
drop the Words which I have heard him speak, and observe
upon his Tenderness towards her.

Fidelia on her Part, as I was going to say, as accomplished
as she is, with all her Beauty, Wit, Air, and Mien, employs
her whole Time in Care and Attendance upon her Father.
How have I been charmed to see one of the most beauteous
Women the Age has produced on her Knees helping on an old
Man's Slipper. Her filial Regard to him is what she makes her
Diversion, her Business, and her Glory. When she was asked
by a Friend of her deceased Mother to admit of the Courtship
of her Son, she answer'd, That she had a great Respect and
Gratitude to her for the Overture in Behalf of one so near to
her, but that during her Father's Life she would admit into
her heart no Value for any thing that should interfere with
her Endeavour to make his Remains of Life as happy and
easie as could be expected in his Circumstances. The Lady
admonished her of the Prime of Life with a Smile; which
Fidelia answered with a Frankness that always attends unfeigned Virtue. *It is true, Madam, there is to be sure very great
Satisfactions to be expected in the Commerce of a Man of Honour,
whom one tenderly loves; but I find so much Satisfaction in the
Reflection, how much I mitigate a good Man's Pains, whose
Welfare depends upon my Assiduity about him, that I willingly
exclude the loose Gratifications of Passion for the solid Reflections
of Duty. I know not whether any Man's Wife would be allowed,
and (what I still more fear) I know not whether I, a Wife, should
be willing to be as officious as I am at present about my Parent.*
The happy Father has her Declaration that she will not marry
during his Life, and the Pleasure of seeing that Resolution
not uneasie to her. Were one to paint filial Affection in its
utmost Beauty, he could not have a more lively Idea of it than
in beholding *Fidelia* serving her Father at his Hours of Rising,
Meals, and Rest.

When the general Crowd of Female Youth are consulting
their Glasses, preparing for Balls, Assemblies, or Plays; for a
young Lady, who could be regarded among the foremost in
those Places, either for her Person, Wit, Fortune, or Conversation, and yet contemn all these Entertainments, to sweeten
the heavy Hours of a decrepid Parent, is a Resignation truly
heroic. *Fidelia* performs the Duty of a Nurse with all the
Beauty of a Bride; nor does she neglect her Person, because

of her Attendance on him, when he is too ill to receive Company, to whom she may make an Appearance.

Fidelia, who gives him up her Youth, does not think it any great Sacrifice to add to it the Spoiling of her Dress. Her Care and Exactness in her Habit, convince her Father of the Alacrity of her Mind; and she has of all Women the best Foundation for affecting the Praise of a seeming Negligence. What adds to the Entertainment of the good old Man is, that *Fidelia*, where Merit and Fortune cannot be overlook'd by Epistolary Lovers, reads over the Accounts of her Conquests, plays on her Spinet the gayest Airs, (and while she is doing so, you would think her formed only for Gallantry) to intimate to him the Pleasures she despises for his Sake.

Those who think themselves the Pattern of good Breeding and Gallantry, would be astonished to hear that in those Intervals when the old Gentleman is at Ease, and can bear Company, there are at his House, in the most regular Order, Assemblies of People of the highest Merit; where there is Conversation without Mention of the Faults of the Absent, Benevolence between Men and Women without Passion, and the highest Subjects of Morality treated of as natural and accidental Discourse; All which is owing to the Genius of *Fidelia*, who at once makes her Father's Way to another World easie, and her self capable of being an Honour to his Name in this.

'*Mr.* SPECTATOR,

I was the other Day at the *Bear-Garden*, in hopes to have seen your short Face; but not being so fortunate, I must tell you by way of Letter, That there is a Mystery among the Gladiators which has escaped your Spectatorial Penetration. For being in a Box at an Ale-house near that renowned Seat of Honour abovementioned, I overheard two Masters of the Science agreeing to quarrel on the next Opportunity. This was to happen in the Company of a Set of the Fraternity of Basket-Hilts, who were to meet that Evening. When this was settled, one asked the other, Will you give Cuts or receive? the other answered, Receive. It was replied, Are you a passionate Man? No, provided you cut no more nor no deeper than we agree. I thought it my Duty to acquaint you with this, that the People may not pay their Mony for Fighting, and be Cheated.

Your humble Servant,

T   Scabbard Rusty.'

No. 450.
[STEELE.]   Wednesday, August 6.

> . . . *Quaerenda pecunia primum est,*
> *Virtus post nummos.*

'*Mr.* SPECTATOR,

ALL Men, through different Paths, make at the same common thing, *Mony*; and it is to her we owe the Politician, the Merchant, and the Lawyer; nay, to be free with you, I believe to that also we are beholden for our *Spectator*. I am apt to think, that could we look into our own Hearts, we should see Mony ingraved in them in more lively and moving Characters than Self-Preservation; for who can reflect upon the Merchant hoisting Sail in a doubtful Pursuit of her, and all Mankind sacrificing their Quiet to her, but must perceive that the Characters of Self-Preservation (which were doubtless originally the brightest) are sullied, if not wholly defaced; and that those of Mony (which at first was only valuable as a Mean to Security) are of late so brightened, that the Characters of Self-Preservation, like a less Light set by a greater, are become almost imperceptible? Thus has Mony got the Upper Hand of what all Mankind formerly thought most dear, *viz.* Security; and I wish I could say she had here put a Stop to her Victories; but, alas! common Honesty fell a Sacrifice to her. This is the Way Scholastick Men talk of the greatest Good in the World; but I, a Tradesman, shall give you another Account of this Matter in the plain Narrative of my own Life. I think it proper, in the first Place, to acquaint my Readers, that since my setting out in the World, which was in the Year 1660, I never wanted Mony; having begun with an indifferent good Stock in the Tobacco-Trade, to which I was bred; and by the continual Successes, it has pleased Providence to bless my Endeavours with, am at last arrived at what they call a *Plumb*. To uphold my Discourse in the Manner of your Wits or Philosophers, by speaking fine Things, or drawing Inferences, as they pretend, from the Nature of the Subject, I account it vain; having never found any thing in the Writings of such Men, that did not favour more of the Invention of the Brain, or what is stiled Speculation, than of sound Judgment, or profitable Observation. I will readily grant indeed, that there is what the Wits call Natural in their Talk; which is the utmost those curious Authors can assume to themselves, and is indeed all they endeavour at, for they are but lamentable Teachers. And, what, I pray, is Natural? That which is Pleasing and Easie: And what are pleasing and Easie? Forsooth, a new Thought or Conceit dressed up in smooth quaint Language, to make you smile and wag your Head, as being what you never imagined before, and yet wonder why you had not; meer frothy Amusements! fit only for Boys or silly Women to be caught with.

It is not my present Intention to instruct my Readers in the Methods of acquiring Riches; that may be the Work of another Essay; but to exhibit the real and solid Advantages I have found by them in my long and manifold Experience; nor yet all the Advantages of so worthy and valuable a Blessing, (for who does not know or imagine the Comforts of being warm or living at Ease? and that Power and Preheminence are their inseparable Attendants?) but only to instance the great Supports they afford us under the severest Calamities and Misfortunes; to shew that the Love of them is a special Antidote against Immorality and Vice, and that the same does likewise naturally dispose Men to Actions of Piety and Devotion: All which I can make out by my own Experience, who think my self no ways particular from the rest of Mankind, nor better nor worse by Nature than generally other Men are.

In the Year 1665, when the Sickness was, I lost by it my Wife and two Children, which were all my Stock. Probably I might have had more, considering I was married between 4 and 5 Years; but finding her to be a teeming Woman, I was careful, as having then little above a Brace of thousand Pounds to carry on my Trade and maintain a Family with. I loved them as usually Men do their Wives and Children, and therefore could not resist the first Impulses of Nature on so wounding a Loss; but I quickly rouzed my self, and found Means to alleviate, and at last conquer my Affliction, by reflecting how that she and her Children having been no great Expence to me, the best Part of her Fortune was still left; that my Charge being reduced to my self, a Journeyman, and a Maid, I might live far cheaper than before; and that being now a childless Widower, I might perhaps marry a no less deserving Woman, and with a much better Fortune than she brought, which was but 800*l.* And to convince my Readers that such Considerations as these were proper and apt to produce such an Effect, I remember it was the constant Observation at that deplorable Time, when so many Hundreds were swept away daily, that the Rich ever bore the Loss of their Families and Relations far better than the Poor; the latter having little or nothing before-hand, and living from Hand to Mouth, placed the whole Comfort and Satisfaction of their Lives in their Wives and Children, and were therefore inconsolable.

The following Year happened the Fire; at which Time, by good Providence, it was my Fortune to have converted the greatest Part of my Effects into ready Mony, on the Prospect of an extraordinary Advantage which I was preparing to lay Hold on. This Calamity was very terrible and astonishing, the Fury of the Flames being such, that whole Streets, at several distant Places, were destroyed at one and the same Time, so that (as it is well known) almost all our Citizens were burnt out of what they had. But what did I then do? I did not stand gazing on the Ruins of our noble Metropolis; I did not shake my Head, wring my Hands, sigh and shed Tears; I considered with myself what could this avail; I fell a plodding what Advantages might be made of the ready Cash I had, and immediately bethought myself that wonderful Penny-worths might be bought of the Goods that were saved out of the Fire. In short, with about 2000*l.* and a little Credit, I bought as much Tobacco as raised my Estate to the value of 10000*l.* I then *looked on the Ashes of our City, and the Misery of its late In- habitants, as an Effect of the just Wrath and Indignation of Heaven towards a sinful and perverse People.*

After this I married again, and that Wife dying, I took another; but both proved to be idle Baggages, the first gave me a great deal of Plague and Vexation by her Extravagancies, and I became one of the Bywords of the City. I knew it would be to no manner of Purpose to go about to curb the Fancies and Inclinations of Women, which fly out the more for being restrained; but what I could I did. I watched her narrowly, and by good Luck found her in the Embraces (for which I had two Witnesses with me) of a wealthy Spark of the Court-end of the Town; of whom I recovered 15000 Pounds, which made me Amends for what she had idly squandered, and put a Silence to all my Neighbours, taking off my Reproach by the Gain they saw I had by it. The last died about two Years after I married her, in Labour of three Children. I conjecture they were begotten by a Country Kinsman of hers, whom, at her Recommendation, I took into my Family, and gave Wages to as a Journeyman. What this Creature expended in De- licacies and high Diet with her Kinsman (as well as I could compute by the Poulterer's, Fishmonger's, and Grocer's Bills) amounted in the said two Years to one hundred eighty six Pounds, four shillings, and five Pence Half-penny. The fine Apparel, Bracelets, Lockets and Treats, etc. of the other, according to the best Calculation, came in three Years and about three Quarters to seven hundred forty four Pounds, seven Shillings and nine Pence. After this I resolved never to marry more, and found I had been a Gainer by my Marriages, and the Damages granted me for the Abuses of my Bed, (all Charges deducted) eight thousand three hundred Pounds within a Trifle.

I come now to show the good Effects of the Love of Mony

on the Lives of Men towards rendring them honest, sober, and religious. When I was a young Man, I had a Mind to make the best of my Wits, and over-reached a Country Chap in a Parcel of unsound Goods; to whom, upon his upbraiding, and threatning to expose me for it, I returned the Equivalent of his Loss; and upon his good Advice, wherein he clearly demonstrated the Folly of such Artifices, which can never end but in Shame, and the Ruin of all Correspondence, I never after transgressed. Can your Courtiers, who take Bribes, or your Lawyers or Physicians in their Practice, or even the Divines who intermeddle in worldly Affairs, boast of making but one Slip in their Lives, and of such a thorough and lasting Reformation? Since my coming into the World I do not remember I was ever overtaken in Drink, save nine times, one at the Christening of my first Child, thrice at our City Feasts, and five times at driving of Bargains. My Reformation I can attribute to nothing so much as the Love and Esteem of Mony, for I found my self to be extravagant in my Drink, and apt to turn Projector and make Rash Bargains. As for Women, I never knew any, except my Wives: For my Reader must know, and it is what he may confide in as an excellent Recipe, That the Love of Business and Mony is the greatest Mortifier of inordinate Desires Imaginable, as employing the Mind continually in the careful Oversight of what one has, in the eager Quest after more, in looking after the Negligences and Deceits of Servants, in the due Entring and Stating of Accounts, in hunting after Chaps, and in the exact Knowledge of the State of Markets; which Things whoever thoroughly attends, will find enough and enough to employ his Thoughts on every Moment of the Day: So that I cannot call to Mind, that in all the Time I was a Husband, which off and on, was about twelve Years, I ever once thought of my Wives but in Bed. And, lastly, for Religion, I have ever been a constant Churchman, both Forenoons and Afternoons on *Sundays*, never forgetting to be thankful for any Gain or Advantage I had had that Day; and on *Saturday* Nights, upon casting up my Accounts, I always was grateful for the Sum of my Week's Profits, and at *Christmas* for that of the whole Year. It is true, perhaps, that my Devotion has not been the most fervent; which, I think, ought to be imputed to the Evenness and Sedateness of my Temper, which never would admit of any Impetuosities of any Sort: And I can remember that in my Youth and Prime of Manhood, when my Blood ran brisker, I took greater Pleasure in Religious Exercises than at present, or many Years past, and that my Devotion sensibly declined as Age, which is dull and unwieldy, came upon me.

I have, I hope, here proved, that the Love of Mony prevents all Immorality and Vice; which if you will not allow, you must, that the Pursuit of it obliges Men to the same Kind of Life as they would follow if they were really virtuous: Which is all I have to say at present, only recommending to you, that you would think of it, and turn ready Wit into ready Mony as fast as you can. I conclude,

Your Servant,

T   Ephraim Weed.'

No. 451.
[ADDISON.]   Thursday, August 7.

> . . . *Jam saevus apertam*
> *In rabiem coepit verti jocus, & per honestas*
> *Ire domos impune minax.* . . .

THERE is nothing so scandalous to a Government, and detestable in the Eyes of all good Men, as Defamatory Papers and Pamphlets; but at the same time there is nothing so difficult to tame, as a Satyrical Author. An angry Writer, who cannot appear in Print, naturally vents his Spleen in Libels and Lampoons. A gay old Woman, says the Fable, seeing all her Wrinkles represented in a large Looking-glass, threw it upon the Ground in a Passion, and broke it into a thousand Pieces; but as she was afterwards surveying the Fragments with a spiteful kind of Pleasure, she could not forbear uttering her self in the following Soliloquy. What have I got by this revengeful Blow of mine, I have only multiplied my Deformity, and see an hundred ugly Faces, where before I saw but one.

It has been proposed, *to oblige every Person that writes a Book, or a Paper, to swear himself the Author of it, and enter down in a Publick Register his Name and Place of Abode.*

This, indeed, would have effectually suppressed all printed Scandal, which generally appears under borrowed Names, or under none at all. But it is to be feared, that such an Expedient would not only destroy Scandal, but Learning. It would operate promiscuously, and root up the Corn and Tares together. Not to mention some of the most celebrated Works of Piety, which have proceeded from Anonymous Authors, who have made it their Merit to convey to us so great a Charity in secret: There are few Works of Genius that come out at first with the Author's Name. The Writer generally makes a Tryal of them in the World before he owns them; and, I believe, very few, who are capable of Writing, would set Pen to Paper, if they knew, before-hand, that they must not publish their

Productions but on such Conditions. For my own part, I must declare the Papers I present the Publick are like Fairy Favours, which shall last no longer than while the Author is concealed.

That which makes it particularly difficult to restrain these Sons of Calumny and Defamation is, that all Sides are equally guilty of it, and that every dirty Scribbler is countenanced by great Names, whose Interests he propagates by such vile and infamous Methods. I have never yet heard of a Ministry, who have inflicted an exemplary Punishment on an Author that has supported their Cause with Falshood and Scandal, and treated in a most cruel manner, the Names of those who have been looked upon as their Rivals and Antagonists. Would a Government set an everlasting Mark of their Displeasure upon one of those infamous Writers who makes his Court to them by tearing to Pieces the Reputation of a Competitor, we should quickly see an End put to this Race of Vermin, that are a Scandal to Governnent, and a Reproach to Human Nature. Such a Proceeding would make a Minister of State shine in History, and would fill all Mankind with a just Abhorrence of Persons who should treat him unworthily, and employ against him those Arms which he scorn'd to make use of against his Enemies.

I cannot think that any one will be so unjust as to imagine, what I have here said, is spoken with Respect to any Party or Faction. Every one who has in him the Sentiments either of a Christian or Gentleman, cannot but be highly offended at this wicked and ungenerous Practice which is so much in use among us at present, that it is become a kind of National Crime, and distinguishes us from all the Governments that lie about us. I cannot but look upon the finest Strokes of Satyr which are aimed at particular Persons, and which are supported even with the Appearances of Truth, to be the Marks of an evil Mind, and highly Criminal in themselves. Infamy, like other Punishments, is under the direction and distribution of the Magistrate, and not of any private Person. Accordingly we learn from a Fragment of *Cicero*, that tho' there were very few Capital Punishments in the twelve Tables, a Libel or Lampoon which took away the good Name of another, was to be punished by Death. But this is far from being our Case. Our Satyr is nothing but Ribaldry, and *Billingsgate*. Scurrility passes for Wit; and he who can call Names in the greatest Variety of Phrases, is looked upon to have the shrewdest Pen. By this Means the Honour of Families is ruined, the highest Posts and greatest Titles are rendered cheap and vile in the Sight of the People; the noblest Virtues, and most exalted

Parts, exposed to the Contempt of the Vicious and the Ignorant. Should a Foreigner, who knows nothing of our Private Factions, or one who is to act his Part in the World, when our present Heats and Animosities are forgot, should, I say, such an one form to himself a Notion of the greatest Men of all Sides in the *British* Nation, who are now living, from the Characters which are given them in some or other of those abominable Writings which are daily published among us, what a Nation of Monsters must we appear!

As this cruel Practice tends to the utter Subversion of all Truth and Humanity among us, it deserves the utmost Detestation and Discouragement of all who have either the Love of their Country, or the Honour of their Religion at Heart. I would therefore earnestly recommend it to the Consideration of those who deal in these pernicious Arts of Writing; and of those who take pleasure in the Reading of them. As for the first, I have spoken of them in former Papers, and have not stuck to rank them with the Murderer and Assassin. Every honest Man sets as high a Value upon a good Name, as upon Life it self; and I cannot but think that those who privily assault the one, would destroy the other, might they do it with the same Secrecy and Impunity.

As for Persons who take Pleasure in the reading and dispersing of such detestable Libels, I am afraid they fall very little short of the Guilt of the first Composers. By a Law of the Emperors *Valentinian* and *Valens*, it was made Death for any Person not only to write a Libel, but if he met with one by chance, not to tear or burn it. But because I would not be thought singular in my Opinion of this matter, I shall conclude my Paper with the words of Monsieur *Bayle*, who was a Man of great Freedom of Thought, as well as of exquisite Learning and Judgment.

'I cannot imagine, that a Man who disperses a Libel, is less desirous of doing Mischief than the Author himself. But what shall we say of the Pleasure which a Man takes in the reading of a Defamatory Libel? Is it not an heinous Sin in the Sight of God? We must distinguish in this Point. This Pleasure is either an agreeable Sensation we are affected with, when we meet with a witty Thought which is well expressed, or it is a Joy which we conceive from the Dishonour of the Person who is defamed. I will say nothing to the first of these Cases; for perhaps some would think that my Morality is not severe enough, if I should affirm that a Man is not Master of those agreeable Sensations, any more than of those occasioned by Sugar or Honey when they touch his Tongue; but as to the second, every one will own that Pleasure to be a heinous Sin.

The Pleasure in the first Case is of no continuance; it prevents our Reason and Reflection, and may be immediately followed by a secret Grief, to see our Neighbour's Honour blasted.   If it does not cease immediately, it is a Sign that we are not displeased with the Ill-nature of the Satyrist, but are glad to see him defame his Enemy by all kinds of Stories; and then we deserve the Punishment to which the Writer of Libel is subject. I shall here add the Words of a Modern Author.   *St.* Gregory *upon excommunicating those Writers who had dishonoured* Castorius, *does not except those who read their Works; because,* says he, *if Calumnies have always been the delight of their Hearers, and a gratification of those Persons who have no other Advantage over honest Men, is not he who takes Pleasure in reading them as guilty as he who composed them?* It is an uncontested Maxim, that they who approve an Action would certainly do it if they could; that is, if some Reason of Self-love did not hinder them.   There is no difference, says *Cicero*, between advising a Crime, and approving it when committed.   The *Roman* Law confirmed this Maxim, having subjected the Approvers and Authors of this Evil to the same Penalty.   We may therefore conclude, that those who are pleased with reading Defamatory Libels, so far as to approve the Authors and Dispersers of them, are as guilty as if they had composed them; for if they do not write such Libels themselves, it is because they have not the Talent of Writing, or because they will run no Hazard.'

The Author produces other Authorities to confirm his Judgment in this Particular.   C

No. 452.
[ADDISON.]   Friday, August 8.

Est natura hominum novitatis avida.—Plin. apud Lillium.

THERE is no Humour in my Countrymen, which I am more enclined to wonder at, than their general Thirst after News. There are about half a Dozen Ingenious Men, who live very plentifully upon this Curiosity of their Fellow-Subjects.   They all of them receive the same Advices from abroad, and very often in the same Words; but their way of Cooking it is so different, that there is no Citizen, who has an Eye to the publick Good, that can leave the Coffee-house with Peace of Mind, before he has given every one of them a Reading. These several Dishes of News are so very agreeable to the Palate of my Countrymen, that they are not only pleased with them when they are served up hot, but when they are again set cold before them, by those penetrating Politicians, who oblige the Publick with their Reflections and Observations upon every Piece of Intelligence that is sent us from abroad. The Text is given us by one Sett of Writers, and the Comment by another.

But notwithstanding we have the same Tale told us in so many different Papers, and if Occasion requires in so many Articles of the same Paper; notwithstanding in a Scarcity of Foreign Posts we hear the same Story repeated, by different Advices from *Paris*, *Brussels*, the *Hague*, and from every great Town in *Europe*; notwithstanding the Multitude of Annotations, Explanations, Reflections, and various Readings which it passes through, our Time lies heavy on our Hands till the Arrival of a fresh Male; We long to receive further Particulars, to hear what will be the next Step, or what will be the Consequences of that which has been already taken. A Westerly Wind keeps the whole Town in Suspence, and puts a stop to Conversation.

This general Curiosity has been raised and inflamed by our late Wars, and, if rightly directed might be of good Use to a Person who has such a Thirst awakened in him. Why should not a Man, who takes Delight in reading every thing that is new, apply himself to History, Travels, and other Writings of the same kind, where he will find perpetual Fuel for his Curiosity, and meet with much more Pleasure and Improvement, than in these Papers of the Week? An honest Tradesman, who languishes a whole Summer in expectation of a Battel, and perhaps is balked at last, may here meet with half a dozen in a Day. He may read the News of a whole Campain, in less time than he now bestows upon the Product of any single Post. Fights, Conquests and Revolutions lye thick together. The Reader's Curiosity is raised and satisfied every moment, and his Passions disappointed or gratified, without being detained in a State of Uncertainty from Day to Day, or lying at the Mercy of Sea and Wind. In short, the Mind is not here kept in a perpetual Gape after Knowledge, nor punished with that eternal Thirst, which is the Portion of all our modern News-mongers and Coffee-house Politicians.

All Matters of Fact, which a Man did not know before, are News to him; and I do not see how any Haberdasher in *Cheapside* is more concerned in the present Quarrel of the Cantons, than he was in that of the League. At least, I believe every one will allow me, it is of more Importance to an *Englishman* to know the History of his Ancestors, than that of his Contemporaries who live upon the Banks of the *Danube* or the *Borysthenes*. As for those who are of another Mind, I shall recommend to them the following Letter, from a Projector, who is willing to turn a Penny by this remarkable Curiosity of his Countrymen.

' *Mr.* SPECTATOR,

You must have observed, that Men who frequent Coffee-houses, and delight in News, are pleased with every thing that is Matter of Fact, so it be what they have not heard before. A Victory, or a Defeat, are equally agreeable to them. The shutting of a Cardinal's Mouth pleases them one Post, and the opening of it another. They are glad to hear the *French* Court is removed to *Marli*, and are afterwards as much delighted with its return to *Versailles*. They read the Advertisements with the same Curiosity as the Articles of publick News; and are as pleased to hear of a Pye-bald Horse that is stray'd out of a Field near *Islington*, as of a whole Troop that have been engaged in any Foreign Adventure. In short they have a Relish for every thing that is News, let the Matter of it be what it will; or to speak more properly, they are Men of a Voracious Appetite, but no Taste. Now, Sir, since the great Fountain of News, I mean the War, is very near being dried up; and since these Gentlemen have contracted such an in-extinguishable Thirst after it; I have taken their Case and my own into Consideration, and have thought of a Project which may turn to the Advantage of us both. I have thoughts of Publishing a daily Paper, which shall comprehend in it all the most remarkable Occurrences in every little Town, Village and Hamlet that lye within ten Miles of *London*, or in other Words, within the Verge of the Penny - post. I have pitched upon this Scene of Intelligence for two Reasons; first because the Carriage of Letters will be very cheap; and secondly, because I may receive them every Day. By this means my Readers will have their News fresh and fresh, and many worthy Citizens who cannot Sleep with any Satisfaction at present, for want of being informed how the World goes, may go to Bed contentedly, it being my Design to put out my Paper every Night at Nine-a-Clock precisely. I have already established Correspondencies in these several Places, and received very good Intelligence.

By my last Advices from *Knights-bridge*, I hear that a Horse was clapped into the Pound on the third Instant, and that he was not released when the Letters came away.

We are informed from *Pankridge*, that a dozen Weddings were lately celebrated in the Mother Church of that Place, but are referred to their next Letters for the Names of the Parties concerned.

Letters from *Brompton* advise, That the Widow *Blight* had received several Visits from *John Milldew*, which affords great matter of Speculation in those Parts.

By a Fisherman which lately touched at *Hammersmith*, there is Advice from *Putney*, that a certain Person well known in that Place, is like to lose his Election for Church-warden; but this being Boat News, we cannot give entire Credit to it.

Letters from *Paddington* bring little more, than that *William Squeak*, the Sow-gelder, passed through that Place the fifth Instant.

They advise from *Fulham*, that things remained there in the same State they were. They had Intelligence, just as the Letters came away, of a Tub of excellent Ale just set abroach at *Parsons Green*; but this wanted Confirmation.

I have here, Sir, given you a Specimen of the News with which I intend to entertain the Town, and which, when drawn up regularly in the Form of a News Paper, will, I doubt not, be very acceptable to many of those Public-Spirited Readers, who take more delight in acquainting themselves with other People's Business than their own. I hope a Paper of this kind, which lets us know what is done near home, may be more useful to us, than those which are filled with Advices from *Zug* and *Bender*, and make some Amends for that Dearth of Intelligence, which we may justly apprehend from times of Peace. If I find that you receive this Project favourably, I will shortly trouble you with one or two more; and in the mean time am, most worthy Sir, with all due respect,

> *Your most Obedient,*
> *and most Humble Servant.'*

No. 453.
[ADDISON.] Saturday, August 9.

Non usitata nec tenui ferar
Penna . . .—Hor.

THERE is not a more pleasing Exercise of the Mind than Gratitude. It is accompanied with such an inward Satisfaction, that the Duty is sufficiently rewarded by the Performance. It is not like the Practice of many other Virtues, difficult and painful, but attended with so much Pleasure, that were there no positive Command which enjoined it, nor any Recompence laid up for it hereafter, a generous Mind would indulge in it, for the natural Gratification that accompanies it.

If Gratitude is due from Man to Man, how much more from Man to his Maker? The Supream Being does not only confer upon us those Bounties which proceed more immediately from his Hand, but even those Benefits which are conveyed to us by others. Every Blessing we enjoy, by what Means soever it may be derived upon us, is the Gift of him who is the great Author of Good, and Father of Mercies.

If Gratitude, when exerted towards one another, naturally produces a very pleasing Sensation in the Mind of a grateful Man; it exalts the Soul into Rapture, when it is employed on this great Object of Gratitude; on this Beneficent Being who has given us every thing we already possess, and from whom we expect every thing we yet hope for.

Most of the Works of the Pagan Poets were either direct Hymns to their Deities, or tended indirectly to the Celebration of their respective Attributes and Perfections. Those who are acquainted with the Works of the *Greek* and *Latin* Poets which are still extant, will upon Reflection find this Observation so true, that I shall not enlarge upon it. One would wonder that more of our Christian Poets have not turned their Thoughts this way, especially if we consider, that our Idea of the Supream Being is not only Infinitely more Great and Noble than what could possibly enter into the Heart of an Heathen, but filled with every thing that can raise the Imagination, and give an Opportunity for the Sublimest Thoughts and Conceptions.

Plutarch tells us of a Heathen who was singing an Hymn to *Diana* in which he celebrated her for her delight in human Sacrifices, and other Instances of Cruelty and Revenge; upon which a Poet who was present at this piece of Devotion, and seems to have had a truer Idea of the Divine Nature, told the Votary by way of reproof, that in recompence for his Hymn, he heartily wished he might have a Daughter of the same Temper with the Goddess he celebrated. It was indeed impossible to write the Praises of one of those false Deities, according to the Pagan Creed, without a Mixture of Impertinence and Absurdity.

The *Jews*, who before the Times of Christianity were the only People that had the Knowledge of the True God, have set the Christian World an Example how they ought to employ this Divine Talent of which I am speaking. As that Nation produced Men of great Genius, without considering them as inspired Writers, they have transmitted to us many Hymns and Divine Odes, which excel those that are deliver'd down to us by the Ancient *Greeks* and *Romans* in the Poetry, as much as in the Subject, to which it was consecrated. This I think might easily be shewn, if there were occasion for it.

I have already communicated to the Publick some Pieces of Divine Poetry, and as they have met with a very favourable

Reception, I shall from time to time publish any Work of the same Nature which has not yet appeared in Print, and may be acceptable to my Readers.

I.

When all thy Mercies, O my God,
My rising Soul surveys;
Transported with the View, I 'm lost
In Wonder, Love, and Praise.

II.

O how shall Words with equal Warmth
The Gratitude declare,
That glows within my Ravish'd Heart!
But thou canst read it there.

III.

Thy Providence my Life sustain'd
And all my Wants redrest,
When in the silent Womb I lay,
And hung upon the Breast.

IV.

To all my weak Complaints and Cries,
Thy Mercy lent an ear,
Ere yet my feeble Thoughts had learnt
To form themselves in Pray'r.

V.

Unnumber'd Comforts to my Soul
Thy tender Care bestow'd,
Before my Infant Heart conceiv'd
From whom those Comforts flow'd.

VI.

When in the slipp'ry Paths of Youth
With heedless Steps I ran,
Thine Arm unseen convey'd me safe
And led me up to Man;

VII.

Through hidden Dangers, Toils, and Deaths,
It gently clear'd my Way,
And through the pleasing Snares of Vice,
More to be fear'd than they.

VIII.

When worn with Sickness, oft hast thou
With health renew'd my Face,
And when in Sins and Sorrows sunk
Revived my Soul with Grace.

IX.

Thy bounteous Hand with worldly Bliss
Has made my Cup run o'er,
And in a kind and faithful Friend
Has doubled all my Store.

X.

Ten thousand thousand precious Gifts
My Daily Thanks employ,
Nor is the least a chearful Heart,
That tastes those Gifts with Joy.

XI.

Through ev'ry Period of my Life
Thy Goodness I 'll pursue,
And after Death in distant Worlds
The glorious Theme renew.

XII.

When Nature fails, and Day and Night
Divide thy Works no more,
My Ever-grateful Heart, O Lord,
Thy Mercy shall adore.

XIII.

Through all Eternity to Thee
A joyful Song I 'll raise,
For oh! Eternity 's too short
To utter all thy Praise.

C

No. 454.
[STEELE.]   Monday, August 11.

Sine me, vacivom tempus ne quod dem mihi
Laboris.—Ter. *Heau.*

IT is an inexpressible Pleasure to know a little of the World,
and be of no Character or Significancy in it. To be ever unconcerned, and ever looking on new Objects with an endless
Curiosity, is a Delight known only to those who are turned for

Speculation: Nay, they who enjoy it, must value things only as they are the Objects of Speculation, without drawing any worldly Advantage to themselves from them, but just as they are what contribute to their Amusement, or the Improvement of the Mind. I lay one Night last Week at *Richmond*; and being restless, not out of Dissatisfaction, but a certain busie Inclination one sometimes has, I arose at Four in the Morning, and took Boat for *London*, with a Resolution to rove by Boat and Coach for the next Four and twenty Hours, till the many different Objects I must needs meet with should tire my Imagination, and give me an Inclination to a Repose more profound than I was at that time capable of. I beg People's Pardon for an odd Humour I am guilty of, and was often that Day, which is saluting any Person whom I like, whether I know him or not. This is a Particularity would be tolerated in me, if they considered that the greatest Pleasure I know I receive at my Eyes, and that I am obliged to an agreeable Person for coming abroad into my View, as another is for a Visit of Conversation at their own Houses.

The Hours of the Day and Night are taken up in the Cities of *London* and *Westminster* by People as different from each other as those who are Born in different Centuries. Men of Six-a-Clock give way to those of Nine, they of Nine to the Generation of Twelve, and they of Twelve disappear, and make Room for the fashionable World, who have made Two-a-Clock the Noon of the Day.

When we first put off from Shoar, we soon fell in with a Fleet of Gardiners bound for the several Market-Ports of *London*; and it was the most pleasing Scene imaginable to see the Chearfulness with which those industrious People ply'd their Way to a certain Sale of their Goods. The Banks on each Side are as well Peopled, and beautified with as agreeable Plantations, as any Spot on the Earth; but the *Thames* it self, loaded with the Product of each Shoar, added very much to the Landskip. It was very easie to observe by their Sailing, and the Countenances of the ruddy Virgins, who were Super-cargos, the Parts of the Town to which they were bound. There was an Air in the Purveyors for *Covent-Garden*, who frequently converse with Morning Rakes, very unlike the seemly Sobriety of those bound for *Stocks-Market*.

Nothing remarkable happened in our Voyage; but I landed with Ten Sail of Apricock Boats at *Strand-Bridge*, after having put in at *Nine-Elmes*, and taken in Melons, consigned by Mr. *Cuffe* of that Place, to *Sarah Sewell* and Company, at their Stall in *Covent-Garden*. We arrived at *Strand-Bridge* at Six of the Clock, and were unloading; when the Hackney-Coach-

men of the foregoing Night took their Leave of each other at
the *Dark-House*, to go to Bed before the Day was too far spent.
Chimney-Sweepers pass'd by us as we made up to the Market,
and some Raillery happened between one of the Fruit-Wenches
and those black Men, about the Devil and *Eve*, with Allusion
to their several Professions. I could not believe any Place
more entertaining than *Covent-Garden*; where I strolled from
one Fruit-shop to another, with Crowds of agreeable young
Women around me, who were purchasing Fruit for their
respective Families. It was almost Eight of the Clock before
I could leave that Variety of Objects. I took Coach and
followed a young Lady, who tripped into another just before
me, attended by her Maid. I saw immediately she was of the
Family of the *Vainloves*. There are a Sett of these, who of all
things affect the Play of *Blindman's-Buff*, and leading Men
into Love for they know not whom, who are fled they know not
where. This sort of Woman is usually a janty Slattern; she
hangs on her Cloaths, plays her Head, varies her Posture,
and changes place incessantly, and all with an Appearance of
striving at the same time to hide her self, and yet give you to
understand she is in Humour to laugh at you. You must have
often seen the Coachmen make Signs with their Fingers as they
drive by each other, to intimate how much they have got that
Day. They can carry on that Language to give Intelligence
where they are driving. In an Instant my Coachman took
the Wink to pursue, and the Lady's Driver gave the Hint that
he was going through *Long-Acre* towards St. *James*'s: While
he whipp'd up *James-Street*, we drove for *King Street*, to save
the Pass at St. *Martin's-Lane*. The Coachmen took care to
meet, justle, and threaten each other for Way, and be in-
tangled at the End of *Newport-Street* and *Long-Acre*. The
Fright, you must believe, brought down the Lady's Coach
Door, and obliged her, with her Mask off, to enquire into the
Bustle, when she sees the Man she would avoid. The Tackle
of the Coach-Window is so bad she cannot draw it up again,
and she drives on sometimes wholly discovered, and sometimes
half-escaped, according to the Accident of Carriages in her
Way. One of these Ladies keeps her Seat in a Hackney-
Coach as well as the best Rider does on a managed Horse. The
laced Shooe on her Left Foot, with a careless Gesture, just
appearing on the opposite Cushion, held her both firm, and in
a proper Attitude to receive the next Jolt.

As she was an excellent Coach-Woman, many were the
Glances at each other which we had for an Hour and an Half
in all Parts of the Town by the Skill of our Drivers; till at last
my Lady was conveniently lost with Notice from her Coachman

to ours to make off, and he should hear where she went. This Chace was now at an End, and the Fellow who drove her came to us, and discovered that he was ordered to come again in an Hour, for that she was a Silk-Worm. I was surprized with this Phrase, but found it was a Cant among the Hackney Fraternity for their best Customers, Women who ramble twice or thrice a Week from Shop to Shop, to turn over all the Goods in Town without buying any thing. The Silk-Worms are, it seems, indulged by the Tradesmen; for tho' they never buy, they are ever talking of new Silks, Laces and Ribbands, and serve the Owners in getting them Customers, as their common Dunners do in making them pay.

The Day of People of Fashion began now to break, and Carts and Hacks were mingled with Equipages of Show and Vanity; when I resolved to walk it out of Cheapness; but my unhappy Curiosity is such, that I find it always my Interest to take Coach, for some odd Adventure among Beggars, Ballad-Singers, or the like, detains and throws me into Expence. It happened so immediately; for at the Corner of *Warwick-Street*, as I was listening to a new Ballad, a ragged Rascal, a Beggar who knew me, came up to me, and began to turn the Eyes of the good Company upon me, by telling me he was extream Poor, and should die in the Streets for want of Drink, except I immediately would have the Charity to give him Six-pence to go into the next Ale-House and save his life. He urged, with a melancholy Face, that all his Family had died of Thirst. All the Mob have Humour, and two or three began to take the Jest; by which Mr. *Sturdy* carried his Point, and let me sneak off to a Coach. As I drove along it was a pleasing Reflection to see the World so prettily chequered since I left *Richmond*, and the Scene still filling with Children of a new Hour. This Satisfaction encreased as I moved towards the City; and gay Signs, well disposed Streets, magnificent publick Structures, and wealthy Shops, adorned with contented Faces, made the Joy still rising till we came into the Centre of the City, and Centre of the World of Trade, the *Exchange* of *London*. As other Men in the Crowds about me were pleased with their Hopes and Bargains, I found my Account in observing them, in Attention to their several Interests. I, indeed, looked upon my self as the richest Man that walked the *Exchange* that Day; for my Benevolence made me share the Gains of every Bargain that was made. It was not the least of the Satisfactions in my Survey, to go up Stairs, and pass the Shops of agreeable Females; to observe so many pretty Hands busie in the Foldings of Ribbands, and the utmost Eagerness of agreeable Faces in the Sale of Patches, Pins, and Wires, on each Side the

Counters, was an Amusement, in which I should longer have
indulged my self, had not the dear Creatures called to me to
ask what I wanted, when I could not answer, only *To look at
you.* I went to one of the Windows which opened to the Area
below, where all the several Voices lost their Distinction, and
rose up in a confused Humming; which created in me a Reflection that could not come into the Mind of any but of one a
little too studious; for I said to my self, with a kind of Punn in
Thought, *What Nonsense is all the Hurry of this World to those
who are above it?* In these, or not much wiser Thoughts, I
had like to have lost my Place at the Chop-House; where every
Man, according to the natural Bashfulness or Sullenness of our
Nation, eats in a publick Room a Mess of Broth, or Chop of
Meat, in dumb Silence, as if they had no Pretence to speak to
each other on the Foot of being Men, except they were of each
other's Acquaintance.

I went afterwards to *Robin*'s and saw People who had
dined with me at the Five-penny Ordinary just before, give
Bills for the Value of large Estates; and could not but behold
with great Pleasure, Property lodged in, and transferred in a
Moment from such as would never be Masters of half as much
as is seemingly in them, and given from them every Day they
live. But before Five in the Afternoon I left the City, came
to my common Scene of *Covent-Garden*, and passed the Evening at *Will*'s in attending the Discourses of several Sets of
People, who relieved each other within my Hearing on the
Subjects of Cards, Dice, Love, Learning and Politicks. The
last Subject kept me till I heard the Streets in the Possession
of the Bell-man, who had now the World to himself, and cryed,
Past Two of Clock. This rous'd me from my Seat, and I went
to my Lodging, led by a Light, whom I put into the Discourse
of his private Oeconomy, and made him give me an Account
of the Charge, Hazard, Profit and Loss of a Family that depended upon a Link, with a Design to end my trivial Day
with the Generosity of Six-pence, instead of a third Part of
that Sum. When I came to my Chambers I writ down these
Minutes; but was at a Loss what Instruction I should propose
to my Reader from the Enumeration of so many Insignificant
Matters and Occurrences; and I thought it of great Use, if they
could learn with me to keep their minds open to Gratification,
and ready to receive it from any thing it meets with. This
one Circumstance will make every Face you see give you the
Satisfaction you now take in beholding that of a Friend; will
make every Object a pleasing one; will make all the Good
which arrives to any Man, an Encrease of Happiness to your
self.   T

No. 455.
[STEELE.]   Tuesday, August 12.

> . . . *Ego apis Matinae*
>   *More modoque*
> *Grata carpentis thyma per laborem*
> *Plurimum* . . .

THE following Letters have in them Reflections which will seem of Importance both to the Learned World and to Domestick Life. There is in the first an Allegory so well carry'd on, that it cannot but be very pleasing to those who have a Taste of good Writing; and the other Billets may have their Use in common Life.

'*Mr.* SPECTATOR,

As I walked t'other Day in a fine Garden, and observed the great Variety of Improvements in Plants and Flowers beyond what they otherwise would have been, I was naturally led into a Reflection upon the Advantages of Education, or modern Culture; how many good Qualities in the Mind are lost, for want of the like due Care in nursing and skilfully managing them, how many Virtues are choaked, by the Multitude of Weeds which are suffered to grow among them; how excellent Parts are often starved and useless, by being planted in a wrong Soil; and how very seldom do these moral Seeds produce the noble Fruits which might be expected from them, by a Neglect of proper Manuring, necessary Pruning, and an artful Management of our tender Inclinations and first Spring of Life: These obvious Speculations made me at length conclude, that there is a sort of vegetable Principle in the Mind of every Man when he comes into the World. In Infants the Seeds lie buried and undiscovered, 'till after a while they sprout forth in a kind of rational *Leaves*, which are *Words*; and in a due Season the *Flowers* begin to appear in Variety of beautiful Colours, and all the gay Pictures of youthful Fancy and Imagination; at last the Fruit knits and is formed, which is green, perhaps, first, and soure, unpleasant to the Taste, and not fit to be gathered; 'till ripened by due Care and Application it discovers it self in all the noble Productions of Philosophy, Mathematicks, close Reasoning, and handsome Argumentation: And these Fruits, when they arrive at a just Maturity, and are of a good Kind, afford the most vigorous Nourishment to the Minds of Men. I reflected further on the intellectual Leaves beforementioned, and found almost as great a Variety among them as in the vegetable World. I could easily observe the smooth shining *Italian* Leaves; the nimble *French* Aspen, always in Motion; the *Greek* and *Latin* Ever-greens, the *Spanish* Myrtle, the *English* Oak, the *Scotch* Thistle, the *Irish* Shambrogue, the prickly *German* and *Dutch* Holy, the *Polish* and *Russian* Nettle, besides a vast Number of Exoticks imported from *Asia, Africk,* and *America.* I saw several barren Plants, which bore only Leaves, without any Hopes of Flower or Fruit: The Leaves of some were fragrant and well-shaped, of others ill-scented and irregular. I wonder'd at a Set of old whimsical Botanists, who spent their whole Lives in the Contemplation of some withered *Aegyptian, Coptick, Armenian,* or *Chinese* Leaves, while others made it their Business to collect in voluminous Herbals all the several Leaves of some one Tree. The Flowers afforded a most diverting Entertainment, in a wonderful Variety of Figures, Colours and Scents; however, most of them withered soon, or at best are but *Annuals.* Some professed Florists make them their constant Study and Employment, and despise all Fruit; and now and then a few fanciful People spend all their Time in the Cultivation of a single Tulip, or a Carnation: But the most agreeable Amusement seems to be the well chusing, mixing, and binding together these Flowers, in pleasing Nosegays to present to Ladies. The Scent of *Italian* Flowers is observed, like their other Perfume, to be too strong, and to hurt the Brain; that of the *French* with glaring, gaudy Colours, yet faint and languid; *German* and *Northern* Flowers have little or no Smell, or sometimes an unpleasant one. The Ancients had a Secret to give a lasting Beauty, Colour, and sweetness to some of their choice Flowers, which flourish to this Day, and which few of the Moderns can effect. These are becoming enough and agreeable in their Season, and do often handsomely adorn an Entertainment, but an Over-fondness of them seems to be a Disease. It rarely happens to find a Plant vigorous enough, to have (like an Orange-Tree) at once beautiful shining Leaves, fragrant Flowers, and delicious nourishing Fruit.

Sir, Yours, &c.'

'*Dear* SPEC,   *August* 6, 1712.

You have given us in your *Spectator* of *Saturday* last, a very excellent Discourse upon the Force of Custom, and its wonderful Efficacy in making every thing pleasant to us. I cannot deny but that I received above Two penny-worth of Instruction from your Paper, and in the General was very well pleased with it; but I am without a Complement, sincerely troubled that I cannot exactly be of your Opinion, That it makes every thing pleasing to us. In short, I have the Honour to be yoked to a young Lady, who is, in plain *English*, for her Standing, a very eminent Scold. She began to break her Mind very freely both to me and to her Servants about two Months after our Nuptials; and tho' I have been accustomed to this Humour of hers this three Years, yet, I do not know what's the Matter with me, but I am no more delighted with it than I was at the very first. I have advised with her Relations about her, and they all tell me that her Mother and her Grandmother before her were both taken much after the same Manner; so that since it runs in the Blood, I have but small Hopes of her Recovery. I should be glad to have a little of your Advice in this Matter: I would not willingly trouble you to contrive how it may be a Pleasure to me; if you will but put me in a Way that I may bear it with Indifference, I shall rest satisfied.

Dear SPEC,

Your very Humble Servant.

P.S. I must do the poor Girl the Justice to let you know that this Match was none of her own chusing (or indeed of mine either); in consideration of which I avoid giving her the least Provocation; and indeed we live better together than usually Folks do who hated one another when they were first joined: To evade the Sin against Parents, or at least to extenuate it, my *Dear* rails at my Father and Mother, and I curse hers for making the Match.'

'*Mr.* SPECTATOR,

I like the Theme you lately gave out extremely, and should be as glad to handle it as any Man living: But I find my self no better qualified to write about Mony, than about my Wife: for, to tell you a Secret, which I desire may go no further, I am Master of neither of those Subjects.

Yours,

Aug. 8, 1712. Pill Garlick.'

'*Mr.* SPECTATOR,

I desire you would print this in *Italick*, so as it may be generally taken Notice of. It is designed only to admonish all Persons, who speak either at the Bar, Pulpit, or any publick Assembly whatsoever, how they discover their Ignorance in the Use of Similes. There are in the Pulpit it self, as well as in other Places, such gross Abuses in this Kind, that I give this Warning to all I know. I shall bring them for the future before your Spectatorial Authority. On *Sunday* last, one, who shall be nameless, reproving several of his Congregation for standing at Prayers, was pleased to say, *One would think,* like the Elephant, *you had no knees:* Now I myself saw an Elephant in *Bartholomew Fair* kneel down to take on his Back the ingenious Mr. *William Pinkethman.*

T   *Your most Humble Servant.'*

No. 456.
[STEELE.]   Wednesday, August 13.

De quo libelli in celeberrimis locis proponuntur, huic ne perire quidem . . . tacite . . . conceditur.—Tull.

Otway, in his Tragedy of *Venice preserv'd,* has described the Misery of a Man, whose Effects are in the Hands of the Law, with great Spirit.   The Bitterness of being the Scorn and Laughter of base Minds, the Anguish of being insulted by Men hardened beyond the Sense of Shame or Pity, and the injury of a Man's Fortune being wasted, under Pretence of Justice are excellently aggravated in the following Speech of *Pierre* to *Jaffier.*

> *I pass'd this very Moment by thy Doors,*
> *And found them guarded by a Troop of Villains;*
> *The Sons of publick Rapine were destroying.*
> *They told me, by the Sentence of the Law,*
> *They had Commission to seize all thy Fortune:*
> *Nay more, Priuli's cruel Hand had sign'd it.*
> *Here stood a Ruffian with a horrid Face,*
> *Lording it o'er a Pile of massy Plate,*
> *Tumbled into a Heap for publick Sale,*
> *There was another making villainous Jests*
> *At thy Undoing: He had ta'en Possession*
> *Of all thy antient most domestick Ornaments;*
> *Rich Hangings intermix'd and wrought with Gold;*
> *The very Bed, which on thy Wedding-Night*
> *Receiv'd thee to the Arms of* Belvidera,
> *The Scene of all thy Joys, was violated*
> *By the coarse Hands of filthy Dungeon Villains.*
> *And thrown amongst the common Lumber.*

Nothing indeed can be more unhappy than the Condition of Bankruptcy.   The Calamity which happens to us by ill Fortune, or by the Injury of others, has in it some Consolation; but what arises from our own Misbehaviour or Error, is the State of the most exquisite Sorrow.   When a Man considers not only an ample Fortune, but even the very Necessaries of Life, his Pretence to Food it self, at the Mercy of his Creditors, he cannot but look upon himself in the State of the Dead, with his Case thus much worse, that the last Office is performed by his Adversaries instead of his Friends. From this Hour the cruel World does not only take Possession of his whole Fortune, but even of every thing else, which had no Relation to it. All his indifferent Actions have new Interpretations put upon them; and those whom he has favoured in his former Life, discharge themselves of their Obligations to him, by joining in the Reproaches of his Enemies. It is almost incredible that it should be so; but it is too often seen that there is a Pride mixed with the Impatience of the Creditor, and there are who would rather recover their own by the Downfall of a prosperous Man, than be discharged to the common Satisfaction of themselves and their Creditors. The wretched Man who was lately Master of Abundance, is now under the Direction of others; and the Wisdom, Oeconomy, good Sense and Skill in human Life before, by reason of his present Misfortune, are of no Use to him in the Disposition of any thing. The Incapacity of an Infant or a Lunatick is designed for his Provision and Accommodation; but that of a Bankrupt, without any Mitigation in respect of the Accidents by which it arrived, is calculated for his utter Ruin, except there be a Remainder ample enough after the Discharge of his Creditors to bear also the Expense of rewarding those by whose Means the Effect of all his Labour was transferred from him. This Man is to look on and see others giving Directions upon what Terms and Conditions his Goods are to be purchased, and all this usually done not with an Air of Trustees to dispose of his Effects, but Destroyers to divide and tear them to Pieces.

There is something sacred in Misery to great and good Minds; for this Reason all wise Law-givers have been extremely tender how they let loose even the Man who has Right on his Side, to act with any Mixture of Resentment against the Defendant. Virtuous and modest Men, though they be used with some Artifice, and have it in their Power to avenge themselves, are slow in the Application of that Power, and are ever constrained to go into rigorous Measures. They are careful to demonstrate themselves not only Persons injured, but also that to bear it longer would be a Means to make the Offender injure others, before they proceed. Such Men clap their Hands upon their Hearts, and consider what it is to have at their Mercy the Life of a Citizen. Such would have it to say to their own Souls, if possible, That they were merciful when they could have destroyed, rather than when it was in their Power to have spared a Man, they destroyed. This is a Due to the common Calamity of Human Life, due in some measure to our very Enemies. They who scruple doing the least Injury, are cautious of exacting the utmost Justice.

Let any one who is conversant in the Variety of Human Life reflect upon it, and he will find the Man who wants Mercy has a Taste of no Enjoyment of any Kind. There is a natural Disrelish of every thing which is good in his very Nature, and he is born an Enemy to the World. He is ever extremely partial to himself in all his Actions, and has no Sense of Iniquity but from the Punishment which shall attend it. The Law of the Land is his Gospel, and all his Cases of Conscience are determined by his Attorney. Such Men know not what it is to gladden the Heart of a Miserable Man, that Riches are the Instruments of serving the Purposes of Heaven or Hell, according to the Disposition of the Professor. The Wealthy can torment or gratifie all who are in their Power, and chuse to do one or other as they are affected with Love or Hatred to Mankind. As for such who are insensible of the Concerns of others, but merely as they affect themselves, these Men are to be valued only for their Morality, and as we hope better Things from their Heirs. I could not but read with great Delight a Letter from an eminent Citizen, who has failed, to one who was intimate with him in his better Fortune, and able by his Countenance to retrieve his lost Condition.

'*Sir*,

It is in vain to multiply Words, and make Apologies for what is never to be defended by the best Advocate in the World, the Guilt of being Unfortunate. All that a Man in my Condition can do or say, will be received with Prejudice by the Generality of Mankind, but I hope not with you: You have been a great Instrument in helping me to get what I have lost, and I know (for that Reason as well as Kindness to me) you cannot but be in Pain to see me undone. To shew you I am not a Man incapable of bearing Calamity, I will, though a poor Man, lay aside the Distinction between us, and talk with the Frankness we did when we were nearer to an Equality: As all I do will be received with Prejudice, all you do will be looked upon with Partiality. What I desire of you, is, that you, who are courted by all, would smile upon me who am shunned by all. Let that Grace and Favour which your Fortune throws upon you, be turned to make up the Coldness and Indifference that is used toward me. All good and generous Men will have an Eye of Kindness for me for my own Sake, and the rest of the World will regard me for yours. There is an happy Contagion in Riches, as well as a destructive one in Poverty; the Rich can make rich without parting with any of their Store, and the Conversation of the Poor makes Men Poor, though they borrow nothing of them. How this is to be accounted for I know not; but Men's Estimation follows us according to the Company we keep. If you are what you were to me, you can go a great Way towards my Recovery; if you are not, my good Fortune, if ever it returns, will return by slower Approaches.

> *I am, Sir,*
> > *Your affectionate Friend,*
> > > *and humble Servant.'*

This was answered with a Condescension that did not, by long impertinent Professions of Kindness, insult his Distress, but was as follows.

> '*Dear* Tom,
>
> I am very glad to hear that you have Heart enough to begin the World a second time. I assure you, I do not think your numerous Family at all diminished (in the Gifts of Nature for which I have ever so much admired them) by what has so lately happened to you. I shall not only countenance your Affairs with my Appearance for you, but shall accommodate you with a considerable Sum at common Interest for three Years. You know I could make more of it; but I have so great a Love for you, that I can wave Opportunities of Gain to help you: For I do not care whether they say of me after I am dead, that I had an hundred or fifty thousand Pounds more than I wanted when I was living.

T   *Your obliged humble Servant.'*

No. 457.

[ADDISON.]   Thursday, August 14.

> . . . *Multa & praeclara minantis.*—Hor.

I SHALL this Day lay before my Reader a Letter, written by the same Hand with that of last *Friday*, which contained Proposals for a Printed News-Paper, that should take in the whole Circle of the Penny-post.

> '*Sir,*
>
> The kind Reception you gave my last *Friday's* Letter, in which I broached my Project of a News-Paper, encourages me to lay before you two or three more; for, you must know, Sir, that we look upon you to be the *Lowndes* of the learned World, and cannot think any Scheme practicable or rational before you have approved of it, tho' all the Mony we raise by it is on our own Funds, and for our private Use.
>
> I have often thought that a *News-Letter of Whispers*, written

every Post, and sent about the Kingdom, after the same manner as that of Mr. *Dyer*, Mr. *Dawkes*, or any other Epistolary Historian, might be highly gratifying to the Publick, as well as beneficial to the Author. By Whispers I mean those Pieces of News which are communicated as Secrets, and which bring a double Pleasure to the Hearer; first, as they are private History, and in the next place, as they have always in them a Dash of Scandal. These are the two chief Qualifications in an Article of News, which recommend it in a more than ordinary Manner, to the Ears of the Curious. Sickness of Persons in high Posts, Twilight Visits paid and received by Ministers of State, Clandestine Courtships and Marriages, Secret Amours, Losses at Play, Applications for Places, with their respective Successes or Repulses, are the Materials in which I chiefly intend to deal. I have two Persons, that are each of them the Representative of a Species, who are to furnish me with those Whispers which I intend to convey to my Correspondents. The first of these is *Peter Hush*, descended from the ancient Family of the *Hushes*. The other is the old Lady *Blast*, who has a very numerous tribe of Daughters in the two great Cities of *London* and *Westminster*. *Peter Hush* has a whispering Hole in most of the great Coffee-Houses about Town. If you are alone with him in a wide Room, he carries you up into a Corner of it, and speaks in your Ear. I have seen *Peter* seat himself in a Company of seven or eight Persons, whom he never saw before in his Life; and after having looked about to see there was no one that over-heard him, has communicated to them in a low Voice, and under the Seal of Secrecy, the Death of a great Man in the Country, who was perhaps a Fox-hunting the very moment this Account was given of him. If upon your entring into a Coffee-house you see a Circle of Heads bending over the Table, and lying close by one another, it is ten to one but my Friend *Peter* is among them. I have known *Peter* publishing the Whisper of the Day by eight a Clock in the Morning at *Garraway*'s, by twelve at *Will*'s, and before two at the *Smyrna*. When *Peter* has thus effectually launched a Secret, I have been very well pleased to hear People whispering it to one another at second Hand, and spreading it about as their own; for you must know, Sir, the great Incentive to Whispering is the Ambition which every one has of being thought in the Secret, and being looked upon as a Man who has Access to greater People than one would imagine. After having given you this Account of *Peter Hush*, I proceed to that virtuous Lady, the old Lady *Blast*, who is to communicate to me the private Transactions of the Crimp Table, with all the *Arcana* of the fair Sex. The Lady *Blast*, you must understand, has such a particular Malignity in her Whisper, that it blights like an Easterly Wind, and withers every Reputation that it breaths upon. She has a particular knack at making private Weddings, and last Winter married above five Women of Quality to their Footmen. Her Whisper can make an innocent young Woman big with Child, or fill an healthful young Fellow with Distempers that are not to be named. She can turn a Visit into an Intrigue, and a distant Salute into an Assignation. She can beggar the Wealthy, and degrade the Noble. In short, she can whisper Men Base or Foolish, Jealous or Ill-natured, or if occasion requires, can tell you the Slips of their Great Grandmothers, and traduce the Memory of honest Coach-men that have been in their Graves above these hundred Years. By these, and the like helps, I question not but I shall furnish out a very handsome News-Letter. If you approve my Project, I shall begin to Whisper by the very next Post, and question not but every one of my Customers will be very well pleased with me, when he considers that every Piece of News I send him is a Word in his Ear, and lets him into a Secret.

Having given you a Sketch of this Project, I shall, in the next place, suggest to you another for a Monthly Pamphlet, which I shall likewise submit to your Spectatorial Wisdom. I need not tell you, Sir, that there are several Authors in *France*, *Germany*, and *Holland*, as well as in our own Country, who Publish every Month, what they call *An Account of the Works of the Learned*, in which they give us an Abstract of all such Books as are Printed in any Part of *Europe*. Now, Sir, it is my Design to Publish every Month, *An Account of the Works of the Unlearned*. Several late Productions of my own Country-men, who many of them make a very Eminent Figure in the Illiterate World, encourage me in this Undertaking. I may, in this Work, possibly make a Review of several Pieces which have appeared in the Foreign *Accounts* above-mentioned, tho' they ought not to have been taken Notice of in Works which bear such a Title. I may, likewise, take into Consideration such Pieces as appear, from time to time, under the Names of those Gentlemen who Complement one another in Publick Assemblies, by the Title of the *Learned Gentlemen*. Our Party-Authors will also afford me a great Variety of Subjects, not to mention Editors, Commentators, and others, who are often Men of no Learning, or what is as bad, of no Knowledge. I shall not enlarge upon this Hint; but if you think any thing can be made of it, I shall set about it with all the Pains and Application that so useful a Work deserves.

I am ever,
Most worthy Sir, &c.'

C

No. 458.
[ADDISON.]   Friday, August 15.

Αἰδὼς οὐκ ἀγαθὴ . . . .—Hes.
. . . *Pudor malus* . . .—Hor.

I COULD not but Smile at the Account that was Yesterday
given me of a modest young Gentleman, who being invited to
an Entertainment, tho' he was not used to drink, had not the
Confidence to refuse his Glass in his Turn, when on a sudden
he grew so flustered, that he took all the Talk of the Table into
his own Hands, abused every one of the Company, and flung
a Bottle at the Gentleman's Head who treated him. This has
given me Occasion to reflect upon the ill Effects of a vicious
Modesty, and to remember the saying of *Brutus*, as it is quoted
by *Plutarch*, that *the Person has had but an ill Education, who
has not been taught to deny any thing*. This false kind of
Modesty has, perhaps, betrayed both Sexes into as many Vices
as the most abandoned Impudence, and is the more inexcusable
to Reason, because it acts to gratifie others rather than it self,
and is punished with a kind of Remorse, not only like other
vicious Habits when the Crime is over, but even at the very
time that it is committed.

Nothing is more amiable than true Modesty, and nothing is
more contemptible than the false. The one guards Virtue,
the other betrays it. True Modesty is ashamed to do any
thing that is repugnant to the Rules of right Reason: False
Modesty is ashamed to do any thing that is opposite to the
Humour of the Company. True Modesty avoids every thing
that is criminal, false Modesty every thing that is unfashionable. The latter is only a general undetermined Instinct; the
former is that Instinct, limited and circumscribed by the
Rules of Prudence and Religion.

We may conclude that Modesty to be false and vicious, which
engages a Man to do any thing that is ill or indiscreet, or which
restrains him from doing any thing that is of a contrary Nature.
How many Men, in the common Concerns of Life, lend Sums
of Mony which they are not able to spare, are Bound for
Persons whom they have but little Friendship for, give Re-
commendatory Characters of Men whom they are not acquainted with, bestow Places on those whom they do not
esteem, live in such a Manner as they themselves do not
approve, and all this meerly because they have not the Confidence to resist Solicitation, Importunity or Example?

Nor does this false Modesty expose us only to such Actions
as are indiscreet, but very often to such as are highly Criminal.
When *Xenophanes* was called timorous, because he would not

venture his Mony in a Game at Dice: *I confess*, said he, *that I am exceeding timorous, for I dare not do any ill thing.* On the contrary, a Man of vicious Modesty complies with every thing, and is only fearful of doing what may look singular in the Company where he is engaged. He falls in with the Torrent, and lets himself go to every Action or Discourse, however unjustifiable in it self, so it be in Vogue among the present Party. This, tho' one of the most common, is one of the most ridiculous Dispositions in human Nature, that Men should not be ashamed of speaking or acting in a dissolute or irrational Manner, but that one who is in their Company should be ashamed of governing himself by the Principles of Reason and Virtue.

In the second place we are to consider false Modesty, as it restrains a Man from doing what is good and laudable. My Reader's own Thoughts will suggest to him many Instances and Examples under this Head. I shall only dwell upon one Reflection, which I cannot make without a Secret Concern. We have in *England* a particular Bashfulness in every thing that regards Religion. A well-bred Man is obliged to conceal any Serious Sentiment of this Nature, and very often to appear a greater Libertine than he is, that he may keep himself in Countenance among the Men of Mode. Our Excess of Modesty makes us shame-faced in all the Exercises of Piety and Devotion. This Humour prevails upon us daily; insomuch, that at many well-bred Tables, the Master of the House is so very Modest a Man, that he has not the Confidence to say Grace at his own Table: A Custom which is not only practised by all the Nations about us, but was never omitted by the Heathens themselves. *English* Gentlemen who Travel into Roman Catholick Countries, are not a little surprized to meet with People of the best Quality kneeling in their Churches, and engaged in their private Devotions, tho' it be not at the Hours of Publick Worship. An Officer of the Army, or a Man of Wit and Pleasure in those Countries, would be afraid of passing not only for an Irreligious, but an ill-bred Man, should he be seen to go to Bed, or sit down at Table, without offering up his Devotions on such Occasions. The same Show of Religion appears in all the Foreign Reformed Churches, and enters so much in their Ordinary Conversation, that an *Englishman* is apt to term them Hypocritical and Precise.

This little Appearance of a Religious Deportment in our Nation, may proceed in some measure from that Modesty which is natural to us, but the great occasion of it is certainly this. Those Swarms of Sectaries that overran the Nation in the time of the great Rebellion, carried their Hypocrisie so high, that they had converted our whole Language into a

Jargon of Enthusiasm; insomuch that upon the Restoration Men thought they could not recede too far from the Behaviour and Practice of those Persons, who had made Religion a Cloak to so many Villanies. This led them into the other Extream, every Appearance of Devotion was looked upon as Puritanical, and falling into the Hands of the Ridiculers who flourished in that Reign, and attacked every thing that was Serious, it has ever since been out of Countenance among us. By this means we are gradually fallen into that Vicious Modesty which has in some measure worn out from among us the Appearance of Christianity in Ordinary Life and Conversation, and which distinguishes us from all our Neighbours.

Hypocrisie cannot indeed be too much detested, but at the same time is to be preferred to open Impiety. They are both equally destructive to the Person who is possessed with them; but in regard to others. Hypocrisie is not so pernicious as bare-faced Irreligion. The due Mean to be observed is to be sincerely Virtuous, and at the same time to let the World see we are so. I do not know a more dreadful Menace in the Holy Writings, than that which is pronounced against those who have this perverted Modesty, to be ashamed before Men in a Particular of such unspeakable Importance.   C

No. 459.
[ADDISON.]   Saturday, August 16.

. . . *Quicquid dignum sapiente bonoque est.*—Hor.

RELIGION may be considered under two General Heads. The first comprehends what we are to believe, the other what we are to practise. By those things which we are to believe, I mean whatever is revealed to us in the Holy Writings, and which we could not have obtained the Knowledge of by the Light of Nature; by the things which we are to practise, I mean all those Duties to which we are directed by Reason or Natural Religion. The First of these I shall distinguish by the Name of Faith, the Second by that of Morality.

If we look into the more Serious Part of Mankind we find many who lay so great a Stress upon Faith, that they neglect Morality; and many who build so much upon Morality, that they do not pay a due Regard to Faith. The perfect Man should be defective in neither of these Particulars, as will be very evident to those who consider the Benefits which arise from each of them, and which I shall make the Subject of this Day's Paper.

Notwithstanding this general Division of Christian Duty into Morality and Faith, and that they have both their peculiar Excellencies, the first has the Pre-eminence in several Respects.

First, Because the greatest part of Morality (as I have stated the Notion of it,) is of a fixt Eternal Nature, and will endure when Faith shall fail, and be lost in Conviction.

Secondly, Because a Person may be qualified to do greater Good to Mankind, and become more beneficial to the World, by Morality without Faith, than by Faith without Morality.

Thirdly, Because Morality gives a greater Perfection to human Nature, by quieting the Mind, moderating the Passions, and advancing the Happiness of every Man in his private Capacity.

Fourthly, Because the Rule of Morality is much more certain than that of Faith, all the Civilized Nations of the World agreeing in the great Points of Morality, as much as they differ in those of Faith.

Fifthly, Because Infidelity is not of so malignant a Nature as Immorality, or to put the same Reason in another Light, because it is generally owned, there may be Salvation for a virtuous Infidel, (particularly in the Case of Invincible Ignorance) but none for a vicious Believer.

Sixthly, Because Faith seems to draw its Principal, if not all its Excellency, from the Influence it has upon Morality; as we shall see more at large, if we consider wherein consists the Excellency of Faith, or the Belief of Revealed Religion; and this I think is,

First, In explaining, and carrying to greater Heights, several Points of Morality.

Secondly, In furnishing new and stronger Motives to enforce the Practice of Morality.

Thirdly, In giving us more amiable Ideas of the Supreme Being, more endearing Notions of one another, and a truer State of our selves, both in regard to the Grandeur and Vileness of our Natures.

Fourthly, By shewing us the Blackness and Deformity of Vice, which in the Christian System is so very great, that he who is possessed of all Perfection and the Sovereign Judge of it, is represented by several of our Divines as hating Sin to the same Degree that he loves the Sacred Person who was made the Propitiation of it.

Fifthly, In being the ordinary and prescribed Method of making Morality effectual to Salvation.

I have only touched on these several Heads, which every one who is conversant in Discourses of this Nature will easily enlarge upon in his own Thoughts, and draw Conclusions from them which may be useful to him in the Conduct of his Life. One I am sure is so obvious, that he cannot miss it, namely that a Man cannot be perfect in his Scheme of Morality, who does not strengthen and support it with that of the Christian Faith.

Besides this, I shall lay down two or three other Maxims which I think we may deduce from what has been said.

First, That we should be particularly cautious of making any thing an Article of Faith, which does not contribute to the Confirmation or Improvement of Morality.

Secondly, That no Article of Faith can be true and authentick, which weakens or subverts the practical part of Religion, or what I have hitherto called Morality.

Thirdly, That the greatest Friend of Morality, or Natural Religion, cannot possibly apprehend any Danger from embracing Christianity, as it is preserved pure and uncorrupt in the Doctrines of our National Church.

There is likewise another Maxim which I think may be drawn from the foregoing Considerations, which is this, that we should in all dubious Points, consider any ill Consequences that may arise from them, supposing they should be Erroneous, before we give up our Assent to them.

For Example, In that disputable Point of Persecuting Men for Conscience Sake, besides the imbittering their Minds with Hatred, Indignation, and all the Vehemence of Resentment, and ensnaring them to profess what they do not believe; we cut them off from the Pleasures and Advantages of Society, afflict their Bodies, distress their Fortunes, hurt their Reputations, ruin their Families, make their Lives painful, or put an End to them. Sure when I see such dreadful Consequences arising from a Principle, I would be as fully convinced of the Truth of it, as of a Mathematical Demonstration, before I would venture to act upon it, or make it a Part of my Religion.

In this Case the Injury done our Neighbour is plain and evident, the Principle that puts us upon doing it, of a dubious and disputable Nature. Morality seems highly violated by the one, and whether or no a Zeal for what a Man thinks the true System of Faith may justifie it, is very uncertain. I cannot but think, if our Religion produces Charity as well as Zeal, it will not be for shewing it self by such Cruel Instances. But, to conclude with the Words of an Excellent Author, *We have just enough Religion to make us hate, but not enough to make us love one another.*   C

No. 460.
[STEELE.] Monday, August 18.

Decipimur specie recti . . .—Hor.

Our Defects and Follies are too often unknown to us; nay, they are so far from being known to us, that they pass for Demonstrations of our Worth. This makes us easie in the Midst of them, fond to shew them, fond to improve in them, and to be esteemed for them. Then it is that a thousand unaccountable Conceits, gay Inventions, and extravagant Actions must afford us Pleasures, and display us to others in the Colours which we ourselves take a Fancy to glory in: And indeed there is something so amusing for the Time in this State of Vanity and ill-grounded Satisfaction, that even the wiser World has chosen an exalted Word to describe its Enchantments, and called it *the Paradise of Fools*.

Perhaps the latter Part of this Reflection may seem a false Thought to some, and bear another Turn than what I have given; but it is at present none of my Business to look after it, who am going to confess that I have been lately amongst them in a Vision.

Methought I was transported to a Hill, green, flowery, and of an easie Ascent. Upon the broad Top of it resided squint-eyed *Errour*, and popular *Opinion* with many Heads; two that dealt in Sorcery, and were famous for bewitching People with the Love of themselves. To these repaired a Multitude from every Side, by two different Paths which lead towards each of them. Some who had the most assuming Air, went directly of themselves to *Errour*, without expecting a Conductor; others of a softer Nature went first to popular *Opinion*, from whence as she influenced and engaged them with their own Praises, she delivered them over to his Government.

When we had ascended to an open Part of the Summit where *Opinion* abode, we found her entertaining several who had arrived before us. Her Voice was pleasing; she breathed Odours as she spoke: She seemed to have a Tongue for every one; every one thought he heard of something that was valuable in himself, and expected a Paradise which she promised as the Reward of his Merit. Thus were we drawn to follow her, 'till she should bring us where it was to be bestowed: And it was observable, that all the Way we went, the Company was either praising themselves for their Qualifications or one another for those Qualifications which they took to be conspicuous in their own Characters, or dispraising others for wanting theirs, or vying in the Degrees of them.

At last we approached a Bower, at the Entrance of which

Errour was seated. The trees were thick-woven, and the Place where he sat artfully contrived to darken him a little. He was disguised in a whitish Robe, which he had put on, that he might appear to us with a nearer Resemblance to *Truth*: And as she has a Light whereby she manifests the Beauties of Nature to the Eyes of her Adorers, so he had provided himself with a magical Wand, that he might do something in Imitation of it, and please with Delusions. This he lifted solemnly, and muttering to himself, bid the Glories which he kept under Enchantment to appear before us. Immediately we cast our Eyes on that Part of the Sky to which he pointed, and observed a thin blue Prospect, which cleared as Mountains in a Summer Morning when the Mists go off, and the Palace of *Vanity* appeared to Sight.

The Foundation hardly seemed a Foundation, but a Set of curling Clouds, which it stood upon by magical Contrivance. The Way by which we ascended was painted like a Rainbow; and as we went the Breeze that played about us bewitched the Senses. The Walls were gilded all for Show; the lowest Set of Pillars were of the slight Fine *Corinthian* Order, and the Top of the Building being rounded, bore so far the Resemblance of a Bubble.

At the Gate the Travellers neither met with a Porter, nor waited 'till one should appear; every one thought his Merit a sufficient Passport, and pressed forward. In the Hall we met with several Phantoms, that roved amongst us, and ranged the Company according to their Sentiments. There was decreasing *Honour*, that had nothing to shew in but an old Coat of his Ancestors Atchievements; There was *Ostentation*, that made himself his own constant Subject, and *Gallantry* strutting upon his Tip-toes. At the upper End of the Hall stood a Throne, whose Canopy glitter'd with all the Riches that Gayety could contrive to lavish on it; and between the gilded Arms sat *Vanity*, deck'd in the Peacock's Feathers, and acknowledged for another *Venus* by her Votaries. The Boy who stood beside her for a *Cupid*, and who made the World to bow before her, was called *Self-Conceit*. His Eyes had every now and then a Cast inwards, to the Neglect of all Objects about him; and the Arms which he made use of for Conquest, were borrowed from those against whom he had a Design. The Arrow which he shot at the Soldier, was fledged from his own Plume of Feathers; the Dart he directed against the Man of Wit, was winged from the Quills he writ with; and that which he sent against those who presumed upon their Riches, was headed with Gold out of their Treasuries: He made Nets for Statesmen from their own Contrivances; he took Fire from the Eyes of Ladies, with which he melted their Hearts; and Lightning from the Tongues of the Eloquent, to enflame them with their own Glories. At the Foot of the Throne sat three false Graces; *Flattery* with a Shell of Paint, *Affectation* with a Mirrour to practise at, and *Fashion* ever changing the Posture of her Cloaths. These applied themselves to secure the Conquests which *Self-Conceit* had gotten, and had each of them their particular Polities. *Flattery* gave new Colours and Complections to all things, *Affectation* new Airs and Appearances, which, as she said, were not vulgar, and *Fashion* both concealed some home Defects, and added some foreign external Beauties.

As I was reflecting upon what I saw, I heard a Voice in the Crowd, bemoaning the Condition of Mankind, which is thus managed by the Breath of *Opinion*, deluded by *Errour*, fired by *Self-Conceit*, and given up to be trained in all the Courses of *Vanity*, 'till *Scorn* or *Poverty* come upon us. These Expressions were no sooner handed about, but I immediately saw a General Disorder, 'till at last there was a parting in one Place, and a grave old Man, decent and resolute, was led forward to be punished for the Words he had uttered. He appeared inclined to have spoken in his own Defence, but I could not observe that any one was willing to hear him. *Vanity* cast a scornful Smile at him; *Self-Conceit* was angry; *Flattery*, who knew him for *Plain-dealing*, put on a *Vizard*, and turned away; *Affectation* tossed her Fan, made Mouths, and called him *Envy* or *Slander*; and Fashion would have it, that at least he must be *Ill-Manners*. Thus slighted and despised by all, he was driven out for abusing People of Merit and Figure; and I heard it firmly resolved, that he should be used no better wherever they met with him hereafter.

I had already seen the Meaning of most part of that Warning which he had given, and was considering how the latter Words should be fulfilled, when a mighty Noise was heard without, and the Door was blackned by a numerous Train of Harpies crowding in upon us. *Folly* and *Broken Credit* were seen in the House before they entered, *Trouble, Shame, Infamy, Scorn* and *Poverty* brought up the Rear. *Vanity*, with her *Cupid* and *Graces*, disappeared; her Subjects ran into Holes and Corners; but many of them were found and carried off (as I was told by one who stood near me) either to Prisons or Cellars, Solitude, or little Company, the mean Arts or the viler Crafts of Life. But these, added he with a disdainful Air, are such who would fondly live here, when their Merits neither matched the Lustre of the Place, nor their Riches its Expences. We have seen such Scenes as these before now; the Glory you saw will all return when the Hurry is over. I thanked him for his

Information, and believing him so incorrigible as that he would stay 'till it was his Turn to be taken, I made off to the Door, and overtook some few, who, though they would not hearken to *Plain-dealing*, were now terrified to good purpose by the Example of others: But when they had touched the Threshold, it was a strange Shock to them to find that the Delusion of *Errour* was gone, and they plainly discerned the Building to hang a little up in the Air without any real Foundation. At first we saw nothing but a desperate Leap remained for us, and I a thousand times blamed my unmeaning Curiosity that had brought me into so much Danger. But as they began to sink lower in their own Minds, methought the Palace sunk along with us, 'till they were arrived at the due Point of *Esteem* which they ought to have for themselves; then the Part of the Building in which they stood touched the Earth, and we departing out, it retired from our Eyes. Now, whether they who stayed in the Palace were sensible of this Descent, I cannot tell; it was then my Opinion that they were not. However it be, my Dream broke up at it, and has given me Occasion all my Life to reflect upon the fatal Consequences of following the Suggestions of *Vanity*.

'*Mr.* Spectator,

I write to you to desire, that you would again touch upon a certain Enormity, which is chiefly in Use among the politer and better-bred Part of Mankind: I mean the Ceremonies, Bows, Curtsies, Whisperings, Smiles, Winks, Nods, with other familiar Arts of Salutation, which take up in our Churches so much Time, that might be better employed, and which seem so utterly inconsistent with the Duty and true Intent of our entring into those Religious Assemblies. The Resemblance which this bears to our indeed proper Behaviour in Theatres, may be some Instance of its Incongruity in the above-mentioned Places. In *Roman* Catholick Churches and Chappels abroad, I my self have observed, more than once, Persons of the first Quality, of the nearest Relation, and intimatest Acquaintance, passing by one another unknowing as it were, and unknown, and with so little Notices of each other, that it looked like having their Minds more suitably and more solemnly engaged; at least it was an Acknowledgment that they ought to have been so. I have been told the same even of the *Mahometans*, with relation to the Propriety of their Demeanour in the Conventions of their erroneous Worship: And I cannot but think either of them sufficient and laudable Patterns of our Imitation in this Particular.

I cannot help upon this Occasion remarking on the excellent

Memoirs of those Devotionists, who upon returning from Church shall give a particular Account how two or three hundred People were dressed; a Thing, by reason of its Variety, so difficult to be digested and fixed in the Head, that 'tis a Miracle to me how two poor Hours of Divine Service can be Time sufficient for so elaborate an Undertaking, the Duty of the Place too being jointly and, no doubt, oft pathetically performed along with it. Where it is said in Sacred Writ, that *the Woman ought to have a Covering on her Head, because of the Angels,* that last Word is by some thought to be metaphorically used, and to signifie young Men. Allowing this Interpretation to be right, the Text may not appear to be wholly foreign to our present Purpose.

When you are in a Disposition proper for writing on such a Subject, I earnestly recommend this to you, and am,

Sir,

T   *Your very humble Servant.'*

No. 461.
[STEELE.]   Tuesday, August 19.

. . . Sed non ego credulus illis.—Virg.

For want of Time to substitute something else in the Room of them, I am at present obliged to publish Compliments above my Desert in the following Letters. It is no small Satisfaction, to have given Occasion to ingenious Men to employ their Thoughts upon sacred Subjects from the Approbation of such Pieces of Poetry as they have seen in my *Saturday's* Papers. I shall never publish Verse on that Day but what is written by the same Hand; yet shall I not accompany those Writings with *Eulogiums*, but leave them to speak for themselves.

' For the SPECTATOR.

Mr. SPECTATOR,

You very much promote the Interests of Virtue, while you reform the Taste of a profane Age, and perswade us to be entertained with Divine Poems. While we are distinguished by so many thousand Humours, and split into so many different Sects and Parties, yet Persons of every Party, Sect, and Humour are fond of conforming their Taste to yours. You can transfuse your own Relish of a Poem into all your Readers, according to their Capacity to receive; and when you recommend the pious Passion that reigns in the Verse, we seem to feel the Devotion, and grow proud and pleas'd inwardly, that we have Souls capable of relishing what the SPECTATOR approves.

Upon reading the Hymns that you have published in some late Papers, I had a mind to try Yesterday whether I could write one. The 114th *Psalm* appears to me an admirable Ode, and I began to turn it into our Language. As I was describing the Journey of *Israel* from *Egypt*, and added the Divine Presence amongst them, I perceived a Beauty in the *Psalm* which was entirely new to me, and which I was going to lose; and that is, that the Poet utterly conceals the Presence of God in the Beginning of it, and rather lets a possessive Pronoun go without a Substantive, than he will so much as mention any thing of Divinity there. Judah *was his Sanctuary, and* Israel *his Dominion or Kingdom.* The Reason now seems evident, and this Conduct necessary: For if God had appeared before, there could be no Wonder why the Mountains should leap and the Sea retire; therefore that this Convulsion of Nature may be brought in with due Surprise, his Name is not mentioned till afterward, and then with a very agreeable Turn of Thought God is introduced at once in all his Majesty. This is what I have attempted to imitate in a Translation without Paraphrase, and to preserve what I could of the Spirit of the sacred Author.

If the following Essay be not too incorrigible, bestow upon it a few Brightenings from your Genius, that I may learn how to write better, or to write no more.

Your daily Admirer,
and humble Servant, &c.'

PSALM CXIV.

I.

When Israel, freed from Pharaoh's *Hand,*
Left the proud Tyrant and his Land,
The Tribes with chearful Homage own
Their King, and Judah *was his Throne.*

II

Across the Deep their Journey lay,
The Deep divides to make them Way;
The Streams of Jordan *saw, and fled*
With backward Current to their Head.

III.

The Mountains shook like frighted Sheep,
Like Lambs the little Hillocks leap;
Not Sinai *on her Base could stand,*
Conscious of Sovereign Power at hand.

IV.

What Power could make the Deep divide?
Make Jordan *backward roll his Tide?*
Why did ye leap, ye little Hills?
And whence the Fright that Sinai *feels?*

V.

Let every Mountain, every Flood
Retire, and know th' approaching God,
The King of Israel: *See him here;*
Tremble thou Earth, adore and fear.

VI.

He thunders, and all Nature mourns;
The Rock to standing Pools he turns;
Flints spring with Fountains at his Word,
And Fires and Seas confess their Lord.

' *Mr.* Spectator,

There are those who take the Advantage of your putting an Half-penny Value upon your self above the rest of our daily Writers, to defame you in publick Conversation, and strive to make you unpopular upon the Account of the said Half-penny. But if I were you, I would insist upon that small Acknowledgment for the superior Merit of yours, as being a Work of Invention. Give me Leave therefore to do you Justice, and say in your Behalf what you cannot your self, which is, That your Writings have made Learning a more necessary Part of good Breeding than it was before you appeared: That Modesty is become fashionable, and Impudence stands in need of some Wit, since you have put them both in their proper Lights. Profaneness, Lewdness, and Debauchery are not now Qualifications, and a Man may be a very fine Gentleman, tho' he is neither a Keeper nor an Infidel.

I would have you tell the Town the Story of the *Sibyls,* if they deny giving you Two-pence. Let them know, that those sacred Papers were valued at the same Rate after two Thirds of them were destroyed, as when there was the whole Set. There are so many of us who will give you your own Price, that you may acquaint your Non-Conformist Readers, That they shall not have it, except they come in within such a Day, under Three-pence.   I don't know but you might bring in the *Date Obolum Bellisario* with a good Grace.   The Witlings come in Clusters to two or three Coffee-houses which have left you off, and I hope you will make us, who fine to your Wit, merry with their Characters who stand out against it.

I am your most humble Servant.

P.S. I have lately got the ingenious Authors of Blacking for Shooes, Powder for colouring the Hair, Pomatum for the Hands, Cosmetick for the Face, to be your constant Customers; so that your Advertisements will as much adorn the outward Man, as your Paper does the inward.'   T

No. 462.
[STEELE.]   Wednesday, August 20.

Nil ego contulerim jucundo sanus amico.—Hor.

PEOPLE are not aware of the very great Force which Pleasantry in Company has upon all those with whom a Man of that Talent converses.   His Faults are generally over-looked by all his Acquaintance, and a certain Carelessness that constantly attends all his Actions, carries him on with greater Success, than Diligence and Assiduity does others who have no Share of this Endowment.   *Dacinthus* breaks his Word upon all Occasions both trivial and important; and when he is sufficiently railed at for that abominable Quality, they who talk of him end with, *After all he is a very pleasant Fellow.   Dacinthus* is an ill-natured Husband, and yet the very Women end their Freedom of Discourse upon this Subject, *But after all he is very pleasant Company.   Dacinthus* is neither in point of Honour, Civility, good Breeding, or good Nature unexceptionable, and yet all is answer'd, *For he is a very pleasant Fellow.*   When this Quality is conspicuous in a Man who has, to accompany it, manly and virtuous Sentiments, there cannot certainly be any thing which can give so pleasing Gratification as the Gaiety of such a Person; but when it is alone, and serves only to gild a Crowd of ill Qualities, there is no Man so much to be avoided as your pleasant Fellow.   A very pleasant Fellow shall turn your good Name to a Jest, make your Character contemptible, debauch your Wife or Daughter, and yet be received by the rest of the World with Welcome where-ever he appears.   It is very ordinary with those of this Character to be attentive only to their own Satisfactions, and have very little Bowels for the Concerns or Sorrows of other Men; nay, they are capable of purchasing their own Pleasures at the Expence of giving Pain to others. But they who do not consider this Sort of Men thus carefully, are irresistibly expos'd to his Insinuations. The Author of the following Letter carries the Matter so high, as to intimate that the Liberties of *England* have been at the Mercy of a Prince merely as he was of this pleasant Character.

'*Mr.* SPECTATOR,

There is no one Passion which all Mankind so naturally give into as Pride, nor any other Passion which appears in such different Disguises: It is to be found in all Habits and all Complections. Is it not a Question, Whether it does more Harm or Good in the World? And if there be not such a Thing as what we may call a virtuous and laudable Pride?

It is this Passion alone, when misapplyed, that lays us so open to Flatterers; and he who can agreeably condescend to sooth our Humour or Temper, finds always an open Avenue to our Soul; especially if the Flatterer happen to be our Superior.

One might give many Instances of this in a late *English* Monarch, under the Title of *The Gayeties of King* Charles II. This Prince was by Nature extreamly familiar, of very easie Access, and much delighted to see and be seen; and this happy Temper, which in the highest Degree gratified his People's Vanity, did him more Service with his loving Subjects than all his other Virtues, tho' it must be confessed he had many. He delighted, tho' a mighty King, to give and take a Jest, as they say; and a Prince of this fortunate Disposition, who were inclined to make an ill Use of his Power, may have any thing of his People, be it never so much to their Prejudice. But this good King made generally a very innocent Use, as to the Publick, of this ensnaring Temper; for, 'tis well known, he pursued Pleasure more than Ambition: He seemed to glory in being the first Man at Cock-matches, Horse-races, Balls, and Plays; he appeared highly delighted on those Occasions, and never failed to warm and gladden the Heart of every Spectator. He more than once dined with his good Citizens of *London* on their Lord-Mayor's Day, and did so the Year that Sir *Robert Viner* was Mayor. Sir *Robert* was a very Loyal Man, and if you will allow the Expression, very fond of his Sovereign; but what with the Joy he felt at Heart for the Honour done him by his Prince, and thro' the Warmth he was in with continual toasting Healths to the Royal Family, his Lordship grew a little fond of his Majesty, and entered into a Familiarity not altogether so graceful in so publick a Place. The King understood very well how to extricate himself on all kinds of Difficulties, and with an Hint to the Company to avoid Ceremony, stole off, and made towards his Coach, which stood ready for him in *Guildhall* Yard: But the Mayor liked his Company so well, and was grown so intimate, that he pursued him hastily, and catching him fast by the Hand, cried out with a vehement Oath and Accent, *Sir, you shall stay and take t'other Bottle.* The airy Monarch looked kindly at him over his Shoulder, and with a Smile and graceful Air, (for I saw him at the Time, and do now) repeated this Line of the old Song:

He that's drunk is as great as a King.

and immediately returned back and complied with his Landlord,

I give you this Story, Mr. SPECTATOR, because as I said, I saw the Passage; and I assure you it's very true, and yet no common one; and when I tell you the Sequel, you will say I have yet a better Reason for't. This very Mayor afterwards erected the Statue of his merry Monarch in *Stocks-Market*, and did the Crown many and great Services; and it was owing to this Humour of the King, that his Family had so great a Fortune shut up in the Exchequer of their pleasant Sovereign. The many good-natured Condescensions of this Prince are vulgarly known; and it is excellently said of him by a great Hand which writ his Character, *That he was not a King a Quarter of an Hour together in his whole Reign.* He would receive visits even from Fools and half Mad-men, and at Times I have met with People who have box'd, fought at Back-sword, and taken Poison before King *Charles* II. In a Word, he was so pleasant a Man, that no one could be sorrowful under his Government. This made him capable of baffling, with the greatest Ease imaginable, all Suggestions of Jealousie, and the People could not entertain Notions of any thing terrible in him, whom they saw every way agreeable. This Scrap of the familiar Part of that Prince's History I thought fit to send you, in compliance to the Request you lately made to your Correspondents.

I am, Sir,

T   *Your most Humble Servant.*'

No. 463.

[ADDISON.]   Thursday, August 21.

> *Omnia quae sensu volvuntur vota diurno,*
> *Pectore sopito reddit amica quies.*
> *Venator defessa toro cum membra reponit,*
> *Mens tamen ad silvas & sua lustra redit.*
> *Judicibus lites, aurigae somnia currus,*
> *Vanaque nocturnis meta cavetur equis. . . .*
> *Me quoque Musarum studium sub nocte silenti*
> *Artibus assuetis sollicitare solet.*—Claud.

I WAS lately entertaining myself with comparing *Homer's* Ballance, in which *Jupiter* is represented as weighing the Fates of *Hector* and *Achilles*, with a Passage of *Virgil*, wherein that Deity is introduced as weighing the Fates of *Turnus* and *Aeneas*. I then considered, how the same way of thinking prevailed in the Eastern Parts of the World, as in those noble Passages of Scripture, wherein we are told, that the great King of *Babylon*, the Day before his Death, had been weighed in the Ballance, and been found wanting. In other Places of the Holy Writings, the Almighty is described as weighing the Mountains in Scales, making the weight for the Winds, knowing the Ballancings of the Clouds, and, in others, as weighing the Actions of Men, and laying their Calamities together in a Ballance. *Milton*, as I have observed in a former Paper, had an Eye to several of these foregoing Instances, in that beautiful Description wherein he represents the Arch-Angel and the Evil Spirit as addressing themselves for the Combat, but parted by the Ballance which appeared in the Heavens and weighed the Consequences of such a Battel.

> *Th' Eternal to prevent such horrid fray,*
> *Hung forth in Heav'n his golden Scales, yet seen*
> *Betwixt Astrea and the Scorpion Sign,*
> *Wherein all things created first he weigh'd,*
> *The pendulous round Earth with ballanc'd Air*
> *In counterpoise, now ponders all events,*
> *Battles and Realm; in these he put two weights,*
> *The sequel each of parting and of fight:*
> *The latter quick up flew, and kickt the beam:*
> *Which* Gabriel *spying, thus bespake the Fiend.*

> Satan *I know thy Strength, and thou know'st mine,*
> *Neither our own, but giv'n; what folly then*
> *To boast what Arms can do, since thine no more*
> *Than Heav'n permits, nor mine, tho' doubled now*
> *To trample thee as more: For proof look up,*
> *And read thy Lot in yon coelestial Sign,*

Where thou art weigh'd and shown how light, how weak,
If thou resist. The Fiend look'd up, and knew
His mounted Scale aloft; nor more; but fled
Murm'ring, and with him fled the Shades of Night.

These several amusing Thoughts having taken Possession of my Mind some time before I went to sleep, and mingling themselves with my ordinary Ideas, raised in my Imagination a very odd kind of Vision. I was, methought, replaced in my Study, and seated in my Elbow Chair, where I had indulged the foregoing Speculations, with my Lamp burning by me, as usual. Whilst I was here meditating on several Subjects of Morality, and considering the Nature of many Virtues and Vices, as Materials for those Discourses with which I daily entertain the Publick; I saw, methought, a Pair of Golden Scales hanging by a Chain of the same Metal over the Table that stood before me; when on a sudden, there were great Heaps of Weights thrown down on each side of them. I found, upon examining these Weights, they shewed the Value of every thing that is in Esteem among Men. I made an Essay of them, by putting the Weight of Wisdom in one Scale, and that of Riches in another, upon which the latter, to shew its comparative Lightness, immediately *flew up and kickt the Beam.*

But, before I proceed, I must inform my Reader, that these Weights did not exert their Natural Gravity, 'till they were laid in the Golden Ballance, insomuch that I could not guess which was light or heavy, whilst I held them in my Hand. This I found by several Instances, for upon my laying a Weight in one of the Scales, which was inscribed by the Word Eternity; tho' I threw in that of Time, Prosperity, Affliction, Wealth, Poverty, Interest, Success, with many other Weights, which in my Hand seemed very ponderous, they were not able to stir the opposite Ballance, nor could they have prevailed, tho' assisted with the Weight of the Sun, the Stars, and the Earth.

Upon emptying the Scales, I laid several Titles and Honours, with Pomps, Triumphs, and many Weights of the like Nature, in one of them, and seeing a little glittering Weight lie by me, I threw it accidentally into the other Scale, when, to my great Surprize, it proved so exact a Counterpoise, that it kept the Ballance in an Equilibrium. This little glittering Weight was inscribed upon the Edges of it with the Word *Vanity.* I found there were several other Weights which were equally Heavy, and exact Counterpoises to one another; a few of them I tried, as Avarice and Poverty, Riches and Content, with some others.

There were likewise several Weights that were of the same Figure, and seemed to Correspond with each other, but were entirely different when thrown into the Scales; as Religion and Hypocrisie, Pedantry and Learning, Wit and Vivacity, Superstition and Devotion, Gravity and Wisdom, with many others.

I observed one particular Weight lettered on both sides, and upon applying my self to the Reading of it, I found on one side, written, *In the Dialect of Men*, and underneath it *CALA-MITIES;* on the other side was written, *In the Language of the Gods*, and underneath *BLESSINGS*. I found the intrinsick Value of this Weight to be much greater than I imagined, for it over-powered Health, Wealth, Good Fortune, and many other Weights, which were much more ponderous in my Hand than the other.

There is a Saying among the *Scotch*, that an Ounce of Mother-Wit is worth a Pound of Clergy; I was sensible of the Truth of this Saying, when I saw the difference between the Weight of Natural Parts, and that of Learning. The Observation which I made upon these two Weights opened to me a new Field of Discoveries, for notwithstanding the weight of Natural Parts was much heavier than that of Learning, I observed that it weighed an hundred times heavier than it did before, when I put Learning into the same Scale with it. I made the same Observation upon Faith and Morality; for notwithstanding the latter out-weighed the former separately, it received a thousand times more additional weight from its Conjunction with the former, than what it had by it self. This odd Phaenomenon shewed it self in other Particulars, as in Wit and Judgment, Philosophy and Religion, Justice and Humanity, Zeal and Charity, Depth of Sense and Perspicuity of Stile, with innumerable other Particulars too long to be mentioned in this Paper.

As a Dream seldom fails of dashing Seriousness with Impertinence, Mirth with Gravity, methought I made several other Experiments of a more ludicrous Nature, by one of which I found that an *English* Octavo was very often heavier than a *French* Folio; and by another, that an old *Greek* or *Latin* Author weighed down a whole Library of Moderns. Seeing one of my *Spectators* lying by me, I laid it into one of the Scales and flung a two-penny Piece into the other. The Reader will not enquire into the Event, if he remembers the first Tryal which I have recorded in this Paper. I afterwards threw both the Sexes into the Ballance; but as it is not for my Interest to disoblige either of them, I shall desire to be excused from telling the Result of this Experiment. Having an Opportunity of this Nature in my Hands, I could not forbear throwing into one Scale the Principles of a Tory, and into the other those of a Whig; but as I have all along declared this to be a Neutral

Paper, I shall likewise desire to be silent under this Head also, tho' upon examining one of the Weights, I saw the Word *TEKEL* Engraven on it in Capital Letters.

I made many other Experiments, and tho' I have not room for them all in this Day's Speculation, I may perhaps reserve them for another. I shall only add, that upon my awaking I was sorry to find my Golden Scales vanished, but resolved for the future to learn this Lesson from them, not to despise or value any Things for their Appearances, but to regulate my Esteem and Passions towards them according to their real and intrinsick Value.   C

No. 464.
[ADDISON.]   Friday, August 22.

> *Auream quisquis mediocritatem*
> *Diligit, tutus caret obsoleti*
> *Sordibus tecti, caret invidenda*
> *Sobrius aula.*—Hor.

I am wonderfully pleased when I meet with any Passage in an old *Greek* or *Latin* Author, that is not blown upon, and which I have never met with in a Quotation. Of this kind is a Beautiful Saying in *Theognis. Vice is covered by Wealth, and Virtue by Poverty*; or to give it in the Verbal Translation, *Among Men there are some who have their Vices concealed by Wealth, and others who have their Virtues concealed by Poverty.* Every Man's Observation will supply him with Instances of Rich Men, who have several Faults and Defects that are overlooked, if not entirely hidden, by means of their Riches; and, I think, we cannot find a more Natural Description of a Poor Man, whose Merits are lost in his Poverty, than that in the Words of the Wise Man. *There was a little City, and few Men within it; and there came a great King against it, and besieged it, and built great Bulwarks against it: Now there was found in it a poor Wise Man, and he, by his Wisdom, delivered the City; yet no Man remembred that same poor Man. Then said I, Wisdom is better than Strength; nevertheless, the poor Man's Wisdom is despised, and his Words are not heard.*

The middle Condition seems to be the most advantageously situated for the gaining of Wisdom. Poverty turns our Thoughts too much upon the supplying of our Wants, and Riches upon enjoying our Superfluities; and as *Cowley* has said in another Case, *It is hard for a Man to keep a steady Eye upon Truth, who is always in a Battel or a Triumph.*

If we regard Poverty and Wealth, as they are apt to produce Virtues or Vices in the Mind of Man, one may observe that there is a Set of each of these growing out of Poverty, quite different from that which rises out of Wealth. Humility and Patience, Industry and Temperance, are very often the good Qualities of a poor Man. Humanity and Good-nature, Magnanimity, and a Sense of Honour, are as often the Qualifications of the Rich. On the contrary, Poverty is apt to betray a Man into Envy, Riches into Arrogance; Poverty is too often attended with Fraud, vicious Compliance, Repining, Murmur and Discontent. Riches expose a Man to Pride and Luxury, a foolish Elation of Heart, and too great a Fondness for the present World. In short, the middle Condition is most eligible to the Man who would improve himself in Virtue; as I have before shown, it is the most advantageous for the gaining of Knowledge. It was upon this Consideration that *Agur* founded his Prayer, which for the Wisdom of it is recorded in Holy Writ. *Two things have I required of thee, deny me them not before I dye. Remove far from me Vanity and Lies; give me neither Poverty, nor Riches; feed me with Food convenient for me. Lest I be full and deny thee, and say, who is the Lord? or lest I be poor and steal, and take the name of my God in vain.*

I shall fill the remaining Part of my Paper with a very pretty Allegory, which is wrought into a Play by *Aristophanes* the *Greek* Comedian. It seems originally designed as a Satyr upon the Rich, though, in some Parts of it, 'tis like the foregoing Discourse, a Kind of Comparison between Wealth and Poverty.

Chremylus, who was an old and a Good Man, and withal exceeding Poor, being desirous to leave some Riches to his Son, consults the Oracle of *Apollo* upon the Subject. The Oracle bids him follow the first Man he should see upon his going out of the Temple. The Person he chanced to see was to Appearance an old sordid blind Man, but upon his following him from Place to Place, he at last found by his own Confession, that he was *Plutus* the God of Riches, and that he was just come out of the House of a Miser. *Plutus* further told him, that when he was a Boy he used to declare, that as soon as he came to Age he would distribute Wealth to none but virtuous and just Men; upon which *Jupiter*, considering the pernicious Consequences of such a Resolution, took his Sight away from him, and left him to strole about the World in the Blind Condition wherein *Chremylus* beheld him. With much ado *Chremylus* prevailed upon him to go to his House, where he met an old Woman in a tattered Raiment, who had been his Guest for many Years, and whose Name was *Poverty*. The old Woman refusing to turn out so easily as he would have her, he threatned to banish her not only from his own House, but out of all *Greece*, if she made any more Words upon the Matter. *Poverty* on this Occasion pleads her Cause very notably, and represents to her old Landlord, that should she be driven out of the Country, all their Trades, Arts and Sciences would be driven out with her; and that if every one was Rich, they would never be supplied with those Pomps, Ornaments and Conveniencies of Life which made Riches desirable. She likewise represented to him the several Advantages which she bestowed upon her Votaries, in Regard to their Shape, their Health, and their Activity, by preserving them from Gouts, Dropsies, Unwieldiness, and Intemperance. But whatever she had to say for her self, she was at last forced to Troop off. *Chremylus* immediately considered how he might restore *Plutus* to his Sight; and in order to it conveyed him to the Temple of *Esculapius*, who was famous for Cures and Miracles of this Nature. By this means the Deity recovered his Eyes, and begun to make a right use of them, by enriching every one that was distinguished by Piety towards the Gods, and Justice towards Men; and at the same time by taking away his Gifts from the Impious and Undeserving. This produces several merry Incidents, 'till in the last Act *Mercury* descends with great Complaints from the Gods, that since the Good Men were grown Rich they had received no Sacrifices, which is confirmed by a Priest of *Jupiter*, who enters with a Remonstrance, that since this late Innovation he was reduced to a Starving Condition, and could not live upon his Office. *Chremylus*, who in the beginning of the Play was Religious in his Poverty, concludes it with a Proposal which was relished by all the Good Men who were now grown Rich as well as himself, that they should carry *Plutus* in a Solemn Procession to the Temple, and Install him in the place of *Jupiter*. This Allegory instructed the *Athenians* in two Points; first, as it vindicated the Conduct of Providence in its ordinary Distributions of Wealth; and in the next place, as it showed the great Tendency of Riches to corrupt the Morals of those who possessed them.   C

No. 465.

[ADDISON.]   Saturday, August 23.

> *Qua ratione queas traducere leniter aevum :*
> *Ne te semper inops agitet vexetque cupido,*
> *Ne pavor & rerum mediocriter utilium spes.*—Hor.

HAVING endeavoured in my last *Saturday*'s Paper to shew the great Excellency of Faith, I shall here consider what are the

proper Means of strengthning and confirming it in the Mind
of Man. Those who delight in reading Books of controversie,
which are written on both sides of the Question in Points of
Faith, do very seldom arrive at a fixed and settled Habit of it.
They are one Day entirely convinced of its important Truths,
and the next meet with something that shakes and disturbs
them. The Doubt which was laid revives again, and shews
it self in new Difficulties, and that generally for this Reason,
because the Mind which is perpetually tost in Controversies
and Disputes, is apt to forget the Reasons which had once set
it at rest, and to be disquieted with any former Perplexity,
when it appears in a new Shape, or is started by a different
Hand. As nothing is more laudable than an Enquiry after
Truth, so nothing is more irrational than to pass away our
whole Lives, without determining our selves one way or other
in those Points which are of the last Importance to us. There
are indeed many things from which we may with-hold our
Assent; but in Cases by which we are to regulate our Lives, it
is the greatest Absurdity to be wavering and unsettled, without closing with that Side which appears the most safe and
the most probable. The first Rule therefore which I shall lay
down is this, that when by Reading or Discourse we find ourselves thoroughly convinced of the Truth of any Article, and
of the Reasonableness of our Belief in it, we should never after
suffer ourselves to call it into question. We may perhaps
forget the Arguments which occasioned our Conviction, but
we ought to remember the Strength they had with us, and
therefore still to retain the Conviction which they once produced. This is no more than what we do in every common
Art or Science, nor is it possible to act otherwise, considering
the Weakness and Limitation of our intellectual Faculties.
It was thus, that *Latimer*, one of the glorious Army of Martyrs
who introduced the Reformation in *England*, behaved himself
in that great Conference which was managed between the
most learned among the Protestants and Papists in the Reign
of Queen *Mary*. This venerable old Man knowing how his
Abilities were impaired by Age, and that it was impossible for
him to recollect all those Reasons which had directed him
in the Choice of his Religion, left his Companions who were
in the full Possession of their Parts and Learning, to baffle
and confound their Antagonists by the Force of Reason. As
for himself he only repeated to his Adversaries the Articles in
which he firmly believed, and in the Profession of which he was
determined to die. It is in this manner that the Mathematician
proceeds upon Propositions which he has once demonstrated,
and though the Demonstration may have slipt out of his

Memory, he builds upon the Truth, because he knows it was demonstrated. This Rule is absolutely necessary for weaker Minds, and in some measure for Men of the greatest Abilities; but to these last I would propose, in the second place, that they should lay up in their Memories, and always keep by them in a readiness, those Arguments which appear to them of the greatest Strength, and which cannot be got over by all the Doubts and Cavils of Infidelity.

But, in the third place, there is nothing which strengthens Faith more than Morality. Faith and Morality naturally produce each other. A Man is quickly convinced of the Truth of Religion, who finds it is not against his Interest that it should be true. The Pleasure he receives at present, and the Happiness which he promises himself from it hereafter, will both dispose him very powerfully to give Credit to it, according to the ordinary Observation that *we are easie to believe what we wish.* It is very certain, that a Man of sound Reason cannot forbear closing with Religion upon an impartial Examination of it; but at the same time it is certain, that Faith is kept alive in us, and gathers Strength from Practice more than from Speculation.

There is still another Method which is more Persuasive than any of the former, and that is an habitual Adoration of the Supreme Being, as well in constant Acts of Mental Worship, as in outward Forms. The Devout Man does not only believe but feels there is a Deity. He has actual Sensations of him; his Experience concurs with his Reason; he sees him more and more in all his Intercourses with him, and even in this Life almost loses his Faith in Conviction.

The last Method which I shall mention for the giving Life to a Man's Faith, is frequent Retirement from the World, accompanied with religious Meditation. When a Man thinks of any thing in the Darkness of the Night, whatever deep Impressions it may make in his Mind, they are apt to vanish as soon as the Day breaks about him. The Light and Noise of the Day, which are perpetually solliciting his Senses, and calling off his Attention, wear out of his Mind the Thoughts that imprinted themselves in it, with so much Strength, during the Silence and Darkness of the Night. A Man finds the same difference as to himself in a Crowd and in a Solitude; the Mind is stunned and dazzled amidst that variety of Objects which press upon her in a great City. She cannot apply her self to the Consideration of those things which are of the utmost Concern to her. The Cares or Pleasures of the World strike in with every Thought, and a Multitude of vicious Examples give a kind of Justification to our Folly. In our Retirements every thing disposes us to be serious. In Courts and Cities we are entertained with the Works of Men, in the Country with those of God. One is the Province of Art, the other of Nature. Faith and Devotion naturally grow in the Mind of every reasonable Man, who sees the Impressions of Divine Power and Wisdom in every Object on which he casts his Eye. The Supream Being has made the best Arguments for his own Existence, in the Formation of the Heavens and the Earth, and these are Arguments which a Man of Sense cannot forbear attending to, who is out of the Noise and Hurry of human Affairs. *Aristotle* says, that should a Man live under Ground, and there converse with Works of Art and Mechanism, and should afterwards be brought up into the open Day, and see the several Glories of the Heav'n and Earth, he would immediately pronounce them the Works of such a Being as we define God to be. The Psalmist has very beautiful Strokes of Poetry to this purpose, in that exalted Strain; *The Heavens declare the Glory of God; And the Firmament sheweth his handy Work. One Day telleth another: And one Night certifieth another. There is neither Speech nor Language: But their Voices are heard among them. Their Sound is gone out into all Lands: And their Words into the Ends of the World.* As such a bold and sublime Manner of Thinking furnishes very noble Matter for an Ode, the Reader may see it wrought into the following one.

I.

The Spacious Firmament on high,
With all the blue Etherial Sky,
And spangled Heav'ns, a Shining Frame,
Their great Original proclaim:
Th' unwearied Sun, from Day to Day,
Does his Creator's Power display,
And publishes to every Land
The Work of an Almighty Hand.

II.

Soon as the Evening Shades prevail,
The Moon takes up the wondrous Tale,
And nightly to the listning Earth
Repeats the Story of her Birth:
Whilst all the Stars that round her burn,
And all the Planets in their turn,
Confirm the Tidings as they rowl,
And spread the Truth from Pole to Pole.

III.

What though, in solemn Silence, all
Move round the dark terrestrial Ball?
What tho' nor real Voice nor Sound
Amid their radiant Orbs be found?
In Reason's Ear they all rejoice,
And utter forth a glorious Voice,
For ever singing, as they shine,
'The Hand that made us is Divine.'

C

No. 466.
[STEELE.]   Monday, August 25.

 . . . *Vera incessu patuit dea.*—Virg.

WHEN *Aeneas*, the Hero of *Virgil*, is lost in the Wood, and a
perfect Stranger in the Place on which he is landed, he is
accosted by a Lady in an Habit for the Chace. She enquires
of him, Whether he has seen pass by that Way any young
Woman dressed as she was? Whether she were following the
Sport in the Wood, or any other way employed, according
to the Custom of Huntresses? The Hero answers with the
Respect due to the beautiful Appearance she made; tells her,
He saw no such Person as she enquired for; but intimates that
he knows her to be of the Deities, and desires she would conduct a Stranger. Her Form from her first Appearance mani-
fested she was more than Mortal; but tho' she was certainly a
Goddess, the Poet does not make her known to be the Goddess
of *Beauty* till she moved: All the Charms of an agreeable Person
are then in their highest Exertion, every Limb and Feature
appears with its respective Grace. It is from this Observation,
that I cannot help being so passionate an Admirer as I am of
good Dancing. As all Art is an Imitation of Nature, this is an
Imitation of Nature in its highest Excellence, and at a Time
when she is most agreeable. The Business of Dancing is to
display Beauty, and for that Reason all Distortions and
Mimickries, as such, are what raise Aversion instead of Pleasure: But Things that are in themselves excellent, are ever
attended with Imposture and false Imitation. Thus, as in
poetry there are laborious Fools who write Anagrams and
Acrosticks, there are Pretenders in Dancing, who think merely
to do what others cannot, is to excel. Such Creatures should
be rewarded like him who had acquired a Knack of throwing
a Grain of Corn through the Eye of a Needle, with a Bushel
to keep his Hand in Use. The Dancers on our Stages are very
faulty in this Kind; and what they mean by writhing them-

selves into such Postures, as it would be a Pain for any of the Spectators to stand in, and yet hope to please those Spectators, is unintelligible. Mr. *Prince* has a Genius, if he were encouraged, would prompt him to better Things. In all the Dances he invents, you see he keeps close to the Characters he represents. He does not hope to please by making his Performers move in a Manner in which no one else ever did, but by Motions proper to the Characters he represents. He gives to Clowns and Lubbards clumsie Graces, that is, he makes them practise what they would think Graces: And I have seen Dances of his, which might give Hints that would be useful to a Comick Writer. These Performances have pleas'd the Taste of such as have not Reflection enough to know their Excellence, because they are in Nature; and the distorted Motions of others have offended those, who could not form Reasons to themselves for their Displeasure, from their being a Contradiction to Nature.

When one considers the inexpressible Advantage there is in arriving at some Excellence in this Art, it is monstrous to behold it so much neglected. The following Letter has in it something very natural on this Subject.

'Mr. SPECTATOR,

I am a Widower with but one Daughter; she was by Nature much enclined to be a Romp, and I had no Way of Educating her, but commanding a young Woman, whom I entertained to take Care of her, to be very watchful in her Care and Attendance about her. I am a Man of Business, and obliged to be much abroad. The Neighbours have told me, that in my Absence our Maid has let in the spruce Servants in the Neighbourhood to Junketings, while my Girl played and romped even in the Street. To tell you the plain Truth, I catched her once, at eleven Years old, at Chuck-Farthing among the Boys. This put me upon new Thoughts about my Child, and I determined to place her at a Boarding-School, and at the same time gave a very discreet young Gentlewoman her Maintenance at the same Place and Rate, to be her Companion. I took little Notice of my Girl from Time to Time, but saw her now and then in good Health, out of Harm's way, and was satisfied. But by much Importunity, I was lately prevailed with to go to one of their Balls. I cannot express to you the Anxiety my silly Heart was in, when I saw my Romp, now fifteen, taken out: I never felt the Pangs of a Father upon me so strongly in my whole Life before; and I could not have suffered more, had my whole Fortune been at Stake. My Girl came on with the most becoming Modesty I had ever seen, and casting a respectful Eye, as if she feared me more than all the Audience, I gave a Nod, which, I think, gave her all the Spirit she assumed upon it, but she rose properly to that Dignity of Aspect. My Romp, now the most graceful Person of her Sex, assumed a Majesty which commanded the highest Respect; and when she turned to me, and saw my Face in Rapture, she fell into the prettiest Smile, and I saw in all her Motion that she exulted in her Father's Satisfaction. You, Mr. SPECTATOR, will, better than I can tell you, imagine to your self all the different Beauties and Changes of Aspect in an accomplished young Woman, setting forth all her Beauties with a Design to please no one so much as her Father. My Girl's Lover can never know half the Satisfaction that I did in her that Day. I could not possibly have imagined, that so great Improvement could have been wrought by an Art that I always held in it self ridiculous and contemptible. There is, I am convinced, no Method like this, to give young Women a Sense of their own Value and Dignity; and I am sure there can be none so expeditious to communicate that Value to others. As for the flippant insipidly Gay, and wantonly Forward, whom you behold among Dancers, that Carriage is more to be attributed to the perverse Genius of the Performers, than imputed to the Art it self. For my Part, my Child has danced her self into my Esteem, and I have as great an Honour for her as ever I had for her Mother, from whom she derived those latent good Qualities which appeared in her Countenance, when she was dancing; for my Girl, tho' I say it my self, shewed in one Quarter of an Hour the innate Principles of a modest Virgin, a tender Wife, a generous Friend, a kind Mother, and an indulgent Mistress. I 'll strain hard but I will purchase for her an Husband suitable to her Merit. I am your Convert in the Admiration of what I thought you jested when you recommended; and if you please to be at my House on *Thursday* next, I make a Ball for my Daughter, and you shall see her Dance, or, if you will do her that Honour, Dance with her.

I am, Sir, Your most humble Servant,

PHILIPATER.'

I have some Time ago spoken of a Treatise written by Mr. *Weaver* on this Subject, which is now, I understand, ready to be published. This Work sets this Matter in a very plain and advantageous Light; and I am convinced from it, that if the Art was under proper Regulations, it would be a mechanick way of implanting insensibly in Minds, not capable of receiving it so well by any other Rules, a Sense of good Breeding and Virtue.

Were any one to see *Mariamne* Dance, let him be never so sensual a Brute, I defie him to entertain any Thoughts but of the highest Respect and Esteem towards her. I was shewed last Week a Picture in a Lady's Closet, for which she had an hundred different Dresses, that she could clap on round the Face, on purpose to demonstrate the force of Habits in the diversity of the same Countenance. Motion, and change of Posture and Aspect, has an Effect no less surprising on the Person of *Mariamne* when she Dances.

Chloe is extreamly pretty, and as silly as she is pretty. This Ideot has a very good Ear, and a most agreeable Shape; but the Folly of the Thing is such, that it Smiles so impertinently, and affects to please so sillily, that while she Dances you see the Simpleton from Head to Foot. For you must know (as trivial as this Art is thought to be) no one ever was a good Dancer, that had not a good Understanding. If this be a Truth, I shall leave the Reader to judge from that Maxim, what Esteem they ought to have for such Impertinents as fly, hop, caper, tumble, twirl, turn round, and jump over their Heads, and, in a word, play a thousand Pranks which many Animals can do better than a Man, instead of performing to Perfection what the human Figure only is capable of Performing.

It may perhaps appear odd, that I, who set up for a mighty Lover, at least, of Virtue, should take so much Pains to recommend what the soberer Part of Mankind look upon to be a Trifle; but, under Favour of the soberer Part of Mankind, I think they have not enough considered this Matter, and for that Reason only disesteem it. I must also, in my own Justification say, that I attempt to bring into the Service of Honour and Virtue every Thing in Nature that can pretend to give elegant Delight. It may possibly be proved, that Vice is in it self destructive of Pleasure, and Virtue in it self conducive to it. If the Delights of a free Fortune were under proper Regulations, this Truth would not want much Argument to support it; but it would be obvious to every Man, that there is a strict Affinity between all Things that are truly laudable and beautiful, from the highest Sentiment of the Soul, to the most indifferent Gesture of the Body. **T**

No. 467.

Tuesday, August 26.

> . . . *Quodcunque meae poterunt audere Camoenae,*
> **Seu tibi par poterunt, seu, quod spes abnuit, ultra,**
> *Sive minus, certeque canent minus, omne vovemus*
> *Hoc tibi, nec tanto careat mihi nomine charta.*
> —Tibull. ad Messalam.

THE Love of Praise is a Passion deeply fixed in the Mind of every extraordinary Person, and those who are most affected with it, seem most to partake of that Particle of the Divinity which distinguishes Mankind from the inferior Creation. The Supream Being it self is most pleased with Praise and Thanksgiving; the other Part of our Duty is but an Acknowledgment of our Faults, whilst this is the immediate Adoration of his Perfections. 'Twas an excellent Observation, That we then only despise Commendation when we cease to deserve it; and we have still extant two Orations of *Tully* and *Pliny*, spoken to the greatest and best Princes of all the *Roman* Emperors, who, no doubt, heard with the greatest Satisfaction, what even the most disinterested Persons, and at so large a Distance of Time, cannot read without Admiration. *Caesar* thought his Life consisted in the Breath of Praise, when he profess'd he had lived long enough for himself when he had for his Glory; others have sacrificed themselves for a Name which was not to begin till they were dead, giving away themselves to purchase a Sound which was not to commence till they were out of hearing: But by Merit and superior Excellencies not only to gain, but, whilst living, to enjoy a great and universal Reputation, is the last Degree of Happiness which we can hope for here. Bad Characters are dispers'd abroad with Profusion, I hope for Example Sake, and (as Punishments are designed by the Civil Power) more for the deterring the Innocent, than the chastising the Guilty. The Good are less frequent, whether it be that there are indeed fewer Originals of this Kind to copy after, or that, thro' the Malignity of our Nature, we rather delight in the Ridicule than the Virtues we find in others. However, it is but just, as well as pleasing, even for Variety, sometimes to give the World a Representation of the bright Side of human Nature, as well as the dark and gloomy: The Desire of Imitation may, perhaps, be a greater Incentive to the Practice of what is good, than the Aversion we may conceive at what is blameable; the one immediately directs you what you should do, whilst the other only shews you what you should avoid: And I cannot at present do this with more Satisfaction, than by endeavouring to do some Justice to the Character of *Manilius*.

It would far exceed my present Design, to give a particular Description of *Manilius* thro' all the Parts of his excellent Life: I shall now only draw him in his Retirement, and pass over in Silence the various Arts, the courtly Manners, and the undesigning Honesty by which he attained the Honours he has enjoyed, and which now give a Dignity and Veneration to the Ease he does enjoy. 'Tis here that he looks back with Pleasure on the Waves and Billows thro' which he has steered to so fair an Haven; he is now intent upon the Practice of every Virtue, which a great Knowledge and Use of Mankind has discovered to be the most useful to them. Thus in his private domestick Employments he is no less glorious than in his publick; for 'tis in Reality a more difficult Task to be conspicuous in a sedentary inactive Life, than in one that is spent in Hurry and Business; Persons engaged in the latter, like Bodies violently agitated, from the Swiftness of their Motion have a Brightness added to them, which often vanishes when they are at rest; but if it then still remain, it must be the Seeds of intrinsick Worth that thus shine out without any foreign Aid or Assistance.

His Liberality in another might almost bear the Name of Profusion; he seems to think it laudable even in the Excess, like that River which most perfect enriches when it overflows: But *Manilius* has too perfect a Taste of the Pleasure of doing good, ever to let it be out of his Power; and for that Reason he will have a just Oeconomy, and a splendid Frugality at home, the Fountain from whence those Streams should flow which he disperses abroad. He looks with disdain on those who propose their Death as the time when they are to begin their Munificence; he will both see and enjoy (which he then does in the highest Degree) what he bestows himself; he will be the living Executor of his own Bounty, whilst they who have the Happiness to be within his Care and Patronage at once, pray for the Continuation of his Life, and their own good Fortune. No one is out of the reach of his Obligations; he knows how, by proper and becoming Methods, to raise himself to a Level with those of the Highest Rank; and his good Nature is a sufficient Warrant against the want of those who are so unhappy as to be in the very lowest. One may say of him, as *Pindar* bids his Muse say of *Theron*.

> *Swear, that* Theron *sure has sworn,*
> *No one near him should be Poor.*
> *Swear that none e'er had such a graceful Art*
> *Fortune's Free-Gifts as freely to impart,*
> *With an unenvious Hand, and an unbounded* **Heart.**

Never did *Atticus* succeed better in gaining the universal Love and Esteem of all Men, nor steer with more Success betwixt the Extreams of two contending Parties. 'Tis his peculiar Happiness, that while he espouses neither with an intemperate Zeal, he is not only admired, but, what is a more rare and unusual Felicity, he is beloved and caressed by both; and I never yet saw any Person, of whatsoever Age or Sex, but was immediately struck with the Merit of *Manilius*. There are many who are acceptable to some particular Persons, whilst the rest of Mankind look upon them with Coldness and Indifference, but he is the first whose entire good Fortune it is ever to please and to be pleased, where-ever he comes to be admired, and where-ever he is absent to be lamented. His Merit fares like the Pictures of *Raphael*, which are either seen with Admiration by all, or at least no one dare own he has no Taste for a Composition which has received so universal an Applause. Envy and Malice find it against their Interest to indulge Slander and Obloquy. 'Tis as hard for an Enemy to detract from, as for a Friend to add to his Praise. An Attempt upon his Reputation is a sure lessening of one's own; and there is but one Way to injure him, which is to refuse him his just Commendations, and be obstinately silent.

It is below him to catch the Sight with any Care of Dress; his outward Garb is but the Emblem of his Mind, it is genteel, plain, and unaffected, he knows that Gold and Embroidery can add nothing to the Opinion which all have of his Merit, and that he gives a Lustre to the plainest Dress, whilst 'tis impossible the richest should communicate any to him. He is still the principal Figure in the Room: He first engages your Eye, as if there were some Point of Light which shone stronger upon him than on any other Person.

He puts me in mind of a Story of the famous *Bussy d'Amboise*, who at an Assembly at Court, where every one appeared with the utmost Magnificence, relying upon his own superior Behaviour, instead of adorning himself like the rest, put on that Day a plain Suit of Cloaths, and dressed all his Servants in the most costly gay Habits he could procure: The Event was, that the Eyes of the whole Court were fixed upon him, all the rest looked like his Attendants, whilst he alone had the Air of a Person of Quality and Distinction.

Like *Aristippus*, whatever Shape or Condition he appears in, it still sits free and easie upon him; but in some Part of his Character, 'tis true, he differs from him; for as he is altogether equal to the Largeness of his present Circumstances, the Rectitude of his Judgment has so far corrected the Inclinations of his Ambition, that he will not trouble himself with either the

Desires or Pursuits of any thing beyond his present Enjoyments.

A thousand obliging Things flow from him upon every Occasion, and they are always so just and natural, that it is impossible to think he was at the Least pains to look for them. One would think it were the Daemon of good Thoughts that discovered to him those Treasures, which he must have blinded others from seeing, they lay so directly in their Way. Nothing can equal the Pleasure is taken in hearing him speak, but the Satisfaction one receives in the Civility and Attention he pays to the Discourse of others. His Looks are a silent Commendation of what is good and praise-worthy, and a secret Reproof to what is licentious and extravagant. He knows how to appear free and open without Danger of Intrusion, and to be cautious without seeming reserved. The Gravity of his Conversation is always enlivened with his Wit and Humour, and the Gaiety of it is tempered with something that is instructive, as well as barely agreeable. Thus with him you are sure not to be merry at the Expence of your Reason, nor serious with the Loss of your good Humour; but by a happy Mixture in his Temper, they either go together, or perpetually succeed each other. In fine, his whole Behaviour is equally distant from Constraint and Negligence, and he commands your Respect, whilst he gains your Heart.

There is in his whole Carriage such an engaging Softness that one cannot perswade one's self he is ever actuated by those rougher Passions, which, where-ever they find Place, seldom fail of shewing themselves in the outward Demeanour of the Persons they belong to: But his Constitution is a just Temperature between Indolence on one Hand and Violence on the other. He is mild and gentle, wherever his Affairs will give him Leave to follow his own Inclinations; but yet never failing to exert himself with Vigour and Resolution in the Service of his Prince, his Country or his Friend. Z

No. 468.
[STEELE.]   Wednesday, August 27.

Erat homo ingeniosus, acutus, acer, & qui plurimum . . . & salis haberet & fellis, nec candoris minus.—Plin. Epist.

My Paper is in a kind a Letter of News, but it regards rather what passes in the World of Conversation than that of Business. I am very sorry that I have at present a Circumstance before me which is of very great Importance to all who have a Relish for Gaiety, Wit, Mirth, or Humour; I mean the Death of poor

Dick Eastcourt. I have been obliged to him for so many Hours of Jollity, that it is but a small Recompence, tho' all I can give him, to pass a Moment or two in Sadness for the Loss of so agreeable a Man. Poor *Eastcourt!* the last Time I saw him, we were plotting to shew the Town his great Capacity for acting in its full Light, by introducing him as dictating to a Set of young Players, in what Manner to speak this Sentence, and utter t'other Passion. . . . He had so exquisite a Discerning of what was defective in any Object before him, that in an Instant he could shew you the ridiculous Side of what would pass for beautiful and just, even to men of no ill Judgment, before he had pointed at the Failure. He was no less skilful in the Knowledge of Beauty; and, I dare say, there is no one who knew him well, but can repeat more well-turned Compliments, as well as smart Repartees of Mr. *Eastcourt*'s, than of any other man in *England*. This was easily to be observed in his inimitable Faculty of telling a Story, in which he would throw in natural and unexpected Incidents to make his Court to one Part, and rally the other Part of the Company: Then he would vary the Usage he gave them, according as he saw them bear kind or sharp Language. He had the Knack to raise up a pensive Temper, and mortifie an impertinently gay one, with the most agreeable Skill imaginable. There are a thousand things which crowd into my Memory, which make me too much concerned to tell on about him. *Hamlet* holding up the Skull which the Grave-digger threw to him, with an Account that it was the Head of the King's Jester, falls into very pleasing Reflections, and cries out to his Companion.

Alas, poor Yorick! *I knew him,* Horatio, *a Fellow of infinite Jest, of most excellent Fancy; he hath born me on his Back a thousand times: And how abhorred my Imagination is now, my Gorge rises at it. Here hung those Lips that I have kiss'd I know not how oft. Where be your Gibes now, your Gambols, your Songs, your Flashes of Merriment, that were wont to set the Table on a Roar: Not one now to mock your own Jeerings, quite Chop-fallen! Now get you to my Lady's Chamber, and tell her, Let her paint an Inch thick, to this Favour she must come. Make her laugh at that.*

It is an Insolence natural to the Wealthy to affix, as much as in them lies, the Character of a Man to his Circumstances. Thus it is ordinary with them to praise faintly the good Qualities of those below them, and say it is very extraordinary in such a Man as he is, or the like, when they are forced to acknowledge the Value of him whose Lowness upbraids their Exaltation. It is to this Humour only, that it is to be ascribed that a quick Wit in Conversation, a nice Judgment upon any

Emergency that could arise, and a most blameless inoffensive Behaviour, could not raise this Man above being received only upon the Foot of contributing to Mirth and Diversion. But he was as easie under that Condition, as a Man of so excellent Talents was capable; and since they would have it, that to divert was his Business, he did it with all the seeming Alacrity imaginable, tho' it stung him to the Heart that it was his Business. Men of Sense, who could taste his Excellencies, were well satisfied to let him lead the Way in Conversation, and play after his own Manner; but Fools who provoked him to Mimickry, found he had the Indignation to let it be at their Expence who called for it, and he would shew the Form of conceited heavy Fellows as Jests to the Company at their own Request, in Revenge for interrupting him from being a Companion to put on the Character of a Jester.

What was peculiarly excellent in this memorable Companion, was, that in the Accounts he gave of Persons and Sentiments, he did not only hit the Figure of their Faces, and Manner of their Gestures, but he would in his Narration fall into their very Way of Thinking, and this when he recounted Passages, wherein Men of the best Wit were concerned, as well as such wherein were represented Men of the lowest Rank of Understanding. It is certainly as great an Instance of Selflove to a Weakness, to be impatient of being mimick'd, as any can be imagined. There were none but the Vain, the Formal, the Proud, or those who were incapable of amending their Faults, that dreaded him; to others he was in the highest Degree pleasing; and I do not know any Satisfaction of any indifferent Kind I ever tasted so much, as having got over an Impatience of my seeing my self in the Air he could put me when I have displeased him. It is indeed to his exquisite Talent this way, more than any Philosophy I could read on the Subject, that my Person is very little of my Care; and it is indifferent to me what is said of my Shape, my Air, my Manner, my Speech, or my Address. It is to poor *Eastcourt* I chiefly owe, that I am arrived at the Happiness of thinking nothing a Diminution to me, but what argues a Depravity of my Will.

It has as much surprized me as any thing in Nature, to have it frequently said, that he was not a good Player: But that must be owing to a Partiality for former Actors in the Parts in which he succeeded them, and judging by comparison of what was liked before, rather than by the Nature of the Thing. When a Man of his Wit and Smartness could put on an utter Absence of common Sense in his Face, as he did in the Character of *Bullfinch* in the *Northern Lass*, and an Air of insipid Cunning and Vivacity in the Character of *Pounce* in the *Tender Hus-*

band, it is Folly to dispute his Capacity and Success, as he was an Actor.

Poor *Eastcourt!* let the Vain and Proud be at Rest; they will no more disturb their Admiration of their dear selves, and thou art no longer to drudge in raising the Mirth of Stupids, who know nothing of thy Merit, for thy Maintenance.

It is natural for the Generality of Mankind to run into Reflections upon our Mortality, when Disturbers of the World are laid at Rest, but to take no Notice when they who can please and divert are pulled from us: But for my part, I cannot but think the Loss of such Talents as the Man of whom I am speaking was Master of, a more melancholly Instance of Mortality, than the Dissolution of Persons of never so high Characters in the World, whose Pretensions were that they were noisie and mischievous.

But I must grow more succinct, and, as a SPECTATOR, give an Account of this extraordinary Man, who, in his Way, never had an Equal in any Age before him, or in that wherein he lived. I speak of him as a Companion, and a Man qualified for Conversation. His Fortune exposed him to an Obsequiousness towards the worst Sort of Company, but his excellent Qualities rendered him capable of making the best Figure in the most refined. I have been present with him among Men of the most delicate Taste a whole Night, and have known him (for he saw it was desired) keep the Discourse to himself the most Part of it, and maintain his good Humour with a Countenance, in a Language so delightful, without Offence to any Person or Thing upon Earth, still preserving the Distance his Circumstances obliged him to; I say I have seen him do all this in such a charming Manner, that I am sure none of those I hint at will read this, without giving him some Sorrow for their abundant Mirth, and one Gush of Tears for so many Bursts of Laughter. I wish it were any Honour to the pleasant Creature's Memory, that my Eyes are too much suffused to let me go on——   T

No. 469.
[ADDISON.]   Thursday, August 28.

Detrahere aliquid alteri, & hominem hominis incommodo suum augere commodum, magis est contra naturam, quam mors, quam paupertas, quam dolor, quam cetera quae possunt aut corpori accidere, aut rebus externis.—Tull.

I AM persuaded there are few Men, of generous Principles, who would seek after great Places, were it not rather to have an

Opportunity in their Hands of obliging their particular Friends, or those whom they look upon as Men of Worth, than to procure Wealth and Honour for themselves. To an honest Mind the best Perquisites of a Place are the Advantages it gives a Man of doing Good.

Those who are under the great Officers of State, and are the Instruments by which they Act, have more frequent Opportunities for the Exercise of Compassion, and Benevolence, than their Superiors themselves. These Men know every little Case that is to come before the Great Man, and if they are possessed with honest Minds, will consider Poverty as a Recommendation in the Person who applies himself to them, and make the Justice of his Cause the most powerful Sollicitor in his behalf. A Man of this Temper, when he is in a Post of Business, becomes a Blessing to the Publick; He patronizes the Orphan and the Widow, assists the Friendless, and guides the Ignorant: He does not reject the Person's Pretensions, who does not know how to explain them, or refuse doing a good Office for a Man because he cannot pay the Fee of it. In short, tho' he regulates himself in all his Proceedings by Justice and Equity, he finds a thousand Occasions for all the good-natured Offices of Generosity and Compassion.

A Man is unfit for such a Place of Trust, who is of a sower untractable Nature, or has any other Passion that makes him uneasie to those who approach him. Roughness of Temper is apt to discountenance the Timorous or Modest. The proud Man discourages those from approaching him, who are of a mean Condition, and who most want his Assistance. The impatient Man will not give himself time to be informed of the Matter that lies before him. An Officer with one or more of these unbecoming Qualities, is sometimes looked upon as a proper Person to keep off Impertinence and Solicitation from his Superior; but this is a kind of Merit, that can never attone for the Injustice which may very often arise from it.

There are two other vicious Qualities which render a Man very unfit for such a Place of Trust. The first of these is a Dilatory Temper, which commits innumerable Cruelties without Design. The Maxim which several have laid down for a Man's Conduct in ordinary Life, should be inviolable with a Man in Office, never to think of doing that to Morrow which may be done to Day. A Man who defers doing what ought to be done, is guilty of Injustice so long as he defers it. The Dispatch of a good Office is very often as beneficial to the Sollicitor as the good Office it self. In short, if a Man compared the Inconveniencies which another suffers by his Delays, with the trifling Motives and Advantages which he himself may reap by such a Delay, he would never be guilty of a Fault which very often does an irreparable Prejudice to the Person who depends upon him, and which might be remedied with little Trouble to himself.

But in the last place, there is no Man so improper to be employed in Business, as he who is in any degree capable of Corruption; and such an one is the Man, who upon any Pretence whatsoever, receives more than what is the stated and unquestioned Fee of his Office. Gratifications, Tokens of Thankfulness, Dispatch Mony, and the like specious Terms, are the Pretences under which Corruption very frequently shelters it self. An honest Man will however look on all these Methods as unjustifiable, and will enjoy himself better in a moderate Fortune that is gained with Honour and Reputation, than in an overgrown Estate that is cankered with the Acquisitions of Rapine and Exaction. Were all our Offices discharged with such an inflexible Integrity, we should not see Men in all Ages, who grow up to exorbitant Wealth with the Abilities which are to be met with in an ordinary Mechanick. I cannot but think that such a Corruption proceeds chiefly from Men's employing the first that offer themselves, or those who have the Character of shrewd worldly Men, instead of searching out such as have had a liberal Education, and have been trained up in the Studies of Knowledge and Virtue.

It has been observed, that Men of Learning who take to Business, discharge it generally with greater Honesty than Men of the World. The chief Reason for it I take to be as follows. A Man that has spent his Youth in Reading, has been used to find Virtue extolled, and Vice stigmatized. A Man that has past his Time in the World, has often seen Vice triumphant, and Virtue discountenanced. Extortion, Rapine, and Injustice, which are branded with Infamy in Books, often give a Man a Figure in the World; while several Qualities which are celebrated in Authors, as Generosity, Ingenuity and Good-Nature, impoverish and ruin him. This cannot but have a proportionable Effect on Men, whose Tempers and Principles are equally Good and Vicious.

There would be at least this Advantage in employing Men of Learning and Parts in Business, that their Prosperity would fit more gracefully on them, and that we should not see many worthless Persons shot up into the greatest Figures of Life. C

No. 470.

[ADDISON.] Friday, August 29.

Turpe est difficiles habere nugas,
Et stultus labor est ineptiarum.—Mart.

I HAVE been very often disappointed of late Years, when upon examining the new Edition of a Classick Author, I have found above half the Volume taken up with various Readings. When I have expected to meet with a Learned Note upon a doubtful Passage in a *Latin* Poet, I have only been informed, that such or such ancient Manuscripts for an *et* write an *ac*, or of some other notable Discovery of the like Importance. Indeed, when a different Reading gives us a different Sense, or a new Elegance in an Author, the Editor does very well in taking Notice of it; but when he only entertains us with the several ways of Spelling the same Word, and gathers together the various Blunders and Mistakes of twenty or thirty different Transcribers, they only take up the Time of the learned Reader, and puzzle the Minds of the Ignorant. I have often fancied with my self how enraged an old *Latin* Author would be, should he see the several Absurdities in Sense and Grammar, which are imputed to him by some or other of these various Readings. In one he speaks Nonsense; in another makes use of a Word that was never heard of: And indeed there is scarce a Solecism in Writing which the best Author is not guilty of, if we may be at Liberty to read him in the Words of some Manuscript, which the laborious Editor has thought fit to examine in the Prosecution of his Work.

I question not but the Ladies and pretty Fellows will be very curious to understand what it is that I have been hitherto talking of; I shall therefore give them a Notion of this Practice, by endeavouring to write after the manner of several Persons who make an eminent Figure in the Republick of Letters. To this end we will suppose, that the following Song is an old Ode which I present to the Publick in a new Edition, with the several various Readings which I find of it in former Editions, and in Ancient Manuscripts. Those who cannot relish the various Readings, will perhaps find their Account in the Song, which never before appeared in Print.

My Love was fickle once and changing,
Nor e'er would settle in my Heart;
From Beauty still to Beauty ranging,
In ev'ry Face I found a Dart.

> *'Twas first a Charming Shape enslaved me;*
> *   An Eye then gave the fatal Stroke:*
> *'Till by her Wit* Corinna *sav'd me,*
> *   And all my former Fetters broke.*

> *But now a long and lasting Anguish*
> *   For* Belvidera *I endure;*
> *Hourly I Sigh and hourly Languish,*
> *   Nor hope to find the wonted Cure.*

> *For here the false unconstant Lover,*
> *   After a thousand Beauties shown,*
> *Does new surprising Charms discover,*
> *   And finds Variety in One.*

Various Readings.

Stanza the First, Verse the First. *And changing.*] The *ana* in some Manuscripts is written thus, *&*, but that in the *Cotton* Library writes it in three distinct Letters.

Verse the Second. *Nor e'er would.*] *Aldus* reads it *ever would;* but as this would hurt the Metre, we have restored it to its genuine Reading, by observing that *Synaeresis* which had been neglected by ignorant Transcribers.

Ibid. *In my Heart.*] *Scaliger* and others, *on my Heart.*

Verse the Fourth. *I found a Dart.*] The *Vatican* Manuscript for *I* reads *it,* but this must have been the Hallucination of the Transcriber, who probably mistook the Dash of the *I* for a *T.*

Stanza the Second, Verse the Second. *The fatal Stroke.*] *Scioppius, Salmasius,* and many others, for *the* read *a,* but I have stuck to the usual Reading.

Verse the Third. *'Till by her Wit.*] Some Manuscripts have it *his Wit,* others *your,* others *their Wit.* But as I find *Corinna* to be the Name of a Woman in other Authors, I cannot doubt but it should be *her.*

Stanza the Third, Verse the First. *A long and lasting Anguish.*] The *German* Manuscript reads *a lasting Passion,* but the Rhyme will not admit it.

Verse the Second. *For* Belvidera *I endure.*] Did not all the Manuscripts reclaim, I should change *Belvidera* into *Pelvidera; Pelvis* being used by several of the ancient Comick Writers for a Looking-Glass, by which means the Etymology of the Word is very visible, and *Pelvidera* will signifie a Lady who often looks in her Glass, as indeed she had very good reason, if she had all those Beauties which our Poet here ascribes to her.

Verse the Third. *Hourly I sigh and hourly languish.*] Some for the Word *hourly* read *daily*, and others *nightly*; the last has great Authorities of its side.

Verse the Fourth. *The wonted Cure.*] The elder *Stevens* reads *wanted Cure*.

Stanza the Fourth, Verse the Second. *After a thousand Beauties.*] In several Copies we meet with a *Hundred Beauties* by the usual Error of the Transcribers, who probably omitted a Cypher, and had not taste enough to know, that the Word *Thousand* was ten Times a greater Compliment to the Poet's Mistress than an *Hundred*.

Verse the Fourth. *And finds Variety in one.*] Most of the ancient Manuscripts have it *in two*. Indeed so many of them concur in this last Reading, that I am very much in doubt whether it ought not to take place. There are but two Reasons which incline me to the Reading, as I have Published it; First, because the Rhime, and, Secondly, because the Sense is preserved by it. It might likewise proceed from the Oscitancy of Transcribers, who, to dispatch their Work the sooner, used to write all Numbers in Cypher, and seeing the Figure 1 followed by a little Dash of the Pen, as is customary in old Manuscripts, they perhaps mistook the Dash for a second Figure, and by casting up both together, composed out of them the Figure 2. But this I shall leave to the Learned, without determining any thing in a Matter of so great Uncertainty. C

No. 471.
[ADDISON.]   Saturday, August 30.

'Εν ἐλπίσιν χρὴ τοὺς σοφοὺς ἔχειν βίον.—Euripid.

THE *Time present* seldom affords sufficient Employment to the Mind of Man. Objects of Pain or Pleasure, Love or Admiration, do not lie thick enough together in Life to keep the Soul in constant Action, and supply an immediate Exercise to its Faculties. In order, therefore to remedy this Defect, that the Mind may not want Business, but always have Materials for thinking, she is endowed with certain Powers, that can recall what is passed, and anticipate what is to come.

That wonderful Faculty, which we call the Memory, is perpetually looking back, when we have nothing present to entertain us. It is like those Repositories in several Animals, that are filled with Stores of their former Food, on which they may ruminate when their present Pasture fails.

As the Memory relieves the Mind in her vacant Moments, and prevents any Chasms of Thought by Ideas of what is *past*, we

have other Faculties that agitate and employ her upon what *is
to come*. These are the Passions of Hope and Fear.

By these two Passions we reach forward into Futurity, and
bring up to our present Thoughts Objects that lie hid in the
remotest Depths of Time. We suffer Misery, and enjoy Happiness, before they are in Being; we can set the Sun and Stars
forward, or lose sight of them by wandring into those retired
Parts of Eternity, when the Heavens and Earth shall be
no more.

By the way, who can imagine that the Existence of a
Creature is to be circumscribed by Time, whose Thoughts are
not? But I shall, in this Paper, confine my self to that
particular Passion which goes by the Name of Hope.

Our Actual Enjoyments are so few and transient, that Man
would be a very miserable Being, were he not endowed with
this Passion, which gives him a Taste of those good Things
that may possibly come into his Possession. *We should hope
for every thing that is good*, says the old Poet *Linus, because
there is nothing which may not be hoped for, and nothing but
what the Gods are able to give us.* Hope quickens all the still
Parts of Life, and keeps the Mind awake in her most Remiss
and Indolent Hours. It gives habitual Serenity and good
Humour. It is a kind of Vital Heat in the Soul, that cheers
and gladdens her, when she does not attend to it. It makes
Pain easie, and Labour pleasant.

Beside these several Advantages which rise from *Hope*, there
is another which is none of the least, and that is, its great
Efficacy in preserving us from setting too high a Value on
present Enjoyments. The Saying of *Caesar* is very well known.
When he had given away all his Estate in Gratuities among his
Friends, one of them asked what he had left for himself; to
which that great Man replied, *Hope.* His Natural Magnanimity hindred him from prizing what he was certainly possessed
of, and turned all his Thoughts upon something more valuable
than he had in View. I question not but every Reader will
draw a Moral from this Story, and apply it to himself without
my Direction.

The old Story of *Pandora*'s Box (which many of the Learned
believe was formed among the Heathens upon the Tradition
of the Fall of Man) shews us how deplorable a State they
thought the present Life, without Hope. To set forth the
utmost Condition of Misery they tell us, that our Forefather,
according to the Pagan Theology, had a great Vessel presented
him by *Pandora*: Upon his lifting up the Lid of it, says the
Fable, there flew out all the Calamities and Distempers incident
to Men, from which 'till that Time, they had been altogether

exempt. *Hope,* who had been enclosed in the Cup with so much bad Company, instead of flying off with the rest, stuck so close to the Lid of it, that it was shut down upon her.

I shall make but two Reflections upon what I have hitherto said. First, that no kind of Life is so happy as that which is full of Hope, especially when the Hope is well grounded, and when the Object of it is of an exalted kind, and in its Nature proper to make the Person happy who enjoys it. This Proposition must be very evident to those who consider how few are the present Enjoyments of the most happy Man, and how insufficient to give him an entire Satisfaction and Acquiescence in them.

My next Observation is this, that a Religious Life is that which most abounds in a well-grounded Hope, and such an one as is fixed on Objects that are capable of making us entirely happy. This Hope in a Religious Man, is much more sure and certain than the Hope of any Temporal Blessing, as it is strengthened not only by Reason, but by Faith. It has at the same time its eye perpetually fixed on that State, which implies in the very Notion of it the most full and the most complete Happiness.

I have before shewn how the influence of Hope in general sweetens Life, and makes our present Condition supportable, if not pleasing; but a Religious Hope has still greater Advantages. It does not only bear up the Mind under her Sufferings, but makes her rejoice in them, as they may be the Instruments of procuring her the great and ultimate End of all her Hope.

Religious Hope has likewise this Advantage above any other kind of Hope, that it is able to revive the *dying* Man, and to fill his Mind not only with secret Comfort and Refreshment, but sometimes with Rapture and Transport. He triumphs in his Agonies, whilst the Soul springs forward with Delight to the great Object which she has always had in view, and leaves the Body with an expectation of being re-united to her in a glorious and joyful Resurrection.

I shall conclude this Essay with those emphatical Expressions of a lively Hope, which the Psalmist made use of in the midst of those Dangers and Adversities which surrounded him, for the following Passage had its present and personal, as well as its future and prophetick Sense. *I have set the Lord always before me: Because he is at my right hand I shall not be moved. Therefore my heart is glad, and my glory rejoiceth; my flesh also shall rest in hope. For thou wilt not leave my Soul in Hell, neither wilt thou suffer thine holy One to see Corruption. Thou wilt shew me the path of life: in thy presence is fullness of joy, at thy right hand there are pleasures for evermore.* C

No. 472.

[STEELE.]   Monday, September 1.

. . . *Voluptas*
Solamenque mali . . .—Virg.

I RECEIVED some time ago a Proposal, which had a Preface to it, wherein the Author discoursed at large of the innumerable Objects of Charity in a Nation, and admonished the Rich, who were afflicted with any Distemper of Body, particularly to regard the Poor in the same Species of Affliction, and confine their Tenderness to them, since it is impossible to assist all who are presented to them. The Proposer had been relieved from a Malady in his Eyes by an Operation performed by Sir *William Read;* and being a Man of Condition, had taken a Resolution to maintain three poor blind Men during their Lives, in Gratitude for that great Blessing. This Misfortune is so very great and unfrequent, that one would think, an Establishment for all the Poor under it might be easily accomplished, with the Addition of a very few others to those Wealthy who are in the same Calamity. However, the Thought of the Proposer arose from a very good Motive, and the parcelling of our selves out, as called to particular Acts of Beneficence, would be a pretty Cement of Society and Virtue. It is the ordinary Foundation for Men's holding a Commerce with each other, and becoming familiar, that they agree in the same Sort of Pleasure; and sure it may also be some Reason for Amity, that they are under one common Distress. If all the rich who are lame in the Gout, from a Life of Ease, Pleasure, and Luxury, would help those few who have it without a previous Life of Pleasure, and add a few of such laborious Men, who are become lame from unhappy Blows, Falls, or other Accidents of Age or Sickness; I say, would such gouty Persons administer to the Necessities of Men disabled like themselves, the Consciousness of such a Behaviour would be the best Julep, Cordial, and Anodine in the feverish, faint, and tormenting Vicissitudes of that miserable Distemper. The same may be said of all other, both bodily and intellectual Evils. These Classes of Charity would certainly bring down Blessings upon an Age and People; and if Men were not petrify'd with the Love of this World, against all Sense of the Commerce which ought to be among them, it would not be an unreasonable Bill for a poor Man in the Agony of Pain, aggravated by Want and Poverty, to draw upon a sick Alderman after this Form.

Mr. Basil Plenty,

   Sir,

      You have the Gout and Stone, with Sixty thousand Pound

> *Sterling; I have the Gout and Stone, not worth one Far-*
> *thing: I shall pray for you, and desire you would pay the*
> *Bearer Twenty Shillings for Value received from*

Cripple-Gate,   Sir,
Aug. 29, 1712.   Your humble Servant,
                                    Lazarus Hopefull.

The Reader's own Imagination will suggest to him the
Reasonableness of such Correspondences, and diversifie them
into a thousand Forms; but I shall close this as I began upon
the Subject of Blindness. The following Letter seems to be
written by a Man of Learning, who is return'd to his Study
after a Suspence of an Ability to do so. The Benefit he reports
himself to have received, may well claim the handsomest Encomium he can give the Operator.

'*Mr.* SPECTATOR,

Ruminating lately on your admirable Discourses on the
Pleasures of the Imagination, I began to consider to which of
our Senses we are obliged for the greatest and most important
Share of those Pleasures; and I soon concluded that it was to
the *Sight*: That is the Sovereign of the Senses, and Mother of
all the Arts and Sciences, that have refined the Rudeness of
the uncultivated Mind to a Politeness that distinguishes the
fine Spirits from the barbarous *Gout* of the *great* Vulgar and the
small. The Sight is the obliging Benefactress that bestows on
us the most transporting Sensations that we have from the
various and wonderful Products of Nature. To the Sight we
owe the amazing Discoveries of the Height, Magnitude, and
Motion of the Planets; their Several Revolutions about their
common Centre of Light, Heat, and Motion, the *Sun*. The
Sight travels yet farther to the fix'd Stars, and furnishes the
Understanding with solid Reasons to prove, that each of them
is a *Sun* moving on its own Axis, in the Centre of its own Vortex
or Turbillion, and performing the same Offices to its dependant
Planets, that our glorious Sun does to this. But the Enquiries
of the *Sight* will not be stopp'd here, but make their Progress
through the immense Expanse of the *Milky Way*, and there
divide the blended Fires of the *Galaxy* into infinite and different
Worlds, made up of distinct Suns, and their peculiar Equipages
of Planets; till unable to pursue this Track any farther, it
deputes the Imagination, to go on to new Discoveries, till it
fill the unbounded Space with endless Worlds.

The *Sight* informs the Statuary's Chizel with Power to give
Breath to lifeless Brass and Marble, and the Painter's Pencil to
swell the flat Canvas with moving Figures actuated by ima-

ginary Souls. Musick indeed may plead another Original, since *Jubal*, by the different Falls of his Hammer on the Anvil discovered by the Ear the first rude Musick that pleas'd the Antediluvian Fathers; but then the *Sight* has not only reduc'd those wilder Sounds into artful Order and Harmony, but conveys that Harmony to the most distant Parts of the World without the Help of Sound. To the *Sight* we owe not only all the Discoveries of Philosophy, but all the divine Imagery of Poetry that transports the intelligent Reader of *Homer*, *Milton*, and *Virgil*.

As the Sight has polish'd the World, so does it supply us with the most grateful and lasting Pleasure. Let Love, let Friendship, paternal Affection, filial Piety, and conjugal Duty, declare the Joys the *Sight* bestows on a Meeting after Absence. But it would be endless to enumerate all the Pleasures and Advantages of *Sight*; every one that has it, every Hour he makes use of it, finds them, feels them, enjoys them.

Thus as our greatest Pleasures and Knowledge are deriv'd from the Sight, so has Providence been more curious in the Formation of its Seat, the Eye, than of the Organs of the other Senses. That stupendous Machine is composed in a wonderful Manner of Muscles, Membranes, and Humours. Its Motions are admirably directed by the Muscles; the Perspicuity of the Humours transmit the Rays of Light; the Rays are regularly refracted by their Figure; the black Lining of the Sclerotes effectually prevents their being confounded by Reflection. It is wonderful indeed to consider how many objects the Eye is fitted to take in at once, and successively in an Instant, and at the same Time to make a Judgment of their Position, Figure, and Colour. It watches against our Dangers, guides our Steps, and lets in all the visible Objects, whose Beauty and Variety instruct and delight.

The Pleasures and Advantages of Sight being so great, the Loss must be very grievous; of which *Milton*, from Experience, gives the most sensible Idea, both in the third Book of his *Paradise Lost*, and in his *Sampson Agonistes*.

To Light in the former.

> . . . *Thee I revisit safe,*
> *And feel thy sovereign vital Lamp; but thou*
> *Revisit'st not these Eyes, that roul in vain*
> *To find thy piercing Ray, but find no Dawn.*

And a little after.

> *Seasons return, but not to me returns*
> *Day, or the sweet Approach of Ev'n and Morn,*
> *Or Sight of vernal Bloom, or Summer's Rose,*
> *Or Flocks or Herds, or human Face divine;*

But Cloud instead and ever-during Dark
Surround me: From the chearful Ways of Men
Cut off; and for the Book of Knowledge fair,
Presented with an universal Blank
Of Nature's Works, to me expung'd and raz'd,
And Wisdom at one Entrance quite shut out.

Again, in *Sampson Agonistes.*

. . . But Chief of all,
O Loss of Sight! of thee I most complain;
Blind among Enemies! O worse than Chains,
Dungeon, or Beggary, or decrepid Age!
Light, the prime Work of God, to me 's extinct,
And all her various Objects of Delight
Annull'd . . .

. . . Still as a Fool,
In Power of others, never in my own,
Scarce half I seem to live, dead more than Half;
O dark! dark! dark! amid the blaze of Noon:
Irrecoverably dark, total Eclipse,
Without all Hopes of Day!

The Enjoyment of Sight then being so great a Blessing, and the Loss of it so terrible an Evil; how excellent and valuable is the Skill of that Artist which can restore the former, and redress the latter? My frequent Perusal of the Advertisements in the publick News-Papers (generally the most agreeable Entertainments they afford) has presented me with many and various Benefits of this Kind done to my Countrymen by that skilful Artist Dr. *Grant*, Her Majesty's Oculist Extraordinary, whose happy Hand has brought and restored .. Sight several Hundreds in less than Four Years. Many have received Sight by his means who came blind from their Mother's Womb, as in the famous Instance of *Jones* of *Newington*. I my self have been cured by him of a Weakness in my Eyes next to Blindness, and am ready to believe any thing that is reported of his Ability this way; and know that many, who could not purchase his Assistance with Mony, have enjoy'd it from his Charity. But a List of Particulars would swell my Letter beyond its Bounds, what I have said being sufficient to comfort those who are in the like Distress, since they may conceive Hopes of being no longer miserable in this Kind, while there is yet alive so able an Oculist as Dr. *Grant*.

I am,

The SPECTATOR'S
humble Servant,

PHILANTHROPUS.'

T

No. 473.

[STEELE.]   Tuesday, September 2.

Quid? si quis vultu torvo ferus & pede nudo
Exiguaeque togae simulet textore Catonem,
Virtutemne repraesentet moresque Catonis?—Hor.

' To the SPECTATOR.

Sir,

I AM now in the Country, and employ most of my Time in reading, or thinking upon what I have read. Your Paper comes constantly down to me, and it affects me so much, that I find my Thoughts run into your Way; and I recommend to you a Subject upon which you have not yet touched, and that is the Satisfaction some Men seem to take in their Imperfections, I think one may call it Glorying in their Insufficiency; a certain great Author is of Opinion it is the contrary to Envy, tho' perhaps it may proceed from it. Nothing is so common, as to hear Men of this sort speaking of themselves, add to their own Merit (as they think) by impairing it, in praising themselves for their Defects, freely allowing they commit some few frivolous Errors, in order to be esteemed Persons of uncommon Talents and great Qualifications. They are generally professing an injudicious Neglect of Dancing, Fencing and Riding, as also an unjust Contempt for Travelling and the modern Languages; as for their Part (they say) they never valued or troubled their Head about them. This panegyrical Satyr on themselves certainly is worthy of your Animadversion. I have known one of these Gentlemen think himself obliged to forget the Day of an Appointment, and sometimes even that you spoke to him; and when you see 'em, they hope you 'll pardon 'em, for they have the worst Memory in the World. One of 'em started up t'other Day in some Confusion, and said, Now I think on 't, I 'm to meet Mr. *Mortmain* the Attorney about some Business, but whether it is to Day or to Morrow, faith, I can't tell. Now to my certain Knowledge he knew his Time to a Moment, and was there accordingly. These forgetful Persons have, to heighten their Crime, generally the best Memories of any People, as I have found out by their remembring sometimes through Inadvertency. Two or three of them that I know can say most of our modern Tragedies by Heart. I asked a Gentleman the other Day that is famous for a good Carver (at which Acquisition he is out of Countenance, imagining it may detract from some of his more essential Qualifications) to help me to something that was near him; but he excused himself, and blushing told me, Of all things he could never carve in his Life; tho' it can be proved upon him, that he

III—Q   166 cuts up, disjoints, and uncases with incomparable Dexterity. I would not be understood as if I thought it laudable for a Man of Quality and Fortune to rival the Acquisitions of Artificers, and endeavour to excel in little handy Qualities; No, I argue only against being ashamed at what is really Praiseworthy. As these Pretences to Ingenuity shew themselves several Ways, you 'll often see a Man of this Temper ashamed to be clean, and setting up for Wit only from Negligence in his Habit. Now I am upon this Head, I can't help observing also upon a very different Folly proceeding from the same Cause. As these above mentioned arise from affecting an Equality with Men of greater Talents from having the same Faults, there are others that would come at a Parallel with those above them, by possessing little Advantages which they want. I heard a young Man not long ago, who has Sense, comfort himself in his Ignorance of Greek, Hebrew, and the Orientals: At the same Time that he published his Aversion to those Languages, he said that the Knowledge of 'em was rather a Diminution than an Advancement of a Man's Character, tho' at the same Time I know he languishes and repines he is not Master of them himself. Whenever I take any of these fine Persons, thus detracting from what they don't understand, I tell them I will complain to you, and say I am sure you will not allow it an Exception against a thing, that he who contemns it is an Ignorant in it.

> *I am, Sir,*
> *Your most humble Servant,*
>
> S. P.'

'*Mr.* SPECTATOR,

I am a Man of a very good Estate, and am honourably in Love. I hope you will allow, when the ultimate Purpose is honest, there may be, without Trespass against Innocence, some Toying by the Way. People of Condition are perhaps too distant and formal on those Occasions; but, however that is, I am to confess to you, that I have writ some Verses to attone for my Offence. You profess'd Authors are a little severe upon us, who write like Gentlemen: But if you are a Friend to Love, you will insert my Poem. You cannot imagine how much Service it will do me with my Fair one, as well as Reputation with all my Friends, to have something of mine in the *Spectator*. My Crime was, that I snatch'd a Kiss, and my Poetical Excuse as follows:

I.

> Bellinda, *see from yonder Flowers*
> *The Bee flies loaded to its Cell;*
> *Can you perceive what it devours?*
> *Are they impair'd in Shew or Smell?*

II.

So, tho' I robb'd you of a Kiss,
Sweeter than their Ambrosial Dew,
Why are you angry at my Bliss?
Has it at all impoverish'd **you***?*

III.

'Tis by this Cunning I contrive,
In spite of your unkind Reserve,
To keep my famish'd Love alive,
Which you inhumanly would starve.

I am,
Sir,
Your humble Servant,
Timothy Stanza.'

'*Sir*,   *Aug.* 23. 1712.

Having a little Time upon my Hands, I could not think of
bestowing it better, than in writing an Epistle to the SPECTA-
TOR, which I now do, and am,

Sir,
Your humble Servant,
BOB SHORT.

P.S. If you approve of my Stile, I am likely enough to
become your Correspondent. I desire your Opinion of it. I
design it for that Way of Writing called by the Judicious the
Familiar.'

T

The End of the Sixth Volume.

NOTES

A. = Original Daily Issue

B. I. = Biographical Index.

322. PAGE 3. *Motto.* Horace, *Ars Poetica*, 110.

323. PAGE 5. *Motto.* Ovid, *Metamorphoses*, iv. 280. It is said in the folio and octavo to be from Virgil; and Chalmers, who could not find it, endeavoured to explain it as a misquotation of *Aeneid*, vi. 448.

    Mohock. See next paper.

PAGE 6. *A new Head.* See i. 555 and ii. 495.

PAGE 7. *Fontange.* See i. 555.

    Not at home. Probably a very early use of the phrase in this sense.

PAGE 8. *Indamora.* The 'Captive Queen' in Dryden's *Aureng-Zebe*.

    A Lady in the Front Box. See i. 549.

    Nicolini. See i. 17; ii. 446: and *B. I.*

    Ancora. Cf. Toby Rentfree's letter, ii. 446–7.

    The dumb Man was a Duncan Campbell, much in repute as a fortune-teller. He is alluded to in No. 31 (i. 530) and again, at greater length, in No. 474 (q.v.).

PAGE 9. *An uncertain Author.* Formerly ascribed to Ben Jonson, but now given to William Browne, author of *Britannia's Pastorals*.

324. *Motto.* Persius, *Satires*, ii. 61. The motto in *A* is ' *Saevis inter se convenit ursis.*—Juv.'

    Mohocks. Contemporary literature, and especially the epistolary literature of this month, is full of references to this 'race of rakes' (as Swift called them), 'that play the devil about this town every night.' They carried on the traditions of the *Muns*, the *Tityre-tus*, the *Hectors*, and the famous *Scowrers* of the seventeenth century (i. 532: see also Shadwell's *Scowrers*, i), and in their reputation for brutality had quite eclipsed their immediate predecessors the *Nickers* and *Hawcubites*. Their name and that of their leader ('Emperor of the Mohocks') seem to have been suggested by the title of one of the four Indian kings who had been on a visit to England (i. 540). They are further discussed in subsequent numbers of the *Spectator* (see by index). Cf. also Swift's *Journal to Stella*, March 8, 12, 16, 18, 22, and 26, 1712; Gay's *Trivia*, iii. 326 et sqq. Austin Dobson quotes an interesting passage from a letter of Lady Wentworth, of 14th March 1712: 'I am very much frighted with the fyer, but much more with a gang of Devils that call themselves Mohocks; they put an old woman into a hogshead, and rooled her down a hill, they cut of som nosis, others hands, and several barbarass tricks, without any provocation. They are said to be

464

young gentlemen, they never take any money from any; instead of setting fifty pound upon the head of a highwayman, sure they would doe much better to sett a hundred upon thear heads.' (*Wentworth Papers*, 1883, 277–8.) Gay, in the passage referred to above, describes

> How matrons, hoop'd within the hogshead's womb,
> Were tumbled furious thence.

(Cf. the name of *Tumblers*, in this essay and in No. 347.) These miscreants were afterwards found to be but common thieves. Lord Chesterfield has said, 'The Society of Mohocks never existed.' In No. 349 (*A*) is advertised: '*The Mohocks. A Tragi-Comical Farce. As it was Acted near the Watch-house in Covent-Garden. By Her Majesty's Servants. Printed for Bernard Lintott.*' See also D'Urfey's verses on the Mohocks in his *Pills to Purge Melancholy* (vi. 336).

PAGE 11. *The rest is torn off.* The continuation will be found in the original paper No. 328 (*A*) printed at the foot of this page. 'This letter,' says Percy, 'was really conveyed in the manner here mentioned to a Mrs. Cole, the wife of a churlish attorney in or near Northampton, who would not suffer her to correspond with anybody. It was written by a substantial freeholder in Northamptonshire, whose name was Gabriel Bullock, and given to Steele by his friend, the ingenious antiquary, Mr. Brown Willis.'

325. *Motto.* Ovid, *Metamorphoses*, iii. 432–6.

PAGE 12. *Mr. Dryden in his Ovid. The Story of Acis, Polyphemus and Galatea, from the Thirteenth Book of Ovid's Metamorphoses*, line 30.

326. PAGE 14. *Motto.* Horace, *Odes*, III. xvi. 1–5.

Your subsequent Discourse. See No. 311 (ii. 436).

PAGE 15. *Reconnoitring.* See i. 500; and note, ii. 501.

327. PAGE 17. *Motto.* Virgil, *Aeneid*, vii. 44.

PAGES 20, 21. Addison does not hesitate to name Le Bossu when he chooses to disagree with him. See note, ii. 496–7.

PAGE 22, line 4. *Imagination.* So in *A*; 'Indignation' in the octavo edition.

328. PAGE 23. *Motto.* Horace, *Epodes*, xvii. 24.

This paper takes the place in the octavo edition of the following, which was published as No. 328 in *A*:

> '*Delecta illa urbanitate tam stulta.*—Petron. Arb.

That useful Part of Learning which consists in Emendations, Knowledge of different Readings, and the like, is what in all Ages Persons extremely wise and learned have had in great Veneration. For this reason I cannot but rejoyce at the following Epistle, which lets us into the true Author of the Letter to Mrs. *Margaret Clark*, part of which I did myself the Honour to publish in a former Paper. I must confess I do not naturally affect critical Learning; but finding my self not so much regarded as I am apt to flatter my self I may deserve from some professed Patrons of Learning, I could not but do my self the Justice to shew I am not a Stranger to such Erudition as they smile upon, if I were duly encouraged. However this only to let the World see what I could do; and shall not give my Reader any more of this kind, if he will forgive the Ostentation I shew at present.

"*Sir*, *March* 13, 1712.

Upon reading your Paper of Yesterday, I took the Pains to look out a Copy I had formerly taken, and remembered to be very like your last Letter: Comparing them, I found they were the very same, and have underwritten sent you that Part of it which you say was torn off. I hope you will insert it, that Posterity may know 'twas *Gabriel Bullock* that made Love in that natural Stile of which you seem to be fond. But, to let you see I have other Manuscripts in the same way, I have sent you enclosed three Copies, faithfully taken by my own Hand from the Originals, which were writ by a *Yorkshire* gentleman of a good estate to Madam *Mary*, and an Uncle of her's, a Knight very well known by the most ancient Gentry in that and several other Counties of *Great Britain*. I have exactly followed the Form and Spelling. I have been credibly informed that Mr. *William Bullock*, the famous Comedian, is the descendant of this *Gabriel*, who begot Mr. *William Bullock's* great grandfather on the Body of the above-mention'd Mrs. *Margaret Clark*. But neither *Speed*, nor *Baker*, nor *Selden*, taking notice of it, I will not pretend to be positive; but desire that the letter may be reprinted, and what is here recovered may be in Italick.

I am, Sir,

Your daily Reader.

To her I very much respect, Mrs. Margaret Clark.

Lovely, and oh that I could write loving Mrs. *Margaret Clark*, I pray you let Affection excuse Presumption. Having been so happy as to enjoy the Sight of your sweet Countenance and comely Body, sometimes when I had Occasion to buy Treacle or Liquorish Powder at the Apothecary's Shop, I am so enamoured with you, that I can no more keep close my flaming Desire to become your Servant. And I am the more bold now to write to your sweet self, because I am now my own Man, and may match were I please; for my Father is taken away; and now I am come to my Living, which is Ten Yard Land, and a House; and there is never a Yard of Land in our Field but is as well worth ten Pound a Year, as a Thief's worth a Halter; and all my Brothers and Sisters are provided for: Besides I have good Household-stuff, though I say it, both Brass and Pewter, Linnens and Woollens; and though my House be thatched, yet if you and I match, it shall go hard but I will have one half of it slated. If you shall think well of this Motion, I will wait upon you as soon as my new Cloaths is made and Hay-Harvest is in. I could, though I say it, have good *Matches in our Town*;

but my Mother (God's Peace be with her) charged me upon her Death-Bed to marry a Gentlewoman, one who had been well trained up in Sowing and Cookery. I do not think but that if you and I can agree to marry, and lay our Means together, I shall be made Grand-Jury-man e'er two or three Years come about, and that will be a great Credit to us. If I could have got a Messenger for Sixpence, I wou'd have sent one on purpose, and some Trifle or other for a Token of my Love ; but I hope there is nothing lost for that neither. So hoping you will take this Letter in good part, and answer it with what care and speed you can, I rest and remain,

Yours, if my own,

Mr. *Gabriel Bullock,*

Swepson, Leistershire.   now my father is dead.

When the Coal Carts come, I shall send oftener; and may come in one of them my self.

For Sir William to go to london at westminster, remember
a parlement.

Sir,
William, i hope that you are well. I write to let you know that i am in troubel about a lady you noase; and I do desire that you will be my frend; for when i did com to see her at your hall, i was mighty Abuesed. i would fain a see you at topecliff, and thay would not let me go to you; but i desire that you will be our frends, for it is no dishonor neither for you nor she, for God did make us all. i wish that I might see you, for thay say that you are a good man; and many doth wounder at it, but madam norton is abuesed and ceated two i beleive. i might a had many a lady, but i con have none but her with a good consons, for there is a God that know our harts. if you and madam norton will come to York, there i shill meet you if God be willing and if you pleased. so be not angterie till you know the trutes of things.

George Nillson.   I give my to me lady, and to Mr. Aysenby, and to madam norton. March, the 19th; 1706.

This is for madam mary norton disforth Lady she went to York.

Madam Mary. Deare loving sweet lady, i hope you are well. Do not go to london, for they will put you in the nunnery; and heed not Mrs. Lucy what she saith to you, for she will ly and ceat you. go from to another Place, and we will gate wed so with speed. mind what i write to you, for if they gate you to london they will keep you there; and so let us gate wed, and we will both go. so if you go to london, you rueing your self. so heed not what none of them saith to you. let us gate wed, and we shall lie to gader any time. i will do any thing for you to my poore. i hope the devill will faile them all, for a hellish Company there be. from there cursed trick and mischiefus ways good lord bless and deliver both you and me.

I think to be at york the 24 day.

This is for madam mary norton to go to london for a lady that belongs to dishforth.

Madam Mary, i hope you are well. i am soary that you went

away from York. deare loving sweet lady, i writt to let you know that i do remain faithfull; and if can let me know where i can meet you, i will wed you, and i will do any thing to my poor; for you are a good woman, and will be a loving Misteris. i am in troubel for you, so if you will come to york i will wed you. so with speed come, and i will have none but you. so, sweet love, heed not what to say to me, and with speed come: heed not what none of them say to you; your Maid makes you believe ought.

So deare love think of Mr. george Nillson with speed; i sent you 2 or 3 letters before.

I gave misteris elcock some nots, and thay put me in pruson all the night for me pains, and non new whear i was, and i did gat cold.

But it is for mrs. Lucy to go a good way from home, for in York and round about she is known; to writ any more her deeds, the same will tell hor soul is back within, hor corkis stinks of hell.

March 19th, 1706."'

A portion of the letter to Mrs. Clarke is printed in No. 324 (page 11 of this volume). Chalmers states, on the authority of a MS. note by Dr. Birch, that a paper in the original folio (probably this one) was withdrawn in the octavo edition on the remonstrance of a family who conceived themselves injured by it.

PAGE 24. *Charles Mather*, a toy-dealer in Fleet Street.

Persico. In No. 335 (*A*) and subsequent numbers, one Paul Girard, at the 3 Flower de Luces, at Charing Cross, advertises distilled waters from Italy 'of the 4 most select Sorts, Millefleur, Orangiat, Burgamot, and Persicot.'

329. PAGE 25. *Motto.* Horace, *Epistles*, I. vi. 27.

Baker's Chronicle. See note, i. 534.

PAGE 26. *Sir Cloudsly Shovel.* Cf. the passage in No. 26 (i. 79-80).

Dr. Busby, head master of Westminster School from 1640 to 1695. See ii. 443 and note.

PAGE 27. *The little Chappel*, of St. Edmund.

That Martyr to good Housewifry. Elizabeth Russell.

330. PAGE 28. *Motto.* Juvenal, *Satires*, xiv. 47.

In *A* the paper concludes with this note, bearing on the original paper, No. 328 (given in the note, page 465):

' *Mr.* SPECTATOR,   *March the* 18*th.*

The Ostentation you shew'd Yesterday wou'd have been pardonable, had you provided better for the two Extremities of your Paper, and plac'd in one the Letter R, in the other *Nescio quid meditans nugarum, et totus in illis.* A Word to the Wise.

I am your most humble Servant,
T. Trash.

According to the Emendation of the above Correspondent, the Reader is desired in the Paper of the 17th to read R for T.'

331. PAGE 31. *Motto.* Persius, *Satires,* ii. 28.
    Aelian. Variae Historiae, xi. 10.
    Zoilus. See note, ii. 499.
  PAGE 33. *Hudibras,* I. i. 241–6.
    They already appear in Huts, etc. Cf. No. 104 (i. 319 and note).

332. *Motto.* Horace, *Satires,* I. iii. 29–30.

333. PAGE 36. *Motto.* Virgil, *Aeneid,* vi. 172.
    Paradise Lost, i. 44–9; i. 128–9, 134–7, 169–77.
  PAGE 37. *Paradise Lost,* ii. 165–8. The second quotation is from the *second* book, lines 988–98.
  PAGE 38. *Longinus. On the Sublime,* viii. The passage in Homer is in the *Odyssey* (xi. 314).
  PAGE 39. *Lord Roscommon's Essay.* Cf. No. 253 (ii. 254).
  PAGE 41. *My Bow,* etc. Later texts read:

> My bow and thunder, my almighty arms,
> Gird on, and sword upon thy puissant thigh.

    All Heaven, etc. More correctly:

> All Heaven
> Resounded; and, had Earth been then, all Earth
> Had to her centre shook.

334. PAGE 42. *Motto.* Cicero, *De Oratore,* I. lxi. 258.
  PAGE 43. *Booth in the Character of Pyrrhus.* In Philips's *Distrest Mother,* referred to in the next paper.
    The following letter. Probably by John Weaver, being an epitome of portion of his *Essay towards the History of Dancing,* octavo, 1712. John Essex's *Treatise of Choreography* (3rd ed.) is advertised in No. 336.
  PAGE 44. *Terence.* In the prologue to *Hecyra.*
  PAGE 45. *Macrobius. Somnium Scipionis,* ii (near the beginning).
335. *Motto.* Horace, *Ars Poetica,* 317–18.
    Sir Roger's visit to the play may be compared with Mr. Bickerstaff's, which is the subject of the 122nd *Tatler.*
    The new Tragedy. The Distrest Mother. See No. 290 and note thereon (ii. 500). The leading parts were taken as follows: Orestes, Mr. Powell (see No. 346, page 85); Pyrrhus, Mr. Booth (see preceding paper); Andromache, Mrs. Oldfield (see No. 341, page 65); Hermione, Mrs. Porter. The play was, according to Genest, acted about nine times. It was published by Buckley, on Friday 28th March (see advt. in this number, *A*). It was burlesqued by Fielding in his *Covent Garden Tragedy* (1732).
  PAGE 46. *The Committee,* by Sir Robert Howard, had great vogue after the Restoration, on account of its political character. See Pepys's *Diary* (12th June 1663).
    Mohocks. See page 464.
336. PAGE 48. *Motto.* Horace, *Epistles,* II. i. 80–5.
  PAGE 49. *So these three Men.* Job, xxxii.

337. **PAGE 51.** *Motto.* Horace, *Epistles*, I. ii. 63–4.
 PAGE 53. *Says Horace. Satires*, I. iv.
 Xenophon. Cyropaedia, I. ii. 6.
 Apuleius. Florida, vi.
 PAGE 54. *The Archbishop of Cambray.* Fénelon. See i. 555.

338. **PAGE 55.** *Motto.* Horace, *Satires*, I. iii. 18–19.
 Is publish'd to Day. So, too, the advertisement in *A*.
 Author of the Prologue. See note, ii. 500.
 Gentleman who writ the Epilogue. See ii. 500.
 'The propriety of epilogues in general, and consequently of this,' says Johnson in his *Life of Ambrose Philips*, 'was questioned by a correspondent of the *Spectator*, whose Letter was undoubtedly admitted for the sake of the answer, which soon followed, written with much zeal and acrimony [No. 341]. The attack and defence equally contributed to stimulate curiosity and continue attention. It may be discovered in the defence, that Prior's Epilogue to *Phaedra* had a little excited jealousy; and something of Prior's plan may be discovered in the performance of his rival.
 'Of this distinguished Epilogue the reputed author was the wretched Budgell, whom Addison used to denominate "the man who calls me cousin"; and when he was asked how such a silly fellow could write so well, replied, "The Epilogue was quite another thing when I saw it first." It was known in Tonson's family, and told to Garrick, that Addison was himself the author of it, and that, when it had been at first printed with his name, he came early in the morning, before the copies were distributed, and ordered it to be given to Budgell, that it might add weight to the solicitation which he was then making for a place.'

 PAGE 56. *Mrs. Oldfield* as *Andromache*. See note to page 45.

 PAGE 57. *Paul Lorrain.* Ordinary of Newgate. Cf. *Tatler*, No. 63: 'Most Writers, like the Generality of Paul Lorrain's Saints' seem to place a peculiar Vanity in dying hard.' He published accounts of the chief criminals whom he had executed. Cf. Bolingbroke to Swift (*Pope's Letters*, edited by Elwin, vii. (ii). 67).

339. *Motto.* Virgil, *Eclogues*, vi. 33–6. In the original it is ascribed to Ovid.
 Longinus. On the Sublime, viii.

 PAGE 58. *The Critick above-mentioned. On the Sublime*, xiv; and, again, ix.

 PAGE 59. *And behold there came*, etc. Zechariah, vi. 1.

 PAGE 62. Line 29. 'Resounded' in the later texts of *Paradise Lost*. *A Poem which has lately appear'd. The Creation*, by Blackmore (see note, i. 519). It first appeared on 28th February 1712.

340. **PAGE 63.** *Motto.* Virgil, *Aeneid*, iv. 10–11.
 The Prince. Eugene of Savoy. See note, ii. 497.

 PAGE 64. *Of that Stature.* Cf. Swift's *Journal to Stella*, especially under 13th January 1712.

PAGE 64. *His Action and Address*, etc. Cf. Burnet's *History of his Own Time*, 1734, ii. 590: 'He has a most unaffected Modesty, and does scarcely bear the Acknowledgments, that all the World pay him: He descends to an easy Equality with those, with whom he converses; and seems to assume nothing to himself, while he reasons with others.'

PAGE 65. *Never was equalled but by one Man.* The Duke of Marlborough.

341. *Motto.* Virgil, *Aeneid*, i. 203–4.

Some of the editors have commented on the bitterness of this epistle, but the writers of this letter and that in No. 338 (q.v.) are less serious in their critical anger than in drawing the attention of the public to their friend's piece. See the note on page 470.

PAGE 66. *In a Tragedy where there is not only a Death*, etc., i.e. in Dryden's *Tyrannic Love or The Royal Martyr* (1669). Nell Gwyn ('Mrs. Ellen') played Valeria, daughter of Maximin, and Mrs. Boutell, St. Catherine, Princess of Alexandria. The concluding lines of the Epilogue run:

> Here *Nelly* lies, who, though she lived a Slater'n,
> Yet dy'd a princess, acting in *S. Cathar'n*.

This may explain the Spectator's slip.

Phaedra and Hippolitus. See i. 526. The Epilogue was written by Prior.

PAGE 67. *Orestes and Lubin.* Probably in Racine's *Andromaque* and Molière's *George Dandin ou Le Mari confondu*.

The Rehearsal. 'Now, Gentlemen, I would fain ask your opinion of one thing. I have made a Prologue and an Epilogue, which may both serve for either (do you mark?): nay, they may both serve too, I gad, for any other Play as well as this' (I. i).

The Knight of the Sorrowful Countenance. Don Quixote.

342. PAGE 68. *Motto.* Cicero, *De Officiis*, I. xxviii. 99.

343. PAGE 71. *Motto.* Ovid, *Metamorphoses*, xv. 165–8.

Sir Paul Rycaut. His *Present State of the Ottoman Empire* appeared in 1669.

344. PAGE 74. *Motto.* Juvenal, *Satires*, XI. ii.

PAGE 76. *Taking Snuff.* See note, i. 547.

345. *Motto.* Ovid, *Metamorphoses*, i. 76–8.

PAGE 81. Dryden's *State of Innocence and Fall of Man*, II. ii.

346. PAGE 82. *Motto.* Cicero, *De Officiis*, II. xviii. 63.

PAGE 83. *My beloved Author.* Cicero. Cf. i. 466, 476, and note, i. 517. The reader (and the editor) can appreciate Steele's admission.

PAGE 84. *The Practice of some wealthy Men.* See note, ii. 491 (No. 248).

PAGE 85. *York-Buildings.* See ii. 494. It was a general name applied to the blocks of houses erected on the site of York House.

Pepys resided there for a short time towards the close of his life. See Globe edition, pages xxii, xxiii.

PAGE 85. *George Powell*. See i. 524. He played Falstaff this night at Drury Lane.

347. *Motto*. Lucan, *Pharsalia*, i. 8.

The 'Emperor's' technicalities are explained in the letter printed in No. 332.

348. PAGE 88. *Motto*. Horace, *Satires*, II. iii. 13.

349. PAGE 90. *Motto*. Lucan, *Pharsalia*, i. 459–62.

PAGE 91. *St. Evremont*. See i. 99, etc. Addison here refers to Saint-Evremond's *Life and Character of Petronius Arbiter*, which appeared with the translation of 1708.

PAGE 92. *The Abbot de Vertot*. René Aubert de Vertot d'Auboeuf, author of a *History of the Revolutions of Portugal*.

Don Sebastian. This tale is the plot of the old play *The Battle of Alcazar* (1594), and of Dryden's tragedy *Don Sebastian* (1690).

350. PAGE 93. *Motto*. Cicero, *De Officiis*, I. xix. 62.

PAGE 95. *A French Author*, etc. Le Bossu, *Du Poéme épique*, IV. x (towards the end).

351. *Motto*. Virgil, *Aeneid*, xii. 59.

PAGE 96. *Heus etiam*, etc. Virgil, *Aeneid*, vii. 116.

PAGE 99. . . . Some cursed fraud

Of enemy hath beguiled thee . . .

Paradise Lost, ix. 905–6.

352. PAGE 101. *Motto*. Cicero, *De Officiis*, III. viii. 55.

353. PAGE 104. *Motto*. Virgil, *Georgics*, iv. 6.

PAGE 105. *Two Persons*. Chalmers suggests that this may be a reference to Swift and his friend Mr. Stratford, the Hamburg merchant, who is referred to very frequently in the *Journal to Stella*.

354. PAGE 107. *Motto*. Juvenal, *Satires*, vi. 168–9.

Questions and Commands. Cf. ii. 226; *The Vicar of Wakefield*, xi (2nd paragraph).

PAGE 108. *Xenophon*. *On the Polity of Lacedaemon*.

PAGE 109. *Red Breeches*, etc. Wycherley, The *Plain Dealer*, II. i. *Otway*. *Friendship in Fashion*, III. i.

355. PAGE 110. *Motto*. Ovid, *Tristia*, ii. 563.

Epictetus. *Enchiridion*, xlviii, lxiv.

PAGE 111. *Balzac*. Balzac's *Letters* were first translated into English by W. Tirwhyt, in 1634. Sir Richard Baker added two volumes of *New Epistles* in 1638. An enlarged edition was published in one volume in 1654.

PAGE 112. *Boccalini*. See note, ii. 500.

356. *Motto*. Juvenal, *Satires*, x. 349–50.

PAGE 113. *Catastrophe of this Day*. Good Friday.

In plain and apt Parable. It would appear that from this

point the paper is a reprint, with some alterations, of the concluding portion of the second chapter of Steele's early work *The Christian Hero.*

357. PAGE 115. *Motto.* Virgil, *Aeneid,* ii. 6, 8.

PAGE 121. *Homer . . . represents Sleep. Iliad,* xiv.

PAGE 122. *Strength and Necessity.* Aeschylus, *Prometheus Bound, Before him went the Pestilence.* Habakkuk, iii. 5.

358. *Motto.* Horace, *Odes,* IV. xii. 28.

    Charles Lillie. See i. 539.

    Mosaick Work. Steele's allusion to the Stonesfield mosaic is best explained by an advertisement in No. 349 et sqq. (*A*): 'Whereas about nine Weeks since there was accidentally discovered by an Husbandman at Stimsfield [Stunsfield], near Woodstock in Oxfordshire, (a large Pavement of rich Mosaick Work of the Ancient Romans, which is adorn'd with several Figures alluding to Mirth and Concord, in particular that of Bacchus seated on a Panther). This is to give Notice, that an exact Delineation of the same is Engraven and Imprinted on a large Elephant Sheet of Paper; which are to be sold at Mr. Charles Lillie's, Perfumer, at the corner of Beauford Buildings, in the Strand, at 1s. N.B. There are to be had at the same Place at one Guinea each on superfine Atlas Paper, some painted with the same variety of Colours that the said Pavement is beautified with; this piece of Antiquity is esteemed by the Learned to be the most considerable ever found in Britain.' The engraver was Vertue.

PAGE 124. *And one perhaps.* Probably a reference to one of Sir Charles Sedley's frolics.

    Estcourt. See note, ii. 495.

    Ancient Pantomime. Pantomime is here used in its older and more correct sense. The word is defined in Blount's *Glossary* (edition of 1674), as 'an actor of many parts in one play.' Cf. Johnson in his *Dictionary,* where he quotes *Hudibras,* III. ii. 1287-90.

PAGE 125. *Love for Love.* Congreve's play is advertised in *A* for Tuesday, 22nd April.

359. *Motto.* Virgil, *Eclogues,* ii. 63-4.

PAGE 127. *Pocket Milton.* Perhaps a friendly reference to the pocket edition so frequently advertised by Buckley in the *Spectator* (*A*).

    Paradise Lost, x. 888-908. Usually:

> O, why did God,
> Creator wise, that peopled highest heaven.

360. *Motto.* Horace, *Epistles,* I. xvii. 43-4.

    Silence of our Poverty. Cf. ii. 286 (foot) and 336 (top).

PAGE 128. *The Christian Hero.* In Chapter III. See the note to page 113 *supra,*

PAGE 130. *A Fellow of no Mark. 1 Henry IV,* III. ii. 45.

361. *Motto.* Virgil, *Aeneid*, vii. 514–15. Addison had changed it to *Omnis contremuit domus.*

The Humorous Lieutenant, by Beaumont and Fletcher. See also ii. 292.

PAGE 132. *Mr.* * * *. In *A*, at the end, is added: `Not being yet determined with whose Name to fill up the Gap in this Dissertation, which is marked with Asterisks, I shall defer it till this Paper appears with others in a Volume.`

Mr. Collier. The passage will be found on page 24 of part ii of his *Essays upon Several Moral Subjects* (1697).

Almanzor. See i. 566 and ii. 488.

362. PAGE 133. *Motto.* Horace, *Epistles*, I. xix. 6.

Celebrated Yesterday. 23rd April was Queen Anne's coronation day (1702), and also St. George's Day.

Brooke and Hellier. See note, ii. 504. This paper on bad wine recalls No. 131 of the *Tatler*, which exposes the 'Chymical Operators' who, 'by the Power of Magical Drugs and Incantations,' raise 'under the Streets of London the choicest Products of the Hills and Valleys of France.' Steele there speaks of the adulteration of port, and of 'the Lands in Herefordshire' being 'raised Two Years Purchase since the Beginning of the War.' He denounces the operators 'as no better than a kind of Assassins and Murderers within the Law.' The advertisements of protestation, in the columns of the original *Spectator*, show that the fraud was well known to the vintners of Steele's day.

Cully Mully Puff. See ii. 245, and note.

363. PAGE 136. *Motto.* Virgil, *Aeneid*, ii. 368–9.

They forthwith. This is adapted from *Paradise Lost*, x. 1086–90. The other quotations in this paper show several variations from the accepted text.

PAGE 141. *Jamque mare*, etc. Ovid, *Metamorphoses*, I. 291–2.

364. PAGE 143. *Motto.* Horace, *Epistles*, I. ii. 28–9.

'This letter on travelling,' says Chalmers, 'was written by Mr. Philip Yorke, afterwards Earl of Hardwicke, who was likewise the author of another paper in the *Spectator*, which his son could not particularly remember. This information is given on the authority of Dr. Thomas Birch, in a letter dated June 15, 1764.'

PAGE 145. *Exactness.* After this word the text of *A* continues: 'I can't quit this Head without paying my Acknowledgments to one of the most entertaining Pieces this Age has produc'd, for the Pleasure it gave me. You will easily guess, that the Book I have in my head is *Mr. A——'s Remarks upon Italy.* That Ingenious gentleman has with so much Art and Judgment applied his exact Knowledge of all the Parts of Classical Learning to illustrate the several occurrences of his Travels, that his Work alone is a pregnant Proof of what I have said. No Body that had a Taste this way, can read him going from *Rome* to *Naples*, and making *Horace* and *Silius Italicus* his Chart, but he must feel some Uneasiness in himself to Reflect that he was not in his Retinue. I am sure I wish'd it Ten Times in every Page, and that not without a secret Vanity to think in what State I should have travelled the *Appian* Road with *Horace* for a Guide, and in company with a Countryman of my own, who of all Men living knows best how to follow his Steps.

'But I have wandered. . . .'

PAGE 146. *The Amorous Widow or The Wanton Wife*, a comedy based on Molière's *George Dandin* (see note, page 471), first played at Lincoln's Inn Fields in 1670. Mrs. Porter had taken the part of Philadelphia at the revival at the Haymarket on 19th November 1709. See Genest, i. 108.

365. Motto. Virgil, *Georgics*, iii. 272.
    Menagiana. See i. 185 and note.

PAGE 147. *Dryden. Palamon and Arcite*, ii. 53–6; i. 176–9: 'break their *sluggard* sleep.'

PAGE 148. *Paradise Lost*, iv. 268–71.
    Snake in the Grass. Virgil, *Eclogues*, iii. 92–3.

366. PAGE 149. Motto. Horace, *Odes*, i. xxii. 17–18, 23–4.

PAGE 150. Scheffer's *History of Lapland* is the Oxford translation (1674) of his Latin account, entitled *Lapponia* (1673). Scheffer, a native of Strasburg (died 1679), was librarian to Queen Christina of Sweden and a professor in the university of Upsala. The version of this translation in the *Spectator* is by Ambrose Philips, whose translations from Sappho had been printed in Nos. 223 and 229 (see note, ii. 487). Another song in Scheffer's book is rendered in No. 406.

367. PAGE 152. Motto. Juvenal, *Satires*, i. 18.

PAGE 154. *The new Edition . . . of Caesar's Commentaries.* This is the beautiful folio edited by Samuel Clarke, and published by Tonson. The Preface is dated 4th December 1711.

368. Motto. Cicero, *Tusculan Disputations*, i. xlviii. 115.

369. PAGE 157. Motto. Horace, *Ars Poetica*, 180–1.

PAGE 158. *Haec tum*, etc. Virgil, *Aeneid*, vi. 777.

PAGE 161. *Bossu.* See i. 216, and note. Cf. also Johnson: 'Bossu is of opinion that the poet's first work is to find a moral, which his fable is afterwards to illustrate and establish' (*Life of Milton*). See the notes on Addison's use of Le Bossu, ii. 495, 500, and page 465 of this volume.

PAGE 163. This paper concludes Addison's weekly critiques of *Paradise Lost*. With all due appreciation of the literary merits of Addison's work in this matter, one is forced to the conclusion that it is unsatisfactory as a piece of systematic criticism. Its influence was undoubtedly great (see note, ii. 496), but its true merit lies in the success which it achieved for the reputation of Milton. The papers took the public fancy, as Addison's bookseller was glad to testify, and were the innocent cause of much exaggerated praise, of which Eusden's verses in Steele's *Miscellany* (1727) are a typical example. An excellent critique of Addison's papers will be found in a note by Richard Hurd:

'It gives one pain to refuse to such a writer, as Mr. *Addison*, any *kind* of merit, to which he appears to have laid claim, and which the generality have seemed willing to allow him. Yet it must not be dissembled, that *criticism* was, by no means, his talent. His taste was truly elegant; but he had neither that vigour of understanding, nor chastised, philosophical spirit, which are so essential to this character, and which we find in hardly any of the antients, besides Aristotle, and but in a very few of the moderns. For what concerns his *Criticism on Milton* in particular, there was this accidental benefit arising from it, that it occasioned an admirable poet to be read, and his excellencies to be observed. But for the merit of the work itself, if there be any thing just in the *plan*, it was because Aristotle and Bossu had taken the same route before him. And as to his *own* proper observations, they are for the most part, so general and indeterminate, as to afford but little instruction to the reader, and are, not unfrequently, altogether frivolous. They are of a kind with those, in which the French critics (for I had rather instance in the defects of *foreign* writers than of our *own*) so much abound; and which good judges agree to rank in the worst sort of criticism.' (*Q. Horatii Flacci Epistolae ad Pisones et Augustum*, etc., third edition, Cambridge, 1757, ii. 94.)

370. *Motto.* See text of paper.

This paper is a companion to No. 182 of the *Tatler*. Steele there says: 'It may possibly be imagined by severe Men, that I am too frequent in the mention of the Theatrical Representations,' and he proceeds to make a comparison between Robert Wilks and Colley Cibber in the terms of the present paper. 'Wilks has a singular Talent in representing the Graces of Nature, Cibber the Deformity in the affectation of them. . . . Cibber, in another Light, hits exquisitely the flat Civility of an affected Gentleman-Usher, and Wilks the easy Frankness of a Gentleman. If you would observe the Force of the same Capacities in higher Life, Can any Thing be more ingenuous, than the Behaviour of Prince Harry when his Father checks him? Any Thing more exasperating, than that of Richard, when he insults his Superiors? To beseech gracefully, to approach respectfully, to pity, to mourn, to love, are the Places wherein Wilks may be made to shine with the utmost Beauty: To rally pleasantly, to scorn artfully, to flatter, to ridicule, and to neglect, are what Cibber would perform with no less Excellence.'

PAGE 164. *The Trip to the Jubilee.* The second title of Farquhar's *Constant Couple* (1700). Sir Harry Wildair is the 'Young Man of Good-nature.'

An artful Servant. Mosca in Ben Jonson's *Volpone or The Fox.*

Eastcourt. See page 473.

Lord Foppington. In Colley Cibber's popular play *The Careless Husband.*

Dogget. Cf. ii. 199. See *B. I.*

PAGE 164. *Corbacchio*. Corbaccio was Johnson's part in Ben Jonson's *Volpone*.

William Penkethman, See i. 530. Cibber's *Love Makes a Man or The Fop's Fortune* is advertised in *A* for his benefit that evening. He took the part of Don Lewis, *alias* Don Choleric Snap Shorto de Testy, and the author that of Clodio, *alias* Don Dismallo Thick-Scullo de Half Witto.

PAGE 165. *Mrs. Bicknell* took her benefit in Farquhar's *Constant Couple* (*supra*). Mrs. Oldfield took the part of *Lady Lurewell*. The bill of the play adds: 'Dancing by Mr. Prince, Mr. Thurmond, and Mrs. Bicknell' (advertisement in *A*). See *B. I*.

371. *Motto*. Juvenal, *Satires*, x. 28–9.

One of the Wits of the last Age. Perhaps Buckingham, author of *The Rehearsal*.

372. PAGE 168. *Motto*. Ovid, *Metamorphoses*, i. 758–9.

Ralph Bellfry refers to the letter in No. 14 (i. 44).

PAGE 169. *Mr. Powell at the Bath*. See the *Tatler*, Nos. 44, 50 (containing Powell's reply from Bath), 77, and 115; also note in vol. i of the *Spectator*, page 524.

373. PAGE 171. *Motto*. Juvenal, *Satires*, xiv. 109.

Locke's Treatise. II. x. xi.

374. PAGE 173. *Motto*. Lucan, *Pharsalia*, ii. 657. Some texts read 'Nil actum credens, cum quid . . .' Steele translates it in the essay.

375. PAGE 175. *Motto*. Horace, *Odes*, iv. 45–50.

A noble Saying of Seneca. See the first paragraph of No. 39 (i. 116).

376. PAGE 179. *Motto*. Persius, *Satires*, vi. 11.

377. PAGE 181. *Motto*. Horace, *Odes*, ii. xiii. 13–14.

Oroondates. See ii. 91 and note.

PAGE 182. *Porcupine*. Cowley's *Anacreontiques*, iii

> They are all Weapon, and they dart
> Like Porcupines from every Part.

The Ring. See i. 539.

PAGE 183. *The Trip to the Jubilee*. See note, page 476.

378. *Motto*. Virgil, *Eclogues*, iv. 48.

This is the first appearance of the *Messiah*, which Pope had written at Binfield. Steele printed it in *A* as he received it, and on 1st June wrote to the author: 'I have turned to every verse and chapter, and think you have preserved the sublime heavenly spirit throughout the whole, especially at *Hark a glad voice*, and *The Lamb with wolves shall graze*. There is but one line which I think below the original,

He wipes the tears for ever from our eyes.

You have expressed it with a good and pious, but not so exalted and poetical a spirit as the prophet, *The Lord God will wipe away tears from off all faces*. If you agree with me in this, alter it by way of paraphrase or otherwise, that when it comes into a volume it may be amended. Your poem is already better than the Pollio.' Pope accepted the advice, and altered the line in the octavo edition (see page 184, last line but two). The poem (with Introduction and Notes) will be found in the first volume of Elwin and Courthope's edition.

379. PAGE 186. *Motto.* Persius, *Satires*, i. 27.

PAGE 187. *There is still extant.* Aulius Gellius, *Noctes Atticae*, xx. 5.

Gratian. See note, ii. 500.

Cowley. Several Discourses by Way of Essays, x ('The Danger of Procrastination').

PAGE 188. A book entitled *Le Comte de Gabalis*, by the Abbé Villars, dealing with the Rosicrucian mysteries, was at this time much read and talked about in England. It was translated from the French by Ozell. Pope derived from it his notion of the machinery of the sylphs, which he incorporated in the revised version of *The Rape of the Lock*.

380. *Motto.* Ovid, *Ars Amatoria*, ii. 539.

PAGE 191. *You were so kind to recommend.* See ii. 378.

381. *Motto.* Horace, *Odes*, II. iii. 1–4.

382. PAGE 194. *Motto.* Cicero, *Pro Ligario.*

383. PAGE 197. *Motto.* Juvenal, *Satires*, i. 75. In the original it is ascribed to Horace.

Spring-Garden. Also known as Vauxhall ('Fox-hall' on page 198). See Austin Dobson's *Eighteenth Century Vignettes*, i.

PAGE 198. *La Hogue.* '*Bantry Bay*' in *A*.

384. PAGE 199. *Motto.* As there noted.

PAGE 200. *My Lord Bishop of St. Asaph* (William Fleetwood) published *Four Sermons* in 1712, to which he prefixed the Preface here reprinted by Steele. The House of Commons having condemned the book, because of its Whig principles, Steele by this editorial ruse gave it a wide circulation (fourteen thousand copies were said to have been sold). He delayed publication till twelve o'clock, so that it might go direct to the queen's breakfast-table without risk of suppression by the court officials. Mr. Spectator here, and in the case of the Duke of Marlborough, had forgotten his vow not to meddle with politics. See Johnson's *Life of Addison*.

385. PAGE 203. *Motto.* Ovid, *Tristia*, I. iii. 66.

386. PAGE 205. *Motto.* Cicero, *Oratio pro M. Caelio*, vi. 13.

387. PAGE 208. *Motto.* Horace, *Epistles*, I. xviii. 102. This paper and Nos. 388 and 390 are wrongly numbered in *A*.

388. PAGE 211. *Motto.* Virgil, *Georgics*, ii. 174–5.

There is an editorial tradition that verse renderings of a chapter of Proverbs and of another portion of the Old Testament were by a Mr. Parr, a dissenting minister at Moretonhampstead in Devonshire. The passage in Addison's paper which sug-

gested the present exercise will be found in No. 327. The last
lines in the first and second stanzas read in *A*, respectively:

> And their united Beauties shall be less than mine.
>
> And stands among ten thousand eminently bright.

389. PAGE 214. *Motto.* ? Horace.
　　A small Book, etc. This copy of Giordano Bruno's work
was purchased in 1711 by Mr. Walter Clavel at public auction
for twenty-eight pounds. (In *A* the sum is given as *fifty*
pounds.) See the note in Chalmers's edition.

　　PAGE 216. *Vanini.* Lucilio Vanini was burned at Toulouse in
1619. *Casimir Lyszynski* suffered at Warsaw in 1689. See
Chalmers's notes.

390. PAGE 217. *Motto.* Cicero, *De Oratore*, I. xxvi. 120.

　　PAGE 218. *The best, said he.* Spenser, *Faerie Queene*, VI. vi. 14.

391. PAGE 219. *Motto.* Persius, *Satires*, ii. 3–13.

　　PAGE 221. *An Ephesian Widow.* Cf. i. 34 and ii. 193.

392. PAGE 222. *Motto.* Petronius Arbiter, cxviii. The passage runs:
'Sed per ambages, deorumque ministeria, et fabulosum senten-
tiarum tormentum, praecipitandus est liber spiritus.'

　　PAGE 223. Line 6. '. . . that it produced so odd a Dream, that
no one but the SPECTATOR could believe that the Brain, clogged
in Sleep, could furnish out such a regular Wildness of Imagination' (*A*).

393. PAGE 224. *Motto.* Virgil, *Georgics*, i. 412.

　　PAGE 225. *Paradise Lost*, iv. 148–56.

394. PAGE 227. *Motto.* Cicero, *De Officiis*, II. xvi.

395. PAGE 233. *Motto.* Ovid, *Remedia Amoris*, 10.
　　The Advice I gave. See Budgell's previous paper, No. 365.
　　PAGE 234. *Valetudinarians.* See i. 528.
　　Long she flourished, etc. Said by Chamont in Otway's
Orphan, IV. ii.

396. PAGE 235. *Motto.* A familiar aid to the 'logical' memory.
　　Clenching. See No. 61.
　　PAGE 236. *Philobrune.* See ii. 355.
　　Dr. T—— W——. Percy suggested that the reference was
to Thomas Woolston, author of *The Old Apology of the Truth for
the Christian Religion against the Jews and Gentiles revived* (1705),
and of the more notorious discourses on the miracles (1727–9).
Henry Morley names a Cambridge M.D., Thomas Winston,
who settled in London in 1607.
　　Belch. A slang term for poor beer.
　　PAGE 237. *Mr. W——n.* William Whiston. See B. I.
　　Mr. L——y it is difficulty to identify. If John Lacy, the
actor and dramatist, who died in 1681, is intended, why is his
name disguised? Steele's reference to the criticism of the
'Gentlemen of the *Bon Goust* in the Pit' recalls in a striking way

the Prologue to his play *The Old Troop*, where he appeals to the 'gods' against the critics in 'box and pit.' (See Ward's *Dramatic Literature*, iii. 449, note.) Or he may be the John Lacy whom Chalmers traced in the advertisements of the *Post-Boy* (3rd August 1714): 'This day is published, The Steeleids, or the Trial of Wits, a poem in three cantos. By John Lacy.

> Quo propius stet, te capiat magis.
>
> Then will I say, swell'd with poetic rage,
> That I, John Lacy, have reform'd the age.

Printed and sold by John Morphew, Pr. 1s.'

PAGE 237. *Peter de Quir*, i.e. Orator Henley. See Henley, John, in *B. I.* In No. 518 he subscribes as 'Tom Tweer.'

397. *Motto.* Ovid, *Metamorphoses*, xiii. 228–9.

Epictetus. See Stanhope's *Epictetus*, xxii. 153 (third edition, 1704). Cf. *ante*, i. 541.

398. PAGE 240. *Motto.* Horace, *Satires*, II. iii. 271.

PAGE 241. *Favoured.* Resembled in features.

399. PAGE 243. *Motto.* Persius, *Satires*, iv. 23.

PAGE 244. *Who can*, etc. Psalm xix. 12.

Plutarch has written. Cf. No. 125 (i. 380) and note (ib. 560).

400. PAGE 246. *Motto.* Virgil, *Eclogues*, iii. 93.

Sidley has, etc. The same passage is quoted in No. 91. See i. 284, and note on page 553. Eight days earlier (1st June) Steele wrote to Pope: 'I am at a solitude, an house between Hampstead and London, wherein Sir Charles Sedley died. The circumstance set me a-thinking and ruminating upon the employments in which men of wit exercise themselves. It was said of Sir Charles, who breathed his last in this room, "Sedley has that . . ." [Here follow the lines given in the text.]' Steele evidently liked these lines much, and found solace in quoting them in his 'solitude,' for which, says Nichols, 'there were too many pecuniary reasons' (Steele's *Epistolary Correspondence*, i. 236).

PAGE 247. *Her Gallery*, etc. Dryden's *All for Love*, III. i.

Breathe soft, etc. Ambrose Philips's *Pastorals*, vi. 69–72.

PAGE 248. *When Lucy decks*, etc. Ib. 89–92, 73–6. Line 92 reads, in the 1748 edition of the *Pastorals*, 'nor *herds*, nor pasture.'

PAGE 249. *Sexes very often find.* 'Sexes, for want of other Amusement, often study Anatomy together; and what is worse than happens in any other friendship, they find' (*A*).

401. *Motto.* Terence, *Eunuchus*, i. 14–16 (59–61).

402. PAGE 251. *Motto.* Horace, *Ars Poetica*, 181–2. This punning motto does not appear in the original sheet.

403. PAGE 254. *Motto.* Horace, *Ars Poetica*, 142.

St. James's. See note, i. 514.

PAGE 255. *Jenny Man's.* See note, i. 557.

Will's. See note, i. 513.

404. PAGE 257. *Motto.* Virgil, *Eclogues*, viii. 63. In *A* the motto was from the *Georgics* (i. 60).

405. PAGE 260. *Motto.* Homer, *Iliad*, i. 472–4.

    Nicolini. Referred to *ante*, i. 17, 40, etc., and note, page 523. See *B. I.* In the *Poetical Miscellanies . . . published by Sir Richard Steele* (second edition, 1727) there is included a piece *On Nicolini's leaving the Stage* (page 36).

406. PAGE 262. *Motto.* Cicero, *Pro Archia*, vii. 16.

    PAGE 263. *Seneca says.* 'Itaque hoc quod apud Pomponium legi, animo mandabitur: Quidam adeo in latebras refugerunt, ut putent in turbido esse quidquid in luce est' (*Epistles*, iii).

    Companion of Obscurity. Cowley's *Essays* (iii, 'Of Obscurity,' 31):

> Here wrapt in th' arms of quiet let me lye;
> Quiet, companion of obscurity.

    Scheffer. See *ante*, pages 150–1 and note, page 475.

407. PAGE 265. *Motto.* Ovid, *Metamorphoses*, xiii. 127. With No. 407 cf. *Tatler*, No. 70.

    PAGE 266. *Laterum contentio.* See Pliny, XXVI. xiii. 85, and Cicero, *De Oratore*, I. lx and lxi.

    The anecdote of the *Counsellor* recalls the story of young Walter Scott and the button (Lockhart's *Life*, Chapter III).

408. PAGE 267. *Motto.* Cicero, ? *De Finibus.*

409. PAGE 270. *Motto.* Lucretius, i. 933.

    Gratian. Cf. No. 293 (ii. 373 and note) and No. 379 (*ante*, page 187). Baltasar Gracian in his *Agudeza y Arte del Ingenio* reduced to an exact system the literary mannerism (*conceptismo*) of his predecessor Góngora, the Spanish representative of the style associated with the name of Marini in Italy and of Lyly in England.

    PAGE 273. *I entertained the Town.* Nos. 58–63 (i. 176–98). *I have likewise examined.* See the 'Saturday' papers from No. 266 (ii. 291) to No. 369 (*ante*, page 163).

410. *Motto.* Terence, *Eunuchus*, v. iv. 12–18 (933–40).

    PAGE 274. *Your late Papers.* See page 211, and note.

411. PAGE 276. *Motto.* Lucretius, i. 925–7.

    The essays on the Imagination, of which this is the first, were originally a single essay, perhaps written at Oxford in Addison's undergraduate days. The first draft has been preserved, though not in its entirety. See *Some Portions of Essays contributed to the Spectator by Mr. Joseph Addison*, printed for J. Dykes Campbell (the owner of the MS.), Glasgow, 1864. A comparison of the text of this pamphlet with that of the *Spectator* shows that Addison had made considerable emendations.

    Akenside's *Pleasures of Imagination* was inspired by these papers: see the reference in the 'Design' prefixed to the first version of the poem. This paper and Nos. 412, 413, and 414

supply in Blair's *Rhetoric* the material of four lectures on the
'Critical Examination of the Style of Mr. Addison.'   The worthy
professor made a specious excuse for his dreary discourse on
Addison's style by saying that he was urged to it 'by the
circumstances of that part of the kingdom where these Lectures
were read: where the ordinary spoken language often differs
much from what is used by good English authors.'

412. PAGE 279. *Motto*.   Martial, *Epigrams*, IV. lxxxii. 8.

   PAGE 281. The Latin verses are by Addison.   We learn this from
   the MS. referred to above, in which the verses appear with a
   number of corrections in the essayist's hand.   In the duo-
   decimo edition of the *Spectator*, published in 1744, the following
   translation is added:

> The feather'd Husband to his Partner true,
> Preserves connubial Rites inviolate.
> With cold Indifference every Charm he sees,
> The milky Whiteness of the stately Neck,
> The shining Down, proud Crest, and purple Wings;
> But cautious with a searching Eye explores
> The female Tribes, his proper Mate to find,
> With kindred Colours mark'd: Did he not so,
> The Grove with painted Monsters wou'd abound,
> Th' ambiguous Product of unnatural Love.
> The Black-bird hence selects her sooty Spouse;
> The Nightingale her musical Compeer,
> Lur'd by the well-known Voice: the Bird of Night,
> Smit with her dusky Wings and greenish Eyes,
> Woos his dun Paramour.   The beauteous Race
> Speak the chaste Loves of their Progenitors;
> When, by the Spring invited, they exult
> In Woods and Fields, and to the Sun unfold
> Their Plumes, that with paternal Colours glow.

413. PAGE 282. *Motto*.   Ovid, *Metamorphoses*, iv. 287.

   In *A* the following letter is printed after the essay:

'*Mr.* SPECTATOR,   *June* 24, 1712

   I would not divert the Course of your Discourses, when you
seem bent upon obliging the World with a train of Thinking,
which, rightly attended, may render the Life of every Man who
reads it, more easy and happy for the future.   The Pleasures or
the Imagination are what bewilder Life, when Reason and
Judgment do not interpose; It is therefore a worthy Action in
you, to look carefully into the Powers of Fancy, that other Men,
from the Knowledge of them, may improve their Joys, and
allay their Griefs, by a just use of that Faculty: I say, Sir, I
would not interrupt you in the progress of this Discourse; but,
if you will do me the Favour of inserting this Letter in your
next Paper, you will do some Service to the Publick, tho' not
in so noble a way of Obliging, as that of improving their Minds.
Allow me, Sir, to acquaint you with a Design (of which I am
partly Author) though it tends to no greater a Good than that
of getting Mony.   I should not hope for the Favour of a
Philosopher in this Matter, if it were not attempted under all
the Restrictions which you Sages put upon private Acquisitions.

The first Purpose which every good Man is to propose to himself, is the Service of his Prince and Country; after that is done, he cannot add to himself, but he must also be beneficial to them. This Scheme of Gain is not only consistent with that End, but has its very Being in Subordination to it, for no Man can be a Gainer here, but at the same time he himself, or some other, must succeed in their Dealings with the Government. It is called the *Multiplication Table*, and in so far calculated for the immediate Service of Her Majesty, that the same Person who is fortunate in the Lottery of the State, may receive yet further Advantage in this Table. And I am sure nothing can be more pleasing to Her gracious Temper, than to find out additional Methods of encreasing their good Fortune who adventure any thing in Her Service, or laying Occasions for others to become capable of serving their Country who are at present in too low Circumstances to exert themselves. The manner of executing the Design is, by giving out Receipts for half Guineas received, which shall entitule the fortunate Bearer to certain Sums in the Table, as is set forth at large in the Proposals Printed the 23rd instant. There is another Circumstance in this Design which gives me hopes of your Favour to it, and that is what Tully advises, to wit, that the Benefit is made as diffusive as possible. Every one that has half a Guinea is put into a possibility from that small Sum to raise himself an easie Fortune; when these little parcels of Wealth are, as it were, thus thrown back again into the Redonation of Providence, we are to expect that some who live under Hardship or Obscurity, may be produced to the World in the Figure they deserve by this means. I doubt not but this last Argument will have Force with you, and I cannot add another to it, but what your Severity will, I fear, very little regard, which is that

> *I am, Sir,*
> *Your greatest Admirer,*
> Richard Steele.'

For the sequel to this letter see the note to No. 417 (page 484).

414. PAGE 284. *Motto.* Horace, *Ars Poetica*, 410–11.

PAGE 285. Horace, *Epistles*, II. ii. 77.

Virgil, *Georgics*, ii. 467–70.

PAGE 286. *British Gardeners.* See note, i. 519. Addison's thesis is that of Pope in the *Moral Essays*, iv. Cf. also Pope's letter to Lord Bathurst, 23rd September 1719 (Elwin and Courthope, viii. 327).

415. PAGE 287. *Motto.* Virgil, *Georgics*, ii. 155.

PAGE 289. *I have seen . . . in a French Author.* Addison here, as on many other occasions of a like character, is a little disingenuous. The passage is an almost verbatim transcript from John Evelyn's book, entitled *A Parallel of the Antient Architecture with the Modern . . . Written in French by Roland Freart, Sieur de Chambray ; made English for the Benefit of Builders.* London, 1664 (pages 10, 11).

416. PAGE 290. *Motto.* Lucretius, iv. 754.

417. PAGE 293. *Motto.* Horace, *Odes*, IV. iii. 1-4, 10--12.

    PAGE 295. Homer, *Iliad*, i. 528-30.

        Dixit, etc. Virgil, *Aeneid*, i. 402-5.

        Lumenque, etc. Virgil, *Aeneid*, i. 590-1.

    The following advertisement appears in *A*: 'Whereas the Proposal called the Multiplication-Table is under an Information from the Attorney-General, in Humble Submission and Duty to Her Majesty the said Undertaking is laid down, and Attendance is this Day given at the last House on the left Hand in Ship-Yard in Bartholomew-lane in order to repay such Sums as have been paid into the said Table without Deduction.' Such was the summary ending of the proposal made by Steele in his letter in No. 413 (*A*), note *supra*. Swift makes an ill-natured allusion in his *Journal to Stella* (1st July 1712): 'Steele was arrested the other day for making a lottery directly against an act of Parliament. He is now under prosecution; but they think it will be dropped out of pity. I believe he will very soon lose his employment, for he has been mighty impertinent of late in his Spectators; and I will never offer a word in his behalf.' It is quite possible that Swift's gossip of an 'arrest' is but an improvement on the notorious facts of Steele's pecuniary embarrassments. There is no reference to the affair in Steele's correspondence, unless, *perhaps*, in a letter to 'Dear Prue,' dated next day (*Epistolary Correspondence*, 240).

418. PAGE 296. *Motto.* Virgil, *Eclogues*, iii. 89.

    PAGE 298. *Informe cadaver*, etc. Virgil, *Aeneid*, viii. 264-7.

419. PAGE 299. *Motto.* Horace, *Epistles*, II. ii. 140.

        The Fairy Way of Writing. Cf. Dryden's *Apology for Heroic Poetry* (Scott and Saintsbury, v. 121).

    PAGE 300. *Sylvis*, etc. Horace, *Ars Poetica*, 244-6.

420. PAGE 302. *Motto.* Horace, *Ars Poetica*, 100.

421. PAGE 304. *Motto.* Ovid, *Metamorphoses*, iv. 294-5.

    PAGE 306. *Eumenidum*, etc. Virgil, *Aeneid*, iv. 469-73. The octavo reads: 'Cum *videt*, ultricesque . . .'

422. PAGE 309. *Motto.* Cicero, *Epistolae ad Familiares*, vii. i.

    Callisthenes. Chalmers suggests that in this sketch there may be a reference to Addison, and Austin Dobson quotes the following passage from Swift's *Character of Mrs. Johnson* (Stella): 'She was never positive in arguing; and she usually treated those who were so in a manner which well enough gratified that unhappy disposition; yet in such a sort as made it very contemptible, and at the same time did some hurt to the owners. Whether this proceeded from her easiness in general, or from her indifference to persons, or from her despair of mending them, or from the same practice which she much liked in Mr. Addison, I cannot determine; but when she saw any of the company very warm in a wrong opinion, she was more inclined to confirm them in it than oppose them.' (See *Selections from*

Steele, page 454.) Pope seems to refer to the same trait in the familiar lines on 'Atticus' in the *Prologue of the Satires*.

PAGE 311. *Mr. Congreve's Doris.* In the Dedication *To Mr. Congreve*, prefixed to the *Poetical Miscellanies* (referred to on page 481, Steele wrote: 'I cannot but instance Your inimitable DORIS, which excels, for Politeness, fine Raillery, and courtly Satyr, any Thing we can meet with in any Language . . . I cannot leave my Favourite DORIS, without taking Notice how much that short Performance discovers a True Knowledge of Life. DORIS is the Character of a Libertine Woman of Condition, and the Satyr is work'd up accordingly: For People of Quality are seldom touched with any Representation of their Vices, but in a Light which makes them Ridiculous.'

423. PAGE 312. *Motto.* Horace, *Odes*, III. xxvi. 1.

424. PAGE 315. *Motto.* Horace, *Epistles*, I. xi. 30.
   Sir Roger's Country-Seat. See Nos. 106 and 107 (i. 323–9).

PAGE 316. *As Tully speaks.* 'Nam mira sum alacritate ad litigandum' (*Epistolae ad Atticum*, II. vii).

425. PAGE 317. *Motto.* Horace, *Odes*, IV. vii. 9–12.

PAGE 318. *Milton.* Il Penseroso, 61–72, 147–154.

426. PAGE 321. *Motto.* Virgil, *Aeneid*, iii. 56–7.
   Basilius Valentinus. Cf. i. 554.
   'This tale is from the Description of the memorable Sea and Land Travels through Persia to the East Indies, by Johann Albrecht von Mandelslo, translated from the German of Olearius, by J. B. B. Bk. v. p. 189' (H. Morley's edition of the *Spectator*).

427. PAGE 324. *Motto.* Cicero, *Pro M. Caelio*, iii. 8.

PAGE 325. *Cicero in one of his Pleadings.* *Oratio pro Cn. Plancio*, xxiii. 57.

PAGE 326. *The Statue in Rome.* See note, i. 528.

428. PAGE 327. *Motto.* Horace, *Ars Poetica*, 417.

PAGE 328. *Author of Strops for Razors.* In No. 449 (*A*) there is an advertisement of the 'Famous Original Venetian Strops, neatly fix'd on Boards.'

429. PAGE 329. *Motto.* Horace, *Odes*, II. ii. 19–21.
   Institution of an Infirmary. See page 316.

430. PAGE 333. *Motto.* Horace, *Epistles*, I. xvii. 62.

PAGE 335. *For higher*, etc. *Paradise Lost*, viii. 598–9.

431. *Motto.* Cicero?

432. PAGE 338. *Motto.* Virgil, *Eclogues*, ix. 36.

> nec dicere Cinna
> Digna, sed argutos inter strepere anser olores.

Different Cocks. Cf. No. 129 (i. 392, 393).
Patches. See note, i. 500.
Head-dresses. Ib. and ii. 289.
The White or the Red Hood. See No. 265 (ii. 290–1).
Fine Odes . . . in Lapland. A reference to the pieces in Nos. 366 (page 150) and 406 (page 264).

433. PAGE 341. *Motto.* Martial, *Epigrams*, XIV. clxxxiii.

434. PAGE 343. *Motto.* Virgil, *Aeneid*, xi. 659–63.

435. PAGE 345. *Motto.* Ovid, *Metamorphoses*, iv. 378–9.

PAGE 346. *Female Cavaliers.* See i. 556.

PAGE 347. *Fashion . . . from France.* Cf. i. 160.

436. PAGE 348. *Motto.* Juvenal, *Satires*, iii. 36–7.

    Hockley-in-the-Hole. See note, i. 530.

    For *Millar*, [*S*]*parkes*, and *Preston* see *B. I.*

PAGE 351. *Tully speaks. Tusculan Disputations*, II. xvi. 41.

437. *Motto.* Terence, *Andria*, v. iv. 7–10.

PAGE 354. Steele had satirized the ladies' 'Affectation of Nakedness' in No. 215 of the *Tatler*, in 'the humble Petition of the Company of Linendrapers.'

    Gatty. See note to No. 515; also the *Tatler*, Nos. 24, 52, and 206.

438. *Motto.* Horace, *Epistles*, I. ii. 62–3.

    One of the greatest Souls. See note to Dedication of volume i.

PAGE 355. *Nat Lee.* The passage occurs in Act III, scene i of *The Rival Queens or Alexander the Great.* A line and a half are omitted after the third in the quotation. The words are spoken by Roxana, *not* by Alexander.

PAGE 356. *At a French Bookseller's.* 'This scene passed in the shop of Mr. Vaillant, late Mr. Elmsly's, and now Mr. Collingwood's, in the Strand; and the subject of it was (for it is still in remembrance) a volume of Massillon's Sermons' (Note repeated in Chalmers's edition). 'Chapman' is here used in the now obsolete sense of 'purchaser' or 'customer.'

439. PAGE 357. *Motto.* Ovid, *Metamorphoses*, xii. 57–8.

    Palace of Fame. Ib., 39 et sqq.

    Curse not the King. Ecclesiastes, x. 20.

PAGE 358. The anecdote from the 'Italian Author' is probably taken from Bayle. Cf. that of Gil Blas and the archbishop.

PAGE 359. *By the Earl of Clarendon.* A sketch of Lord Treasurer Weston, Earl of Portland.

440. PAGE 360. *Motto.* Horace, *Epistles*, II. ii. 213.

441. PAGE 362. *Motto.* Horace, *Odes*, III. iii. 7–8.

442. PAGE 365. *Motto.* Horace, *Epistles*, II. i. 117.

443. PAGE 367. *Motto.* Horace, *Odes*, III. xxiv. 32.

PAGE 368. *Those complaisant Lines.* The first stanza (without four lines at the end) of the 'Irregular Ode' *On Mrs. Arabella Hunt Singing*, which will be found in Congreve's *Works*, iii. 225–6 (edition of 1730).

PAGE 369. *Camilla.* Mrs. Tofts. See note, i. 526.

PAGE 370. *F. B.* 'Francis Beasniffe is said to have been the author of this last letter' (Edd.).

444. PAGE 370. *Motto.* Horace, *Ars Poetica*, 139. The motto in *A* was line 138.

PAGE 371. Steele has here deleted the greater portion of the advertisement of this quack, which appears *in extenso* in *A*. 'Gandice' (for 'jaundice') is an orthographic eccentricity of the said quack, whose spelling and grammar in the suppressed portion are not of the best.

445. PAGE 373. *Motto*. Martial, *Epigrams*, I. cxvii. 18.

The Stamp Act of 1712 (10 Anne, c. 19), which imposed a tax of one halfpenny on each half-sheet, was included in a bill levying duties on soap (cf. *Spectator*, No. 488), paper, parchment, silk, etc. It came into force next day, 1st August. Swift writes in his *Journal to Stella* (7th August 1712): 'Do you know that Grub Street is dead and gone last week? No more ghosts or murders now for love or money. I plied it pretty close the last fortnight, and published at least seven penny papers of my own, besides some of other people's: but now every simple half-sheet pays a halfpenny to the Queen. The *Observator* is fallen; the *Medleys* are jumbled together with the *Flying Post*; the *Examiner* is deadly sick; the *Spectator* keeps up, and doubles its price; I know not how long it will hold. Have you seen the red stamp the papers are marked with? Methinks it is worth a halfpenny, the stamping it.' No. 488 discusses the effect of the enhanced price on the circulation of the *Spectator*. The stamp (which was finely cut) bore, over the word *Halfpenny*, the motto *Semper eadem* surmounted by a twined rose and thistle under a crown.

PAGE 374. *How is it possible for me to write so clear of Party ?* Mr. Spectator protests overmuch, for, despite his constant vows of neutrality, he showed a growing inclination to disturb the peace of over-sensitive Tories.

Among the advertisements in *A* we read: 'Florinda, the Letter you was desirous to know, was received,' which must be a very early example of the literature of the agony column.

446. PAGE 375. *Motto*. Horace, *Ars Poetica*, 308.

With an Eye to some of these degenerate Compositions. Steele had the same thesis in No. 51, where he courteously makes an 'awful example' of one of his own comedies. Cf. among others, Nos. 65 and 502. The *Spectator* papers are the gentler notes of the war of words which had been waging since the publication of Jeremy Collier's book in 1698. Addison and Steele escaped the Vanbrughian dislike of the

> Dread Reformers of an Impious Age,
> You awful Catta-nine-Tailes to the Stage.
> > *The False Friend*, Prologue.

but they were to be commended by Parson Adams. 'I never heard of any plays fit for a Christian to read, but *Cato*, and the *Conscious Lovers*; and, I must own, in the latter there are some things almost solemn enough for a sermon' (*Joseph Andrews*, III. xi).

PAGE 376. *Martial*. *Epigrams*, I (opening lines).

PAGE 377. *Dogget*. Cf. ii. 109, and page 164 *ante*. See *B. I.*

447. PAGE 378. *Motto.* Another extract from Winterton's *Poetae Minores Graeci* (page 469). It is a fragment of Evenus Parius.

Dr. Robert Plot published his *Natural History of Staffordshire* in folio in 1686. He was the first keeper of the Ashmolean Museum.

PAGE 379. *One of the greatest Geniuses this Age has produced.* Dr. Atterbury (Edd.).

Optimum, etc. Probably from some Latin version of the eighth book of Diogenes Laertius.

PAGE 380. *Said Hesiod. Works and Days,* i. 287–8.

PAGE 381. *Dr. Scott.* John Scott, D.D., canon of Windsor (died 1694), author of a popular book, *The Christian Life.* The first edition appeared in 1681 and the ninth in 1712.

448. *Motto.* Juvenal, *Satires,* ii. 82.

449. PAGE 385. *Motto.* Martial, *Epigrams,* iii. lxviii. 1.

PAGE 387. Scabbard Rusty's letter may be read in connection with No. 436 (*ante,* page 348).

450. PAGE 388. *Motto.* Horace, *Epistles,* I. i. 53–4.

Ephraim Weed's letter is Steele's satirical sequel to his proposal in No. 442 (*ante,* page 367).

A Plumb. £100,000.

451. PAGE 392. *Motto.* Horace, *Epistles,* II. i. 148–50.

PAGE 393. *Fragment of Cicero. De Republica,* iv. 7.

Billingsgate. Cf. No. 247 (ii. 232 and 491).

PAGE 394. *Words of Monsieur Bayle.* See the dissertation upon defamatory libels in the *Dictionary* (x. 330 et sqq.).

452. PAGE 395. *Motto.* Pliny the elder, *Natural History,* xii. 5. Addison quotes it from Lily's Latin Grammar (*Brevissima Institutio*) where (page 76, Cambridge edition, 1681) it is cited in illustration of the genitive after certain adjectives. Cf. ii. 486.

PAGE 396. *Any Haberdasher in Cheapside.* Cf. i. 148 and note.

PAGE 397. *Pankridge*—i.e. Pancras, the church then in repute for 'fashionable' weddings.

453. PAGE 398. *Motto.* Horace, *Odes,* II. xx. 1–2.

PAGE 399. *Pieces of Divine Poetry. Ante,* Nos. 378 (page 183), 388 (page 211), 410 (page 275), and 441 (page 364).

PAGE 401. *And in a kind and faithful Friend.* Editors persist in seeing in this a reference by Addison to his colleague. As Henry Morley puts it: 'Was it not Steele whom he felt near to him at the Mercy-seat?'

454. *Motto.* Terence, *Heautontimorumenos,* I. i. 38–9.

PAGE 402. *Stocks-Market* was on the site of the Mansion House. See also page 429 and note. The 'ruddy virgins' of this place and Covent Garden (same paragraph) appear again in Fielding's burlesque lines (quoted in *Selections from Steele,* page 491):

> Oh! my Kissinda! Oh! how sweet art thou!
> Not Covent-Garden nor Stocks-Market knows
> A flower like thee.

PAGE 404. *A Silk-Worm.* Cf. Swift in his *Description of a City Shower (Tatler,* No. 238):

> To Shops in Crowds the daggled Females fly,
> Pretend to cheapen Goods, but nothing buy.

or, in better illustration, as Austin Dobson has pointed out:

> Miss, the mercer's plague, from shop to shop,
> Wandering, and littering with unfolded silks
> The polished counter, and approving none,
> Or promising with smiles to call again.
>
> Cowper's *Task*, VI.

PAGE 405. *Robin's* Coffee-house, in Exchange Alley. Swift frequented it, and he complains in a note to Stella, written there, 'I am here ever interrupted' (*Journal to Stella,* 20th Sept. 1710).

455. PAGE 406. *Motto.* Horace, *Odes,* IV. ii. 27–30.

PAGE 409. *Mr. William Pinkethman.* See note, i. 530.

456. *Motto.* Cicero, *Pro Quintio,* xv. 50.

    I pass'd, etc. Otway's *Venice Preserved,* I. i.

457. PAGE 412. *Motto.* Horace, *Satires,* II. iii. 9.

    William Lowndes was Secretary of the Treasury. See Swift's *Journal to Stella* (21st May 1711), and Pope's letter to Gay, 8th November 1717 (Elwin and Courthope's edition, vii. 420).

PAGE 413. *Mr. Dyer, Mr. Dawkes.* See note, i. 537; and cf. Anthony Alsop's *Ode* (Nichols, *Literary Anecdotes,* i. 3):

> Quid habent novorum
> *Dawks*que *Dyer*que,

and *Tatler,* No. 18: 'I remember Mr. Dyer, who is justly look'd upon by all the Fox-hunters in the Nation as the greatest Statesman our Country has produced, was particularly famous for dealing in Whales; insomuch that in Five Months time (for I had the curiosity to examine his Letters on that Occasion) he brought three into the Mouth of the River Thames, besides Two Porpusses and a Sturgeon. The judicious and wary Mr. I. Dawks hath all along been the rival of this great Writer, and got himself a Reputation from Plagues and Famines, by which, in those days, he destroyed as great multitudes as he has just lately done by the Sword. In every Dearth of News, Grand Cairo was sure to be unpeopled.'

    Garraway's. See note, i. 514.

458. PAGE 415. *Mottos.* The first, which does not appear in *A,* is from Hesiod's *Works and Days,* i. 315; the second is from Horace's *Epistles,* I. xvi. 24.

    Xenophanes. Taken from Plutarch's *Morals* ('Of Bashfulness'). In *A* it is printed *Xenophon,* in error.

459. PAGE 417. *Motto.* Horace, *Epistles,* I. iv. 5.

PAGE 419. *An Excellent Author.* The reference may be to Tillotson, with whom this sentiment was something of a favourite.

460 PAGE 420. *Motto.* Horace, *Ars Poetica*, 25.

   The allegorical sketch is said to be by Thomas Parnell.

   PAGE 423. *A certain Enormity.* Cf. *ante*, Nos, 259, 270, 344, etc.

   PAGE 424. *In Sacred Writ.* 1 Corinthians, xi. 10.

461. *Motto.* Virgil, *Eclogues*, ix. 34.

   PAGE 425. The author of this hymn is Dr. Isaac Watts.

   PAGE 426. *An Half-penny Value.* The price was raised to *2d.*, or double the original price. Half of the increase was paid to Government under the new Stamp Act (*ante*, page 487).

   PAGE 427. The advertisements in the earlier numbers (*A*) give point to the jocular Postscript, for there are frequent insertions regarding 'The famous Spanish Blacking for Gentlemen's Shoes,' and 'The famous Bavarian Red Liquor, which gives a delightful blushing Colour to the Cheeks of those that are White or Pale.'

462. *Motto.* Horace, *Satires*, I. v. 44.

   PAGE 429. *Stocks-Market.* See note, page 488. The statue had a curious history. It is said to have originally represented Sobieski on horseback over the conquered Turk, but it was converted into the effigy of the Merry Monarch subduing Oliver Cromwell, who continued to wear the turban of the eastern potentate (see Stowe's *Survey of London*, ii. 199, edition of 1720). Cf. the following passage in the *Tatler* (No. 18) : 'Had I not come by the other Day very early in the Morning, there might have been Mischief done; for a worthy North-Britain was swearing at Stocks-market, that they would not let him in at his Lodgings; but I knowing the Gentleman, and observing him look often at the King on Horse-back, and then double his Oaths, that he was sure he was right, found he mistook that for Charing-Cross, by the erection of the like Statue in each Place.' The statue was removed about 1735, to make way for the erection of the present Mansion House on the site of Stocks Market.

   A great Hand. Sheffield, Duke of Buckingham.

463. PAGE 430. *Motto.* Claudian, xxvii (*De Sexto Consulatu Honorii Augusti, Praefatio*), 1–6, 11–12.

   Homer, *Iliad*, viii, 69; Virgil, *Aeneid*, xii. 725.

   Milton, *Paradise Lost*, iv. 996–1015.

   PAGE 432. *A Saying among the Scotch.* All the editions omit '-Wit.'

   A two-penny Piece. See note to page 426.

   PAGE 433. *Tekel.* Daniel, v. 27.

464. *Motto.* Horace, *Odes*, II. x. 5–8.

   There was a little City. Ecclesiastes, ix. 14–16.

   PAGE 434. *Two things,* etc. Proverbs, xxx. 7–9.

   A Play by Aristophanes. The *Plutus.*

465. PAGE 435. *Motto.* Horace, *Epistles*, I. xviii. 97–9.

   PAGE 438. *The Heavens,* etc. Psalm xix. 1–4.

466. PAGE 439. *Motto.* Virgil, *Aeneid*, i. 405.

PAGE 439. *Admirer as I am.* Cf. Nos. 66, 67, 334, 370, 376.
  Anagrams and Acrostics. Cf. No. 60.

PAGE 440. *Mr. Prince.* See *B. I.*

PAGE 441. *Mr. Weaver.* See No. 334 (page 43 and note, page 469).

467. PAGE 443. *Motto.* Tibullus, *Elegies*, IV. i. 24–7.
  The greatest Princes. Caesar and Trajan.

PAGE 444. *Pindar.* Cowley's *Second Olympique Ode of Pindar*,
  175–9.

PAGE 445. *Bussy d'Amboise.* The story will be found in de Thou;
  but the writer of the essay may have gone no further than Bayle.
  Chapman wrote two plays, *Bussy d'Ambois* (1607) and *The Revenge of Bussy d'Ambois* (1613). The first opens with a soliloquy
  by d'Ambois, who is clad in simple garb. This play was
  recast by D'Urfey and played in 1691.

  This paper has been ascribed to John Hughes, and Chalmers
  suggests that 'Manilius' is his patron, Lord Cowper.

468. PAGE 446. *Motto.* Pliny, *Epistles*, III. xxi. 1.

PAGE 447. *Dick Eastcourt.* See i. 521, ii. 494; also pages 124, 164
  of this volume. See *B. I.* Colley Cibber said in his *Apology*:
  'This Man was so amazing and extraordinary a Mimick, that
  no Man or Woman, from the Coquette to the Privy-Counsellor,
  ever mov'd or spoke before him, but he could carry their Voice,
  Look, Mien, and Motion, instantly into another Company'
  (edition of 1740, page 69). 'Estcourt was buried in the South
  Aisle of St. Paul's, Covent Garden, on the day this paper was
  issued' (*Eighteenth Century Essays*, edited by Dobson, page 271).

PAGE 448. *Bullfinch.* In Richard Brome's *Northern Lass.* See
  ii. 60.
  Pounce, the lawyer in Steele's comedy, *The Tender Husband
  or The Accomplished Fools.*

PAGE 449. The following paragraph appears in *A*, after 'go on—':
  'It is a felicity his friends may rejoyce in, that he had his Senses,
  and used them as he ought to do, in his last Moments. It is
  remarkable, that his Judgment was in its calm Perfection to the
  utmost Article; for when his Wife, out of her Fondness, desired
  that she might send for a certain illiterate Humourist (whom he
  had accompanied in a thousand mirthful Moments, and whose
  Insolence makes Fools think he assumes from conscious Merit)
  he answered, "*Do what you please, but he won't come near me.*"
  Let poor Eastcourt's Negligence about this Message, convince
  the unwary of a triumphant Empyrick's Ignorance and Inhumanity.' This attack is said to have been levelled against
  the eccentric Dr. Radcliffe (founder of the infirmary and Radcliffe Library at Oxford), whose careless manner was matter
  of public scandal.

469. *Motto.* Cicero, *De Officiis*, iii. 5.

470. PAGE 452. *Motto.* Martial, *Epigrams*, ii. lxxxvi. 9–10.
  Following Song is an. 'Following Song, which, by the way,

is a beautiful Descant upon a single Thought, like the Compositions of the best Ancient Lyrick Poets, I say we will suppose this song is an' (*A*).

471. PAGE 454. *Motto.* Euripides, *Ino*, Fragment 7.

PAGE 455. *Linus.* Stobaeus, *Florilegium*, cx. 1:

> Ἐλπεσθαι χρὴ πάντ'· ἐπεὶ οὐκ ἔστ' οὐδὲν ἀέλπτον·
> ῥάδια πάντα θεῷ τελέσαι, καὶ ἀρήνυτον οὐδέν.

PAGE 456. *I have set the Lord.* Psalm xvi. 8–11.

472. PAGE 457. *Motto.* Virgil, *Aeneid*, iii. 660–1.
Sir William Read. 'My very worthy friend' (*Tatler*, No. 224). See *B. I.*

PAGE 458. *Pleasures of the Imagination.* See pages 276 et sqq.

PAGES 459–60. *Paradise Lost*, iii. 21–4, 41–50; *Samson Agonistes*, 66–72, 77–82.

PAGE 460. *Dr. Grant.* See *B. I.*
Jones of Newington. See the pamphlet *A Full and True Account of a Miraculous Cure of a young Man in Newington.* 1709.

473. PAGE 461. *Motto.* Horace, *Epistles*, i. xix. 12–14.